Second Edition

STRATEGIC STAFFING

Jean M. Phillips
Rutgers University

Stanley M. Gully
Rutgers University

Prentice Hall

Boston   Columbus   Indianapolis   New York   San Francisco   Upper Saddle River
Amsterdam   Cape Town   Dubai   London   Madrid   Milan   Munich   Paris   Montreal   Toronto
Delhi   Mexico City   Sao Paulo   Sydney   Hong Kong   Seoul   Singapore   Taipei   Tokyo

Editorial Director: Sally Yagan
Editor in Chief: Eric Svendsen
Director of Editorial Services: Ashley Santora
Editorial Project Manager: Meg O'Rourke
Editorial Assistant: Carter Anderson
Director of Marketing: Patrice Lumumba Jones
Marketing Manager: Nikki Ayana Jones
Marketing Assistant: Ian Gold
Senior Managing Editor: Judy Leale
Production Manager: Meghan DeMaio

Creative Director: Jayne Conte
Cover Designer: Suzanne Behnke
Cover Art: Fotolia
Media Editor: Denise Vaughn
Media Project Manager: Lisa Rinaldi
Full-Service Project Management/Composition:
  Hemalatha/Integra Software Services, Ltd.
Printer/Binder: Edwards Brothers
Cover Printer: Lehigh-Phoenix Color
Text Font: Times

Credits and acknowledgments borrowed from other sources and reproduced, with permission, in this textbook appear on appropriate page within text.

Library of Congress Cataloging-in-Publication Data
Phillips, Jean
  Strategic staffing/Jean M. Phillips, Stanley M. Gully.—2nd ed.
    p. cm.
  Includes bibliographical references and index.
  ISBN-13: 978-0-13-610974-7
  ISBN-10: 0-13-610974-8
  1. Personnel management. 2. Employee selection. 3. Strategic planning. I. Gully, Stanley Morris.
II. Title.
  HF5549.P4597 2012
  658.3'01—dc22

                                                                                2010036083

10 9 8 7 6 5 4 3 2 1

Prentice Hall
is an imprint of

www.pearsonhighered.com

ISBN 10:   0-13-610974-8
ISBN 13: 978-0-13-610974-7

CONTENTS

PREFACE

Strategic Staffing

Prepares all current and future managers to take a strategic and modern approach to the identification, attraction, selection, deployment, and retention of talent

It is well accepted that talent is a source of competitive advantage. Employees are what set organizations apart and drive their performance. In today's competitive business environment, an organization's ability to execute its business strategy and maintain a competitive edge depends even more on the quality of its employees. The quality of a company's employees is directly affected by the quality of its staffing systems. Because hiring managers are involved in the staffing process, hiring managers and human resource professionals need to be familiar with strategic staffing techniques.

The practice of staffing has changed significantly over the past 10 to 15 years. Organizations increasingly realize that their employees are the key to executing their business strategies. The war for talent has made the identification and attraction of high-performing employees essential for companies to compete and win in their marketplaces. The Internet and other technologies have also changed the ways firms identify, attract, hire, and deploy their talent.

Our goal in writing *Strategic Staffing* was to create a text that is grounded in research, communicates practical staffing concepts as well as the role of staffing in organizational performance, and is engaging to read. The second edition of *Strategic Staffing* continues to present current staffing theories and practices in an interesting, engaging, and easy-to-read format. As one professor who uses the book so clearly said, "It's practical and can be applied immediately by students on their jobs." We have tried to be responsive to reviewers and users of this text. Some of the more substantial changes are:

- Replacement of three chapter opening vignettes with new ones on Caribou Coffee, Hilton, and Osram Sylvania
- Revision of the legal chapter (Chapter 3) to address current changes in legislation and court decisions including independent contractor misclassification cases, I-9 forms, EEOC claims, and the Genetic Information Nondiscrimination Act
- Addition of figures and supplement to the measurement chapter (Chapter 8) for more advanced treatment
- Addition of new exercises throughout the book on Caribou Coffee, Hilton, and Osram Sylvania as well as a new job offer negotiation exercise
- Updated citations and many new company examples throughout the text, including the examples of Google, 3M, Qualcomm, IBM, Yahoo!, and Silly Bandz
- The addition of current tools and techniques including Twitter and Facebook for using technology for sourcing and managing staffing systems
- Provision of new and additional material for instructors in the Instructor's Manual

This is a partial list of the changes in this edition. For a more detailed list please see below.

We treat staffing as an integrated process that begins with an understanding of a company's business strategy and continues through planning, sourcing, recruiting, selecting, negotiating, socializing, career planning, retaining, and transitioning the workforce. These stages enable organizations to meet hiring objectives and ensure that talent is in the right place at the right time. Although the book is research based, we include many company examples to illustrate the material. *Strategic Staffing* describes how to:

- Develop a staffing strategy that reinforces business strategy
- Forecast talent needs and labor supply and plan accordingly
- Conduct a job or competency analysis and a job rewards analysis
- Strategically source potential recruits
- Recruit and select the right people
- Negotiate with and hire top candidates
- Socialize, deploy, and retain talent

- Manage turnover
- Use staffing metrics and conduct staffing system evaluations
- Leverage technology throughout the staffing system
- Integrate the staffing system with the other human resource functions of training, compensation, and performance management
- Ensure the legal compliance of the staffing system

NEW TO THE SECOND EDITION

Here is a chapter-by-chapter list of the changes in the second edition.

Chapter 1

- New opening vignette about Caribou Coffee
- New SAS and Mattel examples
- New exercise on Caribou Coffee

Chapter 2

- New P&G and 3M examples

Chapter 3

- Updated legal information, including information on misclassifying independent contractors, the WARN Act, and the legal use of assessment test results
- Updated examples and statistics
- Added information on leased employees
- Added information on the Genetic Information Nondiscrimination Act of 2008
- Updated information on I-9s and E-Verify

Chapter 4

- New The Richards Group example

Chapter 5

- New Corning and Saudi Aramco examples

Chapter 6

- New examples of Google, Genentech, Aricent, Accenture, Silly Bandz, and Qualcomm
- Expanded discussion of the advantages of informal versus formal recruiting sources
- X-raying, Twitter, and an updated discussion of Internet sourcing techniques
- Expanded discussion of global sourcing

Chapter 7

- New examples of Wachovia Bank, Advanced Technology Services, National City Corporation, Tesco, Schlumberger, and IBM
- Expanded discussion of organizational image
- Expanded discussion of realistic job previews

Chapter 8

- New examples of PeopleAnswers and AmeriPride,
- Added new figures to illustrate concepts, including Figure 8–3 showing diagrams for correlations, Figure 8–5 showing diagrams of multiple regression, Figure 8–6 illustrating deficiency, contamination, and relevance, and Figure 8–8 showing unreliability and correlation
- Added a discussion of the Taylor-Russell tables
- Added new chapter supplement covering more technical information and formulae, including coverage of attenuation due to unreliability and range restriction
- Added computational exercises in the chapter supplement
- Added new data set for more advanced computational practice
- Included Excel commands/formulas for computations

Chapter 9

- New examples of Luxottica Group, Sunglass Hut, Planned Cos., Adobe Systems, Deloitte Consulting, and National City Corporation
- New discussion of how stereotype threat can reduce the accuracy of employment tests
- Discussion of the STAR technique in responding to structured interviews
- Expanded discussion of behavioral interviews

Chapter 10

- New examples of job bidding
- New Figure 10–2 of a succession management database

Chapter 11

- Updated example of reneging
- Expanded discussion of issues involved in rejecting internal candidates
- New job offer negotiation exercise

Chapter 12

- New opening vignette about Hilton
- New examples of Southwest Airlines, Ritz-Carlton, Macy's, Cisco, Capital One, Aviva, Chipotle Mexican Grill, Deloitte, Boeing, and Wynn Resorts
- Expanded discussion of orientation programs
- Expanded discussion of exit interviews
- New discussion of clarifying promotion paths
- New exercise about Hilton

Chapter 13

- New opening vignette about Osram Sylvania
- New example of Nokia
- New discussion of the storage requirements of employees' medical information
- New exercise about Osram Sylvania

Appendix–Chern's Case

- Modified Boolean search assignment to match changing technology
- Improved applicant and résumé information for the case
- Revised and clarified description of assessment tools
- Revised applicant assessment scores and scoring key for final decision

We have also updated citations and references throughout the book so they are as current as possible. This edition continues to discuss modern strategic staffing theories and practices including, for example, integrating staffing strategy with business strategy, aligning staffing with other human resource management functions, using technology in recruiting and staffing system management, downsizing strategies, and current legal issues. Of course, traditional staffing concepts including forecasting and planning, recruiting, assessment, and selection are covered as well. Throughout the book, staffing concepts being discussed are "brought to life" through organizational examples.

We also strive to develop staffing skills in addition to conveying staffing theories and concepts. The *Develop Your Skills* feature in each chapter covers topics including job offer negotiation tips, Boolean sourcing techniques, online résumé tips, and making your own career development plan help translate the book's concepts into real skills.

BOOK FEATURES

- We provide *learning objectives* at the beginning of each chapter to provide an advance organizer of the material covered by the chapter.
- Each chapter leads off with a *vignette* describing a staffing challenge faced by a real organization. At the end of the chapter, the vignette concludes and integrates the relevant staffing concepts used by the company to address the challenge.

- Every chapter has a *Develop Your Skills* feature that extends a topic in the chapter and develops a personal skill related to staffing.
- *Discussion questions* at the end of each chapter provide the opportunity to check understanding of chapter material.
- A brief *case study* at the end of each chapter encourages problem solving and the application of chapter material by stimulating in-class discussions or focusing on individual solutions.
- *Three interactive exercises* at the end of each chapter bring the material to life. One exercise is tied to the opening vignette, one is linked to the chapter's Develop Your Skills feature, and one integrates the chapter's staffing concepts with business strategy.
- A *book-long active learning project* applies the breadth of the textbook material to a specific job in an organization. This active learning project develops strategic staffing skills in addition to developing tacit knowledge about the strategic staffing process.
- A *book-long case study* contained in the Appendix provides the experience of evaluating the staffing strategy and staffing system for sales associates in a hypothetical high-end retail store called Chern's. The case also provides practice planning, budgeting, and evaluating the return on the investment of the staffing choices made. Online videos accompanying the case illustrate both structured and unstructured interviews and provide the experience creating an assessment plan, scoring job interviews, and making a hiring decision from among eight candidates.
- A humorous *video* is available online that illustrates what *not* to do in an interview.

ORGANIZATION OF THE BOOK

The book is broken into four sections.

Section 1, "The Staffing Context," contains Chapters 1 through 4. Chapter 1, "Strategic Staffing," considers the importance of staffing for organizational success. We define *strategic staffing*, explore the strategic staffing process, and discuss key staffing outcomes and goals. We describe and illustrate the difference between traditional and strategic staffing and highlight the impact staffing can have on the other human resource management functions.

Chapter 2, "Business and Staffing Strategies," covers how the organization's business strategy and competitive advantage influence the organization's human resource strategy, as well as the organization's talent strategy and philosophy. We discuss how business strategy and competitive advantage connect with human resource strategy and the organization's talent strategy and philosophy. This chapter also explains how staffing can create value for a firm, and introduces the various strategic staffing decisions that must be made during any staffing effort.

Chapter 3, "The Legal Context," describes the legal environment in which staffing must operate. Laws and regulations are changing yet they play an important role in determining how an organization recruits, hires, promotes, and terminates employees. We discuss specialized employment relationships, such as independent contractors and temporary workers, and summarize relevant laws and regulations. We describe legal theories including negligent referral and negligent hiring, and discuss barriers to legally defensible recruiting and hiring. We address current topics, such as definitions of *applicant* in an Internet world.

Chapter 4, "Strategic Job Analysis and Competency Modeling," covers job analysis, future-oriented job analysis, job rewards analysis, and competency modeling. We discuss the linkage between business strategy and employee competencies, styles, and traits. We present a basic job analytic technique applicable to most jobs that is also appropriate for the book-long active learning project.

Section 2, "Planning, Sourcing, and Recruiting," addresses the identification, attraction, and recruitment of job applicants in addition to staffing planning. Because people who never apply for a position cannot become employees, sourcing and recruiting qualified and interested applicants is a critical step in the strategic staffing process. This section contains Chapters 5 through 7.

Chapter 5, "Forecasting and Planning," describes how organizations derive business forecasts that are then translated into estimates of future labor demand. Labor supply forecasts are also made, and when combined with labor demand estimates, they help to identify where the organization needs to focus attention to ensure that it has the right talent in the right place at the right time. We present techniques for forecasting labor supply and labor demand, action planning, and discuss issues regarding the planning of a recruiting and hiring initiative.

Chapter 6, "Sourcing: Identifying Recruits" discusses applicant sourcing, or the identification and attraction of recruits, including the use of different types of Internet searches. We describe many different recruiting sources and discuss how to develop a sourcing plan and evaluate recruitment source effectiveness.

Chapter 7, "Recruiting," describes employer branding and image, and the importance of addressing applicant reactions. Methods of targeting recruits, crafting an effective recruiting message, and persuading people to apply for jobs are described. We also discuss considerations in choosing the appropriate form and content of the recruiting message.

Section 3, "Selecting," covers the assessment of job candidates and the evaluation of their fit with the job and organization. This section contains Chapters 8 through 10.

Chapter 8, "Measurement," describes some of the issues regarding candidate assessment. The concepts of central tendency, variability, scatter plots, correlation, regression, and practical and statistical significance are introduced along with explanations of reliability, validity, and validity generalization. The material in this chapter provides the foundation for some of the material in Chapters 9 through 13.

Chapter 9, "Assessing External Candidates," discusses methods of assessing the qualifications of external job candidates. We review interviews, work samples, personality testing, cognitive ability testing, and other methods, and describe their effectiveness.

Chapter 10, "Assessing Internal Candidates," discusses methods of assessing the qualifications of employees being considered for a different position in the company. Performance reviews, the GE nine box method, and peer and supervisor ratings are some of the methods reviewed.

Strategic staffing involves the movement of employees into and through an organization. Section 4, "Managing the Staffing System," covers the final choice and socializing of new employees, including the negotiation and hiring process. This section also discusses managing the flow of talent through the organization using career planning and succession planning, and by conducting separations, such as layoffs, terminations, and downsizing. We describe the use of technology in the staffing process, managing employee retention, and the evaluation of the staffing process. This section contains Chapters 11 through 13.

Chapter 11, "Choosing and Hiring Candidates," describes the process of deciding which job candidate(s) should receive job offers, subsequently negotiating those offers, and socializing new hires. Methods of combining candidate assessment scores into a single score that can be used to compare candidates are described. We describe candidate choice methods including banding, ranking, cut scores, and grouping. We discuss tactics for negotiating hiring agreements and persuading job offer recipients to join the company, along with inducements. The perspectives of both the candidate and the organization on the negotiating process are considered.

Chapter 12, "Managing Workforce Flow," discusses the management of talent through the organization, including new hire socialization, career planning, succession planning, and leadership development. Separation decisions, such as layoffs, terminations, and downsizing, are also reviewed. The chapter also covers different types of turnover, the causes of turnover, and methods of retaining valued talent.

Chapter 13, "Staffing System Evaluation and Technology," covers the importance of evaluating a staffing system's effectiveness. We cover other metrics and evaluation methods in other chapters when appropriate. We describe the staffing system evaluation process and present specific staffing system metrics. This chapter also discusses the ways in which technology has changed and shaped strategic staffing systems. Technology can enable strategic execution, and many organizations are leveraging technology, such as applicant tracking systems, to enhance their recruitment and selection efforts. Internet recruiting, the role of a company's own Web site, résumé screening software, and HRIS systems are discussed. Use of technology as an aid to collecting data that can be used to evaluate the effectiveness of a staffing system is also covered.

TEACHING AND LEARNING SUPPORT

Strategic Staffing continues to be supported with an extensive supplement package for both students and faculty.

Instructor Resource Center

http://www.pearsonhighered.com/educator is where instructors can access a variety of print, media, and presentation resources available with this text in downloadable, digital format.

Once you register, you will not have additional forms to fill out, or multiple usernames and passwords to remember to access new titles and/or editions. As a registered faculty member, you can log in directly to download resource files, and receive immediate access and instructions for installing Course Management content to your campus server.

Our dedicated Technical Support team is ready to assist instructors with questions about the media supplements that accompany this text. Visit http://247pearsoned.custhelp.com for answers to frequently asked questions and toll-free user support phone numbers.

To download the supplements available with this, please visit http://www.pearsonhighered .com/educator.

Instructor's Manual

- Includes interviewing, résumé, negotiation, and firing/layoff tips
- Includes new data set and computations for supplement in Chapter 8
- Provides a "User's Guide" for managing the Chern's case and for using associated interview videos
- Provides support for Chern's assessment data (located on Companion Website) for easy cut-and-paste response to students

Test Item File

This Test Item File contains multiple-choice, true/false, and essay questions. Each question is followed by the correct answer, the learning objective to which it correlates, page reference, AACSB category, question type (concept, application, critical thinking, or synthesis), and difficulty rating. It has been thoroughly reviewed by assessment experts. The Test Item File is available for download by visiting www.pearsonhighered.com/irc.

TestGen

Pearson Education's test-generating software is available from www.pearsonhighered.com/irc. The software is PC/MAC compatible and preloaded with all of the Test Item File questions. You can manually or randomly view test questions and drag and drop to create a test. You can also add or modify test-bank questions as needed.

PowerPoints

This edition offers accompanying PowerPoints. The PowerPoints offer helpful instructional support by highlighting and clarifying key concepts. The PowerPoints are available for download from www.pearsonhighered.com/irc.

Companion Website

In addition to chapter quizzes and videos, The companion website (www.pearsonhighered .com/phillips) contains a new data set for Chapter 8 as well as corresponding exercises. Faster streaming of interview videos facilitates an improved viewing experience.

CourseSmart eTextbook

CourseSmart eTextbooks were developed for students looking to save on required or recommended textbooks. Students simply select their eText by title or author and purchase immediate access to the content for the duration of the course using any major credit card. With a CourseSmart eText, students can search for specific keywords or page numbers, take notes online, print out reading assignments that incorporate lecture notes, and bookmark important passages for later review. For more information or to purchase a CourseSmart eTextbook, visit http://www.coursesmart.com

REVIEWERS

We also thank the terrific panel of reviewers whose many comments and suggestions improved the book.

Nancy E. Day, University of Missouri

Robert Eder, Portland State University

John Hausknecht, Cornell University

Jeanie Kellas, Columbia College

Lois Kurowski, Michigan State University

Kimberly Lukaszewski, State University of New York at New Paltz

Val Miskin, Washington State University

Barbara Rau, University of Wisconsin–Oshkosh

Thomas Stone, Oklahoma State University

Mary Trottier, Nichols College

Karl Kelley, North Central College

Kimberly O'Brien, Wayne State University

Ronald S. Landis, University of Memphis

PERSONAL ACKNOWLEDGEMENTS

We would like to thank our sons, Ryan and Tyler, for their patience and support while we wrote this book. We dedicate it to them and could not have done it without the joy and inspiration they give us. We also gratefully acknowledge the superb Prentice Hall team for their contributions to this revision. Jennifer Collins, Meg O'Rourke, Susie Abraham, and Nikki Jones were true partners in the effort. Pete Troost and Hébert Peck of Rutgers University's iTV Studio did a terrific job shooting and producing the interview videos. We thank J. Allen Suddeth for his skill in casting and directing the video, and Beth Wicke for her efforts in assembling and motivating a terrific cast. We also appreciate the talented engineering work of Alex Fahan, Thomas Sanitate's sound expertise, Steve Barcy's skilled camera work, and Debra Andriano's administrative help. We appreciate Rutgers University's Eric Polino and Jim Drumheller for allowing us to use their interview bloopers video in conjunction with this book. We also thank the many people who shared their stories and staffing tools and allowed us to include them for your benefit.

We firmly believe that learning should be fun and not boring, and wrote the book with this goal in mind. We hope you enjoy reading it, and welcome your feedback at phillipsgully@gmail.com!

Jean Phillips and Stan Gully

ABOUT THE AUTHORS

Jean Phillips is a professor in the School of Management and Labor Relations at Rutgers University. For over 15 years, she has taught classroom and hybrid classroom/online courses to executive, professional, and full-time students in staffing, strategic human resource management, organizational behavior, management, and teams and leadership in the United States and in Singapore.

Dr. Phillips earned her BA and PhD in business administration and organizational behavior from Michigan State University. Her research interests focus on recruitment and staffing, leadership and team effectiveness, and issues related to learning organizations. Her work has appeared in *Academy of Management Journal, Journal of Applied Psychology, Organizational Behavior and Human Decision Processes, Personnel Psychology, Small Group Research, Journal of Business and Psychology, International Journal of Human Resource Management*, and *HR Magazine*.

Dr. Phillips was among the top 5 percent of published authors in *Journal of Applied Psychology* and *Personnel Psychology* during the 1990s and received the 2004 Cummings Scholar Award from the Organizational Behavior Division of the Academy of Management. She has served on the editorial boards of *Journal of Applied Psychology, Journal of Management*, and *Personnel Psychology*. Dr. Phillips is also a member of the Academy of Management and the Society for Industrial and Organizational Psychology. Her consulting work includes creating and evaluating strategic staffing programs, coaching on enhancing leadership performance and the effectiveness of work teams, strategic human resource management, and developing employer value propositions.

Stan Gully is a professor in the Department of Human Resource Management in the School of Management and Labor Relations at Rutgers University. He has authored or presented numerous papers, research articles, and book chapters on a variety of topics. His work has appeared in *Research in Personnel and Human Resources Management, Journal of Applied Psychology, Organizational Behavior and Human Decision Processes, Journal of Organizational Behavior, Organizational Research Methods*, and *Advances in Interdisciplinary Studies of Work Teams*, among other outlets.

Dr. Gully earned his master's and PhD in industrial/organizational psychology from Michigan State University. He has taught courses at the undergraduate, master's, doctoral, and executive master's level covering content such as organizational learning and innovation, recruiting and staffing, human resource management, performance management, training and development, and leadership. He has taught using traditional and hybrid technologies in the United States, Singapore, and Indonesia. Dr. Gully has won awards for the quality of his research, teaching, and service, and he has served on the editorial boards of *Journal of Applied Psychology, Academy of Management Journal, Journal of Management,* and *Journal of Organizational Behavior.*

His applied work includes, but is not limited to, management at a major parcel delivery firm, assessment of the effectiveness of an employer branding initiative, design of various training programs, development of guidelines for training leaders of interdependent work teams, evaluation of recruiting source effectiveness, and implementation of a multisource feedback system. His research interests include strategic recruiting, leadership and team effectiveness, training, and organizational learning.

1

Strategic Staffing

Outline

LEARNING OBJECTIVES
After studying this chapter, you should be able to:

- Understand why staffing is critical to an organization's performance.

- Define *strategic staffing* and contrast it with less strategic views of staffing.

- Describe the seven components of strategic staffing.

- Understand staffing goals.

- Describe how staffing influences and is affected by the other functional areas of human resource management.

IMPROVING STORE PERFORMANCE AT CARIBOU COFFEE[1]

After establishing their first coffee house in 1992, Caribou Coffee Company cofounders John and Kim Puckett quickly grew the company. Headquartered in Minneapolis, Minnesota, Caribou Coffee Company is now the nation's second largest specialty coffee company with over 500 stores. The company also sells its coffee, equipment, and other goods through the Caribou Coffee Web site and various retail partners.

Caribou's leaders logically assumed that customer service was the reason customers returned to their stores. This made sense, particularly given the company's emphasis on the customer service skills of all of its employees, including district managers who were responsible for eight to fourteen locations. But the fact that store success varied more across district managers than within a single district manager's stores created a puzzle: If there was an across-the-board focus on customer service, why was the performance of each district manager's stores so similar, but the performance of each district manager different? Did the higher-performing district managers communicate more effectively to customers and associates? Were they better at developing employees? What exactly accounted for the difference?

Imagine that Caribou Coffee approaches you for ideas as to what its highest-performing district managers must be doing or offering to consistently outperform the others. After reading this chapter, you should have some good ideas.

People's efforts, talents, knowledge, and skills matter to organizations. If you don't believe this is true, then fire all your organization's employees and replace them with cheaper labor. Few successful organizations would accept this challenge because they understand that their people are the key to their performance and survival. A *competitive advantage* is something that a company can do differently from its rivals that allows it to perform better, survive, and succeed in its industry. Sometimes an organization's competitive advantage is defined by its technology. Other times, innovative product lines, low-cost products, or excellent customer-service drive competitive advantage. In each case, the company's employees create, enhance, or implement the company's competitive advantage.

How do people make a difference? At companies like Microsoft and Google, key technology is devised, implemented, and updated by the people who create and use it. Employees at Apple Computer, Pfizer, and 3M create and sell new and innovative product lines. Employees identify and implement the manufacturing system improvements that create low-cost, high-quality automobiles at Hyundai. Finally, the service at Starbucks is all about employee–customer interactions and experiences. In each of these cases, employees influence and implement the key drivers of the success of the business. From where do these employees come? It all begins with the staffing process.

Effective staffing is the cornerstone of successful human resource (HR) management—it lays the foundation for an organization's future performance and survival. Why is it so important? Staffing is important because its outcomes determine who will work for and represent a company, and what its employees will be willing and able to do. As a result, staffing influences the success of future training, performance management, and compensation programs as well as the organization's ability to execute its business strategy.

Perhaps no other single activity has the potential to have as great an impact on employees' capabilities, behaviors, and performance as identifying and obtaining the talent that the organization will ultimately use to produce its products or services. Reflecting this understanding, many successful companies give employee recruitment, retention, and motivation the same high-level attention as their other core business functions, such as marketing, finance, and research and development.

Research has confirmed that staffing practices are positively related to both profitability and profit growth.[2] Effective staffing can also enhance the performance of an organization's shares in the stock market. A survey by a large consulting firm found that a strong staffing function led to greater shareholder return. In particular, companies that had a clear idea of whom they wanted to hire and that judged applicants against clear criteria outperformed companies with weaker staffing functions.[3]

By collaborating with hiring managers and influencing the flow of talent into, through, and out of an organization, staffing professionals play an important strategic role in organizations. Effective staffing requires a partnership between hiring managers and staffing professionals in the human resource management department. Staffing professionals bring expertise to the workforce planning and staffing processes, including evaluating what a job requires; identifying what competencies, skills, personalities, and so forth, are required for job success; and assessing those characteristics in job applicants. As the expert in the job itself, the hiring manager provides input throughout the process and typically makes the final hiring decision after the staffing specialist generates and screens a much larger pool of applicants. In addition to promoting the goals of their firms, staffing professionals promote the goals of society by helping match people with jobs and organizations in which they are able to be successful and happy.

This chapter begins with an explanation of the context in which staffing operates, followed by a definition of strategic staffing. We then discuss how strategic staffing is different from less strategic ways of looking at staffing, what strategic staffing entails, and why it matters. We then describe the importance of integrating staffing with the other areas of human resource management (i.e., training, compensation, performance management, career development, and succession management). Finally, we explain our plan for the rest of the book and describe some of the core ideas that we will present in each chapter. After reading this chapter, you should understand why a company's staffing practices must be consistent with its business strategy and with the other areas of human resource management if they are to support the larger goals of the organization.

THE STAFFING CONTEXT

There are over 7 million employers in the United States,[4] employing anywhere from one to hundreds of thousands of employees. Over 145 million people were employed in the United States in February of 2007,[5] and an additional 7.4 million were actively looking for work.[6] Millions of employees are hired or separated every month, making staffing a multibillion-dollar business.[7]

Many forces in an organization's environment influence its staffing activities. For example, as globalization expands, companies are increasingly searching the world for talent. This has resulted in greater competition for top talent and has made it more difficult for firms to hire the best workers. Global competition for a firm's products and services also influences staffing because the increased competition can lower the company's profit margins and leave fewer resources available for its staffing activities.

Technological changes have also dramatically influenced the ways in which firms hire and manage their employee relationships. Technology has made it easier for firms to track and develop their employees' skills as well as recruit and hire new employees. The Internet has changed the way organizations recruit and hire, and changed the ways many people now look for jobs. Similarly, database software systems have greatly facilitated the staffing evaluation process, making it easier to evaluate a staffing system and address any underperforming parts.

Many different legal and societal forces shape firms' staffing activities, too. For example, firms face antidiscrimination laws and laws that hold them responsible for the damaging actions of their employees if they fail to exercise reasonable care in hiring these people. Applicants responding negatively to the firm's recruiting or selection methods, employees demanding greater work-life balance, or customers no longer buying the products of a firm that lays off domestic workers and hires cheaper labor abroad—all of these factors can influence a firm's future staffing choices as well.

Together these forces drive the way organizations identify, attract, assess, and integrate talent into the workforce. **Talent management** is the implementation of integrated strategies or systems designed to increase workplace productivity by developing improved processes for attracting, developing, retaining, and utilizing people with the required skills and aptitude to meet current and future business needs.[8] As one expert put it, "The ability to execute business strategy is rooted in the ability to attract, retain, and develop key talent. Successful talent management creates the most enduring competitive advantage. No company can afford to be unprepared for both the best and worst of times."[9] This book addresses the role that staffing can play in the talent management process.

talent management
attracting, developing, retaining, and utilizing people with the required skills and aptitudes to meet current and future business needs

DEFINING STRATEGIC STAFFING

Strategic staffing is the process of staffing an organization in future-oriented, goal-directed ways that support the business strategy of the organization and enhance its effectiveness.[10] This involves the movement of people into, through, and out of the organization.

strategic staffing
the process of staffing an organization in future-oriented, goal-directed ways that support the business strategy of the organization and enhance its effectiveness

This definition differs from the way companies often staff themselves. For example, too many organizations still fill a job opening by putting the same job announcement they have been using for years in one or two recruiting sources, such as a job board or newspaper, and make a hiring decision based on a gut feeling they get during an interview. In other words, they don't put sufficient thought or planning into hiring in the way that best helps the firm execute its business strategy with an eye toward the future.[11] The focus of strategic staffing is the integration of staffing practices with business strategy and with the other areas of human resource management to enhance organizational performance.

HOW STRATEGIC STAFFING DIFFERS FROM TRADITIONAL STAFFING

strategy
a long-term plan of action to achieve a particular goal

A **strategy** is a long-term plan of action to achieve a particular goal. Traditional staffing tends to focus on quickly and conveniently filling an opening rather than on aligning the staffing effort with the long-term strategic needs of the organization. By contrast, strategic staffing entails both short- and long-term planning. The process involves acquiring, deploying, and retaining the right number of employees with the appropriate talents to effectively execute this strategy. When done strategically, staffing can enable a company to acquire a sustainable competitive advantage that allows it to successfully fulfill its mission and reach its goals. To illustrate what we mean by strategic staffing and how it differs from "less strategic" ways of thinking about staffing, let's consider how two hypothetical organizations fill job openings. The first company, Treds, has a less-strategic staffing process.

As the store manager of Treds, a popular shoe store in a local shopping mall, Ron knows he cannot afford to be understaffed during the upcoming holiday season. As soon as his assistant manager, Sandy, tells him she is quitting, Ron reaches into his file drawer and pulls out the job description (description of the job requirements) and person specification (description of the qualifications and competencies required of a person performing the job description) he used to hire her two years earlier. He quickly scans it, decides that it would be all right to use it again without making any changes, and forwards it to his regional manager along with a job requisition to get permission to hire a replacement.

When Lee, who is in Treds's human resource department, receives the approved job requisition and job description from Ron's boss, she checks how the company typically finds assistant managers. She sees that when it last hired an assistant manager, the firm posted an ad in the local paper. Lee can't tell from the company's records how many people had applied after seeing the ad. However, she decides that if it worked before, it should work again. So, she places the same "help wanted" ad in the store's local paper.

After two weeks, seven people have responded to the recruitment ad and submitted their résumés. Three of them lack the previous retail experience Lee sees as a minimum qualification for the position. After reading the other four résumés, Lee sets up telephone interviews with all four of them. She never gets back to the three applicants who lack retail experience to let them know that they are not being considered further.

After interviewing the four candidates over the phone about how interested they are in the job and confirming they have appropriate education and experience, Lee decides that three of them merit an interview and schedules them to meet with Ron at the store. At that point, Lee does not let the rejected candidate know that she is no longer being considered for the position.

Ron asks the three candidates individually about their work history and what they are looking for from the job and decides to hire Alex. Alex seems eager to start as soon as possible. Although he doesn't have a lot of retail management experience, Ron hopes he will be able to learn quickly on the job even though Treds doesn't have a formal training program. Alex receives a job offer contingent upon his passing a drug test and background check. After the background report and drug tests come back favorably, Alex accepts the job offer.

Ron sends Alex a copy of Treds's policy manual and schedules, and he reports to work the following Monday. The other finalists are not informed that the position has been filled until they call Ron to follow up.

The second company, Soles, illustrates a better strategic staffing process.

Amy, the manager of popular shoe retailer Soles, has to replace her departing assistant manager, Ken, who has worked with her for the past two years. To be prepared for the upcoming holiday season, Amy would like to replace Ken as quickly as possible. She sets aside some time in her busy day to think about what she needs in an assistant manager.

Amy goes to her computer and reviews the job description she used when hiring Ken two years ago. "It is a good description of the job," she thinks, "but it seems like something is missing." Amy thinks about how the store's competitive landscape has changed over the past few years. When she first started working at Soles four years ago, there was only one other shoe retailer in the mall in which it is located. Now there are five, and two of them offer lower prices on shoes that compete with some of Soles's key product lines. Amy knows that her company can't lower its prices, but she feels that if her store offers excellent customer service, her customers will be willing to pay higher prices for her store's shoes. Also, Soles is increasing its Web-based reporting by stores, so having an assistant manager with technological skills would also be useful.

Amy calls her human resource representative, Mike, to get some assistance in analyzing what her new assistant manager should be able to do. After determining what the job requires, Amy sends a revised job description to her regional manager along with a job requisition to get permission to hire a replacement.

After receiving hiring approval, Mike gives some thought to the qualifications and competencies Amy listed for the position. He tries to figure out where people with those qualifications might be so that he can find a way to let them know about the job opportunity. Mike realizes that the company's salary is competitive with the other stores in the mall but not different enough to particularly attract applicants. He thinks about the other aspects of the job that could appeal to a talented potential recruit. The company has good benefits, a good performance assessment and training program, and tries to promote from within. Although he probably won't be able to hire a very experienced assistant manager in light of the salary he can offer, the opportunity should appeal to someone with at least some experience—someone who would like to advance through Soles's managerial ranks.

Mike reviews the data about how the company has been most successful in hiring past assistant managers. He then brainstorms with Amy about where they might find qualified and interested people. He also decides to visit some of the other stores in the mall to evaluate their employees and see if any of them might be suited for the job. While at the stores, he pays particular attention to how the assistant managers there interact with customers and evaluates the strength of their customer service skills. In addition, Mike posts a job advertisement on the job board of a local college that offers a degree in fashion design. The ad emphasizes that Soles is searching for someone with managerial experience, fashion knowledge, technological skills, and excellent customer service skills.

Within two weeks, Mike has recruited five promising mall employees to apply for the position and received 15 applications from the college's job board. He screens the résumés for retail and managerial experience, and identifies three mall employees and seven candidates from the college who appear to be promising candidates. He immediately sets up phone meetings with all ten of them, and asks them each a series of questions designed to assess their knowledge of retail management and their customer service orientation. He then evaluates their answers and invites five of them to take a written test that assesses their management skills and intellectual curiosity (which the company has identified as being related to better customer interactions, service performance, and continuous learning on the job). The five applicants who are not being considered further are sent a letter thanking them for their interest in the position and explaining that they are not being considered further.

During the testing phase, the five candidates are given instructions and asked to perform several timed tasks using the Internet. Mike then shows them around the company's regional headquarters and answers their questions about the company and the job opportunity. He schedules the three top scorers to meet with Amy at the store, and calls the other two to let them know that they are no longer being considered for the position.

Amy goes online to the company's hiring resource center and downloads a series of questions the company has developed to assess the competencies needed for the job and some questions the company uses to assess customer service skills. She completes the brief online training refresher module on conducting and scoring the interviews, and meets with the three candidates. She finds all three impressive but feels that Jose is most qualified for the position. After passing a drug test and background check as well as some additional screening, Jose accepts the job.

Before Jose works in the store, he reviews the company's policies online and receives a copy of the store's policy manual. He is introduced to the assistant managers at several other Soles locations, given their contact information, and encouraged to call them if he has any questions about the job. Amy meets with Jose to review the company's performance expectations and answer any questions he has. She also schedules him to work with her for a few shifts to help him quickly learn his new job.

Mike contacts the other two finalists to let them know that although they did not get the job, he feels that they would be very competitive for other assistant manager positions. He then asks if they would be interested in being considered for other job opportunities that come up in the next few months. Mike knows that the turnover of assistant managers is typically 20 percent a year. Consequently, he expects to have three more openings within a month or two. The two finalists say yes, giving Mike two very strong candidates for his next openings.

Mike then ensures that the data on each of the job applicants is successfully entered into Soles's staffing evaluation database, including the recruiting source that produced them, and whether they were hired or not. He knows that this will be useful for future recruiting purposes.

Which company is likely to perform better as a result of its staffing process? Good strategic staffing systems incorporate:

- longer-term planning,
- alignment with the firm's business strategy,
- alignment with the other areas of human resources,
- alignment with the labor market,
- targeted recruiting,
- sound candidate assessment on factors related to job success and longer-term potential, and
- the evaluation of staffing outcomes against preidentified goals.

Clearly, this better describes Soles's staffing process.

Both companies would say they engage in the staffing process as mapped in Figure 1–1. Both planned, decided where to advertise the job opening, recruited applicants, and selected who should receive a job offer, but clearly they did so in very different ways. Mike's decision to seek out local college students was aligned with his need to hire people with fashion knowledge and a willingness to learn, and who likely have retail experience. Getting back to rejected applicants to let them know that they are no longer being considered helps keep them feeling positive about the company so they will be willing to shop at Soles and apply for jobs with it again in the future.

Figure 1–1 illustrates the general staffing process and identifies whether the applicant, human resource department, or hiring manager is responsible for each stage. The staffing process begins when a hiring manager determines there is a need for a position, which could be due to turnover or the creation of a new job. If necessary, the human resource department conducts a job analysis, and the hiring manager gets a job requisition approved that authorizes him or her to fill the position. Human resource personnel then recruit appropriate applicants and advertise the job opportunity. Applicants apply for the job, and the human resource department screens them to identify those to consider further. By further assessing the remaining candidates, the department screens out applicants who are a poor fit for the job and identifies the finalists for the position. The hiring manager subsequently interviews them and determines who should receive a job offer. The firm then makes a job offer contingent upon the candidate passing any background check, drug test, or other tests. If the candidate chosen turns down the offer, another candidate receives a contingent job offer until someone is hired. The organization begins socializing the new employee to familiarize him or her with the job and the organization and to help the new employee become productive as quickly as possible.

Companies also differ in how proactively they manage their existing workforce. Software company SAS developed an employee retention program that crunches data on the skills, profiles, studies, and friendships of employees who have quit in the past five years and then finds current employees with similar patterns. Another SAS program identifies the workers most likely to experience accidents.[12]

Our goal in this book is to help you understand how to design and better strategically execute the staffing process in ways that will lead to higher-quality staffing decisions and enhanced organizational performance. We will not only describe the strategic staffing process, but also discuss how to make it more effective in helping a firm meet its goals. When we use the term *staffing* in this book we are referring to *strategic staffing*.

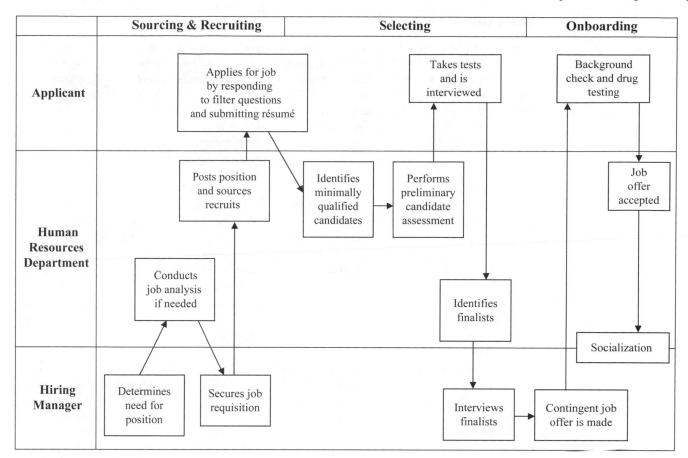

FIGURE 1–1   A Flowchart of the Staffing Process

THE COMPONENTS OF STRATEGIC STAFFING

There are seven staffing activities that, if done well strategically, create a staffing system that supports business strategy and organizational performance. The seven activities are planning, sourcing, recruiting, selecting, acquiring, deploying, and retaining talent. Table 1–1 summarizes how each of the seven is important strategically. We next discuss each of these seven activities in more detail.

TABLE 1–1	Seven Components of Strategic Staffing

1. *Workforce Planning:* strategically evaluating the company's current lines of business, new businesses it will be getting into, businesses it will be leaving, and the gaps between the current skills in the organization and the skills it will need to execute its business strategy
2. *Sourcing Talent:* locating qualified individuals and labor markets from which to recruit
3. *Recruiting Talent:* making decisions and engaging in practices that affect either the number or types of individuals willing to apply for and accept job offers
4. *Selecting Talent:* assessing job candidates and deciding who to hire
5. *Acquiring Talent:* putting together job offers that appeal to chosen candidates, and persuading job offer recipients to accept those job offers
6. *Deploying Talent:* assigning people to appropriate jobs and roles in the organization to best utilize their talents
7. *Retaining Talent:* keeping successful employees engaged and committed to the firm

Workforce Planning

workforce planning
the process of predicting an organization's future employment needs and the availability of current employees and external hires to meet those employment needs and execute the organization's business strategy

Workforce planning is the process of predicting an organization's future employment needs and assessing its current employees and the labor market to meet those needs. This means that the firm's managers and HR personnel have to evaluate the company's current lines of business, new businesses it will be getting into, lines of business it will be leaving, and the gaps that exist between the current skills of its workforce and the skills the workforce will need in the future. For example, if a manufacturing business is planning to expand, then it will likely need to hire more people in areas like sales and production. If the company is planning to automate some of its production activities, then it will likely need fewer employees, but the employees it already has may need new skills related to the new technologies.

Workforce planning usually involves the joint efforts of both the hiring manager and a staffing specialist. The staffing specialist looks at the organization's forecasted business activities and determines the *number and types of people* needed by the organization. The staffing specialist then uses the organization's business strategy to specify further the *competencies and talents* the organization will need to execute its business strategy. To plan for expected job openings, the staffing specialist assesses both the organization's current employees and the external labor market of potential new hires to gauge the availability of desired talent. The specialist then secures the resources needed to engage in an appropriate staffing effort. After working with the hiring manager to identify the talent profiles most appropriate for an open position, the staffing specialist develops recruitment and selection strategies to obtain the desired talent.

Without first identifying the competencies and behaviors the firm needs to execute its business strategy, it is difficult, if not impossible, to develop effective recruiting, staffing, and retention plans to meet those needs. Identifying and securing necessary resources, delegating responsibilities, and creating a timeline are also important outcomes of the planning stage. Planning activities can be *short-term* and focus on an immediate hiring need, or *long-term* and focus on the organization's needs in the future. Workforce plans are more strategic if they better address both the firm's short- and long-term needs. The plans can also address how a firm will address demographic issues, such as an aging workforce and diversity issues.

Sourcing and Recruiting Talent

sourcing
locating qualified individuals and labor markets from which to recruit

Sourcing is a component of recruiting that focuses on locating qualified individuals and labor markets from which to recruit. For example, a sourcing specialist responsible for identifying potential applicants for pharmaceutical sales representative positions may learn that experienced nurses make excellent pharmaceutical salespeople because of their ability to communicate with physicians, and persuade them to prescribe the firm's drugs. The sourcing specialist then identifies where nurses can be found and how best to reach them, perhaps by targeting nursing publications for recruiting advertisements.

recruiting
all organizational practices and decisions that affect either the number or types of individuals willing to apply for and accept job offers

Recruiting refers to all organizational practices and decisions that affect either the number or types of individuals willing to apply for and accept job offers.[13] Recruiting is how firms of all sizes generate a sufficiently large group of applicants from which to select qualified individuals for available jobs.[14] Sourcing focuses on identifying desirable people and finding ways to reach them; recruiting converts these people into actual applicants. Many organizations consider sourcing to require different skills than recruiting. Consequently, they hire both sourcing specialists and recruiting specialists. Because people who don't apply can't be hired, sourcing and recruiting are critical to an effective staffing effort.

Recruiting practices include evaluating which recruiting sources generate greater proportions of high-performing employees who do well in their jobs[15] and improve the firm's performance.[16] A firm's recruiters, their behavior, the messages they send, and the sources from which they recruit affect whether people choose to become or remain applicants of the firm and accept its job offers.[17] The primary goal of recruiting is to get the right people interested in working for an organization or in a specific job, persuade them to apply for it, and then ultimately accept the job offer if it's extended.

If recruiting is done poorly, few people will apply for a job with the company, and more of those who do apply will drop out of the hiring process. In other words, organizations that disrespect job candidates or who fail to meet their information-gathering needs during the recruiting process will be less able to hire them. As a result, more of the company's job offers will be rejected, and the people who end up being hired might not be as committed to the job or the company as they would if a better recruiting job had been done. Moreover, applicants with a bad recruiting experience are likely to tell others about it, making it harder for the organization to recruit people in the future. Because they are unlikely to apply for future jobs with the company, the company is likely to lose the opportunity to hire unhappy job applicants for future jobs as well.

Both organizations and individuals use a screening process when forming an employment relationship. Applicants can select themselves out of consideration for a job at any time. It is thus important that recruitment activities continue during the candidate assessment and selection process to maintain candidates' interest in the job and organization.

Another component of recruiting is *employer branding*, or creating a favorable image in desired applicants' minds about the organization being a good place for them to work. For example, Royal Philips Electronics tells potential employees that the company gives them an opportunity to work in an environment where "you can touch lives every day."[18] When potential applicants are considering whether to apply to a particular organization, they evaluate factors including whether the organization is a place they would like to work. Because most applicants do not know very much about what different organizations are like as employers, many companies proactively craft employer brands for themselves through marketing and advertising. For example, Federated Department Stores created an employment brand and recruitment Web site called Retailology.com. Starbucks has employed a "Program Manager for Employer Branding," whose job it is to promote the coffee chain as a great place to work.

Selecting Talent

The **selection** process involves putting applicants through activities, such as skills tests and employment interviews to evaluate their capabilities and qualifications so that the organization can choose whom to hire. The methods an organization uses to assess and select job candidates will determine how well the firm's new hires, and thus the company as a whole, will perform.[19]

selection
assessing job candidates and deciding whom to hire

Of course, the effectiveness of the selection process depends in part on recruitment. If a recruiting effort generates 1,000 applicants but only a few of them are qualified, this bogs down the selection process.

Targeted recruiting practices that prescreen applicants can result in fewer but higher quality applicants than can general recruiting practices. For example, if a pharmaceutical sales position requires a certain amount of medical knowledge that nurses with certain credentials have, then the recruiting effort should prescreen applicants by locating nurses with the required credentials. Prescreening saves the organization both time and money because it does not have to sift through as many underqualified applicants during the selection process.

In contrast, if recruitment efforts fail to generate qualified applicants, then it is impossible for any selection system to identify them. It is not surprising that the effectiveness of various selection practices, such as interviews and skill testing, vary dramatically with a firm's recruitment practices.[20] Historically, organizations have tried to maximize the quality of their new hires by focusing on recruiting a large number of applicants, then relying on various applicant assessment methods to identify the highest quality candidates. However, it is important to note that there is no guarantee that the appropriate qualifications will be present in any applicant pool, regardless of its size.

The goal of strategic recruiting, therefore, is to attract a greater percentage of applicants who are likely to meet minimum hiring requirements and reduce the burden on the selection system. It is also very possible that the hiring gains will come with a reduced administrative burden and lower cost per hire, even if the initial cost of the recruiting system is higher.

When we examine staffing and retention from these perspectives, it is easy to see why many companies make the search for the right talent their top priority. As a manager of one high-technology company stated, "The quality of our talent is as important as our technologies. The quality of our talent is how we win in our business."[21] The same is true for most nontechnology-oriented businesses as well. Says Andy Spade, the cofounder of the fashion design company Kate Spade, "Your people are your product. They are the vehicle through which everything happens, and they define what you put out."[22]

Acquiring Talent

Acquiring talent involves putting together job offers that appeal to chosen candidates and persuading job offer recipients to accept those job offers. Although many job offers are presented on a take-it-or-leave-it basis, organizations sometimes *negotiate* job offer terms with the candidates they want to hire. Job offers can include salary, health care, retirement contributions, vacation time, relocation expenses, housing allowances, and other benefits. The *employment contract*, or written offer to the candidate, then formalizes the outcomes of the negotiations. In addition to specifying the job's compensation, such as salary, bonus, long-term accounting, and stock-based compensation, the employment contract addresses other aspects of the relationship between the employee and the firm—for example, retirement or severance payments, procedures governing conflict resolution, and restrictions on the employee's ability to engage in other activities, such as doing similar work for other firms.

Although the terms of an employment contract help to align a new hire's behavior with the firm's business strategy, many companies do not have comprehensive explicit (written) employment agreements or they have an explicit agreement that covers only limited aspects of their relationships. A case in point: At the beginning of 2000, less than half of S&P 500 firms had an explicit agreement with their CEOs.[23] In lieu of an explicit agreement, these firms and their CEOs rely on implicit contracts through which the CEO is employed "at will." We will discuss employment contracts in greater detail in Chapter 3.

Deploying Talent

deployment
assigning talent to appropriate jobs and roles in the organization

Deployment involves assigning talent to appropriate jobs and roles in the organization. The deployment of new talent and the redeployment of existing employees as needed are both relevant to optimally leveraging an organization's talent. For example, assigning a technically capable programmer who dislikes interacting with people to a sales position would be a talent deployment mistake.

Socialization is the process of familiarizing newly hired and promoted employees with their jobs, work groups, and the organization as a whole. It is an important step in terms of getting these people up to speed quickly.[24] Some organizations simply give new hires a manual of company policies and show them to their desks. Instead, it is critical to take the time to help them form appropriate expectations about the company's corporate culture, suggest ways for them to adjust and perform well in their new jobs, provide them with the emotional support they need to improve their satisfaction and job success, and increase their commitment to the firm.[25]

Over time, firms can develop employees' skills and capabilities, resulting in a broader set of deployment options. Through *succession management* and *career development*, employees can acquire new skills and be prepared to assume different and higher-level positions in the organization. Internal talent development sometimes enables faster transitions and higher performance than does external hiring because existing employees are familiar with the organization's culture, customers, and how employees get work done (i.e., they understand how the firm's internal systems work and the strengths and weaknesses of people in key positions).

Retaining Talent

Succession management and career development are also effective tools for retaining high-performing employees. It can be frustrating to locate and hire the right talent only to watch these people leave after a short time. Turnover is expensive, especially when it is the best performers who are leaving. Of course, the turnover of poor performers can be beneficial; however, the departure of key employees can be devastating. Losing excellent employees to a competitor is an even greater loss. Retaining successful employees also means that the organization spends less time and fewer resources filling job vacancies.

Matchmaking Process

Strategic staffing is a matchmaking process that involves much more than simply generating applications for an open position. Recruiting and selection are interdependent, two-way processes in which both employers and recruits try to look appealing to the other while learning as much as they can about their potential fit. Although applicants choose organizations as much as organizations choose applicants, too often organizations focus exclusively on selection at the expense of effective recruitment. Because applicants can drop out of the hiring process at any time, recruitment does not end when the employment application is submitted. The applicant is no longer a recruit only when either side is no longer interested in pursuing an employment relationship. Recruitment continues throughout the selection and acquisition process until the person is no longer a viable job candidate, or until a job offer is accepted and the person reports for work. Some firms even try to continuously "recruit" employees to maintain their attractiveness as an employer and enhance retention.

THE GOALS OF STRATEGIC STAFFING

Identifying Staffing Goals

Creating hiring goals that are clearly linked to organizational strategies and objectives guides the strategic staffing process. *Process goals* relate to the hiring process itself, including how many of what quality applicants apply, attracting appropriate numbers of diverse applicants, and meeting hiring timeline goals, such as completing interviews within two weeks and making job offers within one week of the final interview. *Outcome goals* apply to the product of the hiring effort and include the number and quality of people hired, the financial return on the staffing investment, and whether the staffing effort improved organizational effectiveness. Table 1–2 presents a sampling of the many possible staffing goals.

Not all these goals will be relevant in every hiring situation. Different goals are likely to take priority at different times. It is also common for staffing goals to conflict. For example, it can be challenging to hire top performers who will stay with the organization for many years while simultaneously filling jobs quickly and minimizing staffing costs.

Firms that do not staff strategically are often focused on goals such as the time it takes to fill an opening, the number of hires a recruiter produces in a period of time, and the cost per hire. Although these can be useful goals for improving the *efficiency* of the staffing process, they are

---

TABLE 1–2 Examples of Staffing Goals[26]

Process Goals
- Attracting sufficient numbers of appropriately qualified applicants
- Complying with the law and any organizational hiring policies
- Fulfilling any affirmative action obligations
- Meeting hiring timeline goals
- Staffing efficiently

Outcome Goals
- Hiring individuals who succeed in their jobs
- Hiring individuals who will eventually be promoted
- Reducing turnover rates among high performers
- Hiring individuals for whom the other human resource functions will have the desired impact (e.g., who will benefit from training, and who will be motivated by the firm's compensation package)
- Meeting stakeholder needs
- Maximizing the financial return on the organization's staffing investment
- Enhancing the diversity of the organization
- Enabling organizational flexibility
- Enhancing the business's strategy execution

not necessarily aligned with improving the *strategic performance* of the staffing system. For example, if executing the firm's strategy requires hiring top-tier talent, the company's recruiting goals should emphasize the quality of applicants versus hiring speed. For some positions, hiring top talent that will stay with the organization for a long time might be critical (perhaps if the positions are in management, long-term research and development projects, or sales). There may be other positions for which average talent and moderate turnover is acceptable (perhaps administrative positions).

The key objectives of the staffing effort[27] can change over time and be different for different positions, too. Because, over time, jobs change and different technologies emerge, the people best able to do a job as it exists today may be less able to do the job in a few years. And because different organizations pursue different business strategies, each organization's staffing goals are likely to be different as well. Furthermore, differences usually exist in a single organization's staffing goals across positions and over time because positions change, and different positions require different talents.

Each organization needs to identify what its staffing goals are for any position, recognizing that its goals may change over time as the organization changes its strategy or faces changes in its labor or product markets. These goals should be based on the priorities of the organization as well as the needs of the hiring managers. Table 1–3 contains some key questions managers and human resource personnel need to ask themselves before setting strategic staffing goals.

Believe it or not, planning the "churn" of employees can also be an organizational goal. In some cases, particularly when technology is changing rapidly, organizations prefer a steady supply of new hires whose skills are as current as possible rather than continually retraining their existing employees. If the skill sets of employees who have been with the company for several years become inferior to those of new hires, planning for regular churn is a better strategic choice. For example, a small software development firm that does not have a lot of money to invest in training might plan to replace most of its programmers every two to four years and offer two-year contracts to its workers. Other organizations, like SAS, the world's largest privately held software company, value long employee tenure with the company and prefer to invest in ongoing employee development. If building and maintaining customer relationships is important, if unique organizational knowledge is critical for getting the firm's work done, or if the company plans to develop its future leaders from within, then a more appropriate staffing goal may be a reduction in turnover.

The goals of the firm's staffing effort should also be consistent with the goals of the firm's other stakeholders, including the individual hiring managers to whom new hires will report. Each work group and supervisor differs with regard to the type of person wanted to fill a job. Identifying these differences is important. One of the key roles of the recruiter is to partner with hiring managers to assess their underlying needs in this regard. For example, if a firm's Web site development function is being outsourced, then hiring someone with Web site development skills might not be what the hiring manager really needs—even if an employee with these skills has left recently. As we have said, jobs change, and the talent mixes of work groups change. Because hiring managers don't always recognize changing talent needs or know what they need in a new hire, they should see recruiters as partners in this process.

The ultimate goal for a staffing system is to hire people who can perform well, contribute to the execution of the company's business strategy, and increase profits. Doing so as quickly as

---

TABLE 1–3	Questions to Ask When Setting Staffing Goals

- Is it more important to fill the position quickly or fill it with someone who closely matches a particular talent profile?
- What levels of which competencies, styles, values, and traits are really needed for job success and to execute the business strategy?
- What is the business's strategy and what types of people will it need 1, 5, and 10 years from now?
- What talents must new hires possess rather than be trained to develop?
- What are the organization's long-term talent needs? Is it important for the person hired to have the potential to assume leadership roles in the future?

possible and experiencing a good return on the time and resources invested in the staffing effort are also important. Staffing goals should be identified in the early stages of staffing planning, and the staffing system should be evaluated to ensure that it is meeting these goals. (Evaluating the staffing system is discussed in the next section.)

Many resources exist to help staffing professionals stay current and informed. This chapter's Develop Your Skills feature lists several Internet staffing resources.

Evaluating the Staffing System

Linking the goals of a staffing effort directly to the evaluation criteria the firm will use in assessing the staffing system is key to its success. For example, if filling positions quickly is an important goal, then the time it takes to fill each position should be tracked and evaluated for each recruiting source. However, it should be recognized that filling positions quickly may require the recruiter to make a trade-off against the quality of the talent pool that will be quickly accessible. If recruiting high-quality applicants is an important goal, then the quality of recruits from different recruiting sources should also be tracked and evaluated. Because a firm's staffing goals should be closely aligned with the organization's business strategy, it is important to evaluate the staffing system to be sure these goals are being met.

INTEGRATING THE FUNCTIONAL AREAS OF HUMAN RESOURCE MANAGEMENT

In addition to laying the foundation for a firm's strategic execution, staffing impacts the effectiveness of the other human resource management practices within the firm. Because the various functional areas of human resource management (e.g., staffing, training, performance management, and compensation) interact with each other,[28] getting enough people with the right qualifications and competencies to apply for jobs with the organization in the first place will impact these functions. That is, the firm's ability to train, motivate, and retain its employees will be affected. Therefore, it is critical for all human resource functional areas to be aligned with each other.[29]

When Robert Eckert became CEO of toy giant Mattel, he developed a staffing and workforce management strategy that supported the company's new strategic objectives of improving productivity, globalizing and extending the firm's brand name, and creating new brands. His goal was to change Mattel's culture to motivate employees to work together, give them more discipline, and improve their skills as well as their internal mobility and retention. Eckert did this by

---

DEVELOP YOUR SKILLS
Internet Staffing Resources

The Equal Employment Opportunity Commission (www.eeoc.gov)—provides information about the laws enforced by the EEOC and compliance guidance

Electronic Recruiting Exchange (www.ere.net)—has information and articles related to recruiting and employer branding

Hrmetrics.org (http://hrmetrics.org)—contains information about and examples of recruiting and staffing metrics

Human Resource Planning Society (http://hrps.com)—provides information, publications, and resources on staffing and talent management

*O*Net Center* (http://online.onetcenter.org)—a government site that provides labor and occupational market information useful for doing a job analysis

Recruiting.com (www.recruiting.com)—provides resources and information on recruiting and Internet recruiting

Corporate Executive Board's Recruiting Roundtable (www.recruitingroundtable.com)—provides information, best practices, tools, metrics, and networking for recruiting executives

Society for Human Resource Management (www.shrm.org)—provides articles and other resources on staffing including *Staffing Management* magazine articles

Staffing.org (www.staffing.org)—has information and resources about staffing processes, practices, tools, and metrics

Workforce Management (http://workforce.com)—contains articles and resources on staffing and legal issues pertaining to staffing

World at Work (www.worldatwork.org)—a not-for-profit professional association focusing on attracting, motivating, and retaining employees

creating employee development programs that would generate a more skilled and competitive workforce, establishing metrics to understand how the workforce was performing, and developing a systematic succession strategy that would enable the company to retain the valuable talent it developed.[30] "The institutionalization of people development is what I would love my legacy to be," Eckert says, "so that nobody necessarily remembers who I am, but that there is a people development machine that lives on forever."[31] Today, Mattel's staffing, performance measurement, and training programs support each other and reinforce the firm's corporate goals, too.

If even a single functional area reinforces goals that are different from the other functional areas, executing the company's strategy will be much more difficult. Let's now look at the other HR functions and how they are affected by the firm's staffing system.

Training

Strategic staffing ensures that new hires are ready and able to benefit from the organization's training and development programs. Training is often expensive; therefore, one of the first things to consider in terms of developing a staffing strategy is to decide whether new hires should already possess certain competencies at the time they are hired or whether the firm will help them develop those competencies via training. If the staffing function fails to hire candidates with appropriate qualifications, training them may be an organization's only option. Even if the firm chooses to train its new hires, they need to possess at least the minimum qualifications and motivation needed to succeed in the training or the effort is likely to be futile.[32] It is also important to identify how long employees tend to stay with the company. Training might not be the right choice if employees tend to leave the organization before it recoups the cost of training them. For example, some retailers have turnover rates approaching 200 percent. If a retailer wants to invest significant time and resources training its employees, it should focus on identifying and hiring employees who are likely to remain with the organization to recoup training investments.

Compensation

The level of pay an organization is willing and able to invest in salaries can both determine and be determined by its ability to hire people with the necessary qualifications. If an organization is willing to pay premium wages, its staffing effort can focus on identifying and attracting the most qualified candidates. If an organization would like to pay lower wages, but is unable to hire the candidates it would like at its preferred salary levels, then it may be forced to raise its salaries to be competitive in the labor market or to make investments in training and development. When the labor supply is tight, the firm might need to increase its salaries just to be able to hire candidates with minimum skill levels and qualifications. For example, professors in engineering and business are able to command higher wages in today's market because there is a shortage of people with the qualifications they have. If higher pay is not an option, recruiting from nontraditional sources might allow the organization to overcome its compensation challenges. For example, Marriott hotels created a six-week life and occupational skills training program to help it employ people on public assistance in its hotels and resorts.[33] If hiring from nontraditional labor pools is unsuccessful, automating the job, increasing the training the organization provides its employees, or reducing the required qualifications of new hires may be the only alternatives.

The success of incentive pay programs can also be influenced by hiring outcomes. An organization that wishes to motivate its employees to be more productive by using a pay-for-performance or merit pay system will not be able to fully leverage its programs if the skills of the workforce are lacking. Performance incentives are only effective if the individuals have the potential to perform well in the first place. Ensuring that new hires have the potential to succeed is one of the primary goals of staffing.

Consider an organization that has developed a comprehensive merit pay compensation system. The organization pays employees an above-market base salary, plus up to a 20 percent bonus if they meet or exceed their performance goals. But suppose the labor market is tight, so the organization hires several new employees who do not have the skills or experience to perform at the expected levels. In this case, their performance levels will not be consistent with their above-market base compensation. They also will earn no bonuses, which will tend to cause them to further underperform. To avoid this situation, organizations need to assess the availability of their sought-after competencies in the labor market and use recruitment and effective selection practices to ensure that new hires have the requisite skills, background, and motivation so the firm's compensation system works as it's intended. It should be noted, too, that paying top dollar to hire the highest quality candidates is not always the best strategy if the company doesn't really need top talent and average talent will do. In other words, sometimes the greater productivity of the most talented applicants is not enough to offset their higher salaries. For example, does every employee in a research unit really need a PhD?

Performance Management

Performance management involves setting goals, appraising and evaluating past and current performance, and providing suggestions for improvement. Without this information, employees will be unable to adjust their behavior. Staffing influences the effectiveness of a performance management system by providing the raw talent that the system will manage. Even the best performance management system cannot replace important capabilities that employees must have to do their jobs well.

Conversely, performance management systems affect a staffing system's effectiveness. Without performance goals, employees will not know what aspects of their jobs to focus on nor the performance levels expected of them. As a result, they will tend to underperform, and some will quit or need to be replaced, potentially bogging down the staffing system. Even if highly talented employees are hired, they won't perform at their best if they get no or inaccurate performance feedback. If they perceive that the feedback they've been given about their performance is unfair, they will not be motivated to contribute as much as they could.

Career Development and Succession Management

The future success of any organization depends on its next generation of leaders. An organization is likely to flounder and perhaps even go out of business if it is lacking qualified successors to manage the business after the inevitable departure of its current leaders. When Yahoo!'s chief technology officer Farzad Nazem announced that he was leaving the company, there was immediate investor concern that the company might not be able to retain key talent.[34] Citigroup directors didn't start identifying a possible new CEO until after CEO Charles Prince stepped down, leaving the company rudderless at a time when it had already fallen behind rivals and was facing huge mortgage-related losses.[35] Succession management and career development activities can help to ensure that an organization has people ready to assume leadership positions when they become available.

Staffing practices can influence and be influenced by an organization's career development activities and the career advancement opportunities that exist in the company. An organization unable to offer employees opportunities for challenging work and career advancement is likely to have a low job offer acceptance rate. In addition, high-potential new hires who do actually go to work for the company are likely to quit sooner as a result of their being overqualified and underchallenged. This might prompt staffing personnel to recruit less qualified individuals who are less likely to quit but who may also be lower performers. Obviously, this is an even larger problem if the people being hired for current jobs are intended to be the employees upon whom the firm focuses its succession efforts. So, if the firm's current hiring efforts fail to produce employees with the potential for promotion, the organization's future leadership capabilities are likely to be compromised. Thus, organizations that rely on internal recruiting and promoting as part of their succession plans need to consider the long-term potential of candidates they hire from outside of the firm as well as their ability to perform the jobs they're currently applying for.

THE ORGANIZATION OF THIS BOOK

This book is broken into four sections. Section 1, "The Staffing Context," contains Chapters 1 through 4. In Chapter 2, "Business and Staffing Strategies," we discuss how the organization's business strategy and competitive advantage influence the organization's human resource strategy and staffing strategy. We next discuss how to design a firm's staffing strategy to reinforce its business strategy. Chapter 3, "The Legal Context," describes the legal environment in which staffing must operate. Laws and regulations play an important role in determining how an organization recruits, hires, promotes, and terminates employees. Barriers to legally defensible recruiting and hiring are also discussed. Chapter 4, "Strategic Job Analysis and Competency Modeling," covers job analysis, job rewards analysis, and competency modeling. To identify the best person to hire, the job and its role in the execution of the business strategy must first be understood.

Section 2, "Planning, Sourcing, and Recruiting," explains how job applicants are identified, attracted, and recruited. Planning is the first step in the strategic staffing process. It involves estimating the numbers and types of employees the company will need based on its strategy, what the hiring timeline is, and what the firm's staffing budget will allow. Because people who never apply for a position cannot become employees, sourcing and recruiting qualified and interested applicants are the next critical steps in the strategic staffing process. Chapter 5, "Forecasting and Planning," describes how organizations translate business forecasts into future labor demand estimates. Labor supply forecasts are then compared with labor demand estimates to identify where the organization needs to focus attention to ensure it has the right talent in the right place at the right time. Techniques for forecasting labor supply and labor demand are presented. We also discuss issues regarding the planning of a recruiting and hiring initiative. Chapter 6, "Sourcing: Identifying Recruits," discusses applicant sourcing, or the identification and targeting of recruits. Chapter 7, "Recruiting," focuses on getting the people identified through sourcing to apply to the organization and accept job offers if extended.

Section 3, "Selecting," covers the assessment of job candidates and the evaluation of their fit with the job and organization. Chapter 8, "Measurement," describes some of the issues regarding candidate assessment. We present basic staffing-related statistical concepts in an easy-to-understand way. Chapter 9, "Assessing External Candidates," discusses methods of assessing the qualifications of people who do not currently work for the company. Chapter 10, "Assessing Internal Candidates," covers the methods used to assess the qualifications of current employees being considered for other positions in the firm, including career planning and performance appraisal.

Strategic staffing involves the movement of employees into and through an organization. Section 4, "Managing the Staffing System," covers choosing whom to hire, negotiating the employment contract, and socializing new employees. Chapter 11, "Choosing and Hiring Candidates," describes the process of deciding which job candidate(s) should receive job offers and subsequently negotiating those offers. Persuading job-offer recipients to join the company and negotiating hiring agreements with them is an important part of talent acquisition. If the right people apply to an organization but ultimately turn down job offers, the staffing effort cannot be considered effective. Chapter 12, "Managing Workforce Flow," covers socializing new hires, different causes and types of turnover, and methods of retaining valued talent. It also discusses terminations, downsizings, and layoffs. In Chapter 13, "Staffing System Evaluation and Technology," we describe the ways in which many organizations are leveraging technology to enhance their staffing systems, the importance of evaluating a staffing system's effectiveness, the staffing system evaluation process, and specific staffing system metrics.

IMPROVING STORE PERFORMANCE AT CARIBOU COFFEE[36]

Caribou Coffee wanted to know what accounted for the differences in average store performance for its district managers. It assumed that customer service had a lot to do with it, but wanted to objectively evaluate what its best performing district managers did so that it would know for sure and could use this information to improve the future staffing of its district manager positions.

Caribou discovered that its district managers' skills did vary. Some were really customer focused, as it expected. But the sales figures of those stores were not always the best. Caribou discovered that the most important district manager competency was his or her ability to effectively staff the store manager position. When a district manager took the time to find the best replacement for a store manager instead of automatically promoting the shift supervisor with the most tenure, the results had a strong impact on revenue.

Caribou's ability to show its district managers concrete evidence that hiring the right store managers positively impacts sales has been critical in focusing district managers on the careful staffing of its store manager positions. Not only have sales increased in the previously underperforming stores, the district managers appreciated the information and assistance as well in improving their own performance.

Summary

Strategic staffing is a complex process of planning, acquiring, deploying, and retaining talent that enables the organization to meet its hiring objectives and to execute its business strategy. This process supports the movement of talent into, through, and out of the organization in a way that enables the organization to compete successfully in its marketplace. Because an organization's people are central to its development of a competitive advantage and the execution of its business strategy, strategic recruitment and staffing activities are a cornerstone of organizational effectiveness.

A strategic staffing effort focuses on first understanding the organization's mission and objectives as well as its business strategy. Subsequently, the nature and requirements of the job are identified and potential recruits who are likely to meet or exceed the minimum personal and technical requirements of the position are identified. Recruiting then focuses on attracting these people to apply, retaining qualified applicants in the candidate pool, and finally on enticing the chosen candidates to ultimately accept job offers. Efforts are then made to retain valuable employees. This type of strategic staffing effort is likely to produce a greater proportion of successful hires and a greater proportion of higher-performing employees as well.

Takeaway Points

1. Staffing is critical to an organization's performance because it is the means through which the firm acquires, deploys, and retains the talent needed to execute its business strategies and perform well. Staffing is the cornerstone of effective human resource management because it generates the talent that is supported and fostered by a company's other HR functions.
2. Strategic staffing is the process of staffing an organization in future-oriented, goal-directed ways that support the organization's business strategy and enhance its effectiveness. Strategic staffing moves people into, through, and out of the organization in ways that maximize the organization's performance and ability to compete. It requires long-term planning, as well as aligning the staffing function with the firm's business strategy and the other areas of HR. Strategic staffing involves assessing the labor market, targeting recruits, assessing candidates based on job-related success factors and the candidates' longer-term potential, and evaluating staffing outcomes against preidentified goals.
3. The seven components of strategic staffing are planning, sourcing, recruiting, selecting, acquiring, deploying, and retaining talent.
4. The ultimate goal for a staffing system is to hire people who can perform well and contribute to the execution of the company's business strategy. Doing so as quickly as possible and experiencing a good return on the time and resources invested in the staffing effort are also important. Other staffing goals might involve the quality of new hires, their retention rates, how quickly openings are filled, the company's return on the training new hires receive, and the promotion rates of new hires. Staffing goals should be identified in the early stages of staffing planning, and the staffing system should be evaluated to ensure that it is meeting these goals.
5. Staffing both influences and is affected by performance management, training, and compensation. Staffing practices can influence the options available to and the effectiveness of the rest of the human resource function. It is critical that the goals and practices of all of the human resource functional areas be in alignment with each other in support of the firm's human resource and business strategies.

Discussion Questions

1. Relate a hiring experience you have had as a job seeker to the process illustrated in Figure 1–1. What could the organization you applied to have done to improve your experience?
2. Assume that your organization wants to pursue a staffing strategy of acquiring the best talent possible. Give an example of how the firm's ability to provide only average pay can affect the success of this staffing strategy.
3. Why is staffing so important to store performance as discussed in the chapter vignette?
4. Recruiting and selection are interdependent, two-way processes in which both employers and recruits try to look appealing to the other while learning as much as they can about their potential fit. Impression management is the process through which people and employers each try to control the impressions others form of them. How do applicants and employers try to look appealing to each other during the staffing process?
5. If your CEO asked you why she should invest more money in the organization's staffing systems, what would you tell her?

Exercises

1. *Strategy Exercise:* Working alone for five minutes, take notes about how you might design a staffing flowchart for your own job. If you have no work experience, choose a job with which you are familiar. Next, form a group of three to four students, choose one of the jobs just identified by your group members, and design a staffing flowchart for it. Be prepared to share your ideas with the class.
2. *Opening Vignette Exercise:* This chapter's opening vignette described how Caribou Coffee discovered the importance of carefully staffing its store manager positions. Working in a group of three to five students, address the following questions. Feel free to use the Internet or other resources if you need additional information. Be prepared to share your ideas with the class.

a. Describe three staffing goals that would reinforce Caribou's desire to hire the best store managers.

b. How else can Caribou Coffee ensure that its staffing strategy for store managers is integrated with the firm's other HR functional areas?

3. *Develop Your Skills Exercise:*   Go to http://online.onetcenter.org and click on the "Skills Search" button. Identify the skills that you have and the skills that you plan to acquire in the next two years and click on the "Go" button. Next, choose one of the occupations that match the skills you identified. Scroll to the bottom of the summary report and identify a state in the "State and National" section. Click on the "Go" button and read the occupation profile. View the career video if one is provided. Write a one-page report describing how you think this resource could be used by staffing professionals.

CASE STUDY

Strategic Staffing at DSM

DSM is a diversified multinational manufacturing company that concentrates on nutrition and pharmaceutical ingredients, performance materials, and industrial chemicals. Headquartered in Heerlen, The Netherlands, DSM has approximately 22,000 employees located across 200 sites in more than 45 countries.[37] DSM's business strategy focuses on market-driven growth and innovation. The firm's goals include increasing its global presence, streamlining and standardizing its business processes, and improving its profitability.[38]

Supporting continuous learning, DSM maintains a formalized management development program.[39] The development program has also positively impacted productivity and retention. DSM Executive of Sourcing and Corporate Recruitment Bas van Buijtenen states, "Individual people are the key to the success of any organization, which is why DSM has a strong tradition in Management Development. Management Development starts with the recruitment process. We try to ensure that there is a good match between the candidate and the job, creating a solid foundation for [the person's] development opportunities and long-term career prospects."[40]

Because DSM needs entrepreneurial and flexible people, candidates that apply with the company must demonstrate leadership, entrepreneurship, and a results orientation. DSM Chairman Peter Elverding adds, "Investing in talent is crucial for DSM. Our increased global presence means we need to find world-class professionals and managers capable of leading us successfully into the future."[41]

DSM carefully aligned its selection and career development processes.[42] van Buijtenen states, "... We have a process that better matches candidates with jobs, creating a solid foundation for development opportunities and career prospects. We prescreen, assess, hire, deploy, and redeploy the candidates best suited for our culture and the needs of the open positions."[43]

QUESTIONS

1. How has DSM integrated its staffing function with employee training and development?

2. Do you agree with van Buijtenen's comment that "development starts with the staffing process?" Why or why not?

3. What would you suggest DSM do to further enhance the alignment between its staffing function and the other areas of HR?

Semester-Long Active Learning Project

This project will enhance your analytical skills and allow you to apply the concepts in this textbook to a real-world situation. Your project team will select an organization about which your team has some interest or knowledge and about which you can acquire additional information. The goal of your report is to align the staffing system for a key position in this organization with the organization's business strategy. Your team will analyze how effectively the target organization is staffing a key position and make recommendations for improvement. At the end of each chapter is an assignment requiring you to apply that chapter's material to your chosen job.

Your report should target the company's executive management team. Your job is to persuade them that your recommendations will lead to a positive return on investment (ROI) for the firm and better enable it to execute its business strategy. Assume that the team does not have a working knowledge of staffing terminology. As a result, you need to write your report so that a layperson can easily understand what you are communicating.

Your task the first week is to form teams of four to five students, exchange contact information, and brainstorm jobs that at least one team member has access to. It can be a job one of you currently holds or has held in the past, or a job a family member or friend has. Ideally, you will need about 30 minutes of time from a person who currently works or who has worked in the job and 30 minutes of his or her supervisor's time. If you cannot get the supervisor to participate, using one or two current or previous jobholders is acceptable. Before leaving class, you should identify at least two positions that your group would like to use for the project and choose one to pursue. Before the next class, you should confirm that you will have access to the job experts and solidify the job and organization your team will use for the project.

You will also need to identify realistic long-term and short-term process and outcome goals for your chosen position. Table 1–2 gives examples of both types of staffing goals, and Table 1–3 gives you some questions to consider in setting appropriate staffing goals.

Case Study Assignment: Chern's

See the appendix at the back of the book for this case study assignment.

Endnotes

1. Heide, C., and Sevy, B., "The Key to Competency Success at Caribou," *Talent Management Magazine*, March 2010: 38; "Caribou Coffee—Case Study," InterDyn BMI, 2010, http://www.interdynbmi.com/files/cariboucasestudy_000.pdf. Accessed April 7, 2010; "District Manager," Caribou Coffee, 2010, http://www.cariboucoffee.com/page/1/district-manager.jsp. Accessed April 7, 2010.

2. Terpstra, D. E., and Rozell, E. J., "The Relationship of Staffing Practices to Organizational Level Measures of Performance," *Personnel Psychology*, 46, 1 (1993): 27–48.

3. Donnelly, G., "Recruiting, Retention, and Returns," *CFO Magazine*, March 2002.

4. U.S. Census Bureau, *Statistics About Business Size (including Small Business) from the U.S. Census Bureau*, May 10, 2006, www.census.gov/cpcd/www/smallbus.html. Accessed March 15, 2007.

5. Bureau of Labor Statistics, *Employment Situation Summary*, March 9, 2007, www.bls.gov/news.release/empsit.nr0.htm. Accessed March 15, 2007.

6. U.S. Department of Labor Bureau of Labor Statistics, *Labor Force Statistics from the Current Population Survey*, March 15, 2007, www.bls.gov/webapps/legacy/cpsatab1.htm. Accessed March 15, 2007.

7. Ruiz, G., "Russell Tapped to Head Adecco General Staffing USA," Workforce.com, January 29, 2007. Accessed March 15, 2007.

8. *SHRM HR Glossary of Terms*, www.shrm.org. Accessed March 15, 2007.

9. Mucha, R. T., "The Art and Science of Talent Management," *Organization Development Journal,* 22, 4 (Winter 2004): 96–101.

10. Olian, J. D., and Rynes, S. L., "Organizational Staffing: Integrating Practice with Strategy," *Industrial Relations,* 23, 2 (Spring 1984): 170–183; Sonnenfeld, J. A., and Peiperl, M. A., "Staffing Policy as a Strategic Response: A Typology of Career Systems," *Academy of Management Review,* 13 (1988): 588–600; Sonnenfeld, J. A., "Career System Profiles and Strategic Staffing," In M. B. Arthur, D. T. Hall, and B. S. Lawrence (eds.), *Handbook of Career Theory*, Cambridge: Cambridge University Press, 1990.

11. Schneider, B., "Interactional Psychology and Organizational Behavior," In L. L. Cummings and B. M. Staw (eds.), *Research in Organizational Behavior*, Vol. V, Greenwich, CT: JAI Press, 1983, 1–31.

12. Baker, S, "Data Mining Moves to Human Resources," *BusinessWeek*, March 12, 2009, http://www.businessweek.com/magazine/content/09_12/b4124046224092.htm?campaign_id=rss_daily. Accessed April 6, 2010.

13. Rynes, S. L., "Recruitment, Job Choice, and Post-Hire Consequences," In M. D. Dunnette and L. M. Hough (eds.), *Handbook of Industrial and Organizational Psychology* (2nd ed.), Palo Alto, CA: Consulting Psychologists Press, 1991, 399–444.

14. Buford, J. A., Jr., Bedeian, A. G., and Lindner, J. R., *Management in Extension* (3rd ed.), Columbus: Ohio State University Extension, 1995.

15. Breaugh, J. A., "Relationships Between Recruiting Source and Employee Performance, Absenteeism, and Work Attitudes," *Academy of Management Journal,* 24 (1981): 142–147; Breaugh, J. A. and Mann, R. P., "Recruiting Source Effects: A Test of Two Alternative Explanations," *Journal of Occupational Psychology,* 57 (1984): 261–267; Kirnan, J. P., Farley, J. A., and Geisinger, K. E., "The Relationship Between Recruiting Source, Applicant Quality, and Hire Performance: An Analysis by Sex, Ethnicity, and Age," *Personnel Psychology,* 42 (1989): 293–308.

16. "Effective Recruiting Tied to Stronger Financial Performance," Watson Wyatt Worldwide, August 22, 2005, www.watsonwyatt.com/news/press.asp?id=15018. Accessed July 13, 2006.

17. Taylor, M. S., and Giannantonio, C. M., "Forming, Adapting, and Terminating the Employment Relationship: A Review of the Literature from Individual, Organizational, and Interactionist Perspectives," *Journal of Management,* 19, 2 (1993): 461–515; Bretz, R. D., Jr., and Judge, T., "The Role of Human Resource Systems in Job Applicant Decision Processes," *Journal of Management,* 20 (1994): 548–549.

18. Overman, S., "Show Off Your Brand," *Staffing Management,* 2 (April–June 2006): 2, http://www.shrm.org/Publications/StaffingManagementMagazine/EditorialContent/Pages/0604_cover.aspx. Accessed July 11, 2006.

19. Hunter, J. E., and Hunter, R. E., "Validity and Utility of Alternative Predictors of Job Performance," *Psychological Bulletin,* 96 (1984): 72–98.

20. Boudreau, J. W., and Rynes, S. L., "Role of Recruitment in Staffing Utility Analysis," *Journal of Applied Psychology*, 70, 2 (1985): 354–366.

21. Soper, N. A., *Recruitment & Retention Lessons from Industry and High Tech Organizations: Winning the War for Scientists and Engineers,* Air Force Research Laboratory, Space Vehicles Directorate, Kirtland Air Force Base, 2001.

22. "Andy Spade on Branding," *Fast Company*, March 2001: 46.

23. Gillan, S. L., Hartzell, J. C., and Parrino, R., "Explicit vs. Implicit Contracts: Evidence from CEO Employment Agreements," American Finance Association Meetings, Boston, March 30, 2006, http://wintersd.ba.ttu.edu/Seminar%20Papers/GHP_TT.pdf. Accessed June 21, 2006.

24. Wanous, J. P., *Organizational Entry: Recruiting, Selection, and Socialization of Newcomers* (2nd ed.), Reading, MA: Addison-Wesley, 1992.

25. Chao, G. T., O'Leary-Kelly, A. M., Wolf, S., Klein, H. J., and Gardner, P. D., "Organizational Socialization: Its Content and Consequences," *Journal of Applied Psychology*, 79, 5 (1994): 730–743; Wanous, J. P., and Colella, A., "Organizational Entry Research: Current Status and Future Directions," In G. R. Ferris and K. M. Rowland (eds.), *Research in Personnel and Human Resources Management* (7th ed.), Greenwich, CT: JAI Press, 1989, 59; Van Maanen, J., and Schein, E. H., "Toward a Theory of Organizational Socialization," In B. M. Staw (ed.), *Research in Organizational Behaviour*, Greenwich, CT: JAI Press, 1979, 209; Wanous, J. P., *Organizational Entry: Recruitment, Selection, Orientation, and Socialization of Newcomers* (2nd ed.), Reading, MA: Addison-Wesley, 1992.

26. Breaugh, J. A., *Recruitment: Science and Practice*, Boston, MA: PWS-Kent Publishing Company, 1992; Qualigence, "Recruiting Metrics—the Rules Have Changed," HR Management, 8, http://www.hrmreport.com/article/Recruiting-Metrics—the-Rules-Have-Changed/. Accessed September 17, 2010; Earle, D. "What's Your Revenue Per Hire? Staffing.org, October 28, 2009, http://www.staffing.org/library_ViewArticle.asp?ArticleID=471. Accessed September 17, 2010.

27. Rynes, S. L., and Barber, A. E., "Applicant Attraction Strategies: An Organizational Perspective," *Academy of Management Review,* 15 (1990): 286–310.

28. Lepak, D. P., Liao, H., Chung, Y., and Harden, E., "A Conceptual Review of Human Resource Management Systems in Strategic Human Resource Management Research," In J. Martocchio (ed.), *Research in Personnel and Human Resources Management*, Vol. 25, Stamford CT: JAI Press, 2006.

29. Baird, L., and Meshoulam, I., "Managing Two Fits of Strategic Human Resource Management," *Academy of Management Review,* 13 (1988): 116–128; Becker, B. E., Huselid, M. A., and Ulrich, D., *The HR Scorecard: Linking People, Strategy, and Performance*, Boston, MA: Harvard Business School Press, 2001.

30. Ruiz, G., "Shaking Up the Toy Shop," *Workforce Management*, June 26, 2006: 26–34, http://www.workforce.com/section/hr-management/feature/shaking-up-toy-shop/index.html.

31. Ruiz, G., "Shaking Up the Toy Shop."

32. Goldstein, I. L., and Ford, J. K., *Training in Organizations: Needs Assessment, Development, and Evaluation*, Belmont, CA: Wadsworth Thomson Learning, 2002.

33. CSRWire, "Marriott's Welfare-to-Work Program, Pathways to Independence, Reaches 10-year Milestone," December 18, 2000, www.csrwire.com/News/521.html. Accessed April 10, 2007.

34. Helft, M., "For Yahoo, An Ordeal Of Discord," *The New York Times*, June 12, 2007, http://query.nytimes.com/gst/fullpage.html?res=9C00E6D9173FF931A25755C0A9619C8B63. Accessed September 17, 2010.

35. Hymowitz, C., "Too Many Companies Lack Succession Plans, Wasting Time, Talent," *The Wall Street Journal Online*, November 26, 2007, http://online.wsj.com/article/SB119603502237903423.html. Accessed December 1, 2007.

36. Heide, C., and Sevy, B., "The Key to Competency Success at Caribou," *Talent Management Magazine*, March 2010: 38; "Caribou Coffee—Case Study," InterDyn BMI, 2010, http://www.interdynbmi.com/files/cariboucasestudy_000.pdf. Accessed April 7, 2010; "District Manager," Caribou Coffee, 2010, http://www.cariboucoffee.com/page/1/district-manager.jsp. Accessed April 7, 2010.

37. "Company Profile," DSM.com, www.dsm.com/en_US/html/about/company_profile_2006.htm. Accessed July 5, 2006.

38. "Vision and Strategy," DSM.com, www.dsm.com/en_US/html/about/vision_2010.htm. Accessed July 5, 2006.

39. "DSM Implements Taleo to Standardize Its Staffing Process & Effectively Manage Its Global Workforce," Taleo.com, www.taleo.com/customers/media/pdf/15_US-DSM-Case-Study.pdf. Accessed June 28, 2006.

40. "DSM Goes Live on Recruitsoft's Enterprise Staffing Management Solutions," Taleo.com, November 5, 2002, www.taleo.com/news/press-detail.php?id=76. Accessed July 5, 2006.

41. "DSM Implements Taleo to Standardize Its Staffing Process & Effectively Manage Its Global Workforce," http://www.taleo.com/customers/media/pdf/CS_US-DSM.pdf. Accessed July 5, 2006.

42. Ibid.

43. Ibid.

Business and Staffing Strategies

Outline

LEARNING OBJECTIVES

After studying this chapter, you should be able to:

- Explain how different staffing strategies support different business strategies.
- Describe the resource-based view of the firm and how staffing can contribute to a company's sustainable competitive advantage.
- Explain when an organization would use talent-oriented rather than job-oriented staffing.

- Describe human capital advantage and human process advantage and the differences between them.
- Describe the strategic staffing decisions any organization must make.

Starbucks's Staffing Strategy

Starbucks, the Seattle-based premium coffee company named after the first mate in Herman Melville's *Moby Dick,* has expanded from just 84 stores in 1990 to over 100 times that number today. Starbucks's ability to get high prices for its coffee drinks depends on the firm hiring the right employees able to provide high-quality customer service. A guiding principle in the company's mission statement is, "We always treat each other with respect and dignity."[1] Reflecting its focus on its employees, Starbucks refers to all employees as "partners." Starbucks even calls its human resource function "Partner Resources."[2]

Another guiding principle at Starbucks is to develop enthusiastically satisfied customers. More than coffee, Starbucks sells an experience—and that experience is completely dependent on the partners who greet and serve over 30 million customers around the world every day.[3] The challenge facing Starbucks as it pursues its aggressive global growth strategy is to find enough qualified and desirable candidates to increase its current workforce of over 85,000 partners over the coming years. Because Starbucks depends on the skills and personalities of its people, it is a daunting challenge for it to continue to successfully recruit and staff its global workforce. As Jim Donald, Starbucks's president, states, "My biggest fear isn't the competition, although I respect it. It's having a robust pipeline of people to open and manage the stores who will also be able to take their next steps with the company."[4]

How can Starbucks use staffing to pursue its growth strategy and maintain its competitive advantage? What kind of staffing strategy would you recommend Starbucks pursue to help it continue to hire the right people? After reading this chapter, you should have some good ideas to share with Starbucks.

Why does one company succeed and another company fail? Most people believe a company must focus on its strategic, financial, and technological capabilities to compete successfully. We now know that these important capabilities must be supplemented with organizational capabilities generated by attracting, retaining, motivating, and developing talented employees. Therefore, staffing plays a central role in creating and enhancing any organization's competitive advantage. As Steve Ballmer, the CEO of Microsoft, said, "You may have a technology or a product that gives you an edge, but your people determine whether you develop the next winning technology or product."[5]

Organizations that pursue different competitive strategies require different staffing strategies to execute them. For example, companies like Procter & Gamble, which must continually introduce new and improved products like multiblade razors and tooth-whitening toothpaste to stay competitive, need to foster creativity and risk taking among certain employees. By contrast, companies that focus on delivering the best quality or value to customers need to focus more on operations and improving their work processes to reduce costs and improve product quality. These companies are more likely to need team players who are trainable and able to follow standardized procedures.

Acquiring, developing, and retaining the right talent helps businesses create the organizational capability and intellectual capital driving their strategy execution. This potential is well known by companies such as Time, Inc., the world's largest magazine publisher. Kerry Bessey, Time's senior vice president of human resources (HR), states, "HR's mission is building capability for Time's business. . . . Our executives view us as management partners because we recognize this business is about talent—it's what drives the quality of products that connect to readers."[6]

This chapter first describes the resource-based view of the firm and then explains how the business strategy and competitive advantage of a firm affect its staffing needs. We describe what we mean by an organization's "talent philosophy" and discuss how talent philosophies influence human resource strategy and staffing strategy. We also discuss nine strategic staffing decisions all firms must make. After reading this chapter, you should understand the role staffing plays in terms of creating and sustaining a competitive advantage for the firm as it attempts to execute different types of business strategies.

A RESOURCE-BASED VIEW OF THE FIRM

Most organizations recognize that a large budget and state-of-the-art facilities do not guarantee success. Success really depends on employees' motivations, competencies, and skills. The resource-based view of the firm describes how employees' motivations, competencies, and skills can help it create a sustained competitive advantage.

What Is the Resource-Based View of the Firm?

The **resource-based view of the firm** proposes that a company's resources and competencies can produce a sustained competitive advantage by creating value for customers by lowering costs, providing something of unique value, or some combination of the two.[7] To create value, the hiring programs, policies, and practices of an organization must either lower the costs of the organization's products or services, enhance the differentiation of the organization's products or services in the eyes of customers, or both. To the extent that staffing influences who has the opportunity and desire to pursue an employment relationship with the organization, staffing serves as a "gatekeeper" by influencing the level and composition of an organization's talent. In short, the resource-based view of the firm focuses attention on the quality of the skills of a company's workforce at various levels, and on the quality of the motivational climate created by management.[8]

resource-based view of the firm
proposes that a company's resources and competencies can produce a sustained competitive advantage by creating value for customers by lowering costs, providing something of unique value, or some combination of the two

Requirements of a Competitive Advantage

Jay Barney, a professor and business strategy expert, has identified the five criteria (shown in Table 2–1) that a resource must meet to provide an organization with a sustainable competitive advantage.[9] Research shows that resources such as a firm's employees meet the criteria when they add value to the firm, are rare, cannot be imitated, and cannot easily be substituted with other things. The company must also be organized in a way that enables the resource to be exploited.[10] Companies cannot necessarily replicate another firm's capabilities just by imitating the competitor's human resource practices. Thus, good human resource management is valued not only for its ability to *implement* a given competitive strategy but also for its ability to *generate* strategic capabilities for the firm.[11]

THE RESOURCE MUST BE VALUABLE   Staffing activities can create value for a firm in that they can help it to exploit opportunities and/or neutralize threats. The return on staffing investments and the retention and performance of employees can be increased by rigorously evaluating the effectiveness of various staffing practices and targeting staffing activities to identify and attract the best types of applicants for the organization's needs. Providing applicants with realistic information about the job and organization can also help reduce employee turnover, cut overall labor costs, and improve the firm's productivity.[12] Hiring people who do a better job for the same pay is also a way that staffing investments can create value.

The potential of strategic staffing to create value and a sustainable competitive advantage for an organization has been recognized by investors as well. An Ernst & Young study found that institutional investors' decisions to buy a company's stock are based in part on the company's ability to attract talent. Because the quality of a company's staffing practices can differentiate it to investors,[13] staffing appears to meet the value requirement of creating a competitive advantage.

TABLE 2–1	Requirements a Resource Must Meet to Give a Firm a Competitive Advantage

1. The resource must be *valuable* to the firm by exploiting opportunities and/or neutralizing threats in an organization's environment.
2. The resource must be *rare* among the company's current and future competition.
3. The resource must *not be easily imitated* by other firms.
4. The resource must *not be easily substituted or replaced with another resource*.
5. The company *must be organized to be able to exploit the resource*.

THE RESOURCE MUST BE RARE   Value creation alone is not enough to produce a sustainable competitive advantage. For a company to outperform competitors, its staffing practices must also result in a set of workforce attributes that are rare. The ability to identify and attract rare talent varies across organizations. For example, some organizations, such as Google and the warehouse club Costco, are able to hire and retain the best talent at a greater rate than their competitors. Strategic staffing practices are what allow firms such as these to meet the rarity requirement for gaining a competitive advantage.[14] They have the potential to create organizations that are more intelligent and flexible than their competitors, and that exhibit superior levels of cooperation and performance as well.[15]

THE RESOURCE MUST NOT BE EASILY IMITATED   If an organization's strategic staffing practices can be easily copied by a competitor, the organization's resulting talent will not be distinct from the talent of its competitors. But the fact is that this is not always easy to do. A firm's staffing competencies are, in part, determined by the unique, or rare, talent attributes available in the labor market and the firm's ability to identify staffing practices that contribute to the acquisition of this talent. However, the competencies are also due, in part, to the company's deeply ingrained social relationships and its recruiting networks (such as the relationship it has with its employees, customers, and the community who can provide it with candidates) as well as its long-standing relationships with its talent sources, such as employment agencies, universities, and professional recruiters.

An organization's unique history and resulting reputation and culture can also influence competitors' abilities to copy an organization's staffing practices.[16] Imagine if an established company highly respected for its integrity and community philanthropy simply passed out business cards at a community function that read, "We're Hiring!" and provided an Internet address for people to go to for further information. The organization is likely to receive a more favorable response to such a recruiting initiative than would a start-up company with little visibility and no reputation. In other words, companies that try the same staffing initiative may not experience the same response. To the extent that many interrelated factors contribute to the success of an organization's staffing effort, it will be difficult for a competitor to copy all of them exactly. Thus, staffing meets the inimitability requirement for providing a competitive advantage.

THE RESOURCE MUST NOT BE EASILY SUBSTITUTED   A staffing practice should have minimal substitutability. In other words, for it to provide a competitive advantage, there can be no good substitute for it.[17] If one company successfully recruits students via e-mail from a university known for its technological capabilities but a competitor can effectively reach the same students by handing out recruiting brochures to them on campus, then neither company will experience a staffing advantage relative to the other. Similarly, if a competitor can find a substitute for the type of talent another organization has acquired, neither organization will realize a competitive advantage. Technology is also unlikely to serve as a substitute for the talents employees contribute. Why? Because no machine can duplicate the intelligence, judgment, and innovation human beings are able to bring to their jobs. Thus, superior staffing meets the competitive advantage criteria of nonsubstitutability as well.[18]

THE COMPANY MUST BE ORGANIZED TO EXPLOIT THE RESOURCE   For talent to be a source of a sustained competitive advantage, a company must be organized to take full advantage of the value-creating, rare, and inimitable talent it employs.[19] For example, if a firm's human resource activities—its recruitment, selection, compensation, and training systems—are disorganized or inconsistent with one another, the firm won't be able to fully leverage its talent. To illustrate, suppose an organization is able to recruit and select the top candidates it is pursuing but can offer them only a below-market rate of pay. If this is the case, it is unlikely the firm will be able to hire or retain them despite the success of its recruiting and selection functions. Likewise, if an organization successfully hires lower-skilled people with the intention of training them in the necessary job skills but the training program is poor, the organization won't be fully able to capitalize on its effective staffing system. This is why a firm's staffing practices have to be integrated with the company's human resource and other functions as well as be consistent with its policies and practices.

THE FIRM'S BUSINESS STRATEGY

A company's **business strategy** defines how the firm will compete in its marketplace.[20] The strategy should reflect what the organization's customers want, what the firm wants, and what the firm can cost-effectively deliver. Business strategies are likely to differ across multiple business units in a diversified corporation. Procter & Gamble, IBM, and General Electric take different strategic approaches to ensure the success of their various business lines. This involves making different choices about which products and services to offer, and which strategies to pursue to gain a competitive advantage. Both, of course, will hinge on a company's capabilities, strengths, and weaknesses in relation to its competitors. In other words, for a company to execute its business strategy, not only must its human resource management policies and practices fit with its strategy, but also its business strategy must square with the firm's competitive environment and the immediate business conditions it faces.[21]

> **business strategy**
> *how a company will compete in its marketplace*

Because it is an organization's *people* who are responsible for gaining and keeping a competitive advantage, hiring and retaining the right people are critical to business strategy execution. Researchers Michael Treacy and Fred Wiersma have identified many sources of competitive advantage, including having the best-made or cheapest product, providing the best level of customer service, being more convenient to buy from, having shorter product development times, and having a well-known brand name.[22] Warehouse retailer Costco's strong and loyal customer base, access to a broad range of high-quality products for a low price, and committed employees give it a competitive advantage over smaller and lesser-known retailers. Although Costco pays its employees substantially more than its closest competitor, Sam's Club, it has similar financial returns on its labor costs due to lower turnover and higher levels of employee productivity.[23] This, in turn, results in a better-qualified workforce and a higher-quality customer experience. According to management expert Michael Porter, to have a competitive advantage, a company must ultimately be able to give customers *superior value for their money* (a combination of quality, service, and acceptable price)—a better product that is worth a premium price or a good product at a lower price can both be a source of competitive advantage.[24] Table 2–2 lists some possible sources of competitive advantage.

Types of Business Strategies

A company can create value based on price, technological leadership, customer service, or some combination of these and other factors. Its business strategy not only involves the issue of how to compete but also encompasses:

- The strategies of different functional areas in the firm
- How changing industry conditions, such as deregulation, product market maturity, and changing customer demographics, will be addressed
- How the firm as a whole will address the range of strategic issues and choices it faces

Business strategies are partially planned and partially reactive to changing circumstances. A large number of possible strategies exist for any organization, and an organization may pursue different strategies in different business units. Companies may also pursue more than one strategy at a particular time. Porter proposes that a business can compete successfully by being

---

TABLE 2–2 Sources of a Competitive Advantage

Innovation: develop new products, services, and markets and improving current ones
Cost: be the lowest-cost provider
Service: provide the best customer support before, during, or after the sale
Quality: provide the highest-quality product or service
Branding: develop the most positive image
Distribution: dominate distribution channels to block competition
Speed: excel at getting your product or service to consumers quickly
Convenience: be the easiest for customers to do business with
First to market: introduce products and services before competitors

the cheapest producer, by making unique products valued by consumers, or by applying its expertise in a narrow market segment to meet that segment's particular product or service needs.[25] Companies can also make a strategic choice to grow the business. Next, we discuss each of these strategies and their implications for what is required of the staffing function.

cost-leadership strategy
be the lowest cost producer for a particular level of product quality

A COST-LEADERSHIP STRATEGY   Firms pursuing a **cost-leadership strategy** strive to be the lowest-cost producer in an industry for a particular level of product quality. These businesses are typically good at designing products that can be manufactured efficiently (e.g., designing products with a minimum number of parts needing assembly) and at engineering efficient manufacturing and distribution processes to keep production costs and customer prices low. Walmart is a good example of a firm pursuing a cost-leadership strategy.

operational excellence
maximizing the efficiency of the manufacturing or product development process to minimize costs

Because organizations pursuing a cost-leadership strategy focus on keeping costs and prices low, they try to develop a competitive advantage based on **operational excellence**. Employees in these firms need to identify and follow efficient processes and engage in continuous improvement practices. Manufacturing and transportation companies frequently adopt this approach. These organizations continually look for ways to reduce their costs and lower their prices while offering a desirable product that competes successfully with competitors' products. Dell Computers, FedEx, and Walmart are good examples of companies whose competitive advantage is based on operational excellence.

Most firms striving for operational excellence want trainable and flexible employees who are able to focus on shorter-term production objectives, avoid waste, and lower the company's production costs. As a result, hiring employees who have high salary expectations is not necessarily desirable.[26] Because organizations pursuing this strategy operate with tight margins and tend to rely more on work teams, it is not as helpful to pay the high price required to attract top talent. The return on this investment is not high enough, and the resulting pay disparity among employees can hinder their effective teamwork. Instead, the staffing goals for such an organization's core production workforce are likely to include hiring people who are adaptable, efficiency oriented, team oriented, trainable, and willing to follow standardized procedures.

differentiation strategy
developing a product or service that has unique characteristics valued by customers

A DIFFERENTIATION STRATEGY   When a firm pursues a **differentiation strategy** it attempts to develop products or services that have unique characteristics valued by customers—products and services for which the firm may be able to charge a premium price. The dimensions along which a firm can differentiate include the image of the firm's products (Rolex watches are an example), product durability (Carter's children's clothing), quality (Lexus automobiles), safety (the Volvo brand name), and usability (Apple Computers). As we mentioned earlier, companies can pursue more than one strategy at a time. Southwest Airlines is both a cost leader and a differentiator. In addition to being a low-cost, no-frills airline, Southwest Airlines differentiates itself from its competitors by creating an unconventional atmosphere for customers.

product innovation
developing new products or services

Organizations pursuing a differentiation strategy often try to develop a competitive advantage based on **product innovation**. This requires employees to continually develop new products and services to create an organization's advantage in the market. These companies create and maintain an environment that encourages employees to bring new ideas into the company. These companies then listen to and consider these ideas, however unconventional they might be. For these companies, the frequent introduction of new products is key to staying competitive. This strategy is common in technology and pharmaceutical companies. Johnson & Johnson, Nike, and 3M are good examples of organizations whose competitive advantage is based on product innovation.

Product innovators must protect their entrepreneurial corporate culture. To that end, they recruit, hire, and train employees to fit their innovative culture. That means that instead of selecting job candidates based only on their related experience, they also assess whether a candidate can work cooperatively in teams and whether she or he is open-minded and creative.[27] An organization with a product innovation competitive advantage would likely seek a core workforce of research and development employees who have an entrepreneurial mind-set, longer-term focus, high tolerance for ambiguity, and an interest in learning and discovery. Employees who need stability and predictability would not fit in as well. Individuals able to sift through large amounts of information to identify ideas that lead to new products or services would also be valuable to innovative companies. Firms pursuing a differentiation strategy based on innovation would likely make greater investments in their human resources and focus on hiring highly skilled workers for key research positions than would companies pursuing a cost-leadership strategy.[28]

Being first to market with the best new products is usually the highest priority of product innovators. As a result, cost is less of a barrier when it comes to acquiring top talent for the firm's key research and development positions. Individual contributions are important for this type of organization. Consequently, new hires who are motivated by pay-for-performance systems and who accept that pay disparities will exist among employees depending upon their contributions to new product development are likely to be good employees. Innovative organizations also need employees with a wider range of aptitudes and abilities than do organizations pursuing low-cost strategies in relatively stable markets.[29]

A SPECIALIZATION STRATEGY   Businesses pursuing a **specialization strategy** focus on a narrow market segment or niche—a single product, a particular end use, or buyers with special needs—and pursue either a differentiation or cost-leadership strategy within that market segment. Successful businesses following a specialist strategy know their market segment very well, and often enjoy a high degree of customer loyalty. This strategy can be successful if it results in either lower costs than competitors serving the same niche or an ability to offer customers something other competitors cannot, say, nonstandard products and parts, for example. Red Lobster and Starbucks are examples of companies pursuing a specialization strategy. Seiko is another example. It sells a variety of relatively inexpensive, but innovative, specialty watches with features including compasses and altimeters.

specialization strategy
focusing on a narrow market segment or niche and pursuing either a differentiation or cost-leadership strategy within that market segment

Organizations pursuing a specialization strategy often try to develop a competitive advantage based on **customer intimacy** and try to deliver unique and customizable products or services to meet their customers' needs and increase their loyalty. This approach involves dividing markets into segments or niches and then tailoring the company's offerings to meet the demands of those niches. Creating customer loyalty requires employees to have operational flexibility as well as detailed knowledge about what their customers want so they can respond quickly to meet their needs, from customizing products to fulfilling special requests. Consulting, retail, and banking organizations often pursue customer intimacy strategies. High-end retailer Nordstrom is known for the high-quality customer service it provides customers. Employees in primary contact with customers would likely receive particular staffing attention due to their key role in obtaining customer intimacy.

customer intimacy
delivering unique and customizable products or services that better meet customers' needs and increase customer loyalty

Most service-quality experts say that hiring is not only the first but also the most critical step in building a customer-oriented company.[30] Hiring active learners with good customer relations skills and emotional resilience under pressure would complement a firm's customer intimacy competitive advantage. It would also help ensure that the organization continually enhances its ability to deliver on promises to customers.[31] Employee cooperation and collaboration are important to developing customer intimacy, so firms pursuing this strategy should focus on identifying and attracting adaptable team players with good people skills.

Starbucks is an example of a firm that pursues this strategy. The company is able to command a high price for a cup of coffee because it focuses on its relationship with customers. But imagine if Starbucks replaced its workforce with cheaper labor, including people who don't enjoy interacting with customers or people or who have weak communication skills. Soon Starbucks's competitive advantage would begin to erode, and its brand would lose its luster. Quickly Starbucks would have to reduce the price of its coffee to keep customers coming back. Eventually, Starbucks could find itself pursuing a cost-leadership strategy rather than a specialization strategy because it failed to recruit and hire the right types of people.

A GROWTH STRATEGY   A **growth strategy** involves expanding the company to either increase the firm's sales or allow the company to achieve economies of scale. The success of a growth strategy depends on the firm's ability to find and retain the right number and types of employees to sustain its intended growth. The growth can be *organic*, happening as the organization expands from within by opening new factories or stores. If it is, it requires an investment in recruiting, selecting, and training the right people to expand the company's operations. This is what Starbucks has had to do as it regularly opens new stores.

growth strategy
a strategy to expand the company either organically or via acquisitions

Firms can also pursue growth strategies through *mergers and acquisitions*. Mergers and acquisitions have been a common way for organizations to achieve growth and expand internationally. In addition to expanding the organization's business, mergers and acquisitions can also be a way for an organization to acquire the quality and amount of talent it needs to execute its business strategy.

For example, an organization whose growth strategy requires it to hire thousands of additional experienced information technology consulting specialists may seek to acquire a company that already employs this talent. It is not unusual for organizations to acquire other companies solely for their talent and subsequently discontinue the business the acquired company was initially in. Employees in redundant positions or in jobs not needed by the merged organization are reassigned or let go and the targeted talent is incorporated into the acquiring company's ranks. Assuming the targeted talent stays with the merged organization, which is not guaranteed, this strategy can be effective in expanding an organization's talent base. It is important to consider the match between organizational cultures, values, talent philosophy, and human resource practices when using mergers and acquisitions as a way to implement a growth strategy. Mismatches between merged or acquired organizations can result in the loss of talented employees. Mergers and acquisitions often fail because of people issues rather than technical or financial issues. For example, a culture clash prevented the merged DaimlerChrysler from achieving the anticipated synergies.[32]

Table 2–3 illustrates the staffing implications of the different sources of competitive advantage.

TABLE 2–3 Staffing Implications of the Different Sources of Competitive Advantage		
Source of Competitive Advantage	**Description**	**Staffing Implications**
Operational Excellence (Low Cost)	• Focus is on the efficient production and delivery of products and/or services	• Efficiency focus
		• Adaptable
		• Trainable
	• Objective is to lead industry in both price and convenience	• Willing to follow standardized procedures
Product Leadership (Innovation)	• Provide a continuous stream of new cutting-edge products and services	• Top research talent
		• Entrepreneurial mind-set
		• Creativity
	• Objective is the fast commercialization of new ideas	• High tolerance for ambiguity
		• Interested in and motivated by learning and discovery
Customer Intimacy (Customization)	• Tailor and shape products and services to fit each customer's needs	• Adaptable
		• Learning oriented
	• Objective is long-term customer loyalty and long-term customer profitability	• Networking skills
		• Customer relations skills
		• Emotional resilience
Growth	• Expand the company to either increase the firm's sales or allow the company to achieve economies of scale	• Fit with company culture
		• Future oriented
		• Flexible (willing to assume multiple roles)
		• Willing to take controlled risks

Making Changes to the Firm's Business Strategy—and Staffing

Strategy implementation and strategic change require large-scale organizational changes, one of the largest of which may be the nature of the competencies, values, and experiences required of employees. Depending on the nature of a strategic change, some employees are likely to lack the willingness or even the ability to support the new strategy. Targeting the staffing effort to hire people who will be willing and able to implement a new strategy may help the strategy to take hold and ultimately influence its effectiveness.

Imagine an organization currently manufacturing semiconductor chips. The competitive environment is such that the organization must compete on cost. The organization is focused on operational efficiencies to control expenses, and tries to hire the best labor it can at the lowest wages possible. Its focus is on keeping hiring and training costs contained, and the organization promotes from within, when possible, to help achieve these goals. Now consider what would change if the organization identifies a better competitive position by specializing in designing new and innovative computer chips and outsourcing their production. The organization's recruiting focus would now be on identifying and attracting the best and brightest research and development talent to join the organization, and the cost of doing so would be less of a factor. External hires would be more prevalent despite their higher cost because the need for the top chip design skills would require the firm to invest in new, more expensive talent. The return on the larger staffing investment would be much greater than under the old low-cost producer strategy. Intel went through this type of transformation in the early 1970s when it moved from being a producer of semiconductor memory chips to programmable microprocessor chips.

Because staffing influences the skills, motivations, and interests of the organization's employees, unintended strategies may emerge in an organization as employees exercise their interests and skills. These emergent strategies can actually create new market opportunities for the firm and influence future business strategy. For example, an organization intending to become a leader in pharmaceutical drug research and development may alter its course toward genomics research because it finds that many of the scientists it has hired to do traditional research have skills and expertise in this area as well.

How the Organizational Life Cycle Affects Staffing

The *organizational and product life cycle* can also influence a firm's choice of strategy. As a firm or a particular product ages, it grows, matures, declines, and dies. A firm's strategies often change to adjust to the different stage in the life cycle. During the *introduction* stage when a company is forming, attracting top technical and professional talent is often a priority, often requiring the company to meet or exceed market compensation rates. Firms that lack the resources they need to attract the talent they require to get off the ground sometimes offer applicants ownership in the company (company stock, generally). During the *growth* stage, new companies or products must set themselves apart from competitors to gain customers and market share by pursuing innovation or differentiation strategies. Because they are less established and thus higher-risk employers, they often need to invest more money and resources in staffing to attract the talent they need to grow. They usually lack a large and strong internal talent pool, and they need to hire new employees externally as they grow. Because of their rapid growth, employees are likely to be promoted or transferred to other positions faster than during the other stages of an organization's life cycle.

During the *maturity* stage of the life cycle, the firm's products and services have fully evolved, and their market share has become established. The company's focus then shifts to maintaining or obtaining further market share via a cost-leadership strategy. Companies achieve this by streamlining operations and focusing on efficiency. Because mature companies have a larger pool of internal talent from which to draw, the talent focus becomes more internal during this stage, and promotion opportunities can decrease unless the turnover of lower performers is managed carefully. Many companies also restructure during their mature years, which requires employees to be more adaptable and mobile as the company's needs for workers and skills change.

Companies in *decline* are facing shrinking markets and weaker business performance. A company in decline can pursue a cost-leadership strategy and allow the decline to continue until the business is no longer profitable. Alternatively, it can try to make changes to revive its product or service. If it chooses to try to change its product or service, the firm typically adopts a specialization or differentiation strategy.

Up to this point, we have discussed how a firm's business strategy shapes its staffing needs and influences the characteristics it looks for in its new hires. A firm's human resource strategy and its talent philosophy influence a company's staffing strategy as well. We discuss this next.

THE FIRM'S TALENT PHILOSOPHY

talent philosophy
a system of beliefs about how a firm's employees should be treated

An organization's **talent philosophy** is a system of beliefs about how its employees should be treated. Typically shaped by its founders, it reflects how an organization thinks about its employees. For example, some organizations view employees as partners and key stakeholders in the company, whereas others view employees as more expendable and easily replaceable. A company's business strategy can also influence how a company interacts with its employees, which then affects how it decides to manage the movement of people into, through, and out of the company.

human resource strategy
the linkage of the entire human resource function with the company's business strategy

A firm's **human resource strategy** links the entire human resource function with the firm's business strategy. Strategic human resource management aligns a company's values and goals with the behaviors, values, and goals of employees as well as influences the substrategies of each of the firm's human resource functions, including its staffing, performance management, training, and compensation functions. The alignment of these separate functions creates an integrated human resource management system supporting the execution of the business strategy, guided by the talent philosophy of the organization.

staffing strategy
the constellation of priorities, policies, and behaviors used to manage the flow of talent into, through, and out of an organization over time

An organization's overall **staffing strategy** is the constellation of priorities, policies, and behaviors used to manage the flow of talent into, through, and out of an organization over time. An organization's talent strategy thus encompasses its approaches to acquiring, deploying, and retaining its talent, and the choice of jobs to which it devotes greater or lesser resources. A firm's staffing strategy ultimately reflects its business strategy, human resource strategy, and talent philosophy. We next look more closely at how a company's talent philosophy shapes its staffing strategy.

If not created intentionally, a firm's talent philosophy evolves on its own as the personal values of high-level managers are expressed in their hiring and talent management decisions and actions. Over time, these values and perspectives become those of the organization. Johnson & Johnson's articulates its talent philosophy as part of the company credo.[33]

The four core questions to answer in developing a talent philosophy are summarized in Table 2–4. We will discuss each of the questions next.

Filling Vacancies or Hiring for Long-Term Careers

An organization's talent philosophy can focus on a short- or long-term horizon. Some organizations fill open positions with people able to do the open job without also considering their likelihood of advancement. The only concern is getting a qualified person in the vacant job as soon as possible. Other organizations, including Nokia, believe in hiring people with the ability to both fill the vacant job successfully as well move into other positions in the organization over time.

If a company's talent philosophy is to hire employees for long-term careers, it should focus on hiring people with both the potential and the desire to eventually be promoted. This increases the likelihood that employees will be able to take advantage of the training and career advancement opportunities the organization makes available. Such a company should also invest more heavily in the staffing system for its entry-level positions, as this is also the source of the company's future

TABLE 2–4	Questions Addressed by an Organization's Talent Philosophy

1. Do we want people to contribute to the company over long-term careers or do we want to focus on filling vacancies in the short term?
2. Do we value the ideas and contributions of people with diverse ideas and perspectives?
3. Do we see our employees as assets to be managed or employees as investors who choose where to allocate their time and efforts?
4. What are our ethical principles when it comes to our employees?

leaders. P&G hires less than one-half of 1 percent of the 400,000 people who apply each year for its entry-level management positions, placing strong emphasis on candidates' values, empathy, and leadership and innovation skills.[34] The company's staffing investment is worth it as 95 percent of its talent starts at the entry level and progresses throughout the organization.[35]

If a company has high turnover, a better strategic choice might be to focus on filling vacancies quickly and hiring people who can hit the ground running. Why? Because any training costs are unlikely to be recovered if a new hire leaves quickly. If turnover is low and the company invests a lot of money and time developing employees, then the better strategic choice might be to hire employees for long-term careers. Similarly, if the company's business involves long-term projects, or higher-level managers need a substantial amount of knowledge about how the company works to be effective, then hiring employees for long-term careers makes sense.

The Firm's Commitment to Diversity

Another component of an organization's talent philosophy is its commitment to diversity. A firm can proactively recruit a diverse mix of people and strive to incorporate diversity into its workplace. Alternatively, the company can more passively let diversity "happen on its own" to the extent that it occurs. In light of the many laws and regulations we will cover in Chapter 3, actively managing diversity through staffing is usually the better strategic choice.

Diversity is important for more than legal reasons. Years of research have shown that well-managed, heterogeneous groups will generally outperform homogeneous groups in problem solving, innovation, and creative solution building, which are critical to business success in today's fast-paced global marketplace.[36] Organizations also benefit from diversity because their customers are diverse. In the United States today, African Americans, Hispanics, Asian Americans, and Native Americans have an estimated combined spending power of more than $1.3 trillion.[37] Diverse employees may also be better able to understand and negotiate with different suppliers and customers.

An organization's staffing strategy reflects its commitment to diversity. For example, 3M values diversity, innovation, and long-term commitment on the part of its employees. Consequently, it focuses on attracting and hiring intelligent and intellectually curious individuals. As stated on its Web site, "At 3M, our recruiting efforts are first and foremost dedicated to identifying talent. With that goal in mind, we look for individuals from all walks of life that share our commitment to innovation and excellence."[38]

An organization proactively seeking diversity is likely to establish relationships with recruiting sources of diverse people, and actively create a culture of inclusion. For example, the commitment the law firm Mintz Levin has made to diversity is reflected in how it recruits. In addition to hosting an Annual Mock Interview Workshop for minority law students, the firm regularly participates in minority job fairs. Mintz Levin attorneys also mentor women and minority law students by speaking at diversity and recruiting symposia.[39]

This chapter's Develop Your Skills feature will help you to assess your organization's climate for diversity.

Applicants and Employees as Either Assets or Investors

Another important way organizations differ in their talent philosophies is in viewing their job applicants and employees as either assets (i.e., "human capital") or as investors. If applicants and employees are thought of as *assets*, the staffing focus is on managing costs and controlling the asset (as is the case with managing other assets, such as land, equipment, or steel). As a result, the goal tends to focus on the acquisition and deployment of labor as cheaply and quickly as possible.

By contrast, if applicants and employees are thought of as *investors* rather than expenses, the focus is on establishing a mutually beneficial relationship in which employees are recognized as investing their resources (time, talents, energy, and so forth) in the organization in exchange for a return on that investment (a supportive culture, good pay and benefits, professional development, opportunities, and so on). Because talented employees (as investors) can choose not to invest in the company (by not applying for or accepting a job) or to discontinue their investment in the organization (by leaving) at any time, an organization with this philosophy does its best to be as attractive as possible to potential and current employees. When viewing applicants and employees as investors, the goal is to give them a return on their personal investment in the organization.

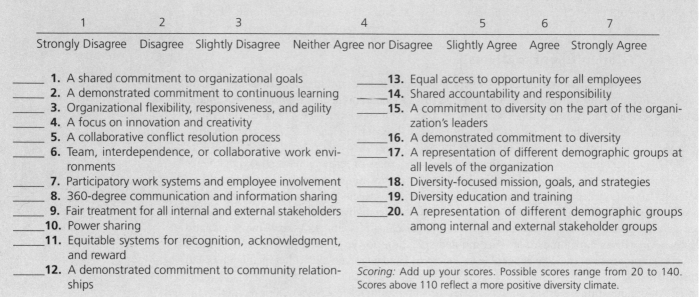

An organization's staffing strategy reflects whether it looks at its employees as assets or investors. Viewing employees as an asset to be managed generally leads to a low-cost approach to staffing. A dominant staffing goal of an organization such as this would be to acquire as quickly and cheaply as possible employees who can perform the duties of a job. Recruiting sources and selection methods requiring the firm to invest a large amount of time or money would be less likely to be used. Although an asset-based talent philosophy is unlikely to generate a high degree of employee commitment,[41] it can be an effective approach for organizations pursuing a low-cost strategy in which high levels of skill are not required, and high levels of turnover are not disruptive or prohibitively expensive.

By contrast, organizations that rely on the development of new products are likely to find that the commitment and efforts of its employees are key drivers of their success. Organizations such as Corning, Pfizer, Whirlpool, and Genentech, for example, may find themselves handicapped if they embrace an asset-based philosophy of talent. An asset-based philosophy will make it harder for them to attract top talent, retain good employees, and inspire their best performance.

The Firm's Commitment to Ethical Behavior

An organization's philosophy toward ethical issues including fairness, honesty, and integrity is reflected in its talent philosophy and staffing strategy as well. A firm with a talent philosophy focused on maintaining high ethical standards is more likely to explain to applicants its hiring process—that is, how the firm will make its hiring decision and the reasoning behind the assessment methods it uses to evaluate job candidates. Communications with candidates are likely to be more frequent, and delays minimized. By contrast, firms whose staffing philosophies are less focused on ethics will be more prone to emphasizing hiring expediency and low recruiting and staffing costs at the expense of building trust with its job applicants and employees. Johnson & Johnson is a company that applies its core ethical values to its staffing and other HR practices. The company respectfully and honestly explains its hiring process on its Web site, for example, and describes how it invests in the development and evaluation of its employees.[42]

Numerous government agencies, professional organizations, and societies have developed guidelines to help organizations establish good standards for staffing and address many of the ethical issues and the grey areas of the law related to it. Some of the best sources for staffing related standards and ethical guidelines include:

- *The American Psychological Association (APA).*
  - Publishes a document that describes test takers' rights and responsibilities. (Available online at www.apa.org/science/ttrr.html.)
  - Publishes the *Standards for Educational and Psychological Testing* (1999) along with the American Educational Research Association, American Psychological Association, and the National Council on Measurement in Education. (Available for purchase online at www.apa.org/science/standards.html.)
  - Publishes reports to address emerging staffing issues, such as the APA's position on good and ethical Internet testing practice[43] and test user qualifications.[44] (Many of these reports are free on the APA's Web site located at www.apa.org/science/testing.html.)
  - Publishes ethical guidelines to help staffing experts. (Available online at www.apa.org/ethics/code2002.html.)
- *The Society for Industrial and Organizational Psychology.*
  - Publishes *The Principles for the Validation and Use of Personnel Selection Procedures* (2003). (Available online at www.siop.org/_Principles/principlesdefault.aspx.)
  - Publishes a report on record keeping and defining job applicants.[45]
- *The Uniform Guidelines on Employee Selection Procedures* (1978)—although this publication doesn't cover Internet-related staffing issues, it provides a uniform set of legal standards governing the use of employee selection procedures and validation standards generally accepted by the psychological profession. (Available online at www.dol.gov/dol/allcfr/ESA/Title_41/Part_60-3/toc.htm.)
- *The Society for Human Resource Management (SHRM)* represents over 200,000 human resource practitioners. The organization provides numerous resources and publications on its Web site (www.shrm.org). SHRM's code of ethics for its members is also available online at www.shrm.org/ethics/code-of-ethics.asp.
- *Academy of Management*—founded in 1936, the organization is a leading professional association for scholars dedicated to creating and disseminating knowledge about management and organizations (www.aom.pace.edu). The code of ethics for members can be found at www.aomonline.org/aom.asp?id=14&page_id=235.

Table 2–5 offers some examples of how a firm's staffing strategy is influenced by its HR strategy and talent philosophy.

DERIVING THE FIRM'S STAFFING STRATEGY

Having an appropriate and high-potential strategy is useless unless it is executed properly. This usually poses the biggest strategic challenge for organizations. For example, when Lou Gerstner first became the CEO of IBM in 1993, employees resisted the changes he tried to implement. Gerstner found that his biggest challenge was not deciding which direction to take the company, but figuring out how to execute the strategy.[46] Staffing is a key step toward strategy execution.

Ultimately, a firm's business strategy depends on employees' willingness and ability to execute it. Leaders with a talent mind-set generally share Allied Signal CEO Larry Bossidy's conviction that "At the end of the day, we bet on people, not strategies."[47] Leaders like Bossidy believe that building their talent pool leads to a competitive advantage in and of itself. Therefore, it is an important part of their jobs.

An organization's staffing strategy should be derived from and be clearly supportive of its human resource strategy, which, as we have said, links the entire human resource function to the execution of the organization's overall business strategy.[48] It addresses the question, "how will the organization's talent acquisition and retention, training, compensation, and performance management functions contribute to the organization's competitive advantage and help it successfully compete."

TABLE 2–5	How a Firm's Talent Philosophy Affects Its Human Resource Strategy and Staffing Strategy	
Talent Philosophy	**Human Resource Strategy**	**Staffing Strategy**
Wants employees to contribute to the firm over long-term careers	Acquires, develops, and retains talent able to contribute to the firm over time	*Hiring*: Recruits and hires talent able to perform now and in future jobs
		Deploying: Uses succession planning, career planning, and career development to take advantage of employees' potential over time
		Retaining: Retains top performers and high-potential employees
Values the ideas and contributions of people with diverse ideas and perspectives	Acquires and retains a diverse workforce; creates and maintains a culture of inclusion and respect to leverage diversity	*Hiring*: Recruits and hires diverse people
		Deploying: Creates mentoring programs
		Retaining: Rewards and promotes diversity "champions"
Views applicants and employees as investors of their time and effort	Develops mutually beneficial relationships with its employees; respects applicants and employees	*Hiring*: Attracts and hires employees who fit the firm's culture and values; responds quickly to applicant inquiries
		Deploying: Puts employees in jobs that match their interests and abilities
		Retaining: Allows flexible work arrangements to meet employees' needs
Has high ethical standards regarding the treatment of its applicants and employees	Treats applicants and employees with fairness, honesty, and integrity	*Hiring*: Explains the hiring decision-making process and the uses of all assessment methods; hires based on merit; complies with laws
		Deploying: Gives honest performance feedback
		Retaining: Promotes based on merit

As we have noted, there are many ethical issues related to staffing that human resource professionals have to consider. We will continue to discuss them throughout the book.

For example, RMB Holdings is the holding company of some of South Africa's leading financial services companies. RMB's human resource strategy is to "recruit, build and retain the best people from South Africa's diverse population base. In particular, it seeks people with an entrepreneurial attitude and encourages an owner-manager culture. People are empowered, held accountable for their actions, and are rewarded appropriately."[49] Likewise, the human resource strategy for Metso, an organization whose core businesses are fiber and paper technology, rock and mineral processing, and automation and control technology, is reflected by the following:

The aim of Metso's human resource strategy is to ensure the availability of skilled and committed personnel needed by Metso's businesses and to develop such human resource policies that allow utilizing the intellectual capital in achieving common goals. The goals of the human resource strategy further involve directing the transformation in Metso towards a new type of knowledge environment, staying up-to-date with the surrounding world and anticipating changes affecting human resource policies.

The role of the human resource function is to safeguard the development of knowledge and competencies, as well as the development of leadership required for a motivating working atmosphere and the desired personnel structure. The tasks of the human resource function further involve providing support to networking and establishment of sustainable ways of operation. Moreover, we ensure for our part that Metso is an attractive and respected employer to both existing and future Metso professionals.[50]

The primary staffing strategies for both of these organizations are easily derived from their broader human resource strategies.

As we have explained, if a business wishes to pursue a low-cost strategy, it will need to focus on controlling labor costs, reducing expensive turnover, and hiring people willing to work for market or below market wages. Its training programs will likely be streamlined and focus narrowly on currently needed behaviors and skills. And rather than rewarding innovation, the company's performance management system is likely to reward performance. This, in turn, directly affects its recruiting and staffing functions. As we will cover extensively in Chapter 4, consistently doing a job analysis will translate every position in the organization into a set of employee competencies, styles, and traits to which applicants can be matched. The goal is to hire people who have the talents necessary to execute the business strategy. To do this managers need to determine: (1) the investment that needs to be made to staff each job; (2) whether to recruit people for only the present job opening or future, advanced openings; and (3) the skill levels needed by new hires. Identifying these and other goals establishes a critical link between the organization's business strategy and its HR (and staffing) function. At a minimum, an organization's business strategy is likely to influence (1) its talent philosophy, (2) the type of people the organization recruits, (3) the type of information communicated during the hiring process, (4) the type of recruiter used, and (5) the type of recruitment media used to publicize openings.[51]

Because staffing activities are not the only human resource activities an organization undertakes, it is also important that the strategies of each functional area of human resources complement each other as well as the organization's higher-level human resource strategy. For example, a staffing strategy of hiring people with the potential to fill higher-level positions over time would be unlikely to work without well-designed and implemented training and development systems. A broad understanding of the role of the organization's human resource systems and functions that support the business strategy guides the development of more specific strategies for each of the functional areas.

THE FIRM'S STRATEGIC STAFFING DECISIONS

As we have explained, a company's talent philosophy reflects how it thinks about its employees and influences its staffing strategy. Organizations have to make several decisions when it comes to developing and executing their staffing strategies. The nine decisions that influence a company's staffing strategy are summarized in Table 2–6 and will be discussed in greater detail next.

Should We Establish a Core or Flexible Workforce?

An organization's **core workforce** consists of people who are perceived by the organization to be regular employees who are central to what the organization does or produces. These workers are considered to be important, longer-term contributors to the company. Therefore, the company tries to retain them for longer periods.

core workforce
longer-term, regular employees

Flexible workers, or contingent workers, have less job security than the firm's core workforce. These people may be temporary, leased, part-time, or contract workers. Typically, they have a formal contract with the organization that specifies the nature of their relationship. When a firm's business slows down, flexible workers are usually let go before core workers. When the firm's business expands, flexible workers are added sometimes to the workforce before core workers are until it's clear the expansion will be permanent. In other words, a flexible

flexible workers
temporary, leased, part-time, or contract workers, or independent contractors employed for shorter periods by firms as needed

TABLE 2–6	Nine Elements of the Staffing Strategy

1. Do we want a core or flexible workforce?
2. Do we prefer to hire internally or externally?
3. Do we want to hire for or train and develop needed skills?
4. Do we want to replace or retain our talent?
5. What levels of which skills do we need where?
6. Will we staff proactively or reactively?
7. Which jobs should we focus on?
8. Is staffing treated as an investment or a cost?
9. Will staffing be centralized or decentralized?

workforce also allows a company to adjust quickly to volatile changes in demand for its products or services, thereby decreasing the likelihood it will have to lay off its core workforce when demand shifts again later.

Companies like Kelly Services, Accountemps, and Manpower provide temporary workers on an as-needed basis to help a firm adjust its workforce to its production needs. Eighty percent of employers use some form of nontraditional staffing arrangement, and many use more than one.[52] 3M uses a wide range of contingent workers to meet its varying workforce needs and to create a feeder pool for future hires.[53] Mail-order companies and shipping companies like UPS and FedEx regularly use temporary workers to ramp up for busy holiday periods.

Flexible arrangements can also be used to help meet a company's workforce needs. Flexible job arrangements that allow people to work outside of the traditional nine-to-five schedule include job sharing, allowing employees to work part-time or work from home, and taking extended periods of time off to, say, attend school or raise children. Some flexible workers would prefer to be core workers and have greater job stability—especially if their companies offer better health, retirement, and vacation benefits to core workers. Other flexible workers like the arrangement, believing it helps them better balance their work and nonwork responsibilities, such as school and family life. In fact, in recent surveys, the majority of working women say working part-time would be the ideal employment arrangement for them.[54] Moreover, some people would be unable to work at all if their schedules weren't flexible. Thus, having a flexible workforce can help an organization tap underutilized, high-quality talent.

Organizations need to determine which jobs are best for core and flexible workers, and the appropriate mix of each. Traditionally, firms have been more willing to allow flexible arrangements for employees in supporting functions than those in jobs more central to the organization's strategic execution. However, this may be changing—especially as employers search for talent worldwide in order to become more globally competitive. As one IBM executive said about his company's employees, who often work from home: "We don't care where and how you get your work done. We care that you get your work done."[55]

Should Our Talent Focus Be Internal or External?

internal talent focus
a preference for developing employees and promoting from within to fill job openings

external talent focus
a preference for filling jobs with new employees hired from outside the organization

One aspect of an organization's talent philosophy concerns its preference for developing, retaining, and promoting employees, which is an **internal talent focus**, versus hiring new employees for higher-level jobs, which is an **external talent focus**. Which is the better choice? The answer depends on the organization's business strategy; talent philosophy; the quality of its employee assessment, training, and development programs; and the quality and cost of talent available in the labor market. On the one hand, a video game producer might be constantly looking for new talent representative of its customers' current tastes. This type of company would be less focused on recruiting internally. Focusing on hiring people from outside the company would help it continually acquire fresh talent with skills in the most recent technologies and trends. On the other hand, a firm with a customer service strategy might need to retain long-term employees who have developed relationships with customers and understand how the company can best meet their needs. An external talent focus could undermine such a strategy. For example, if the firm always looked externally to fill advanced positions, it would likely lead to high turnover among its customer service representatives and hamper its ability to create and maintain quality relationships with its customers.

Indeed, some organizations focus solely on developing their own talent via succession planning and career development rather than hiring new employees for higher-level jobs. Nonetheless, both approaches can be effective depending on the organization's strategies and needs. Most companies use a mixed strategy that includes both internal and external hiring. Many companies consider internal candidates first. If they cannot find suitable internal candidates, then they look externally. Alternatively, a firm can conduct internal and external searches simultaneously, giving preference to internal candidates.

An internal talent focus requires hiring people with the capability to perform well in currently open positions, who have the capability to perform well in the organization's training and development programs, and who have the potential to assume leadership positions in the organization later. It also requires a firm to invest in training and employee development to ensure it has a sufficient pool of qualified internal job candidates available. An external talent focus often requires paying a premium to acquire talent with the existing skills and experience to perform well in the organization's currently open positions. If the firm cannot find appropriate talent outside the firm, it will have to develop and promote from within, find a way to substitute technology for the scarce skills, or do without those skills. Table 2–7 summarizes reasons organizations pursue each focus.

Should We Hire People with the Skills We Need or Train Them to Develop Those Skills?

Another strategic staffing decision is whether the organization prefers to hire people who already possess the desired skills and competencies or whether it is willing to hire people without those skills and train them instead. McDonald's founder Ray Kroc once said, "If we are going to go anywhere, we've got to have talent. And, I'm going to put my money in talent."[56]

TABLE 2–7	Internal and External Talent Focuses

Why organizations prefer to hire internally:
- Internal hiring sends employees the message that loyalty and good performance can be rewarded with a promotion, thereby enhancing their motivation and retention levels.
- One promotion could generate the opportunity for others to be promoted to fill the jobs left vacant.
- Greater information is known about candidates who already work for the organization, so a more accurate assessment about their fit with the job can be made.
- Internal hires are likely to get up to speed in their new jobs faster because they are already familiar with the organization.
- Jobs can be filled faster.
- The return on the company's investment in terms of training lower-level employees can be increased when more of them are ultimately promoted.
- The higher training and development expenses associated with internal hiring can be offset by lower turnover, recruiting, and hiring expenses.
- Smaller or lesser-known organizations sometimes have a more difficult time attracting external talent they desire.
- Organizations with a strong, positive organizational culture sometimes find that internal hires reinforce and strengthen their existing cultures more than external hires do.

Why organizations prefer to hire externally:
- The firm lacks qualified internal candidates.
- External hiring can enhance an organization's diversity.
- Focusing on external hires can increase the size and quality of the candidate pool.
- External hires can inject new ideas and perspectives into the organization.
- The firm's cost of developing and maintaining internal training and development programs is greater than its cost of hiring externally.
- Internal promotions can be disruptive because they lead to other open positions that must be filled (creating additional promotion opportunities can also be a desirable outcome as listed previously).
- Too much internal movement can create instability and cause delays in the completion of projects.

Supporting this philosophy, McDonald's created a worldwide management training center called Hamburger University, which has trained over 80,000 McDonald's managers since its founding in 1961.[57]

Companies unable to pay competitive wages and, therefore, attract skilled workers might find it necessary to hire people willing and able to learn the job and train them instead. For jobs that are unique to an organization, skilled workers may not exist, which would make it necessary to hire people and put them through a company-developed training program. If a company does not have an appropriate training budget or program, if there is no time to train new hires, or if the job needs to be filled immediately, the better decision would be to hire people already able to do the job who can hit the ground running.

Should Talent Be Replaced or Retained?

Organizations can choose to try to minimize their turnover or accept whatever turnover occurs and hire replacements as openings occur. The advantages of letting turnover occur include receiving a more frequent infusion of new ideas and talent, which can be useful for companies in fast-changing industries. For example, some biotechnology or computer software companies may find that their employees' talents are obsolete within a few years. Unless they are willing to invest in retraining their employees, it might be beneficial to encourage them to leave after a few years and replace them with new graduates trained in the latest technology. When there is an abundant supply of people with the qualifications a firm seeks, replacing employees might also be less expensive than retaining current employees for certain jobs. The advantages of retaining workers include a more loyal and committed workforce with a better understanding of the company's products, services, and processes, and decreased staffing costs. If a position is of particular importance to the running of the company, or if the talent needed by a particular position is difficult to find, focusing on retention can help to ensure that the position is rarely vacant.

Which Skills and What Level of Them Should We Seek?

One of the most critical staffing decisions concerns the types of skills a new hire should possess and the appropriate level of those skills. Although hiring managers often request "top talent," most jobs do not require top skills in all areas. Objectively analyzing the job to determine exactly what is required for an incumbent to perform well is key to making this determination. This process is called job analysis and is described in more detail in Chapter 4.

Some organizations' staffing goal is to hire only the highest-ability individuals. To do this, the organization must first be able to recruit high-ability individuals and then be able to identify and hire the highest-ability applicants. Because there is a limited number of high-ability people, for many organizations this is an extremely difficult goal. Although this approach can be very appropriate for some organizations, such as top consulting firms or other businesses relying on knowledge workers to create new products, for many organizations it is not the best approach.

It is often more strategic to try to identify attributes that are difficult to change through training, and that effectively differentiate among applicants, and to hire people who already possess them. For example, technology services company EDS has a saying that they "hire the traits and train the skills."[58] Indeed, in a rapidly changing business environment like the one firms face today, focusing on applicants' current skills is often insufficient. Employees need to also learn quickly, adapt to change, communicate effectively, and work well with others. Some jobs stay the same for long periods, and others change rapidly. Even clerical jobs, which we often don't think of as rapidly changing, went through a period of rapid change in the 1980s and 1990s, when computers and word processing became mainstream. During this time, for many organizations hiring an office assistant skilled only at manual typing would not have been as strategic as hiring an office assistant able to use both a typewriter and a computer.

Should We Pursue Proactive or Reactive Staffing?

proactive staffing
done before situations or issues arise
reactive staffing
done in response to situations or issues

Proactive staffing is done before situations or issues come up, rather than in response to them, as is the case with **reactive staffing**. An organization can staff its positions proactively or reactively in regard to diversity as well as talent quality. Proactive diversity decisions would include recruiting from sources known to be diverse, tracking the diversity of hires produced by each recruiting source, and constantly monitoring the firm's progress toward its diversity goals. This is generally better than making reactive staffing decisions following a specific event, such as being sued for hiring discrimination. Reactive organizations take a more "wait-and-see" approach to staffing, while proactive organizations try to identify practices or situations that could be problematic and work to improve them before they become problems.

Organizations typically recruit when they need to fill a specific job opening, which is **job-oriented staffing**. However, when labor markets are tight and good recruits are hard to find, organizations must pursue **talent-oriented staffing** and pursue scarce talent constantly—not just when a vacancy occurs. This alternative philosophy encourages people within the firm to identify where its future skill gaps are going to be well in advance of its actual needs. This way the firm can inject a continuous stream of talent into the staffing pipeline to ensure there are always qualified people in various stages of the hiring process. For example, in the last chapter, Mike, a human resource professional with Soles, kept two job finalists in the pipeline for future openings. Similarly, because of the nursing shortage in many areas of the country, some hospitals are partnering with local high schools to encourage students to go into nursing.

Some firms create unique, or *idiosyncratic,* jobs for people with talents the organization can put to use. Idiosyncratic jobs are created around a current or new employee's unique experience, knowledge, skills, interests, and abilities.[59] Rather than focusing on whether there is currently an opening before evaluating available talent, the person is hired and then a job is created to exploit the individual's strengths. For example, when someone steps down from a position in the White House, it is common for a consulting or lobbying firm to hire him or her in a "consulting" role to take advantage of their connections.

An additional advantage of a talent-oriented philosophy is that it can speed up the hiring process and decrease the amount of time jobs stay unfilled. With qualified job candidates already in the advanced stages of the hiring process, hiring will be faster when a position opens. Because more time is taken to generate qualified job candidates, a deeper pool of candidates is usually created as well. This approach to filling jobs can be a better strategic choice than the traditional approach of waiting for a position to open. In fact, at The Container Store, store managers are required to invest two to three hours per week interviewing job candidates. The idea is to help the company attain its goal of never having to place a job ad anywhere! Prescreened job candidates exist before the next job opening even occurs. By maintaining a roster of qualified candidates to call on, even when seasonal employees need to be hired, the home office's two-person recruiting staff does not need to get involved.[60]

Whether an organization's talent philosophy is talent oriented or job oriented influences its staffing strategy. A talent-oriented philosophy often requires organizations to recruit regionally or nationally, and to assess how candidates can meaningfully contribute to the company rather than evaluating candidates against predefined job requirements. A job-oriented philosophy has a better chance of attracting the active, local job seeker who is considering a job change or is currently unemployed than attracting top talent who could really add value to the organization but who perhaps are already employed or would have to relocate.[61]

Whether a firm's staffing is proactive or reactive will also depend on the degree to which staffing is considered an important contributor to the company's business strategy. If the firm develops its business strategy without considering the staffing issues related to it, the staffing is reactive. If the firm considers its staffing issues in conjunction with its business strategy, then the staffing decisions are proactive and strategic.

Which Jobs Should We Focus On?

Another aspect of a successful talent strategy involves identifying key jobs on which to focus additional attention and resources because of their importance to the company's performance and execution of its business strategy. Not all jobs warrant equal investment in recruitment or staffing activities. A company's key jobs are those that in some way create value for the organization by contributing to the generation or retention of clients' business or the creation of new capabilities or products for the organization. Whenever there is performance variability among people working in the same position, there is the potential to improve that position's contribution

job-oriented staffing
hiring to fill a specific job opening

talent-oriented staffing
recruiting and even hiring without a specific job opening

to the organization by raising the average performance level of those employees. For example, if some salespeople sell substantially more of a company's product than do others, staffing improvements may be identified that result in the hiring of a greater number of higher-performing salespeople and fewer lower-performing salespeople.

The company must identify which jobs and roles are critical to obtaining its competitive advantage. Focusing on better staffing the identified positions should help the company execute its business strategy and enhance its competitive advantage. If, for example, FedEx executives are asked which would have a greater impact on profitability, a 15 percent improvement in their pilots or a 15 percent improvement in their couriers, they will identify the couriers. This illustrates the fact that it is not necessarily the employees who are paid the most money who deserve the most attention—it is the employees who are a key component of value creation.[62]

Imagine a group of Dell Computer customer service representatives responsible for answering customers' questions about the company's products and solving product problems. This is a key position because the people in it are responsible for marketing the company's products and keeping customers satisfied with their purchases. Some of the customer service representatives are extremely effective at communicating with callers to understand their issues, and they provide clear and correct answers and solutions. Other customer service representatives are much less effective, taking much longer to understand callers' questions and problems, and sometimes providing them with incorrect or ineffective answers and solutions. Callers to these lower-performing customer service representatives are unhappy with the company's inability to address their needs and are less likely to buy the product again or recommend it to others than are callers speaking to the higher-performing representatives.

Because employees in this position create wealth for Dell by retaining its customers and selling them additional products, the staffing practices related to the job are worth investing in. If Dell can improve its staffing system to recruit and select better customer service representatives who will be more effective, the firm is even more likely to retain its customers, experience better word-of-mouth advertising, and generate additional business. If the average productivity of the customer service representatives also increases because of the new staffing system, fewer customer service representatives may be needed.

Is Staffing an Investment or a Cost?

It is common for an organization's average cost per hire to be many thousands of dollars. A study by a major human resource firm found that the average organization spent 41 days and $5,708 to fill an open position.[63] Staffing activities can be expensive. However, it's a mistake to view the expense purely as a cost to be minimized. The investments made in recruiting, staffing, and retaining employees can lead to financial returns in terms of higher performance and productivity for the firm, stronger future leaders, lower training costs, and lower recruiting and staffing expenditures due to fewer vacancies. Just as effective investments in marketing and advertising can lead to a larger and more profitable customer base, investments in sourcing and recruiting can generate a greater number of higher-quality job applicants who are interested in joining and contributing to the company.

If there can be meaningful performance differences among workers in the same job, staffing is a good investment. Consider the results of a study of Bell Labs's "star" performers: The study found that the "stars" were 8 times more productive than average computer programmers.[64] Even in jobs of medium complexity, top performers have been found to be 12 times more productive than lower performers, and 85 percent more productive than an average performer. In the most complex jobs—the jobs insurance salespeople and account managers hold, for example—a top performer is 127 percent more productive than an average performer.[65] These are not pie-in-the-sky numbers. Other research has shown that higher-quality employees can generate even larger dollar value differences in performance than in our illustration.[66]

In addition to boosting productivity, staffing systems also have the potential to enhance employee retention.[67] Thus, any benefits from better staffing last over the longer tenure of the new hires' employment with the firm, further increasing the company's return on its staffing investment. For most companies, investing a little more money recruiting, hiring, and retaining better employees is likely to lead to a good return if the new system results in the consistent hiring of star employees.

This is not to say that staffing costs are unimportant. Organizations must strike a balance between making a long-run investment and achieving their short-term cost goals. Most companies, particularly smaller ones, cannot pay unlimited amounts for optimal staffing systems. To illustrate the possible return on investment for a staffing system, assume an organization has to hire 1,000 salespeople in the next year and that it has a choice of two different staffing systems. Both systems have similar, but not identical, capabilities. One system costs $900,000 while another costs $1.3 million. Because human resource expenditures are treated typically as a cost, many managers and businesses would opt for the cheaper system. But which system is the better strategic choice? Assume the latter system generates employees who average $10,000 more in sales per employee per year than the cheaper system and 30 percent of those sales is profit. In the very first year, the $400,000 investment in the more expensive staffing system would yield $3 million more in profit ($10,000 $\times$ .3 $\times$ 1,000), before taxes. This simple example illustrates how decisions may differ when viewing staffing as an investment rather than as an expense.

Technology and a looser labor market can reduce the average hiring cost for an organization. However, the costs still amount to a considerable investment for most companies. That said, the cost of the system is not what is most important. The most important issue is to determine the return on investment, which we just did with our previous calculations. Unfortunately, many companies don't take the time to quantify the cost–benefit trade-offs when it comes to their staffing decisions. Maximizing the company's return on that investment requires the staffing function to prioritize its goals and make appropriate trade-offs among them.

Should Our Staffing Function Be Centralized or Decentralized?

Who should manage the staffing process? This is a key aspect of a firm's staffing philosophy. A staffing function is *centralized* when an organization that has multiple business units has one staffing unit responsible for meeting at least some of the needs of all the company's business units. Each business informs the centralized staffing function when it needs to hire, and the staffing unit then sources, recruits, and prescreens candidates. The local business unit is still responsible for making a final hiring decision from the group of candidates or finalists sent to it by the staffing unit.

Centralized staffing is a situation in which all of an organization's staffing activities are channeled through one unit. Sometimes called *shared services staffing*, it allows for greater economies of scale. Multiple positions can be filled from the same candidate pool, and optimal hiring practices can be leveraged across the organization. By centralizing its staffing, a firm can quickly reallocate its resources to meet the company's changing business priorities. Centralized staffing also tends to result in policies and procedures that provide some level of uniformity for the organization. The firm can "brand" its image as an employer by ensuring consistency in how the organization presents itself and its job opportunities.

centralized staffing
a situation in which all of an organization's staffing activities are channeled through one unit

Decentralized staffing occurs when the different business units of a company each house their own staffing functions. Decentralized staffing gives units more localized control over their recruiting and staffing activities. Given local control, a recruiter can improve his or her understanding of what type of person will be most successful in a particular unit. The structure also gives recruiters greater flexibility to source and recruit in the best way for their location and labor markets. A decentralized staffing function is also more responsive to the needs of hiring managers because the staffing specialists report directly to them versus someone at the company's headquarters. However, with decentralized staffing, the firm's staffing metrics are less likely to be tracked or consolidated. This can result in the units duplicating the company's staffing efforts and result in higher costs. For example, a good applicant who ultimately isn't hired by one unit might never be considered by another unit of the company.

decentralized staffing
the different business units of a company each house their own staffing functions

Some organizations use a combination of centralized and decentralized approaches. Some areas of the staffing function are shared, and others are decentralized and tailored to meet the needs of each business unit. The **combined approach** can maximize each business unit's flexibility as well as standardize the staffing metrics used throughout the company, minimize redundancies, and leverage technology and best practices. A combined approach can

combined approach
a combination of centralized and decentralized staffing

also help staffing personnel build a more credible and productive relationship with the firm's hiring managers by giving them more hiring discretion than they would have under a centralized structure.

Consider Hewitt Associates, a provider of human resource outsourcing and consulting. Although recruiting activity is decentralized at Hewitt, its business-unit recruiters have access to a variety of data and resources at the company's central office. The central office is responsible for developing policies, sourcing strategies, and metrics, and providing advice if needed. But because the recruiting is dedicated to a particular business unit, the recruiters have a richer understanding of the business and skills for which they are recruiting.[68]

ACHIEVING A COMPETITIVE TALENT ADVANTAGE

human capital advantage
acquiring a stock of quality talent that creates a competitive advantage

human process advantage
superior work processes that create a competitive advantage

An organization's talent can create a competitive advantage by influencing the quality of the organization's stock of talent or the superiority of its work processes.[69] Resource stock and process capabilities reflect the difference between human capital advantage and human process advantage. The organization can generate **human capital advantage** by hiring and retaining outstanding people, and producing a stock of exceptional talent.

A **human process advantage** is obtained when the firm's work gets done in a superior way. The phenomenon can be thought of as a function of complex processes that evolve over time as a result of learning, cooperation, and innovation on the part of employees. Human process advantages are very difficult to imitate.[70] For example, a firm might have very smart and capable managers (high-quality talent stock) but fail to fully utilize their talents—perhaps because the politicking and infighting between the firm's departments are excessive (poor work processes). Thus, an organization achieves a competitive talent advantage if it has a better stock of employees working with better processes.

Given that any competitive advantage erodes over time, an organization must do what it can to defend its current position by regularly undertaking new strategic initiatives. These initiatives can include broadening the company's product line or customer support (e.g., offering free or low-cost training to product users), patenting alternative technologies, further reducing costs and prices, and acquiring talent ahead of the company's present needs to keep them from being hired by potential competitors. Indeed, getting the right people on board *before* they are needed can defensively prevent them from being hired by the competition and offensively ensure they will be available when the organization needs them. For example, Praxair, a worldwide provider of industrial gasses, believed that it could not afford to wait for the firm's future growth to finance its human resources. Knowing the talent had to be in place before the company could be successful, it made acquiring new talent and developing employees a top spending priority.[71] An economic downturn is often an excellent time for organizations to build up their talent reserves because the looser labor market makes it easier to hire good people at an affordable cost. When an industry is in an upswing, the labor pool becomes tighter, and the competition for talent heats up.

STARBUCKS'S STAFFING STRATEGY

How can Starbucks use staffing to pursue its growth and differentiation strategies and maintain its competitive advantage? Starbucks needs to offer premium service if it is to command premium prices for its products. Maintaining a high level of customer service while the company expands and opens hundreds of new stores is a big challenge. Because the quality of its customer service depends on the efforts of its employees, who it calls "partners," Starbucks tries to hire people who are adaptable, self-motivated, passionate, and creative team players.[72]

To keep them committed, Starbucks treats its partners as investors by also investing in them, which helps it to retain its valued talent. The company's strong mission and values statement emphasizes creating a respectful and positive work environment, which also helps keep its partners satisfied. Even though two-thirds of its employees work part-time,[73] Starbucks's frequent appearance on the list of *Fortune*'s Best Places to Work reflects its reputation as an employer that cares about its people.[74] This, too, helps it continue to recruit good people. Starbucks offers competitive wages and good benefits, including comprehensive health benefits for full- and part-time employees, tuition reimbursement, vacation, a 401(k) plan, and stock options. The generous benefits reflect its philosophy of creating a respectful and positive work environment, help keep turnover low, and generate a ready pool of experienced employees who can assist in its expansion efforts.

In addition to having a reputation for treating employees well, Starbucks is also known for its social responsibility initiatives, including outreach programs into communities both where stores operate and where its coffee is grown. Dave Pace, executive vice president for partner resources, explains, "We do it because it's the right thing to do....But from my perspective it's also a terrific recruiting and retention tool."[75] By living its values and mission statement, Starbucks is able to attract people who share its values.

To bring in new partners, Starbucks has implemented a staffing strategy that is both centralized and decentralized. According to Sheri Southern, vice president of partner resources for Starbucks North America, Starbucks's staffing strategy is, "To have the right people hiring the right people." Experienced store managers often make initial contact with potential recruits in the stores and at job fairs. Word-of-mouth and the company's Web site also generate leads. Hiring managers receive hiring guidelines containing questions that help reveal whether recruits have the core competencies necessary for the job. The company also encourages recruits to self-select out of the hiring process by clearly stating in its hiring advertisements and on its Web site that it wants people who are adaptable, dependable, passionate team players. Starbucks also maintains a database of hundreds of thousands of online candidates who have answered preliminary informational and skills-based questions. This gives the company a head start on the hiring process, allowing it to staff more quickly.[76]

Summary

A firm's talent philosophy and business strategy influence the human resource strategy that guides its staffing strategy. Its talent philosophy reflects how it thinks about its employees. Its business strategies are created to leverage the firm's resources and capabilities in ways that result in superior value creation compared to their competitors. Its competitive advantage depends on its ability to leverage the resources and capabilities that derive from the talent it is able to hire and retain. How it positions itself to compete in the marketplace determines the competitive advantage it needs to create and the staffing strategies it needs to pursue to acquire and retain the appropriate talent. A company's choice and execution of its staffing strategy influence the number and types of people it hires, and thus its ability to maintain a competitive talent advantage as a result of its human capital and processes.

Takeaway Points

1. If a firm seeks to achieve a competitive advantage, its staffing strategy should support its business strategy. Different strategies require different types of employees. A cost-leadership strategy requires trainable and flexible employees who are able to focus on shorter-term production objectives and avoid waste, and who are concerned about production costs. The goal in this case is to develop a competitive advantage based on operational excellence. A differentiation strategy based on innovation requires employees who fit the firm's innovative culture. A company pursuing a specialization strategy based on customer intimacy would need to hire adaptable, active learners with good people and customer relations skills, and emotional resilience under pressure.

2. The resource-based view of the firm proposes that a company's resources and competencies can produce a sustained competitive advantage by creating value for customers by lowering costs, providing something of unique value, or some combination of the two. Because the talent resources created by staffing can be valuable, rare, inimitable, and nonsubstitutable, staffing has the potential to create a competitive advantage for a firm. Acquiring the right talent is not enough, however. The company must be appropriately organized to take full advantage of its talent resources.

3. An organization would use job-oriented staffing when it needs to fill a specific job opening. It would pursue talent-oriented staffing when labor markets are tight and good recruits are hard to find, or to address anticipated skill gaps in advance of actual needs.

4. A firm can achieve a human capital advantage by hiring a stock of quality talent and retaining outstanding people. A human process advantage occurs when the firm's work gets done in a superior way as a result of effective processes that evolve over time, such as learning, cooperation, and innovation on the part of its employees. Human process advantages are very difficult to imitate.

5. Strategic staffing decisions include whether to: have an internal or external talent focus, establish a core or flexible workforce, hire people with the skills the firm needs or train them to develop those skills, replace or retain talent, and pursue proactive or reactive staffing. It is also important to address what levels of which skills should be sought and which jobs should be focused on, as well as whether staffing should be viewed as an investment or a cost and should be centralized or decentralized.

Discussion Questions

1. What are the three most important ethical principles that you feel organizations should adhere to in terms of their staffing philosophies? Why?
2. What is the difference between treating employees as assets and as investors? When is it appropriate for an organization to treat employees as investors? When is it appropriate for an organization to treat job applicants and employees as assets?
3. Suppose you were in charge of recruiting and staffing the software engineers who would work for Google. Do you think that a company like Google should hire software engineers with the skills it needs or train them to develop those skills? Why?
4. In what situations would position-oriented staffing be preferable to talent-oriented staffing?
5. List the costs and benefits of having an internal staffing focus. Then list the cost and benefits of having an external staffing focus. What are the trade-offs between the two approaches?

Exercises

1. *Strategy Exercise:* Form a small group of four to five students. Identify a business that you could start. What type of business would you propose? What business strategy would you follow? What staffing strategies would you use and why? How does the resource-based view inform your thinking?
2. *Opening Vignette Exercise:* Working individually or in a small group, reread the chapter vignette on Starbucks and address the following questions. Be prepared to share your answers with the class after 20 minutes.
   (a) What staffing issues would create the biggest obstacles to Starbucks's ability to execute its growth and specialization strategies?
   (b) What would you recommend Starbucks do to overcome the obstacles you identified?
3. *Develop Your Skills Exercise:* Think of an organization that you currently work for or have worked for in the past as you complete the "Measuring Your Firm's Climate for Diversity" assessment in the Develop Your Skills feature. How well do you think the organization's climate-for-diversity score reflects its talent philosophy?

CASE STUDY

Integrating McDonald's Business, Human Resource, and Staffing Strategies

People are McDonald's most important asset. The company's success depends on the satisfaction of its customers, which begins with workers who have the attitudes and abilities required to work efficiently and provide good customer service. To execute its growth strategy, McDonald's has identified people as one of its three global corporate strategies. McDonald's claims that as an employer, it wants "to be the best employer in each community around the world."[77] It also makes a "people promise" to its employees that "we value you, your growth, and your Contributions."[78] Its five "people principles" reflected by its human resource strategy are respect and recognition; values and leadership behaviors; competitive pay and benefits; learning, development, and personal growth; and ensuring that employees have the resources needed to get the job done.[79]

McDonald's has executed its operational excellence strategy well by tracking key indicators of product and service quality, speed, and accuracy. The company has also identified its people practices and approaches that substantially impact the firm's turnover, productivity, customer satisfaction, sales, and profitability. This has allowed it to develop a business model that emphasizes not only financial and operational factors but also people factors that improve the company's results by improving employee commitment, retention, productivity, and customer loyalty.[80]

Because its business strategy relies on providing customers quality, cleanliness, quick service, and value, McDonald's works hard at hiring people who want to excel in delivering outstanding service. Many of its restaurant employees are teenagers, and McDonald's is their first employer. The company tries to recruit and hire the best people, retain them by offering them ongoing training,[81] and then promote from within to fill its managerial positions. To ensure that it is recruiting the right people, the company has identified important skills and behaviors that it looks for in applicants. McDonald's has found that the best way of hiring quality crew members is to advertise inside the restaurant and attract local people and/or friends of existing employees. McDonald's also recruits at local job centers and career fairs, using hiring material with a clear message targeted at its intended audience. As McDonald's CEO Steve Easterbrook says, "If you get the people part right, the rest will follow."[82]

QUESTIONS

1. How would you describe McDonald's business strategy? What are the foundations of its competitive advantage (what are the sources of its success)?
2. How has McDonald's aligned its business, human resource, and staffing strategies?
3. What are some possible talent-related threats that could eat away at McDonald's competitive advantage? Would higher turnover or a tight labor market in which it is difficult to find talented people be a problem? What would you recommend the company do to maintain its competitive advantage over the next five years?

Semester-Long Active Learning Project

You should have a list of jobs and companies that your team will have access to for the project. You now need to decide which job and organization to use for the semester project and begin collecting information on the company, its business strategy and competitive advantage, and how it currently sources, recruits, and selects for the position you identified. You also need to identify how the position is strategic for the company in some way. Before the next class, you should confirm that you will have access to one or two job experts and solidify the job and organization your team will use for the project.

Specifically, you need to include the following in your report:

1. A brief summary of the organization, its business strategy, and its culture.

2. An explanation of why the position you chose is strategic for the company. (Why should attention be given to improving how it is staffed? What are the implications of having low versus high performers in the job?) Describe the strategic context of your future proposal for recruiting and selecting for this job—what must future hires be able to do to help the company execute its business strategy?

3. Responses to each of the nine strategic staffing decisions presented in Table 2–6 and a justification for each of your recommendations. *It is a good idea to read the applied case assignments for the rest of the chapters to guide your research and identify how your job experts might provide useful information for future sections of the project.*

Case Study Assignment: Strategic Staffing at Chern's

See the appendix at the back of the book for this chapter's Case Study Assignment.

Endnotes

1. "Starbucks Mission Statement," Starbucks.com, http://www. starbucks.com/about-us/company-information/mission-statement. Accessed September 19, 2010.
2. "Career Center," Starbucks.com, www.starbucks.com/aboutus/jobcenter.asp. Accessed July 7, 2006.
3. Weber, G., "Preserving the Starbucks' Counter Culture," *Workforce Management*, February 2005: 28–34.
4. Ibid.
5. Copeland, M. V., "My Golden Rule," *Business 2.0*, December 1, 2005, http://money.cnn.com/magazines/business2/business2_archive/2005/12/01/8364598/index.htm. Accessed June 27, 2006.
6. Center for Advanced Human Resource Studies, "Time, Inc.," *hrSPECTRUM* (March–April 2004): 4, http://www.ilr.cornell.edu/cahrs/research/pubs/hrspectrum/upload/HRSpec04-04.pdf.
7. Porter, M. E., *Competitive Advantage: Creating and Sustaining Superior Performance*, New York: Free Press, 1985.
8. Taylor, M. S., and Collins, C. J., "Organizational Recruitment: Enhancing the Intersection of Research and Practice," In G. L. Cooper and E. A. Locke (eds.), *Industrial and Organizational Psychology: What We Know About Theory & Practice*, Oxford, UK: Blackwell Business, 2000, 304–330.
9. Barney, J., "Firm Resources and Sustained Competitive Advantage," *Journal of Management,* 17 (1991): 99–120; Barney, J., and Wright, P. M., "On Becoming a Strategic Partner: The Role of Human Resources in Gaining Competitive Advantage," *Human Resource Management* (Spring 1998): 31–46.
10. Wright, P., McMahan, G., and McWilliams, A., "Human Resources and Sustained Competitive Advantage: A Resource-Based Perspective," *International Journal of Human Resource Management,* 5 (1994): 301–326.
11. Barney, "Firm Resources and Sustained Competitive Advantage."
12. Taylor and Collins, "Organizational Recruitment: Enhancing the Intersection of Research and Practice."; Phillips, J. M., "Effects of Realistic Job Previews on Multiple Organizational

Outcomes: A Meta-Analysis," *Academy of Management Journal,* 41 (1998): 673–690.
13. Grant, L., "Happy Workers, High Returns," *Fortune*, January 12, 1998: 81–95.
14. Taylor and Collins, "Organizational Recruitment: Enhancing the Intersection of Research and Practice."
15. Grant, R., "The Resource-Based Theory of Competitive Advantage: Implications for Strategy Formation," *California Management Review,* 33 (1991): 114–135.
16. Taylor and Collins, "Organizational Recruitment: Enhancing the Intersection of Research and Practice."
17. Barney, "Firm Resources and Sustained Competitive Advantage."
18. Taylor and Collins, "Organizational Recruitment: Enhancing the Intersection of Research and Practice."
19. Barney and Wright, "On Becoming a Strategic Partner."
20. Pfeffer, J., *The Human Equation: Building Profits by Putting People First*, Boston, MA: Harvard Business School Press, 1998.
21. Olian, J. D., and Rynes, S. L., "Organizational Staffing: Integrating Practice with Strategy," *Industrial Relations,* 23, 2 (Spring 1984): 170–183.
22. Treacy, M., and Wiersma, F., *The Discipline of Market Leaders*, Massachusetts: Perseus Books, 1997.
23. Holmes, S., and Zellner, W., "The Costco Way," *BusinessWeek Online*, April 12, 2004, www.businessweek.com/magazine/content/04_15/b3878084_mz021.htm.
24. Porter, M. E., *Competitive Advantage*, New York: Free Press, 1985.
25. Ibid; Porter, M. E., *Competitive Strategy: Techniques for Analyzing Industries and Competitors*, New York: Free Press, 1998.
26. Beatty, R. W., and Schneier, C. E., "New HR Roles to Impact Organizational Performance: From 'Partners' to 'Players'," *Human Resource Management,* 36 (1997): 29–37; Deloitte & Touche, LLP, *Creating Shareholder Value Through People: The Human Capital ROI Study*, New York: Deloitte & Touche, LLP, 2002; Treacy, M., and Wiersema, F., "Customer Intimacy and

Other Value Disciplines," *Harvard Business Review,* 71 (1993): 84–94.

27. Ibid.

28. Schuler, R., and Jackson, S., "Linking Competitive Strategies and Human Resource Management Practices," *Academy of Management Executive,* 1, 3 (1987): 207–219.

29. Olian and Rynes, "Organizational Staffing: Integrating Practice with Strategy."

30. Kiger, P. J., "Why Customer Satisfaction Starts with HR," *Workforce,* May 2002: 26–32.

31. Beatty and Schneier, "New HR Roles to Impact Organizational Performance."; Deloitte & Touche, LLP, *Creating Shareholder Value Through People*; Treacy and Wiersema, "Customer Intimacy and Other Value Disciplines."

32. Baker, D., "DaimlerChrysler's Culture Needs Retooling," *Business Review,* March 16, 2001, http://albany.bizjournals.com/albany/stories/2001/03/19/editorial4.html. Accessed September 6, 2007.

33. Available online at: http://www.jnj.com/connect/about-jnj/jnj-credo/.

34. Crockett, R. O., "How P&G Finds and Keeps a Prized Workforce," *BusinessWeek,* April 9, 2009, http://www.businessweek.com/magazine/content/09_16/b4127055263615.htm?chan=magazine+channel_in%3A+inside+innovation. Accessed April 6, 2010.

35. "Culture," P&G, 2009, http://www.pg.com/en_US/careers/culture.shtml. Accessed April 6, 2010.

36. E. E. Hubbard, "Diversity Leadership by the Numbers: Implementing Diversity Management Strategies for Measurable Return on Investment (ROI) Performance," *News Brief of the MultiCultural Development Center,* May 25, 2006, http://view.exacttarget.com/?ffcb10-fe8e1277776d047f72-fdf017777d61057b76127273-ff 2d17767060. Accessed March 23, 2007.

37. Ibid.

38. "Career Opportunities," 3M Worldwide, http://cms.3m.com/cms/CA/en/1-30/criRrFN/view.jhtml. Accessed July 12, 2006.

39. Levin, M, "Embracing Diversity," www.mintz.com/about/diversity/default.cfm. Accessed June 13, 2006.

40. Roberson, Q. M., "Disentangling the Meanings of Diversity and Inclusion in Organizations," *Group and Organization Management,* 31 (April 2006): 212–236.

41. Dyer, L., and Holder, J., "A Strategic Perspective of Human Resource Management," In L. Dyer (ed.), *Human Resource Management: Evolving Roles and Responsibilities,* Washington, D.C.: American Society for Personnel Administration/Bureau of National Affairs, 1988, 1–35.

42. The Ayers Group, "J&J Chairman Weldon Opens Ayers' Leadership Series," *The Ayers Report,* 2004: 2, http://ayers.com/Summer_2004.pdf. Accessed June 6, 2006.

43. Naglieri, J. A., Drasgow, F., Schmit, M., Handler, L., Prifitera, A., Margolis, A., and Velasquez, R., "Psychological Testing on the Internet: New Problems, Old Issues," *American Psychologist,* 59 (2004): 150–162.

44. Turner, S. M., DeMers, S. T., Fox, H. R., and Reed, G. M., "APA's Guidelines for Test User Qualifications: An Executive Summary," *American Psychologist,* 56 (2001): 1099–1113.

45. Reynolds, D., "EEOC and OFCCP Guidance on Defining a Job Applicant in the Internet Age: SIOP's Response," *The Industrial-Organizational Psychologist,* 42 (2004): 127–138.

46. Sager, I., "Lou Takes the Gloves Off," *BusinessWeek,* November 18, 2002: 64–70.

47. Chambers, E. G., Foulon, M., Handfield-Jones, H., Hankin, S. M., and Michaels, E. G. III, "The War for Talent," *The McKinsey Quarterly,* 3 (1998): 44–57.

48. Baird, L., and Meshoulam, I., "Managing Two Fits of Strategic Human Resource Management," *Academy of Management Review,* 13 (1988): 116–128; Lepak, D. P., Liao, H., Chung, Y., and Harden, E., "A Conceptual Review of Human Resource Management Systems in Strategic Human Resource Management Research," In J. Martocchio (ed.), *Research in Personnel and Human Resources Management,* Vol. 25, Stamford, CT: JAI Press, 2006; Huang, T. C., "The Effects of Linkage Between Business and Human Resource Management Strategies," *Personnel Review,* 30 (2001): 132–151.

49. RMB Holdings, www.rmbh.co.za/sustainability_overview.htm.

50. Metseo, www.metso.com/reports/personnel/henkilosto_1_2.html. Accessed July 7, 2006. Reprinted with permission from Metso Corporation.

51. Olian and Rynes, "Organizational Staffing: Integrating Practice with Strategy."

52. Houseman, S. N., *Flexible Staffing Arrangements: A Report on Temporary Help, On-Call, Direct-Hire Temporary, Leased, Contract Company, and Independent Contractor Employment in the United States,* W. E. UpJohn Institute for Employment Research, August 1999.

53. Sriram, S. R., "3M Looks to a VMS to Transform Its Temporary Workforce Program," *Workforce Management Online,* March 2009, http://www.workforce.com/section/recruiting-staffing/feature/3m-looks-vms-transform-temporary-workforce/index.html. Accessed September 19, 2010.

54. Fletcher-Stoeltje, M., "Working Moms Fully in Favor of Going Part Time," *Fort Worth Star Telegram,* August 30, 2007: E1–E9.

55. Stark, B., "The Future of the Workplace: No Office, Headquarters in Cyberspace," ABCnews.com, August 27, 2007, http://abcnews.go.com/WN/story?id=3521725&page=1. Accessed December 1, 2007.

56. "Hamburger University—McDonald's Center of Training Excellence," McDonald's, www.mcdonalds.com/corp/career/hamburger_university.html. Accessed July 12, 2006.

57. Ibid.

58. Solomon, C. M., "Stellar Recruiting for a Tight Labor Market," *Workforce,* 77 (August 1998): 66–71.

59. Miner, A., "Idiosyncratic Jobs in Formal Organizations," *Administrative Science Quarterly,* 32 (1987): 327–351.

60. Krell, E., "Recruiting Outlook: Creative HR for 2003," *Workforce,* 81 (December 2002): 40–45.

61. Soper, N. A., *Recruitment & Retention Lessons from Industry and High Tech Organizations: Winning the War for Scientists and Engineers,* Air Force Research Laboratory, Space Vehicles Directorate, Kirtland Air Force Base, 2001.

62. NACE, "2009 Recruiting Benchmarks Survey," October 2009. Available online at: http://www.naceweb.org/Research/Recruiters/2009_Recruiting_Benchmarks_Survey.aspx. Accessed March 26, 2010.

63. PricewaterhouseCoopers, *Saratoga 2005–2006 Human Capital Index Report.*

64. Kelley, R., and Caplan, J., "How Bell Labs Create Star Performers," *Harvard Business Review* (July–August 1993): 128–139.

65. Hunter, J. E., Schmidt, F. L., and Judiesch, M. K., "Individual Differences in Output Variability as a Function of Job Complexity," *Journal of Applied Psychology,* 75 (1990): 28–42.

66. Boudreau, J. W., "Utility Analysis for Decisions in Human Resource Management," In M. D. Dunnette and L. M. Hough (eds.), *Handbook of Industrial and Organizational Psychology*, 2, Palo Alto, CA: Consulting Psychologists Press, 1991: 601–617.

67. Phillips, "Effects of Realistic Job Previews on Multiple Organizational Outcomes."

68. Martinez, M. N., "Recruiting Here and There," *HR Magazine*, September 2002: 95–100.

69. Lado, A. A., and Wilson, M. C., "Human Resource Systems and Sustained Competitive Advantage: A Competency-Based Perspective," *Academy of Management Review,* 19, 4 (1994): 699–727.

70. Boxall, P., "The Strategic Human Resource Management Debate and the Resource-Based View of the Firm," *Human Resource Management Journal,* 6 (1996): 59–75.

71. Harris, B. R., Huselid, M. A., and Becker, B. E., "Strategic Human Resource Management at Praxair," *Human Resource Management,* 38 (1999): 315–320.

72. "Career Center," Starbucks.com, www.starbucks.com/aboutus/jobcenter.asp. Accessed July 18, 2007.

73. "Part-time Workers Lag in Benefit Coverage," *Workforce Management*, February 2005: 34.

74. "*Fortune* 100 Best Companies to Work For 2006: Starbucks," http://money.cnn.com/magazines/fortune/bestcompanies/snapshots/1267.html. Accessed July 7, 2006.

75. Weber, G., "The Recruiting Payoff of Social Responsibility," *Workforce Management*, January 2005, http://www.workforce.com/section/recruiting-staffing/article/recruiting-payoff-social-responsibility.html. Accessed September 17, 2010.

76. Weber, "Preserving the Starbucks' Counter Culture."

77. "McDonald's People Vision," McDonald's Corporation, www.rmhc.org/corp/values/ppromise/people_vision.html. Accessed July 10, 2006.

78. "McDonald's People Promise," McDonald's Corporation, www.rmhc.org/corp/values/ppromise/people_promise.html. Accessed July 10, 2006.

79. "McDonald's Commitment to Our Employees," McDonald's Corporation, www.rmhc.org/corp/values/ppromise/our_commitment. html. Accessed July 10, 2006.

80. Moore, D., Landa, A., and Nelson, S., "I-O Psychologists' Roles in HR Systems," *Industrial-Organizational Psychologist*, July 2001, http://siop.org/tip/backissues/TipJul01/17barney.aspx. Accessed July 10, 2006.

81. "World Class Service," http://www.aboutmcdonalds.com/mcd/franchising/us_franchising/why_mcdonalds/world_class_service.html, Accessed September 17, 2010.

82. Fuller, G., "The Burger Meister: McDonald's CEO Steve Easterbrook's View from the Top," Personnel Today, October 10, 2006. http://www.personneltoday.com/articles/2006/10/10/37557/the-burger-meister-mcdonalds-ceo-steve-easterbrooks-view-from-the-top.html. Accessed September 17, 2010.

Outline

LEARNING OBJECTIVES

After studying this chapter, you should be able to:

▪ Explain why complying with staffing laws can be strategic.

▪ Discuss different types of employment relationships.

▪ Describe different types of staffing-related lawsuits.

▪ Discuss the role affirmative action and equal employment opportunity play in a firm's staffing processes.

▪ Describe various barriers to legally defensible staffing.

Recruiting and Hiring to Promote a Brand Image

To appeal to its target market of 18- to 22-year-old college students, clothing retailer Abercrombie & Fitch wanted to project an all-American, collegiate image and make its store employees part of its marketing strategy. Paralleling the predominantly white, youthful, and attractive models used in Abercrombie's marketing materials, the company's salespeople, also called "brand representatives," were also mostly good-looking, white, young adults.

Abercrombie & Fitch Investor Relations and Communications Director Lonnie Fogel once commented that the company was "very particular about recruiting certain kinds of people to work as brand representatives in our store."[1] To the company, this meant limiting its recruiting to certain fraternities and sororities known for their attractive, predominantly white members.[2] One former Abercrombie manager said that a poster with images of the ideal Abercrombie white male and female hung in her office containing bullet points of the qualities an Abercrombie employee should possess. Qualities for a male included being a fraternity member who likes sports, partying, and girls. A female should like to have fun, shop, and be a sorority member.[3]

The company asks your opinion about the legality of the recruiting and staffing practices it has adopted to reinforce its brand image and marketing strategy featuring predominantly white, attractive, young people. After reading this chapter, you should have some good insights to tell Abercrombie & Fitch.

Complying with staffing laws is obviously a good idea from a moral, ethical, and legal perspective, but as you learned in the last chapter, doing so can also be strategic. In addition to avoiding the expense of lawsuits and the negative public relations that comes with litigation, legal compliance allows companies to capitalize on the strengths of diversity. This allows them to perform better because they focus more on performance and merit, and are better able to hire quality people from all segments of the labor force. Proactive and strategic firms often go beyond legal compliance in recruiting and retaining diverse employees.

Employment laws and regulations exist for several reasons. Because the employer decides the structure of the employment relationship and the principles that will guide employees' pay, promotions, and so forth, the firm usually has more power than employees do. Laws and regulations help to limit the employer's power as well as prohibit unfair discrimination and provide equal employment opportunities for everyone. Unfair discrimination happens when employment decisions are not based on job-relevant knowledge, skills, abilities, and so forth, but on factors such as age, sex, race, religion, ethnicity, or a person's disabilities (or lack of them). **Unlawful (discriminatory) employment practices** are those that unfairly discriminate against people with characteristics protected by law. The legal foundation for workplace diversity recognizes that workforce barriers exist based on people's characteristics including their race, gender, age, ethnicity, and religion. However, because the law alone does not provide the tools to recognize and break down these barriers, proactively managing diversity is important.

unlawful or discriminatory employment practices
employment practices that unfairly discriminate against people with characteristics protected by law

Because employment laws and the courts' interpretations of them identify what is expected and required of every employer, they clarify what is permissible. They also help employers hire strategically by promoting the hiring of the most qualified people. This enhances the quality of the firm's hiring decisions and, thus, the performance of the organization. Avoiding unfair discrimination helps companies better execute their strategies and reach their goals. In short, complying with employment laws:

- Enhances the quality of the firm's hiring decisions
- Enhances the company's reputation and image as an employer

- Promotes the perception of fairness among job candidates
- Reduces the negative public relations firms experience when people feel they were discriminated against and tell others about their experience
- Reinforces an ethical culture
- Enhances an organization's performance by ensuring that people are hired or not hired based on their qualifications, not biases
- Promotes diversity, which can enhance an organization's ability to appeal to a broader customer base.

Given that entire books have been written on employment law, this chapter's coverage of the major government regulations and legal issues involving staffing cannot cover every detail. This book is not intended as a legal reference, and it does not constitute legal advice. The purpose of this chapter is to provide an overview of some of the key laws and legal issues surrounding staffing and to identify resources for additional information. The chapter will also give you a good understanding of how to prevent discriminatory or illegal staffing practices. Laws change and differ from state to state, and they evolve over time, so you should always consult legal counsel to ensure compliance with current local, state, and federal regulations.

In this chapter, we first discuss various types of employment relationships, their legal implications, and the influence of labor unions. Next, we cover some of the primary laws and regulations regarding staffing, different enforcement agencies, and different types of staffing-related lawsuits. Finally, we discuss barriers to legal recruitment and hiring. After reading this chapter, you should have a good understanding of how to create a legal staffing system.

THE TYPES OF EMPLOYMENT RELATIONSHIPS

Employers use different types of employment relationships to strategically manage their workforce and ensure that they have the number of workers with the skills they need ready to work when they need them. Let's look at these different employment relationships and their legal implications.

Types of Employees

employee

someone hired by another person or business for a wage or fixed payment in exchange for personal services, and who does not provide the services as part of an independent business

EMPLOYEES   An **employee** is someone hired by another person or business for a wage or fixed payment in exchange for personal services, and who does not provide the services as part of an independent business. A job offer is made that must be accepted as presented, or the employer and employee negotiate the terms and conditions of their relationship and create an employment contract. Every employee has an employment contract. If a written agreement does not exist, there is often an oral contract in place that in most instances is just as enforceable as a formal written agreement. Even if a written or verbal **explicit employment contract** does not exist, there is an **implicit employment contract** reflecting a common understanding between the employer and employee.[4] We discuss employment contracts in more detail in Chapter 11.

explicit employment contract

specific written or verbal employment contract

implicit employment contract

an understanding that is not part of a written or verbal contract

The employer must withhold employee payroll taxes (income taxes and Social Security taxes) from the paychecks of employees and pay certain taxes (unemployment insurance and the employer's share of Medicare and Social Security). In addition, employers must abide by the many laws and regulations that govern the employment relationship, and they are liable for the acts of their employees during their time of employment.

at-will employment

an employment relationship in which either party can terminate the employment relationship at any time for just cause, no cause, or any cause that is not illegal with no liability as long as there is no contract for a definite term of employment

AT-WILL EMPLOYEES   **At-will employment** is an employment relationship in which either party can terminate the employment relationship at any time for just cause, no cause, or even a cause that is morally wrong as long as it is not illegal with no liability as long as there is no contract for a definite term of employment. At-will employment allows an employee to quit for any reason. Firms call upon it most often when they want to fire an employee for any legal reason or for no reason at all. In most states (except Montana), if a formal contract does not govern a company's employment relationships, these relationships are governed by the "employment-at-will" doctrine.

Although the courts generally have upheld the right to terminate at will, this does not mean that employers should casually terminate employees without giving a reason or without following normal policies and procedures. Companies should follow their formal discipline and termination procedures whenever possible to help avoid discrimination and wrongful termination claims. The at-will clause is best used as a legal defense by organizations when they feel it's not in their interests to follow their own policies inflexibly.[5] For example, at-will employment allows an employer to immediately dismiss an employee who is behaving dangerously. Case law establishing when or if firms can rely on the at-will nature of the relationship varies from state to state.

It is important to note that employment-at-will does not offer blanket protection to employers for all employee discharges. Existing contracts, of course, create exceptions to employment-at-will provisions. These contracts include tenure systems, such as those that exist between universities and tenured professors, formalized (written) employment contracts, and union contracts. "Just cause" clauses in union contracts protect most unionized workers from arbitrary firings and prohibit employers from firing workers unless they can show that a person should reasonably (due to "a just cause") be terminated. Federal laws, such as equal employment legislation and the National Labor Relations Act, protect employees from being retaliated against—fired or punished, for example—for engaging in a protected activity, such as filing a discrimination charge, opposing unlawful employer practices, or filing a valid worker's compensation claim, regardless of an employee's at-will status.

Certain state laws also limit employment-at-will provisions. Most states recognize that an implied employment contract exists between employers and employees that creates an exception to at-will employment. An implied employment contract occurs when an employer's personnel policies, handbooks, or other materials indicate that it will only fire an employee for good cause or specify a procedural process for firing. If an employee is fired in violation of an implied employment contract, the employer may be found liable for breach of contract.

A few states have also recognized that a breach of an implied covenant of good faith and fair dealing is an exception to at-will employment. This covenant presumes that employers are generally obligated to deal fairly and in good faith with all of their employees. For example, firing an employee solely to deny the employee an earned bonus that has not yet been received, or to prevent him or her from soon vesting in the firm's pension plan is unlawful in some states. Like the federal government, all U.S. states also recognize that a retaliatory discharge is an exception to at-will employment.

The best way to ensure that an employment-at-will message has been adequately communicated to employees is by publishing the policy on something employees sign. Signing an employment application or to acknowledge reading an employee handbook produces a written record that an employee has read and understood the policy. Table 3–1 describes how to develop an at-will employment statement.

CONTINGENT WORKERS In 1989 the Bureau of Labor Statistics defined **contingent work** as "any job in which an individual does not have an explicit or implicit contract for long-term employment."[6] In other words, a contingent worker is anyone who has a job of limited duration. Contingent workers are outside of a company's core workforce. The average percentage of work done by contingent labor grew from 6 percent in 1989 to more than 27 percent in 2009.[7]

contingent work
any job in which an individual does not have a contract for long-term employment

TABLE 3–1	Developing an At-Will Statement

Most courts will find an employment-at-will relationship if the following criteria are met:[8]

- The at-will statement is written in clear, understandable language and thoroughly explains what the at-will relationship means.
- The at-will statement clearly states that no company representative may change the at-will relationship through oral or written promises.
- The at-will statement explains that the organization's policies and practices are not intended to create a contract.
- The at-will statement is prominently displayed, such as in bold type, a separate introductory policy, or set apart in other policies.
- The at-will statement is repeated where appropriate in other policies and handbooks, particularly those outlining work rules and disciplinary procedures.
- The at-will statement is contained in other employment documents, such as application forms and offer letters.

A company can engage a contingent worker in two ways. It can hire the worker directly, or it can contract with another employer that has hired the worker. One of the primary benefits of contingent workers is that they can be quickly brought on board by placing a request with a temporary staffing firm or an employee-leasing firm. This allows a firm to adjust its staffing levels quickly without having to fire or lay off employees, which can increase a firm's unemployment insurance premiums and hurt morale. Next, we will discuss several types of contingent workers.

temporary workers
nonpermanent workers who can be supplied by staffing agencies or directly hired by the company

TEMPORARY WORKERS   As we discussed in the last chapter, **temporary workers** are contingent workers supplied by staffing agencies or directly hired by the company in which they work. Contract workers are a type of temporary worker who provide more specific, advanced, technical, and professional skills than do temporary workers. These people tend to have assignments lasting several months to a year or more. Temporary and contract workers are paid by the hour and are only paid for hours actually on the job. Temporary workers often do not receive the health and other benefits given to full-time employees, and, unlike employees, they do not raise a firm's unemployment insurance if they are dismissed. Because of the lower cost and nonpermanent nature of their relationship with the firm, it can be strategic for the firm to utilize temporary workers until it is clear that the additional talent will be needed for the long term. Microsoft, Delphi, and FedEx make extensive use of temporary workers.

When using a staffing agency, the agency can be considered the temporary worker's employer of record rather than the company's. But this is only the case if the company using the agency has the right to control or direct *only the result of the work* done by the worker, and *not the means and methods of accomplishing the result*. This can shield a company using an agency from charges of age, race, or sex discrimination for the staffing agency's workers. The agency must also provide performance feedback and scheduling functions or else both the company and the agency may be determined to be *co-employers*, both subject to the employment laws governing the employer–employee relationship.

It is important to note that firms cannot always legally exclude temporary workers from benefits, such as health insurance. In *Burrey v. Pacific Gas & Electric*[9] the court concluded that employees of temporary agencies working at an unrelated company's place of business, *unless specifically excluded* from the firm's employee benefit plan coverage, are to be treated as the company's common-law employees for employee benefit plan purposes. Therefore, employers need to have a clearly written benefits policy that specifically excludes temporary workers if that is their intention.

leased workers
employees of a company (also called a professional employer organization) who take on the operation of certain functions, or staff an entire location on a contractual basis for a client company

LEASED WORKERS   **Leased workers** are employees of a company who take on the operation of certain functions, or staff an entire office or factory on a contractual basis for a client company. The workers are employees of the contractor and are considered leased workers by the company for which they perform the work. Because the employee-leasing company and the client company are co-employers, both are liable for payment of payroll taxes and workers' compensation premiums, and compliance with government regulations.[10]

Leased workers are typically assigned to projects lasting at least a year that require professional and technical expertise. Many smaller firms use employee-leasing companies as a human resource partner. The firm recruits, screens, and hires its own workers, then puts them on the leasing company's payroll. The agency then "leases" the workers back to the company for a fee. This allows smaller businesses with limited resources to transfer the responsibility for administering payroll and benefits from themselves to the leasing company. Because the employee-leasing agency employs more workers, it can offer better health insurance and retirement benefits at lower cost than small businesses with only a few employees.

PART-TIME AND SEASONAL WORKERS   Part-time workers work less than a full workweek and can be contingent workers, but do not have to be. Seasonal employees are employees hired to work only during a particular part of the year. For example, when UPS hires more workers during the busy holiday season, and when growers hire laborers to harvest fruit, they are hiring seasonal workers.

UNIONIZED WORKERS In the United States, **labor unions** legally represent workers, organizing employees and negotiating the terms and conditions of their employment. In addition to wages and benefits, labor unions bargain over virtually all aspects of the staffing process, including working conditions, facility locations, staffing levels, job descriptions and classifications, promotion and transfer policies, layoff and termination policies, hiring pools, employment discrimination protections, grievance procedures, and seniority provisions. The terms and conditions of employment are contained in a contract called a *collective bargaining agreement* or a *collective employment agreement*. The inability of management and the union to reach an agreement may culminate in either a labor strike or a management lockout.

labor unions
legally represent workers, organizing employees and negotiating the terms and conditions of union members' employment

Congress approved the National Labor Relations Act[11] (NLRA) in 1935 to encourage a healthy relationship between private-sector workers and their employers. The NLRA was designed to curtail work stoppages, strikes, and general labor strife. It extends many rights to workers who wish to form, join, or support unions or labor organizations; to workers who are already represented by unions; and to workers who join as a group of two or more nonunionized employees seeking to modify their wages or working conditions. Employers also may not discriminate against pro-union applicants.

U.S. companies that employ workers with a union operate on several different models:

- A *closed shop* exclusively employs people who are already union members. An example is a compulsory hiring hall, where the employer must recruit directly from the union. In 1947, the Taft-Hartley Labor Act declared the closed shop illegal. Although the NLRA permits construction employers to enter into prehire agreements to draw their workforces exclusively from a pool of employees dispatched by the union, construction employers are under no legal obligation to enter into such agreements.
- A *union shop* employs both union and nonunion workers, but new employees must join the union or begin paying dues to the union within a specified time limit.
- An *agency shop* requires nonunion workers to pay a fee to the union for its services in negotiating their contracts.
- An *open shop* does not discriminate based on union membership in employing or keeping workers. Some workers benefit from a union or the collective bargaining process despite not contributing to the union.

A collective bargaining agreement specifying that promotions will be based on seniority rather than merit influences the types of competencies the firm should hire. Seniority-based promotions make leadership competencies important hiring criteria even for lower-level positions because these lower-level hires are likely to become the company's future leaders. Even in nonunion companies, the effects from competitors' union agreements can occur as the nonunion companies adjust their pay, benefits, and terms and conditions of employment to successfully compete for new hires and prevent current employees from leaving to work for a competitor.

Although the influence of labor unions has declined significantly in some sectors of the U.S. economy, this is not the case abroad. In many countries, collective labor enjoys a strong presence. In some countries, collective representation differs radically from the United States in that collective agreements often legally apply to an entire industry sector, making even nonunion workers covered by the agreements, and effectively "unionized." For example, in Brazil, all workers have to be in unions. Europe and Indonesia require employee representative bodies, called works councils, to offer workers a second level of representatives beyond unions.

Independent Contractors

An **independent contractor** performs services wherein the employer controls or directs only the *result* of the work. Anyone who performs services for a company is legally an employee if the company controls *what is done and how it is done*. Independent contractors must make their own Social Security contributions, pay various employment taxes, and report their income to state and federal authorities. From a legal perspective, whether a worker is an employee or an independent contractor with respect to the company determines the obligations the company has to the worker. If an employee is incorrectly classified as an independent contractor instead of an employee, the company can be liable for employment taxes for that worker, plus a penalty.[12]

independent contractor
performs services wherein the employer controls or directs only the result of the work

The Internal Revenue Service (IRS) gives the example of Vera Elm, an electrician, who submits a job estimate to a housing complex for 400 hours of electrical work at $16 per hour. Elm is to receive $1,280 every two weeks for the next 10 weeks, which is not an hourly payment. No matter how long it takes her to complete the work, Vera will receive $6,400. She also performs additional electrical installations for other companies under contracts that she obtained through advertisements. The IRS classifies Vera as an independent contractor.[13]

Companies can strategically use independent contractors to help control costs, temporarily increase capabilities, and bring in needed talents quickly. They can thus be particularly useful for companies competing through innovation or low-cost strategies. Independent contractors often receive a higher salary than do regular employees but do not receive benefits, which can make them cost-effective. Because independent contractors are often highly skilled, they may prefer to work on a project basis for many firms rather than be a single company's employee. Independent contractors also have greater control over the work they take on and the hours they work, which can enable people to work despite responsibilities preventing them from working traditional hours.

Some companies have tried to reduce costs by wrongly classifying regular employees as independent contractors, and workers have become more reluctant to challenge these practices in the tough job market. But federal and state officials, many facing record budget deficits exacerbated by the lost unemployment insurance and workers' compensation insurance revenue resulting from this misclassification, are starting to aggressively pursue companies trying to claim that regular employees are independent contractors.[14] In 2009, the Illinois Department of Labor imposed $328,500 in penalties on a home improvement company for misclassifying 18 workers by pressing them to incorporate as separate business entities.[15]

Outsourcing

An alternative to contingent work is *outsourcing* the work to another firm. This typically involves contracting with an outside firm that has a particular expertise to assume complete responsibility for a specific contracted service—not just to supply workers. Firms often outsource their noncore functions, such as their payroll, landscaping, and food service activities.

Offshore outsourcing by opening a location in another country or outsourcing work to an existing company abroad has become increasingly popular for many organizations seeking productivity gains. In 2005, nearly two-thirds of all Fortune 500 companies used offshore outsourcing. Some of these companies saved over 70 percent in labor costs by doing so.[16] Offshore outsourcing can be successful if the work is relatively minor or intermittent; for example, if the firm is updating a software module or developing new Web pages. The risks involved with outsourcing are primarily the result of conducting work in two countries having different cultures, different intellectual property laws, and conflicting legal systems. A company must consider the nature of the other country's judicial system, local laws, and what would happen if the offshore company goes bankrupt. In addition, the company should ensure that an accepted dispute resolution procedure is in the outsourcing contract, including where the case would be filed if a conflict arises.[17]

LAWS AND REGULATIONS

Social pressures often lead to legislation, such as wage and hour laws and equal employment opportunity legislation, with which employers must comply. Common law, or court-made law, is the body of case-by-case decisions made by the courts that over time determines what is legal and what remedies are appropriate. Each state develops its own common law in response to federal and state legislation and the nature of the specific cases brought before its courts. Over time, these decisions establish the permissibility of various staffing practices as well as appropriate remedies for impermissible practices. For example, workplace tort cases, or civil wrongs in which an employer violates a duty owed to its customers or employees, and employment-at-will cases are treated at the state level. Because case law differs across states, it is necessary to be familiar with the case law in the states in which an organization is operating.

Although most employment discrimination lawsuits are brought under federal statutes, state laws can sometimes be even more restrictive. (A state's Attorney General's office can provide you with information about that state's fair employment practice laws.[18]) Some laws extend similar protection as provided by the federal acts to employers who are not covered by those statutes. Other statutes provide protection to groups not covered by the federal acts and protection for individuals who are performing civil or family duties outside of their normal employment. The District of Columbia protects workers from family responsibilities discrimination. In Alaska, workers are protected from discrimination based on parental status, and a similar executive order covers federal workers and contractors.[19]

Local, state, and federal legislative bodies pass statutory laws as well as create agencies, such as the Department of Labor and the Equal Employment Opportunity Commission, to interpret, administer, and enforce specific laws. Constitutional law supersedes all other sources of laws and regulations, and applies particularly to the due process rights of public employees.

The Laws Relevant to Staffing

There are several major federal laws that broadly apply to employers. Whether or not an employer is covered by a particular law depends on its number of employees and whether the company is a federal contractor. Table 3–2 summarizes some of the federal antidiscrimination laws that allow individuals to sue an employer for failure to hire, and we will discuss each of these laws next.

TABLE 3–2	Summary of Federal Laws Relevant to Staffing		
Law or Executive Order	**Who is Covered**	**General Provisions**	**Further Information**
Title VII of the Civil Rights Act of 1964 (Amended in 1991)	Private employers with at least 15 employees Labor unions, employment agencies, and educational institutions Local, state, and federal governments	Prohibits discrimination on the basis of race, color, religion, sex (both women and men), or national origin	http://www.eeoc.gov/ policy/ http://www.eeoc.gov/ facts/qanda.html http://www.dol.gov/ oasam/regs/statutes/2 000e-16.htm http://www.eeoc.gov/ eeoc/history/35th/1990s /civilrights.html
Executive Order 11246 of 1965 and Executive Order 11375 of 1967	Federal contractors with contracts exceeding $10,000	Prohibits discrimination and establishes affirmative action to promote diversity in race, color, religion, sex, or national origin	http://www.dol.gov/ compliance/laws/com p-eeo.htm http://www.dotcr.ost. dot.gov/documents/ ycr/eo11246.htm http://www.dotcr.ost. dot.gov/documents/ ycr/eo11375.htm
Pregnancy Discrimination Act of 1978	Private employers with at least 15 employees Labor unions, employment agencies, and educational institutions Local, state, and federal governments	Pregnancy, childbirth, or related medical conditions (Defines pregnancy as a temporary disability that requires accommodation)	www.eeoc.gov/facts/ fs-preg.html
Americans with Disabilities Act of 1990	Private employers with at least 15 employees Local, state, and federal governments	Qualified individual with or perceived as having a disability	http://www.eeoc.gov/ policy/ http://www.eeoc.gov/ laws/types/ disability.cfm www.usdoj.gov/crt/ ada/ www.eeoc.gov/ada/ amendments_ notice.html

(Continued)

TABLE 3–2 (Continued)

Law or Executive Order	Who is Covered	General Provisions	Further Information
Title II of the Genetic Information Nondiscrimination Act of 2008	Private employers with at least 15 employees Labor unions, employment agencies, and educational in-stitutions Local, state, and federal gov-ernments	Prohibits discrimination on the basis genetic information	http://www.eeoc.gov/laws/types/genetic.cfm
Rehabilitation Act of 1973	Federal contractors with contracts exceeding $2,500 must engage in affirmative action	Individuals with a handicap	http://www.eeoc.gov/laws/types/disability.cfm
Age Discrimination in Employment Act of 1967	Private employers with at least 20 employees	Protects people 40 years of age or older	www.eeoc.gov/policy/adea.html http://www.eeoc.gov/laws/types/age.cfm
Immigration Reform and Control Act of 1986	Employers with at least 4 employees must verify the employment eligibility of everyone hired	Citizens, U.S. nationals, and aliens authorized to work in the United States are eligible for employment	https://www.oig.lsc.gov/legis/irca86.htm
Worker Adjustment and Retraining Notification Act (WARN) of 1988	Employers with at least 100 employees not including employees who have worked less than 6 months in the last 12 months and not including employees who work less than 20 hours per week Private, public, quasi-public entities which operate in a commercial context Regular local, federal, and state government entities that provide public services are *not* covered	Must provide 60 days advance notice of covered plant closings and covered mass layoffs of 50 or more people (excluding part-time workers)	www.doleta.gov/layoff/warn.cfm
The Uniformed Services Employment and Reemployment Rights Act (USERRA) of 1994	All members of the uniformed services (including non-career National Guard and Reserve members, as well as active duty personnel)	Ensures that members of the uniformed services are entitled to return to their civilian employment after their service	www.dol.gov/elaws/userra.htm
Vietnam Era Veterans' Readjustment Assistance Act of 1974 (VEVRAA) (Amended in 2002 by the Jobs for Veterans Act)	Any contractor or subcontractor with a contract of $25,000 or more with the federal gov-ernment	Prohibits discrimination against and requires affirmative action for disabled veterans as well as other categories of veterans	http://www.dol.gov/compliance/laws/comp-vevraa.htm http://www.doleta.gov/Seniors/html_docs/docs/veteransjobs.cfm

TABLE 3–2	(Continued)		
Law or Executive Order	**Who is Covered**	**General Provisions**	**Further Information**
Consumer Credit Reporting Reform Act of 1996	Employers who conduct credit checks for employment purposes (e.g., if an employee handles money, which may require being bonded)	Employers must disclose in advance the company's intention to obtain a credit report and obtain written permission from the applicant or employee. The applicant or employee must receive a copy of the report and a written description of their rights under this Act before action is taken based on the report	www.ftc.gov/os/ statutes/03.1224fcra. pdf

TITLE VII OF THE CIVIL RIGHTS ACT OF 1964   Title VII of the Civil Rights Act of 1964, amended in 1991, prohibits employment discrimination based on race, color, religion, sex, or national origin. Title VII prohibits not only intentional discrimination, but also practices that have the effect of discriminating against individuals because of their race, color, national origin, religion, or sex. Title VII explicitly states that race can never be used as a bona fide occupational qualification when making hiring decisions.

Under Title VII, it is an unlawful employment practice for an employer:[20]

1. "to fail or refuse to hire or to discharge any individual, or otherwise to discriminate against any individual with respect to his compensation, terms, conditions, or privileges of employment, because of such individual's race, color, religion, sex, or national origin"; or
2. "to limit, segregate, or classify his employees or applicants for employment in any way which would deprive or tend to deprive any individual of employment opportunities or otherwise adversely affect his status as an employee, because of such individual's race, color, religion, sex, or national origin."

Congress established that intentional discrimination was established "when a complaining party demonstrates that race, color, religion, sex or national origin was a motivating factor for any employment practice, even though other factors also motivated the practice."[21] The Civil Rights Act of 1991 is enforced by the Equal Employment Opportunity Commission and provides monetary damages in cases of intentional employment discrimination.

The largest employment discrimination lawsuit filed to date is a widely publicized discrimination lawsuit against Walmart and Sam's Club. Thousands of female employees filed a class-action suit over alleged denial of advancement, denial of equal pay, and a denial of promotions and raises based on the fact that they were women.[22] The suit was settled in 2010 for more than $11.7 million.[23]

EXECUTIVE ORDER 11246 OF 1965 AND EXECUTIVE ORDER 11375 OF 1967   Executive Orders 11246 and 11375 apply to employers with a federal contract exceeding $10,000. Among other things, these Executive Orders establish that an employer with a federal contract exceeding $10,000:[24]

...will not discriminate against any employee or applicant for employment because of race, color, religion, sex, or national origin. The contractor will take affirmative action to ensure that applicants are employed, and that employees are treated during employment, without regard to their race, color, religion, sex, or national origin. Such action shall include, but not be limited to the following:

employment, upgrading, demotion, or transfer; recruitment or recruitment advertising; layoff or termination; rates of pay or other forms of compensation; and selection for training, including apprenticeship. The contractor agrees to post in conspicuous places, available to employees and applicants for employment, notices to be provided by the contracting officer setting forth the provisions of this nondiscrimination clause.

Affirmative action is required by the executive orders, which are enforced by the U.S. Department of Labor.

THE PREGNANCY DISCRIMINATION ACT OF 1978   The Pregnancy Discrimination Act of 1978 prohibits private employers with at least 15 employees, labor unions, employment agencies, educational institutions, and local, state, and federal governments from discriminating on the basis of pregnancy, childbirth, or related medical conditions. Pregnancy, childbirth, and related medical conditions must be treated the same way as other temporary illnesses or conditions are treated.[25]

THE AMERICANS WITH DISABILITIES ACT (ADA) OF 1990   The Americans with Disabilities Act (ADA) of 1990 and the Americans with Disabilities Act Amendments Act that became effective on January 1, 2009, apply to private employers with at least 15 employees as well as to local, state, and federal governments. The ADA guarantees equal opportunity for individuals with disabilities or perceived as having disabilities and grants similar protections to those provided on the basis of race, color, sex, national origin, age, and religion. A person is to be considered disabled regardless of whether or not any form of treatment or corrective device (other than contact lenses or glasses) is used to ameliorate or control the condition. The Equal Employment Opportunity Commission enforces the ADA.

THE GENETIC INFORMATION NONDISCRIMINATION ACT (GINA) OF 2008   The Genetic Information Nondiscrimination Act prohibits employers from discriminating against individuals based on the results of genetic testing when making hiring, firing, job placement, or promotion decisions. Genetic testing is a type of testing that can identify people genetically susceptible to certain diseases that could result from exposure to toxic substances, such as chemicals or radiation, in the workplace. However, few diseases or conditions are due to a single gene or even several genes acting alone. Most are due to a combination of factors such as stress, diet, and environmental pollutants so genetic tests can't reliably predict whether someone will develop a particular condition.

HR professionals should ensure that job applications do not ask questions that can discriminate based on genetic makeup. In addition no employment decisions can be made based on genetic information. Hiring managers must also be trained to not ask about genetic information or family health issues on interviews, while making hiring or any employment decisions. HR departments must also ensure that they update labor posters and handbooks to reflect this law.

THE REHABILITATION ACT OF 1973   The Rehabilitation Act of 1973 requires federal contractors with contracts exceeding $2,500 to engage in affirmative action to promote the hiring of individuals with a disability. The Act protects qualified individuals from discrimination based on a disability. As with the ADA, qualified individuals with disabilities are defined as persons who, with reasonable accommodation, can perform the essential functions of the job for which they have applied or have been hired to perform. **Reasonable accommodation** means an employer is required to take reasonable steps to accommodate a disability unless it would cause the employer undue hardship.[26]

reasonable accommodation
reasonable steps to accommodate a disability that do not cause the employer undue hardship

THE AGE DISCRIMINATION IN EMPLOYMENT ACT (ADEA) OF 1967   The Age Discrimination in Employment Act (ADEA) prohibits employers with more than 20 employees from discriminating against any worker with respect to compensation or the terms, conditions, or privileges of employment because he or she is age 40 or older. Specifically related to staffing, it is unlawful for an employer:[27]

1. "to fail or refuse to hire or to discharge any individual or otherwise discriminate against any individual with respect to his compensation, terms, conditions, or privileges of employment, because of such individual's age"; or

2. "to limit, segregate, or classify his employees in any way which would deprive or tend to deprive any individual of employment opportunities or otherwise adversely affect his status as an employee, because of such individual's age."

The Supreme Court has held that the ADEA does not apply to claims of "reverse discrimination" where "young" older workers receive less favorable treatment than "older" older workers. As a result, employers may provide more favorable benefits (formal phased retirement programs, for example) to older workers within the over-40 age group.[28]

Some states have expanded the ages protected from employment discrimination. In New Jersey it is illegal to discriminate against employees between the ages of 18 and 70.[29]

THE IMMIGRATION REFORM AND CONTROL ACT OF 1986 Under the Immigration Reform and Control Act, employers must use an I-9 verification form to verify the employability status of every new employee within three days of their being hired. This form requires documentation verifying a new hire's eligibility, identity, and authorization to work in the United States. To avoid the appearance of discrimination on the basis of national origin, it is a good idea to make the job offer contingent on proof of employment eligibility.

For privacy reasons, I-9s must be kept in a folder where managers cannot see them. Training recruiters and hiring managers on I-9 compliance is also important.[30] The voluntary and free Internet-based E-Verify system operated by the Homeland Security Department in partnership with the Social Security Administration can help employers determine a person's eligibility to work in the United States.[31]

Rather than conducting workplace raids to pick up undocumented workers, Immigration and Customs Enforcement policy has shifted to the criminal prosecution of businesses for workplace immigration law violations. In 2007, Immigration and Customs Enforcement made 863 work-site criminal arrests of corporate officers, managers, and contractors, up from 25 in 2002, and 4,077 administrative arrests, up from 485 in 2002.[32] It is a good idea to keep I-9 records clean and error free and regularly conduct internal I-9 workforce audits to identify and correct problems on your own.

THE WORKER ADJUSTMENT AND RETRAINING NOTIFICATION ACT (WARN) OF 1988 In brief, the WARN Act is a federal law requiring employers of 100 or more full-time workers who have worked at least six of the last 12 months and an average of 20 hours or more per week to give employees 60 days' advance notice of closing or major layoffs.[33] Hourly, salaried, managerial, and supervisory employees are all entitled to notice under WARN, although business partners, workers participating in strike actions, and contract employees are not. More details about what is covered are available on the Department of Labor's Web site.[34]

Some states have passed their own WARN-type Acts expanding this coverage. California requires a WARN notice when a company cuts at least 50 workers in one place. New York requires 90 days' notice when laying off 250 or more workers at a site.

THE UNIFORMED SERVICES EMPLOYMENT AND REEMPLOYMENT RIGHTS ACT (USERRA) OF 1994 The Uniformed Services Employment and Reemployment Rights Act of 1994 (significantly updated in 1996 and 1998) prohibits employers from discriminating against job applicants who may be called into military service or who volunteer for military service. The act seeks to ensure that members of the uniformed services are entitled to return to their civilian employment upon completion of their service with the seniority, status, and rate of pay they would have obtained had they remained continuously employed by their civilian employer. The law also protects individuals from discrimination in hiring, promotion, and retention on the basis of present and future membership in the armed services. The Department of Labor enforces the USERRA.

VIETNAM ERA VETERANS' READJUSTMENT ASSISTANCE ACT (VEVRAA) OF 1974 (AMENDED IN 2002 BY THE JOBS FOR VETERANS ACT) The Vietnam Era Veterans' Readjustment Assistance Act (VEVRAA) prohibits discrimination against protected veterans and it requires federal government contractors and subcontractors with a contract of $25,000 or more with the federal government to take affirmative action to employ and advance in employment the veterans protected by VEVRAA and its amendments. VEVRAA requires that contractors and subcontractors list their employment openings with the appropriate employment service delivery system, and that covered veterans receive priority in referral to such openings. Further, VEVRAA requires that federal contractors and subcontractors track and submit annually the number of current employees who are covered veterans.

THE CONSUMER CREDIT REPORTING REFORM ACT OF 1996   Under the Consumer Credit Reporting Reform Act of 1996, an employer must disclose in advance its intention to obtain an applicant's or employee's credit report and obtain written permission from the individual. The applicant or employee must receive a copy of the report and a written description of their rights under this act before action is taken based on the report.

Bona Fide Occupational Qualification (BFOQ)

bona fide occupational qualification (BFOQ)
a characteristic that is essential to the successful performance of a relevant employment function

business necessity
an important business objective of the employer

protected class
a group of people who share a particular characteristic that is protected by federal and/or state employment discrimination laws

There are situations in which a protected characteristic can be considered a **bona fide occupational qualification (BFOQ)** and legally be used to make employment decisions. A BFOQ means that the characteristic is essential to the successful performance of a relevant employment function. As established in the Supreme Court case *Diaz v. Pan Am World Airways*,[35] only a qualification that affects an employee's ability to perform the job can be considered a BFOQ. BFOQs do not apply to all jobs, and race and color can never be considered BFOQs. One example of how sex can be a BFOQ is in relation to employment in a setting, such as a locker room, that is exclusively used by members of one sex.

It is important to develop a specific job description outlining the requirements and duties of the position and a job specification detailing the corresponding qualifications of the individual needed for the position before beginning a recruitment effort. BFOQs must be based only on the actual inability of individuals with some protected characteristic (e.g., their sex) to perform job duties, not on stereotyped characterizations.

Asking about protected characteristics that are not BFOQs during employment interviews is a mistake made by many uninformed hiring managers. This chapter's Develop Your Skills feature contains several taboo interview questions and an explanation of why they should be avoided.

DEVELOP YOUR SKILLS
Improper Interview Questions

Court rulings and Equal Employment Opportunity Commission guidelines prohibit the use of all preemployment inquiries that disproportionately screen out members of protected classes, are not valid predictors of on-the-job performance success, or cannot be justified by "business necessity."[36] A protected class is a group of people who share a particular characteristic protected by federal and/or state employment discrimination laws. A business necessity is an important business objective of the employer.

Although interview questions in and of themselves are not illegal, questions that can have an illegal impact in terms of a firm's hiring should be avoided. The following are five interview questions that are likely to have a discriminatory effect on employment and that should be avoided:[37]

1. *How many children do you have?* Questions regarding an applicant's marital status, children, and childcare arrangements can be construed as being discriminatory. Title VII of the Civil Rights Act makes it illegal to deny a female applicant employment because she has or is planning to have children.

2. *What is your native language?* If an English-language skill is not a job requirement but the employer requires English-language proficiency, an adverse effect upon a minority group may result, violating Title VII. Inquiring how an applicant acquired the ability to read, write, or speak a foreign language is also inappropriate.

3. *What clubs or organizations do you belong to?* The courts may view this question as seeking information that is not job related and that could result in discrimination based on a person's gender, national origin, or religion in violation of Title VII.

4. *What is your height? What is your weight?* Minimum height and weight requirements have been found to be illegal under Title VII if they screen out a disproportionate number of minorities or women and the employer cannot show that these standards are essential to the safe performance of the job(s) in question.[38]

5. *Are you able to work on Christmas Day?* An employer can be accused of religious discrimination in violation of Title VII if its interviewers ask about an applicant's willingness to work any particular religious holiday.

Global Issues

Employment laws vary across countries. For example, Mexican workers not only enjoy a right to severance pay, they also benefit from laws that give them absolute caps on the number of hours they can work, paid vacations at premium-pay rates, paid holidays, paid weekends, paid maternity leave, employer-funded housing, annual profit-sharing bonuses, and annual 13th-month pay bonuses. None of these practices exists under U.S. law. Mexico's constitution also grants affirmative action–related employment rights and bans noncompete agreements.[39]

U.S. multinational companies operating in Europe must also comply with the employment laws of their European host countries. Although many European nations have statutes or constitutional clauses prohibiting employment discrimination, unlike U.S. laws, many of these laws lack provisions by which government agencies can enforce them or private litigation can be pursued. But this situation is changing because Europeans are concerned that due to the formation of the European Union, people's employment rights and working conditions will deteriorate to the point where they mirror the lowest levels of protection afforded by a particular member-nation. This concern has resulted in European Union–level legislation requiring member nations to strengthen their legal provisions.[40]

EQUAL EMPLOYMENT OPPORTUNITY, AFFIRMATIVE ACTION, AND QUOTAS

Equal employment opportunity, affirmative action, and staffing quotas are frequently misunderstood and often the subjects of debate. Next, we discuss each of them.

Equal Employment Opportunity

Equal employment opportunity (EEO) means that a firm's employment practices must be designed and used in a "facially neutral" manner. Facially neutral means that all employees and applicants are treated consistently regardless of their protected characteristics, such as their sex and race. EEO laws require firms to make an unbiased assessment and interpretation of applicants' job qualifications. The consistent administration of staffing practices is thought to create an equal opportunity for everyone to obtain a job or promotion, not just members of protected classes. A person cannot be discriminated against (i.e., he or she would fall into a protected class) based on the following characteristics:[41]

equal employment opportunity (EEO)
employment practices designed and used in a "facially neutral" manner

- Age
- Disability
- National origin
- Pregnancy
- Race
- Religion
- Sex

EEO laws also prohibit employees from retaliatory discharge and from being sexually harassed. In addition, the laws prohibit employers from paying employees more than other employees based upon their sex or discriminating against employees based on the fact that they are pregnant.

Affirmative Action

You might have wondered at some point in your lifetime what exactly affirmative action consists of. **Affirmative action**[42] refers to the proactive efforts of the U.S. government to eliminate discrimination and its past effects. Affirmative action programs began in the 1970s to improve the outcome of the Civil Rights Act of 1964, which prohibited race discrimination in employment. As President Lyndon Johnson put it in 1965: "We seek . . . not just equality as a right and a theory but equality as a fact and equality as a result." Out of concern that ending formal discrimination would not eliminate racism by employers, President Johnson issued Executive Order 11246 in September 1965, requiring employers who received federal contracts to take extra steps—affirmative action, that is—to integrate their workforces. Executive Order 11246 requires contractors with federal contracts of at least $50,000 and 50 or more employees to have an affirmative action plan.

affirmative action
the proactive effort to eliminate discrimination and its effects, and to ensure nondiscriminatory results in employment practices in the future

The goal of affirmative action is to provide employment opportunities to groups formerly underrepresented in employment. These groups, particularly blacks, Native Americans, Asian Americans, Hispanic Americans, and women, have been identified by the U.S. Department of Labor as "protected classes." Affirmative action is also required for handicapped persons, disabled veterans, and Vietnam War veterans. Although Executive Order 11246 requires that federal contractors set goals for hiring minorities and females, there are currently no laws or regulations requiring they set goals for hiring other protected classes (handicapped persons and Vietnam veterans).

AFFIRMATIVE ACTION PLANS   An *affirmative action plan* describes in detail the actions to be taken, procedures to be followed, and standards to be adhered to when it comes to establishing an affirmative action program. Affirmative action plans can include, but are not limited to, adhering to provisions for nondiscriminatory recruitment, training, and promotion. Procedures for internal record keeping, internal compliance auditing, and reporting are often included to measure the success of the plans. Employers adhere to affirmative action plans because they want to, because a court orders them to, because they are federal contractors, or because they agree to them as a remedy for discrimination that occurred in the past.

Affirmative action programs can temporarily give preferential treatment to qualified applicants from underrepresented protected groups. Preferential treatment is only allowable in cases settled by courts in contexts of discrimination claims. (A firm cannot legally decide to give preferential treatment on its own, in other words.) Numerical benchmarks are usually established based on the availability of qualified applicants in the job market or qualified candidates in the employer's workforce. These numerical goals do not create quotas for specific groups, nor are they designed to guarantee proportional representation or equal results. In most cases, the plans identify voluntary goals and timetables for integrating workers from underrepresented groups into the workplace. In other words, the plans give employers a framework to use as they develop their recruiting, hiring, and promotion strategies. Moreover, a contractor's failure to attain its goals is not in and of itself an affirmative action violation. However, failing to make a good faith effort to attain the goals is.[43] Affirmative action plans should be temporary and be discontinued when the workforce is representative of the available population, and should be formally stated in writing.

The practice of affirmative action (making an effort to undo the results of discrimination that has occurred in the past) tends to be controversial. Nonetheless, since the establishment of affirmative action programs, women and minorities have experienced significant employment gains. In the first 25 years following the government's affirmative action efforts, the participation by blacks in the workforce increased 50 percent, and the percentage of blacks holding managerial positions jumped fivefold.[44] But the result has been far from perfect. For example, in 2006, only 20 of the Fortune 1000 CEOs were women.[45]

It is important to understand some of the key factors that determine the legal defensibility of an affirmative action plan, particularly if it requires giving preferential treatment to any subgroup. Several federal court decisions[46] have helped to clarify some of the factors that are important in determining whether an affirmative action plan that involves preferential treatment is in violation of Title VII. These are summarized in Table 3–3 [47] Rather than giving any protected group preferential treatment, it may be better for employers to identify the business-related characteristic they are seeking (e.g., a goal to hire people with knowledge of and influence in the African American community) and use it in making hiring decisions rather than using the protected characteristic itself.

In addition to hiring decisions, affirmative action implications extend to layoffs as well. In 1986, *Wygant v. Jackson Board of Education*[48] challenged a school board's policy of protecting minority employees by laying off nonminority teachers first, even though they had seniority. The Supreme Court ruled against the school board, saying that the injury suffered by the nonminorities affected could not justify the benefits to minorities: "We have previously expressed concern over the burden that a preferential-layoffs scheme imposes on innocent parties. In cases involving valid hiring goals, the burden to be borne by innocent individuals is diffused to a considerable extent among society generally. Though hiring goals may burden some innocent individuals, they simply do not impose the same kind of injury that layoffs impose. Denial of a future employment opportunity is not as intrusive as loss of an existing job."

TABLE 3–3	Affirmative Action Plans Involving Preferential Treatment[49]

- **Affirmative action plans should be remedial in nature.** Employers found guilty of discrimination can be forced to implement an affirmative action plan to remedy the discrimination. Employers that have an imbalanced workforce but that have not been found guilty of discrimination may be able to justify an affirmative action plan to remedy the imbalance. Employers whose workforce is representative of the available workforce will have a difficult time justifying an affirmative action plan.
- **An affirmative action plan should not exclude all nonminorities.** Exactly how restrictive any subgroup quotas can be is unclear, but an affirmative action plan that excludes all members of a nonminority group would likely be found to be illegal.
- **An affirmative action plan should be temporary.** Discontinue the plan after meeting the affirmative action goals.
- **An affirmative action plan should be formalized.** Actions taken under informal affirmative action plans (i.e., those lacking formal goals or a formal statement of the actions to be taken under the plan) have been found to be discriminatory.

An equal opportunity/affirmative action statement should be included in all recruitment communications. Most organizations use phrases or acronyms such as *EOE/AA* (Equal Opportunity Employer/Affirmative Action), *Equal Opportunity Employer*, or *An Equal Opportunity/Affirmative Action Institution*. If these statements are ineffective in recruiting the quality and range of applicants desired, the employer can create a more explicit and proactive statement, such as the following: "Applicants from underrepresented groups are strongly encouraged to apply." An excellent sample affirmative action program has been created by the Equal Employment Opportunity Commission and is available at www.dol.gov/esa/regs/compliance/ofccp/pdf/sampleaap.pdf.

Quotas

Staffing quotas establish specific requirements that certain percentages of disadvantaged groups be hired. Staffing quotas are generally illegal. The goal of quotas is often to equalize the proportional representation of underrepresented groups in the company's workforce with their proportions in the organization's relevant labor market. The size and location of a firm's relevant labor market depends on the nature of the job. As an illustration, for faculty positions, the relevant labor market is usually defined as national. For management and professional positions, the relevant labor market is generally defined as regional. For staff and laborer positions, the relevant labor market is usually defined as local.

staffing quotas
establish specific requirements that certain numbers of people from disadvantaged groups be hired

By the late 1970s, flaws in affirmative action policy began to arise, and *reverse discrimination*, or discrimination against white males, became an issue. The landmark 1978 *Bakke* case made numerical quotas illegal in college admissions programs. Allan Bakke, a white male, had been rejected two years in a row by a medical school that had accepted less-qualified minority applicants. The school had a separate admissions policy for minorities and reserved 16 out of 100 slots for minority students. The Supreme Court outlawed inflexible quota systems in affirmative action programs. In the same ruling, however, the Court upheld the legality of affirmative action per se. *Regents of University of California v. Bakke*[50] prohibited schools from considering race as a factor in admissions to promote racial diversity unless race is considered alongside other factors and on a case-by-case basis. In 2003, the Supreme Court ruled in *Grutter v. Bollinger*[51] and *Gratz v. Bollinger*[52] that a school can make action-based admission decisions if it treats race as one factor among many for the purpose of achieving a "diverse" student population. In other words, each applicant must be reviewed individually, and an affirmative action policy is unconstitutional if it automatically increases an applicant's chances over others simply because of his or her race.[53] Although these school admissions cases are not Title VII cases, similar mechanisms are applied to them.

Employers are not required to have a proportional representation in their workforce as long as they can show that they are not engaging in discrimination. However, they are more open to lawsuits if they do not. Although affirmative action, preferential treatment policies, and quotas are not required by law, they are not prohibited either. Because numerical quota systems allow less-qualified members of protected groups to be hired over more-qualified candidates, there are limitations on their features and usage. A quota is most often used as a court-imposed remedy for past discrimination or as part of a voluntary affirmative action plan.

ENFORCEMENT AGENCIES

Legislative bodies at the local, state, and federal levels have the power to create, amend, and eliminate laws and regulations, including those pertaining to staffing and employment. Legislative bodies also create agencies for the purposes of interpreting, administering, and enforcing these laws. The two most important federal agencies in terms of staffing are the Equal Employment Opportunity Commission (EEOC) and the Department of Labor's Office of Federal Contract Compliance Programs.

The Equal Employment Opportunity Commission (EEOC)

When the EEOC was established by Title VII of the Civil Rights Act of 1964, its primary responsibility was to receive and investigate charges of unlawful employment practices and, for those charges found to be of "reasonable cause," to try to resolve the disputes. The agency's responsibilities have expanded with the enactment of new and amended legislation, and in 1972, the commission was given the power to enforce certain laws. Currently, the EEOC enforces the following federal statutes:

- Title VII of the Civil Rights Act of 1964
- The Age Discrimination in Employment Act of 1967 (ADEA)
- Pregnancy Discrimination Act of 1978
- Title I and Title V of the Americans with Disabilities Act of 1990 (ADA)
- Sections 501 and 505 of the Rehabilitation Act of 1973
- Sections 102 and 103 of the Civil Rights Act of 1991
- The Equal Pay Act of 1963
- The Genetic Information Nondiscrimination Act of 2008 (GINA)

The EEOC receives over 90,000 charges each year,[54] and recently increased its staff to help resolve a backlog of charges.[55] Even companies with large, sophisticated staffing functions are vulnerable. In 2006, the EEOC filed a lawsuit against United Parcel Service on behalf of a Rastafarian who was told he had to shave his beard if he wanted to be hired as a driver's helper. The EEOC also filed a national class-action sex discrimination lawsuit against Lawry's Restaurants Inc. on behalf of male applicants who alleged they were systematically rejected for jobs as food servers.[56]

In addition to enforcing equal employment laws, the EEOC encourages and facilitates voluntary compliance via tailored programs that meet the needs of employers, including small business and federal-sector employers, and via programs to educate the public on EEO laws. Another good reason to ensure that recruiters and hiring managers rely on objective standards and comply with antidiscrimination laws is that the EEOC is pursuing more systemic discrimination cases, which can generate judicial damage awards that run into hundreds of millions of dollars.[57]

The remedies available to the EEOC for employment discrimination, intentional or not, include:

- Back pay, or the pay a plaintiff is entitled to up to the time the court rendered its judgment
- Hiring, promotion, or job reinstatement
- Front pay, or pay a plaintiff is entitled to between the time the judgment is reached and the time the worker returns to the place of employment
- Reasonable accommodation
- Other actions that will make an individual "whole" (i.e., in the condition he or she would have been if not for the discrimination).

When the EEOC finds that a firm has intentionally discriminated, it can award the victims compensatory damages for their actual past and future monetary losses as well damages for their mental anguish and inconvenience. It can also award punitive damages as a deterrent or punishment if an employer acted with malice or reckless indifference (although punitive damages cannot be levied against federal, state, or local government employers). The years 2008 and 2009 saw the highest level of EEOC workplace discrimination charges to date, averaging more than 94,000 claims and $376 million recovered each year.[58] The employer can also be required to take corrective or preventive actions to cure the source of the identified discrimination and minimize the chance of its recurrence.[59] The EEOC's compliance manual, updated in 2006, can be found at www.eeoc.gov.

All employers with 15 or more employees are required to keep employment records. Some large employers are also required to file an EEO-1 report annually depending on the number of employees and federal contracts they have.[60] A sample EEO Standard Form 100 used for this reporting can be found at www.eeoc.gov/stats/jobpat/eeo1.pdf.

The Office of Federal Contract Compliance Programs (OFCCP)

The Office of Federal Contract Compliance Programs (OFCCP) is part of the U.S. Department of Labor [61] and is responsible for administering and enforcing three equal employment opportunity programs that apply to federal contractors and subcontractors: Executive Order 11246 (later expanded by Executive Order 11375), Section 503 of the Rehabilitation Act of 1973, and the affirmative action provisions of the Vietnam Era Veteran's Readjustment Assistance Act of 1974. The primary mission of the OFCCP is to ensure that federal contractors with at least 50 employees and who receive $50,000 or more in grants, goods, and services take affirmative action to promote equal employment opportunity and annually file appropriate affirmative action plans with the agency. The OFCCP systemically reviews employers' employment practices to make sure firms are complying with U.S. discrimination laws.[62] In 2006, the OFCCP conducted almost 4,000 compliance evaluations. However, the office focuses to a greater extent on class-action discrimination. In 2006, it recovered $51.5 million on behalf of workers subjected to unlawful discrimination. This was an increase of 14 percent from 2005, and 78 percent from 2001.[63]

The OFCCP undertakes compliance reviews for contractors flagged by a software program as having below average participation rates for minorities or women. The OFCCP also conducts reviews of contractors selected randomly and those identified through complaints. If it finds a violation of affirmative action or antidiscrimination requirements, the OFCCP attempts to reconcile with the contractor before referring the case for formal administrative enforcement. The OFCCP gives Exemplary Voluntary Efforts (EVE) and Opportunity 2000 awards to those companies that demonstrate significant achievement in terms of their equal opportunity and affirmative action. Although a contractor in violation of Executive Order 11246 may have its federal contracts terminated or suspended, such administrative actions are rare, and the contractor gets sufficient due process before this happens.[64]

HOW DOES THE OFCCP DEFINE AN "APPLICANT"?   Because they must track the gender, race, and ethnicity of applicants and analyze whether hiring practices, policies, or procedures have a "disparate impact" on minority and women applicants, the definition of an applicant is particularly important to federal government contractors. The OFCCP's record-retention regulations under Executive Order 11246 require federal contractors to retain paper résumés and applications for two years if the contractor has at least 150 employees and a government contract of at least $150,000. Contractors with less than 150 employees or no contract of at least $150,000 must retain paper applications and résumés for one year. The OFCCP's regulations also require government contractors to identify the gender, race, and ethnicity of each applicant, where possible.[65] The legal definition of an applicant is particularly important because only "applicants" can allege that unlawful discrimination has occurred with regard to a firm's hiring decisions under state and federal discrimination statutes. Understanding the definition of an applicant can help employers minimize risk and protect themselves from costly audit defense.

INTERNET APPLICANTS   To help federal contractors and subcontractors manage the burdens created by the Internet, which can generate thousands of applicants for a single position, in 2005, the OFCCP published a revised definition of what constitutes an "Internet applicant."[66] By "Internet and related electronic technologies" the OFCCP includes e-mail, résumé databases, job banks, electronic scanning technology, applicant tracking systems, applicant service providers, and applicant screeners. The OFCCP's 2005 definition applies only to data collection and record-keeping requirements under Executive Order 11246 (data related to race, color, religion, national origin, and sex).[67] A person applying via the Internet and related technologies is an "applicant" if all four of the following criteria are satisfied:

1. The individual expresses an interest in a job via the Internet or related electronic data technologies;
2. The contractor considers the individual for employment in a particular position;

3. The individual's expression of interest indicates that he or she possesses the basic qualifications for the position; and

4. The individual at no point in the contractor's selection process, prior to receiving an offer of employment from the contractor, removes himself or herself from further consideration or otherwise indicates that he or she is no longer interested in the position.

Consider a contractor who wants to hire a bilingual manufacturing supervisor and searches an Internet job database containing 30,000 résumés for two basic qualifications: a four-year business degree and fluency in English and Spanish. The initial screen for these two basic qualifications narrows the pool to 5,000 people. The contractor then adds a third, preestablished basic qualification of two years of management experience, which reduces the pool to 1,500. Finally, the contractor adds a fourth, preestablished basic qualification of experience in a manufacturing environment, which results in a pool of 85 job seekers. Under the rule, only the 85 job seekers meeting all four basic qualifications would be Internet applicants, assuming they met the other three prongs of the "Internet applicant" definition.

Contractors are allowed to use data management techniques, such as random sampling or absolute numerical limits, to reduce the number of people who express interest in their jobs as long as the techniques are facially neutral and the applicants aren't individually assessed for their qualifications. For example, if the contractor receives a large number of applicants expressing interest, it can decide that it will only consider the first 200.

Contractors must retain records "identifying job seekers contacted regarding their interest in a particular position," and, with respect to internal résumé databases, retain the following:

- a record of each résumé added to the database,
- a record of the date each résumé was added to the database,
- the position for which each search of the database was made, and
- for each search, the substantive search criteria used and the date of the search.

With respect to external résumé databases, the contractor must maintain the following:

- a record of the position for which each search of the database was made,
- the substantive search criteria used,
- the date of the search, and
- the résumés of job seekers who met the basic qualifications for the particular position who are considered by the contractor, even if they do not qualify as Internet applicants.

Contractors must also keep all documents related to the Internet job seekers it contacts regarding their interest in a particular position, the applicants' tests and test results, interview notes, and records identifying their race, gender, and ethnicity.[68] The OFCCP requires contractors to maintain only (1) those records relating to the analyses of the impact of employee selection procedures on Internet applicants, and (2) the impact of employment tests (without regard of whether the tests were administered to Internet applicants) because the OFCCP does not consider employment tests to be basic qualifications. Although the OFCCP generally will use labor force statistics and census data to determine whether basic qualifications have an adverse impact on race, gender, or ethnicity, contractors should consider performing their own analyses.[69]

As we have explained, the OFCCP's definition of an Internet applicant applies only to people applying for jobs with federal contractors via the Internet and related technologies. For noncontractors and for people applying for jobs through nonelectronic means, the Uniform Guidelines on Employee Selection Procedures[70] states that "The precise definition of the term 'applicant' depends upon the user's recruitment and selection procedures. The concept of an applicant is that of a person who has indicated an interest in being considered for hiring, promotion, or other employment opportunities. This interest might be expressed by completing an application form, or might be expressed orally, depending on the employer's practice."[71]

The information collected allows the organization to provide the documentation it needs to justify its selection decisions and defend those decisions against any legal challenges. Much of the information can also be used by firms to evaluate their staffing systems. For example, applicants' assessment scores cannot only be used as evidence in a legal proceeding to show the firm acted in an unbiased way, but to evaluate the quality of the firm's various recruiting sources. Care must be taken to ensure that records on protected characteristics are not easily accessible during the selection process so that charges of discrimination cannot be made.

THE BASES FOR EMPLOYMENT LAWSUITS

Faulty recruiting, hiring, promotion, and termination procedures can all generate lawsuits. Employees who initiate lawsuits often reach all the way back to the hiring process to show that a firm's practices systematically discriminated against them.[72] Next, we discuss several different types of staffing-related lawsuits and what is required for them to succeed in court.

Disparate Treatment

Disparate treatment is intentional discrimination based on a person's protected characteristic. If the employment decision (hiring or firing) would change if the applicant's race, religion, national origin, color, sex, disability, or age were different, disparate treatment has taken place. Disparate treatment can be *direct*, as when it results from a company's policy to not hire older workers. It can also be *inferred* from situational factors or result from a combination of permissible and prohibited factors, both of which we discuss next.

disparate treatment
intentional discrimination based on a protected characteristic

AN INFERRED DISPARATE TREATMENT CASE   Disparate treatment can be inferred from situational factors. To establish this type of case of discrimination, the plaintiff must show:[73]

1. That he or she belongs to a group protected from discrimination (race, gender, etc.).
2. That he or she applied for the job and was qualified for the job for which the employer was seeking applicants.
3. That despite being qualified, he or she was rejected. (The plaintiff does not need to prove that he or she was rejected because of his or her protected status, only that despite his or her qualifications, he or she was rejected.)
4. That after being rejected, the position remained open, and the employer continued to seek applicants whose qualifications were similar to those of the plaintiff.

Once these four aspects are established, the burden shifts to the employer to show that the hiring decision was the result of a BFOQ based on business necessity. Demonstrable evidence of a business necessity is required. The defendant can offer as evidence statistical reports, validation studies, expert testimony, prior successful experience, and other evidence to that effect.[74]

If the defendant is successful in establishing a BFOQ defense, the plaintiff then has the opportunity to present evidence showing that the employer's stated reason for the rejection was false and merely a pretext. To establish a case allowed to go to court, the plaintiff need not prove that discrimination was the motivating factor in the hiring or promotion decision, only raise an inference that such misconduct occurred.

A MIXED MOTIVE CASE   A **mixed motive** case of disparate treatment is one in which the employer is accused of having both a legitimate and an illegitimate reason for making the employment decision. Under the 1991 Civil Rights Act, a plaintiff can establish an unlawful employment practice by showing that a protected characteristic (such as race, sex, color, religion, or national origin) was a motivating factor in an employment decision, even if other legitimate factors—for example, the fact that the plaintiff was tardy, frequently absent, or violated the company's rules—also motivated the decision. A plaintiff only needs to prove that race and/or gender was *a motivating factor*—one of the reasons for the decision—no matter how small a role it played. If the plaintiff satisfies the burden of proof that discrimination was a motivating factor in the employer's action, the employer is found liable. The burden of proof then shifts to the employer to cut off or reduce a plaintiff's monetary damages by proving to the jury that it would have made the same employment decision in the absence of the discriminatory motive. Under the mixed motive analysis, the burden of proof is on the defendant to show that the decision would have been the same despite the plaintiff's race or sex. Under the disparate treatment method, the burden of proof is on the plaintiff to disprove the same thing.

mixed motive
when an employer is accused of having both a legitimate and an illegitimate reason for making an employment decision

The Supreme Court has ruled that plaintiffs do not need a "smoking gun" or direct evidence in showing a protected characteristic to be a motivating factor but can rely on "circumstantial evidence" that does not have to be linked directly to the employment decision.[75] This includes circumstances from which the jury can infer a discriminatory motive—for example, providing evidence that a black employee who had three unexcused absences was fired whereas a white employee with the same number of unexcused absences was not.

Adverse (or Disparate) Impact

Adverse (disparate) impact occurs when an action has a disproportionate effect on a protected group, regardless of its intent. Employment practices that are facially neutral in their treatment of different groups but that have a significantly adverse effect on a protected group when compared with other practices can be legally challenged. The only defense for adverse impact is when it can be justified by a business necessity or job relatedness.

The seminal adverse impact case is the Supreme Court's 1971 decision in *Griggs v. Duke Power Co.* The Court held that if the Duke Power Company could not show a "business necessity" for requiring applicants to possess a high-school diploma or pass off-the-shelf intelligence tests, due to the difference in pass rates for white and minorities, the employer would be in violation of Title VII. Examples of practices that may be subject to an adverse impact challenge include written tests, educational requirements, height and weight requirements, strength requirements (e.g., being able to carry at least 50 pounds), and subjective procedures, such as interviews. In larger organizations, the probability of adverse impact taking place somewhere in the company is greater because of the larger numbers of jobs and job families, or clusters of jobs in the same general areas.

Assessment scores cannot be altered or changed to reduce the adverse impact on protected groups. According to the Civil Rights Act of 1991, it is an unlawful employment practice "to adjust the scores of, use different cutoff scores for, or otherwise alter the results of employment related tests on the basis of race, color, religion, sex, or national origin." This means that *race norming*, or comparing an applicant's scores only to members of his or her own racial subgroup and setting separate passing or cutoff scores for each subgroup, is unlawful.

STATISTICS There are three types of statistics relevant for showing adverse impact: stock statistics, flow statistics, and concentration statistics. **Stock statistics** compare the percentage of men, women, or minorities employed in a job category with their availability in the relevant population of qualified people interested in the position. This is also called a *utilization analysis*. If the employment rate of men, women, or minorities is less than what would be expected based on their availability, they are said to be *underutilized*.

To properly conduct a utilization analysis, employers must compile stock statistics by job group (a group of related jobs) and do them separately for women and minorities. Usually firms compile these statistics as a starting point when developing affirmative action programs. Although it is relatively easy to identify the number of people in each subgroup employed by the firm, it can be difficult to accurately identify each subgroup's availability in the relevant population. The percentage of women or minorities in the recruitment area who have the required skills must be taken into account as well as the percentage of women or minorities among those promotable, transferable, and trainable within the organization—both of which can be difficult to estimate or measure. Different utilization rates do not demonstrate adverse impact; they only show that there is a reason to further investigate an employer's staffing practices to see why the underutilization is occurring. Economists are often hired to conduct utilization analyses. Firms are also advised to seek legal assistance when compiling stock statistics and developing affirmative action plans.

Table 3–4 identifies a firm's utilization rates of women in the clerical job group relative to their availability in the relevant population. In the table, we see that females are 80 percent and males are 20 percent of the company's clerical workers. We see from the right column that females make up 60 percent of the available clerical workers and males 40 percent. This suggests that males may be underutilized in the clerical job category because they are employed at a rate (20 percent) that is less than their availability (40 percent).

TABLE 3–4	Stock Statistics

Job Category: Clerical Workers		
	Current Clerical Workers (%)	**Availability in Relevant Population (%)**
Females	80	60
Males	20	40

Flow statistics compare protected groups' *selection rates*, or the percentage of applicants hired from different subgroups, to determine if the rates are significantly different from each other. If a significant difference is found, adverse impact is demonstrated. This is the only one of the three statistics that can establish adverse impact by itself. The Uniform Guidelines on Employee Selection Procedures,[76] which are on the Internet at www.uniformguidelines.com/uniformguidelines.html, address the requirements for computing and interpreting flow statistics. These guidelines state that:

flow statistics
statistics that compare the percentage of applicants hired from different subgroups to determine if they are significantly different from each other

- Organizations must keep records so the relevant selection rates (also called applicant flow statistics) can be calculated.
- Selection rates must be calculated
  - for each job category,
  - for both internal and external selection decisions,
  - for each step in the selection process, and
  - by applicant race and sex.

- The 80 percent (or 4/5) rule determines whether or not companies' procedures have an adverse impact. The 80 percent rule states that "a selection rate for any race, sex, or ethnic group which is less than four-fifths (4/5) (or 80 percent) of the rate for the group with the highest rate will generally be regarded by federal enforcement agencies as evidence of adverse impact, while a greater than four-fifths rate will generally not be regarded by federal enforcement agencies as evidence of adverse impact."[77]
- The 80 percent rule is only a guideline, and exceptions to it can be made based on issues surrounding the statistical and practical significance of the differences in selection rates (such as small sample sizes).

Statistics are no longer sufficient to show adverse impact. In the 2009 case of *Ricci v. DeStefano*,[78] the U.S. Supreme Court ruled that the results of assessment tests cannot be ignored simply because they have an adverse impact on a protected group. Once an employer has established the selection or promotion process and selection criteria, invalidating the test results without strong evidence of an impermissible adverse impact amounts to racial preference, which is counter to the Title VII notion of a workplace where individuals are guaranteed equal opportunity regardless of race.

The courts have also found that adverse impact occurs if the difference between the number of members of the protected class selected and the number that could be reasonably anticipated to be selected in a random selection system is more than two or three standard deviations. We will discuss this in greater detail in Chapter 8.

In Table 3–5 we see the different selection rates (the percentage of applicants hired) of women and men for the sales associate job category. To apply the four-fifths, or 80 percent, rule to determine if adverse impact has occurred, we start by identifying the most favorable subgroup selection rate. In this example we see that men were hired at the higher rate, and that 50 percent of male applicants were hired (100/200). Four-fifths (or 80 percent) of 50 percent is 40 percent (.80 × 50%). So if females were selected at a rate of less than 40 percent, then the subgroup selection rates differ enough to suggest that the selection method is discriminatory. We see that women were selected at a 25 percent rate, which is less than 40 percent, suggesting the possibility that sex discrimination has occurred.

The 80 percent rule highlights why targeted recruiting is important. If an organization was to simply target a particular subgroup for recruiting with little or no attention to talent, skills, and quality in that pool, then it could unintentionally create a situation in which it would be likely to violate the rule. Simply increasing the size of the pool without maintaining or improving its quality can reduce the selection rate of certain protected subgroups, thereby violating the rule.

TABLE 3–5 Flow Statistics: An Example

Job Category: Sales Associates

	Number of Applicants	Number Hired	Selection Rate (%)
Men	200	100	50
Women	100	25	25

TABLE 3–6	Concentration Statistics: An Example		
	Job Category		
	Sales (%)	**Clerical (%)**	**Management (%)**
Whites	30	15	80
Blacks	50	20	15
Hispanics	20	65	5

concentration statistics

statistics that compare the percentages of men, women, or minorities in various job categories to see if men, women, or minorities are concentrated in certain workforce categories

Concentration statistics compare the percentages of people in various job categories to see if men, women, or minorities are concentrated in certain workforce categories. For example, 50 percent of an organization's total employees may be female, but if women tend to comprise 90 percent of the clerical workforce and men tend to comprise 90 percent of the managerial workforce, then women may be underutilized in managerial positions and men underutilized in clerical positions. Concentration statistics do not establish adverse impact by themselves, but they can give the EEOC a reason to investigate an employer's staffing practices further to see why the differences are occurring.

In Table 3–6, we see that the concentration of blacks in the sales positions is 50 percent, and that the concentration of Hispanics in the clerical positions is 65 percent. By contrast, the concentration of whites in management positions is 80 percent. This suggests that racial subgroups do tend to be concentrated in certain job categories and may suggest discrimination.

ESTABLISHING A LEGAL CASE   The steps in establishing an adverse impact case are:

1. The plaintiff must prove, generally through statistical comparisons, that the challenged practice or selection device has a substantial adverse impact on a protected group.[79] The defendant can then criticize the statistical analysis or offer different statistics.
2. If the plaintiff establishes adverse impact, the employer must prove that the challenged practice is "job-related for the position in question and consistent with business necessity."[80]

Even if the employer proves business necessity, the plaintiff can still prevail by showing that the employer has refused to adopt an alternative employment practice that would satisfy the employer's legitimate interests without having an adverse impact on a protected class.[81]

Defending Failure-to-Hire Lawsuits

Lawsuits for failure to hire can be difficult to defend. In wrongful termination or failure-to-promote lawsuits, personnel records can help establish that the decision to terminate or not promote a person was based on a legitimate, nondiscriminatory reason. But when a company is sued for failure to hire, the employer frequently has no history with the employee on which to rely. Providing an accurate job description to all recruits and using a standardized and well-documented recruitment and screening process is, therefore, very important for the employer. This will be the foundation of the employer's defense. Screening candidates using objective, job-relevant criteria and archiving all recruiter and interviewer notes, test and interview scores, and so forth for each applicant can help the employer defend its hiring decisions in court.[82]

One of the best ways for an organization to reduce the chances of being sued for failure to hire is to reduce the desire of an aggrieved individual to file a lawsuit. On the one hand, if an organization proactively and genuinely tries to generate applicants from diverse groups and subsequently treats all recruits fairly and with respect, rejected applicants may be less likely to engage in legal action. On the other hand, if an organization makes no effort to recruit from diverse groups and treats some applicants differently than others, or treats all applicants unfairly or with disrespect, those who are not hired may be more motivated to sue. The large number of jobs at a big organization increases the chances that adverse impact is occurring somewhere in the company. Although important for all organizations, using proactive recruitment practices and attending to applicant reactions to the recruitment and hiring processes are even more important for larger organizations wishing to avoid lawsuits.

Fraudulent Recruitment

Fraudulent recruitment or *fraudulent inducement* involves misrepresenting the job or organization to a recruit. In a tight job market or during periods of low unemployment among people with the skills they are seeking, employers may be tempted to exaggerate the benefits of their jobs or make unrealistic promises to attract new hires. If they fall prey to this temptation, they risk being hit with a tort lawsuit filed by employees based on a theory of fraudulent inducement to hire. A *tort* involves a claim that someone was harmed by a wrongful but not necessarily criminal act of another party and does not require the existence of a contract. Damages must generally go beyond the loss of employment in order for a plaintiff to make such a claim. If an employer intentionally exaggerates what a job offers, it could be vulnerable to a charge of fraud. Although employment fraud cases are not common or easy to prove, they are becoming more frequent. In addition to sizable jury awards (one plaintiff won $10 million in a breach-of-contract case having claimed that an oil company never intended to keep the promises it made while recruiting him), the damage to a company's reputation as an employer can compromise its future recruiting efforts.[83]

fraudulent recruitment
misrepresenting the job or organization to a recruit

In one fraudulent recruitment case, the Colorado Court of Appeals upheld a $250,000 jury award against a company for concealing information from a candidate during the recruitment process. The company presented a positive picture of itself and of the plaintiff's future with it and concealed its financial losses and the substantial risk that the plaintiff could soon be laid off. The court ruled that an organization may not have to divulge its financial condition to every applicant, but that full disclosure is required if statements are made to an applicant that would create a "false impression" about the employer's outlook and the applicant's future employment prospects.[84]

Statements made to convince a job applicant to accept a position can be legally binding on the employer, even when no employment contracts are involved and even if the contract states that no promises about employment have been made. In other words, an employment-at-will arrangement will not preclude an employee from making a fraudulent recruitment claim.[85] Moreover, any actions that adversely affect a recently hired employee's compensation or status can make it look like the employer acted in bad faith and potentially give rise to a fraudulent recruitment claim. To defend itself, the employer would have to show that intervening circumstances after the person was hired justified the action.

To win a case involving an allegation of fraudulent recruitment and hiring, the plaintiff must prove five things:[86]

1. that the employer made a false representation of a material fact;
2. that the employer knew or believed the representation was false or that there was an insufficient basis for asserting that it was true;
3. that the employer intended the employee to rely on the representation;
4. that the employee justifiably relied on the representation; and
5. that the employee suffered damages as a result of doing so, such as costs related to relocating, resigning from the firm, or rejecting other offers.

A variation on fraudulent hiring occurs when an employer uses fraud to keep an employee from resigning. In one instance, following the purchase of a controlling interest in another company, a man's employer assured him that "absolutely no changes would be made" that could hurt his job security. The man stayed with the firm, was soon subjected to a pay cut, and eventually laid off. In this case, the court allowed the man's claim for fraudulent misrepresentation to go to trial.[87]

Employers can reduce the likelihood of being faced with such lawsuits by instructing all individuals involved in recruiting and hiring not to make any statements about the company or the job that they know are not true, and not to make any promises concerning a job's functions, pay, benefits, or job security that the employer does not intend to keep. Although it is only natural to want to present the job in a positive light, it is a good idea to qualify such statements so they are not taken as guarantees. Any written employment agreement should clearly spell out the terms of employment, including the temporary nature of the employment if the job is not permanent, and state that the written agreement supersedes all prior agreements or understandings concerning the employment. Written reminders that employment is at will can also refute future employees' claims of having been promised long-term job security.[88]

Negligent Hiring

Negligent hiring is a relatively new tort claim based on the common law concept that an employer has a general obligation not to hire an applicant it knows or should have known could harm a third party. Essentially, an organization is considered responsible for the damaging actions of its employees if it failed to exercise reasonable care in hiring the employee who caused the harm. These issues are particularly important when the employee will have a lot of contact with the public, customers, patients, or children, or when the firm is hiring employees whose jobs would give them access to homes and apartments—installers, maintenance workers, delivery drivers, and the like.

A company can be found legally liable for negligent hiring if it fails to uncover a job applicant's incompetence or unfitness by checking his or her references, criminal records, or general background. In order for a customer, employee, or other third party to win a negligent hiring suit against an employer, the following must generally be shown:[89]

1. the existence of an employment relationship between the employer and the worker,
2. the employee's unfitness,
3. the employer's actual or constructive knowledge of the employee's unfitness (failing to investigate an employee's background can lead to a finding of constructive knowledge),
4. the employee's act or omission caused the third party's injuries, and
5. the employer's negligence in hiring the employee was the most likely cause of the plaintiff's injuries.

An employer's obligation to its employees and third parties for negligent hiring depends upon whether that employer acted as a reasonable prudent employer would when hiring its employees. Preemployment background checks are often the responsibility of recruiters. Because the law also requires organizations to respect applicants' privacy, candidates' backgrounds should be researched as thoroughly as possible without violating their privacy rights. Background checks should seek to identify the felony convictions of would-be employees, but not prior arrests that didn't result in convictions since these arrest records are generally protected by privacy laws. Employers should contact all previous employers of the people they want to hire and keep a written record of all of their investigation efforts. Applicants should also be required to explain any gaps in their employment histories. If the organization can afford it, outsourcing background checks to qualified professionals can help the firm refute later claims that it failed to make a reasonable effort to learn about the employee's history.[90] Performing background checks routinely and consistently can also help the firm defend itself against other suits filed, for example, on the basis of disparate treatment and adverse impact. *Negligent retention* is similar to negligent hiring, but it focuses on situations in which a company knowingly retains employees who have a high risk of injuring themselves or others.[91]

Negligent Referral

A growing number of states recognize **negligent referral** as being the basis for a claim. Negligent referral involves misrepresenting or failing to disclose complete and accurate information about a former employee. An employee's former employer can be sued for negligent referral if the employee is involved in some incident at his or her new workplace that might have been predicted based on prior behavior. For example, suppose an employee of Company A is a poor performer or has violent tendencies and the company wants the employee to leave. The employee then applies for a job with Company B, who calls Company A for a reference on the employee. Company A provides either minimal information about the employee or gives a positive reference, so Company B hires the employee who subsequently injures someone in his new position. Not only could Company B end up in court for negligent hiring, Company A could also find itself defending a negligent referral claim brought by Company B or the person injured.[92] Unfortunately, there have been several incidents in the United States in which nurses killed their patients and then moved on to do the same thing at new hospitals. How could this have happened? It happened because administrators at the nurse's former hospitals failed to disclose the information during their reference checks for fear of being sued for defamation.[93] *Defamation* is defined as "an unprivileged publication of false statements to third parties that tends to harm the reputation of the plaintiff in the community."[94]

Clearly, checking a person's references is an important part of conducting a thorough background check as well as establishing an applicant's credentials and potential fit with the organization and position. But many employers provide only dates of employment, salary, and title, fearing that revealing more information about former employees could expose them to defamation suits by disgruntled former employees unable to find new employment. To promote safe workplaces, over 30 states have passed laws providing varying degrees of immunity to former employers who provide honest references about their former employees. It is too early to tell whether the immunity given to employers under these laws will sufficiently protect former employers from defamation. Defamation is currently the most common cause of action used by former employees to challenge a reference given by a former employer. Virtually unheard of prior to the 1990s, defamation in wrongful-termination lawsuits has become a growing trend.[95] Basically, recruiters can be trained to obtain information the firm needs to know about a candidate, but it can still be difficult for them to learn all the firm would like to know about a candidate from a reference check.

Certainly, it is wise for managers to exercise caution in giving references for former employees, even in the states that currently have laws granting immunity to employers for giving references. However, a blanket policy of providing only cursory referral information to avoid being sued for defamation claims can result in a company's failure to disclose certain information about former employees that it should. This, too, could lead to a lawsuit for the company. Some experts believe that the best advice is to say as little as possible except in those situations where the employee's behaviors could endanger others in the new workplace. Saying nothing or providing a good reference for a bad employee could be riskier than simply telling the truth.[96]

Managers should also be trained in the company's policy about giving references on social networking sites like LinkedIn. If managers' comments about former employees are inconsistent with the reason for their termination, the employee might be able to prove that the company's reason for termination was a pretext. For example, a lawyer representing Jamie Sky, who was terminated for poor performance, will be thrilled to find a LinkedIn recommendation by Jamie's former manager stating that Jamie was the best employee she ever had.[97]

Trade Secret Litigation

Under the Uniform Trade Secrets Act, which has been adopted by most state legislatures, *trade secrets* can be any type of information, process, idea or "know how" that is not generally known and gives the possessor an advantage in the marketplace. Trade secrets include a wide range of confidential business or proprietary information, such as chemical formulas, industrial processes, business strategies, and, under certain circumstances, customer lists. Almost all organizations have trade secrets they must protect. To maintain business information as a trade secret, companies must take reasonable precautions including requiring employees to sign confidentiality, noncompete, and nondisclosure agreements to prevent them from disclosing the information to competitors. In 2006, a sunroom manufacturer was ordered to pay $8.6 million for interfering with the noncompete contract of a competitor's employee and subsequently stealing a business plan.[98]

Trade secret litigation can take place after an employee is hired by a competitor, or during the interview process. In 2000, Intel accused Broadcom of conducting job interviews of Intel employees to obtain confidential information. A judge determined that Broadcom had attempted to extract trade secrets during the interviews and granted a preliminary injunction against Broadcom. The company was later ordered to change its interviewing and training processes so that new employees are neither encouraged nor permitted to disclose the trade secrets of their previous employers.[99] Even asking a candidate to list the customers with whom he or she regularly does business, or whom the candidate could bring over as new customers, could lead to an accusation of wrongful conduct. Virtually any employee may be in possession of confidential information.

The best defense from trade secret litigation may be to prevent job candidates from disclosing protected information about other companies. Interviewers need to know what information is protected and how to question job candidates. Candidates should be warned at the beginning of an interview not to share a previous employer's proprietary information. When requesting a general description of the interviewee's job responsibilities and capabilities, ask the candidate to omit the specifics of accomplishments, which might include details that could reveal a trade secret. An example of a carefully worded interview question would be, "Without telling me anything about the actual recipe for a particular product, what role do you play in terms of developing new food products for your company?" It is also possible to ask the candidate before the interview to acknowledge in writing that he or she has been asked to avoid discussing confidential or trade secret information.[100]

Sexual Harassment

Under Title VII, the ADA, and the ADEA, harassment on the basis of race, color, religion, sex, national origin, disability, or age is illegal, as is retaliation against an individual for filing a charge of discrimination, participating in an investigation, or opposing discriminatory practices. Denying employment opportunities to a person because of marriage to, or association with, an individual of a particular race, religion, national origin, or an individual with a disability is also illegal.[101]

Title VII's broad prohibitions against sex discrimination specifically cover sexual harassment, which includes practices ranging from direct requests for sexual favors to workplace conditions that create a hostile environment for persons of either gender, including same-sex harassment. The "hostile environment" standard also applies to harassment conducted on the basis of race, color, national origin, religion, age, and disability. Sexual harassment is recognized as intentional discrimination, and companies may be subject to punitive and compensatory damages by a jury if found guilty of it.

EEOC BEST PRACTICES

In addition to enforcing EEO laws, the EEOC provides programs to educate the public and employers on EEO laws and EEO compliance. One of the ways they do this is by identifying specific examples of good EEO and diversity programs and deriving examples of "best practices" that other companies might successfully emulate.[102] The EEOC defines a best staffing practice as one that:[103]

- complies with the law,
- promotes equal employment opportunity,
- addresses one or more barriers that adversely affect equal employment opportunity,
- manifests management commitment and accountability,
- ensures management and employee communication,
- produces noteworthy results, and
- does not cause or result in unfairness.

This general set of key elements that support successful EEO programs corresponds to the acronym SPLENDID:[104]

- **S**tudy—know the laws and standards, remove EEO barriers, and seek assistance from the EEOC, professional consultants, associations or groups, etc.
- **P**lan—know the relevant workforce and demographics, define the problem(s), propose solutions, and develop strategies for achieving them.
- **L**ead—have all levels of management champion the cause and provide leadership for EEO implementation at all organizational levels.
- **E**ncourage—link pay and performance for how employees interact, support, and respect each other.
- **N**otice—monitor the impact of EEO practices, ensure that unfairness does not occur as a result of a corrective strategy.
- **D**iscuss—communicate and reinforce the message that diversity is a business asset.
- **I**nclude—bring all employees and groups into the analysis, planning, and implementation process.
- **D**edicate—assign needed resources and stay persistent; an investment in EEO may take a little while to pay off.

BARRIERS TO LEGALLY DEFENSIBLE STAFFING

Strategically responding to the legal context surrounding staffing requires leveraging laws and guidelines to employ and retain the employees who will best help the firm compete and execute its business strategy. In addition to obeying staffing laws, it is critical that organizations identify and reduce the barriers that exist to legally defensible staffing and provide equal employment opportunities.

Many barriers to equal employment opportunity exist. Some of these barriers tend to be specific to a particular employer, rather than being societal or cultural in nature. Other general barriers based in societal or cultural practices or norms tend to be external to the employer. Next, we describe some of the general and specific barriers to equal employment opportunity.

General Barriers

A report by the EEOC has identified the most common equal employment opportunity barriers that tend to exist.[105] Because understanding and proactively addressing these barriers can minimize their impact and reduce the chances that an organization is discriminating unintentionally or intentionally in its staffing practices, we discuss each next.

THE "LIKE ME" BIAS   People tend to associate with other people who they perceive to be like themselves. This bias is part of human nature, and may be conscious or unconscious. Although it can create a higher comfort level in working relationships, it can lead to the discrimination of people based on protected characteristics, such as their race, sex, a disability, or age. Perceived cultural and religious differences and ethnocentrism can compound the "like me" bias and result in equal employment opportunities being denied people.

Because the "like me" bias can influence the assessment of performance norms, there may be a perception that someone "different" is less able to do the job and that someone "like me" is more able to do the job. For example, a male scientist who tends to believe that women make poor scientists is unlikely to hire a female scientist. This perception can influence a firm's targeted recruiting efforts and further reduce equal employment opportunities.

STEREOTYPES   A *stereotype* is a belief about an individual or a group based on the idea that everyone in a particular group will behave the same way. For example, "all men are athletic," "all women are nurturing," and "people who look a certain way are dangerous" are all examples of stereotypes. Stereotypes are harmful because they judge an individual based solely on his or her being part of a particular group, regardless of his or her unique identity.

People may have stereotypes of other individuals based on their race, color, religion, national origin, sex, disability, or age. Stereotypes are often negative and erroneous, and thus adversely affect the targeted individuals.[106] Because stereotypes can breed subtle racism, sexism, prejudice, and discomfort, they must be addressed in the EEO context. Recruiters and hiring managers may have stereotypes of what makes a good employee that, if they are the underlying beliefs and attitudes that form the bases of the firm's recruiting decisions, can adversely affect people's equal employment opportunities.

A common example of stereotyping occurs when rejecting an applicant as "overqualified." An employer might assume that a highly experienced person will have no interest in a lower-paying position, or will soon leave for something better. Although this assumption might be true, case law says that a person who is overqualified is, by definition, qualified. So, he or she cannot be rejected on that basis. Also, if a person is truly qualified but not hired, the candidate might erroneously assume that age discrimination occurred. The best solution is to ask the candidates why they are interested in the position—they may honestly be looking to change careers or seeking a job with less responsibility. If there is evidence that the individual has done a lot of job-hopping, the interviewer is no longer simply speculating about whether the person will stay in the job and has a more solid basis for rejecting them.[107]

IGNORANCE   Some employers, particularly smaller organizations, are not aware of all of the EEOC's requirements and discriminate against people out of ignorance. Although it is not an effective legal defense, organizations may not know how the law applies to them because they have received poor or inaccurate advice. Even the largest employers may have individual hiring managers and recruiters who are not well versed in employment laws. As noted by the EEOC, to a large degree, stereotyping feeds on ignorance, but the repercussions of ignorance go much farther than stereotyping.[108]

PREJUDICE   It is also possible that outright bigotry still occurs on the part of an employer or its management for or against a targeted group, despite Title VII now having been in existence for over 40 years.[109] Even if an organization has a strong commitment to equal employment opportunity, it is possible that the beliefs and actions of the firm's individual hiring managers or recruiters are inconsistent with the organization's policies and values. Organizations can help to reduce the occurrence of prejudice by carefully selecting and training hiring managers and recruiters, evaluating their performance, and tracking the diversity of the candidates recruited and hired by different recruiters and hiring managers to identify possible discriminatory trends that warrant further investigation and attention.

THE PERCEPTION OF LOSS BY PERSONS THREATENED BY EEO PRACTICES   As voluntary efforts are made by companies to address EEO and fairness concerns, individuals of groups who traditionally have been the predominant employees of a particular workforce or occupation may grow anxious or angry, believing they are "losing out" on employment opportunities. Some of these people may feel that they need to protect their own prospects by impeding the prospects of others.[110] This can influence employees' willingness to refer diverse candidates for a position, objectively screen diverse recruits, and help persuade them to accept the job offers extended to them.

HIRING MANAGERS   Hiring managers often lack an understanding of employment laws and may be unaware that the same antidiscrimination laws that apply to employees apply equally to applicants. In one successful discrimination case, the U.S. Court of Appeals for the Seventh Circuit found that a car dealership's hiring managers had never been trained concerning bias laws. The court wrote, "Leaving managers with hiring authority in ignorance of the basic features of the discrimination laws is an 'extraordinary mistake' for a company to make."[111]

Hiring managers are also often untrained and unprepared to ask the right kinds of questions during an interview. The most common problematic types of questions they ask are questions related to child care and child rearing. If a hiring manager is concerned that someone might not be able to come to work because of child care issues, instead of asking about the candidate's child care arrangements, the manager should ask the candidate directly how often he or she misses work. Asking questions related to attendance and productivity is entirely appropriate.[112]

Specific Barriers

Unlike the general barriers just discussed, there are additional barriers to equal employment opportunity that tend to be specific to an employer. In Table 3–7, we summarize some of the more common specific barriers identified by the U.S. Equal Employment Opportunity Commission.[113]

RECRUITING AND HIRING TO PROMOTE A BRAND IMAGE

In June 2003, a lawsuit was filed by the EEOC that alleged that Abercrombie & Fitch violated Title VII of the Civil Rights Act of 1964. The EEOC contended that Abercrombie's recruiting and staffing practices to reinforce its brand image and marketing strategy by featuring predominantly white, attractive young people limited the number of minority and female employees hired. The lawsuit began when several black, Hispanic, and Asian plaintiffs complained that when they applied for jobs, they were steered away from sales positions and into low-visibility jobs, such as stocking and cleaning.[114] Ultimately, about 20,000 people joined the class-action suit.[115]

The consent decree required Abercrombie to abandon its practice of recruiting employees from predominantly white fraternities and sororities—a practice that helped it develop its trademark look. As part of the settlement, Abercrombie agreed to hire 25 diversity recruiters and set benchmarks for hiring women and minorities. Abercrombie was also required to "reflect diversity, as reflected by the major racial/ethnic minority populations of the United States, in its marketing materials (taken as a whole)."[116] So, not only did Abercrombie have to change its recruitment and hiring practices, it also had to avoid the appearance of discrimination in its marketing materials. Diverse models are now used in the company's quarterly magazines and on shopping bags, store posters, and other advertising to encourage minorities to apply for jobs with Abercrombie.[117] Although the firm did not admit it was guilty, it also agreed to hire a monitor, to provide diversity training to all hiring managers, and to make its managers' progress toward their diversity goals a factor in their bonuses and compensation.[118]

Trying to create a particular "look" for a sales force is not inherently unlawful. "But if recruiters use a subjective or 'creative' component in the hiring process, the employer must carefully review the results for adverse impact," warns Eric Dreiband, the general counsel for the EEOC. "The company needs to consider whether this 'creative' component breeds discrimination. At Abercrombie, it created a group of employees who were young, lily-white males."[119] Dreiband also stated, "businesses cannot discriminate against individuals under the auspice of a marketing strategy or a particular 'look.' Race and sex discrimination in employment are unlawful."[120]

The damage to Abercrombie's reputation likely exceeded the $40 million financial cost of the settlement. "When a discrimination charge is filed, applicants are making one of the most serious charges anyone can make short of a criminal accusation," notes Dreiband. "They are charging that their civil rights have been violated. . . . A discrimination charge goes to the integrity and reputation of the employer."[121] At the same time, one retail analyst felt that the settlement might ultimately improve Abercrombie's performance by forcing the firm to change its image to include minorities to whom the brand will now better appeal.[122]

TABLE 3–7 Barriers to Equal Employment Opportunity Identified by the EEOC[123]

Barriers to Recruiting:

- The failure to advertise widely in order to attract diverse applicants.
- Recruiting practices that overlook or fail to seek all qualified individuals.
- An over-reliance on informal networks for recruitment (such as the "good old boy" network).
- A lack of or no formal systems for recruitment.

Barriers to Advancement and Promotion:

- Deficient feedback, performance evaluation, and promotion processes of employees.
- A lack of access to informal networks of communication by employees of protected classes.
- Different standards of performance used for different classes of employees.
- A lack of equal access to assignments that provide key career experiences, visibility, and interaction with senior managers.
- Equal opportunity HR personnel excluded from the recruiting process when it comes to the firm's higher-level positions.

Barriers in Terms and Conditions:

- Unequal pay.
- Counterproductive behavior and harassment in the workplace.
- Employer policies that are not family-friendly.
- Inflexible working hours and working conditions.
- Failure to provide reasonable accommodation to qualified individuals with disabilities.

Barriers in Termination and Downsizing:

- Unfair standards used to make layoff decisions; different benefits given to different types of employees.
- Inadequate planning for the layoff.
- A lack of adequate incentives to encourage voluntary separations.
- A lack of communication between employers and employees.
- The failure to provide counseling, job placement assistance, and training to laid-off employees.

Summary

Given the many federal and state regulations affecting staffing practices, it is clear that those involved in staffing activities need to thoroughly understand them. A firm's failure to comply with government regulations, even if it is unintentional, can have adverse consequences. Fortunately, the government has tried to help organizations to comply with the regulations by providing "best practice" suggestions and encouraging organizations to be proactive when it comes to resolving any underrepresentation that might exist in their workforces. In addition to avoiding legal trouble, many organizations also realize the benefits of an expanded candidate pool and better quality hires when legal compliance leads to greater recruitment and selection of previously overlooked sources of talent.

Takeaway Points

1. Complying with staffing laws is obviously a good idea from a moral, ethical, and legal perspective, but doing so can also be strategic for firms. In addition to avoiding the expense of lawsuits and the negative public relations associated with litigation, legal compliance allows companies to capitalize on the strengths of diversity and perform better by appealing to a broader customer base.
2. Employees, independent contractors, and contingent workers have different types of employment relationships with firms. Employment relationships may also be "at will," meaning that either party can terminate the employment relationship at any time, for any legal reason, with no liability as long as there is no contract for a definite term of employment.
3. Disparate treatment is intentional discrimination based on a person's protected characteristic. Adverse impact occurs when an action has a disproportionate effect on a protected group, regardless of its intent or actual disparate treatment. Fraudulent recruitment is the misrepresentation of the job or organization to an applicant. Negligent hiring occurs when an applicant is hired that the company knew or should have known poses a risk of harm to third parties, and the person harms another person. Negligent referral is misrepresenting or failing to disclose complete and accurate information about a former employee. Trade secret litigation occurs when confidential information from another company is acquired after an employee is hired by a competitor, or during the interview process.
4. Equal employment opportunity in staffing means that the firm's employment practices are designed and used in a "facially neutral manner"—in other words, they clearly do not illegally favor some applicants over others. Affirmative action is the proactive effort to eliminate discrimination and to ensure nondiscriminatory results in the workforce. Affirmative action plans describe in detail the staffing procedures and standards an employer will take to remedy the underemployment of certain groups. Affirmative action plans can include, but are not limited to, provisions for nondiscriminatory recruitment, training, and promotion.
5. Various barriers to legally defensible staffing exist. Some barriers tend to be specific to a particular employer, rather than being societal or cultural in nature. The "like me" bias, stereotypes, ignorance, and prejudice are common barriers, as are uneducated hiring managers. Other general barriers based in societal or cultural practices or norms tend to be external to the employer.

Discussion Questions

1. Do laws prohibiting certain kinds of hiring discrimination benefit only job seekers? Or do companies benefit from the enforcement of discrimination laws? If so, how?
2. What is meant by "at-will employment" and what advice would you give an organization considering this type of employment relationship?
3. What is the difference between flow, stock, and concentration statistics? How is each type of statistic used?
4. What is affirmative action? What is an affirmative action plan? Do you feel that affirmative action is a good way to remedy past discrimination? Why or why not?
5. Which three general barriers to legally defensible staffing do you feel are most common? What can companies do to remove these barriers?

Exercises

1. *Strategy Exercise:*   Analyzing Adverse Impact
   Mary was recently hired as an HR generalist at Super Foods, an organic grocery chain. One of her first assignments is to review the store's data on its cashiers to identify if its hiring and promotion practices have had an adverse (disparate) impact on men or women. Mary generated the following reports from the company's employee database to use in her analyses.

   Working in groups of three to four students, use this information to determine whether there is evidence of sex discrimination for cashiers. Write a brief report explaining why there is or is not

Stock Statistics		Job Category: Cashiers
	Current Cashiers(%)	Availability in Relevant Population(%)
Males	30	50
Females	70	50

Flow Statistics   **Job Category: Cashiers**

	Number of Applicants	Number Hired	Selection Rate(%)
Men	200	100	50
Women	150	75	50

Concentration Statistics   **Job Category:**

	Cashiers(%)	Stockers(%)	Cleaners(%)
Men	30	70	65
Women	70	30	35

adverse impact. If there is, try to identify what might be happening and suggest ways the firm can reduce it.

2. *Opening Vignette Exercise:*   The opening vignette describes how Abercrombie & Fitch engaged in "creative" recruiting to fill sales jobs with candidates who matched the company's carefully constructed marketing image. The high-profile clothing retailer staffed its stores with good-looking young white men and women and touched off a lawsuit that ultimately cost the company $40 million and a barrage of bad publicity.

Working alone or in a group of three to five students, answer the following questions. Be prepared to share your answers with the class.

a. Do you think Abercrombie should be allowed to staff its stores in a way that reinforces its marketing image? Why or why not?

b. What are some alternative ways Abercrombie can staff its stores legally and still project a desirable image?

3. *Develop Your Skills Exercise:*   The best test of any question posed to a job applicant is whether the employer can demonstrate a job-related necessity for asking the question. Because both the intent behind the question and how the information is to be used by the employer are important, an employer should consider whether the answers to the question, if used to make the hiring decision, will adversely affect and screen out minorities or members of one sex.

This chapter's Develop Your Skills feature presented five improper interview questions (provided again here), along with an explanation of why each question should be avoided. Working with a partner, identify what the employer really wants to know by asking each question, and come up with an alternative way to find out the same information.[124]

1. How many children do you have?
2. What is your native language?
3. To what clubs or organizations do you belong?
4. What is your height? What is your weight?
5. Are you able to work on Christmas Day?

CASE STUDY

When Chicago Bulls's forward Eddy Curry experienced an irregular heartbeat before a basketball game, the team's management immediately sent him to the country's best cardiologists, who diagnosed him with a benign arrhythmia, or an irregularity in the heart's natural rhythm.[125] The arrhythmia could be due to factors including heart disease, high blood pressure, smoking, stress, and caffeine, but the condition could also be congenital. Concerned about his fitness for the sport and before sinking an additional $5 million into him by signing him on for another season, the Bulls's executives offered to hire Curry if he would agree to undergo a DNA test, which it hoped would identify whether the condition was life-threatening. Curry's own cardiologist cleared him to play and said that a DNA test would reveal nothing conclusive or definite.

Curry refused to take the DNA test, and his lawyer argued that the Bulls would be violating multiple state privacy and federal employment laws if it performed the test. The lawyers also argued that if employers were allowed to test for this type of predisposition, they may base hiring decisions on the test results. A few months later, the Bulls traded Curry to the New York Knicks, which did not ask for a DNA test.

QUESTIONS

1. Do you think that DNA testing should become a required part of the physical professional athletes are required to undergo?

2. Which laws are relevant to this situation? What does the law say about the Bulls's requirements with regard to Eddy Curry?

3. Do you think that it is ethical for an employer to request an employee to undergo a DNA test?

4. Would you consider it ethical for an employer to request an employee to undergo a DNA test if the employee was piloting a plane or operating dangerous machinery?

Semester-Long Active Learning Project

You should have finalized your choice of job and organization and begun collecting information about it from the organization, the Internet, and from http://online.onetcenter.org. This week, finish your background research on the job and organization, and add to your report a description of the existing staffing systems for the job.

Case Study Assignment: Strategic Staffing at Chern

See the appendix at the back of this book for this chapter's Case Study Assignment.

Endnotes

1. Marino-Nachison, D., "TMF Interview with Abercrombie & Fitch Investor Relations and Communications Director Lonnie Fogel," The Motley Fool, June 7, 1999, www.fool.com/ foolaudio/transcripts/1999/stocktalk990607_abercrombie.htm. Accessed August 15, 2010.

2. Gerstein, J., "Suit Charged Company Discriminated Against Minorities, Women," New York Sun, April 15, 2005, National section, 7; Hansen, F., "Recruiting on the Right Side of the Law," Workforce Management Online, May 2006, www.workforce.com/section/06/feature/24/38/12. Accessed August 15, 2010.

3. Stumpf, V., "Abercrombie & Fitch to Pay $40 Million in Settled Lawsuit," Californiaaggie.com, November 30, 2004: 1, www.californiaaggie.com/media/storage/paper981/news/2004/1 1/30/FrontPage/Abercrombie.Fitch.To.Pay.40.Million.In.Settled. Lawsuit-1318914.shtml?norewrite200607191309&sourcedomain=www.californiaaggie.com. Accessed July 19, 2006. "AF Justice Media Center," http://www.afjustice.com/media.htm. Accessed August 15, 2010.

4. See Mende, B., "Controlling Risk with Employment Contracts," CareerJournal.com, January 26, 1998, http://www. careerjournaleurope.com/salaryhiring/negotiate/19980126-mende.html. Accessed August 15, 2010.

5. Personnel Policy Service, Inc. "Use At-Will to Defend Your Policies, Not as a Reason to Terminate," 2004, www. ppspublishers.com/articles/gl/atwill_terminate.htm. Accessed August 15, 2010.

6. See Polivka, A. E., and Nardone, T., "On the Definition of 'Contingent Work,'" Monthly Labor Review, December 1989: 9–16.

7. Sullivan, J., "Managing Contingent Labor Strategically," ERE.net, March 15, 2009, http://www.ere.net/ 2009/03/15/managing-contingent-labor-strategically/#more-6927. Accessed March 11, 2010.

8. Ibid.

9. Burrey v. Pacific Gas & Electric, 159 F.3d 388, 98 D.A.R. 10924 (9th Cir. 1998).

10. Bahls, J. E., "Lease on Life? Leasing Workers Can Reduce Your Paperwork, But Don't Forget Your Legal Obligations to Those Employees," Entrepreneur, November 2004, available online at: http://www.entrepreneur.com/magazine/entrepreneur/2004/november/73188.html. Accessed August 15, 2010.

11. See www.nlrb.gov.

12. Internal Revenue Service, "Independent Contractors Versus Employees," Accessed August 15, 2010.

13. Ibid.

14. Greenhouse, S., "U.S. Cracks Down on 'Contractors' As a Tax Dodge," The New York Times, February 18, 2010: A1.

15. Ibid.

16. Petershack, R., "Consider the Legal Issues Before Outsourcing Offshore," Wisconsin Technology Network, July 18, 2005, http://wistechnology.com/articles/2007/. Accessed August 15, 2010.

17. Ibid.

18. See also http://www.hrtools.com/resources.aspx?type=State%20 Laws for a description of employment laws in different states.

19. Stephenson, C. E., "Family Responsibilities Discrimination Claims on the Upswing," Lawyers Weekly, July 7, 2007, www.lawyersweeklyusa.com. Accessed September 7, 2007.

20. See Sec. 2000e-2. [Section 703] of the Civil Rights Act of 1964, www.eeoc.gov/policy/vii.html.

21. Sec. 703 (m) of Title VII.

22. Glater, J. D., "Attention Wal-Mart Plaintiffs: Hurdles Ahead," New York Times, June 27, 2004, http://select.nytimes.com/ gst/abstract.html?res=F00B13FD3D5C0C748EDDAF0894DC 404482&n=Top%2fNews%2fBusiness%2fCompanies%2fWal %2dMart%20Stores %20Inc%2e. Accessed August 15, 2010.

23. EEOC , Walmart to Pay More Than $11.7 Million to Settle EEOC Sex Discrimination Suit, U.S. Equal Employment Opportunity Commission, March 1, 2010, http://www.eeoc. gov/eeoc/newsroom/release/3-1-10.cfm.

24. See, U.S. Department of Labor, "Executive Order 11246, As Amended," http://www.dotcr.ost.dot.gov/documents/ycr/eo11246.htm. Accessed August 15, 2010.

25. U.S. Equal Employment Opportunity Commission, "Federal Laws Prohibiting Job Discrimination Questions and Answers," www.eeoc.gov/facts/qanda.html. Accessed August 15, 2010.

26. Office for Civil Rights, "Your Rights Under Section 504 of the Rehabilitation Act," United States Department of Health and Human Services, www.hhs.gov/ocr/504.html. Accessed August 15, 2010.

27. U.S. Equal Employment Opportunity Commission, "The Age Discrimination in Employment Act of 1967," http://www. eeoc.gov/laws/types/age.cfm. Accessed August 15, 2010.

28. Georgetown University Law Center, "Laws Impacting Workplace Flexibility," Workplace Flexibility 2010, www.law. georgetown.edu/workplaceflexibility2010/law/adea.cfm. Accessed August 15, 2010.

29. See http://www.state.nj.us/lps/dcr/downloads/fact_age.pdf.

30. Hansen, F., "Compliance Issues Put Recruiters on the Hot Seat," Workforce Management Online, February 2008, http://www.workforce.com/section/06/feature/25/36/79/index.h tml. Accessed March 15, 2010.

31. See http://www.dhs.gov/files/programs/gc_1185221678150.shtm for more information about E-Verify.

32. Hansen, F., "Compliance Issues Put Recruiters on the Hot Seat," Workforce Management Online, February 2008, http://www.workforce.com/section/06/feature/25/36/79/index.h tml. Accessed March 15, 2010.

33. "The Worker Adjustment and Retraining Notification Act," U.S. Department of Labor Employment and Training Administration Fact Sheet, available online at: http://www .doleta.gov/programs/factsht/warn.htm. Accessed December 28, 2009.

34. See http://www.doleta.gov/programs/factsht/warn.htm.

35. Diaz v. Pan Am World Airways, 442 F.2d 385 (5th Cir. 1971).

36. *Griggs v. Duke Power Co.*, 401 U.S. 424 (1971).

37. Based on Kucler, D. G., "Interview Questions: Legal or Illegal?" Workforce.com, www.workforce.com/archive/ feature/22/23/74/ index.php. Accessed July 29, 2010; KFDS General Assistance Center, "Legal/Illegal Interview Questions," Office of Human Resources Management, University at Albany, http:// hr.albany.edu/content/legalqtn.asp. Accessed July 25, 2010; "Legal Issues in Employment Interviewing," University of Kansas Medical Center, Equal Opportunity Office, www.kumc.edu/eoo/ interview.html. Accessed July 25, 2010; "Conducting a Lawful Employment Interview,"State of Idaho Department of Labor, http://labor.idaho.gov/ lawintvw3.htm#_Toc426425135. Accessed July 29, 2010.

38. See *Davis v. County of Los Angeles*, 655 F.2d 1334 (9th Cir. 1977), vacated and remanded as moot on other grounds, 440 U.S. 625 (1979); *Dothard v. Rawlinson*, 433 U.S. 321 (1977).

39. Dowling, D. C. Jr., "HR Is Going Global," *National Law Journal,* 26, 41 (June 14, 2004): S1.

40. Adnett, N., "Social Dumping and European Economic Integration," *Journal of European Social Policy,* 5, 1 (1995): 1–12.

41. See www.eeoc.gov.

42. There are many free and fee-based sources of information on EEO and AA laws and regulations. The EEOC (www.eeoc .gov), OFCCP (www.dol.gov/esa/ofccp), and the Department of Labor (www.dol.gov) all offer compliance manuals and policy guidance online. Reference books that review and summarize permissible and impermissible practices as well as the outcomes of relevant court cases can also be useful. Fee-based information services including the Commerce Clearing House (CCH) and the Bureau of National Affairs (BNA) offer numerous employment law products and newsletters. Several professional associations including the Society for Human Resource Management (www.shrm.org) and the International Personnel Management Association (www.ipma-hr.org) also provide legal information to their members. Although some of the material is subscription-based, employment law Web sites such as HR Comply (www.hrcomply.com) and the employment law practice center (www.law.com) also provide employment law news and resources.

43. Office of Federal Contract Compliance, *Affirmative Action Review: The Office of Federal Contract Compliance Programs (DOL)*, 2004, http://clinton4.nara.gov/WH/ EOP/OP/html/aa/ aa06.html. Accessed August 15, 2010.

44. Andre, C., Velasquez, M., and Mazur, T., "Affirmative Action: Twenty-Five Years of Controversy," *Issues in Ethics,* 5, 2 (Summer 1992), www.scu.edu/ethics/publications/iie/v5n2/ affirmative.html. Accessed August 15, 2010.

45. Labor Research Association, "The Growing Power of the *Fortune* 500," *LRA Online,* May 30, 2006, http://www. work-inglife.org/wiki/The+Growing+Power+of+the+Fortune+500+ %28May+30,+2006%29. Accessed August 15, 2010.

46. For example, *Steelworkers v. Weber*, 443 U.S. 193 (1979); *Wygant v. Jackson Board of Education*, 476 U.S. 267 (1986).

47. Based on Breaugh, J. A., *Recruitment: Science and Practice*, Boston, MA: PWS-Kent Publishing Company, 1992.

48. *Wygant v. Jackson Board of Education*, 476 U.S. 267 (1986).

49. Ibid; Kleiman, L. S., and Faley, R. H., "Voluntary Affirmative Action and Preferential Treatment: Legal and Research Implications," *Personnel Psychology,* 41, 3 (1988): 481–496; Rosenfeld, M., *Affirmative Action and Justice: A Philosophical and Constitutional Inquiry*, New Haven: Yale University Press, 1993.

50. *Regents v. Bakke*, 438 U.S. 265 (1978).

51. *Grutter v. Bollinger*, 539 U.S. 306 (2003).

52. *Gratz v. Bollinger*, 539 U.S. 244 (2003).

53. McBride, A, "*Grutter v. Bollinger* and *Gratz v. Bollinger* (2003)," *The Supreme Court*, December 2006, www.pbs.org/ wnet/supremecourt/future/landmark_grutter.html. Accessed March 22, 2007.

54. "U.S. Equal Employment Opportunity Commission: An Overview," U.S. Equal Employment Opportunity Commission, http://www.eeoc.gov/eeoc/index.cfm. Accessed August 15, 2010.

55. Gangemi Law Firm, P.C., "EEOC Releases 2009 Charge Statistics," *New York Employment Attorney Blog*, January 7, 2010, http://www.newyorkemploymentattorneyblog.com/2010/01/ee oc_releases_2009_charge_stat_1.html. Accessed April 6, 2010.

56. Ibid.

57. Ibid.

58. SHRM, "EEOC Charges Remain at Record High," SHRM eLearning, February 12, 2010, http://messaging.shrm.org/ progmarketing/notice-description.tcl?newsletter_id=27005789. Accessed February 12, 2010.

59. U.S. Equal Employment Opportunity Commission, *Filing a Charge of Discrimination*, http://www.eeoc.gov/employees/ charge.cfm. Accessed August 15, 2010.

60. U.S. Equal Employment Opportunity Commission, *EEO-1 Instruction Booklet*, http://www.eeoc.gov/employers/ eeo1sur-vey/2007instructions.cfm. Accessed August 15, 2010.

61. The OFCCP can be found at http://www.dol.gov/OFCCP/.

62. http://www.dol.gov/ofccp/index.htm. Accessed August 15, 2010.

63. Hansen, F., "Avoid Getting Sued: Risks and Rewards in Recruitment Record Keeping," *Workforce Management Online*, February 2007, www.workforce.com/section/ 06/feature/24/ 76/39/index.html. Accessed August 15, 2010.

64. Office of Federal Contract Compliance, *Affirmative Action Review: The Office of Federal Contract Compliance Programs (DOL).*

65. Quarles & Brady and Affiliates, LLP, "Final OFCCP Rule Issued on Recordkeeping and Tracking of Race, Gender, and Ethnicity of 'Internet Applicants'…An In-depth Analysis for Government Contractors, Employment Relations E-Mail Alert," November 2006, www.edatab2b.com/monster/qb.pdf. Accessed August 15, 2010.

66. "Obligation to Solicit Race and Gender Data for Agency Enforcement Purposes," *Federal Register,* 70, 194 (October 7, 2005): 58, 945–958, 963, http://www.dol.gov/regs/ fedreg/fi-nal/2005020176.htm.

67. Hoffman, V. J., and Davis, G. M., "OFCCP's 'Internet Applicant' Definition Requires Overhaul of Recruitment and Hiring Policies," *Society for Human Resource Management* (January/February 2006): 1–5.

68. To narrow the pool of job seekers for which the contractor must solicit gender, race, and ethnicity data, contractors should identify as many basic qualifications as possible in their advertisements or, if not advertising, in their internal basic qualifications record, prior to considering any expressions of interest for that particular position. Although not specifically addressed in the rule, the OFCCP notes in the "Discussion of Comments and Revisions" preceding the rule that it encourages contractors to solicit such information through self-identification methods, such as electronic or traditional tear off sheets.

69. For additional information, visit the OFCCP's Web site, http://www.dol.gov/ofccp/index.htm.

70. "Uniform Guidelines on Employee Selection Procedures," *Federal Register,* 43, 166 (August 25, 1978): 38290–38315, www.dol.gov/dol/allcfr/ESA/Title_41/Part_60-3/toc.htm.

71. Question and Answer No. 15, Adoption of Questions and Answers to Clarify and Provide a Common Interpretation of the UGESP, 44 FR 11998 (March 2, 1979).

72. Hansen, "Recruiting on the Right Side of the Law."

73. This is known as a "McDonnell Douglas analysis." See *McDonnell Douglas v. Green*, 411 U.S. 792, 802 (1973).

74. Civil Rights Act of 1991. See http://www.eeoc.gov/laws/statutes/cra-1991.cfm.

75. *Desert Palace, Inc. v. Costa*, 539 U.S. 90 (2003), No. 02-679.

76. The Uniform Guidelines on Employee Selection Procedures, www.uniformguidelines.com/uniformguidelines.html.

77. Ibid, Section 4(D).

78. http://www.supremecourt.gov/.

79. See 42 U.S.C. § 2000e-2(k)(1)(A)(i).

80. Ibid.

81. 42 U.S.C. § 2000e-2(k)(1)(A)(ii).

82. Eiserloh, L. R., "Hiring, Firing, and Retaliation for Human Resources Personnel," *15th Annual Local Government Seminar: Employment Law Focus,* April 10, 2002, Austin, Texas.

83. Breaugh, *Recruitment: Science and Practice.*

84. Geyelin, M., and Green, W., "Companies Must Disclose Shaky Finances to Some Applicants," *Wall Street Journal,* April 20, 1990: B8.

85. *Agosta v. Astor*, 120 Cal.App.4th 596 (July 12, 2004).

86. Human Resource Advisor, "HR Policies and Practices: Hiring," Hr-esource.com, 2003, www.hresource.com/index.asp? rightframe=hresources/sampleChapters/whrawSampleChapter_03.html. Accessed July 16, 2005; Wren, A. O., Clark, L., and Derison, M., "Employer Beware: Truth-in-hiring May Be the New Standard in Recruiting," Spring 2006, http://www. entrepreneur.com/tradejournals/article/154005369.html. Accessed, August, 15, 2010; Hansen, F. "Avoiding Truth in Hiring Lawsuits," *Workforce Management,* December, 2007, http://www.workforce.com/section/06/feature/25/26/34/. Accessed August 15, 2010.

87. Panus, V., "Make Sure the Picture You Paint Comes True," *The Panus Report: Insights and Developments in the Law,* Summer 2000, Reprinted in *Small Business Monthly,* July 21, 2006, www.kcsmallbiz.com/october-2000/people-power.html. Accessed July 21, 2006.

88. Ibid.

89. Smith, S., Negligent Hiring, http://www.sideroad.com/Human_Resources/negligent_hiring.html. Accessed July 19, 2006.

90. Steingold, F. S., and Bray, I. M., *Legal Guide for Starting and Running a Small Business,* Berkeley, CA: Nolo Press, 2003.

91. "Employee Lawsuits: Negligent Hiring and Retention," USLaw.com, www.uslaw.com/library/article/carel5NegligentHiring.html?area_id=43. Accessed August 15, 2010.

92. Barada, P. W., "How to Avoid Negligent Hiring Litigation," Monster.com, http://career-advice.monster.com/in-the-office/workplace-issues/how-to-avoid-negligent-hiring-litigation/article.aspx. Accessed August 15, 2010.

93. See "Did Hospitals 'See No Evil'?" *CBS News,* August 15, 2004, www.cbsnews.com/stories/2004/04/02/60minutes/main610047.shtml. Accessed August 15, 2010; Robbins, G., "HMC

May Face Suits for Killer's Victims," *Hunterdon County Democrat,* September 6, 2007: A4.

94. McCord, L. B., "Defamation vs. Negligent Referral," *The Graziadio Business Report,* Spring 1999, http://gbr.pepperdine.edu/992/referral.html. Accessed August 15, 2010.

95. Based on McCord, L. B., "Defamation vs. Negligent Referral," *The Graziadio Business Report*, Spring 1999, http://gbr. pepperdine.edu/992/referral.html. Accessed August 15, 2010.

96. Ibid.

97. Hable, S. Z., "The Trouble with Online References," *Workforce Management Online,* February 2010, http://www. workforce.com/archive/feature/26/98/74/index.php. Accessed March 30, 2010.

98. Kahn, R., "Violating a Noncompete Agreement Costs Ohio Firm Millions," *Workforce Management Online,* May 31, 2006, www.workforce.com/section/00/article/24/39/01.html. Accessed August 15, 2010.

99. Thompson, E. C., "Secrets That You Keep," *Security Products,* January 2001: 14–22.

100. Kondon, C., "But It Was Just an Interview!" *Workforce Management,* January 2005: 12–13.

101. U.S. Equal Employment Opportunity Commission, "Federal Laws Prohibiting Job Discrimination Questions and Answers."

102. U.S. Equal Employment Opportunity Commission, *Best Practices For Employers And Human Resources/EEO Professionals,* http://www.eeoc.gov/eeoc/initiatives/e-race/bestpractices-employers.cfm. Accessed August 15, 2010.

103. Ibid.

104. Ibid.

105. Ibid.

106. Federal Glass Ceiling Commission, "Good for Business: Making Full Use of the Nation's Human Capital," *Fact-Finding Report of the Federal Glass Ceiling Commission,* March 1995.

107. Hansen, "Recruiting on the Right Side of the Law."

108. U.S. Equal Employment Opportunity Commission, "Best Practices of Private Sector Employers."

109. Federal Glass Ceiling Commission, "Good for Business: Making Full Use of the Nation's Human Capital."

110. Ibid, 31–32.

111. *Mathis v. Phillips Chevrolet Inc.*, 269 F.3d 771, U.S. App. (7th Cir. 2001), No. 00-1892.

112. Hansen, F. "When Interviews Go Astray," *Workforce Management Online,* June 2006, www.workforce.com/archive/article/24/41/14.php?ht=hiring%20managers%20weak%20link%20hiring%20managers%20weak%20link. Accessed August 15, 2010.

113. U.S. Equal Employment Opportunity Commission, *Best Practices of Private Sector Employers.*

114. Greenhouse, S., "Abercrombie & Fitch Bias Case Is Settled," *New York Times,* November 17, 2004, Section A, Column 4, National Desk, 16.

115. Gerstein, "Suit Charged Company Discriminated Against Minorities, Women."

116. Consent Decree, Case Nos. 03-2817 SI, 04-4730 and 04-4731, http://afjustice.com/pdf/20041116_consent_decree.pdf. Accessed August 15, 2010.

117. Ibid.

118. Greenhouse, "Abercrombie & Fitch Bias Case Is Settled."

119. Hansen, "Recruiting on the Right Side of the Law."

120. "Clothier Settles Lawsuit over Bias," *Washington Times,* November 17, 2004, www.washtimes.com/national/20041116-115217-2037r.htm. Accessed August 15, 2010.

121. Hansen, "Recruiting on the Right Side of the Law."

122. Greenhouse, "Abercrombie & Fitch Bias Case Is Settled."

123. Ibid.

124. Kucler, D. G., "Interview Questions: Legal or Illegal?" Workforce.com, www.workforce.com/archive/ feature/22/23/74/index.php. Accessed July 29, 2010; KFDS General Assistance Center, "Legal/Illegal Interview Questions," Office of Human Resources Management, University at Albany, http://hr.albany.edu/content/legalqtn.asp. Accessed July 25, 2010; University of Kansas Medical Center, Equal Opportunity Office, "Legal Issues in Employment Interviewing," www.kumc.edu/eoo/interview.html. Accessed July 25, 2010; State of Idaho Department of Labor, "Conducting a Lawful Employment Interview,"http://labor.idaho.gov/lawintvw3.htm#_Toc426425135. Accessed July 29, 2010; see also *Griggs v. Duke Power Co.*, 401 U.S. 424 (1971).

125. This case is based on Krishna, D., "DNA Testing for Eddy Curry?" http://www.law.upenn.edu/ journals/conlaw/articles/volume9/issue4/Krishna9U.Pa.J.Const.L.1105%282007%29.pdf. Accessed August 15, 2010; Litke, J., "Curry's DNA Fight With Bulls 'Bigger Than Sports World' " *Associated Press*, September 29, 2005, http://sports.espn.go.com/nba/news/story?id= 2174877. Accessed August 15, 2010; "Tell-tale Heart," *SI Vault*, October 10, 2005, http://sportsillustrated.cnn.com/vault/article/magazine/MAG1106476/index.htm. Accessed August 15, 2010.

4

Strategic Job Analysis and Competency Modeling

Outline

LEARNING OBJECTIVES

After studying this chapter, you should be able to:

- Explain why doing a job analysis can be strategic.
- Describe the different types of job analyses, and for what they are used.
- Define *job description* and *person specification,* and describe how they are used.
- Describe the advantages and disadvantages of different job analysis methods.
- Describe how to plan a job analysis.
- Describe how to conduct a job analysis.

Job Descriptions at Red Lobster

Red Lobster operates over 670 casual-dining seafood restaurants in the United States and Canada, employing more than 63,000 people.[1] When Red Lobster developed a new business strategy to focus on value and improve its image, it established a new vision, mission, and goals for the company.[2] The restaurant chain simplified its menu with the highest-quality seafood it could offer at mid-range prices, traded its restaurants' tropical themes for a crisp, clean look with white-shirt-and-black-pants uniforms for its employees, and added Northeastern coastal imagery to its menu and Web site.[3] Executing the new mission and differentiation strategy required hiring fun, hospitality-minded people who shared its values.

Although Red Lobster had not had any problem hiring restaurant managers, the company felt that the managers it hired did not always reflect Red Lobster's strategy, vision, and values. The company also realized that their old job descriptions did not reflect the passion its new strategy needed from its employees.[4] Red Lobster asks your opinion of what it should do in writing its job descriptions to improve the fit between its new management hires and its new business strategy. After reading this chapter, you should have some good ideas you can share with Red Lobster.

What every employee does in an organization should enhance a firm's business strategy execution and positively contribute to the company's effectiveness. Sometimes these behaviors are done when performing a formal **job**, and other times these behaviors result from different **roles** or expected patterns or sets of behaviors people play in a company.[5] Some organizations function best with clearly defined and well-structured jobs, such as positions on a manufacturing line. Other firms function best with employees performing multiple, sometimes changing, roles that do not fit into a single job description. Sometimes jobs are expanded to incorporate a new hire's talents in areas unrelated to the initial job description.

job
a formal group or cluster of tasks

role
an expected pattern or set of behaviors

Young organizations often need their few employees to each wear many hats and to perform duties spanning the finance, human resources, product development, sales, and marketing functions. Rigid, formal job descriptions can be too restrictive for the needs of these organizations. Organizations that require employees to be flexible in what they do, including consulting firms like Accenture and Proxicom, often prefer employees to be flexible and rely less on formal job descriptions. Many organizations rely on formal job descriptions for some positions, such as administrative or staff jobs, and on less structured roles for creative or leadership positions. Procter & Gamble usually hires people with no clear position in mind, focusing on bringing in people with soft skills and talent who have the potential to grow with the company. Only 20 percent of the company's yearly openings are for specific jobs.[6]

Regardless of whether a company relies on jobs or roles, the person hired must have the competencies and motivation to do what the firm needs done. Understanding what is and what will be required to do a job well is necessary if companies are to hire the right people. Job analysis is the process that staffing professionals use to first identify the tasks required by a job, and then evaluate what is required to perform each of the tasks that comprise the job. The process can be a strategic tool that results in a competitive advantage if it aligns the requirements of a job with the company's business strategy, taking into account what is required to perform the job today as well as in the future. Imagine the job of corporate marketing in the late 1990s, when the Internet was beginning to have business impact. If a company planned to begin using the Internet as a marketing tool within the next year or two, hiring a marketing person unable to use technology could have been a poor strategic choice. A job analysis identifies the type of people to recruit and on what characteristics to evaluate them. It can also help to identify career paths and pinpoint turnover risk factors.

When CitiFinancial conducted a job analysis of its loan officer position, it identified three different levels associated with the job as well as the top 10 skills and abilities needed for each of the three. This allowed CitiFinancial to hire based on the specific skills and specific abilities needed for each level.[7]

Jobs performed in a consistent, predictable manner can be readily analyzed. However, this doesn't work so well for organizations that are structured around networks, teams, and roles rather than around individuals performing well-defined jobs.[8] Because the roles in the groups change and are unique to each employee, a job analysis often cannot adequately define them.

Thus, evaluating the broader roles played by people in these positions rather than specific jobs can better capture the responsibilities and requirements of flexible, team-based work.[9] One procedure that looks at roles rather than jobs is *competency modeling*, which analyzes the broader competencies needed to perform well in roles as opposed to jobs. For example, Nordstrom's customer service strategy means that it needs to hire people with the competencies of having a customer focus and good interpersonal skills as well as good sales skills. Walmart's low-cost strategy means that it needs to hire people who are efficiency oriented. It is important to consider how the job can best contribute to strategy execution, not just what tasks need to be done. Because competency modeling identifies these "extra" behaviors and characteristics, it often augments job analysis, even when a job is well defined.

Job analysis can enhance the execution of strategy. General Electric (GE) performed a job analysis on its sales force and found that salespeople were spending 80 percent of their time on bureaucratic duties, not directly toward activities driving sales. This insight allowed GE to reorganize the functions of its sales representatives to better align their activities with the mission of the organization.[10]

In this chapter, you will learn the fundamentals of doing both job analysis and competency modeling. After reading this chapter, you should have a good understanding of how to identify the essential elements of a job and determine what employees need to do to execute the firm's business strategy and to give the company a competitive advantage.

JOB ANALYSIS AND THE STRATEGY BEHIND IT

Types of Job Analyses

job analysis
the systematic process of identifying and describing the important aspects of a job and the characteristics a worker needs to do it well

A **job analysis** is the systematic process of identifying and describing the important aspects of a job and the characteristics a worker needs to do it well. It identifies the job's important tasks and working conditions as well as the tools and technologies people doing the job use. It also involves making judgments about what an employee needs to do to perform a job well given the specific business strategy and culture of an organization. It does not necessarily mean profiling the job incumbent to hire someone similar. The goal is to define the ideal individual for a job from the perspective of the company, its strategy, and the employees with whom the new hire will work.

Job analyses are used for multiple purposes, including:

- Determining a job's entry requirements
- Developing a strategic recruiting plan for the firm
- Selecting individuals for employment
- Developing employee training plans
- Designing employee compensation systems
- Developing performance evaluation measures

job family
a grouping of jobs that either call for similar worker characteristics or contain parallel work tasks

Doing a job analysis also helps HR professionals categorize jobs into **job families**, or groupings of jobs that either call for similar worker characteristics or contain parallel work tasks. Job families enhance an organization's flexibility by allowing workers to perform more than just one official job. Grouping jobs into families can also help streamline the staffing process by enabling firms to hire people for different jobs from the same pool of candidates, apply the same selection procedures to them, and provide a systematic procedure for promoting employees. Table 4–1 presents an example of grouping jobs into job families.

TABLE 4–1	Grouping Jobs into Job Families

Job Family	Examples of Jobs Within Job Family
Personnel Recruiters	Recruiter
	Executive Recruiter
	Human Resources Specialist
	Employment Coordinator
Secretaries	Secretary
	Clerk Typist
	Department Secretary
	Administrative Support Assistant
Chemical Engineers	Project Engineer
	Chemical Engineer
	Engineering Scientist
	Scientist

Different purposes require different job analysis techniques. The techniques of interest to us are those used for staffing-related purposes. A staffing-oriented job analysis ultimately aids in the development of valid, or job-related, recruiting plans and selection devices that identify the best candidates for a job. A job analysis that produces a valid selection system identifies characteristics in candidates that:

- distinguish superior from average and unacceptable workers;
- are not easily learned on the job; and
- exist to at least a moderate extent in the applicant pool.

There are many ways of conducting a job analysis, but most involve a job analyst managing the process and collecting information from job experts—typically people who already hold the job and their supervisors—via interviews and written surveys. The job analyst then compiles and summarizes this information, and the job experts check their work for accuracy and thoroughness. Before staffing can be done strategically, it is critical that the contributions of the position to the organization as well as the characteristics and requirements of the job be thoroughly understood. Companies like Oral-B Laboratories and Equistar Chemicals conduct thorough job analyses before deciding how to staff key positions.

Research has shown that firms that engage in effective job analysis financially outperform their competitors in a variety of ways.[11] Unless the way a position contributes to the execution of the business strategy is understood, it is impossible to consistently hire people able to do the job in the manner it needs to be done to reinforce the firm's strategy. For example, a manufacturing company pursuing a specialist business strategy is likely to require sales representatives with advanced degrees or with specific educational and experiential backgrounds—backgrounds that make them best suited to contribute to the organization's market niche. But a manufacturing company pursuing a low-cost strategy may focus on hiring efficiency-minded people who can do their jobs well but are willing to work for lower wages to keep the company's costs down.

A **future-oriented job analysis**[12] is a technique for analyzing new jobs or how jobs will look in the future. Whereas a traditional job analysis focuses on describing jobs as they exist today, a future-oriented job analysis focuses on identifying the skills the company also anticipates needing in the future. Think about the typical administrative assistant job in the 1990s as computers began entering the workplace: Administrative assistants were selected based upon their Dictaphone and shorthand skills. The scenario is clearly different today. In future years, with the increasing use of speech recognition technology, the scenario will be different too: firms might need secretaries who can speak rapidly and articulate clearly. Sometimes the speed at which jobs change can make it difficult to maintain current job profiles cost-effectively. In this case, organizations should focus on key jobs or on jobs they need to fill frequently to maximize the return on their investment.

future-oriented job analysis
a technique for analyzing new jobs or how jobs will look in the future

TABLE 4–2	Components of the Job-Worker Match

Job-Worker

Current and future tasks and responsibilities *match* Characteristics, knowledge, skills, abilities, and competencies

Intrinsic and extrinsic rewards *match* Needs, motivations, and values

Source: Reproduced with permission of Red Lobster.

Table 4–2 illustrates the need for staffing to match the job's current and future tasks and responsibilities with the characteristics and competencies of the worker, and the job's intrinsic and extrinsic rewards with the needs and motivations of the worker.

The Legal and Practical Reasons for Doing a Job Analysis

As we have explained, the job analysis process enables firms to hire the people best able to contribute to the company's organizational effectiveness and performance. However, there are legal reasons for conducting a job analysis as well. The legal reasons relate to the organization's ability to show that its hiring methods are job related. A job analysis helps create an accurate and current list of the essential functions of a job and the required and desired qualifications employees that do it should have. Because an applicant must meet the stated job-related requirements, crafting a job description based on objective standards is a critical step for avoiding and defending future failure to hire and wrongful discharge lawsuits.

Companies are not required by law to conduct job analyses, but they do increase a firm's ability to make staffing decisions based solely on job requirements. For example, under the Americans with Disabilities Act (ADA), as long as disabled applicants can perform the essential functions of a job with reasonable accommodation, they have to be considered for the position.

Doing a job analysis helps staffing specialists systematically identify a position's essential functions, as well as the corresponding knowledge, skills, abilities, and other characteristics (KSAOs) an employee needs to perform those functions. For example, if a job requires climbing stairs, stating this in the job description will help protect an employer from a claim from someone confined to a wheelchair that he or she was discriminated against based on his or her inability to do so.[13] **Essential functions** are defined by the ADA as the fundamental duties or tasks of a position. According to the ADA, a job function may be deemed essential for a number of reasons, including, but not limited to, the following:

essential functions
the fundamental duties or tasks of a position

- Because the reason the position exists is to perform that function.
- Because of the limited number of employees available among whom the performance of that job function can be assigned or distributed.
- Because the function is so highly specialized that the incumbent in the position is hired specifically for his or her expertise or ability to perform the particular function.
- Because of the consequences of not requiring an incumbent to perform the particular function.
- Because of the terms of a collective bargaining agreement.

Therefore, it is critical to complete a job analysis before a recruiting and selection system is developed. To meet legal requirements, a job analysis must:

1. Be valid and identify the worker's knowledge, skills, abilities, and other characteristics necessary to do the job and differentiate superior from barely acceptable workers
2. Be in writing and relevant to the particular job in question
3. Be derived from multiple sources

There are many practical reasons to do a job analysis. In addition to enhancing the effectiveness of staffing efforts, job analysis procedures are useful for other human resource management activities, such as performance management, compensation, training, development, and succession planning. Table 4–3 summarizes some of the reasons related to staffing.

TABLE 4–3	The Practical Reasons for Doing a Job Analysis

- It links the staffing process to the firm's business strategy and to what the firm needs in terms of the position in the future.
- It helps HR personnel write an accurate description of the job's requirements and duties for the purposes of advertising and recruiting for an open position.
- It enables HR personnel to write an accurate description of the type of person the organization wants to recruit.
- It aids in the identification of the best selection methods that should be used to fill a position.
- It clarifies how to present the job's rewards to candidates in the most appealing way to match their needs and interests.
- It helps to identify what to change in the current staffing system for a job.
- It provides a foundation to determine the best way to combine a job candidate's scores on multiple assessment methods to compute a total score for comparison with the scores of the other candidates.
- It assists potential recruits when they are making up their own minds about whether to apply based on their perceived fit with and interest in the requirements and responsibilities of the position.

JOB DESCRIPTIONS AND PERSON SPECIFICATIONS

One of the primary outcomes of a staffing-oriented job analysis is a **job description**, or a written description of the duties and responsibilities associated with a job itself. Job descriptions usually include:

job description
written description of the duties and responsibilities associated with a job

- The size and type of organization
- The department and job title
- The salary range
- Position grade or level
- To whom the employee reports and for whom the employee is responsible
- Brief summary of the main duties and responsibilities of the job
- Brief summary of the occasional duties and responsibilities of the job
- Any special equipment used on the job
- Any special working conditions (shift or weekend work, foreign travel, etc.)
- Purpose and frequency of contact with others
- The statement, "Other duties as assigned" to accommodate job changes and special projects

Job descriptions are typically part of an organization's recruitment materials to inform potential candidates about the requirements and responsibilities of the job being filled. Looking back to this chapter's opening vignette, Red Lobster wrote its job descriptions to capture people's attention and get them excited about the company's management positions. Red Lobster feels that although job descriptions need to identify essential job functions to meet federal legislation guidelines, they don't have to be boring. So the company made its description of essential job functions engaging by incorporating the company's principles, values, and mission statement. Here is an excerpt from a Red Lobster managerial job description from its Web site:

> *Beverage and Hospitality Manager*: Select, hire and train all the folks that'll make sitting at your bar so fun. Then manage their day-to-day shifts. You'll be a constant motivator and strategist—overseeing promotions, supervising bar product inventory, ordering and receiving shipments, and taking charge of sales and costs at the bar.[14]

Compare this against a more typical description of the same job:

> *Beverage and Hospitality Manager*: Key responsibility areas include management of team performance, ordering supplies and beverages, pursuit of increased sales and profitability, establishment of effective cost controls, and development, training and retention of key associates. You will implement policies and set procedures in keeping with corporate goals.

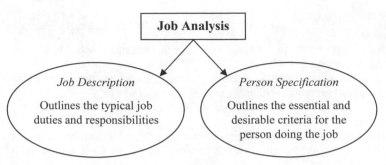

FIGURE 4–1   Outcomes of a Job Analysis

person specification
summarizes the characteristics of someone able to perform the job well

The other primary outcome of a job analysis is a **person specification**, also called a "job specification," that summarizes the characteristics of someone able to do the job well. Based on the job description, the person specification profiles the personal skills, qualifications, abilities, and experiences the organization needs to evaluate in job candidates during the recruitment and selection process. These characteristics should relate directly to the duties of the job, contain the minimum requirements essential to do the job effectively, and should be as specific as possible. These characteristics form the basis of the recruiting strategy to attract qualified applicants. Because it describes the type of person best suited for the job, the person specification helps to identify where and how job openings should be communicated, as well as provide assessment and screening criteria for job applicants.

Person specifications often describe the "ideal" candidate, which is usually someone with many years of experience, high past performance, excellent leadership and teamwork skills, and strong technical skills. In reality, the goal of finding the "perfect" candidate who excels at every job requirement is rarely attainable. Prioritizing the characteristics a person most needs to do the job successfully and being willing to accept a slightly lower degree of performance in less important areas can lead to more appropriate person specifications. The job candidate characteristics that are critical can be categorized as **essential criteria**, and job candidates should be screened for them. Criteria that can enhance the new hire's success on the job but that are not essential can be categorized as **desirable criteria**. To choose among candidates who all possess the essential criteria, a firm can look at their desirable criteria. Figure 4–1 illustrates the relationship between doing a job analysis and sorting out essential and desirable criteria for the job.

essential criteria
job candidate characteristics that are critical to the adequate performance of a new hire

desirable criteria
job candidate criteria that may enhance the new hire's job success, but that are not essential to adequate job performance

It is worthwhile to give some thought to what the "effective performance" of a new hire means when writing person specifications. Arbitrary criteria unrelated to job success should not be included in person specifications. Many person specifications state a minimum number of years of experience, GPA, specific degrees, and other activities or skills. Sometimes these qualifications are not at all relevant to job success. For example, in some jobs, a person's technical skills might be less important than his or her persistence, cooperativeness, interpersonal skills, and conscientiousness. When degrees are required for hiring but are not really necessary to do the job, the risk of adverse impact also increases. Rather than arbitrarily specifying the requirements a new hire must meet, firms need to evaluate job candidates on those criteria that truly predict whether they will be able to do the job successfully.

COMMON JOB ANALYSIS METHODS

Different job analysis methods vary with regard to how job information is collected, analyzed, and documented. Each method requires different amounts of time, resources, and involvement by job experts. As a result, some methods are better at describing the job and some are better at describing the worker. Job analysts typically use more than one method because collecting all the relevant information about a job is usually impossible to do using just one of the methods. It is best to think of each job analysis method as a distinct tool that leads to different insights and information about a job.

Two of the most important features of any job analysis method are that it be *reliable*, or replicable, and *valid*, or accurately measure what it was intended to measure. A reliable job analysis procedure will produce the same results when it (1) is applied to the same job by a different job specialist, (2) when a different group of job experts is used, and (3) when it is done at a different time.

Next, we will discuss five of the most commonly used job analysis methods and then describe a job analysis approach that uses multiple methods and works for many different types of jobs.

The Critical Incidents Technique

The **critical incidents technique**[15] is a job analysis method that identifies extremely effective and ineffective behaviors by documenting critical incidents that have occurred on the job.[16]

critical incidents technique
a job analysis method that identifies extremely effective and ineffective behaviors by documenting critical incidents that have occurred on the job

For each incident, the critical incidents job analysis technique identifies:

1. the *circumstances* leading up to the event, or the sequence of events that occurred;
2. the *action* taken by the worker; and
3. the *consequences* of the action taken.

Critical incidents can be collected through interviews with incumbents and supervisors or by reviewing logbooks or other written records of job events (these are usually more effective for collecting negative critical incidents). Job experts can discuss any events they feel most clearly illustrate effective or poor job performance.

Alternatively, the duties of the job can be collected first. Job experts can then discuss a work event that is an example of particularly good or poor performance on a particular job duty. If the job duties are not predetermined, after recording the incidents, the job analyst reviews them to identify a set of critical job duties (e.g., problem-solving or customer-relations duties), and then identifies the relevant worker characteristics required for the successful performance of these duties.

The critical incidents technique is a particularly useful method for identifying infrequent or unusual work events that may be missed by other job analysis methods (particularly standardized questionnaires). It is relatively inexpensive and is often used in conjunction with other job analysis techniques to capture the "extremes" of job behaviors and, thus, to distinguish superior from average or barely acceptable workers. The critical incidents technique is sometimes used to collect information about "average" job performance as well. Because stories about actual work events are collected, the method is also very good for developing interview questions and other screening types of tests. Doing a critical incidents job analysis can also help a company defend itself against hiring discrimination if it can document that the person ultimately hired demonstrated the capability to do the job under critical circumstances.

The Job Elements Method

The **job elements method**[17] is used primarily with industrial occupations and lesser-skilled jobs. The job elements method focuses on identifying the characteristics of workers who are able to do the job at a satisfactory level. The process involves:

job elements method
a job analysis method that uses expert brainstorming sessions to identify the characteristics successful workers currently have

1. Selecting a group of experts (including incumbents and their supervisors).
2. Conducting brainstorming sessions with them to identify the characteristics successful workers currently have.
3. Assigning weights to each characteristic (element) based on the following criteria:
   a. the proportion of barely acceptable workers who have the job element (or characteristic);
   b. how effective the element is when it comes to picking a superior worker;
   c. the trouble likely to occur if the element is not considered; and
   d. practicality, or the effect that using the job element in screening job candidates will have on the organization's ability to fill job openings.
4. Analyzing the job element data.

The Structured Interview Technique

structured interview technique
a job analysis method in which subject matter experts provide information about the job verbally in structured face-to-face interviews

subject matter expert
a person who exhibits expertise in a job

The **structured interview technique** asks subject matter experts to provide information about the job verbally in structured face-to-face interviews. A **subject matter expert** is a person who exhibits expertise in a job. This method can be a good choice when only a small number of job experts are able to participate in the job analysis effort or if the job analysis must be completed quickly. Because a relatively small amount of data is collected using this technique, a job analysis professional should conduct the interviews to reduce the risk of interviewer bias and ensure participants focus on identifying characteristics that distinguish superior from average or barely acceptable workers. For example, two possible questions that would be asked during a structured job analysis interview for a radio assembler's job are, "What is the sequence of activities you perform in assembling a radio?" and "How much time do you spend on each part of the assembly process?"

The Task Inventory Approach

task inventory approach
a job analysis method in which job experts generate a list of 50 to 200 tasks grouped into categories reflecting the job's major functions; the functions are then evaluated on dimensions relevant for selection purposes

The **task inventory approach** relies on job experts to generate a list of tasks (typically 50 to 200) that are subsequently grouped into categories reflecting the job's major functions. The information is typically collected via a survey. Then the categories are evaluated on dimensions relevant for selection purposes, including the relative importance of each category of tasks and the relative amount of time a worker spends on each one. Because the focus is on identifying what is typical of the job, this technique might not identify worker characteristics that are important but infrequently displayed or those that distinguish superior from average or barely acceptable workers. The task inventory approach can be combined with other approaches to address these limitations.

The Structured Questionnaire Method

structured questionnaire method
a job analysis method that involves using a list of preplanned questions designed to analyze a job

Position Analysis Questionnaire (PAQ)
a copyrighted, standardized job analysis questionnaire that can be used for just about any job

A **structured questionnaire method** is a job analysis method that involves using a list of preplanned questions designed to analyze a job. The **Position Analysis Questionnaire (PAQ)**[18] is a copyrighted, standardized job analysis questionnaire designed to be used for just about any job. It uses 194 questions to assess the information input, mental processes, work output, relationships with other persons, job context, and other job characteristics associated with a position. Because the PAQ is worker oriented, its questions and results are written in terms of what a successful worker must know or be able to do. The PAQ report outlines the job's requirements for the worker's mental, perceptual, psychomotor, and physical abilities, as well as the desirability of certain personality characteristics and interests. This makes the PAQ very useful for designing selection systems. Because the makers of this questionnaire keep all the results in a comprehensive database, purchasers of this technique can also learn about studies done on similar jobs.

The advantages of using structured questionnaires for job analysis include their speed and low cost. The standardized format also allows for a more objective comparison to be done of different jobs. The disadvantages include the fact that some of the questions may be written at a high reading level, and the predetermined questions restrict the job analyst's ability to customize the questionnaire to fit the organization's unique needs.

Multiple approaches to job analysis can be combined to address the limitations of any single approach and to enhance the quality of the information obtained. Because of the time, expertise, and resources required, many small- and medium-sized businesses do not do job analyses, and instead buy CD-ROMs with collections of generic job descriptions or adapt job descriptions found from similar companies online. In addition to not necessarily providing an adequate legal defense, these methods do not do as good a job of integrating a firm's business strategy with its talent needs as a tailored job analysis done from scratch.

Table 4–4 summarizes the five job analysis methods we just discussed and their advantages and disadvantages.

PLANNING A JOB ANALYSIS

By adequately planning and preparing for the job analysis, the results are likely to be more accurate and useful, and the job analysis should take less time and effort. Although the process can be complex in terms of political implications, who does it, and how it is managed, it is

TABLE 4–4	A Summary of the Five Most Commonly Used Job Analysis Methods	
Method	**Advantages**	**Disadvantages**
Critical Incidents: Subject matter experts provide incidents of good and poor performance.	• Examples of particularly effective or ineffective job behaviors are detailed. • The incidents are examples of actual on-the-job behavior.	• Narrative data can be difficult to analyze and use. • It requires a fair amount of time and resources to collect enough critical incidents.
Job Elements: A panel of subject matter experts list and rate the important job elements (worker characteristics that influence success in the job, including the person's knowledge, skills, abilities, and personal characteristics).	• Job experts are involved in every stage and feel ownership over the process. • It is efficient and relatively fast. • A relatively small number of people are needed. • It results in well-organized documentation of the job and the worker.	• It can be difficult to explain and communicate the job elements methodology.
Structured Interview: Verbally in a face-to-face interview, subject matter experts provide information about the job and worker characteristics that distinguish superior from average or poor workers.	• It is fast. • It requires minimal time and resources. • It is good when only a small number of job experts are available and when the job analysis must be completed quickly. • It is objective. • It results in a reliable description of the job.	• Interviews require a job analysis professional to reduce interviewer bias. • If many experts are involved, then the interviews can be time consuming. • Interview data can be difficult to analyze and use.
Task Inventory: A list of tasks (typically 50 to 200) are generated by job experts and then grouped in categories reflecting major work functions. The categories are subsequently evaluated on dimensions relevant for selection.		• It may not identify worker characteristics that are important but infrequently displayed. • It does not identify worker characteristics that distinguish superior from average or barely acceptable workers.
Structured Questionnaire: A written questionnaire that assesses the job's required information input, mental processes, work output, relationships with other persons, job context, and other job characteristics. The characteristics related to the job are then related to worker characteristics (rather than only the job's tasks, or duties being described).	• It is fast. • It is relatively cheap. • It can be used for almost any position. • It is standardized so different jobs can be compared. • It produces estimates of the job requirements for mental, perceptual, psychomotor, and physical abilities, including estimates of the job's requirements for certain personality characteristics.	• A high reading level may be required for some questionnaire items. • Information obtained is limited by the predetermined questions. • It may miss unique aspects of the job or employee context.

important that the information be as accurate as possible. A job analysis should be performed in such a way as to meet the professional and legal guidelines that have been published in the *Uniform Guidelines on Employee Selection Procedures*.[19]

The process of doing a job analysis can become politicized; it is not uncommon for the job experts doing the analysis to try to color the job analyst's interpretation of the job to suit their personal goals and needs. For example, an incumbent good at the interpersonal part of a secretarial job might play up the importance of the job's interpersonal aspects whereas another incumbent who excels at the administrative part of the job might play up the job's administrative requirements. Therefore, it is important to try to identify any conflicting motivations job experts might have in terms of accurately interpreting the job. When people know that job analysis information will be collected from multiple sources, they are often more honest about the information they provide.

Employees can also get very defensive and worried when their jobs are being analyzed. The process should be thoroughly explained to them and the fairness and objectivity of it stressed. Sometimes top managers are reluctant to spend any time on job analyses because it seems pointless to them to collect data on "something everyone already knows." Emphasizing the fact that the process will help identify employee characteristics that will augment the firm's business strategy and increase the company's return on its staffing investment can help gain the support of top managers. Communicating the job analysis system, purpose, and needs to both employees and management is important in securing the buy-in and support that is essential to performing a quality job analysis.

Time and Resources

Determining the amount of time and resources to invest in a job analysis is an important consideration. Although time and money are often important factors, in general, the greater the resources invested in analyzing the job, the greater the validity and legal defensibility the resulting selection system will be. Establishing the desired level of validity and legal defensibility of the job analysis influences the needed timeline and resources. A firm that wants to do the best job it can at hiring the right people will invest more time and resources in the job analysis than a company that merely wants a minimal level of legal defensibility in case it finds itself in court. As featured in this chapter's opening vignette, Red Lobster invested considerable amount of time and resources to ensure that its job analysis accurately captured what it needed from its restaurant managers.

Identifying Job Experts

The third step in the job analysis planning process is to identify the subject matter experts who will be able to participate in the job analysis. These might include current jobholders, customers, and supervisors. Involving as many high-performing employees in the job analysis as possible will help the job analyst identify all of the most important job tasks and worker behaviors.

Identifying Appropriate Job Analysis Techniques

The fourth step is to identify the job analysis technique(s) that will be used. If the job analyst is unfamiliar with the job, it can be a good idea to first observe one or more employees who do the job before choosing a job analysis technique. This is particularly helpful for manufacturing jobs and jobs that are easily described once the job analyst understands the tasks a worker physically does. Asking one or more people who do the job to keep a diary of what they do can also be helpful, but may not be practical for all jobs. Once the analyst has a general understanding of the position, the appropriateness of various job analysis techniques can be better evaluated.

Identifying the nature of the resources and expertise the firm has available is necessary to determine the best job analysis techniques and the resources required to do the job analysis. For example, in smaller organizations, too few job experts may be available for some techniques. In larger organizations, so many job experts might be available that different people can be involved in each stage of the process. A larger number of available job experts can provide a wider range of insights into the position.

Job analysis techniques can be inductive or deductive. *Inductive* means that the main duties and work tasks of the job have not yet been determined. The job analyst is essentially starting from scratch, in other words. *Deductive* means that the duties and sometimes even the work tasks of the job have already been determined. In this case, the job analyst will be able to build on this information. For example, the job of university professor usually has three duties: teaching, research, and service. In a *deductive* job analysis, these three duties are already specified. More specific work tasks and behaviors within each duty might be identified during the job analysis. The deductive job analysis only needs to identify which work behaviors current professors do, how important they each are, and how much of the professors' time they take. Because quite a bit of descriptive job information is already predetermined, to save time, deductive job analyses are usually conducted via questionnaires rather than personal interviews with employees.

CONDUCTING A JOB ANALYSIS

Next, we discuss a job analysis procedure that is adaptable to suit most jobs. We would like to stress that depending on the job or the purpose of the job analysis, other methods might be more appropriate. Table 4–5 lists the 11 steps in performing a typical job analysis.

Get the Support of Top Management

The first and perhaps most important step in a job analysis effort is to secure the support of the firm's managers, especially its top managers. Without it, the appropriate resources are not likely to be provided for the effort, and employees who are asked to participate will not be as likely to take the effort seriously or be given enough time away from their regular job duties to do it. The job analyst is more likely to gain managerial support by explaining that the goals are to better identify what the firm's jobs require so as to improve how the positions are staffed and reduce costly turnover.

Communicate the Purpose of the Job Analysis to All Participants

After securing the support of the firm's top managers, the purpose of the job analysis needs to be communicated to all employees who will participate in the effort. Often it can be helpful for top managers to make an internal announcement about the importance of the effort and how employees can help improve the quality of the information collected by participating honestly and objectively. Explaining why the job analysis is being done and describing how the results will be used can promote cooperation among employees and help reduce their fears that the process might somehow negatively affect their own jobs.

Collect Background Information

The next activity that should be undertaken is a review of the firm's existing documents and information related to the position, including the following:

- *A job family description*, which provides a quick overview of the job family that contains similar jobs.
- *Desk audits*, which involve asking people who currently do the job to walk you through their most important and most frequent tasks. (This can be particularly useful for analyzing clerical and technical positions.)
- *Entry examinations* currently used for the job.
- *Worker logs*, which can provide the job analyst a feel for the tasks done and identify particularly important job functions. The logs might also include critical incidents that can be looked at.
- *Any existing job analyses, job descriptions, person specifications, or job profiles*, which can be a useful starting point for developing task statements and identifying competencies.

TABLE 4–5   The Eleven Steps in Performing a Typical Job Analysis

1. Get the support of top managers and ensure that all managers support the job analysis effort
2. Thoroughly communicate the purpose of the job analysis to all participants and ensure they are diligent about completing the tasks objectively
3. Collect background information and analyze how the job contributes to the execution of the firm's business strategy
4. Generate the task statements
5. Generate the KSAOs
6. Form the job duty and task groupings
7. Link the KSAOs back to the job duties
8. Collect critical incidents
9. Weight the job duties
10. Construct a job requirements matrix
11. Write the job description and person specification

- *Performance reviews* of current and previous occupants of the position, which can provide the job analyst with information about what job behaviors and outcomes are currently considered important.
- *Recruitment information*, such as Internet postings and brochures given to past applicants.
- *Training materials*

Documents such as these will obviously only be available for existing jobs. Before beginning a job analysis for a brand-new job, the people doing it need to understand the reasons why the position is being created and what the managers who have authority over the position perceive its important duties and characteristics to be. If no previous information on the job exists, and if there are no job experts currently performing the job, it is particularly important to gather information from as many people who will be affected by the job as possible. It can also be helpful to establish what job duties will *not* be assigned to the new position to ensure that appropriate boundaries are created. Considering the organization's culture and business strategy and how the target job fits into the broader organization is important, too. This information can help identify appropriate job experts and frame why the position exists and how it contributes to strategy execution and to the company's competitive advantage.

Another helpful source of background information about a current or new job is the government's current online job classification system called the Occupational Information Network (O*NET).[20] O*NET replaced the Dictionary of Occupational Titles, which described what workers did on a job with regard to seven categories: (1) things, (2) data, (3) people, (4) worker instructions, (5) reasoning, (6) math, and (7) language. O*NET contains a variety of information about a wide variety of jobs. Although the job analysis information contained in O*NET must usually be modified and supplemented to fit the particular job and organization, it is a great place to begin gathering background job analysis information and a starting point for identifying a job's requirements. Because O*NET was developed for general occupations, the information will likely need to be made more specific to suit a particular job and organization. The Dictionary of Occupational Titles[21] and Job Analysis Dot Net[22] can also be useful resources.

It is also important at this stage to analyze the organization's culture and business strategy and learn how the target job fits into the broader organization. Why does this position exist in the organization? What do other people in the organization need from the people in the target job? What must people in the target job be able to do to enable the organization's work to be done well and be done consistently with the organization's business strategy? What values and work styles are necessary for effective performance? The answers to these questions can identify important behaviors and tasks that should be included in the job analysis.

This is also a good time to begin identifying any changes anticipated for the position. Incumbents, supervisors, and company executives may all have insights as to how what the company needs from the position might change in ways that affect how the position should be staffed. Job analyses should be future oriented, and conducted in a way that the talent placed in a job will be able to perform the job both now and in the future.

Generate the Task Statements

job task

an observable unit of work with a beginning and an end

The fourth step is to identify in specific behavioral terms the regular duties and responsibilities of a position. A **job task** is an observable unit of work with a beginning and an end. For example, one of the job tasks of a warehouse worker might be to sort a box or complete a purchase order. After consulting the existing materials collected during the literature review, interview multiple job experts, including incumbents, supervisors, and others with a thorough knowledge of the job to generate task statements. Each task statement should describe a discreet, identifiable aspect of the work performed on the target job and describe *what* the worker does, *how* the worker does it, and *for what purpose*. Then combine any related or similar task statements and write them as one statement. Table 4–6 shows examples of task statements and how to format them.

Task statements reveal a lot of information about a job, including:

- the type of knowledge used,
- the amount of supervision exercised and received,
- the decisions made,
- the physical working conditions,

TABLE 4–6	Task Statement Examples		
What? (action verb)	**To Whom/What?**	**How?**	**Why?**
Writes	Advertising copy	Using Microsoft Word	For placement in newspaper and magazine advertisements
Mows	Lawn area	Using rider and push mowers	To maintain appearance of company grounds
Supervises	Assistant store managers	In person and using surveillance cameras	To ensure compliance with company policies
Compares	Unit expenses with budget	Using basic math computations	To ensure budgetary compliance
Drives	Fuel truck containing gasoline to work sites	Following all safety procedures	To refuel construction vehicles

- the physical requirements of the job (e.g., how much lifting, stooping, and bending is conducted and under what conditions),
- the technology used, and
- the necessity of working individually or as a team member.

To comply with the ADA, task statements should focus on *what* needs to be done and not *how* it needs to be done. Try to avoid nondescriptive verbs, such as *prepares* or *conducts,* and be as specific as possible. Here is an example of a poor versus a good task statement:

Poor: Accounts for all cash at the end of a shift.

Good: Balances the cash in register at the end of a shift by counting the money, visually comparing the total with the register tape total, and identifying and correcting errors in order to account for all the cash received.

The physical requirements of a job description must be addressed to ensure ADA compliance. Table 4–7 presents a physical requirements checklist.

Generate the KSAOs

One of the primary goals of a staffing-oriented job analysis is to identify the job-related worker characteristics that need to be present for recruits to be considered minimally qualified for the job, and those characteristics that help to identify the job candidates likely to be most successful on the job. Job-related worker characteristics can be thought of in terms of knowledge (K), skills (S), abilities (A), other characteristics (O) (referred to as a group as KSAOs), and competencies.

Knowledge refers to an organized body of factual or procedural information that can be applied to a task. The knowledge of computer programming languages, foreign languages, and machine operating procedures are examples. A job's knowledge requirements should be stated as specifically as possible. Consider the knowledge requirements a corporate recruiter must have, for example: Instead of stating, "knowledge of staffing-related legal principles and laws is required" it would be more appropriate to state, "knowledge of Equal Employment Opportunity (EEO) and affirmative action guidelines and laws, such as the Americans with Disabilities Act, is required."

A **skill** is the capability to perform tasks accurately and with ease. Skills often refer to psychomotor activities (e.g., activities performed using body movements, such as one's arms and hands, vision, and so forth). When a skill is identified as necessary, a performance standard must also exist for using that skill (e.g., 20/20 vision, typing 120 words per minute with five or fewer errors, and so on).

Skills reflect the ability of people to effectively use their knowledge to perform physical tasks. Driving skills are a good example. It is not only an individual's knowledge about how to drive that's important, but also his or her skill in actually doing so. Imagine, for example, a child knowledgeable about the function and use of a steering wheel, gas pedal, and brake pedal

knowledge
an organized body of factual or procedural information that can be applied to a task

skill
the capability to perform tasks accurately and with ease; skills often refer to psychomotor activities

TABLE 4–7 A Partial Checklist of the Physical Activities and Requirements, Visual Acuity, and Working Conditions of the Position[23]

The physical requirements of the position (Please check only ONE)

- *Sedentary Work:* Exerting up to 10 pounds of force occasionally and/or a negligible amount of force frequently or constantly to lift, carry, push, pull, or otherwise move objects, including the human body. Sedentary work involves sitting most of the time. Jobs are sedentary if walking and standing are required only occasionally and all other sedentary criteria are met.
- *Light Work:* Exerting up to 20 pounds of force occasionally, and/or up to 10 pounds of force frequently, and/or a negligible amount of force constantly to move objects. If the use of arm and/or leg controls requires exertion of forces greater than that for Sedentary work and the worker sits most of the time, the job is rated for Light Work.
- *Medium Work:* Exerting up to 50 pounds of force occasionally, and/or up to 20 pounds frequently, and/or up to 10 pounds of force constantly to move objects.
- *Heavy Work:* Exerting up to 100 pounds of force occasionally, and/or up to 50 pounds of force frequently, and/or up to 20 pounds of force constantly to move objects.
- *Very Heavy Work:* Exerting in excess of 100 pounds of force occasionally, and/or in excess of 50 pounds of force frequently, and/or in excess of 20 pounds of force constantly to move objects.

The physical activity of this position (Please check ALL that apply)

- *Climbing*: Ascending or descending ladders, stairs, scaffolding, ramps, poles, and the like using feet and legs and/or hands and arms. Body agility is emphasized. This factor is important if the amount and kind of climbing required exceeds that required for ordinary locomotion.
- *Balancing:* Maintaining body equilibrium to prevent falling when walking, standing, or crouching on narrow, slippery, or erratically moving surfaces. This factor is important if the amount and kind of balancing exceeds that needed for ordinary locomotion and maintenance of body equilibrium.
- *Stooping:* Bending body downward and forward by bending spine at the waist. This factor is important if it occurs to a considerable degree and requires full use of the lower extremities and back muscles.
- *Kneeling:* Bending legs at knee to come to a rest on knee or knees.
- *Crouching:* Bending the body downward and forward by bending legs and spine.

The conditions the worker will be subject to in this position (Please check ALL that apply)

- *The worker is subject to inside environmental conditions*: Protection from weather conditions but not necessarily from temperature changes.
- *The worker is subject to outside environmental conditions:* No effective protection from weather.
- *The worker is subject to both environmental conditions:* Activities occur inside and outside.
- *The worker is subject to extreme cold:* Temperatures typically below 32 degrees for periods of more than one hour. Consideration should be given to the effect of other environmental conditions, such as wind and humidity.
- *The worker is subject to extreme heat:* Temperatures above 100 degrees for periods of more than one hour. Consideration should be given to the effect of other environmental conditions, such as wind and humidity.
- *The worker is subject to noise:* There is sufficient noise to cause the worker to shout in order to be heard above the ambient noise level.
- *The worker is subject to vibration:* Exposure to oscillating movements of the extremities or whole body.

Source: Reprinted with permission from the North Carolina Office of State Personnel.

but who is clearly unable to actually drive a car. This child would have driving knowledge but no driving skills. Other examples of skills are:

- Depth perception
- Manual dexterity

ability
a more stable and enduring capability to perform a variety of tasks than a skill allows

An **ability** is a more stable and enduring capability to perform a variety of tasks than a skill allows. Abilities can be inherited, acquired, or a combination of both. Unlike skills, abilities reflect more natural talents, including cognitive abilities (e.g., verbal or quantitative abilities), psychomotor abilities (reaction time), sensory abilities (e.g., the ability to see or hear particularly well), and physical abilities (e.g., a person's strength, endurance, or flexibility).

- Mathematical ability
- Perceptual ability
- The ability to lift 50 pounds

"Other" characteristics is typically a catchall category for worker characteristics that do not fall into the knowledge, skill, or ability categories. They include a person's values, interests, integrity, work style, and other personality traits. Additional examples grouped into this category include one's degrees and/or certifications and the ability to work weekends. It is important to note that while some personality traits, such as conscientiousness, are consistently predictive of job performance, their relationship with job performance is not strong enough to base hiring decisions exclusively on them.

After the task statements are generated, the third step is to ask a different group of job experts to identify the KSAOs necessary to perform each task. It is sometimes more efficient to identify the KSAOs *after* conducting the next step, forming job duty and task groupings. The risk is that important, but infrequently used KSAOs may be overlooked. In addition to KSAOs, job experts can identify the competencies needed for a worker in the job to be successful. It is particularly important that this group identify knowledge that a worker needs but that he or she cannot refer to (in manuals or other written instructions) while actively on the job. For example, someone working as a press operator for a newspaper publisher cannot stop the presses to look up operating information. Some tips for writing good KSAOs are to maintain a reasonable balance between being too general and too specific. A common error is to include trivial information when writing KSAOs. Do not simply restate the task statement. Focus on providing new information by identifying what KSAOs employees really need to perform a given task. Of course, as we hinted at in previous chapters, the job expert should also identify whether each KSAO is something that new hires are expected to have before being hired or whether the organization intends to train new hires to develop the KSAOs.

A substantial amount of empirical research has helped us to identify some of the employee characteristics that seem to be related to better job performance in virtually all jobs. For example, intelligence[24] and conscientiousness[25] have consistently been shown to be related to higher job performance. Additionally, a person's emotional stability and extraversion can enhance his or her job performance in many different types of jobs, particularly those involving interpersonal relations.[26] If the goal is to recruit top performers for a dynamic job, focusing on the intelligence and the ability of candidates to learn quickly should help. If honesty and integrity are key, recruiting people who display these traits can result in employees who are less likely to engage in counterproductive behaviors and steal.[27] Table 4–8 summarizes some of the characteristics likely to be important in specific job environments.

"other" characteristics
characteristics that do not fall into the knowledge, skill, or ability categories; they include a person's values, interests, integrity, work style, and other personality traits

TABLE 4–8	The Characteristics Related to Specific Job Requirements
Characteristic	**Job Requirements**
Adaptability: The ability to effectively manage change, delays, or unexpected events	Complex, dynamic jobs (e.g., CEO and research & development jobs)
Emotional Stability: The disposition to be calm, optimistic, well-adjusted	Jobs involving interpersonal interaction (e.g., police and air traffic control jobs)
Conscientiousness: The tendency to be purposeful, dependable, and attentive to detail	Jobs requiring dependability, consistency, and motivation (e.g., quality control jobs)
Extraversion: The tendency to be sociable, assertive, and upbeat	Jobs requiring interpersonal interaction and persuasion (e.g., sales and customer service jobs)
Emotional Intelligence: The ability to control one's emotions, read the emotions of others, and relate to others	Jobs requiring interpersonal interaction, negotiation, and influence (e.g., sales, customer service, and management jobs)
Ethics: One's honesty, willingness to follow rules, and tendency to treat people with respect	Jobs with a high level of discretion or with a high risk of employee theft (e.g., casino and bank jobs, and cashier and accounting jobs)
Team Orientation: The tendency to be oriented toward the achievement of collective goals	Jobs requiring a high degree of teamwork or sharing of resources (e.g., jobs as part of creative or medical teams)

Form the Job Duty Groupings

In the next step, the job analyst groups similar task statements into job duties that reflect broader job responsibilities (e.g., decision making, supervision, and customer relations). A **job duty** is a set of related tasks that are repeated on the job, such as servicing customers or maintaining an office's supplies. The grouping process is subjective, but the goal is to reduce a lengthy list of task statements into a much shorter list—generally to fewer than 12 job duties each containing 6 to 30 task statements. Often the KSAOs required for each task will help the job analyst determine which tasks should be grouped together. Each job duty should then be labeled to reflect the broader tasks it represents. Table 4–9 lists some task statements for the job duty of classroom instruction for a university professor.

Link the KSAOs Back to the Job Duties

In the seventh step, a third set of job experts links the KSAOs associated with the tasks contained in each job duty back to the various job duties. These experts are asked to confirm whether each KSAO is important to the performance of the tasks in each given category. Ideally, the relationship of every KSAO to every task category is rated in terms of its importance. This helps the firm identify which KSAOs should be given priority when it comes to making its recruiting and selection decisions. The step also confirms that each of the KSAOs is critical to the performance of the job.

Collect Critical Incidents

The eighth step is to collect critical incidents to identify the behaviors that differentiate very good from poor job performance. Ask job experts to consider each of the job duties one at a time and imagine instances of particular effective or ineffective performance. Ideally, both good and bad critical incidents will be collected to try to identify the behaviors, competencies, skills, and so on, that differentiate good job performers.

Certain questions can help employees recall the details of an incident. A job analyst might use the following questions to probe for details about a negative critical incident that occurred for a customer service representative:

1. *What were the circumstances leading up to the incident?* Answer: A caller was using abusive language but not communicating what the actual problem was.
2. *What did the worker do that made you think that s/he was a good, average, or poor performer?* Answer: The customer service representative "told off" the caller and angrily hung up.
3. *What were the consequences of the worker's behavior in the critical incident?* Answer: The caller worked for a large customer, which subsequently discontinued its relationship with the firm.

This negative critical incident suggests that patience, the ability to stay calm in the event of a belligerent call, and emotional control are useful screening criteria for a telephone-based customer service representative.

TABLE 4–9   Group Task Statements into a Job Duty

For the job of: *University Professor*
Job Duty: *Classroom Instruction*
Task Statements:
a. Prepare course syllabus using Microsoft Word to inform students of instructor's expectations and grading criteria, provide a reading schedule, and summarize course goals
b. Prepare lectures in advance using appropriate software and media to communicate the course material to students
c. Lecture students verbally to accurately communicate the course materials in an engaging way

An example of a positive critical incident for a customer service representative might be the following:

> A caller was hysterical because the birthday gift she ordered for her child arrived damaged and the birthday was the next day. She yelled incoherently about the incident. The customer service representative talked in a clear, calm voice and persuaded the woman to repackage the damaged product for return. The customer service representative checked to ensure that the product was still available and personally assured the caller that a replacement would immediately be sent for overnight delivery.

This example suggests that the ability to regulate one's emotions, remain calm in the presence of an emotional caller, and be persuasive are useful screening criteria for a customer service representative.

Weight the Job Duties

After finalizing the job duties, task statements, and KSAOs, employees, supervisors, and others familiar with the job weight its duties according to their relative importance to the overall performance of the job and the relative time spent on each. The weights should each add up to 100 percent. Table 4–10 shows how to weight the job duties of an administrative job.

The weights for each job duty's relative importance are used to identify Bona Fide Occupational Qualifications (BFOQs), or the essential qualifications of new hires, and to prioritize the characteristics that will be recruited and screened for. If the optimal weights for each job dimension cannot be determined statistically—a situation that we will discuss further in Chapter 8—the weights for the relative time spent on each job duty are used to prioritize them into essential versus desirable categories.

In Table 4–10, database administration is the most important job dimension for this position although administrative assistants spend most of their time performing clerical duties. Staff administration is the least important relative to the others (although still an important job duty); administrative assistants spend the least amount of time performing these job duties.

The staffing specialist may then determine that database administration will be weighted 45 percent, clerical will be weighted 35 percent, and staff administration will be weighted 20 percent in computing an overall evaluation score. Equally weighting the three duties would misrepresent their relative contribution to the job. Of course, the weights different job experts

TABLE 4–10	Weighting Job Duties by Their Importance and the Relative Time Spent on Each

In the left column, record a number of points between 1 and 100 that reflects the importance of the particular task category to the overall performance of an administrative assistant. The total number of points distributed over the job duties should equal 100. In the right column, indicate what percentage of time is spent on the activities like those represented by the three job duties. Again, the total number of points distributed across the job duties should equal 100.

Relative Importance	Job Duty	Relative Time Spent
45	1. *Database Administration*. Maintaining and developing databases and spreadsheets, including collecting and entering information. Using databases and spreadsheets to obtain summaries and answer questions.	25
35	2. *Clerical*. General clerical activities including answering phone, filing, handling mail, and duplicating.	50
20	3. *Staff Administration*. Record keeping and handling payroll duties, including auditing and resolving discrepancies. Maintaining unit personnel files.	25
100	*Total must equal 100	100

give each job duty will vary. Consequently, the job analyst will have to use good judgment when deciding which weights to actually assign.

When First Hawaiian Bank conducted a job analysis on its customer service positions, it found that 40 percent of a customer service employee's time was being spent on administrative duties, not focusing on customer service. This information prompted First Hawaiian Bank to restructure its customer service department, which resulted in a more efficient workforce.[28]

Construct a Job Requirements Matrix

The tenth step in a job analysis is to construct a job requirements matrix summarizing the information collected so far. Table 4–11 shows what a job requirements matrix looks like.

In addition to looking at a single job description to plan for a particular job, a firm can pool together job analyses from a variety of positions to identify key KSAOs or competencies that are important for multiple jobs. Job analyses for jobs in the same job family, or for jobs that tend to link into career paths for employees, can be used for strategic planning.

Write the Job Description and Person Specification

The final step is the writing of the job description and person specification. At the very minimum, the previous steps should generate a list of tasks and duties with some information regarding their importance to the overall performance of a satisfactory employee, an indication of the frequency these duties are performed, and the job's essential and desirable qualifications. To write the job description, the job analyst should be able to use the tasks and duties to describe the basic functions. The Web site www.jobdescription.com can be a helpful resource for writing job descriptions. After searching to find a desired job title, the wizard can be used to customize the generic job description for this position using the information obtained from the job analysis.

TABLE 4–11	A Job Requirements Matrix for a Project Manager

		Characteristics of the Job		Characteristics of the Worker	
Job Duty	**Tasks**	**Relative Importance of Job Duty (%)**	**Relative Time Spent (%)**	**Competency or KSAO**	**Importance of KSAO or Competency to Task Performance (1 = Low, 10 = High) (E = Essential)**
Project Management	1. Develop and implement plans, schedules, and responsibility charts to ensure adherence to the project's timeline 2. Report the project's progress and results to superiors	35	20	1. Ability to develop plans and schedules 2. Time management skills 3. Knowledge of project management reporting software	8.2 9.1 E 7.6
Supervision	1. Schedule and track team members' work assignments to ensure appropriate progress 2. Acquire the resources the team needs to function	35	30	1. Ability to work with diverse people 2. Ability to delegate 3. Negotiation skills 4. Prioritization skills 5. Leadership ability	5.9 7.6 8.3 8.9 E 7.4
Customer Service	1. Research and understand customers' needs and take actions to ensure their needs are met	30	50	1. Communication skills 2. Listening skills 3. Empathy	8.1 8.8 E 7.9

In addition to precisely specifying the actual job duties that have to be performed from a business or management standpoint, to comply with certain requirements of the ADA, a job description has to be very specific about the physical, ergonomic, environmental, and other requirements of the job. For example, a job description for a sales position should include a specific description of the physical requirements of the job, such as "must stand for significant periods of time without a break" or "must meet with customers outside under all weather conditions." If the job analyst isn't specific in describing every important aspect of the job, then the ADA assumes that the employee can perform the actual job duties any way he or she wants to, regardless of whether or not his or her way complies with company policy.[29]

The person specification summarizes the KSAOs needed to perform the job well as well as the minimum worker qualifications and BFOQs. One way to create a person specification is to look at the job duties and try to identify the most important KSAOs or competencies needed to do the job. The necessary KSAOs should be stated in the most job-related terms possible. The required qualifications and the level of education required for the job should be stated as precisely as possible as well. If the organization intends to train new hires, the required aptitudes or training-readiness criteria should be stated. If related experience is included in the person specification, the quality of a person's experience is often more important than the length of experience. If any qualifications are deemed essential, they should reflect the minimum basic educational requirements necessary to carry out the job to an acceptable standard.

The quality and specificity of the job description and person specification are critical for the recruiting function to match candidates' skills to job requirements. However, rather than simply developing a laundry list of all the tasks required of the position, it is more strategic to consider the business strategy and competitive advantage, a job's performance needs, and what it means to be successful on the job in addition to these base skills. By first defining outstanding performance, the key competencies, styles, and traits desired in a new hire can become more apparent. To comply with the requirements of the ADA, job descriptions must also identify the essential job functions and the physical and mental requirements needed to perform these essential functions.

Consider the position of executive assistant. The job requires filing, answering phones and screening calls, scheduling the executive's time, processing requisitions, and light bookkeeping. As a result, the job posting could describe a need for a person with strong typing, filing, organization, and communication skills, and an understanding of the company's requisition and bookkeeping procedures. A deeper analysis of what has made past incumbents most successful in this position, however, may be their ability to multitask and to not be turned off by the executive's aggressive managing style. The amount of typing required by the job is minimal, and the bookkeeping and requisition processing are easily trained. Focusing the recruiting effort on identifying people who are organized, are good at multitasking, and work well under pressure may be more important in hiring a high performer for this job.

The longer the list of skill requirements in a person specification, the fewer the number of people who will feel qualified and apply. Focusing on the key characteristics to be sought in recruits increases the likelihood of hiring a superior performer. Also, if the person specification calls for qualifications greater than those actually required by the job, problems can arise. Hiring more highly qualified candidates is likely to cost more. Moreover, if the candidates are hired but then begin to feel underchallenged in their positions, their turnover is likely to be higher.[30] Next to analyzing actual performance data for employees with differing levels of qualifications to assess the relationship between qualification level and job performance for that position, the best gauge for specifying required qualification levels is generally the judgment of an experienced manager.

Writing an effective job description can be as much an art as a science. Here are some experts' tips to help you write more effective job descriptions:

- Because the primary objective of a job description is to "sell" the organization and the job to qualified candidates, provide enough information to pique their interest. Describe how the organization is unique by communicating its mission statement, future vision, and why it is meaningful to work in the firm.[31]

ROLE

Be a role model and teacher; create an environment where you and the restaurant crew are living our principles, keeping the promises, and living the non-negotiables by providing leadership to crew members who deliver a great dining experience for our guests by maintaining consistently high standards, modeling a passion for service, and attending to the details.

RESPONSIBILITIES

- Arrive to work on time and ready to work, neat and well groomed, according to RL (Red Lobster) dress and appearance standards.
- Build sales and guest counts through leadership of crew and being involved in the community.
- Maximize sales and profits by teaching, coaching, and upholding sales and service techniques to ensure a great guest experience.
- Clearly communicate priorities concerning restaurant readiness, the menu, and promotions through pre-shift and regularly scheduled monthly departmental meetings with crew.
- Know each crew member's name and genuinely greet and interact with crew throughout every shift.
- Model ways to delight guests and crew member to deliver an excellent guest experience.
- Proactively handle all crew and guest requests or concerns quickly with caring and fairness.
- Maintain consistent staffing levels of well-qualified front of the house & heart of the house crew by using the crew selection process.
- Manage crew performance with clear feedback, recognition, reviews, coach/teach, and discipline.
- Identify and develop crew members for future leadership roles.
- Ensure the restaurant's appearance and cleanliness meets our guests' expectations by upholding the highest standards including QA, sanitation levels, and equipment/facilities maintenance.
- Hold yourself and crew accountable for attitude, behavior, results, and RL standards/systems (such as crew appearance, three table stations, service steps).
- Inventories, orders, and maintains sufficient levels of product, small wares, and the tools necessary to provide an excellent experience for our guests.
- Take pride in making food and beverage look and taste great.

KNOWLEDGE AND SKILLS

- Learn, live, and teach Our Compass' principles and promises, and RL non-negotiables to all crewmates.
- Delegate and get work done through others.
- Learn, teach, and uphold food, beverage and service standards and systems using the RL training system.
- Work well with and communicate with people of different backgrounds, experience levels, and personalities.
- Know the RL menu completely and be able to teach crew members to describe the taste, preparation, ingredients, and prices of all food and beverage items.
- Learn, understand, and use the POS and BOS systems.
- Demonstrate a leadership style that creates a positive working environment and remain calm during stressful and emotional situations.
- Be organized in all areas, for example, in your personnel files, storage areas, side work and scheduling needs.
- Be aware of the laws and RL standards that impact the business.

BASIC REQUIREMENTS

(1) Withstand temperatures of 0 degrees Fahrenheit or less and 100 degrees Fahrenheit or more, (2) move throughout the restaurant for extended periods of time (up to 10-12 hours per day), (3) move 50 lbs. for distances of up to 10 ft., (4) balance and move up to 25 lbs. for distances of up to 50 ft., (5) understand and respond to crew members' and guests' requests in a loud environment, and (6) perform basic math and understand finances and cost management.

EDUCATION/EXPERIENCE REQUIREMENTS

(1) High school equivalency required; college coursework preferred, (2) previous supervisory and hospitality industry experience preferred, (3) proficient communication in English (verbal and in writing), (4) minimum 21 years of age, and (5) proven track record of success as a restaurant manager. This description is not intended and should not be construed to be an exhaustive list of all responsibilities, skills, effort, or work conditions associated with the job. It is intended to be an accurate reflection of the principal job elements essential for making employment decisions.

"Management Crew Positions," Redlobster.com, www.redlobster.com/jobs/management_positions.asp. Accessed April 5, 2007.

FIGURE 4–2 The Job Description for a Red Lobster Restaurant Manager

- Because job descriptions can quickly become outdated, supplement them with regularly negotiated goals and developmental opportunities.[32]
- Write enough flexibility (including something like, "and any other tasks as assigned by the supervisor") into job descriptions so that workers do not think, "That's not my job," and they are comfortable helping coworkers, cross-training, and finding additional ways to contribute to the organization.[33]
- The title of a job is an important part of a job description—job seekers view many job titles, so be sure it is as descriptive as possible.[34]

Figure 4–2 is an actual job description for a Red Lobster restaurant manager.

Both job analyses and competency modeling techniques can be applied in a forward-looking manner to jobs that are evolving or that do not yet exist. In this case, the job or subject matter experts are interviewed and asked to identify the KSAOs and competencies likely to be critical in the future.

OTHER METHODS: COMPETENCY MODELING AND JOB REWARDS ANALYSIS

Competency Modeling

Competency modeling[35] is a job analysis method that identifies the necessary worker competencies for high performance. **Competencies** are more broadly defined components of a successful worker's repertoire of behavior needed to do the job well. Rather than mere job skills, they are the worker characteristics that underlie on-the-job success. Competencies can encompass multiple types of knowledge, skills, attitudes, personalities, and so on.

The differences between KSAOs and competencies can be confusing. One way to think about the difference is to think of competencies as "job-spanning" whereas KSAOs are often limited to an individual job. Also, competencies often come from the top managers of an organization and serve to reinforce the firm's culture. By contrast, KSAO statements are derived mostly by job analysts for staffing purposes.

Because competencies are linked to the organization's business goals, strategy, and values, a person specification resulting from a job description can enhance hiring quality and strategy execution. Because competency modeling may not identify worker characteristics that are important but infrequently displayed, it often supplements other job analysis methods. Because competencies are better linked to the organization's business goals and strategy than traditional KSAOs, competency modeling is gaining in popularity.

A competency-based job description enhances a manager's flexibility in assigning work, lengthens the life of a job description, and can allow firms to group jobs requiring similar competencies under a single job description. Competency modeling allows for greater flexibility in specifying a job's requirements. Because competencies define how to perform a job more broadly than does a traditional job analysis, if the job is changing, then the job analysis will not have to be updated as frequently. The broader description of a job also discourages workers asked to perform a new work task or behavior from saying, "That is not in my job description," unlike workers in a more rigidly specified job.

Therefore, identifying the organization's business strategy, vision, and values is the first step in competency modeling. Job experts with different perspectives on the job, including incumbents, supervisors, and internal and external customers, then identify the characteristics, values, etc., that enable an employee in that position to best execute the strategy and ensure that the company's values are consistently practiced. For example, a strategy based on innovation and fast product development requires employees with a sense of urgency and the ability to innovate. If the organization's strategy requires employees to continually adapt to or apply new or changing technologies, adaptability and the ability to learn quickly can be more important than specific skills. A strategy with a large customer service component requires hiring employees who are committed to integrity and customer service. Low-cost strategies generally require people who are efficient, detail oriented, and committed to reducing waste and enhancing the firm's efficiencies.

competency modeling
a job analysis method that identifies the necessary worker competencies for high performance

competencies
more broadly defined components of a successful worker's repertoire of behavior needed to do a job well

Table 4–12 shows some examples of competencies and jobs that require them.

A good example of linking core competencies, values, and experiences to job descriptions and staffing practices is Dell Computer Corporation. Dell believes that although it can teach its new executives the nuances of the computer industry, it cannot teach them how to be effective in Dell's dynamic environment. After reviewing the performance ratings and compensation levels of Dell vice presidents and directors hired over a three-year period, Dell learned who had been successful, and why. Interviewing the superiors of those executives who had left the company or who had not advanced also provided insights into the competencies required for success at Dell. The research resulted in the identification of five core competencies for executive hires: the ability to learn fast, to thrive in a changing environment, to deliver results, to solve problems, and to build teams. Dell recruiters now use these criteria in determining which candidates to pursue.[36]

Like the other methods, job experts using competency modeling also observe and judge the behaviors displayed by successful employees. Ideally, one group of job experts identifies the competencies, and another group reviews them and offers input. Similar competencies are combined, and a set of from 6 to 12 competencies is generated. It is important not to include too many competencies to ensure the staffing effort focuses on those most important and useful for selection purposes. Accomplishing this goal may require the generation of a longer competency list at first, collecting data over time on employees' performance of the skills and behaviors thought to be important, and analyzing the data to see which actually make the most difference. Although many organizations can brainstorm relatively good lists of key competencies, there is no substitute for taking an objective, data-driven look at which competencies actually matter.

Competency modeling is becoming more popular for a number of reasons: Because competencies are broader than skills, job analysts have greater flexibility in terms of specifying a job's requirements. This can help discourage workers from refusing to undertake certain duties not explicitly written into their job descriptions. Also, if the job is changing, then the job analysis will not have to be updated as frequently. Thus, the method's greater simplicity and flexibility appeals to many organizations with rapidly changing jobs for which traditional job analysis methods are costly and time consuming.

Competency analysis is less useful than most other job analysis techniques for describing technical skills. As a result, it often supplements other job analysis methods. However, it's worth noting that the most important competencies, values, and experiences are likely to vary across business units and departments as well. The competencies required by people in a firm's

TABLE 4–12	Competencies Related to Specific Job Environments
Competency Required	**Job Examples**
Adaptability: The ability to effectively manage change, delays, or unexpected events	Complex, dynamic jobs (the job of the CEO and research & development jobs)
Communication: Includes choosing the appropriate communication medium, presenting verbal and written information clearly and concisely, listening, and giving and receiving feedback	Jobs involving interpersonal interaction (most jobs)
Leadership: Building motivation and a sense of shared purpose in others	Jobs requiring the supervision or influencing of others (managerial jobs and jobs in team settings)
Emotional Intelligence: The ability to control one's emotions, read the emotions of others, and relate to others	Jobs requiring interpersonal interaction, negotiation, and influence (sales, customer service, and managerial jobs)
Problem Solving: Acquiring, analyzing, and integrating information from relevant sources to make timely and appropriate decisions	Jobs requiring analyzing and troubleshooting (customer service, maintenance, and product design jobs)
Creativity: The ability to come up with novel ideas and insights	Jobs requiring original and unique ideas and insights (marketing executive, interior designer, and graphic artist jobs)

accounting department, for example, are likely to differ from those required by the firm's marketing or research and development departments.

Some companies are experimenting with the elimination of multiple job titles to refocus employees on their work rather than their job title. Marketing firm the Richards Group eliminated the titles of its 560 employees and gave all of its 20 executives the same title of principal. The move was welcomed by clients, who didn't care about the title of the people handling their accounts, and seems to have refocused employees on what they do rather than on climbing the corporate ladder.[37]

Because the approach is relatively new, and because the level of rigor and documentation is less than traditional job analysis methods, it is unclear how well the approach will withstand legal challenges.[38] Until it has withstood greater legal scrutiny, it is advisable to combine competency modeling with more traditional job analysis techniques.

Job Rewards Analysis

Another type of job analysis is called a **job rewards analysis**. Job rewards analysis is a job analysis technique that analyzes a job's **intrinsic rewards** that are nonmonetary and derived from the work itself and from the organization's culture as opposed to **extrinsic rewards** that have monetary value. Intrinsic rewards can include the satisfaction of meeting one's personal goals, from engaging in continuous learning activities, and doing meaningful work. Extrinsic rewards include an employee's base pay, bonuses, and benefits. Some jobs provide unique extrinsic rewards like free travel for flight attendants and merchandise discounts for retail employees.[39] Intrinsic and extrinsic rewards together comprise the **total rewards** related to a particular job.

The identified rewards can be used to better match candidates with different jobs, as well as to improve the recruitment process. For example, if a recruiter learns what motivates a job candidate, she or he can identify job rewards that will make the job more appealing to the candidate: A job candidate motivated by money can be told extensively about the company's pay-for-performance system. By contrast, a job candidate motivated by developing his or her skills can be told more about the company's training, development, and continuing education programs.

The **employee value proposition** is the balance between the intrinsic and extrinsic rewards an employee receives by working for a particular employer in return for the employee's job performance. If employees believe they receive rewards equal to or exceeding what they put into the company, they will be more satisfied and less likely to quit. When recruiting or convincing someone to accept his or her job offer instead of a competitor's offer, the recruiter and hiring manager must answer the candidate's most important question, "What's in it for me?" in a manner that makes the job opportunity the most appealing. Answering this question requires a job rewards analysis.

To do a job rewards analysis, one must first determine exactly what attracts job candidates and why incumbents enjoy their work. Then one must craft a message to clearly state what makes the company the obvious choice over the competition. Sometimes the selling points used for different candidates will differ—some are more motivated by financial rewards than others, some prefer a team-based work environment, and so on. The rewards emphasized to each candidate should reflect what motivates them as individuals. To do this, the recruiter and hiring manager need to have a thorough understanding of the intrinsic and extrinsic rewards of the job.

Because even intrinsic rewards often cost money, it is important to balance what a firm can afford with what it would like to offer employees as attractive rewards. This relates to the three criteria for employee value propositions: magnitude, mix, and distinctiveness.[40] *Magnitude* refers to a reward package that is neither too small nor too large in economic terms. Investing too little in a reward package risks offending applicants, discouraging them from applying or accepting job offers, and being noncompetitive. Spending too much on rewards can negatively impact the firm's financial stability, and hurt investors' return on their investment in the firm. *Mix* refers to the composition of the reward package matching the needs and preferences of applicants or employees. Offering stock options that vest in five years to a young, mobile workforce that tends to turn over every three to four years, or free day care to an older workforce might not be consistent with workers' needs and preferences. *Distinctiveness* refers to the uniqueness of a

job rewards analysis
a job analysis technique that identifies the intrinsic and extrinsic rewards of a job

intrinsic rewards
nonmonetary rewards derived from the work itself and from the organization's culture

extrinsic rewards
rewards that have monetary value

total rewards
a combination of the intrinsic and extrinsic rewards related to a particular job

employee value proposition
the balance between the intrinsic and extrinsic rewards an employee receives by working for a particular employer in return for the employee's job performance

reward package. Rewards with no special appeal and that do not set the organization apart as distinctive do not present a compelling value proposition. Some Internet start-ups in the 1990s created distinctive intrinsic rewards by allowing employees to bring their dogs to work and to dress casually.

What a recruiter or hiring manager feels are a job's best selling points may not totally reflect reality. As a result, it is important to confidentially interview job incumbents, hold focus groups, or conduct formal surveys. First conducting a paper survey to identify categories of rewards and identify those employees most often to identify with them, then following up with interviews and focus groups can play each approach to its best advantage. If employees feel free to make honest comments, they are more likely to share their insights. Exit interviews—interviews workers give their employers after having resigned—can also identify job rewards employees tend to be dissatisfied with. In addition, a firm can benchmark its competitors' rewards to see how its own rewards stack up. Survey instruments, such as the Minnesota Job Description Questionnaire[41] and the Job Diagnostic Survey,[42] which are completed by employees and job experts, can also measure a firm's job rewards. This chapter's Develop Your Skills feature illustrates how some of a job's intrinsic rewards can be assessed.

The amount, differential, and stability of each reward can also be a factor.[43] A reward's *amount* refers to how much of it is received (how much pay, what level of task variety the employee is given, and so forth). A reward's *differential* is how consistent the reward is among different employees—whether all employees receive the reward or only a certain number do based on certain criteria, such as their performance ratings. A reward's *stability* is how reliable the reward is. Is the reward the same all the time, or does it change based on the organization's performance or other business financials?

The job rewards associated with a position can be summarized in a *job rewards matrix* like the one presented in Table 4–13.

| TABLE 4–13 | The Job Rewards Matrix for a Purchasing Manager's Position |

Reward	Amount	Differential	Stability	To Whom the Reward Might Appeal
1. Competitive base salary	$32,000/year average	$30,000–36,000/year	Changes based on market conditions and firm performance	Most workers
2. Benefits	Comprehensive health and dental insurance, 401(k), 10 personal days/year	None—all workers receive the same benefits package	Stable	Most workers
3. Performance-based pay	4% average	Ranges from 0 to 15%	Can change based on firm's performance	Workers who value making and being rewarded for individual contributions
4. Promotion opportunities	Average person is promoted within 3 years	Can be as early as 18 months; some never get promoted	Varies depending on the manager's performance and company's needs	Workers who desire career advancement
5. Having individual responsibility for tasks	Above average	Based on skills and job performance	Fairly stable	Workers who value making individual contributions
6. Doing different tasks every day	Above average	Fairly consistent across employees	Fairly stable	Workers seeking skill development

DEVELOP YOUR SKILLS
Assessing a Job's Intrinsic Rewards[44]

The following eight questions are intended for educational purposes to show how a job's intrinsic rewards might be assessed. Many more intrinsic rewards are possible, so professionally developed and validated scales should be used when doing a job rewards analysis.

Please answer each question as it applies to your job using the following scale. Write the number from 1 to 7 that corresponds to your answer in the space to the left of each question number. The intrinsic job reward is in parentheses to the right of each question. Higher scores indicate a greater amount of that reward. Scores of 5 or greater indicate that the intrinsic reward is present in the job.

1	2	3	4	5	6	7
Strongly Disagree	Disagree	Slightly Disagree	Neither Agree nor Disagree	Slightly Agree	Agree	Strongly Agree

1. My manager looks out for me. (management relations)
2. I work closely with customers or coworkers. (interpersonal interaction)
3. I use a variety of types of knowledge, skills, abilities, or competencies every day. (skill variety)
4. My work allows me to complete an entire piece of work, rather than just a part of it. (task identity)
5. The results of my work affect the lives of others. (task significance)
6. I decide how to do my job. (autonomy)
7. I can tell how well I am performing my job just by doing it. (feedback from job)
8. My managers or coworkers communicate how well I am doing my job. (feedback from others)

Job values and desired job rewards differ across individuals and change over time. Job rewards analysis helps a company tailor its employee value proposition and recruiting message to appeal to the needs, values, and motivations of targeted potential applicants and current employees. In 2002, American Express launched a company-wide effort to become more competitive. The company was grappling with increased competition and wanted to make sure it was focusing on the right aspects with regard to its recruiting, among other areas. American Express conducted focus groups of its employees worldwide to find out what they valued most about their corporate culture, and identified eight points that all of the company's 500 recruiters should touch on when talking to job candidates: brand, culture, the company's position within the financial services industry, global opportunities, career paths, compensation, training and development, and location. "Five years ago, when we went to a career fair we would have talked more about the American Express brand and products, but now we are talking more about these eight areas," Murray Coon, director of recruiting for American Express, says. "Now it's more about the industry, the people, and the culture."[45]

The reasons many people join an organization are often the same reasons they stay with that employer. Identifying what makes a company unique, and developing a compelling employee value proposition, helps identify and target candidates who will thrive in the firm and who will be likely to stay.

JOB DESCRIPTIONS AT RED LOBSTER

After articulating its new business strategy of focusing on value and improving the image of its restaurants, Red Lobster needed to analyze how to best align its management positions with the strategy. It wanted to rewrite its job descriptions to improve the fit between the new managers it was hiring and its new business strategy. To do this, the company began an extensive job and competency analysis project that involved both the Red Lobster's executive team and individual restaurant operators. The job analysis team observed people working in the jobs, extensively interviewed managers to identify their priorities and daily activities, and surveyed managers to identify the importance and frequency of the different job responsibilities. The executives helped the team identify not only what it wanted Red Lobster's managers to do, but also what they wanted the jobs to become. The executives also wanted a way to make their expectations very clear to potential new hires and hiring managers.

In terms of its job descriptions, Red Lobster wanted to appeal to job applicants of all ages while emphasizing that it's a great place to work. Because Red Lobster is one of the older casual dining restaurant chains, the firm felt that many potential applicants' images of Red Lobster were old and dated. Consequently, the company modified its image to create a staffing brand that reflected its new strategy, values, and vision. By rewriting the job descriptions to better capture the company's brand, the company hoped to recruit employees who better fit its strategy.

In addition to doing a job analysis, the team identified what managers do day-to-day, and then developed a competency model to link those activities with Red Lobster's business strategy, values, and vision. Because managers were so involved in the process of ensuring that the firm's job descriptions were an accurate reflection of the business, they quickly began using them to make their hiring decisions. As a result, Red Lobster was able to hire one of every six candidates it interviewed. Previously it was able to hire only one of nine. The company attributes this to applicants having a better understanding of the job requirements overall and how well they matched up to them. In addition, managerial turnover fell, which the company attributes to the improved job descriptions and an improved selection process. Red Lobster estimates that the reduction in turnover alone has saved the company about $7 million.

Summary

Job analysis is a process used to identify the tasks required by a job and the characteristics a worker needs to perform each of these tasks. Job analysis can be strategic by aligning the requirements of a job with the company's business strategy and competitive advantage, taking into account what is required to perform the job today as well as in the future. If the job changes, it is important that the people hired to perform a job can also effectively perform the changed job. Competency modeling is a method of analyzing the broader competencies needed to perform well in roles as opposed to jobs. Competency modeling also identifies the factors that align employees with an organization's values and strategy. Job rewards analysis is a job analysis technique that identifies the intrinsic and extrinsic rewards of a job. Its purpose is to analyze a job's intrinsic and extrinsic rewards to identify how to create and sell a compelling employee value proposition to recruits and employees. Job analysis is a key step in determining what employees need to do to enhance the firm's competitive advantage and execute its business strategy.

Takeaway Points

1. A *Job analysis* is the systematic process of identifying and describing the important aspects of a job and the characteristics a worker needs to do it well. It identifies the job's important tasks and working conditions as well as the tools and technologies people doing the job use. The goal is to define the ideal individual for the job from the perspective of the company, its strategy, and the employees with whom the person will work. A job analysis is strategic if it aligns the firm's current as well as future job requirements with the company's business strategy.

2. A *job description* is a written description of the duties and responsibilities of a job. A *person specification* summarizes the characteristics of someone able to perform the job well. Based on the job description, the person specification profiles the personal skills, qualifications, abilities, and experiences the organization needs to evaluate candidates during the recruitment and selection process.

3. Different methods can be used to conduct a job analysis. The *critical incidents* method uses subject matter experts to provide examples of good and poor performance incidents that have occurred on the job. This method helps job analysts identify extreme behaviors but not necessarily typical day-to-day behaviors. The *job elements* method asks a panel of job experts to identify and rate the worker characteristics that influence success on the job. Although the process can be difficult to explain, it is efficient, and relatively fast. The *structured interview* method involves interviewing job experts about the job and the required worker characteristics. Although this method can be quick, the job analyst needs to minimize any political biases imparted by the job experts involved in the process. A *task inventory* is a list of tasks generated by job experts and grouped in categories reflecting major work functions. The functions are then evaluated on dimensions relevant for assessing job candidates. Task inventories are objective and produce reliable descriptions of the job but fail to capture worker characteristics displayed infrequently. Neither do the inventories identify the characteristics that distinguish superior from average or barely acceptable workers. The Position Analysis Questionnaire is a structured job analysis questionnaire that is fast, cheap, and useful for almost any position. Like any structured questionnaire, the predetermined questions limit the information the job analyst can obtain. Also, the reading level of the questionnaires may be too high for job experts providing input on certain positions.

4. The steps in planning a job analysis are to (1) determine the time and resources that can be invested in the job analysis, (2) identify the job experts who will be able to participate, and (3) identify appropriate job analysis techniques to use.

5. The steps in conducting a job analysis are to (1) get the support of top managers; (2) thoroughly communicate the purpose of the job analysis to all participants and ensure they are diligent about completing the tasks objectively; (3) collect background information about the job, the business strategy, and the

organization's culture; (4) generate task statements that describe the work done on the job; (5) generate the KSAOs associated with each task statement; (6) form job duty groupings; (7) link the KSAOs back to the job duties to be sure they are appropriate; (8) collect critical incidents to better distinguish excellent from poor performers; (9) weight the duties of the job; (10) construct a job requirements matrix summarizing the information collected; and (11) write a job description and person specification.

6. Competency modeling involves identifying more broadly defined components of a successful worker's repertoire of behaviors needed to do a job well. Competency modeling often comes from the top of an organization and serves to reinforce an organization's culture. By contrast, KSAO statements are derived mostly by job analysts for staffing purposes. A *job rewards analysis* identifies the intrinsic and extrinsic rewards of a job. The rewards that are identified can be used to recruit candidates and match them with certain jobs.

Discussion Questions

1. Why do you think some organizations choose to not perform job analyses given their benefits? What could be done to increase their willingness to analyze jobs?
2. How can job analysis make staffing more strategic?
3. How do you personally evaluate different job opportunities and decide which to pursue?
4. If supervisors and job incumbents disagreed about the relative importance and weights of various job duties, how would you reconcile their conflicting opinions? For example, if a supervisor emphasized the technical aspects of a customer service representative's job and the representatives emphasized the interpersonal aspects of listening to customers and understanding their problems, what would you do?
5. Some jobs change so rapidly that companies do not feel doing a job analysis is worthwhile because by the time one is done, it's already outdated. What advice would you give such a company to help them take advantage of the benefits a job analysis has to offer without wasting unnecessary time and resources doing a traditional job analysis?

Exercises

1. *Strategy Exercise:*   Imagine that you are a staffing specialist in Vroom, a 10-year-old company that manufactures toy cars. The cars are high quality and receive a premium price. Workers assemble pieces of the cars by hand on an assembly line. Some of the assemblers are great at what they do, but others have trouble keeping up and tend to slow the line down. Vroom wants to keep its labor costs as low as possible. However, it is willing to invest in assessment systems to evaluate job candidates and help it identify the most promising candidates to hire.

   You believe that your staffing system for the assemblers could be improved so there's less performance variability among them. Unfortunately, it has been 10 years since the last job analysis was done for the position, and many of the tools and assembly methods have changed. After asking for money to use in conducting an updated job analysis on the assembler position, your CEO asks you to justify your request. Using what you have learned in this chapter, write a one-page report convincing your CEO to invest the money in the job analysis project and describing what resources you would need to do it.

2. *Develop Your Skills Exercise:*   Working in a group of three to four students, do a job rewards analysis on the job one of your group members holds (or has held). Use the questionnaire in this chapter's Develop Your Skills feature as part of your analysis. Summarize your analysis in a job rewards matrix. Then apply the results and describe the type of potential job applicant to which each reward might appeal.

3. *Opening Vignette Exercise:*   The opening vignette describes Red Lobster's job analysis project and effort to make its job descriptions better appeal to its targeted recruits. Your assignment is to first review the Red Lobster job description in Figure 4–2 and then describe who would find the job description appealing and why. Does your description match Red Lobster's goals as described in the opening vignette? Next, critique the Red Lobster job description in Figure 4–2 and suggest ways it can be further improved so the firm can meet its goals even better.

CASE STUDY

Imagine that you are the recruiting manager for RTMM Inc., a software development company. You have had trouble persuading top candidates to join your firm because it is not yet well known. You have attracted a sufficient number of qualified candidates, but too many of them are turning down your job offers and accepting opportunities with your competitors.

Based on your conversations with job candidates, you think that the key to increasing your job offer acceptance rate is to enhance candidates' understanding of the company and its value proposition. To thoroughly identify the benefits of the job and of working for RTMM, you conducted focus groups with your current software engineers to learn what they valued about their jobs and about the company. This is the job rewards matrix you created through these focus groups:

Reward	Amount	Differential	Stability
Annual bonus	$18,000 average	$0 to $40,000 depending on company and individual performance	Availability is based on company performance
401(k)	9% of base salary	Same for all workers after 1 year of service	Stable
Development opportunities	Depends on the project and skills used	Differs by need and by job performance level	Company annually invests at least $3,000 per employee in its formal training program
Promotion opportunities	Promotion rate averages 3 years	Minimum of 2 years required for promotion; 50% are never promoted	Varies according to company needs and individual performance
Autonomy	Above average	Based on skills and job performance	Stable
Task variety	Above average	Same for all employees	Stable
Fun culture	Above average	Same for all employees	Stable

Your assignment is to identify the types of people who might be attracted to this opportunity, and to write a one-page letter to a hypothetical job offer recipient named Keisha Jackson, persuading her to accept your previously extended, competitive job offer.

Semester-Long Active Learning Project

Perform a job or competency analysis on the job as it exists now and as it will look in the near future. Summarize your findings in a job requirements matrix. Identify which qualifications are essential and which are desirable in new hires. Also do a job rewards analysis and summarize it in a job rewards matrix. Who might find the rewards offered by the job and organization attractive? These insights will help you complete the assignment in Chapter 6.

Case Study Assignment: Strategic Staffing at Chern's

See the appendix at the back of this book for this chapter's Case Study Assignment.

Endnotes

1. "Red Lobster Corporate Fact Sheet," www.redlobster.com/company/pdf/Lobsterfest%202006%20-%20Red%20Lobster%20Fact%20Sheet.pdf. Accessed July 3, 2006.
2. Spielberg, S., "After Some Roller-Coaster Results Darden Reports Red Lobster Now on Smoother Ride," *Nation's Restaurant News*, April 4, 2005, www.findarticles.com/ p/articles/ mi_m3190/ is_14_39/ai_n13593249. Accessed July 6, 2006.
3. Macarthur, K., "Red Lobster Retools as 'Better Seafood' Eatery," *Advertising Age*, August 22, 2005, www. advertisingage.com. Accessed June 8, 2007.
4. Crispin, G., "Conversations with Staffing Leaders: Anita Gutel and Chris Himebauch of Red Lobster," ERE.net, July 14, 2005, podcast, www.ere.net/search/default.asp?Searchmode= ARTCL & USERID=2253182946. Accessed June 29, 2006.
5. Biddle, B. J., *Role Theory: Expectations, Identities and Behaviors*, New York: Academic Press, as cited in Ilgen, D. R. and Hollenbeck, J. R. "The Structure of Work: Job Design and Roles ," In M. D. Dunnette and L. M. Hough (eds.), *Handbook of Industrial/ Organizational Psychology* (2nd ed.), Palo Alto, CA: Consulting Psychologists Press, 1979, 165–207.
6. Mullich, J., "P&G's Innovative Student Recruiting," *Workforce Management Online*, November 2003, www.workforce.com/section/06/feature/23/54/54/. Accessed July 3, 2006.
7. "CitiFinancial," SkillsNet.com, www.skillsnet.com/Customers.aspx. Accessed April 10, 2007.
8. Stewart, G. L., and Carson, K. P., "Moving Beyond the Mechanistic Model: An Alternative Approach to Staffing for Contemporary Organizations," *Human Resource Management Review*, 7, 2 (Summer 1997): 157–184.
9. Morgeson, F., Reider, M., and Campion, M., "Selecting Individuals in Team Settings: The Importance of Social Skills, Personality Characteristics, and Teamwork Knowledge," *Personnel Psychology*, 58 (2005): 583–611.
10. "General Electric," SkillsNet.com, www.skillsnet.com/Customers.aspx. Accessed April 10, 2007.
11. Huselid, M. A., "The Impact of Human Resource Management Practices on Turnover, Productivity, and Corporate Financial Performance," *Academy of Management Journal*, 38, (1985): 635–672.
12. Landis, R. S., Fogli, L., and Goldberg, E., "Future-Oriented Job Analysis: A Description of the Process and Its Organizational

Implications," *International Journal of Selection and Assessment,* 6, 3 (July 1998): 192–198; Schneider, B., and Konz, A., "Strategic Job Analysis," *Human Resource Management,* 28, 1 (1989): 51–63.

13. Hansen, F., "Recruiting on the Right Side of the Law," *Workforce Management Online,* May 2006, www.workforce.com/section/06/feature/24/38/12/. Accessed June 30, 2006.

14. "Beverage and Hospitality Manager," Red Lobster, www.redlobster.com/ jobs/management_positions.asp. Accessed July 3, 2006.

15. Flanagan, J. C., "The Critical Incident Technique," *Psychological Bulletin,* 4, 51 (1954): 327–359.

16. Ibid.

17. Primoff, E. S., *How to Prepare and Conduct Job Element Examinations*, Washington, D.C.: U.S. Government Printing Office, 1975 (GPO No. 006-000-00893-3).

18. McCormick, E. J., Jeanneret, P. R., and Mecham, R. C., "A Study of Job Characteristics and Job Dimensions as Based on the Position Analysis Questionnaire," *Journal of Applied Psychology,* 56 (1972): 347–368; PAQ Services Inc., "Job Analysis Questionnaire," www.paq.com/ index.cfm? FuseAction=bulletins.job-analysis-questionnaire. Accessed July 25, 2007.

19. "Uniform Guidelines on Employee Selection Procedures", *Federal Register*, 43, 166 (August 25, 1978): 38290–38315; available online at: www.dol.gov/dol/allcfr/ESA/ Title_41/Part_60-3/toc.htm.

20. See http://online.onetcenter.org.

21. See www.wave.net/upg/immigration/dot_index.html.

22. See www.job-analysis.net.

23. "Checklist for Physical Activities and Requirements, Visual Acuity, and Working Conditions of the Position," Fayetteville State University Human Resources, www.uncfsu.edu/humres/forms/ADA-Checklist.pdf.

24. Hunter, J. E., "Cognitive Ability, Cognitive Aptitudes, Job Knowledge, and Job Performance," *Journal of Vocational Behavior*, 29 (1986): 340–362.

25. Barrick, M. R., and Mount, M. K., "The Big Five Personality Dimensions and Job Performance: A Meta-Analysis," *Personnel Psychology*, 44 (1991): 1–26.

26. Ibid.

27. Ones, D. S., Viswesvaran, C., and Schmidt, F. L., "Comprehensive Meta-Analysis of Integrity Test Validities: Findings and Implications for Personnel Selection and Theories of Job Performance," *Journal of Applied Psychology,* 78 (1993): 679–703.

28. First Hawaiian Bank, *SkillsNet.com*, www.skillsnet.com/Customers.aspx. Accessed April 10, 2007.

29. Kelleher, C., "Writing Great Job Descriptions," *Entrepreneur.com*, http://smallbusiness.yahoo.com/ r-article-a-2335-m-5-sc-47-writing_great_job_descriptions-i. Accessed March 22, 2007.

30. Fisher, C. D., "Boredom at Work: A Neglected Concept," *Human Relations,* 46 (1993): 395–417; McFarling, L. H., and Heimstra, N. W., "Pacing, Product Complexity and Task Perception in Simulated Inspection," *Human Factors,* 17 (1975): 361–367.

31. "Tips for Writing Job Descriptions," *Society for Industrial and Organizational Psychology*, www.siop.org/Placement/TipsforWritingJobDescriptions.pdf. Accessed July 31, 2006.

32. Heathfield, S. M., "Job Descriptions: Why Effective Job Descriptions Make Good Business Sense," *About Inc.*, http://humanresources.about.com/od/policiesproceduresamples/l/aajob_descrip2.htm. Accessed July 31, 2006.

33. "Recruiting Tips," Recruitmentresources.com, www. recruitmentresources.com/recruiting_tips.html. Accessed July 31, 2006.

34. "Tips for Job Descriptions," Nationjob.com, www. nationjob.com/acce/jobdescguide.html. Accessed July 31, 2006.

35. Several good references for competency modeling are available, including Cooper, K. C., *Effective Competency Modeling and Reporting: A Step-by-Step Guide for Improving Individual and Organizational Performance*, New York: American Management Association, 2000; Shippmann, J. S., Ash, R. A., Battista, M., Carr, L., Eyde, L., Hesketh, B., Kehoe, J., Pearlman, K., Prien, E. P., and Sanchez, J. I., "The Practice of Competency Modeling," *Personnel Psychology,* 53 (2000): 703–740; Green, P. C., *Building Robust Competencies: Linking Human Resource Systems to Organizational Strategies*, New York: Jossey-Bass, 1999.

36. Salter, C., "Talent—Andy Esparza." *Fast Company*, 2001: 216–221.

37. Westcott, S., "What's In a Job Title," Inc., July 1, 2006, http://www.inc.com/magazine/ 20060701/ handson-managing.html.

38. Shippmann et al., "The Practice of Competency Modeling."

39. "10 Jobs with Great Employee Rewards," PayScale, http://blogs.payscale.com/content/2008/08/10-jobs-with-gr.html. Accessed May 12, 2010.

40. Ledford, E. E., and Lucy, M. I., *The Rewards of Work*, Los Angeles, CA: Sibson Consulting, 2003.

41. More information about the Minnesota Job Description Questionnaire can be found at www.psych.umn.edu/ psylabs/vpr/mjdqinf.htm.

42. Hackman, J. R., and Oldham, G. R., "Development of the Job Diagnostic Survey," *Journal of Applied Psychology,* 60 (1975): 159–170.

43. Heneman, H. G., Judge, T. A., and Heneman, R. L., *Staffing Organizations* (3rd ed.), New York: McGraw-Hill/ Irwin, 2000.

44. "Total Rewards" Pitney Bowes, www.pb.com/cgi-bin/pb.dll/jsp/ GenericEditorial.do?catOID=-18255& editorial_id=ed_Benefits &lang=en&country=US. Accessed April 5, 2007.

45. Marquez, J., "When Brand Alone Isn't Enough," *Workforce Management*, March 13, 2006: 1, 39–41, www.workforce.com/archive/feature/24/29/58/index.php?ht=mcdonald%20s%20mcdonald%20s. Accessed July 10, 2006.

5   Forecasting and Planning

Outline

LEARNING OBJECTIVES

After studying this chapter, you should be able to:

- Describe the workforce planning process.
- Discuss how an organization can predict its future business activity.
- Describe how an organization can forecast its demand for workers.
- Explain how to forecast the likely supply of available workers from inside and outside the firm.
- Discuss how to develop action plans to address gaps between labor supply and labor demand.
- Describe the staffing planning process.

Strategic Workforce Planning at TransAlta[1]

TransAlta, a power generation and wholesale marketing company based in Canada, employs approximately 2,800 employees around the world. The company knows that accurate workforce planning is critical to the firm's future effectiveness. The problem is that the Canadian workforce is growing at only half the rate of the overall population and will actually decline in the next 10 years because of retiring baby boomers. As a result, TransAlta expects to face intense competition for the skilled workers it needs to hire.

Although TransAlta is used to long-range forecasting to supply and maintain its 49 power plants, to position itself to execute its growth strategy, it also needs a disciplined and strategic approach to meet its staffing needs. The company's ultimate goal is to find and recruit qualified people, ensure they become productive within the organization as quickly as possible, and retain them by providing them with significant rewards for their ongoing contributions to the firm.

To keep its business sustainable and execute its growth strategy, TransAlta asks for your advice about how it can meet its staffing goals. After reading this chapter, you should have some good ideas to share with the company.

The first four chapters of this book described the staffing context and job analysis. In this part of the book, we will discuss planning, sourcing, and recruiting. Workforce planning, the subject of this chapter, is the foundation of strategic staffing because it identifies and addresses future challenges to a firm's ability to get the right talent in place at the right time. Staffing creates the infrastructure for the firm's strategy execution, and proactive workforce and staffing planning ensures that the firm has the people it needs to execute that strategy successfully.[2]

Staffing experts and managers widely predict that organizations will face a challenging labor situation in the coming years as baby boomers retire and developing countries experience lower birth rates. These two factors will affect jobs ranging from the entry level to the executive suite. As a result, some organizations might have to scale back or pass up expansion opportunities if they are unable to staff their companies. For example, a manufacturing organization that can't hire the workers it needs to execute its labor-intensive strategy might be forced to change its business strategy—say, by adopting slower growth goals or manufacturing products that can be produced by a labor force with more readily available skills. Alternatively, the firm might need to invest in equipment automating the manufacturing processes to reduce its need for skilled workers.

The competition for good employees is particularly fierce for smaller companies, who, despite providing the majority of new jobs in the United States,[3] have a more difficult time hiring in general. Forecasting and planning let firms better manage talent shortages and surpluses. By understanding business cycles, the business needs of their firms, the current talent in their firms, and the pipelines for finding future talent, HR professionals can proactively reduce the impact the greater competition for talent will have.

General Electric (GE) is a case in point: In the late 1970s, GE realized that the rapid changes in its business environment made it necessary for the company to consider its staffing issues earlier in its strategic planning process than it previously had. Realizing that the firm's talent requirements would be different in the future, GE began to invest in a campus presence that would influence the teaching of the skills it felt that it would need in 10 years rather than in the next one to three years. By changing the skills available in the labor market, GE increased its ability to hire the talent it needed.[4]

Despite the clear advantages of forecasting and planning, many organizations respond to their staffing needs reactively rather than proactively. In other words, they do little planning and simply work to fill positions as they open up. Jim Robbins, the former president and CEO of Cox Communications, put it this way: "We spend four months per year on the budget process, but we hardly spend any time talking about our talent, our strengths and how to leverage them, our talent needs and how to build them. Everyone is held accountable for their budget. But no one is held accountable for the strength of their talent pool. Isn't it the talent we have in each unit that drives our results? Aren't we missing something?"[5]

At Corning, a leader in specialty glass and ceramics, talent planning is the "bridge that translates business strategy into talent strategy." [6] Corning knows that its talent portfolio influences its success. Over- or understaffed units affect the company's cost structure, cash flow, and ability to deliver its products. The wrong skill mix can mean missed market opportunities if the workforce is underskilled or, if the workforce is overskilled, cost structures that undermine profitability. To keep its skill mix optimized, every spring Corning models its future talent needs across multiple scenarios and then analyzes strategies to close any gaps.[7]

In this chapter, we discuss the importance of understanding the organization's business strategy, goals, and competitive environment to identify what talents the firm will need. Ensuring that the right people are in place at the right time requires forecasting the firm's labor demand and maintaining an awareness of the relevant pipelines for its labor supply. Action plans can then be developed to address any gaps between the two. After reading this chapter, you will have a good understanding of the workforce forecasting and planning process.

THE WORKFORCE PLANNING PROCESS

The workforce planning process, which is illustrated in Figure 5–1, typically includes five steps:

1. *Identify the firm's business strategy.* A firm's strategic vision, mission, and strategy affect its current and future staffing requirements by influencing the types and numbers of employees needed.
2. *Articulate the firm's talent philosophy and strategic staffing decisions.* As you learned in Chapter 2, firms differ in their commitment to things like promoting workers, retaining workers, and their preferences for hiring people with certain skills or training them after they are hired. Because these factors influence the nature of the firm's future labor supply and the type of workers it will need, they are important to understand when forecasting and planning.
3. *Conduct a workforce analysis.* Forecast both labor demand and labor supply and identify any gaps between the two.
4. *Develop and implement action plans.* Develop action plans to address any gaps between labor demand and labor supply forecasts. The plans should be consistent with the firm's talent philosophy, and can include both short- and long-term recruiting, retention, compensation, succession management, and training and development plans. For example, addressing the issues related to an aging workforce or a workforce with many employees who are roughly the same age might require longer-term action plans.
5. *Monitor, evaluate, and revise the forecasts and action plans.* Evaluate how effective the firm's workforce plan has been in terms of meeting the company's recruiting and hiring goals. As the business environment changes, the firm's forecasts and action plans may need to change, too.

Forecasting is not an exact science, and it is rare for a forecast to be exactly right. Given this uncertainty, it is usually best to construct estimates as a *range*—with low, probable, and high

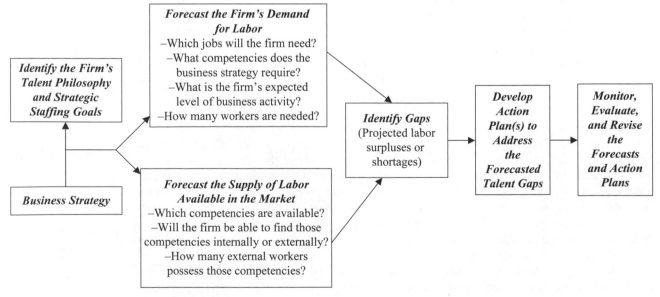

FIGURE 5–1 The Workforce Planning Process

estimates—and then recalculate those estimates as the organization's internal and external environments change, along with the firm's assumptions about its workforce needs. Creating and implementing workforce plans is easier in more stable organizations and more challenging when a company faces rapidly changing conditions. With that said, the firms experiencing rapid changes will find planning the most valuable because it can guide their recruiting and hiring actions in the face of uncertainty.[8]

The time frame for workforce planning should reflect the length of the business planning cycle. Short-term workforce planning involves planning sourcing, recruiting, development, and separation activities the firm needs to do in the coming year. By contrast, long-term workforce planning involves doing the same activities but for a multiyear period.[9]

At the very least, workforce planning should be done for those positions throughout the organization whose execution is considered critical for the success of their units and the firm as a whole. If innovation and intangible assets, such as knowledge or creativity, generate a firm's competitive advantage, then top managers and knowledge workers are essential. If an organization's competitive advantage is based on service, its success depends on the quality and performance of its customer-facing employees[10] The accurate identification of these key positions is extremely important, as their being vacant or poorly staffed can affect the organization's ability to perform. Positions in which top performers significantly outperform average performers can also be important for a firm's workforce planning. Ensuring that the most effective and productive people possible are placed into these positions can positively affect a company's bottom line.

Next, we discuss how an organization can forecast the future demand for its products and services, which, in turn, will affect its demand for labor.

FORECASTING THE FIRM'S LABOR DEMAND

An organization's product demand directly affects its need for labor. On the one hand, if an organization is experiencing growing demand for what it does or makes, unless it plans to increase the automation of its manufacturing processes, it will probably need to hire more people to meet the increased demand. Even if the organization does plan to automate, the process of doing so is likely to increase the firm's demand for people with different *types* of talent—people able to use and maintain the new machinery or technology, for example. On the other hand, if the demand for the organization's products or services is decreasing, the company's need for employees is likely to fall, perhaps to the point that it needs to downsize, or lay off, employees. For example, when the worldwide demand for goods weakened during the 2001 recession, many manufacturers downsized their workforces.[11]

Accurately forecasting business activity requires identifying key business activity factors, identifying quality sources of relevant forecasting information for those factors, and utilizing these sources to compile complete, accurate, and timely data. For example, Cisco, which makes computer routers and switches, diligently seeks out data to predict the products its customers will order in the future as well as the availability of products it needs from its suppliers.[12] This enhances the company's ability to make more accurate projections about its staffing needs.

The time frame for a business activity forecast is at the discretion of the organization. It may make sense for organizations in relatively stable, predictable environments to make five-year or even 10-year forecasts. Organizations in more dynamic, unpredictable environments may have great difficulty making reasonably accurate business forecasts for periods greater than 6 to 12 months out. Forecasts are best treated as dynamic estimates, and should be revisited and updated regularly as assumptions and environmental conditions change. Constructing short-, mid-, and long-range estimates is also useful because long-range forecasts are likely to be less accurate than short-range estimates due to the increased likelihood of environmental and organizational changes in the long term.

There are many external sources of information firms can tap into to forecast the demand for their products. Next, we will discuss five of the most common types of information that can be used to evaluate general business trends in the economy: seasonal factors, interest rates, currency exchange rates, competitive changes, and industry and economic forecasts.

Seasonal Forecasts

For some organizations, business demands are seasonal and predictable. For example, United Parcel Service experiences a sharp increase in shipping volume from November to January every year due to holiday shipping demand. Landscaping firms know that they will need more workers in the spring and summer than in the winter. Because this increased seasonal demand occurs every year, it can be anticipated. For many organizations, business cycles are much less predictable. Occasional spikes and dips in the demand for an organization's products or services can be harder to forecast, but the better an organization can anticipate them, the better it will be able to have an appropriate workforce in place as needed.

Interest Rate Forecasts

Interest rate forecasts can project the likelihood that the organization will need or be able to build new plants and increase production in the near future. Higher interest rates discourage capital investment by making it more expensive for organizations to borrow money to fund their expansion plans. Higher interest rates make it more expensive for consumers to borrow money as well. As a result, product demand tends to decline when interest rates rise. By contrast, when interest rates fall, product demand rises. Rising interest rates generally suggest that the demand for labor will fall, whereas falling interest rates generally suggest that the demand for labor will rise. For example, when interest rates fall, the demand for homes tends to increase, increasing the demand for skilled trade workers and mortgage specialists.

Currency Exchange Rate Forecasts

For many companies, especially global ones, exchange rate forecasts are useful for forecasting business activity. If a country's currency is strengthening against other currencies, it means that one unit of the country's currency translates into greater amounts of the foreign currency than when the country's currency was weaker. This means that the country's companies can import goods and materials more cheaply because one unit of the domestic currency buys more foreign goods than it used to. However, this also means that country's products are more expensive overseas. For example, when the New Zealand dollar strengthened against the U.S. dollar in the early 2000s, Jack Links, a New Zealand beef jerky maker, was forced to cut two-thirds of its workforce because it became cheaper for the company's biggest U.S. customer to buy its jerky from Brazil.[13] Likewise, if a U.S. company does a lot of business internationally, a strengthening U.S. dollar usually translates into lower international demand for the firm's products and lower labor demand for the firm. What do you suppose happens when a country's currency weakens? As a country's currency weakens, the relative prices of its exported goods fall. The international demand for the country's products rises as a result, as does the country's demand for labor. Exchange rates can be volatile and difficult to predict in the long term. The more stable the exchange rate, the more accurate and useful the firm's product demand and labor forecasts will be.

Competition-Based Forecasts

If new competitors enter an industry, customers will have greater product choices, which will tend to dilute the demand for any one company's products or services. For example, in the face of increased competition from foreign carmakers, many U.S. carmakers, including GM and DaimlerChrysler, experienced declining demand for their products and downsized their workforces. Alternatively, if a firm leaves a market, then its surviving competitors might experience greater demand for their products or services.

Industry and Economic Forecasts

The information relevant to making a forecast is likely to differ for different companies and different industries. *The Conference Board's Index of Leading Indicators*, a commonly used barometer of economic activity over three to six months, presents a relatively broad picture of the economy. As such, the index can help identify trends leading to economic recessions or recoveries. The monthly *Conference Board Consumer Confidence Index* measures consumer sentiment by asking survey respondents questions about their perceptions of their job security and willingness to spend money. This index also can help predict future economic activity and thus demand for a company's products or services and associated labor needs.

Additional economic indicators include gross domestic product (GDP), the business inventories and sales ratio tracked by the Department of Commerce, and the Purchasing Managers Index issued monthly by the Institute for Supply Management. Disappointing corporate earnings preannouncements from a firm's own customers can also suggest a declining demand for its products. Industries often have their own forecasts as well. The National Restaurant Association's annual industry forecast is one example. An organization can analyze its past product demand with regard to these indicators to identify which ones tended to accurately predict changes in its business activity, and then use that information to forecast the company's future labor demand.

Other Factors

Additional factors can also indicate changing demand for the organization's products and services and the need for changes in the workforce. Some other factors that often cause companies to change the size of their workforce include:

- An increase or decrease in consumer spending
- An increase or decrease in the unemployment rate
- An increase or decrease in the disposable income of consumers
- Increased or decreased purchases of durable goods
- Increased or decreased housing purchases

Many firms start hiring as soon as the economy begins expanding so that new employees will be well trained and productive by the time the increased economic growth generates increased business activity for the firm. Some information the firm needs to forecast its sales can be generated internally. For example, by tracking a firm's incoming orders, managers can get an idea about what the likely order volume will be in the next month or quarter. Similarly, a company entering or exiting a particular line of business will know that its labor needs are likely to change accordingly. In other words, the firm will generate its forecasts based on its own internal business needs.

Internal Forecasting Tools

A firm can also forecast its labor demand, depending on the goals it has generated internally, which might include the following:

- Achieving the staffing levels the firm needs to generate a given amount of revenue within a particular period of time (e.g., hiring enough salespeople to generate $5 million in revenue within six months)
- Increasing the firm's staffing levels to execute a growth strategy
- Decreasing the firm's staffing levels during a restructuring
- Obtaining the new talent the firm needs to create new products or provide different services

To better size their sales forces in each of their sales channels, companies, like Whirlpool, calculate the investment in human resources required to reach their optimum profit level. Sizing analyses and statistical models can identify if a company is slightly overstaffed in one area or has untapped potential in another. It is a good idea to identify the minimal as well as optimal staffing levels the firm needs to meet its goals.

The most important labor demand forecasts are those for the positions and skills that will be central to the organization's intended strategic direction. For example, assume an organization is experiencing slow growth in its bricks-and-mortar facilities, but it is intending to roll out a new Web-based initiative for selling its product line. The firm's labor forecasts might indicate that its overall hiring will stay relatively flat. However, in light of the new strategic initiative, the company obviously will need experienced IT specialists, computer technicians, and software writers. It will also need customer service employees who are technologically competent. If it cannot hire these people, then the new Web-based initiative is likely to fail.

There are many ways to forecast labor demand, and next, we will discuss four of the most common: ratio analysis, scatter plots, trend analysis, and judgmental forecasting.

staffing ratio
*a mathematical way of calculating
the number of employees a firm needs
to produce certain levels of output*

RATIO ANALYSIS The estimated level of business activity of the firm can be converted into the number of employees the company will need to attain this level of productivity by using past **staffing ratios**. A staffing ratio is a mathematical way of calculating the number of employees a firm needs to produce certain levels of output. A firm can then "index" the number of people it seeks to employ with the business metric. For example, a law firm might index the number of paralegals to the number of attorneys based on a staffing ratio of 3:2. In other words, the firm needs three paralegals for every two attorneys.

A ratio analysis assumes that there is a relatively fixed ratio between the number of employees needed and certain business metrics. Using historical patterns within the firm helps to establish a reasonable range for these ratios. Of course, the process can be used for either justifying new positions or demonstrating the need for layoffs.

For example, assuming that a manufacturing facility has 100 employees and produces $20,000,000 of product annually, then the firm's production-to-employee ratio is $200,000:1. For every additional $200,000 of product the company wants to produce, it should hire an additional worker. Because some economies of scale will result from the expansion that will reduce the number of employees needed, organizations should consider their unique situation and adjust their forecasts accordingly.

Other ratios that can be used in estimating target headcount levels include:

- Revenue per employee
- Managers to employees
- Inventory levels to employees
- Store size to employees
- Number of customers or customer orders to employees
- Labor costs to all production costs
- The percent utilization of production capacity to employees

If an organization expects its employee-productivity ratio to remain stable over the forecasting period, then simply applying the past ratio of employees to the productivity that's been forecasted for the upcoming period can be adequate. However, if the organization is experiencing a change in productivity per employee, due to technology, training, restructuring, and so on, then the application of past ratios such as this is inappropriate. Managers will often have a good idea of how estimates need to be adjusted, and their expertise should be incorporated into the process. In entirely novel situations for which past ratios do not exist, the only way to generate a reasonable staffing forecast is to rely on the judgment of the firm's managers. Although ratio analyses are limited to one predictor of labor demand at a time (labor hours per unit produced, for example), more advanced statistical techniques such as a regression analysis can be used to incorporate multiple predictors. For example, a regression analysis that incorporates sales forecasts, store sizes, mall traffic, and seasonal trends can be used to forecast the number of employees needed in a retail store. Of course, the underlying data used to construct any ratio or regression analysis must be credible and reliable. Otherwise, the forecast will not be accurate.

Forecasting labor demand in small- and medium-size organizations can be more difficult because historical trends are likely to be more variable and because there is typically less historical information from which to draw. Additionally, adding one new person in a 10-employee company means expanding the workforce in 10 percent increments, which may not correspond to the growth rate of the business. Companies of all sizes often prefer to hire temporary or contingent workers until they are sure they need the additional employees.

scatter plots
*a graphic that shows how two different
variables are related*

SCATTER PLOTS **Scatter plots** show graphically how two different variables—say, revenue and salesperson staffing levels—are related. For the purposes of forecasting labor demand, scatter plots help firms determine if a factor has historically been related to staffing levels. This information is then used to determine what staffing levels should be changed as the factor changes. This is related to *correlation coefficients* and *regression analysis*, which are discussed in Chapter 8.

Assume that new housing developments are being built in the area served by Ambulance Express, a private ambulance service. The company wants to forecast its future requirements for ambulance drivers and knows that the more people living in its service area, the more drivers it

TABLE 5–1	The Population Served as It Relates to the Required Number of Ambulance Drivers
Population Served	**Number of Ambulance Drivers**
12,500	2
25,000	5
30,000	5
35,000	6
50,000	10
60,000	11

will need to meet the community's needs. The staffing expert first collects data from six other ambulance services in the state to learn their number of ambulance drivers as well as the populations in their service areas. Table 5–1 summarizes these numbers.

Figure 5–2 shows these two sets of numbers graphically in a scatter plot. The population served by the various ambulance services is indicated on the horizontal axis, and the corresponding number of ambulance drivers employed by each of the companies is indicated on the vertical axis. Each point on the graph reflects one company. Notice that a nearly straight line can be drawn between the points, as we have done on the graph. This leads us to conclude that there is a direct, if not perfect, relationship between the two factors—that is, the number of people that can be served is directly related to the number of ambulance drivers. Therefore, the line can be used to predict the different staffing levels needed to serve the different population levels: Ambulance Express anticipates serving 43,000 people within two years. Starting on the horizontal axis, we located the point that reflects 43,000 people and then drew a dotted vertical line over to the solid diagonal line. From this point on the solid diagonal line, we drew a dotted horizontal line left to the vertical axis. The staffing level at which this horizontal line touches the vertical axis is the estimated number of ambulance drivers Ambulance Express will need. In this example, servicing 43,000 people will require eight drivers.

TREND ANALYSIS   **Trend analysis** involves looking at past employment patterns—the employer's, the industry's, or even the nation's patterns, for example—and using those patterns to predict a firm's future labor needs. For example, if a company has been growing 5 percent annually for the last eight years, it might assume that it will experience the same 5 percent annual growth for the next few years. In other words, any employment trends likely to continue can be useful in terms of forecasting a firm's future labor demand.

trend analysis
using past employment patterns to predict future needs

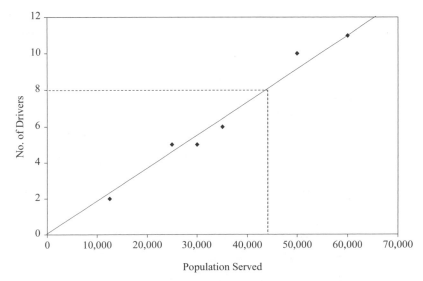

FIGURE 5–2   An Example of a Scatter Plot: The Relationship Between the Population Served and the Number of Ambulance Drivers

Figure 5–3 illustrates a trend analysis using a hypothetical example of a hospital's number of nurses educated internationally versus domestically from 2000 through 2007. The trend lines show that the number of domestically educated nurses has been steadily declining, and the number of internationally educated nurses has been steadily increasing over the last seven years. This suggests that the hospital might need to scale up its international recruiting efforts.

Valero Energy Corporation used historical trends to accurately forecast its talent demand by division and title three years in advance. By putting five years of historical people records into a database, the company developed a series of mathematical algorithms used to do a trend analysis. The analysis allowed the company to predict its turnover by location, position type, salary, employee tenure, and division.[14] Although this example shows that it can be done, trend analysis is rarely used by itself to make labor demand forecasts. So many factors can affect a company's staffing needs, including the firm's competition, economic environment, and changes in how the company gets its work done (automation might improve its productivity, for example), that the method can be difficult to use alone.

judgmental forecasting

relying on the experience and insights of people in the organization to predict a firm's future employment needs

JUDGMENTAL FORECASTING Instead of trying to identify past relationships between staffing levels and various factors as we did with the previous methods, **judgmental forecasting** relies on the experience and insights of people in the organization to predict a firm's future employment needs. Asking managers and supervisors about what they believe future staffing and employee skill levels can be is very insightful. Managers are often aware of what is going on in the lives of their subordinates and may be able to provide reasonably accurate predictions of their future labor supply. Likewise, managers are often aware of the retirement eligibility and intentions of their staff and can use this information to project likely talent losses several years into the future.

Judgmental forecasting can be *top-down*, in which case the organization's leaders rely on their experience and knowledge of their industry and company to make predictions about the firm's future staffing levels needs. The estimates the top managers come up with then become staffing goals for lower-level managers in the organization. In some cases, particularly when companies are facing financial difficulties or restructuring, budgets may determine the firm's "headcount," or number of employees. Bottom-up judgmental forecasting uses the input of lower-level managers to estimate the firm's total staffing requirements. Each manager estimates the number of employees he or she needs to execute the firm's strategy. The estimates are consolidated and modified as they move up the organization's hierarchy to the firm's top managers, who then review and formalize the estimate.

Because historical trends and relationships can change, it is usually best to supplement the more mechanical ratio, scatter plot, and trend forecasting methods with managerial judgment.

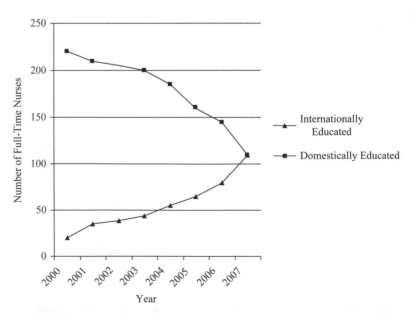

FIGURE 5–3 Domestically and Internationally Educated Nurses (2000–2007)

The mechanical methods can be used as a starting point to make the estimates, and then managers can use their judgment to modify the estimates.

RETURN ON INVESTMENT ANALYSIS   It is possible to estimate the return on investment from adding a new position based on the costs and outcomes resulting from that new hire. The first step is to assign dollar values to the benefits expected from a new hire for the period of time most appropriate for the position and the organization—it could be a month, a quarter, or a year. How much revenue during the period will be directly generated as a result of this position? How much money per period will this position save the organization in terms of increased efficiency, and how much value will it add in greater productivity, quality, or customer service? The sum of these figures is the value of adding this position.

Next, the costs to advertise the position, interview and screen candidates, pay for their travel, and relocate, train, and compensate them is calculated. This is the initial investment the company has made in the new hires, which should then be compared to what they earn for the company to determine the firm's return on its investment.

For example, assume a store's new furniture salespeople generate an average of $60,000 in profit their first year. In addition, the reduced workload on the rest of the sales staff improves their efficiency and ability to provide high-quality customer service by 5 percent. This is worth an additional $15,000 to the company. If the cost of hiring and training a new salesperson is expected to be $7,000, and her salary is $25,000 before commissions, the return on investment of hiring an additional salesperson is predicted to be 234 percent.

$$(\$60,000 + \$15,000)/(\$7,000 + \$25,000) = \$75,000/\$32,000 = 234\% \text{ ROI}$$

Companies can incorporate other human resource data into their models, depending on what they want to forecast. Oil company Saudi Aramco's workforce projections include the corporate resources required to recruit, hire, and train new staff and to mentor employees during their careers.[15]

FORECASTING THE FIRM'S LABOR SUPPLY

Strategic staffing requires firms to keep their fingers on the pulse of their labor markets. Therefore, understanding current and future skill and competency trends in the labor market is crucial. Information about the number and quality of employees likely to be available to an organization when it needs them should be considered while the organization is in the process of formulating its business strategy. For instance, attempting to grow a fiber optics firm by 20 percent a year might not be possible if there aren't a sufficient number of fiber optics engineers and technicians in the labor pool willing to work for salaries the firm is able to pay. It is obviously best for an organization (especially small firms that have a harder time attracting candidates) to have a reasonable estimate of the projected availability of talent for its key positions before developing a strategy that depends on this talent pool. The organization's internal and external labor markets will influence these estimates. We will discuss each one next.

Forecasting the Internal Labor Market

To determine the likely supply of a firm's internal talent at a future point in time, subtract the number of employees the firm anticipates losing via promotions, demotions, transfers, retirements, and resignations from the number of employees in the position at the beginning of the forecasting period. Then add any anticipated talent gains for the position from transfers, promotions, and demotions to the internal labor supply forecast. In tighter labor markets when workers are harder to find, more employees than usual may leave the organization to pursue other opportunities. Fewer employees may leave during looser labor markets when jobs are less plentiful.

Analyzing a company's demographic mix and current turnover rates can help managers forecast how many current employees are likely to still be in the company's workforce at a given forecasting date. An organization that expanded rapidly in the past may find that a particularly large cohort of employees hired at roughly the same time will be retiring at about the same time, for example. This, of course, will mean that the firm will have to hire a large number of new

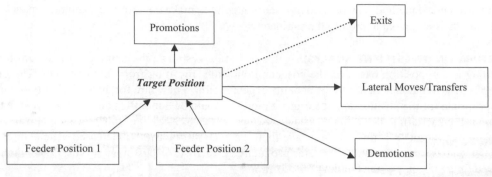

FIGURE 5–4 The Transition Analysis Process Illustrated

employees to replace them. Given their better knowledge of their subordinates, supervising managers may also be able to reasonably estimate the percentage of their current workforce likely to be with the organization at some specified date in the future. Transition analysis, managerial judgment, talent inventories, and replacement charts are some of the methods that can be used to forecast internal talent resources, and will be explained next.

transition analysis

a quantitative technique used to analyze internal labor markets and forecast internal labor supply

TRANSITION ANALYSIS   A quantitative technique called a **transition analysis** (also called Markov analysis) is a simple technique that can be used to analyze a firm's internal labor markets and forecast its internal labor supply. Conducting a transition analysis can also help hiring managers answer applicants' questions about their potential paths for promotion and the firm's upsizing or downsizing plans.

Figure 5–4 shows how a transition analysis works. Managers first identify all of the positions in the company that feed employees into the target position and to which employees in the target position tend to be promoted, demoted, or transferred. Ideally, all of the employees entering and leaving the target job are tracked so that the transition probability matrix is as accurate as possible. The cells in the transition probability matrix contain the percentage of employees staying in the same job, moving to a different job in the company, or exiting the company.

As a numerical example, assume that it is the beginning of 2012, and the company needs to forecast the likely number of customer service representatives its call center will have at the beginning of 2013. Table 5–2 shows the transition probabilities—that is, the likelihood of people staying in their current position or moving—for four jobs reflecting three job levels in the organization based on data from the one-year period from January 1, 2011, to January 1, 2012.

Full-time and part-time customer service representatives are at the entry level, supervisors are at the middle job level, and managers are at the third job level. The last column identifies the number of employees currently working at each job at the beginning of 2012. The transition probabilities are in the third to seventh columns of the matrix, and reflect the probability that an employee who begins the year employed in the job identified to the left will be employed in the job identified at the top of the column or will have exited the organization by the end of the year. The numbers on the diagonal (in bold) reflect the probability that an employee who begins 2012 in the job named to the left will still be in that job one year later.

TABLE 5–2 An Example of a Transition Probability Matrix

| Job Category (1) | Level (2) | Transition Probabilities (2011–2012) | | | | | Current (2012) |
		FTCSR (3) (%)	PTCSR (4) (%)	SUP (5) (%)	MGR (6) (%)	Exit (7) (%)	Number of Employees (8)
Full-Time Customer Service Representative (FTCSR)	1	**40**	10	10	0	40	400
Part-Time Customer Service Representative (PTCSR)	1	20	**50**	5	0	25	150
Supervisor (SUP)	2	5	0	**85**	5	5	75
Manager (MGR)	3	0	0	0	**65**	35	20

A transition probability matrix is presented in Table 5–2. Reading across the first row indicates that 40 percent of the employees who begin 2012 as full-time customer service representatives are likely to still be working as customer service representatives at the beginning of 2013. Ten percent of the employees who begin the year working as a full-time customer service representative are likely to end the year working as a part-time customer service representative, and 10 percent are likely to have been promoted to supervisor. None of the employees beginning the year as a full-time customer service representative can be expected to be a manager by the end of the year. The "Exit" column reflects the percentage of employees in each job that can be expected to have left the company by the end of the year. In this case the turnover rate has been 40 percent among full-time customer service representatives, 25 percent among part-time customer service representatives, 5 percent among supervisors, and 35 percent among managers. When reading the table it is helpful to remember that for each cell the job identified at the beginning of the row is the relevant starting position (at the beginning of the time period captured by the matrix), and the job identified at the top of the column is where employees end up at the end of the time period captured by the matrix.

The bottom row of Table 5–3 shows the forecasted employees in each of the four jobs at the beginning of 2013. The numbers in Table 5–3 come from multiplying the current number of employees in each job by the transition probability in the corresponding cell in Table 5–2. For example, multiplying the 400 current full-time customer service representative employees by .40 (40 percent) gives us an estimate of 160 of those 400 employees being in the same job at the beginning of 2013. Multiplying 400 by .10 (10 percent) gives us an estimate of 40 full-time customer service representatives becoming part-time customer service representatives by 2013, and 40 being promoted to supervisor. None of the 400 are expected to be promoted to a manager's position by 2013 (400×0). In the second row, multiplying the 150 part-time customer service representatives by .20 gives us an estimated 30 still in the same job in 2013, and multiplying 150 by .50 gives us an estimate of 75 of them becoming full-time customer service representatives by 2013. Multiplying 150 by .05 gives us an estimate of approximately eight of the part-time customer service representatives being promoted to supervisor by 2013, perhaps due to the completion of a degree. The numbers in bold on the diagonal reflect the number of people in each job in 2012 expected to be in the same job at the beginning of 2013. In the bottom row of the table are the column sums (in bold), which represent the total number of people forecasted to be in the job identified at the top of the column in 2012. In this case, the company can expect to enter 2013 with 194 full-time customer service representatives, 115 part-time customer service representatives, 112 supervisors, and 17 managers, based on the transition probabilities. A total of 207 employees will have left the organization.

Predicted shortages and surpluses can be easily calculated by subtracting current employee counts from estimated employee counts. If the company expects to maintain its current staffing levels, it is likely to have to hire from outside the organization for three of the four positions (206 full-time customer service representatives, 35 part-time customer service representatives, and three managers). For supervisors, however, the company can anticipate having 112 compared to its current number of 75. This suggests that it may be facing a surplus of 37 supervisors if the firm's internal movements and quit rates continue. This could give the firm the opportunity to

TABLE 5–3	Forecasting Employees Using the Transition Probability Matrix						
		Forecasted Employees for 2013					**Current (2012)**
Job Category (1)	**Level (2)**	**FTCSR (3)**	**PTCSR (4)**	**SUP (5)**	**MGR (6)**	**Exit (7)**	**Number of Employees (8)**
Full-Time Customer Service Representative (FTCSR)	1	**160**	40	40	0	160	400
Part-Time Customer Service Representative (PTCSR)	1	30	**75**	8	0	37	150
Supervisor (SUP)	2	4	0	**64**	4	3	75
Manager (MGR)	3	0	0	0	**13**	7	20
Forecast for 2013		194	115	112	17	207	
		Deficit	**Deficit**	**Surplus**	**Deficit**	**Exits**	

expand because the company will have a surplus of supervisors. Or it could mean that alternative promotion paths have to be considered for them or that their promotion rates need to be reduced to prevent the surplus.

In this example, the transition probabilities are based on the movements of employees for the year 2011 to 2012, but any meaningful period can be used. Some organizations face environments that are relatively stable, and will find that their transition probabilities stay relatively constant over time. In this case, more accurate transition analysis results can be obtained by looking at longer time frames. Other organizations will experience fluctuations in employee movements that make it difficult to identify relevant probabilities. In such a case, the most accurate transition analysis results are likely to come from transition probabilities derived from relatively short periods of a few months rather than a year or more. Because it's hard to make accurate estimates based on small numbers, a transition analysis is most useful for larger employers. It is less effective for very small employers. Managers can also use their judgment to adjust the probabilities based on, say, the company's growth rate. In this case, they would recalculate the employee deficits and surpluses upward or downward by the percentage growth rate they expect the business to experience. For example, if the workforce is expected to grow by 10 percent then the required employee levels for full-time and part-time customer service representatives would be 440 and 165, respectively.

Like any forecasting technique, a transition analysis has some limitations.[16] Multiple moves—for example, a person being promoted twice in the same period—cannot be accounted for. Thus, it is best to keep the time interval used to calculate the transition probabilities to two years or less. If any reason can be identified for why past patterns of employee movements will change, say, due to an expected pay increase or surge in employee retirements, these expectations should be factored into the transition probabilities. In some cases, past trends will not be as accurate as managers' estimates are. This is particularly true if new strategic directions are being considered. Also, if only a few people moved into or out of a job the transition probability estimate might be unstable and subject to error. A transition analysis also assumes that all employees in a job have an equal probability of movement, which of course, isn't likely to be the case.

Despite the limitations we've noted previously, a variety of organizations, including police departments, retail companies, high-tech companies, and the military successfully use the technique to forecast their internal labor supply. Like budgeting, forecasting is an imperfect science. Nonetheless, it is generally useful and certainly far better than doing nothing at all. Again, because of the uncertainties involved with forecasting, entering both conservative and optimistic estimates to produce a forecasted range is likely to be more useful than trying to pinpoint an estimate.

The primary limitation of all forecasting techniques is that they rely on historical patterns and activity levels. If the environment changes, past patterns may no longer hold. For example, if the unemployment rate is increasing, employees may be less likely to leave the company than they were in previous years when it was easier to find another job. On the other hand, decreasing unemployment rates might indicate other employment opportunities exist and lead to an increase in the number of employees quitting their jobs. This may also make it harder for firms to attract sufficient numbers of qualified applicants. In this case, changes in an organization's compensation policy to offer above-market wages can help the firm retain its employees, thereby increasing the organization's internal labor supply. Likewise, if an organization's required competencies change, its ability to meet its future staffing requirements internally will be hampered if its current employees don't possess those competencies.

TALENT INVENTORIES AND REPLACEMENT CHARTS Forecasting the likely *number* of employees that will be available at a given time is only half of the picture. It is also important to identify which current employees might be *qualified* for the anticipated job openings. This requires gathering information about employees' skill sets and qualifications. Although identifying some candidates might be easy, identifying as many qualified employees as possible requires more formal planning.

talent inventories

a detailed record or database that summarizes each employee's skills, competencies, and qualifications

Manual or computerized **talent inventories** are detailed records or databases that summarize each employee's skills, competencies, education, training, languages spoken, previous performance reviews, and chances of being promoted. As such, a talent inventory can be a powerful tool for quickly getting the right talent in the right place when it is needed. The New York State

Department of Taxation and Finance used an inventory system to reassign employees whose jobs were being eliminated. By allowing employees' educational and experiential backgrounds to be quickly matched with the minimum qualifications for jobs in various state agencies, the inventory allowed most displaced employees to be placed in other jobs within six weeks.[17]

Many companies employ immigrants in relatively low-skilled jobs, despite the fact that the employees graduated from universities in their homelands and have higher-level skills. Once their English improves, these employees can often move into more appropriate roles in the company, but only if the firm knows about their qualifications. Talent inventories help to track this information.

Computerized systems and human resource information systems that track the labor supply and talent inventories of firms can make internal labor supply forecasting substantially easier. Software and services allow companies to match employees' expertise and knowledge to business needs and deploy the right people just as assets would be deployed in a supply chain.[18] IBM's Workforce Management Initiative borrows many of the same concepts of supply-chain management, such as capacity planning, supply and demand planning, and sourcing. IBM built a structure that outlines the internal and external skills available to firms and provides a minute-by-minute view of the labor supply chain using a computerized talent inventory. The software catalogs skills, creating common descriptors around what people do, what their competencies are, and what experiences and references they have—information that goes well beyond a basic job description.[19]

IBM's system was tested when a large client based in Washington, D.C., contacted IBM the day before Hurricane Katrina was about to hit its server hub. The client requested 14 employees with specific skills in data analysis, process improvement, logistics management, project management, and information management. A search was placed, and within 24 hours, 14 individuals were in place in the requested locations to support the recovery effort. Tracking down a team without the system would have taken weeks.[20]

Replacement charts are a way to track the potential replacements for particular positions.[21] A replacement chart can be manual or automated. It visually shows each of the possible successors for a job and summarizes their strengths, present performance, promotion readiness, and development needs. Figure 5–5 shows an example of a replacement chart.

replacement chart
visually shows each of the possible successors for a job and summarizes their present performance, promotion readiness, and development needs

EMPLOYEE SURVEYS The availability of internal talent is dependent on turnover rates, which are not always constant. Conducting employee surveys and monitoring indicators of employee dissatisfaction, such as employee absenteeism and grievances, can help to identify the potential for increased turnover in the future. For organizations with a talent philosophy consistent with retaining employees, or for organizations for which turnover is particularly harmful to a firm's strategy execution, staying in touch with the attitudes of the company's employees and managers can be critical. Many firms conduct annual surveys of employee satisfaction and look for declining trends that suggest that turnover rates may rise.

An organization should easily be able to put together an age profile of its workforce, allowing it to forecast how much of its talent in various areas and units it is likely to lose to retirement at various points in the future. Despite the relative ease of compiling this information, a survey by The Conference Board found that 66 percent of participants reported that their companies do not have an age profile of their workforce, suggesting that they lack hard data on

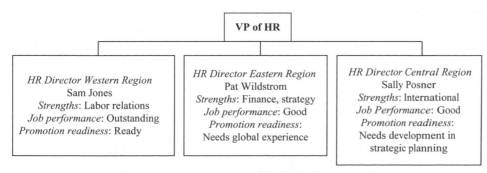

FIGURE 5–5 The Replacement Chart for a Vice President of Human Resources Position

how retirements will affect various divisions and business units. Additionally, despite their obvious usefulness for forecasting, more than 63 percent of survey respondents reported that their organizations did not have an inventory of their employees' skills and talents, and 49 percent did no assessment of their companies' training and development needs.[22] This may be particularly problematic in coming years. According to Development Dimensions International Inc., a global human resource consulting firm, by 2011, 20 percent of large, established companies in the United States will lose 40 percent or more of their top-level talent while the replacement pool of 35- to 44-year-olds declines by 15 percent. This further underscores why it's so important for organizations to develop proactive staffing plans.[23]

Forecasting the External Labor Market

All organizations have to hire from the external labor market at some point. In addition to needing to hire new workers to meet expanding demand, outside people need to replace current employees who retire or leave the organization for other reasons. Organizations monitor the external labor market in two ways. The first is *through their own observations and experiences*. For example, are the quality and quantity of applicants responding to job announcements improving or getting worse? The second way is *by monitoring labor market statistics generated by others*.

The most comprehensive source of free data on conditions in the U.S. labor market is the U.S. Bureau of Labor Statistics (BLS). The BLS Web site (www.BLS.gov) contains information on the nation's productivity, benefits, employment, and unemployment. It also conducts a National Compensation Survey that provides wage and benefit data for over 400 occupations in over 80 metropolitan and nonmetropolitan areas in the United States. Recently the BLS projected that the nation's labor supply and demand would be roughly equal, but that shortages and surpluses would occur in some occupations and industries. This means that firms likely to experience shortages will need to extend their workforce plans three to five years to find alternative sources for hard-to-fill positions and/or train the people hired for them. Firms in industries with sufficient talent can focus on more short-term planning.[24]

This chapter's Develop Your Skills feature contains additional sources of external labor market information.

It can also be helpful to identify and track trends that might affect future labor supply quality or quantity. Companies like Microsoft watch college enrollment trends and have expressed concern about the low number of U.S. students pursuing computer science degrees. Kevin Schofield, the general manager of strategy and communications at Microsoft Research, states, "We want to make sure that there's a rich pipeline of great talent that we can hire to build fantastic products, in our own company and in our partners' companies as well, because it's about the whole industry and not just the products that Microsoft owns itself."[25]

The financial services company Capital One develops three-year labor demand forecasts by anticipating business changes that will impact its headcount needs. Proprietary forecast models determine what the company's maximum sustainable size is in any given market.

DEVELOP YOUR SKILLS
Sources of Labor Market Information

Many sources of labor market information and forecasts exist. Here are some of the most popular sources and their Web addresses:

- Conference Board Help Wanted Advertising Index: www.conference-board.org
- Empire State Manufacturing Survey: www.ny.frb.org
- ISM Report on Business: www.ism.ws
- Labor Market Information by State: www.workforce-security.doleta.gov/map.asp
- Manpower Employment Outlook Survey: www.us.manpower.com

- Monster Employment Index: www.monsterworldwide.com
- NFIB Small Business Poll: www.nfib.com
- SHRM/Rutgers Leading Indicator of National Employment Index: www.shrm.org/line
- TrimTabs Online Jobs Postings Index: www.trimtabs.com
- U.S. Bureau of Labor Statistics: www.bls.gov
- U.S. Census Bureau: www.census.gov
- Local Employment Dynamics from the U.S. Census Bureau: http://lehd.did.census.gov/led

By analyzing multiple factors related to its hiring needs as well as demographic trends, Capital One estimates what percentage of the population is likely to apply with the firm over time. It then determines what percentage of applicants is likely to receive job offers and calculates when its labor reservoir will be depleted to the point that it can't hire enough people. This, in turn, becomes the firm's long-term, maximum sustainable size around which it plans its expansion strategy. Capital One also does a zip code analysis of employees to determine the optimum areas in which to locate so that it doesn't poach its own employees from existing locations.[26]

RESOLVING THE GAPS BETWEEN THE FIRM'S LABOR SUPPLY AND LABOR DEMAND

The next step in the workforce planning process is to compare the firm's forecasted demand for labor in terms of quality, quantity, and skills with its forecasted supply. Perhaps the organization expects to have the amount and quality of labor to meet its future staffing needs. Or perhaps it expects to have a surplus or shortage of labor. If either a labor surplus or labor shortage is forecast, an **action plan** should be developed to proactively address the situation. Action plans should always be consistent with the firm's business strategy, talent philosophy, and HR strategy. For example, layoffs are inconsistent with a talent philosophy of wanting people to contribute to the company over long-term careers and result in negative outcomes for the firm. (In Chapter 12, we discuss some of the alternatives firms can take to avoid laying off employees.)

action plan
strategy to proactively address an anticipated surplus or shortage of employees

Instead of having to lay off employees, some industries are desperate for them. The American Nursing Association created a steering committee to develop an action plan to address the nursing shortage in the United States. Here is a portion of the action plan developed to increase the supply of nurses:[27]

- *Communicate nursing's economic value*—educate the public about the pivotal role nursing plays in the nation's health care system.
- *Improve the work environment*—improve the conditions under which nurses work so that quality patient care is optimized and nursing staff is retained.
- *Communicate the professional nursing culture*—assert nursing's high standards of professional practice, education, leadership, and collaboration to better appeal to potential nurses and enhance the image of the profession.
- *Education*—reshape nursing education to enhance nursing's image.
- *Recruitment/Retention*—enhance professional opportunities to attract and sustain excellent nurses for long, rewarding careers.

Stu Reed, president, Integrated Supply Chain, Motorola Inc., developed an action plan to increase the future supply of supply chain managers. Motorola has identified the likely career path and skills the supply chain professional of the future needs to get to the top job. The company then partnered aggressively with key supply chain schools in North America and internationally. "We validate our model with them and let them know what type of graduates we need for them to provide us," says Reed.[28] In other words, Motorola worked backward to find its supply chain talent.

Whenever changes are observed in labor market conditions, it is important to try to assess whether the change represents a labor market trend that is likely to continue or whether it is a shorter-term fluctuation caused by the business cycle. Understanding the difference is important because different staffing strategies are appropriate for each.[29] We discuss what the basic types of actions plans are next.

Dealing with a Temporary Talent Shortage

What should be done if a shortage of qualified talent is thought to be temporary? Offering hiring incentives such as sign-on and retention bonuses consisting of stock options or cash to be paid after the employee has successfully worked with the company for a certain period of time can help the firm cope with the situation. Because higher salaries cost the organization more money for the duration of the new hire's tenure with the company, it is often better to offer hiring inducements that last only as long as the talent shortage does.[30] When companies find it difficult to hire in a tight labor market, they often turn to more expensive recruiting methods, such as additional advertising and search firms, or they lower their hiring standards so that more recruits are considered qualified for the position. Neither of these strategies is guaranteed to work, and each can produce unwanted consequences.

One short-term solution might be to recruit people currently working for the company. Nonetheless, some positions will likely still have to be filled by new hires. If the root cause of a projected labor shortage is unusually high turnover, the action plan should address the cause of the turnover—for example, low pay, poor supervision, limited career advancement potential, limited training opportunities, and so forth. The firm's HR managers can then try to uncover the cause of the turnover by conducting employee surveys and discuss the situation with the company's managers. In some cases, creativity may be needed to resolve projected labor shortages. For example, when H&R Block had trouble finding workers for its technical support call center in suburban Kansas City, it relocated the facility to the inner city and hired workers who lived downtown.[31]

Business leaders are often attracted to global locations including Mexico and China because of their low labor costs. Labor costs can change quickly, however, making these short-sighted decisions more costly.[32]

Dealing with a Persistent Talent Shortage

If the shortage is likely to last a number of years, an organization must reduce its demand for the talents that will be in short supply and/or increase its supply of employees with the qualifications it needs. Although it can be possible to increase the firm's supply of employees, this is not a fast or practical solution for most organizations. Instead, many organizations try to reduce their need for skills that will be in short supply by increasing their use of automation and technology, and by redesigning jobs so that they need fewer people with the talents that are in short supply.

Although to some extent they have done so for cost-saving purposes, Home Depot, Costco, and many supermarkets are among the companies that have automated jobs by installing self-service checkout lanes. Many callers to customer service departments now receive automated responses to their inquiries. Not all jobs can be automated, but it is frequently an option for companies facing talent shortages or wanting to reduce their labor costs by getting the same work done with fewer employees. However, as we have mentioned, automation can generate the need for new employees with specific types of skills—for example, employees who can maintain the automated equipment. These factors must be considered as well when a company decides to automate some of its functions.

The petroleum industry is facing a severe shortage of petroleum engineers, geologists, and geophysicists, despite automating some processes and reducing the number of workers needed in some jobs from three to one. Despite the decrease due to greater automation, the personnel shortage is so serious that Peter Schwartz, formerly the head of business environment at Royal Dutch/Shell, states that it "will ultimately slow the rate of innovation as we need it more and more. Eventually, it means we'll get less oil."[33]

business process outsourcing
relocating an entire business function to an independent service provider

If talent is hard to find or is too expensive, one option is to outsource the affected business process. **Business process outsourcing** is the relocation of an entire business function, such as production, manufacturing, or customer service, to an independent service provider in the same or a different country. Commonly outsourced business functions include IT and technology services, customer service, and even corporate training. If the firm is able to maintain or improve the quality of the business process being outsourced, the company cannot only reduce its costs but focus more on its core competencies.

The relationship between $3.7 billion transportation services company Penske Corporation and the business process outsourcing firm Genpact involves more than 30 different business processes and illustrates how some companies are engaging in business process outsourcing and leveraging offshore skilled labor. To reduce costs and improve the quality of its operations, independent Genpact essentially acts as Penske's virtual subsidiary. When a Penske truck is leased for an interstate trip, Genpact's staff in India check the customer's credit and acquire permits. If the truck is stopped at a weigh station because it lacks a required fuel permit, Indian workers transmit the necessary document to the weigh station to get the vehicle back on the road within a half hour. After a trip, the driver's log is shipped to a Genpact facility in Juarez, Mexico, where mileage, tax, toll, and fuel data are entered into Penske computers and processed in India. When Penske sells the truck, staff in Mexico record the transaction.[34]

Dealing with a Temporary Employee Surplus

When a firm expects a business slowdown to be temporary, it has several options. If slowdowns are cyclical or happen frequently, using temporary or contingent workers who are the first to be let go when business slows can help buffer key permanent workers and provide them greater employment security. Temporary layoffs are another option to deal with a short-term employee surplus, but they sometimes need to last more than six months to be cost-effective due to severance costs,[35] greater unemployment insurance premiums the firms must pay, temporary productivity declines in the firm's remaining workforce, and the rehiring and retraining process. Losing the investments the organization previously made to hire and train the laid-off workers can also be costly. Alternatives to layoffs include across-the-board salary cuts or a reduction in work hours, or reallocating workers to expanding areas of the business. Some firms offer unpaid vacations, sabbaticals, job sharing, and other creative solutions to temporary surpluses.

Dealing with a Persistent Employee Surplus

Organizations sometimes need to permanently reduce the number of people they employ. Technology changes, the entrance of competitors, and changes in customer preferences can fundamentally change the number and types of workers an organization needs. Early retirement incentives, layoffs, and not filling vacated positions can all reduce an employer's headcount, but not without a cost. Early retirement programs can result in the most skilled and productive employees leaving the organization. Not filling vacated positions can leave key positions in the organization unstaffed or understaffed. Layoffs can damage workforce morale and hurt the firm's reputation as an employer. Action plans to address a persistent employee surplus can also involve reassignments, hiring freezes, and steering employees away from careers in that position to reduce the need for future layoffs. Retraining employees to fill other jobs in the firm can help bring labor supply and demand into balance.

The goal of any staffing strategy is to acquire and retain the most productive employees and remove lower performers. Planning activities that enable an organization to anticipate its future employment needs and scale down gradually rather than abruptly through mass layoffs or dramatic restructuring can help to control the company's restructuring costs and retain top performers.

STAFFING PLANNING

In addition to workforce planning, it is also important to take the time to plan the staffing process. The three questions that need to be answered are:

- How many people should be recruited?
- What resources are needed?
- How much time will it take to hire the employees?

We address each of these questions next.

How Many People Should Be Recruited?

Because some job candidates will usually lose interest in the position before being hired and others will lack appropriate qualifications, it is almost always necessary to generate more applicants than the number of open positions. Additionally, having greater numbers of applicants allows an organization to be more selective. This allows it to identify the candidate who best fits the position rather than hiring the only person who applies. At the same time, recruiting solely to reach numerical applicant targets can result in the firm spending more than it should rather than recruiting only the number of applicants necessary to meet the firm's hiring goals.

The "ideal" number of applicants to recruit for an opening depends on the nature of the organization's staffing and HR strategies. As we have explained, recruiting too small a pool can result in the firm being unable to identify enough qualified candidates to be able to fill its openings. Too large a pool places unreasonable burdens on the recruiting function's administrative systems and wastes time and money but does not guarantee that recruits will have the appropriate qualifications. Plus, the firm risks instilling ill will among the many rejected applicants. The goal is to attract a sufficient number of candidates who meet or exceed the personal and technical requirements of the job.

STAFFING YIELDS   The best source of information for determining how many people to recruit comes from data collected during a company's previous recruiting efforts. One way to start is by looking at the firm's previous **staffing yields**, or the proportion of applicants moving from one stage of the hiring process to the next, and **hiring yields** (also called selection ratios), or the percent of applicants ultimately hired.

For example, as illustrated in Figure 5–6, if three out of four job offers are typically accepted, the company will have to make 100 offers so as to hire 75 employees. If, on average, one job offer is made for every four interviews, then 400 candidates must be interviewed to generate 100 job offers. If four out of five invitations to interview are accepted, then 500 invitations must be issued to produce the 400 interview candidates. If one out of every four applicants is typically invited for an interview, then 2,000 applicants must be generated, resulting in a selection ratio of 3.125 percent (75 hires out of 2,000 applicants). Staffing yield pyramids can be constructed to illustrate these requirements based on the organization's previous experience, and spreadsheets greatly simplify their calculation and application.

Staffing yields are not the same across all jobs, hiring situations, or economic conditions. In fact, they can vary widely within a single industry or even a single firm. For example, Microsoft only hires about 2 percent of its applicants for software positions, which is typical for its industry.[36] On the other hand, organizations like Amway and Discovery Toys hire the majority of their applicants for sales representative positions. Offer acceptance rates are also generally lower for professional and technical candidates than for unskilled and semiskilled workers.

A company's staffing yields tend to be reasonably consistent from year to year, however. Sometimes trends can be identified that add to the accuracy of the firm's labor force prediction when other market conditions are taken into account.[37] For example, if an organization has made its salary levels more competitive or even higher than the market, it can generally expect a larger applicant pool and a lower percentage of applicants hired as a result. At the very least, prior staffing yields can be a good starting point for estimating probable yields and minimum applicant quantity requirements for the current recruiting effort. A primary disadvantage of relying on past staffing yields to forecast a firm's recruiting needs is that ideally an organization will be able to improve on its past yield ratios by analyzing the effectiveness of its different recruiting sources, targeting its recruiting efforts at the most productive sources, and identifying and leveraging the recruiting methods that work best for the given job. However, if the applicant pool an organization attracts in the future is of higher quality than it has been in the past, then the firm can recruit fewer applicants yet enjoy even greater hiring yields and selection ratios. This will allow it to hire a greater percentage of applicants able to do their jobs successfully, thereby improving the average performance level of the company's workforce.

It is important to remember that the key issue is not whether the firm's staffing yields are high or low. What matters is whether the staffing system is producing the right numbers of the right kinds of employees in the right time frame. Although staffing is an investment, not an expense, a key issue for many organizations is the need to control its monetary investment in

staffing yields
the proportion of applicants moving from one stage of the hiring process to the next

hiring yields
the percent of applicants ultimately hired

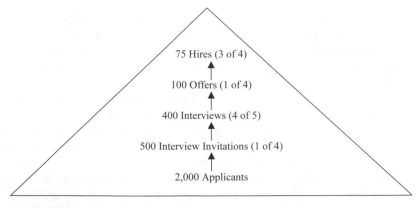

FIGURE 5–6 The Staffing Yield Pyramid

staffing. This can be accomplished by limiting the size of the applicant pool or by more efficiently managing the application process. If the proportion of high-potential applicants increases, the total number of applicants needed to generate the right number of the right quality of new hires decreases. In the past, however, it was widely believed that recruiting a larger applicant pool was always better than recruiting a smaller pool because it would increase the odds of high-potential candidates being in the pool. This assumption does not necessarily hold true. Smaller applicant pools can actually be superior once you consider recruiting yields and costs.

As an example, assume that an organization wants to hire the best talent it can find (say, the top 10 percent of the talent in a given field) and that the organization's applicant assessment methods are able to flawlessly assess the talent of each applicant. In the past, the organization would have probably tried to generate as many applicants as it could and hire one-tenth of them. This would result in a low hiring ratio. In fact, it was thought that the lower selection ratio would actually lead to higher-quality employees being recruited. This could, indeed, occur, but only if the entire spectrum of talent available to the firm applied for the position. For example, if a disproportionate number of undesirable people applied for the position, an even lower hiring ratio would exist. However, the lower ratio wouldn't necessarily lead to higher-quality employees being selected. A better strategy would be to increase the number of high-potential applicants and decrease the number of low-potential applicants. If an organization is able to do this effectively, it will be able to increase the quality of its hires while simultaneously increasing its staffing yields and getting a better return on its recruiting investment.

Increasing the quality of the applicant pool will also lessen the burden placed on the firm's applicant assessment and selection systems because more of the applicants are likely to be successfully hired. The time and financial resources invested in recruiting and evaluating each candidate are also less likely to be wasted if better recruiting results in a greater proportion of applicants being a good fit. Additionally, it is important to remember that even the best applicant assessment system cannot identify potential high performers if they never apply with the organization. Targeted recruiting efforts will increase the probability that the top candidates apply.

Organizations sometimes seek to obtain high yields (hiring a large percentage of applicants) in the recruiting function to keep costs down, but this strategy often doesn't consider the potential dilution of an organization's talent. High hiring yields can be detrimental to the effective recruitment and selection of employees if the quality of the applicants isn't simultaneously considered. However, if an organization leverages the recruiting methods and sources that work best for it, it may be able to alter the talent distribution of its applicant pool to contain only the best of the available talent—for example, the upper 50 percent. In this case, a much higher targeted recruiting yield (say 30 percent) could produce the same quality of new hires as did a lower 10 percent yield under the traditional method when a greater number of undesirable candidates were included in the applicant pool. Clearly, hiring the best 5 of 50 low-quality applicants is less ideal than hiring the best 5 of 20 high-quality applicants.

Evaluating the staffing yields from different recruiting sources can help in this regard. The quantity and quality of hires from various recruiting sources are likely to differ both within and across organizations. One company might be able to hire good performers from newspaper advertisements. But another company or a different division of the same company might find this strategy ineffective. Determining which recruiting sources are the "best" to use generally varies also with the nature of the position and its level within the organization. The Internet might be a very effective recruiting source for recruiting applicants with higher-level information-technology skills, but less effective for recruiting applicants for clerical or manufacturing jobs. Recruiters are likely to differ in their annual hiring rates and the quality of their hires. If an organization needs to hire quickly, it is very helpful for it to know how long it has typically taken to fill positions from a variety of sources so that it can strategically choose among them. The advantages and disadvantages of many different recruiting sources will be discussed in more detail in Chapter 6.

If an organization has failed to collect staffing yield information during its previous staffing efforts, estimating the staffing yield for its current hiring effort will be more challenging but not impossible. Headhunting agencies, college placement offices, and the like might be able to provide the firm with some information on the average yield ratios of their candidates.

The firm can also attempt to benchmark the yields of similar organizations. This information is not ideal, however, because it won't be specific to the actual company doing the hiring or the actual job being hired for. The characteristics of the company itself, including its competitive position, compensation package, image, quality of life, and recreational opportunities where the job is located can dramatically influence staffing yields.

What Resources Are Needed?

According to the Saratoga Institute,[38] there are six basic costs related to external hiring:

1. Advertising expenses
2. Agency and search firm fees
3. Employee referral bonuses
4. Recruiter and applicant travel costs
5. Relocation costs
6. Company recruiter costs (prorated salary and benefits if the recruiter performs duties other than staffing)

These six factors account for 90 percent of hiring costs. (The Saratoga Institute adds an additional 10 percent to cover miscellaneous expenses including testing, reference checking, hiring manager time, and administrative support.[39])

The internal cost per hire calculation is very similar, and includes four elements:[40]

1. Internal advertising costs
2. Travel and interview costs
3. Relocation costs
4. Internal recruiter costs

In addition to these costs, determining the total cost of the firm's staffing effort involves determining the resources and size of the recruiting staff the company will need to hire the employees it is seeking. Next, we discuss two methods of estimating needed resources for a staffing effort: workload-driven forecasting and staffing efficiency–driven forecasting.

workload-driven forecasting

forecasting based on historical data on the average number of hires typically made per recruiter or the average number of recruits processed per recruiter over a given period

WORKLOAD-DRIVEN FORECASTING   **Workload-driven forecasting** uses historical data on the average number of hires typically made per recruiter or the average number of recruits processed per recruiter over a given period of time—for example, a week, month, or year. For example, referring again to Figure 5–6, if an organization's average recruiter can process 100 applicants during a recruiting drive, the company will need a staff of 20 recruiters to process 2,000 applicants. Similar procedures can be used to estimate the amount of additional resources—the telephone costs, advertising costs, photocopying, background checks, medical tests, and so forth—needed for the staffing effort. The amount of money that needs to be budgeted for the staffing effort depends not only on the number of people to be hired but also whether applicants are local or from far away, the recruiting sources used, the selection methods employed, and the tightness of the labor market.

staffing efficiency

the total cost associated with the compensation of the newly hired employees

STAFFING EFFICIENCY–DRIVEN FORECASTING   Another method of forecasting how many recruiters are needed is based on staffing efficiency. **Staffing efficiency**[41] is the total cost associated with the compensation of the newly hired employees—that is, the total starting base pay of all new employees. For example, if a firm's internal and external staffing costs were $100,000, and 10 people were hired, each with a starting base salary of $60,000, the firm's staffing efficiency would be 100,000/600,000 or 16.67 percent. Lower staffing efficiency percentages reflect greater staffing efficiency.

Because the staffing efficiency approach is financially and efficiency driven rather than workload driven, it can be a useful metric for evaluating how well a firm's staffing plans work. The method can also be used to set a budget for an upcoming hiring effort. For example, suppose the firm wants to achieve a staffing efficiency ratio of 15 percent or less, and plans to hire 25 new employees per month at an average starting base salary of $50,000. In this case, the firm will have a budget of $187,500 (25 × $50,000 × 0.15) a month to spend on recruiters and other staffing resources.[42]

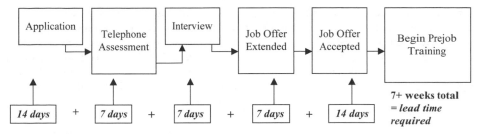

FIGURE 5–7 An Example of a Typical Hiring Timeline

How Much Time Will It Take to Hire the Employees?

Hiring managers, of course, don't want jobs to be vacant any longer than necessary. However, it takes time to find, screen, and negotiate with each new hire. Often it takes longer than expected. Establishing a staffing timeline before beginning the staffing initiative ensures that hiring managers, recruiters, and other staffing specialists know what to expect. Information on the average interval between a candidate's application and interview, interview and offer, offer and hire, and so forth, can be useful for timeline development purposes. By looking at these intervals, HR personnel can identify daily, weekly, and monthly goals for each staffing step.

The length of each staffing stage varies widely across jobs and organizations. In general, higher-level positions take longer to fill than lower-level positions. However, skill shortages and local competition can lengthen the time to fill lower-level positions as well. The staffing technology the firm uses—whether it uses résumé-screening software, accepts job applications over the Internet, and so forth—can greatly impact how long each staffing stage lasts, too.

Figure 5–7 illustrates a typical hiring timeline.

Throughout the staffing process, reliable, accurate progress reports should be prepared and compared to the staffing plan. It could be that some stages of the staffing process take longer or shorter than projected, and the projected timeline should be adjusted accordingly. Maintaining progress reports can also help the firm determine whether it is on track to produce the total number of hires the organization is striving for within the targeted period of time. If the current hiring pace is found to be too slow, the organization might be able to take steps to speed up the process or recruit more people than it had initially intended.

If it is known that job openings are likely to exist, based on historical turnover or hiring patterns, the recruiting staff can begin sourcing and processing candidates before the positions even become open. This can dramatically reduce the time it takes to hire someone to fill an opening because candidates are already in the pipeline. We've described this approach, called *continuous recruiting*, in earlier chapters. The method is particularly useful for positions that turn over relatively quickly—for example, openings will need to be filled throughout the year on a rolling basis. It can also work well for jobs that take a long time to fill, or for jobs that cost the organization a lot of money while they are vacant. Sales jobs are a good example. *Batch recruiting*, in contrast, involves recruiting an entirely new applicant pool every time the organization has one or more positions to fill. Jobs recruited this way typically take a longer time to fill.

If organizations in a particular industry tend to recruit on the same cycle, a job-centric staffing philosophy may reduce the quantity of available talent. For example, if engineering companies tend to start their college recruiting in November and confirm new hires in March, waiting until a job opening occurs in March to begin recruiting for a replacement may mean that an organization is forced to recruit from the other organizations' rejected job candidates. Recruiting after competing organizations do may work for an organization using a low-cost strategy that is not looking for top-tier talent, but other organizations may be unable to identify a sufficient number of quality applicants because they are recruiting out-of-cycle with their competitors.

STRATEGIC WORKFORCE PLANNING AT TRANSALTA[43]

To keep its business sustainable and execute its growth strategy, the Canadian power generation and wholesale company TransAlta knew it needed to engage in workforce planning. The company's strategic workforce planning process began with a review of TransAlta's western

Canadian workforce during the previous seven years. The company examined past attrition rates and hiring profiles to forecast and plan for the next five to ten years. Local community leaders also provided input into the forecasts and plans. By comparing those findings with TransAlta's growth plans and the evolving labor market, TransAlta was able to gauge the balance it would have to strike between recruiting new employees and enhancing the skills of its existing staff—especially given the fact that Canada's workforce is growing at only half the rate of the overall population and that the competition for skilled workers is heating up.

For each of its facilities, TransAlta created action plans for attracting and recruiting new employees; retaining existing employees; maintaining or, preferably, improving productivity; and capturing and transferring key areas of knowledge before people retire. The high cost of living in Fort McMurray, Alberta, where one of the firm's key facilities is located, and the highly competitive compensation packages being offered by other petroleum firms in the area presented special challenges. Because losing experienced employees compromises TransAlta's ability to operate efficiently, retention is an important goal for the company. To enhance the retention of its seasoned employees, Fort McMurray TransAlta is considering strategic measures ranging from providing employees with mortgage assistance to help them afford to buy homes in Fort McMurray to hiring workers earlier than needed to ensure they completely absorb the knowledge of the firm's retiring or resigning staff members. Today, TransAlta focuses a great deal of effort on identifying the talent it will need, when it will need it, and where it will find it. To keep on top of local changes, such as those that are occurring in Alberta, the company also updates all of its recruiting data every two years as part of its regular assets review.

Summary

Forecasting the number, types, and quality of employees needed to execute the business strategy is critical for effective staffing. Setting talent goals and objectives that are consistent with the firm's staffing strategy and talent philosophy are important goals of the planning process. The assessment of the organization's external labor environment and a company's own talent strengths and shortcomings can influence its competitive advantage and the business strategies it is likely to be able to pursue successfully.

It is important to determine the size of the recruiting staff and resources that will be needed and to secure the appropriate budget and resources before the staffing initiative begins. Additionally, it is important for planning purposes that the timeline for the recruiting effort be established to ensure that the correct number of new hires will be ready to start when they are needed. Although this is particularly critical before an expansion effort or the hiring of an unusually large number of people, it is also important to assess needed resources before hiring a single individual to ensure that hiring goals can be met and that the hiring manager understands what to expect from the staffing process.

Takeaway Points

1. The workforce planning process starts with the firm's business strategy. After articulating the firm's talent philosophy and strategic staffing decisions, a workforce analysis is then conducted to forecast both labor demand and labor supply, and to identify any gaps between the two. Action plans consistent with the firm's talent philosophy are then created to address any gaps. The action plans are then monitored, evaluated, and revised as the firm's environment changes.

2. An organization can predict its future business activity by using seasonal forecasts, interest rate forecasts, currency exchange rate forecasts, competitor forecasts, industry and economic forecasts, and other methods, such as whether it is entering or exiting a business.

3. An organization can use ratio analysis, scatter plots, trend analysis, or judgmental forecasting to determine its demand for workers.

4. To forecast its internal labor supply, firms can use transition analysis, judgment, talent inventories and replacement charts, and employee surveys. To forecast its external supply of workers, a firm can rely on their own observations and experiences or monitor labor market statistics generated by others, such as the U.S. Bureau of Labor Statistics.

5. Action plans proactively address anticipated surpluses or shortages of employees and should always be consistent with the firm's business strategy, talent philosophy, and HR strategy.

6. The staffing planning process addresses how many people to recruit, what resources are needed, and how much time it will take to hire.

Discussion Questions

1. If forecasting is rarely exact, why should a firm bother doing it?
2. What labor force trends might influence a firm's staffing planning, in your opinion?
3. How can contingent employees help an organization prepare for anticipated surpluses or shortages of workers?
4. If your boss asked you how investing more resources in forecasting and planning could help the organization compete better, what would you say?
5. What would happen if a firm did not engage in staffing planning?

Exercises

1. *Strategy Exercise:*   Registered nurses are in short supply in the United States—a situation that it is expected to worsen. It is predicted that the demand for U.S. nursing services will exceed supply by nearly 30 percent in 2020.[44] Many registered nurses are approaching retirement age, and the nursing profession is facing difficulties attracting new entrants and retaining existing nurses. In addition, nursing schools have been unable to expand fast enough to supply enough additional nurses.[45]

   Working in a group of three to five students, research the severity of the nursing shortage, if any, in your area. Then develop an action plan to strategically address a nursing shortage in your area (even if one doesn't exist in your area). What are your suggestions for improving the quantity and quality of available nurses over the next two decades? Be prepared to share your answers with the class.

2. *Develop Your Skills Exercise:*   This chapter's Develop Your Skills feature contains numerous Web addresses for different labor supply forecasts. Working alone, use these and any other relevant resources to forecast the supply of labor for a job in your chosen career path. Write a one-page report summarizing your forecast and present a brief action plan to address any forecasted surpluses or shortages for this position.

3. *Opening Vignette Exercise:*   The opening vignette describes the workforce planning process at TransAlta. One of the biggest planning challenges the company identified was retaining its experienced employees, particularly in its Fort McMurray, Alberta, location where the competition for skilled workers is intense. Because experienced employees are critical to TransAlta's ability to operate efficiently, it must retain as many workers as it can, and also ensure that their knowledge is transferred completely to new employees. TransAlta's growth strategy also means that its need for employees is increasing.

   Working in a group of three to five students, develop action plans for TransAlta to both retain its existing employees and ensure the complete transfer of knowledge to its new hires. Be prepared to share your ideas with the class.

CASE STUDY

Sweet Tooth Inc. is experiencing growing demand for its new line of candy and needs to add a new production line of 50 workers. You are the company's newly hired vice president of human resources. Your first task is to develop a staffing plan for this new production line. The company's historical staffing yields for its production line positions are as follows:

- 20 percent of applicants are invited for interviews.
- 80 percent of interview invitations are accepted.
- 15 percent of the people interviewed are extended job offers.
- 50 percent of the people receiving job offers accept them.
- The company's average recruiter can process 100 recruits during a recruiting drive.

- The company's staffing timeline the last time it hired production line employees is given below:

QUESTIONS

1. How many people should Sweet Tooth recruit for its 50 new assembly-line jobs?
2. Using workload-driven forecasting, how many recruiters are needed for the staffing effort?
3. How long will it take to staff the new production line?

Semester-Long Active Learning Project

Continue working on the job analysis and competency model for the position. Also, describe the position's relevant labor market(s) and provide a forecast of the future labor supply for the position. Develop an approximate timeline covering the period from job posting to the new hire beginning work.

Case Study Assignment: Strategic Staffing at Chern's

See the appendix at the back of the book for this chapter's Case Study Assignment.

Endnotes

1. "TransAlta Corporation 2005 Report on Sustainability," TransAlta, 2005, www.transalta.com/2005rs/life-work/working/planning.shtml. Accessed August 3, 2006.
2. Butler, J. E., Ferris, G. R., and Napier, N. K., *Strategy and Human Resources Management*, Cincinnati, OH: South-Western, 1991.
3. Johnson, W. B., and Packer, A. E., *Workforce 2000: Work and Workers for the 21st Century*, Indianapolis, IN: Hudson Institute, Inc, 1987.
4. Butler, Ferris, and Napier, *Strategy and Human Resources Management*.
5. Handfield-Jones, H., Michaels, E., and Axelrod, B., "Talent Management: A Critical Part of Every Leader's Job," *Ivey Business Journal,* 66, 2 (November/December 2001): 53–58.
6. Babcock, P., "Human Capital Planning at Corning: More Than a Head Count," *Society for Human Resource Management,* March 2008, http://www.shrm.org/ema/library_published/nonIC/CMS_025137.asp#TopOfPage. Accessed November 12, 2009.

7. Ibid.

8. Bechet, T. P., and Walker, L. W., "Aligning Staffing with Business Strategy," *Human Resource Planning*, 16, 2 (1993): 1–16.

9. Ibid.

10. Agrawal, V., Manyika, J. M., and Richards, J. E., "Matching People to Jobs," *McKinsey Quarterly*, 4, 2 (2003): 71–79.

11. Brauer, D., "What Accounts for the Decline in Manufacturing Employment?" *Congressional Budget Office Economic and Budget Issue Brief*, February 18, 2004, www.cbo.gov/showdoc .cfm?index=5078&sequence=0. Accessed August 15, 2006.

12. Karpinski, R., "Cisco Attempts to Boost B2B Sales," *InformationWeek*, March 16, 2001, www.internetweek.com/ story/INW20010316S0003.

13. Bond, G., "Jobs Lost as High Dollar Hits Exporters," *New Zealand Herald*, January 24, 2006, www.nzherald.co.nz/ section/story.cfm?c_id=1&objectid=10365097. Accessed August 15, 2006.

14. Schneider, C., "The New Human-Capital Metrics," *CFO Magazine*, February 15, 2006, www.cfo.com/article.cfm/ 5491043/1/c_2984284?f=archives. Accessed August 23, 2006.

15. Minton-Eversone, T., "Report: Employers Refocus on Strategic Workforce Planning as Economy Recovers," *Society for Human Resource Management*, February 22, 2010, http://www.shrm .org/hrdisciplines/staffingmanagement/Articles/Pages/Employers RefocusonWorkforcePlanning.aspx. Accessed March 28, 2010.

16. Heneman, H. G., III., and Sandver, M. H., "Markov Analysis in Human Resource Administration: Applications and Limitations," *Academy of Management Review*, 2 (1977): 535–542.

17. New York State Department of Civil Service, "Management and Mobility: Part III—Using Existing Tools," *Work Force and Succession Planning*, September 2002, www.cs.state.ny.us/ successionplanning/workgroups/ManagementandMobility/skill sinventory.html. Accessed August 15, 2006.

18. Malykhina, E., "Supplying Labor to Meet Demand," *InformationWeek*, March 21, 2005, www.informationweek .com/story/showArticle.jhtml?articleID=159902302. Accessed August 22, 2006.

19. Ibid.

20. Weber, M., "The Labor Pool Becomes a Supply Chain," *Industrial Management*, 48, 4 (2006): 20–25.

21. Werther, W. B., Jr., and Davis, K., *Human Resources and Personnel Management* (5th ed.), New York: McGraw-Hill, 2005.

22. Munson, H., *Valuing Experience: How to Motivate and Retain Mature Workers*, Report #1329-03-RR, The Conference Board, April 2003, www.conference-board.org.

23. Schildhouse, J., "Working Hard to Avoid the Labor Shortage," *Inside Supply Management*, 17, 3 (March 2006): 22.

24. Hansen, F., "Feast and Famine in Recruiting of Professionals," *Workforce Management Online*, April 2006, www.workforce .com/archive/feature/24/34/16/index.php. Accessed August 22, 2006.

25. "Microsoft Listens to College Students, Faculty as Bill Gates Visits Top IT and Engineering Colleges," *Microsoft Press Pass*, October 12, 2005, www.microsoft.com/presspass/features/ 2005/oct05/10-12Campus.mspx. Accessed August 18, 2006.

26. Arend, M., "Campus Culture," *Site Selection Magazine*, June 28, 2001.

27. American Nursing Association, *Nursing's Agenda for the Future*, 2002, http://nursingworld.org/naf. Accessed April 6, 2007.

28. Schildhouse, "Working Hard to Avoid the Labor Shortage."

29. This section is based in part on Director, S. M., and Collison, J., *Staffing Research: Staffing Strategy over the Business Cycle*, SHRM Research Report 05-0551, Alexandria, VA: Society for Human Resource Management, 2005.

30. Ibid.

31. O'Briant, S. M., "Corporate Giving: More Bang for the Buck," *Kiplinger*, August 13, 2001, http://special.kiplinger. com/hr/stories/corporate_giving_br_more_ bang_for_the_ buck.html.

32. Minton-Eversone, T., Report: Employers Refocus on Strategic Workforce Planning as Economy Recovers, Society for Human Resource Management, February 22, 2010. http://www.shrm .org/hrdisciplines/staffingmanagement/Articles/Pages/ EmployersRefocusonWorkforcePlanning.aspx. Accessed March 26, 2010.

33. "Talent Shortage Slows Oil Tech," *Red Herring*, May 14, 2006, www.redherring.com/Article.aspx? a=16854&hed=Talent+ Shortage+Slows +Oil+Tech#. Accessed August 18, 2006.

34. Engardio, P., "Penske's Offshore Partner in India," *Business Week Online*, January 30, 2006, www.businessweek.com/ magazine/content/06_05/b3969414.htm. Accessed September 5, 2006.

35. See Rigby, D., "Look Before You Layoff," *Harvard Business Review*, 80, 4 (2002): 20–21.

36. Matloff, N., "Debunking the Myth of a Desperate Software Labor Shortage," Testimony to the U.S. House Judiciary Committee Subcommittee on Immigration. Presented April 21, 1998, updated September 27, 1999.

37. Hawk, R. H., *The Recruitment Function*, New York: Academy of Management Association, 1967.

38. For more information, see the Saratoga section of the PriceWaterhouseCoopers Web site at www.pwc.com/extweb/ service.nsf/docid/0516c36c9a61714985256eba00702ed5.

39. From Davidson, B., "Hiring an Employee: How Much Does It Cost?" *Workforce*, www.workforce.com/archive/feature/22/ 25/58/223946.php. Accessed August 22, 2006.

40. Ibid.

41. See Staffing.org for additional information on this metric.

42. Burkholder, N., "How Many Recruiters Do We Need and What Happened to Alice?" Staffing.org, April 23, 2003.

43. "TransAlta Corporation 2005 Report on Sustainability."

44. Andrews, D. R., "The Nurse Manager: Job Satisfaction, the Nursing Shortage, and Retention," *Journal of Nursing Management*, 13, 4 (July 2005): 286–295.

45. "AACN Concerned that Recommendations in the President's FY 2008 Budget Request Would Heighten the Nation's Nursing Shortage," American Association of Colleges of Nursing, February 9, 2007, www.aacn.nche.edu/FY08BudgetRequest .htm. Accessed April 6, 2007.

6 Sourcing: Identifying Recruits

Outline

LEARNING OBJECTIVES

After studying this chapter, you should be able to:

- Describe the role of sourcing in the staffing process.
- Explain what makes one recruiting source more effective than another.
- List alternative recruiting sources and match them with specific jobs.
- Create a sourcing plan.
- Explain how to best source nontraditional applicant pools.
- Explain the role geographic targeting plays in the sourcing process.

SOURCING AT VALERO ENERGY CORPORATION

When Dan Hilbert accepted a recruiting leadership role at Valero Energy Corporation, a Fortune 25 company based in San Antonio, Texas, he knew that talent was the key to Valero's performance and future success. But Valero did not have a good understanding of how its different talent sources were performing. Because people who never apply cannot become employees, he focused his attention on improving how the company sourced and identified promising job candidates.

Hilbert wanted to continually evaluate and improve Valero's recruiting function because he knew it would better support Valero's growth strategy and position the company to compete successfully in a tightening labor market.[1] Hilbert asks for your advice about how to devise a better way to evaluate the different recruiting sources Valero can tap for its different job openings. After reading this chapter, you should have some good ideas for him.

After using the job analysis and workforce planning processes to determine what to look for in new hires, the organization needs to find people with the characteristics it wants and convert them into recruits. This is no small task. People who never apply to an organization cannot become employees, making attracting enough of the desired types of applicants one of the most important criteria for an effective staffing system. Great employees are like a gold mine. Just as the skills and activities involved in finding a gold mine differ from the skills and activities required to extract the gold, sourcing quality talent requires a different set of skills and activities than does attracting and recruiting the talent. Because recruiting sources tend to generate different types of applicants, sourcing is the key to finding these employees.

The best applicant sourcing systems identify where the firm can find good potential job applicants who fit the organization and the job requirements and who are likely to be interested in pursuing employment opportunities with the organization. After identifying the objectives of the hiring effort (which might include prehire outcomes, including the number, quality, and diversity of applicants, or posthire outcomes, such as the time to fill the positions, new hire quality and diversity, or a mixture of both) recruiting sources are chosen to help meet these objectives.

One company that takes sourcing very seriously is Cisco Systems. Its strategy of targeting people who are happy and successful in their current jobs prompted it to carefully study this population to understand the nature of their hobbies, when they look for work, whose recommendations they trust regarding a new position, and so forth. Drawing from its research, Cisco relies heavily on the Internet as a recruiting source and supplements this with newspaper advertisements listing the company's Internet address.[2]

Many organizations discount the importance of strategically thinking about "where" to source applicants. Instead, they post the same job advertisement with the same recruiting source they have used for years. Other organizations see their applicant sourcing practices and strategies as a source of competitive advantage, and are reluctant to even talk about them. Genentech identifies targeted candidates early in their campus careers and builds relationships with them throughout their college years.[3] In this chapter, we first explain what sourcing is and what makes a recruiting source effective. We also describe several alternative recruiting sources. Then, we describe how to create a sourcing plan and how to source from nontraditional applicant pools, and discuss global sourcing and geographic targeting. After reading this chapter, you will have a good understanding of the important role sourcing plays in the strategic staffing process, and you will know how to identify good strategic recruiting sources for any job.

WHAT IS SOURCING?

Marketing professionals try to understand who is likely to be interested in purchasing their products and where to find these people. Sourcing professionals do the same thing, but with jobs rather than products. As you learned in Chapter 1, sourcing is a part of the recruiting process. It is done for internal as well as external job candidates, and involves analyzing different possible sources of recruits to identify those best able to meet the firm's staffing goals. For firms that rely on promotions to fill leadership positions, sourcing also affects the quality and depth of a company's future leadership talent. Because the company is likely to have a much better idea of what type of person is the best fit with its needs, it makes sense for the company to identify and reach out to these targeted recruits rather than post a job advertisement and hope that the right people self-select themselves into consideration for the position.

Sourcing strategies differ for different types of recruits. Companies generally find professional employees, including lawyers, doctors, and engineers, differently than they do customer service, manufacturing, or skilled labor workers. Sourcing strategies also differ for recruits who are active as opposed to passive job seekers. **Active job seekers** need a job and are actively looking for information about job openings. Traditional job advertising is usually sufficient to reach these people although the overall quality of this labor market may not be high. **Semi-passive job seekers** are interested in a new position but only occasionally look actively for one. Finding these people requires more proactive and strategic efforts because they are not regularly looking for job information. More high-quality candidates are in this labor market. **Passive job seekers** are currently employed and are not actively seeking another job but could be tempted by the right opportunity. Many high-quality candidates are usually in this group although it can be difficult to find them and interest them in your job opportunity. Because they are not actively seeking out information about other jobs, identifying passive job seekers requires a proactive and strategic effort.

Microsoft sourcers spend about 5 percent of their time on active candidate identification, and 95 percent of their time on passive talent identification.[4] Because semi-passive and passive job seekers are not actively looking at traditional recruitment sources, such as newspaper ads, sourcing is most important for organizations focused on identifying and pursuing them.

Different recruiting sources are good at different things. Next, we discuss what makes a recruiting source more or less effective.

WHAT MAKES A RECRUITING SOURCE EFFECTIVE?

A recruiting source is effective if it helps a company meet its staffing goals for the position being filled. The firm's staffing goals might include speed, cost, and candidate and new hire quality. Given the goal of hiring high-potential employees able to perform well and contribute to a business's strategy execution, attending to the *quality* of the applicant pool is at least as important as attending to the *quantity* of applicants. It doesn't matter how many people apply to an organization if none of them meet the minimum hiring requirements. If the only applicant for a job opening is a perfect fit, accepts the job offer, and performs well, then the sourcing and hiring effort must be considered successful.

Different sources of employees have different strengths. Some sources are:

- Faster
- Cheaper
- Better at acquiring people who fit the corporate culture and work processes
- Better at acquiring high-quality people
- Better at acquiring people more likely to stay with the organization for a long time
- Better at acquiring people with previous work experience
- Better at generating large numbers of hires
- Better at generating professional hires
- Better for long-term needs
- Better for hiring in noncore competency areas of the company
- Better for finding diverse applicants
- Better for finding people not actively looking for a job.

Because recruiting sources differ in their strengths and weaknesses,[5] and because recruiting sources are not equally effective for all positions, it is best to be familiar with a variety of techniques and approaches. Effectively managing your talent supply chain often requires the flexible use of multiple sources and combinations of sources. Many different recruiting sources exist, each with different strengths and weaknesses. Next, we discuss various recruiting sources and how to use each of them.

WHAT RECRUITING SOURCES EXIST?

Recruiting sources can be thought of as being either internal or external to the company. **Internal recruiting sources** locate people who currently work for the company who would be good recruits for other positions. **External recruiting sources** target people outside the firm. Table 6–1 summarizes some of the most common internal and external recruiting sources.

active job seekers
people who need a job and are actively looking for information about job openings

semi-passive job seekers
people who are interested in a new position but only occasionally look actively for one

passive job seekers
people who are currently employed and are not actively seeking another job but could be tempted by the right opportunity

internal recruiting sources
locate people who currently work for the company who would be good recruits for other positions

external recruiting sources
target people outside the firm

TABLE 6–1	Internal and External Recruiting Sources

Internal Recruiting Sources	**External Recruiting Sources**
• Succession management	• Employee referrals
• Talent inventories	• In-house recruiters
• Employee development	• Written advertisements
• Internal job posting systems	• Job and trade fairs
• Employee referrals	• Observation
	• Résumé databases
	• Career sites
	• Online job boards
	• Search firms
	• Professional associations
	• State employment agencies
	• Military transition services
	• Acquisitions and mergers
	• Raiding competitors
	• Internet data mining
	• Networking
	• Schools
	• Previous employees
	• Non-U.S. citizens
	• Walk-ins
	• Creative sourcing

Both internal and external sourcing have strengths and limitations. Internal candidates who don't get promoted may get discouraged and leave the firm, making it critical to discuss with unsuccessful internal job candidates the reasons why they did not get the jobs they were applying for and what they can do to be more successful in the future. A firm that relies on internal sourcing also runs the risk of limiting new ideas and insights. External candidates may be more likely than insiders to see challenges and opportunities in a new way and to bring fresh ideas to the company. External sourcing usually takes longer than internal sourcing and costs more as well.

Internal Recruiting Sources

Internal sourcing often lies at the core of an organization's staffing system. Current employees are usually considered first when a job becomes available, particularly for firms whose talent philosophy supports promotion from within. As we have explained, the skills and talents of internal recruits are better known than external hires. Because current employees can hit the ground running once hired for other positions, many firms first try internal recruiting sources to fill a position, and look outside the firm only if a suitable internal candidate cannot be found.

Succession management, talent inventories, employee development, and internal job posting systems are common internal recruiting sources. Next, we discuss each.

succession management

the ongoing process of recruiting, evaluating, developing, and preparing employees to assume other positions in the firm in the future

SUCCESSION MANAGEMENT **Succession management** is the ongoing process of recruiting, evaluating, developing, and preparing employees to assume other positions in the firm in the future. The goal of succession management is to enhance the firm's bench strength of talent to ensure an ongoing supply of highly qualified people for key jobs. Succession management is grounded in the organization's long-term business strategy and objectives and focuses on addressing employees' developmental needs to prepare them to assume leadership and other key positions in the future. Ideally, at least one current employee is always ready and available to assume every key position in a firm if it should open up.

Obviously, not having the right talent in place can compromise a firm's ability to continue performing if key people leave. It takes time to recruit, hire, and train a replacement, and even longer for the new hire to perform fully in the job. Facing the imminent retirement of baby boomers, increased demands for diversity, and fierce competition for talent, many organizations are using succession management systems to enhance their internal labor supply chains. For example, PanCanadian Energy (now EnCana) looks across the organization for high-potential employees who it can prepare to assume leadership positions in the future.[6] Firms whose staffing strategies involve internal development are likely to use succession management to plan future employee moves and identify employee development opportunities. Succession management will be covered in more detail in Chapter 10.

TALENT INVENTORIES   As discussed in Chapter 5, talent inventories are manual or computerized records of employees' past performances, education and experience, promotability, languages spoken, career interests, and so on. Employees and their managers can be jointly responsible for updating and ensuring the accuracy of the inventories, which help identify employees who are ready and available for promotion or transfer. If they are kept accurate and updated, talent inventories can be a very effective way to quickly and cheaply source qualified internal candidates who can then be contacted to determine their interest in the opportunity. However, if the talent inventories do not contain all of the relevant skills, experiences, talents, and so forth that a company's employees have, some qualified internal candidates will be overlooked.

EMPLOYEE DEVELOPMENT   Employee development is the training of employees to extend their capabilities and prepare them to assume other jobs and roles in the firm. Companies like GE and IBM regularly use developmental activities and assignments to ensure their employees' skills match the organization's needs, and to increase the supply of internal talent available to the company in the future. By tracking employees' performance in these development activities and updating employees' qualifications inventories with their new talents, it is possible to quickly identify which employees have the potential to fill various positions throughout the company.

    Leadership development programs are designed to improve employees' leadership skills. Companies that utilize leadership development programs include Johnson & Johnson, L'Oréal, Raytheon, and GE. These firms use rotational programs that give participants the opportunity to work in a variety of areas. Many firms include training, coaching, developmental project assignments, and mentoring as part of their leadership development programs. Dow Chemical is one of these companies. Dow uses employee development activities including mentoring, coaching, on-the-job learning, and both Web- and university-based training programs to identify and develop promising internal talent. Eli Lilly's developmental tools include individualized developmental plans, 360-degree feedback, job rotation, and a formal mentoring program.[7]

employee development
the training of employees to extend their capabilities and prepare them to assume other jobs and roles in the firm

leadership development programs
a specific type of employee development that develops the leadership skills of employees seen as having leadership potential

INTERNAL JOB POSTING SYSTEMS   Many companies rely on employees to "self-nominate" themselves for openings based on their interest in and perceived fit with other positions in the firm. **Internal job posting systems** publicize open jobs to employees. A posting describes the job's qualifications and requirements as well as information about the work itself, often on the company's intranet or on a bulletin board. An employee wishing to apply for another job in the firm can bid on the job and express their interest in being considered. Then, human resources typically reviews the internal bidder's candidacy and personnel file to confirm that he or she meets the requirements of the vacancy, and the employee is contacted if he or she is considered for the open position.

    Internal job posting systems allow employees to apply for positions they are interested in, reducing the possibility of overlooking qualified internal talent. Internal job posting systems are relatively fast and very inexpensive to use but may miss some qualified recruits because not all qualified employees may look at the postings. Many firms use a combination of internal job postings and qualifications inventories to reduce the chances of missing a qualified internal candidate.

internal job posting systems
systems that publicize a firm's open jobs to the company's employees

EMPLOYEE REFERRALS   Employee referrals involve asking employees to refer coworkers for open positions. Because people are often aware of the talents and career aspirations of their colleagues, and are familiar with their coworkers' job performance and work habits, they can help identify promising internal talent.

    Silicon Valley–based communications product and service provider Aricent's dedicated five-person employee referral team guarantees action within 72 hours of a referral submission.

employee referrals
a practice by which current employees identify and refer promising recruits

Its help desk also guarantees a response to all inquiries within eight hours. Referral program representatives attend employee meetings, social gatherings, workstations, etc., to educate employees about the program and solicit on-the-spot referrals. It also distributes a calendar to keep employees aware of projected needs and events, and at some events it even provides on-the-spot rewards to solicit referrals.[8]

When global consulting firm Accenture realized that the wording it used in job requisitions and postings was much more formal than the language used in day-to-day conversation, it changed it to be more consistent with how friends or colleagues would discuss a role or the company. This made it easier for employees to assess whether they knew anyone who might fit the position. It also lets referring employees monitor the status of their referrals via e-mails, text messages, and RSS feeds.[9] Accenture makes 34 percent of its hires through employee referrals, and estimates it saves over $700,000 in recruiting costs because of the program.[10]

External Recruiting Sources

At some point, all organizations rely on external recruiting sources to bring in needed talent. If a firm is growing or if it lacks needed talent internally, external sourcing can identify high-potential recruits outside the firm. Firms also bring in experienced people to acquire the expertise they need to launch new businesses or to expand into new markets. Next, we discuss a variety of common external recruiting sources and how to use them most effectively.

EMPLOYEE REFERRALS   Asking your best talent to recommend the best people they've worked with in the past or people they feel would be good performers can generate high-quality leads. At Cognizant Technology Solutions in Teaneck, New Jersey, employee referrals account for more than 40 percent of the company's new software engineers and MBA graduates with six to eight years' work experience. Cognizant believes that referral hires remain longer and are a good fit compared to fresh recruits. Referring employees are rewarded with cash or reimbursements for external training after the new hire has successfully completed training.[11] Thomas A. Morelli, vice president of human resources for Solectron, comments, "Around the world, our current employees are our best recruiting source. They understand the soul and spirit of the company."[12]

Not all firms allow nepotism—that is, allow multiple family members to be hired by the firm. However, as part of their referral program, many companies do. James Coblin, Nucor Steel's general manager of personnel services, agrees: "People ask us, 'Do you hire families?' We hire entire clans. We've got brothers, sisters, cousins, husbands, wives."[13] Southwest Airlines actively encourages nepotism and asks employees to recommend family members who might make good employees. The only rule is that one family member can't supervise another.[14]

Referral programs can be an effective way to acquire the names of high-quality potential applicants. Because they are putting their own reputations on the line and because the people they refer will be coworkers, employees generally provide accurate information about the people they refer.[15] Moreover, because they have spoken with people who work at the company, employees hired via referrals are likely to have a more realistic picture of what working at the firm is like.[16]

Employees need to believe the company is a good place to work, or they are not likely to recommend the employer to others. Also, it should be noted that people tend to know and, therefore, refer people who are like themselves. This can result in a firm being relatively homogeneous. Groups underrepresented at a particular company (e.g., women and minorities) could be adversely affected by a heavy reliance on word-of-mouth recruiting, as a result.[17]

Employee referral programs tend to be relatively inexpensive, although some organizations reward employees quite generously for making successful referrals. However, the practice can be relatively fast. Research shows that employees who have been referred have lower turnover early in their tenure with the firm[18] and are better performers.[19]

According to one expert, an excellent internal or external referral program has the following design features:[20]

1. The on-the-job performance of referrals is tracked, and a bonus is given if the employee is rated as a top performer.
2. Referrals for key positions are accepted regardless of whether there is a current opening.
3. Hiring managers have direct access to the candidate referral database.

4. Referrals are proactively sought from the employees most likely to know a top performer.
5. Drawings and contests for prizes are held and guaranteed bonuses given for every hired referral, with the reward varying depending on how critical the job is.
6. New hires in key positions are asked for referrals on their first day on the job.
7. There is an appeal process for individuals who feel they were unfairly denied a referral bonus.

IN-HOUSE SOURCERS Some organizations hire their own **in-house sourcers**—people who rely on their own contacts and research and the organization's database of potential applicants to find recruits. In-house sourcers have a great deal of experience in the fields in which they work and may develop relationships with promising talent to keep them in the pipeline as potential future recruits. In-house sourcers are useful at developing and maintaining a talent pipeline, and their in-depth knowledge of the firm's culture and business strategy can help them generate quality leads. Ernst & Young, Microsoft, Google, and Johnson & Johnson have employees dedicated to sourcing talent. Figure 6–1 shows a Becton Dickinson & Company job posting for such a position.

in-house sourcers
employees who rely on their own contacts and research and the organization's database of potential applicants to source potential recruits

WRITTEN ADVERTISEMENTS Written job advertisements in newspapers, magazines, trade journals, or other printed materials are a good way to attract active job seekers. The ads can also identify some semi-passive job seekers if they are placed outside of the traditional "help wanted" section in newspapers and appear in trade journals instead. Many firms still rely heavily on written advertisements.

For example, skyrocketing demand for Silly Bandz, the fun shaped silicone-rubber bracelets, quickly increased the company's need for new employees. The company effectively recruited people through Craigslist job advertisements to find people to help with ordering, maintaining the Web site, and shipping.[21] Table 6–2 gives some experts' advice on creating effective written job advertisements.

Figure 6–2 shows an example of a more effective and a less effective written job advertisement. The ad on the left is difficult to read, does not stress what is unique or desirable about the bank or present an employer brand, and would not be as effective as the ad on the right is in capturing a reader's attention or persuading them to apply. The ad on the right presents a clear employer brand and value proposition, is easy to read, and gets the reader involved.

Becton Dickinson & Company (BD)—Franklin Lakes, NJ
We are seeking a Recruitment Sourcing Specialist to proactively identify and recruit top talent in a highly competitive employment marketplace. As a Recruitment Sourcing Specialist, you will use your expertise to generate significant pipelines of passive candidates. You will identify, evaluate, and manage proactive sourcing plans, position specific sourcing strategies, initiatives, and tactics including Internet job boards, database mining, referrals, ad response, professional outreach, agencies, and advanced sourcing techniques. You will also maintain the applicant tracking system to ensure data integrity.

You must be a team player with the ability to handle a high volume of sourcing in a fast-paced environment. You will source, and will be responsible for identifying and assessing candidate experiences and skills against critical business needs and core competencies. You will work with all levels of our organization.

Requirements:
    Sources candidates from both internal and external sources.
    Screens candidates for open positions.
    Knowledge of Microsoft Word, Excel, Lotus Notes.
    Proficient in Applicant Tracking Systems such as Taleo, Brassring, or something comparable.
    Knowledge/Experience with major job search engines.
    Experience in sourcing for research and development positions and engineers a strong plus.

Educational Requirements:
BA/BS or equivalent experience

FIGURE 6–1 An Example of a Job Posting for an In-House Sourcer
Source: Reprinted with permission of Becton, Dickinson and Company.

TABLE 6–2	Tips for Creating Effective Written Job Advertisements[22]

The best techniques for writing effective recruitment ads are the same as for other forms of advertising. The job is your product; the readers of the ad are your potential customers. Recruitment ads should follow the AIDA selling format: *Attention, Interest, Desire, and Action*. Good job advertisements must:

- Draw *attention* (from appropriate job seekers).
- Attract relevant *interest* (by establishing relevance in the minds of the ideal candidates).
- Create *desire* (to pursue what looks like a great opportunity).
- Provide a clear instruction for the next *action* or response (contact information).

Writing tips:

- *Use one simple, relevant, and clear headline.* An obvious headline is the job title itself, as this is what people will be looking for. If a different headline is used, have it speak to the job seeker directly. If the organization has a good reputation, display the name prominently.
- *Try to incorporate something innovative, exciting, or challenging.* People are attracted to new things—either in the company or the role. Stress what is unique and special about the job and organization. People want to work for special employers, not boring, ordinary organizations.
- *Get the reader involved.* Refer to the reader as *you* or use the command voice with an implied *you*—as in "Join Our Team." This helps people visualize themselves in the job.
- *Make the ad easy to read.* Use simple language that your reader uses. Use short sentences. More than 15 words in a sentence reduces clarity. Seek out commas and *and*s, and replace them with full stops. Use bullet points and short, "bite-sized" paragraphs.

Common elements to include:

- The job's title and a brief outline of its duties
- The job's location
- The full-time, part-time, permanent, or temporary status of job
- The qualifications or experience required for the job
- The salary and benefits associated with the job
- Response information
- The firm's Web site address
- The firm's corporate brand
- The firm's accreditations or awards
- An EOE statement

Things to avoid:

- All capital letters (this actually decreases readability)
- Too much technical detail about the job or the company
- Too many words or complex language
- Too much focus on the company and not enough on the job seeker

Source: Reprinted with permission from Mary Pomerantz Advertising.

job fairs
sourcing and recruiting events at which multiple employers and recruits meet with each other to discuss employment opportunities

trade fairs
events that gather people from a particular industry to learn about current topics and products in their field

JOB AND TRADE FAIRS   **Job fairs** are sourcing and recruiting events at which multiple employers and recruits meet with each other to discuss employment opportunities. They are common on college campuses. Some cities host them to help match residents with local jobs. Job fairs can be targeted to specific industries or have employers from multiple industries. They can be an effective way to source recruits, but it is important to ensure that the people who will attend the job fair are appropriately qualified.

Job fairs can take place on the Internet as well. Employers can post banner advertisements in a common area. Participants who are interested in learning more about an employer can click the banner and are sent to the firm's virtual area, which contains company literature, descriptions of open positions, and electronic applications. Online career fairs usually run for a limited time to allow potential employers to gather as many inquiries and applications as possible in a short period.[23] Online job fairs tend to be best for contacting active and semi-passive job seekers.

Trade fairs gather people from a particular industry to learn about current topics and products in their field. Attendees are usually their companies' top salespeople, managers, researchers, and technical experts who are sent by their firms to learn about innovations and products in their industry as well as to sell their firms' products. The people attending a trade fair are usually passive or semi-passive job seekers, and their skill levels tend to be higher and more consistent than people attending job fairs.

Big Guy Bank, Inc.

New Jersey's Largest Bank

LARGEST LOAN PORTFOLIO – MOST STATEWIDE BRANCHES – MOST CORPORATE ACCOUNTS

Founded by the Williams brothers in 1936, Big Guy Bank, Inc. has a long history of innovative products and services and commitment to the communities we serve. Since our merger with Jersey First Bancorp in 1967, we have consistently been the largest banking network in the state. Although we have grown in size, we have not forgotten about the small businesses and local communities that form the core of our business. We have also received numerous awards, including: the New Jersey's Favorite Bank Award, the Best Places to Bank in NJ Award, the NJ Fiduciary Responsibility Award, and being named one of America's Top Twenty Banks by the US Banker's Press in 2007.

We currently have openings for:

F/T Loan Officers – Will originate investment quality loans through sales of bank products and services to realtors, builders, homebuyers and others. Responsibilities include: maintaining an understanding of bank products and services, building client relationships with realtors and developers through sales calls and other means, and counseling and pre-qualifying potential home buyers by assembling complete applications and support documentation. Must also negotiate terms and conditions of loans with mortgagors and monitor loan status and ensure conformity with terms. Candidate must stay abreast of trends, rules and regulations in the mortgage market. Requirements include: 2+ years loan officer experience and knowledge of various mortgage lending programs, standard loan products, and underwriting guidelines. Must also have strong Math, accounting, problem solving, and Excel skills.

P/T & F/T Tellers – Duties include selling bank products, processing transactions, and providing superior customer service in a customer oriented, fast-paced professional environment. HS diploma or GED and excellent Math, communication, interpersonal, computer and multi-tasking skills are required; banking experience is preferred. Schedule is flexible but will include some Saturday hours.

P/T Security Guards – Requirements include: HS diploma or GED, successful criminal background check and drug test, good verbal communication and interpersonal skills, and reliable transportation. LTC Class "A" permit and bank security experience is a plus.

Our benefits include: great salaries, free parking, free checking, and comprehensive medical, dental, and vision benefits.

Please send your resume to: John McMurray, Senior New Jersey Recruiter, Human Resources Deparment, Big Guy Bank, Inc., 183 East Maple Lane, Edison, NJ 08837.

For detailed job descriptions and to apply online, visit our website at: www.bigguybanking.com

EOE

BIG GUY BANK, INC.
We're Really, Really Big.

FIGURE 6–2 More Effective and Less Effective Written Job Advertisements

Source: Reprinted with permission from Mary Pomerantz Advertising.

OBSERVATION Observation involves watching people working in similar jobs for other companies to evaluate their potential fit with your organization. One of Nucor Steel's best sources of new steelworkers is the construction workers who build its plants. As managers monitor their construction sites, they also look for workers who demonstrate the work habits they value, and then hire them.[24]

FirstMerit Bank's sourcing strategy for retail positions is founded on the idea that you can't hide great performers in customer-facing positions. To identify and assess potential recruits for its retail bank positions, FirstMerit routinely sends recruiters to visit nonbank retail stores to identify good customer service performers. The bank also sends recruiters to other banks, where they open bank accounts and note whether the people opening the accounts follow up when they say they will.[25] It is important to carefully consider the ethics of engaging in behaviors that cost the other firm money (e.g., the salesperson's or new account representative's time), but many organizations do visit other companies simply to observe and try to identify promising recruits.

RÉSUMÉ DATABASES Résumé databases are searchable collections of prescreened résumés submitted to the company. Many firms maintain a database of promising candidates who were not hired for other jobs or who were generated from continuous recruiting efforts. When a job becomes available, this often proves to be a promising source of candidates who have been preliminarily screened and perhaps thoroughly evaluated for other jobs. Microsoft is a good example of a company that does this. When Microsoft began reaching out to all the candidates in its résumé database—candidates who had previously declined job offers or interviews—to see if they would be interested in discussing opportunities with the firm again, the company's recruiters found that the majority of people were, indeed, interested. This initiative was so successful that it became one of Microsoft's core sourcing strategies.[26]

observation
watching people working in similar jobs for other companies to evaluate their potential fit with your organization

résumé databases
searchable collections of prescreened résumés submitted to the company

career sites
pages on an organization's Web site devoted to jobs and careers within the company

CAREER SITES   **Career sites** are pages on an organization's Web site devoted to jobs and careers within the company. Easy to find links to the career site are often placed on the other pages of the company's Web site. Career sites help current customers and people interested in the company easily learn about what it is like to work for the company, what job openings exist, and how to apply. Some organizations use multiple recruiting sources but require all applicants to apply through their career sites. This makes it easy to assemble a database of all applicants. Although the high volume of responses to a job posting on a career site can be problematic, many firms use applicant questionnaires and brief assessment tools to prescreen applicants and reduce the size of the resulting applicant pool.

Career sites are also very cost-effective, and allow an organization to communicate a lot of information about its values, philosophy, and job requirements to potential applicants. This, in turn, allows them to "self-select" out of the process if they don't feel they are a good fit for the jobs they are applying for. Enterprise Rent-A-Car's career site (www.enterprisealive.com) and Federated Department Stores's site (www.retailogy.com) are excellent examples of how companies are using career sites to source recruits. Federated invests a lot in its career sites. So do Bloomingdales (www.bloomingdalesjobs.com) and Macy's (www.macysjobs.com). The companies' recruiters say their data show that the sites are their most cost-effective and productive recruiting sources.[27]

Internet job boards
Internet sites that allow employers to post jobs and job seekers to post résumés and use a search engine to find one another

INTERNET JOB BOARDS   **Internet job boards** are Internet sites that allow employers to post jobs and job seekers to post résumés and use a search engine to find one another. Job boards are used for both sourcing and recruiting applicants. Sourcing is done by searching the job boards to find qualified people who posted résumés.

Both general (e.g., Jobs.com and Monster.com) and specialty job boards (e.g., Nursing jobs.org, BioSpace.com, and ComputerJobs.com) help employers source promising recruits by searching the résumés that potential applicants have posted. Table 6–3 lists some popular Internet job boards used to source recruits.

search firms
independent companies that specialize in the recruitment and placement of particular types of talent

SEARCH FIRMS   **Search firms** or "headhunters" are independent companies that specialize in the recruitment and placement of particular types of talent. *Contingency firms* present their candidates to a number of organizations and charge a fee when one of them starts the job. Their fee is contingent upon making a successful placement. *Retainer firms* charge employers a fixed fee in advance of the placement. Retainer firms are usually used for senior-management level and technical jobs that need more aggressive sourcing and recruitment methods to identify and generate candidates.

When choosing a search firm, it is important to research the firms being considered and the qualifications of the people who will be doing the work. If you are a recruiter, you should speak with former clients of the search firm to identify their strengths and weaknesses. Find out how quality-oriented the search firm is and what recruiting sources will be targeted and why. Learn when you should expect to see candidates, what form of status reports will be provided to you and when. Find out if the firm will narrow its leads to the list of candidates they actually assess,

---

TABLE 6–3   Internet Sourcing Web Sites

www.jigsaw.com—an online business contact marketplace where marketers, recruiters, and salespeople can buy, sell, and trade business contact information.
www.jobster.com—a place where candidates send information about job openings to their contacts, who forward, recommend, and can even inquire themselves about the positions.
www.monster.com—one of the largest online searchable résumé databases.
www.linkedin.com—users activate links to people they know, which allows them to access information about the people their contacts know; contacts can be asked to introduce a user to someone they don't know (www.linkedin.com/hiring).
www.datafrenzy.com—a "résumé aggregate manager" that searches multiple job boards and a firm's own résumé database for résumés and automatically uploads them into a sortable database.
www.hirediversity.com, www.minorityjobs.net, www.gaywork.com—Web sites that specialize in diversity hiring.

and how they will identify the finalists sent to the company. Also, establish what happens if you are not satisfied with the candidates the search firm presents and/or if the new hire leaves within a short period of time.

In addition, ask about the search firm's placement and retention rate to see if the search firm's previous performance matches your company's needs. Find out if the firm is a member of the Association of Executive Search Consultants, a worldwide professional association for the retained executive search industry. If a search firm is not a member of the organization, ask if it is familiar with the AESC Code of Ethics and if they are willing to abide by it.

Some search firms focus on "raiding" high-ranking talent whose career paths are cut off at their current companies. Targeting the number two or three person on a successful project and offering them a chance for a job with greater responsibility can actually be an effective way to source talent. This practice is known as the "pull-up hire." Search firms often keep files on the bench strength at various organizations, looking for frustrated stars.[28] Because their networks are often very extensive, search firms can tap into a broader pool of talent than smaller or midsize firms. Search firms are not necessarily fast or cheap, but they can greatly improve the quantity and quality of a firm's applicant pool.

PROFESSIONAL ASSOCIATIONS Professionals can often be found through the professional associations to which they belong. The Institute of Electrical and Electronics Engineers Inc. (IEEE) and the American Marketing Association are good examples of professional associations that provide job placement services to their members, including searchable résumé databases on their Web sites. Professional associations often prescreen their members for appropriate credentials, making them a good source of prequalified recruits in that profession. Most professional associations also host conferences for their members, which can be a great way to identify and network with promising leads.

STATE EMPLOYMENT AGENCIES The U.S. Employment Service and affiliated state employment agencies serve both employers and job seekers. State employment agency services can provide outreach, interviewing, counseling, testing, and training to better prepare job seekers for employment. Specialized services for veterans, people with disabilities, youths between the ages of 16 and 22, and older workers also exist.

MILITARY TRANSITION SERVICES Military transition services, such as the Army Career and Alumni Program, give employers access to an extensively trained, diversified group of separating professional and semiprofessional military members, veterans, and family members. The service serves the lowest ranked enlisted members through general officers and provides a Web site (www.acap.army.mil) that allows employers to advertise job vacancies. The service has helped many employers hire highly qualified personnel ranging from skilled mechanics to junior executives. These can also be good sources of hires for people with disabilities who are fully capable of performing difficult and hard-to-fill positions.

ACQUISITIONS AND MERGERS Some firms acquire, or merge, with other companies to acquire their talent, rather than for their products or services. For example, it is not uncommon for big companies to acquire small companies with talented employees and then redeploy them. Rather than wanting the company as a whole, they are acquiring the people and their potential. This is obviously an expensive strategy and not appropriate for an immediate hiring need, but it has been an effective sourcing strategy for pharmaceutical firms and firms such as Microsoft.

RAIDING COMPETITORS **Raiding competitors**, or "poaching," is the practice of hiring top talent away from competitors. Although this can create a vicious cycle of firms within an industry continuously poaching talent from each other, it can be a source of well-trained talent with relevant experience and a proven performance record. Raiding talent is often frowned upon and seen as unethical, and some industries have an informal agreement to not raid each other's talent. Nonetheless, during talent shortages, poaching may become more common. For example, in 2006, when quality oil executives were in short supply, the oil company BP Plc hired a refinery manager from Royal Dutch Shell Plc to run its troubled Texas City plant. This broke an oil industry taboo against "poaching" employees from one's competitors.[29]

raiding competitors
the practice of hiring top talent away from competitors

Poaching outside executives is sometimes seen as a less risky alternative to acquiring an entire company. When AT&T wanted to enter the computer systems integration business, it was concerned about incorporating an entire company into its culture. Instead, AT&T had its recruiters locate the top 50 system integrators in the country. AT&T hired them and started its own systems integration business.[30] When hiring an employee from a rival company, it is important to ensure that the person is not bound by a nondisclosure or noncompete agreement.

Hiring a competitor's top performers does not guarantee that they will perform as well in your company.[31] Differences in culture, business strategy, and coworker skills influence performance and don't move with the employee. In one case, an insurance adjustor moved from a company focused on low costs to one focused on providing high-end insurance with a strong emphasis on customer service. The adjustor couldn't keep himself from "nickel and diming" customers on their claims, even though that behavior was in stark contrast with his new firm's culture and strategy.[32]

Internet data mining

searching the Internet to locate passive job seekers with the characteristics and qualifications needed for a position

Boolean searches

an Internet search technique that allows a search to be narrowed by using special terms before the key words

INTERNET DATA MINING   Some companies have found that over time, the same active job seekers often respond to newspaper ads, job postings on career Web sites, and Internet job boards, and that these methods often fail to attract sufficient numbers of qualified job seekers. **Internet data mining** involves searching the Internet to locate semi-passive and passive job seekers with the characteristics and qualifications needed for a position. Recruiters then try to convert these leads into applicants. In addition to scanning online chat rooms and newsgroups for promising recruits, three techniques for Internet data mining are Boolean searches, flip searching, and using Web crawlers. We discuss each of these next.

Résumés and promising recruiting leads can be identified through the use of complex **Boolean searches**, an Internet search technique that allows a search to be narrowed by using special terms before the key words. Boolean searches allow the inclusion or exclusion of documents containing certain words through the use of operators such as AND, NOT, and OR. Although some Internet search engines do not support this type of searching, Google, AltaVista, and Yahoo do. The syntax may need to be altered for the different search engines. For example, on Google, you might use:

> site:LinkedIn.com ("web designer" or "graphic designer") Chicago and not (eoe)

Whereas on Yahoo you might use:

> site:LinkedIn.com ("web designer" or "graphic designer") Chicago−eoe

One major pharmaceutical company had a very difficult time sourcing doctors until it started using Boolean searching—with Boolean searching it became one of their easiest positions to source. This chapter's Develop Your Skills feature shows how to conduct this type of search.

DEVELOP YOUR SKILLS
Conducting Boolean Searches on the Internet

If you are interested in developing your staffing skills, online courses are available in using Boolean searches to find passive recruits (see www.recruiting-online.com). Some companies offer even more comprehensive in-person and Web-based training and certification on active, Web-based sourcing strategies (see www.airsdirectory.com). Here is an example of how to use the Boolean technique to find Web designers located in the Chicago, Illinois, area able to use JavaScript.

1. Go to www.google.com
2. In the search box, type: site:LinkedIn.com (web designer or graphic designer) (San Francisco) and not (EOE).

The first part of the Boolean search string requests pages in the social networking site LinkedIn.com. The next part requests the skills "web designer" or "graphic designer" (each must be enclosed in quotation marks so it's recognized as a phrase). The last part of the request specifies the San Francisco area and screens out job postings (which typically contain "EOE"). Boolean search syntax is precise. If you encounter problems, check for spelling or punctuation errors and/or missing or extra spaces. Varying search terms with words and phrases job candidates are likely to use can further improve your results.

Some Web sites make this process even easier. Go to www.search4candidates.com and enter your search using key words like "retail sales" and "Atlanta." Then use the "Refine results" section offered on the results page to search specific sites like LinkedIn, Zoominfo, Jobster, Xing, and others.

As the Internet has evolved and privacy concerns have escalated, fewer people are willing to put their résumé, telephone number, or contact information online. Instead, many people are using social networking sites like LinkedIn.com or Facebook to network and look for jobs.

X-raying searches for pages that are all on the same host (like LinkedIn). Putting "site:linkedin.com" or "site:facebook.com" or "site:myspace.com" at the beginning of your Boolean search string limits your results to those on that site (e.g., try "site:linkedin.com (retail or clothing) (sales or professional) (Seattle)" (without the parentheses) to find retail sales professionals in Seattle who are on LinkedIn).

x-raying
searching for pages that are all on the same host site

Flip searching, or *flipping*, identifies people who link to a specific Internet site. If you can identify a Web site often visited by desired recruits, identifying pages that link to the site can identify some of their résumés and personal Web pages. Flipping can be done with some of the major search engines, including Yahoo.com and AltaVista.com.

flip searching
finding people who link to a specific Internet site

If a company is looking for an industrial-organizational psychologist to develop a new employee selection system, this technique can find the various sites and people that link to SIOP.org, the professional association of industrial-organizational psychologists. To do the search, visit a search engine such as Yahoo.com and enter "link:siop.org NY consultant" or "linkdomain:siop.org NY consultant." This searches for possible consultants in the New York area. Scroll through the results to find individual Web pages and résumés. The technique can be used in a variety of ways, including to identify people who currently or previously worked for a competitor. Creating longer Boolean search strings can further streamline the search, and performing the searches on various search engines will give different results.

Recruiters face some ethical issues when they conduct flip searches because the searches can pull up company directories, e-mail lists, and other company related information. In fact, it is sometimes possible to flip search yourself into a company's internal intranet or restricted areas, which is private information and clearly unethical to hack into. Visitors leave an electronic footprint on every page and site visited so intrusions are likely to be noticed. Flip searching has its fans and critics, but clearly all companies should be careful about what content appears on their site.

Web crawlers are Web sites that continually search the Web for information about people with desirable talents and sell access to their database of potential recruits. Some Web sites have capitalized on companies' growing interest in reaching out to more passive job seekers by compiling publicly available information about them—especially company executives and people with in-demand talents. One such firm, ZoomInfo (formerly Eliyon Technologies) continuously searches more than 15 million Web sites for information and sells this information to recruiters. ZoomInfo "reads" news articles, press releases, company Web pages, and SEC fillings, recognizing company and business professional data. In seconds, subscribers can search the over 20 million ZoomInfo profiles and locate top people in U.S. companies, including more than 11 million scientists, engineers, and other professionals. Because ZoomInfo copies Web pages permanently to its database, no link goes dead and both positive and negative information might be accessible forever.[33] Because it helps to identify passive job seekers and provides information on potential candidate's accomplishments, companies such as Merrill Lynch use ZoomInfo for searches for their executive-level candidates.

Web crawlers
Web sites that continually search the Web for information about people with desirable talents and sell access to their database of potential recruits

NETWORKING   **Networking** is the process of leveraging your personal connections to generate applicants. Similar to employee referrals, asking good people who don't work for you for the names of other good people can generate promising recruiting leads.

Networking
the process of leveraging your personal connections to generate applicants

Internet sites like LinkedIn.com, Ryze.com, Tribe.net, Facebook.com, and Spoke.com facilitate sourcing via networking. When a person joins an Internet social networking site, he or she creates a profile that helps him or her find and be found by others. A person's network consists of his or her connections, his or her connections' connections, etc., linking them to thousands of people. To illustrate the power of these connections, when Robert Croak, creator of Silly Bandz, was behind on a deadline, he put up a post on Facebook and 20 people arrived within one hour to help.[34] To contact someone, the information is entered on the social networking site, which checks the person's network to see how he or she connects to your target person. The site usually identifies a number of people who link to the target person, each of whom introduces the searcher to the next, along with an explanation of who he or she is and who he or she is trying to connect with. This gives job seekers a way to tap into broader networks and gives recruiters a way to reach potential recruits. Whenever an application is received, a recruiter can see which of the person's contacts knows people who have worked with the candidate and more easily check their references. Because users' profiles can be viewed by everyone, it is harder for applicants to misrepresent or inflate their credentials.[35] Another benefit of social networking technology is that it can increase the diversity of the talent pool accessible to recruiters. Although it can generate leads to more passive job candidates, social networking technology requires training and does not guarantee that the people identified will be interested in your job opportunity. It is also important to understand a site's privacy policy before searching for applicants or posting information there.

Osram Sylvania, the North American operation of one of the world's largest lighting manufacturers, fills hundreds of positions each year. To fuel its growth, it must be strategic and start filling its talent pipelines well in advance. The company has been very successful using LinkedIn to recruit for positions including chemical engineers. Because the notes associated with the profile for Osram's recruiter on the Web site indicate that she is always looking for chemical engineers, she receives inquiries from people who she would not normally be able to network with.[36] Because the candidates generated by social networking sites are often passive job seekers, the combination of high touch and high tech created by the social networking technology allows recruiters to source faster and gives candidates extra time to consider jobs.

Companies are also increasingly using the free social networking site Twitter.com to source recruits.[37] In addition to getting the word out quickly to targeted people, the message can get re-tweeted and reach an even wider audience. When one legal recruiter received an e-mail one morning that an insurance industry client needed 40 lawyers immediately for a big document review, she quickly sent a tweet to her 150 followers, which was re-twittered by legal blogs that follow her. She had 10 replies waiting for her at the office and filled every post by lunch. She says, "With job boards it takes a couple days before people look. But Twitter is immediate."[38]

Buzzwords can also be searched on Twitter to source recruits with specific skills or who live in a certain area (e.g., using hashtags like #jobs or #RKE for the Roanoke Virginia area). Using unique URLs (shortened to meet Twitter's 140 character maximum using sites like www.bit.ly) that link each open position to a page describing the application process, data can be obtained about who clicks through to job postings and where they are located.[39] Twitter's JobDeck and www.twitjobsearch.com are increasing job seekers' use of Twitter by making it easy to find tweets advertising job openings.

There are downsides to using Twitter, including the possibility that a job posting quickly goes viral on Twitter in a negative way. When using Twitter or any social media recruiting tool it is also important to prevent them from becoming a primary recruiting source for legal reasons as applicant diversity and legal discrimination risks may be negatively affected. Personal photographs on sites including Twitter and Facebook disclose the person's race, gender, age, disability, and possibly other protected categories that the firm otherwise would not have access to at this recruiting stage. Social networking sites also do not include the entire population and are often limited to certain social groups. For example, in 2009, only 5 percent of LinkedIn users were black and only 2 percent were Hispanic.[40] Social networking sites are also better for sourcing for technology-related positions due to the nature of the people using them.

SCHOOLS Colleges and universities are a common recruiting source for both graduates and interns. Companies often source from only a few universities for each job family, focusing on the programs whose graduates best meet the firm's needs. Microsoft tracks the schools from which its best workers come from.[41] Recruiting from a limited number of campuses also allows firms to develop a relationship with the university and its faculty, which can give it greater access to its students. Qualcomm funds labs and faculty research projects on targeted campuses, and has an on-campus ambassador program.[42] Some companies leverage this relationship by asking faculty members to pass along the names of the students who would be the best fits with the companies' needs. The National Association of Colleges and Employers' ethical guidelines for career service professionals and campus sourcers and recruiters, *Principles for Professional Conduct for Career Services and Employment Professionals*, is available online.[43]

Internships can also be an effective source of new hires. Employers get a good look at potential hires during their internships, and the interns get the opportunity to evaluate whether the company is a place they would like to work. Interns become the majority of new hires At J.P.

Morgan and Goldman Sachs.[44] A survey of more than 300 employers found that 30 percent of new college hires came from internship programs, and about 25 percent came from cooperative education programs.[45] Merrill Lynch gives three out of four summer interns a full-time job offer, sourcing them as early as their freshman year to build relationships sooner and increase the probability that it will be able to hire them.[46]

Some firms, including Lockheed Martin, Agilent Technologies, and Deloitte & Touche, have even begun sourcing future hires for hard-to-fill jobs in engineering, accounting, and other areas from high schools. Likewise, the accounting firm Deloitte spends more than $1 million a year sending employees to 45 different high schools to mentor students in how to run virtual businesses. The mentors teach the students the skills and work ethic they will need in the working world, and generate a pipeline of smart, motivated talent.[47] Supermarket chain H.E. Butt Grocery Co. sponsors programs including internships and formal training programs to introduce high school students to its job opportunities. CVS Pharmacy launched Pathways to Pharmacy to expose children from the inner city and rural areas to science and math. The program also trains them in job skills and encourages them to consider a pharmacy career.[48]

PREVIOUS EMPLOYEES   Some organizations make it a point to stay in touch with departing employees and try to rehire them later. Apple Computer and Starbucks did this when they rehired Steve Jobs and Howard Schultz, respectively, as their CEOs. After the September 11 terrorist attacks, the FBI faced a serious challenge when it tried to launch a worldwide investigation. More than 40 percent of its agents around the world had no more than five years on the job.

To regain the experience it would need, the FBI hired dozens of its retired agents on a contract basis as intelligence analysts and evidence examiners.[49] Similarly, because it can't easily or quickly train people with expertise in aircraft engine performance problems, the Navy keeps the addresses of retirees and other past employees in a database for use in the event they are needed.

When the Federal Deposit Insurance Corporation needed to prepare for an increase in failed financial institutions in 2008 it brought back 25 retirees, many of whom worked during the savings-and-loan crisis in the late 1980s and early 1990s.[50] Companies including IBM and KPMG have set up Web sites for their alumni networks to keep in touch with former employees.[51] Software that analyzes the dynamics of each alumnus's connections helped one accounting firm rehire 31 boomerangs through its alumni network.[52]

An employee who voluntarily leaves to pursue other opportunities may find that the new job is not what he or she expected, or the new venture simply may not work out. These "boomerang" employees are already familiar with the job and organization, and the company has a good idea of their talents and fit with the firm. They are also likely to get up to speed quickly, and have enhanced their skills while they were gone. It is a good idea to inquire about how they spent their time away from the company, and how they feel about returning. If they left because they felt mistreated, they may have low morale or an undesirable attitude.[53] One potential drawback is that if returning employees are given better positions than they had when they left, other employees may conclude that the only way to get ahead is to leave the company.

NON-U.S. CITIZENS   Because recruiting globally dramatically increases the pool of available talent, some firms try to source foreign workers and sponsor a visa for them. Because some programs, including the most popular employment-based immigration program, the H-1B visa program, require a new employer to repeat the sponsorship application process if an employee wishes to leave his or her current organization, employees recruited this way often feel more obligated to stay with their employers than people hired domestically do. By increasing the likelihood that its workers will stay with the company for the duration of their visas, the program can increase the stability of a firm's employees and reduce the company's turnover costs.[54]

In the United States, the Immigration and Nationality Act (INA) allows firms to hire only eligible aliens who are specifically authorized to work in the United States. Legal immigrants to the United States can become eligible by applying for a "green card" from the Immigration and Naturalization Service. Employers must verify the eligibility of all of their new employees, and applicants must show proof of their eligibility for U.S. employment by completing an I-9 form. The firm must keep I-9 forms on file for at least three years after the applicant is hired or one year after employment ends, whichever is less.

Other recruits who are not citizens may be approved for hire through the Labor Condition Application and Foreign Labor Certification programs administered by the Department of Labor's Employment and Training Administration. To hire seasonal help, employers must demonstrate that they have tried to hire U.S. citizens without success. Foreign professionals must also be paid the prevailing U.S. wage in their field. Some workers—nurses, for example— must comply with the certification procedures set forth by the Department of Labor. Although the process can take up to two years, it can be worthwhile for companies seeking highly skilled workers. If the hiring organization can show the Department of Labor that qualified workers are not available and that the wages and working conditions offered will not adversely affect those of similarly employed U.S. workers, a regional certifying officer can grant the labor certification. Several types of employment visas exist to meet different employment conditions.

offshore labor
employees living and working in other, usually lower-cost, countries

Offshore labor refers to employees living and working in other, usually lower-cost, countries. Reducing a firm's labor costs is one of the most obvious reasons for offshoring, but the quest for talent is another motivation: By offshoring, companies are able to pursue top talent wherever it is located. Reliable and affordable communication infrastructure has made offshore labor feasible for many jobs. Although not a fast solution to a hiring need, sourcing offshore labor can help acquire quality talent at an affordable price.

Hiring employees is only part of the challenge when a firm offshores. The new workers must also be trained in the company's culture and practices. Because of the negative effects on U.S. jobs, offshoring has been a frequent topic of debate. Bank of America Corporation received negative media attention in recent years when it laid off hundreds of IT workers after requiring some of them to train their Indian replacements. But the company learned from its mistake, and now gives its workers six to eight months' notice before offshoring their jobs, which usually gives them enough time to train for new assignments or hunt for other jobs.[55] Firms must also balance the cost savings of moving some jobs to cheaper locations with the need to protect their sensitive technologies and business secrets. For example, to prevent its technology from being stolen, Symantec, producer of Norton AntiVirus, refuses to offshore or outsource its virus definitions or the engine that works with these definitions to prevent viruses.[56]

walk-ins
people who apply directly with companies

WALK-INS   **Walk-ins** are people who apply directly with companies. Many employers post hiring signs on their properties to encourage people to do just this. Some walk-ins occur even when no openings exist. Walk-in applicants may be asked to complete a job application and given a quick interview to assess their qualifications. Depending on their policies, some organizations only accept walk-in applications for specific positions. Other organizations screen walk-in applications to keep promising recruits on file in case a position opens in the future.

CREATIVE SOURCING   Some firms have utilized creative sourcing strategies, including recruiting at their own training events for employees of other companies, "speed hiring" sessions modeled after speed dating, and reading chat room postings and blogs to locate talented people. Some firms, such as Google, have even held talent competitions and made job offers to the winners.

While pink slips were being handed out at Yahoo's corporate campus, executives from Internet voice and video company Tokbox set up a taco truck across the street, offering affected employees and anyone else who wanted to chat a hot lunch and information about working for Tokbox. The novelty of their efforts generated hundreds of thousands of dollars worth of free PR and employment advertising.[57]

To attract whiz kids, Google posted math puzzles on giant signs in subway stations, and a Web address for where to submit answers. Respondents were then directed to Google's recruitment site and encouraged to apply.[58] Cisco Systems regularly uses creative advertisements and stunts to draw job seekers to its Web site. Cisco sponsors coffee carts at industry conferences, asking patrons to fill out information sheets while waiting for their free coffee.[59] When Cisco learned that members of their targeted applicant pool like to visit antique shows and microbrewery festivals, Cisco's recruiters began attending them to identify potential recruits. Cisco regularly introduces new and innovative recruiting practices to replace old ones every 6 to 12 months.[60]

Table 6–4 summarizes the effectiveness of these external sourcing methods in terms of their speed, cost, and the types of applicants they tend to generate.

TABLE 6–4	The Effectiveness of Various External Sourcing Methods		
Source	**Speed**	**Cost**	**Types of Applicants**
Employee referrals	Fast	Depends on rewards	All
In-house recruiters	Fast	Moderate	All
Written advertisements	Moderate	Moderate	Active
Job and trade fairs	Fast	Low	Active
Observation	Moderate	Low	Passive
Résumé databases	Fast	Low	Active
Career sites	Moderate	Moderate	Active
Online job boards	Moderate	Low	Active
Search firms	Moderate to slow	High	All
Professional associations	Moderate	Low	All
State employment agencies	Moderate	Low	Active
Military transition services	Moderate	Low	Active
Acquisitions and mergers	Slow	High	All
Raiding competitors	Moderate	Moderate	All
Internet data mining	Moderate	Low	Passive
Networking	Moderate	Low	All
Schools	Slow	Moderate	Active
Previous employees	Moderate	Low	All
Non-U.S. citizens	Slow	Moderate	Active
Walk-ins	Fast	Low	Active
Creative sourcing	Depends on the source	Depends on the source	All

CREATING A SOURCING PLAN

A **sourcing plan** prioritizes which recruiting sources should be used to staff a given position to best meet staffing goals that include the cost, speed, and quality of new hires. When creating a sourcing plan, a firm should do the following:

1. Profile desirable employees
2. Analyze the effectiveness of different recruiting sources on an ongoing basis
3. Utilize different recruiting sources based on the firm's staffing goals and employee profiles

Next, we discuss each step in more detail.

sourcing plan
prioritizes which recruiting sources should be used to staff a given position to best meet staffing goals

Profiling Desirable Employees

Just as marketers use customer behavior profiles to better position their products in the marketplace, "employee profiles" help firms identify desirable talent. **Employee profiling** identifies what the firm's successful current employees like to do and how people like them can be recruited. To accomplish this, a firm can use a survey or focus group whereby the firm's top performers are asked about where they like to go, what media they use, what organizations they belong to, what events they attend, and how it's easiest for them to be reached. Identifying how top performers differ from poorer performers can also help a firm prioritize its recruiting sources.[61]

employee profiling
a process that helps a firm identify what its successful current employees like to do and how people like them can be recruited

Anecdotal evidence suggests that employee profiling can be extremely effective. For example, the Minneapolis-based chain Caribou Coffee realized that some of its best performers were women in their thirties who needed a job with flexible hours because of their families. After conducting focus groups of moms currently on staff, the company created a successful, low-cost recruitment campaign to appeal to this applicant pool.[62] When Chiron Corporation, a Silicon Valley biopharmaceutical firm, was having difficulty hiring a pharmacist in a tight labor market, it sent two recruiters to a local Walgreens to ask the pharmacists there for ideas about how they could get in touch with other pharmacists. After providing the recruiters with information about the Web sites pharmacists might go to on the Internet, and how Walgreens would go about hiring another pharmacist, the staffers at the store even offered some leads from their own network of colleagues.[63] Chiron also uses focus groups and other research to profile its most talented employees.[64]

Performing Ongoing Recruiting Source Effectiveness Analyses

There is no one best sourcing strategy in recruitment. What works for one company (or job) might not work for another job, or work for the same company in the future. For these reasons, all of a firm's sourcing strategies, both internal and external, need to be under constant review.

This involves tracking the following metrics:

- How applicants, top candidates, and successful new hires discovered the vacancies for which they applied
- How many recruits each source generated
- What quality of recruits each source generated, and what was the range of the quality from each source
- What were the demographic characteristics of the recruits from each source
- Yield ratios for each source
- Conversion rates from applicant to hire for each source
- Absence and turnover rates by source
- Job performance by source
- Promotion rates by source
- Data relevant to other staffing goals

Table 6–5 shows a hypothetical recruiting source analysis for an engineering position. Additional criteria could be tracked, including demographic information about applicants, hiring rates, and conversion rates from applicant to hire, but we will simplify the analysis for the purposes of demonstration. Assuming that for its engineers, the hiring firm values the quality of its new hires the most, followed by the associated costs of hiring them, and the speed with which they can be hired, the analysis indicates that college hiring has been the best source for new engineers. The time it takes to fill engineering openings from this source is rather long, however. The analysis shows that the second best source has been employee referrals. This method has proven to be relatively fast but modestly expensive due to the referral bonuses paid to employees for their recommendations. The third best source, career sites, is also relatively fast and costs less than the other two methods but produces lower-quality hires.

Yield ratios and other data should be collected for each recruiting source. For example, in Table 6–5, the fact that college hiring yields the best applicants but is slow could mean that another source would be better, or that the yield ratios and time lapse data for each step in the process should be examined to determine how to make each step more efficient.

Human resource professionals analyze *applicant flows* (how many and what type of applicants come from each recruiting source) and *selection ratios* (of the applicants coming from each recruiting source, what proportion of them are hired) to understand the effectiveness of the recruiting sources being used to fill a position. Problems are not likely to be identified or corrected without this information.

TABLE 6–5	A Recruiting Source Analysis for an Engineer's Position		
	Average Speed	**Cost per Hire**	**New Hire Quality**
College Hiring	8 months	$5,500	Very High
Employee Referrals	2 months	$8,000	High
Career Sites	2 months	$2,500	Good
Search Firm	4 months	$15,000	Good
Walk-ins	1 month	$500	OK
Newspaper Ads	2 months	$1,000	Poor

There are two relatively simple analyses of applicant flows and selection ratios that an employer can apply to evaluate its recruiting sources for a particular position. Applicant flow can be tracked using a recruiting yield analysis of the sources producing job applicants. A **recruiting yield analysis** simply tracks the recruiting source(s) that produced each applicant and evaluates each recruiting source on the basis of relevant criteria including the number and proportion of qualified applicants coming from each source and their demographic characteristics.

recruiting yield analysis
tracks the recruiting sources that produced each applicant and evaluates each recruiting source on the basis of relevant criteria including the number and proportion of qualified applicants coming from each source and their demographic characteristics

As an example, imagine that the only recruiting sources a firm used were a newspaper advertisement and word-of-mouth recruiting. Assume that 40 percent of the 500 applicants produced by the newspaper advertisement were hired for positions with the firm (a 40 percent selection ratio), and of them 95 percent were white males, and that 70 percent of the 150 applicants generated through word-of-mouth recruiting were hired, and of them 50 percent were white males. These numbers indicate that word-of-mouth recruiting was more effective in terms of both the quality of applicants and their diversity. Now consider adding a minority job board to the sourcing strategy. If eight of the ten people hired through the job board were minorities and the ad generated 30 applicants, the addition of the minority job board could result in greater diversity even if it generates fewer quality applicants overall.

The proportion of different types of applicants dropping out of the application process at different stages can also be tracked and evaluated. Organizations are well served by diversifying their recruiting methods and tracking each source's effectiveness on whatever criteria are relevant to it, including the quantity, quality, and diversity of applicants as well as the length of time new hires serve with the company, their performance level, and the costs of recruiting them. This information can enable the organization to balance its recruiting sources to increase the probability of the desired distribution of qualified applicants at a reasonable cost. For example, when the bank holding company Wachovia analyzed its past sourcing data, it found that although Internet job boards were the cheapest way to source new hires, the volume of applicants was overwhelming. When Wachovia tracked its sources of new hires in terms of quality of hire rather than number of hires, the analysis led to more limited and shorter-term posting of jobs through job boards.[65]

It is important to note that as an organization begins to recruit differently and its workforce becomes more heterogeneous (diverse), the effectiveness of different recruiting sources can change. For example, as more women and minorities are hired, it will create a number of female and minority employee ambassadors who can recruit other minorities and women via word-of-mouth recruiting. This can improve the effectiveness of word-of-mouth recruiting over time in terms of reaching diverse applicants. If a substantial proportion of successful minority employees applied for the position because they were told that the organization was actively looking to hire women and minorities, then this information could also be actively incorporated into future recruiting efforts. Moreover, research has consistently found that applicants who apply directly for jobs and those who were referred by current employees are more likely to receive and to accept job offers than were applicants recruited via other sources,[66] probably because different recruitment sources tend to reach individuals from different applicant populations.[67]

An additional type of analysis can result in an increased understanding of from where qualified, diverse recruits are likely to come. By tracking the positions and organizations from which successful diverse employees come before being hired by the firm or moving into their current jobs with the firm, an organization can further identify its highest potential applicant pools and devote more resources to better tap them in the future. For example, if 30 percent of the successful minority employees are found to have previously worked in certain jobs elsewhere in the organization and transferred into the target position, the organization might be able to realize a substantial return on its investment by offering training programs to employees such as these who wish to transfer to the target position.

Prioritizing Recruiting Sources

Human resource professionals prioritize their recruiting sources based on the staffing goals of their firms and upon analyzing the effectiveness of their recruiting sources. Referring again to Table 6–5, for some hiring efforts, speed may be more important than for others. In the situation presented in Table 6–5, college hiring channels would not be the first recruiting source used to recruit engineers. Instead, employee referrals would be given priority.

It is important to consider the advantages and disadvantages of each recruiting source before picking which one is most appropriate for a specific business need. At one point, the human resource department of General Telephone and Electronics (GTE) was under pressure to focus on efficiency and lower its costs. To hire applicants faster, recruiters began tapping temporary agencies and job banks rather than graduating college students and experienced professionals. The time to fill positions in one region fell to 50 percent below GTE's company average at a lower cost per hire. But the turnover rate rose to twice the company average and customer service levels fell. An analysis revealed that by changing its sourcing strategy to meet the cost and efficiency goals, the sourcing process became less selective and the recruits' poorer fit with the job and organization led to less-skilled hires, higher training and turnover costs, and lower levels of customer service.[68] In other words, for GTE, the relative importance of different staffing goals influenced the prioritization of different recruiting sources, which dramatically changed the outcomes of the staffing process.

Little research has systematically addressed how organizations can and do make systematic and effective applicant sourcing decisions. From a cost and time perspective, targeting the most active job seekers is usually the best choice. If a company can find sufficient numbers of high-quality active job seekers using job boards or basic employee referral systems, it may be hard to justify doing more than this. But when the company can no longer find enough good people this way, the firm's recruiters might be tempted to try recruiting from these same sources more intensely, which is ill advised. Organizations should have multiple sourcing methods in their arsenal from which to choose depending on the specific needs and goals of each hiring effort.

By having a sourcing plan in place and managing it using appropriate metrics, a company can quickly adjust its sourcing methods when it needs to.[69] Valero Energy Corporation gives each staffing project a risk factor and ranks every applicant source using a dependability index. When critical high-risk projects come in, only sources with high dependability index scores are allowed to work on the project. An automated system automatically assigns positions associated with the staffing project to various sources based on the labor type, job characteristics, speed, cost, quality, and source's dependability.

Informal recruitment sources tend to outperform more formal recruitment sources.[70] In particular, research on the effectiveness of different external recruiting sources has generally found that employees recruited through informal sources, particularly referrals, seem to have the highest rates of job survival and performance.[71] This suggests that if low turnover is a primary goal of a recruiting effort, formal recruiting methods like advertising in print media and simply posting jobs on the Internet may be less effective than informal methods like networking and employee referrals. Despite a modest amount of research on the effects of recruiting source on posthire outcomes, the findings have been relatively weak and inconsistent.[72] Research has suggested that recruiting sources influence job satisfaction, turnover, and absenteeism through realism processes,[73] which could partially explain why informal recruiting sources tend to outperform more formal sources.

SOURCING NONTRADITIONAL APPLICANT POOLS

Research on why and when organizations successfully target alternative labor markets and the short- and long-term consequences of doing so is lacking. That said, many organizations try to gain a competitive staffing advantage by focusing on potential applicants generally overlooked by other employers.[74] "Nontraditional" applicants who differ from typical hires in terms of their educational background, previous employment, age, and so forth can be very good performers. One organization, Microboard Processing, a Connecticut-based assembler of electronic components, sources one-third of its assemblers from high-risk groups including former drug addicts, people with criminal records, and welfare recipients. The recruits are often given simple landscaping jobs first to see how well they do before they are moved to the assembly operation. They are also given a lot of slack during the first few months on the job while they are adapting to the discipline of factory work. The company says that in return, it has hardworking employees who are grateful and loyal to Microboard for giving them a chance.[75]

As another example, during the economic expansion of the late 1990s, many of the top consulting firms were expanding and unable to hire sufficient numbers of the top MBA students from the elite institutions where they had already recruited without compromising their standards. For McKinsey, rather than dipping farther down into the graduating MBA class and hiring from the top 10 percent rather than the top 5 percent, the company widened its candidate search and looked into many disciplines globally for the best talent it could find. These people were bright—many of them had earned PhDs, MDs, and law degrees. As such, they were easily trained to be quality consultants via McKinsey's own mini-MBA program for new hires.[76] By reassessing the value of sourcing from different labor pools, McKinsey successfully adjusted its sourcing strategy to maintain a supply of quality talent. As the projected talent and labor shortage in the United States[77] increases, firms are likely to tap increasingly different applicant sources such as these. Next, we discuss three nontraditional applicant pools: workers with disabilities, older workers, and welfare recipients.

Workers with Disabilities

Qualified persons with disabilities are an underutilized labor source. The unemployment rate for people with disabilities is high, despite the fact that two-thirds of the currently unemployed persons with disabilities would rather be working.[78] The truth is, however, that disabled workers can be as productive as or more productive than nondisabled employees. People with disabilities are often creative problem solvers due to the challenges they face in their daily lives. Some disabilities can even be enabling in particular work contexts. For example, people who are deaf can communicate in noisy environments using American Sign Language.

Employers who look at people's abilities and not their disabilities often benefit from the talents of a diverse workforce. Walgreens proactively created a disability-friendly environment in its distribution division by creating two distribution centers designed specifically to employ people with physical and cognitive disabilities. At one facility, 40 percent of 400 employees have disclosed physical or cognitive disabilities. Because the technology and process changes originally intended to accommodate workers with disabilities improved everyone's jobs, the facility's overall efficiency rose 20 percent since opening.[79]

Temporary staffing agencies are one way to effectively source people with disabilities because they focus on the individual abilities, job skills, and interests of all job seekers. Staffing services use job assessment services, temporary job assignments, and skills training to help individuals with and without disabilities find appropriate employment. These services provide job seekers with opportunities to build a work history, experience different types of jobs, and increase their employment marketability and earning potential.[80]

The Labor Department's Office of Disability Employment Policy[81] facilitates sourcing people with disabilities by distributing a free CD-ROM database in which employers can search from a pool of prescreened applicants in fields including computer sciences, business, communications, and engineering. The federally funded Job Accommodation Network is a free consulting service of the Office of Disability Employment Policy. The network provides employers with suggestions on how their workplaces and equipment can be modified to accommodate disabled employees.[82] Although some employers worry about the cost of accommodating people with disabilities, many affordable technologies exist—80 percent of available accommodations technology costs less than $1,000.[83]

Older Workers

The United States' population and that of the world is aging. The United Nations estimates that by 2050, individuals over age 60 will comprise a larger segment of the population than will those individuals younger than age 15.[84] But the surge in retirement-eligible workers will be a challenge many companies will have to manage long before 2050. According to *The 1999 Annual Report of the Board of Trustees of the Federal Old-Age and Survivors Insurance and Disability Trust Fund*, the percent of U.S. people age 65 and over is expected to reach 16 percent by 2020. According to the Bureau of Labor Statistics, 50 percent of federal employees and 70 percent of federal senior managers will be eligible to retire by 2010.

Facing business-threatening demographic shifts and skill shortages, some organizations have begun recruiting and retaining workers over 50. For example, to more than double its over-55 workforce, which represented 16 percent of the company, CVS drugstore recruiters went to senior centers and pitched the company as a great place for older people to work. "Of the 100 people who came to the presentation, only 10 wanted to work, but those were the 10 we wanted," a CVS manager said.[85] Walmart also makes recruitment pitches at senior centers. Borders bookstores and Home Depot have started "snowbird" programs that allow workers to transfer to stores in warmer regions during the winter. Many organizations are also rethinking ways of retaining older workers by offering them reduced or flexible hours, enhanced benefits packages, and the opportunity to work part-time. The AARP, the advocacy group for retired people, posts on its Web site links to "featured employers," including MetLife, Pitney Bowes, Borders, Home Depot, Principal Financial, and Walgreens—firms that recruit older workers by offering them health benefits, training, and flexible work schedules. Tens of thousands of seniors use the Web site monthly to search for job information.[86]

Some people believe that workers become more costly as they grow older due to more medical problems and more missed workdays. But Dan Smith, senior vice president for human resources at the Borders Group, says that "overall costs are not much different based on the age of employees. Training and recruiting costs are much lower than for younger workers. It all evens out."[87] After years of encouraging workers to take early retirement as a way to cut jobs, many firms are seeking older workers because they have lower turnover rates and, in many cases, perform better. For large organizations, improved retention rates can be worth millions of dollars annually.

Welfare Recipients

Federal and state governments have made moving welfare recipients from the public assistance rolls to employer payrolls a top priority. Business Interface Inc.[88] (www.welfaretowork.org) develops and implements employment strategies and services that directly address employers' reservations about hiring underserved populations. Historically, nontraditional applicant pools, such as welfare-to-work participants, are most likely to be utilized during labor shortages, when the jobs being recruited for are unattractive and the skill levels required for them are flexible.[89] Nonetheless, it is possible for organizations to regularly make use of the people in these pools when the risks associated with their employing workers such as these are relatively low. Retail drug and pharmacy giant CVS has hired over 60,000 low-wage and welfare-to-work participants.[90]

The hotel company Marriott International has a "Pathways to Independence" program, which is a six-week, preemployment, life and occupational skills training program designed to help people receiving public assistance transition to a productive career in the hospitality industry. Marriott's Community Employment and Training Programs Department provides participants with 60 hours of classroom instruction and 120 hours of occupational skills training. Participants learn the importance of job acquisition skills, safety, communication, personal life skills, and job retention. Participants who successfully complete the program receive full-time job offers with benefits from Marriott. The retention rates for Pathways graduates are among the highest in the high-turnover hospitality industry. Eighty percent of participants graduate, 90 percent stay with Marriott for at least 90 days, and over 55 percent stay with the company at least one year.[91]

GLOBAL SOURCING AND GEOGRAPHIC TARGETING

Another issue facing many organizations is the sourcing of recruits wherever they are located in the world. Companies seeking to expand globally also need to source local talent to staff their new operations abroad. International recruiting can be an important part of a company's strategic recruiting effort because it can create a substantially larger pool of talent from which to identify, attract, and hire employees with key skills. Particularly for high-level skills or skills in short supply, recruiting from a global labor market may be necessary in a tight domestic labor market or if an organization wishes to employ the best talent.

In sourcing recruiting internationally, sensitivity to cultural differences is important. Flexibility in the execution of the recruiting strategy is critical, and recruitment methods that work best in each location must be identified. A database of potential candidates who live outside the United States can also be developed from customers, referrals, and people from around the world who contact the organization. It can be helpful to learn as much as possible about targeted recruiting regions and countries, including the kinds of people available and their primary interests and skill levels as well as their motivations and recruiting strategies that particularly appeal to them. It is also important to become knowledgeable about visa requirements and the issues involved in bringing people to the United States to work. It is not necessarily difficult or expensive to do this, but it is important to be aware of the relevant legal and immigration regulations. Next, we discuss some additional issues related to global sourcing.

Global Sourcing

Global sourcing is the sourcing of employees on a global basis. Global sourcing requires planning, developing, implementing, and evaluating staffing initiatives on a worldwide basis to ensure that staffing goals and objectives are met. Sourcing and staffing a global workforce offers a substantially different set of challenges than does sourcing and staffing a domestic workforce. Implementing recruiting and staffing policies across a range of countries, each with its own cultural, legal, economic, and political characteristics, is much more complex.

global sourcing
sourcing employees on a global basis

One of the primary challenges of sourcing and managing a global workforce is the need to strike a balance between two competing objectives: integration and differentiation. *Integration* refers to the coordination of a single global staffing strategy that gives the organization adequate control over its local operations. *Differentiation* refers to the need to acknowledge and respect the diversity of local cultures and a firm's employees' expectations in those cultures. For example, firms need to give some latitude to their local managers to tailor their strategies and practices to meet the needs of their locations.

When analyzing the potential of various international locations, *local employment agencies* can be a useful source of information about the characteristics of the local labor force. These characteristics can include such factors as the local population's skill base, local wage rates, employee turnover rates, and the cultural and legislative issues related to operating in the international location. Companies are wise to analyze whether an international locale has a sufficient amount of talent to support the firm's planned operations and to consider a number of different locations before making a final decision.

After choosing an international location, companies sometimes rely on local employment agencies to staff them. Although the key employees located internationally are likely to be expatriates of the parent country, at least some host-country nationals with local experience are usually hired. The labor markets and the firm's business needs will determine the balance of expatriates and local nationals for global companies, unless the hiring is highly regulated in the new location. (Some countries require international firms to employ a certain percentage of local workers, for example.) Companies can try to attract managers from competitors, or rely on local headhunting companies. Given the difficulty in forecasting demand in the new location, companies often try to keep their labor force as flexible as possible until it is clear that the new venture will succeed. Generally they do this by heavily relying on temporary staffing. Companies can also choose to work with a combination of both local employment agencies and global operators, which can service their requirements in a number of new markets.[92]

Geographic Targeting

Geographic targeting, or sourcing recruits based on where they live, is also commonly done by organizations. Lower-level positions in an organization are typically filled from the local labor market, and the geographic boundaries for a sourcing effort tend to widen as the position moves up the organization's hierarchy. For example, searches for lower-skilled jobs are usually local, and CEO searches are generally national, if not even global in nature. Although very little research has been done on the organizational decision-making processes related to geographic targeting, several studies do indicate that a job's geographic location is very important to applicants. For example, research on the job searches of college graduates indicates that many graduates do not consider job opportunities located outside their preferred geographic areas.[93] The importance of location does not seem to be limited to lower-level employees and college graduates.[94] In fact, experienced employees with greater family obligations and community ties[95] are probably less likely to want to relocate to certain areas than college graduates are.

geographic targeting
sourcing recruits based on where they live

Geographic targeting can be done by focusing on the local labor market, focusing on labor markets in locations similar to the organization's location in terms of city size, cost of living, climate, cultural and recreational opportunities, and other characteristics, or targeting individuals likely to find the organization's location attractive. Individuals tend to have preferences for communities with specific characteristics and are more willing to relocate to areas such as these.[96] Research has also found that when people relocate to areas and communities that are similar to where they previously lived, it's easier for them to adjust.[97] Identifying communities similar to an organization's own location and targeting your recruiting efforts in these areas can be a promising sourcing strategy. For example, because it was difficult for Allied Signal, a multi-national fiber manufacturer, to recruit new production employees in the tight Arizona labor market in 1999, the company (which is now a part of Honeywell Inc.) targeted qualified production workers currently living in cold-weather cities. To recruit them, Allied Signal ran newspaper advertisements that tempted candidates with stories about Arizona's warmth and paid to relocate them.[98] Other companies have moved their manufacturing plants to locations where an abundant and qualified workforce already exists. After a large employer in Lima, Ohio, lost its government defense contract and laid off a large number of skilled manufacturing employees, Siemens Automotive moved one of its manifold assembly plants from Windsor, Ontario, to Lima to take advantage of the availability of talent.[99]

In addition to better sourcing, another advantage of attending to the importance of geography is that it can help an organization to manage its retention rates. A technology company might find that having a location in Silicon Valley allows it to tap into cutting-edge talent. And because the turnover rate is high in Silicon Valley, given the ease with which employees can switch employers, the firm may be able to continually refresh its talent. That said, high turnover could jeopardize a research and development project with a long lead time. In this case, establishing a separate, long-term research facility in a location such as a rural community, in which highly skilled semiconductor employees are not in great demand, can increase employee retention rates. Intersil, a semiconductor designer and manufacturer, is a good example: When the turnover rate in the semiconductor industry was at 20 percent, an Intersil semiconductor facility located in rural Pennsylvania had an average turnover of only 2 percent.[100] Locating a facility in a location where local labor does not have access to many jobs due to transportation limitations can also increase the supply of labor as well as improve retention. Also, people with young families are sometimes interested in relocating to smaller, more rural communities, and may find it hard to leave the area once they have put down roots in those communities. When GE had trouble finding people willing to move to "dreary" Erie, Pennsylvania, the company began sourcing junior military officers. Having been used to working in foxholes, these people found that Erie wasn't such a bad place to be. The program was so successful that GE soon expanded it throughout the company.[101]

SOURCING AT VALERO ENERGY CORPORATION

When Valero Energy wanted to evaluate its different recruiting sources and choose those best suited for its different job openings, it adopted a "talent pipeline model." The model allows Valero to shift rapidly between various "categories" of labor sources, depending on which best fits the business's needs at the time. Dan Hilbert, Valero's director of recruiting, says, "We measure every single source of labor by speed, cost, and efficiency."[102]

Valero categorizes its labor supply channels into four areas: full-time employees, temporary employees, business process outsourcing, and alternative sources. Some of Valero's sources of labor and talent categories include:[103]

- Centralized recruiting
- Succession management
- Employee development
- Employee referrals
- Internal job-posting systems
- Third-party agencies
- Contract labor
- Outsourcing vendors
- Competitor's workforce (for poaching)
- College graduates or interns
- Foreign visa holders
- Software or hardware substitutes for labor

Valero continually and thoroughly evaluates its recruiting sources to improve its recruiting function and best utilize each source. The company creates a weekly "sourcing-channel report" that identifies which sources are having a major impact on the firm's recruiting success. The report identifies cost, time, and quality factors. This allows Valero's recruiting managers to identify problems that might be occurring with its recruiting sources. The company even tracks the results down to the individual-recruiter level.[104]

Valero uses past employment, cost, and employee performance data to predict which sources will be most effective. One month's data showed that of its 30 recruitment sources, Valero got better candidates by advertising on niche industry Web sites than through other sources. The company was able to use the data from these reports to reduce its hiring costs by 60 percent in just two years.[105] By examining historical data, such as from where people were hired, how long they stay employed with Valero, how well they fit in with its corporate culture, and their level of productivity, the company is able to identify the source from which it can recruit the best talent at the most affordable price. For specific projects, Valero can determine whether it is best financially and strategically to recruit full-time, part-time, or contract workers, or to outsource the work entirely.[106]

Summary

Sourcing talent is an important part of the recruitment and staffing process. Because it identifies the talent pools and the people who will eventually become applicants and new hires, it lays the foundation for a successful staffing effort. For firms pursuing quality passive job seekers who are not paying attention to traditional recruitment methods, a well-thought-out sourcing strategy is essential for staffing success. Because effective sourcing improves the quality of the applicant pool, it also decreases the burden placed on the candidate assessment and selection system because more applicants would be good hires. As the competition for talent further intensifies, the ability to source talent is likely to be an increasingly important factor in firms' abilities to find and attract the talent they need to execute their business strategies and maintain a competitive advantage.

A variety of sourcing strategies exist, and firms are getting more creative in identifying quality semi-passive and passive job seekers to target during later recruitment efforts. By profiling desirable employees, performing ongoing recruiting source effectiveness analyses, and prioritizing recruiting sources based on staffing goals and employee profiles, firms can increase the return on their staffing investment and increase the probability of efficiently and effectively finding and hiring the right talent.

Takeaway Points

1. Sourcing is done to identify and locate high-potential people who will later be recruited by the firm. The quality and quantity of a company's new hires and the firm's return on its staffing investment are affected by its sourcing decisions.
2. Recruiting sources differ on many dimensions, including their cost, the quality of the recruits they generate, the time it takes to hire, the number of hires they generate, the types of talent they generate, and the diversity of the applicants and new hires they generate.
3. Different recruiting sources are appropriate for different types of positions. Sourcing executive talent might involve global targeting, search firms, and raiding competitors. Sourcing talent for a manufacturing line might involve local targeting, employee referrals, relationships with local schools, and job fairs.

4. A sourcing plan prioritizes different recruiting sources based on their ability to help the firm reach its staffing goals. Staffing goals aimed at hiring speed and low-cost hiring are likely to result in a sourcing plan that prioritizes newspaper ads and employee referrals over search firms and college recruiting efforts.
5. Sourcing nontraditional applicant pools can require more creative sourcing activities. A key component is identifying where and how people with the desired characteristics can be reached so that a recruitment effort can be developed to effectively target them.
6. Geographic targeting helps firms restrict their sourcing activities to geographic locations likely to generate promising applicant leads. Firms usually source talent in local labor markets to fill lower-level positions. By contrast, the geographic boundaries for a sourcing effort tend to widen the higher up the position is in the organization's hierarchy.

Discussion Questions

1. What could an organization do to be a more appealing employer to people with disabilities?
2. What sourcing strategies do you think would be most effective for finding entry-level managers for an on-campus, fast-food restaurant? Why?
3. If a firm wanted to recruit people like you, how could they best identify you and where could they put a recruiting message where you are likely to see and respond to it?

4. What could go wrong if a firm only sources recruits using one method?
5. How might a company's preferred recruiting sources differ when it is looking for local retail managers versus doing a national search for managerial talent?

Exercises

1. *Strategy Exercise:*   Ringtone and Phones-R-Us are both successful companies in the cellular phone retail sales business. On the one hand, Phones-R-Us pursues a low-cost strategy and has fairly high employee turnover rates. The firm relies on a high volume of phone sales to generate revenue. On the other hand, Ringtone pursues a competitive advantage based on customer intimacy and has very loyal employees. Ringtone sells expensive, high-quality phones and relies on its employees to provide high-quality customer service to generate sales.

   The sales representatives for both companies "bring in the bacon." As such, these people are a key factor to the firms' success. How should each company source recruits for the position?

2. *Develop Your Skills Exercise:*   This chapter's Develop Your Skills feature contains information about performing a Boolean search to identify passive job seekers. Adapt the Boolean terms presented in the feature, and do your own search to identify at least three recruiters in your area.

3. *Opening Vignette Exercise:*   This chapter's opening vignette illustrated how Valero developed its talent pipeline and how it analyzes and prioritizes its recruiting sources. If you had to choose only three metrics for Valero to use to evaluate the effectiveness of its recruiting sources, what would they be? Why did you choose them? If Valero's reports indicate that some of its recruiters are consistently better than others on key metrics, what would you do with this information?

CASE STUDY

The accounting firm Ernst & Young believes that employees who have resigned from the firm are very important to its future success. Many of these people rejoin the firm. In fact, on average, 25 percent of the firm's experienced hires are "boomerangs" who left the company and then returned.[107] The company even has a referral incentive program to reward former employees who send candidates to Ernst & Young.

In addition to maintaining a directory of all of its former employees, Ernst & Young has a Web site dedicated to maintaining relations with them.[108] The Web site contains job postings, news about former employees, and a social events calendar. In addition, the Web site contains information about key industry and business issues, and news pages with updates and firm announcements.

QUESTIONS

1. Do you think that it is a good idea for Ernst & Young to hire previous employees? Why or why not?
2. Think of the previous jobs you have held. Are there any previous employers to which you would consider returning? What would it take for the companies you used to work for to get you to reapply with them?
3. What are some advantages and disadvantages of creating and managing this type of alumni network and Web site?

Semester-Long Active Learning Project

Develop a sourcing plan for the position you have chosen. Critically analyze the recruiting sources currently used to staff the position and recommend other recruiting sources that are likely to work. Be sure to explain why your recommendations are likely to be effective. Using what you learned in Chapter 3, identify how your sourcing plan will enable the company to comply with EEO and other legal requirements.

Then identify a geographic area from which to source the job and perform a Boolean search using the information in this chapter's Develop Your Skills feature. Revise your search until you have identified at least three promising leads for staffing the position. Print out the candidates' résumés or biographies and append them to your report.

Case Study Assignment: Strategic Staffing at Chern's

See the appendix at the back of the book for this chapter's Case Study Assignment.

Endnotes

1. Sullivan, J., "How a Former CEO Built a World-Class Recruiting Department," Electronic Recruiting Exchange, September 19, 2005, http://www.ere.net/2005/09/19/how-a-former-ceo-built-a-world-class-recruiting-department/. Accessed September 17, 2010.
2. Nakache, P., "Cisco's Recruiting Edge," *Fortune*, September 29, 1997: 275–276.
3. Sullivan, J., "Amazing Practices in Recruiting—ERE Award Winners 2009," ERE.net, http://www.ere.net/2009/04/20/amazing-practices-in-recruiting-ere-award-winners-2009-part-2-of-2/#more-7569. Accessed March 15, 2010.
4. McIntosh, R., "Building Creative and Aggressive Sourcing Strategies," October 27, 2005, http://www.ere.net/2005/10/27/building-creative-and-aggressive-sourcing-strategies/. Accessed September 17, 2010.
5. Blau, G., "Exploring the Mediating Mechanisms Affecting the Relationship of Recruitment Source to Employee Performance," *Journal of Vocational Behavior*, 3: 303–320; Griffeth, R. W., Hom, P. W., Fink, L. S., and Cohen, D. J., "Comparative Tests of Multivariate Models of Recruiting Sources Effects, *Journal of Management*, 23 (1997): 19–36.

6. Fulmer, R. M., "Choose Tomorrow's Leaders Today," *Graziadio Business Report*, Winter 2002, Pepperdine University, http://gbr.pepperdine.edu/021/succession.html.Accessed September 1, 2006.

7. Ibid.

8. Sullivan, J., "Best Practices in Recruiting—ERE Excellence Awards 2010," ERE.net, March 29, 2010, http://www.ere.net/2010/03/29/best-practices-in-recruiting-ere-excellence-awards-2010-part-1-of-4/. Accessed March 31, 2010.

9. Ibid.

10. Ibid.

11. Pont, J. "State of the Sector: Recruitment and Staffing," *Workforce Management*, May 2005: 49–56, www.workforce. com/section/06/feature/24/04/85/index.html. Accessed August 31, 2006.

12. Imperato, G., "Gene Pool, Talent Pool: Hiring Is All in the Family," *Fast Company*, August 1996: 81.

13. Carbonara, P., "Hire for Attitude, Train for Skill," *Fast Company*, August 1996: 73.

14. Imperato, "Gene Pool, Talent Pool."

15. "Employee Referrals Improve Hiring," *BNA Bulletin to Management*, March 13, 1997: 88.

16. Moser, K., "Recruitment Sources and Post-Hire Outcomes: The Mediating Role of Unmet Expectations," *International Journal of Selection and Assessment*, 13, 3 (September 2005): 188–197.

17. Hill, R. E., "New Look at Employee Referrals as a Recruitment Channel," *Personnel Journal*, 49 (1970): 144–148.

18. Weller, I., Holtom, B.C., Matiaske, W., and Mellewigt, T., "Level and Time Effects of Recruitment Sources on Early Voluntary Turnover," *Journal of Applied Psychology*, 94 (2009), 1146–1162.

19. Taylor, M. S., and Collins, C. J., "Organizational Recruitment: Enhancing the Intersection of Research and Practice," In C. L. Cooper and E. A. Locke (eds.), *Industrial and Organizational Psychology: Linking Theory with Practice*, Oxford, UK: Blackwell, 2000, 304–330.

20. J. Sullivan, "Assessing Employee Referral Programs: A Checklist," Electronic Recruiting Exchange, September 12, 2005, http://www.ere.net/2005/09/12/assessing-employee-referral-programs-a-checklist/. Accessed September 17, 2010.

21. Berfield, S. "The Man Behind the Bandz," *Bloomberg Businessweek*, June 14–20, 2010: 64–67.

22. Mary Pomerantz Advertising. Used by permission of Mary Pomerantz and Steve Stankievich, April 18, 2007.

23. Frost, M., "Old-fashioned Career Fairs Gain Favor Online," *HR Magazine*, April 1998, http://findarticles.com/p/articles/mi_m3495/is_n5_v43/ai_20633859. Accessed September 6, 2006.

24. Carbonara, "Hire for Attitude, Train for Skill."

25. Sullivan, J., "The Best Practices of the Most Aggressive Recruiting Department," Electronic Recruiting Exchange, July 18, 2005, www.ere.net/ARTICLES/default.asp?cid={251A4E59-6A0C-4E80-8C8C-CEDA95334C2D}. Accessed August 23, 2006.

26. McIntosh, "Building Creative and Aggressive Sourcing Strategies."

27. Zimmerman, E., "Keeping Tabs on Productivity of Recruiting Tools," *Workforce Management Online*, March 2005, www. workforce.com/section/06/feature/23/98/25/index.html. Accessed September 6, 2006.

28. Kaihla, P., "How to Land Your Dream Job," *Business 2.0*, November 1, 2004, http://money.cnn.com/magazines/business2/business2_archive/2004/11/01/8189350/index.htm. Accessed June 27, 2006.

29. "BP Poaches Shell Refinery Boss to Run Texas City," Reuters.com, August 25, 2006. http://today.reuters.com/news/articlebusiness.aspx?type=ousiv&storyID=2006-08-25T152417Z_01_ N25195573_RTRIDST_0_BUSINESSPRO-ENERGY-BP-MANAGER-DC.XML&from=business. Accessed August 31, 2006.

30. Cappelli, P., "A Market-Driven Approach to Retaining Talent," *Harvard Business Review* (January–February 2000): 103–110.

31. Dokko, G., S. L. Wilk and N. P. Rothbard, "Unpacking Prior Experience: How Career History Affects Job Performance." *Organization Science*, 20 (2009): 51–68.

32. Stillman, J., "Experienced Workers Bring Old Issues to New Jobs," BNET1, September 4, 2008, http://blogs.bnet.com/bnet1/?p=576&tag=nl.e713. Accessed March 11, 2010.

33. Kiger, P. J., "Eliyon Steps Up the Search," *Workforce Management*, January 2005: 41–44.

34. Berfield, S. "The Man Behind the Bandz," *Bloomberg Businessweek*, June 14–20, 2010: 64–67.

35. Berkshire, J. C., " 'Social Network' Recruiting," *HR Magazine*, April 2005: 95–98.

36. Hansen, F., "Using Social Networking to Fill the Talent Acquisition Pipeline," *Workforce Management Online*, December 2006, www.workforce.com/section/06/feature/24/60/64/index.html. Accessed December 19, 2006.

37. Fox, A., "Newest Social Medium Has Recruiters All a-Twitter," Society for Human Resource Management, June 24, 2009, http://www.shrm.org/hrdisciplines/staffingmanagement/Articles/Pages/RecruitersandTwitter.aspx. Accessed March 29, 2010.

38. Boyle, M., "Recruiting: Enough to Make a Monster Tremble," *BusinessWeek*, June 25, 2009, http://www.businessweek.com/magazine/content/09_27/b4138043180664.htm. Accessed March 12, 2010.

39. Smith, A., "Twitter Recruiting Raises Legal Concerns," Society for Human Resource Management, February 4, 2010, http://www.shrm.org/LegalIssues/FederalResources/Pages/TwitterRecruiting.aspx. Accessed March 29, 2010.

40. Hansen, F., "Discriminatory Twist in Networking Sites Puts Recruiters in Peril," *Workforce Management Online*, September 2009, http://www.workforce.com/section/06/feature/26/68/67/. Accessed October 12, 2009.

41. Baker, S., "Data Mining Moves to Human Resources," *BusinessWeek*, March 12, 2009, http://www.businessweek.com/magazine/content/09_12/b4124046224092.htm?campaign_id=rss_daily. Accessed April 6, 2010.

42. Sullivan, J., "Amazing Practices in Recruiting—ERE Award Winners 2009," ERE.net, 2009, http://www.ere.net/2009/04/20/amazing-practices-in-recruiting-ere-award-winners-2009-part-2-of-2/#more-7569. Accessed March 15, 2010.

43. See www.naceweb.org/principles/principl.html.

44. "The Top 50," *BusinessWeek*, September 14, 2009: 40.

45. "2006 NACE Experiential Education Survey," *National Association of Colleges and Employers*, Bethlehem, PA: NACE, 2006.

46. Leak, B., "The Draft Picks Get Younger," *BusinessWeek*, May 8, 2006: 96.

47. Byrnes, N., "Get 'Em While They're Young," *BusinessWeek*, May 22, 2006: 86–87.

48. Schoeff, M., Jr., "Skills of Recent U.S. High School Graduates Leave Employers Cold," *Workforce Management*, April 13, 2007, www.workforce.com/section/00/article/24/85/87.html. Accessed April 17, 2007.

49. Mullich, J., "They Don't Retire Them, They Hire Them," *Workforce Management*, December 2003: 49–54.

50. Paletta, D., "FDIC to Add Staff as Bank Failures Loom," *The Wall Street Journal*, February 26, 2008, http://online.wsj.com/article/SB120398607404892133.html?mod=rss_whats_news_us_business. Accessed January 5, 2010.

51. Baker, S., "You're Fired—But Stay in Touch," *BusinessWeek*, May 4, 2009: 54–55.

52. Ibid.

53. "Hiring Workers the Second Time Around," *BNA Bulletin to Management*, January 30, 1997: 40.

54. Based on West, L. A., Jr., and Bogumil, W. A., Jr., "Foreign Knowledge Workers as a Strategic Staffing Option, *Academy of Management Executive,* 14 (2000): 71–83.

55. Kripalani, M., Foust, D., Holmes, S., and Engardio, P., "Five Offshore Practices That Pay Off," *BusinessWeek Online*, January 30, 2006, http://images.businessweek.com/ss/06/01/outsourcing/index_01.htm. Accessed September 5, 2006.

56. Lourie, S., "An Offshore Conversation: Symantec's Dean Lane, Part 2," SearchCIO.com, August 26, 2004. http://searchcio.techtarget.com/qna/0,289202,sid19_ gci1002682,00.html. Accessed September 20, 2007.

57. Sullivan, J., "Recruiting Strategies—Proximity Recruiting Using a Taco Truck," ERE.net, 2008, http://www.ere.net/ 2008/12/15/recruiting-strategies-%e2%80%93-proximity-recruiting-using-a-taco-truck/#more-5345. Accessed March 22, 2010.

58. Zeidner, R., "Recruiters: Work on Massaging the Message," *HR Magazine*, July 2009: 15.

59. Adelson, A., "Robust Online Recruiting at Cisco," *New York Times*, June 7, 2000, http://partners.nytimes.com/library/tech/00/06/biztech/technology/07adel-side1.html. Accessed November 16, 2006.

60. Nakache, "Cisco's Recruiting Edge."

61. Based on Sullivan, J., "Finding Talent Is Easy—Do a Behavior Profile," Electronic Recruiting Exchange, May 2000, http://ourworld.compuserve.com/homepages/gately/pp15s109.htm. Accessed September 6, 2006.

62. Jossi, F., "HR Is Turning Jobs into Brands," *Workforce Online*, July 2002, www.workforce.com/section/06/article/23/25/35.html.

63. Kiger P. J., "Search and Employ," *Workforce*, June 2003: 64–68.

64. Ibid.

65. Zimmerman, "Keeping Tabs on Productivity of Recruiting Tools."

66. Breaugh, J. A., Greising, L. A., Taggart, J. W., and Chen, H., "The Relationship of Recruiting Sources and Pre-Hire Outcomes: Examination of Yield Rations and Applicant Quality," *Journal of Applied Social Psychology,* 33, 11 (2003): 2267–2287.

67. Taylor, M. S., and Schmidt, D.W., "A Process-Oriented Investigation of Recruitment Source Effectiveness," *Personnel Psychology,* 36, 2 (1983): 343–354.

68. Becker, B. E., Huselid, M. A., and Ulrich, D., *The HR Scorecard: Linking People, Strategy, and Performance*, Boston: Harvard Business School Press, 2001, 48.

69. Adler, L., "Sourcing 101," Electronic Recruiting Exchange, May 20, 2005, http://www.ere.net/2005/05/20/sourcing-101/. Accessed September 17, 2010.

70. Barber, A. E., *"Recruiting Employees: Individual and Organizational Perspectives*, Thousand Oaks: Sage, 1998.

71. Wanous, J. P., *Organizational Entry: Recruitment, Selection, Orientation, and Socialization of Newcomers* (2nd ed.), Reading, MA: Addison-Wesley, 1992.

72. Rynes, S. L., and Cable, D. M., "Recruitment Research in the Twenty-first Century," In W. C. Borman, D. R. Ilgen, and R. J. Klimoski (eds.), *Handbook of psychology,* Vol. 12, Hoboken, NJ: John Wiley & Sons, Inc, 2003, 55–76.

73. Griffeth, R. W., Hom, P. W., Fink, L. S., and Cohen, D. J., "Comparative Tests of Multivariate Models of Recruiting Sources Effects," *Journal of Management*, 23 (1997): 19–36.

74. Rynes, S. L., and Barber, A. E., "Applicant Attraction Strategies: An Organizational Perspective," *Academy of Management Review,* 15 (1990): 286–310.

75. Cappelli, P., "A Market-Driven Approach to Retaining Talent," In Harvard Business Review, *Harvard Business Review on Finding and Keeping the Best People*, Boston: Harvard Business School Publishing, 2001, 27–50.

76. "CEO Super Bowl," *Fortune*, August 2, 1999: 238–240.

77. Drucker, P., "The Next Society: A Survey of the Near Future," *Economist*, November 3, 2001: 1–20.

78. "Economic Participation," National Organization on Disability, 2006, www.nod.org/index.cfm? fuseaction=Page.viewPage&pageId=12. Accessed September 6, 2006.

79. Wells, S.J., "Counting on Workers with Disabilities," *HR Magazine*, April 2008, http://www.shrm.org/hrmagazine/articles/0408/0408wells.asp. Accessed December 13, 2009.

80. U.S. Department of Labor, "People with Disabilities—Temporary Employment Options," August 23, 2006, www.dol.gov/odep/pubs/ek99/temp.htm. Accessed September 5, 2006.

81. See www.dol.gov/odep.

82. See www.jan.wvu.edu.

83. Wingender, T., "Beyond Access: Focusing on Abilities Instead of Disabilities Opens Up a Brand New Talent Pool," *Mosaics: SHRM Focuses on Workplace Diversity,* 8, 4 (October 2002): 1–5.

84. United Nations Organization, *Population Ageing: Facts and Figures*, April 8–12, 2003, Second World Assembly on Ageing, Madrid Spain, www.un.org/ageing/prkit/factsnfigures.htm. Accessed April 18, 2007.

85. Mullich, "They Don't Retire Them, They Hire Them."

86. Freudenheim, M., "More Help Wanted: Older Workers Please Apply," *New York Times*, March 23, 2005, http://query.nytimes.com/gst/fullpage.html?res=9C06E5DD163FF930A1550C0A9639C8B63&n=Top%2FReference%2FTimes%20Topics%2FOrganizations%2FA%2FAARP. Accessed April 10, 2007.

87. Ibid.

88. Formerly the Welfare to Work Partnership, home page, www.businessinterfaceinc.com.

89. Rynes and Barber, "Applicant Attraction Strategies: An Organizational Perspective."

90. Pomeroy, A., "For CVS, A Recruiting Resource," *HR Magazine*, February 2008: 37.

91. CSRWire, "Marriott's Welfare-to-Work Program, Pathways to Independence, Reaches 10-Year Milestone," December 18, 2000, www.csrwire.com/News/521.html. Accessed April 10, 2007.

92. Hanson, F., "Regulating the Recruitment Mix in Global Markets," *Workforce Management Online*, August 2006, www.workforce.com/section/06/feature/24/48/08/index.html. Accessed August 24, 2006.

93. Barber, A. E., and Roehling, M. V., "Job Postings and the Decision to Interview: A Verbal Protocol Analysis," *Journal of Applied Psychology,* 78 (1993): 845–856; Osborn, D. P., "A Reexamination of the Organizational Choice Process," *Journal of Vocational Behavior*, 36 (1990): 45–60; Rynes, S. L., and

Lawler, J., "A Policy-Capturing Investigation of the Role of Expectancies in Decisions to Pursue Job Alternatives," *Journal of Applied Psychology,* 68 (1983): 620–631.

94. Barber, A. E., *Recruiting Employees: Individual and Organizational Perspectives*, Thousand Oaks, CA: Sage, 1998.

95. Noe, R. A., Steffy, B. D., and Barber, A. E., "An Investigation of the Factors Influencing Employees' Willingness to Accept Mobility Opportunities," *Personnel Psychology,* 41 (1988): 559–580.

96. Noe, R. A., and Barber, A. E., "Willingness to Accept Mobility Opportunities: Destination Makes a Difference," *Journal of Organizational Behavior,* 14 (1993): 159–175.

97. Brett, J. M., Stroh, L. K., and Reilly, A. H., "Job Transfer," In C. L. Cooper and I. T. Robertson (eds.), *International Review of Industrial and Organizational Psychology,* Chicester, England: Wiley, 1992; Pinder, C. C., and Schroeder, K. G., "Time to Proficiency Following Job Transfers," *Academy of Management Journal,* 30, (1987): 336–353.

98. Siekman, P., "The Hunt for Good Factory Workers," *Fortune*, 1998: 138B–138J.

99. Ibid.

100. Cappelli, "A Market-Driven Approach to Retaining Talent," In Harvard Business Review.

101. Grow, B., "Renovating Home Depot," *BusinessWeek*, March 6, 2006: 50–58.

102. Schneider, C., "The New Human-Capital Metrics," *CFO Magazine*, February 15, 2006, www.cfo.com/article.cfm/5491043/1/c_2984284?f=archives. Accessed August 23, 2006.

103. Sullivan, J., "Best Recruiting Practices from the World's Most Business-like Recruiting Function, Part 5," Electronic Recruiting Exchange, September 19, 2005, http://www.ere.net/2005/09/19/how-a-former-ceo-built-a-world-class-recruiting-department/. Accessed September 17, 2010.

104. Ibid.

105. Zimmerman, "Keeping Tabs on Productivity of Recruiting Tools."

106. Schneider, "The New Human-Capital Metrics."

107. Ernst and Young, "Ernst & Young Alumni Network," 2007, https://ey.alumniprogram.com/jsp/Front/login.jsp. Accessed June 6, 2007.

108. See https://ey.alumniprogram.com/jsp/Front/login.jsp.

Recruiting

Outline

LEARNING OBJECTIVES
After studying this chapter, you should be able to:

- Describe the purpose of recruiting.
- Explain what recruitment "spillover effects" are.
- Understand what makes a recruiter more or less effective.
- Describe the various strategies used to attract applicants.
- Describe how recruiting guides and the EEOC's best recruiting practices promote recruiting consistency and quality.

Recruiting at the Container Store

The Container Store tries to hire self-motivated, team-oriented people with a passion for customer service. Customer service is so important to the company that it characterizes it as the company's core competency. All companies face challenges as they grow, but the central role customer service plays for the Container Store presents more challenges as the company tries to maintain its 20 percent annual store growth rate. Kip Tindell, the Container Store's president and CEO, believes that the company's greatest challenge as it expands isn't financial or finding good locations, but hiring and keeping great customer-oriented people.[1]

Consistently ranked as one of the best companies to work for,[2] one of the company's core principles is "one equals three," meaning that one great person is more valuable than three good people. The firm recruits intensively to help reinforce this principle.[3] Tindell asks for your advice on how to effectively recruit self-motivated, team-oriented people who have the passion for customer service that the firm needs to succeed. After reading this chapter, you should have some good ideas to share with Tindell.

The global consulting firm Watson Wyatt found that an excellent recruiting function increased a firm's total market value (the dollar value of all of its stock) by over 18 percent in 2005.[4] Unfortunately, many companies don't have a formal recruiting strategy. As we have stressed, recruiting the right talent is critical to a firm's performance. As one staffing expert stated, "There are plenty of talented workers out there. It's just that great people already have great jobs. The burden is on companies—both start-ups and established organizations—to become more rigorous and more creative about finding the talented people that they need, and convincing those people to join."[5]

In addition to getting people in the door, recruiting can have an important symbolic aspect. After going through a rigorous recruiting and selection process, a new hire can feel that he or she is joining an elite organization and is one of the few who "made the cut." This creates high performance expectations, and sends the message that people matter.[6]

Recruitment can and should be a source of sustainable competitive advantage. Recruitment is vital to the business model of companies like Enterprise Rent-A-Car, which promote almost entirely from within and regularly open new locations.[7] Valero Energy even calculates how good and bad recruiting affects the company's earnings per share.[8] As two experts stated, "the ultimate cost of failure to attract applicants may be organizational failure."[9]

This chapter will cover recruiting and how applicants react during the recruiting process. We will also discuss what makes recruiters effective and the different strategies companies can use to attract applicants. Finally, we discuss how to make quality recruitment activities more consistent throughout a company. After studying this chapter, you should have a good understanding of the important role recruiters and recruiting activities play in the staffing process.

WHAT IS RECRUITING?

The recruiting function's purpose is to help the organization employ a talented group of employees who contribute to the company's business strategy so the firm can achieve a competitive advantage. As you learned in Chapter 1, recruiting refers to all organizational practices and decisions that affect either the number or types of individuals willing to apply for and accept job offers.[10] This includes converting the leads generated during sourcing into job applicants, generating interest in a company and its jobs, and persuading candidates to accept job offers extended to them. The recruiter is the personal link between the staffing needs of the organization and the labor market and must support the organization's needs and recruiting objectives to be effective. As we discuss next, one of the most important outcomes of any recruiting effort is how applicants react to the recruiting process and to recruiters.

HOW APPLICANTS REACT TO RECRUITING?

An important goal of recruitment is to give every applicant a positive feeling about the organization. Thus, effective recruiting requires considering the applicant's perspective and needs. Because the outcome of recruitment—employment—depends on the results of a series of decisions made by both the organization and the individual, the perspectives of both parties are relevant. Next, we discuss why it's so important for applicants to feel like they were treated fairly during the recruiting process as well as the consequences this can have.

Fairness Perceptions

Organizations expect applicants to be sincere and honest when seeking positions with them. Likewise, applicants expect employers to consider them on their own merits and to make a sincere effort to match their skills with job openings. Both parties expect one another to be professional and conform to commonly accepted hiring practices.[11] In addition to being treated fairly, applicants expect the private information they disclose to employers to be protected.

distributive fairness
the perceived fairness of the hiring or promotion outcome

Three types of perceptions of fairness affect how applicants react to the recruitment and selection process.[12] **Distributive fairness** relates to the perceived fairness of the hiring or promotion outcome. If someone gets the job or promotion, he or she tends to find this outcome fair. If someone does not get the job or promotion, he or she tends to find this outcome less fair. The vast majority of applicants will not receive the job offer or promotion. Consequently, organizations will already have one fairness "strike" against them at the end of a recruiting campaign.

procedural fairness
people's beliefs that the policies and procedures that resulted in the hiring or promotion decision were fair

Procedural fairness relates to people's beliefs that the policies and procedures that produced the hiring or promotion decision were fair. Organizations have much more control over applicants' perceptions of procedural fairness than they do of distributive fairness. Giving job applicants the opportunity to showcase their talents[13] as well as respecting their privacy[14] will improve how fair they believe the process to be. Different screening devices can also be perceived as more or less fair. For example, applicants tend to believe interviews, résumés, and work-sample tests are more procedurally fair than honesty tests and personal referrals, although these beliefs appear to vary across countries.[15] Applicants also tend to react negatively when there are delays in the recruitment process.[16]

interactional fairness
people's perceptions of the interpersonal treatment and amount of information they received during the hiring process

Interactional fairness relates to people's perceptions of the interpersonal treatment and the amount of information they received during the hiring process. Honesty and respectful interpersonal treatment during the recruitment process enhance applicants' perceptions of interactional fairness.[17] A warm and informative recruiter[18] will also tend to have a positive effect on applicants' reactions. Thus, by virtue of how well firms hire and train their recruiters, organizations have a great deal of control over how applicants perceive interactional fairness.

Spillover Effects

spillover effects
the indirect or unintended consequences of an action

Spillover effects are the indirect or unintended consequences of an action. How applicants are treated has spillover effects that extend beyond the recruiting activities they experience. When unhappy job candidates tell potential customers or job applicants about a bad recruiting experience they had, it can have spillover effects on the organization's performance and its ability to recruit candidates effectively in the future. Similarly, if applicants were forced to wait extended periods for prescheduled interviews, met unprepared and distracted interviewers, felt the selection process was unfair, or were made to feel unimportant or unwelcome, would they still want to do business with the company or apply for another job with it in the future? Probably not. Now suppose the applicants were greeted by name, given a quick tour of the facility, treated respectfully, interviewed on time by prepared and enthusiastic recruiters, and heard from the company when it said it would follow up. Most applicants treated this way are likely to reapply with the firm and continue to do business with it.

Addressing how applicants react throughout the hiring process is a critical component of managing any spillover effects of the process. Many firms treat job candidates as if they should feel privileged the firm is even considering them for a position and treat rejected candidates as if it were the end of their relationship with them. The impersonal treatment often given to rejected applicants by many organizations indicates that these potential spillover effects are often overlooked in the recruiting process.[19]

Recruitment (and the spillover effects associated with it) does not end when a job application is received. Until either the organization (or the candidate) removes the person from further consideration, or the individual is hired and reports for work, recruiting keeps him or her interested in pursuing the opportunity. Just because a recruit has formally applied for a job does not mean that she or he will remain interested and see the hiring process to completion. Recruiters should help candidates continually feel excited about the opportunity and ultimately be willing to accept a reasonable job offer.

Recruiters should always treat résumés and employment inquiries with respect and respond to them quickly. Even if a company is not currently hiring, mistreating an applicant could dampen his or her interest in future opportunities with the organization. As obvious as this may seem, it can sometimes be difficult to execute, particularly during periods of rapid expansion when the firm is trying to hire a lot of people. Responding to the large number of people responding to job postings, particularly those posted on the Internet, can be difficult or impossible. For a fee, some Internet businesses will instantly mail an applicant's résumé to over 1,000 headhunters and organizations. The job of sorting through these résumés can be enormous. Worse yet, a large proportion of them don't meet the requirements of the positions posted, increasing the screening burden placed on the organization.

Valero Energy focuses heavily on creating a positive job candidate experience, even when people apply with the company via the Internet. The firm sends at least three personalized e-mails to each candidate throughout the application process. When a candidate is rejected, he or she receives a postcard in the mail after the job is closed.[20] Valero knows that many people not hired for current openings have the potential to become great employees in the future. Sending them follow-up messages and encouraging applicants, who might be a good fit with positions other than the ones to which they applied, to apply for other positions can increase staffing effectiveness.

Although recruiters are often very busy, unresponsive recruiters are often seen as incompetent rather than overworked, risking a negative spillover effect for the company. Wachovia Bank believes that e-mailing candidates quickly when they have been rejected, and giving them the reasons for the rejection, has improved applicants' experiences with Wachovia's hiring process and their perceptions of Wachovia's recruiters.[21]

Next, we turn our attention to what makes recruiters effective.

WHAT MAKES A RECRUITER EFFECTIVE?

The recruiter is usually the first person with whom potential applicants have contact. Thus, he or she is one of the most important players in the hiring process. One study of business and engineering graduates looking for jobs showed that in over one-third of the cases, the primary reason a graduate chose a particular company was because of the firm's recruiter.[22] A potential applicant who is "turned off" by a recruiter might decide not to apply at all. Although currently unemployed people might persist despite a negative encounter with a recruiter, passive job seekers, many of whom are extremely talented, will be less likely to do so. In fact, when it comes to passive job seekers, the missed hiring opportunities experienced by lesser-skilled recruiters can cost firms the most money.

People often have limited information about organizations and jobs. In the absence of information, they will often rely on the traits of the recruiter and the recruiter's behaviors as *signals*. The recruiter's competence, any recruiting delays that occur during the process, and so on—all signal applicants about an organization's characteristics.[23] The type of recruiter deployed also seems to make a difference. For example, a firm can signal that it is demographically diverse by deploying a recruiter from a minority group. Some companies choose people other than recruiters to meet with applicants, which can also send a signal. If an actual hiring manager or the CEO of the company is doing the recruiting, this will send a signal that the job is important to the company. For example, as Microsoft's CEO, Bill Gates spent half his time on recruiting and would personally call college seniors to recruit them to work at Microsoft.[24]

Researchers have concluded that the extent to which recruiters influenced job seekers depended on the degree to which recruiters were seen as reliable signals of what it would be like to work for the company. The signaling function of a recruiter was concluded to be less important when job candidates had considerable information about the organization and/or if the recruiter was from human resources and not from the applicant's functional area. This reinforces the idea that recruiters should be selected and trained to be knowledgeable about the job opening, be effective in communicating this information, be perceived by applicants as trustworthy, and positively reflect what it is like to work for the company.

Another important reason to focus on recruiters is that these people are setting the standard for talent for the company. The caliber of talent they pursue and pass on for further consideration will determine the success potential of the company. For many organizations, frontline recruiters make the vast majority of applicant-screening decisions.

The Recruiter's Characteristics

Individuals may make inferences about the attractiveness of a job or the probability of receiving a job offer based on recruiter characteristics. These inferences can influence the decision to pursue the job. Research suggests that recruiters with the characteristics summarized in Table 7–1 are likely to be more successful. Regardless of whether the recruiter is internal or external to the organization, this core set of competencies seems to be important. When the recruiter is from the applicant's functional area, these effects are even more likely to occur.[25]

Although there is little evidence that recruiters' personal characteristics (e.g., race or sex) are important, recruiter behaviors toward applicants and their perceived knowledge of both the job and the applicant do influence applicant attitudes and behaviors.[26] Recruits often perceive the typical recruiter's preparation as inadequate with respect to knowledge about both characteristics of applicants and characteristics of the position being filled.[27] Recruiters must be familiar with the job, knowledgeable about the job and organization, and be motivated to do a good job recruiting qualified applicants. To accomplish these objectives, the organization can choose a recruiter who has previously worked or currently works in the target position, or it can train a recruiter on the information needed about the job and organization.

Although research has found the largest impact of recruiter behaviors to be on overall applicant impressions of the recruiter rather than on applicant intentions to pursue or accept job offers, the research has overwhelmingly been done with undergraduates who are active job seekers. The costs of lesser-skilled recruiters in terms of missed opportunities to make a good hire are likely larger among more passive job seekers whose initial recruiter experiences are more important in their ultimately becoming applicants at all. A potential recruit who is happy with her current position with another employer is likely to be more put off by a negative experience with a recruiter than a potential recruit who has already decided that the recruiter's organization is where she or he would like to work. Given that recruiter research has generally not directly manipulated recruiter behaviors, it is also possible that the effects of recruiter behaviors in attracting college undergraduates would be stronger in the presence of recruiter training and better recruiters in general.[28] Organizations need to collect their own

TABLE 7–1   Desirable Recruiter Characteristics[29]
• Familiarity with the job and organization
• Good listening skills
• Good communication skills
• Good social skills
• Intelligence
• Self-confidence
• Extroversion
• Enthusiasm about the job and company
• Trustworthiness
• Credibility

data and understand how to leverage their recruiting function to produce new hires who are the best possible fits with the organization's goals.

SIGNALING   Because people often have limited information about organizations and jobs, in the absence of objective information they may rely on traits of the recruiter and the recruiter's behaviors as *signals* of aspects of both the company and the job opportunity. Job candidates often interpret recruiter behavior as a signal of their chances of getting a job offer.[30] Applicants interpret recruitment experiences, including perceived recruiter competence, recruitment delays, and the gender composition of interview panels, as symbolic of broader organizational characteristics.[31] Applicants may form negative impressions of the organization and turn down job offers if a poor recruiter is considered representative of the organization as a whole.

As we discussed, the choice of the person sent to recruit can be taken as a signal of the importance of the job, with higher-level recruiters, the actual hiring manager, and the CEO being considered reflective of more important jobs than staff recruiters. The recruiter may also be a signal of demographic diversity in the organization if the recruiter is a demographic minority. Because recruiter behaviors affect applicant attraction indirectly through influencing applicant perceptions of job and organizational attributes,[32] it seems likely that recruits infer characteristics about the organization from their experiences with the organization's recruiters. The fact that recruits are more put off by poor recruiter behavior when the recruiter is a hiring manager rather than a human resource representative suggests that recruits may make stronger generalizations about the job and organization from experiences with people in the organization who are closely linked to that job, such as the hiring manager. This further emphasizes the point that, as recruiters, hiring managers can have a large impact on the success of a staffing effort.

A RECRUITER'S DEMOGRAPHICS AND ATTITUDES   Does the similarity between the demographic characteristics of the recruiter—including his or her age, gender, race, rank, and function—and the demographic characteristics of the applicant he or she is recruiting affect a job's attractiveness? Consumer marketing research suggests that responses to influence sources (e.g., recruiters) similar to the recruit may be more favorable than responses to dissimilar sources.[33] But do women respond more favorably to female recruiters and men more positively to male recruiters? The data seem to indicate this is not the case. Although studies have tended to look at only a single, or at most a few, demographic characteristics, they indicate that similarity to the recruiter does not necessarily lead to more favorable applicant attitudes toward the job or organization.[34]

However, a recruiter's behavior toward applicants and applicants' perception of the recruiter's knowledge can have a big impact on how attractive a job is.[35] Unfortunately, at least one study found that recruiters were more likely to leave applicants with a *negative* rather than a *positive* impression of an organization.[36] Apparently, applicants seem to believe many recruiters are ill prepared.[37] Recruiters can do a better job if they are familiar with the position and are knowledgeable about the organization. To help them better understand these facets of recruiting, the organization can choose a recruiter who has previously worked or currently works in the target position, or the company can impart this knowledge to the recruiter via training.

Instead of a recruiter's demographics, it's more likely that the key to successful recruiting is the recruiter's *ability to relate to a recruit's value system and motivations*. Recruiting requires persuasion on the part of the recruiter and the ability to sell the organization and its opportunities to the recruit.[38] Research has focused on superficial demographic characteristics when what may be important is the recruiter's ability to relate to and empathize with recruits and to communicate effectively with them by identifying and appealing to what is important to them. Providing preliminary support for this proposition, one study found that management graduates seeking jobs gave higher ratings to recruiters with attitudes similar to their own.[39] Although limited research has been done on this subject, organizations should evaluate for themselves whether or not this seems to be a factor and use this information to hire the best recruiters for different positions. This may mean sending different recruiters to different recruiting events to maximize their ability to establish a rapport with applicants. Some organizations even try to match recruiters' alma maters with the universities from which they are recruiting, and recruiters' hometowns with the hometowns of applicants. The better connection a recruiter can make with applicants, the greater the chances of an organization's job offers being accepted.

Take, for example, the job of recruiting nurses for pharmaceutical sales representative positions. Recruiters who personally relate to the rewards and challenges of nursing and who can communicate in a more compelling way the features of the job are more likely to appeal to nurses than those recruiters who have little understanding of the nursing profession. Profiling information about desired applicants' motivations and value systems can also be used to devise training material for recruiters. If the match between the recruiter and the recruit's value systems can be identified, the recruiters can be trained to better relate to applicants and present the job in the most attractive way.

reviewer profile
a profile of the skills, characteristics, and backgrounds of the most effective recruiters for different positions

DEVELOPING RECRUITER PROFILES Whether a recruiter is internal or external to the organization, understanding the recruiter characteristics most likely to attract desired applicants can enhance recruiting effectiveness. One way to do this is to create a **reviewer profile** of the individual recruiters who have been the most effective in the past. Over time, organizations can track applicant reactions to different recruiting styles and messages, and profile the skills, characteristics, and backgrounds of its most effective recruiters for different positions.

For example, a firm might find after conducting such an analysis that external recruiters do a better job when hiring speed is a priority and the level of the position being filled is relatively high. Internal recruiters might be a better choice when it's more important to keep hiring costs down. When recruiting new graduates with different degrees, recruiters with different backgrounds might be more effective. Analyzing this type of information can help an organization better specify who should do the recruiting and what the job specifications should be for recruiters targeting different positions.

MATCHING THE RECRUITER TO THE TARGETED APPLICANT In some cases, a firm might first identify someone whom they would very much like to hire, then strategize how to best attract them to join the organization. Often the targeted individual is currently employed and not looking to switch jobs. In this situation, it is critical that the choice of recruiter be made after considering whom the targeted individual is likely to best be persuaded by. A cold call by a recruiter from the human resource department is not as likely to stimulate the interest of the individual as well as a professional colleague in the hiring organization, or even the CEO. Persuasion is an important recruiter skill, and in order to persuade an individual to consider leaving a job she or he is happy with, the message must come from a trusted and respected individual to maximize the chances that it be given full consideration.

When the dean of Rutgers's Division of Life Sciences wanted to hire someone who could make Rutgers University preeminent in genetics research, he started by contacting the top people in the field of genetics. These contacts repeatedly recommended the same person. The dean then aggressively recruited the person by tapping a Rutgers agricultural geneticist who had worked with him decades earlier to help convince him that he should join Rutgers. The dean even went so far as to contact the man's best friend from childhood and persuaded him to put in a good word for Rutgers. Ultimately, despite not initially having any interest in returning to the East Coast, where he grew up, the scientist was persuaded to accept the position.[40] Just as a recruiting message should be tailored to best inform and address the needs and concerns of each applicant, the recruiter should be chosen based on his or her ability to communicate with and persuade each recruit to consider the organization as their employer of choice.

The Different Types of Recruiters

So far, we have looked most closely at internal recruiters employed within their firm's human resource departments. However, there are other types of recruiters. Next, we look at some of the different types and the advantages and disadvantages of each.

RECRUITERS FROM OUTSIDE OF THE STAFFING FUNCTION As we have explained, internal recruiters do not have to originate from a firm's human resource department. Research has found that an information source's credibility is influenced by the source's expertise and trustworthiness.[41] Therefore, it may be effective to find technically trained employees who are interested in recruiting and make them recruiters—for example, use engineers to recruit engineers, accountants to recruit accountants, and so forth. This should maximize the recruiter's credibility because the person currently works in the position being filled. It is also often easier to train technically qualified people how to recruit than it is to teach recruiters technical knowledge. By using employees as recruiters, applicants can also better assess their fit and comfort level with the job opportunity.

Some of the top U.S. corporations assign their primary recruiting responsibilities to their line managers rather than human resource professionals. For example, the managing director of the investment-banking firm CS First Boston spends half his time on recruiting. Senior managers at the pharmaceutical giant Merck devote considerable time to recruiting.[42] In addition, as we have indicated, the involvement of an organization's top leaders in its recruiting and selection programs can signal applicants that the company considers recruiting the right people to be a priority and takes its talent seriously. This will obviously increase the organization's attractiveness.

Although using line managers as recruiters can work for many companies, it can be impractical to take employees out of their regular jobs to serve as recruiters. Effective recruiting also requires more than technical job knowledge. Oftentimes recruiters can be trained sufficiently to explain a job to applicants and answer their questions. Compared to line, or hiring, managers, recruiters are also in a better position to answer broader questions about the organization's policies and benefits and identify other positions in the organization for which recruits might be a good fit. By contrast, there may be some highly specialized positions, such as engineering or medical research, that require a recruiter to be well versed in appropriate jargon to fully communicate the job requirements to potential applicants as well as screen candidates. In this case, it is the recruiter's role to help minimize the time the manager has to spend off the job recruiting.

EXTERNAL RECRUITERS   Hiring external recruiters is generally more expensive. However, if an external recruiter can fill a position faster and with a better hire than internal recruiters, the increased cost might be well worth it. External recruiters often have more extensive networks of potential candidates to tap for job openings. Many of these recruiters specialize in particular types of candidates or industries, which can give firms greater access to larger, more highly qualified applicant pools. However, external recruiters generally lack the depth of knowledge about an organization that internal recruiters possess. Obviously, this does not mean that external recruiters are unable to identify good potential applicants. It *does* mean that the firm needs to spend more time communicating recruiting-relevant information to them.

Providing external recruiters with continuous feedback about the quality of their previous hires is an important step toward improving the staffing process. Generally, the longer-term the relationship between an organization and an external recruiter is, the better the recruiter will be able to identify and attract high-potential talent for the company—especially if he or she receives feedback from the firm. Unfortunately, many organizations provide their external recruiters with little feedback.

Other Factors Influencing a Recruiter's Effectiveness

Many factors can influence a recruiter's effectiveness and performance. Some of these factors are controllable by the recruiter, and others are not. There are some situations and some positions for which even the most talented recruiter will have difficulty identifying and attracting qualified applicants. Figure 7–1 illustrates all of the factors that have an impact on the effectiveness of recruiters. Next, we discuss each.

THE LABOR MARKET   Surpluses and shortages of talent can have a large impact on how effective recruiters are. Their skills are likely to be tested when the labor market is tight and job seekers have the luxury of choosing from among multiple job opportunities. In this situation, recruiters will need to "sell" the job and organization to potential applicants. Of course, when jobs are scarce, organizations generally have an easier time attracting quality talent. If a company is the only employer in town, recruiters will also have a much easier time attracting applicants. Even in a loose labor market in which applicants are plentiful, recruiters sometimes find it difficult to attract the right kind of talent. Although the labor market's characteristics can affect the challenge of their assignments, recruiters still have a big impact on the success of most recruiting efforts.

FIGURE 7–1   Factors Influencing a Recruiter's Effectiveness

THE ORGANIZATION'S CHARACTERISTICS   In addition to the state of the labor market, the nature of the organization in terms of its size and visibility can also influence the effectiveness of recruiters. Smaller, lesser-known organizations often have a harder time recruiting, in part because potential applicants have not heard much about the company and either never hear about job opportunities or choose to apply elsewhere. Whether the firm is seen as a desirable place to work will also influence its ability to attract potential applicants. For example, recruiters for an organization that has just been responsible for a large environmental disaster are likely to have a harder time attracting applicants than recruiters for a socially responsible company that engages in philanthropic activities. A recruiter can do a great deal to educate targeted applicants about the nature of the work and organization and put the firm on an applicant's "radar screen," so to speak.

THE CHARACTERISTICS OF THE JOB   The nature of the job being filled can also influence a recruiter's success. Some jobs are less desirable because of the work they involve, their location, hours, and so forth. For example, recruiting for night shifts and repetitive work can be more difficult than recruiting for day shifts and for jobs requiring a variety of skills and activities. Attracting applicants for a position that pays less than comparable positions in the same geographic area will also be harder. Improving job characteristics can often enhance recruiting and retention efforts. Trucking company U.S. Xpress identified poor directions as a top cause of driver dissatisfaction. To better attract and retain its drivers, U.S. Xpress made the job easier to perform by adding global positioning devices to all of its trucks. Clearly, a firm can improve the chances that its recruiters will be successful by improving the characteristics of the jobs they are trying to fill.[43]

HIRING MANAGERS   Once a new employee starts work, his or her boss, coworkers, the work itself, and organizational policies and practices usually assume much greater importance than the recruiter on outcomes such as job performance. Recruiters can only do so much to attract talent. If the hiring managers with whom they work do not reinforce the organization's desirability, the efforts of even the most talented recruiter may be wasted. For example, a promising recruit might be very enthusiastic about a potential opportunity after meeting with a recruiter but be turned off by an unprofessional hiring manager. In fact, applicants seem to be *more* put off by poor recruiting behavior exhibited by hiring managers than by recruiters. Hiring managers must see recruiters as partners and reinforce rather than undermine their efforts.

Hiring managers also need to understand the competencies, styles, and traits the organization is seeking. If hiring managers are screening for characteristics different than those being recruited for, a large number of qualified candidates are likely to be rejected for the wrong reasons. One large U.S. company identified a group of hiring managers that had the highest candidate rejection rates. It turned out the managers had been rejecting qualified candidates due to reasons unrelated to the firm's selection criteria including inappropriate dress, limited eye contact, and poor posture. The company determined that the financial cost of this mistake amounted to over $100,000 in applicant processing and candidate assessment, not including the cost of losing people who would have been good hires.

In addition to qualified candidates not being recruited and hired, if recruiters fail to make hiring managers aware of the basic legal requirements they need to follow during a staffing effort, the firm can be hit with lawsuits. In one of its judgments, the U.S. Court of Appeals for the Seventh Circuit concluded that leaving managers with hiring authority in ignorance of the basic features of discrimination laws is an "extraordinary mistake" for a company to make.[44] Of course, recruiters usually receive legal training with regard to discrimination laws, but hiring managers are sometimes overlooked despite their being integral to the recruiting process.

Because the hiring manager will be the supervisor of new hires, she or he will also play a large role in the applicants' decisions. Enlisting the highest levels of management as recruiters can also help attract top talent. Ralph Larsen, former CEO of Johnson & Johnson, traveled to key college campuses to recruit top talent.[45] In 2006, California Governor Arnold Schwarzenegger called top professors across the United States to offer them a chance to work for the University of California. Because top research talent is difficult to find and attract, California business leaders solicited the governor's help in recruiting top talent that could produce more innovations and products for California's high-tech industries.[46]

COWORKERS   Just as hiring managers can dissuade candidates from accepting job offers, so can the candidates' prospective coworkers. Potential hires often seek out current and past employees to learn about the realities of the job and organization. Thus, every employee and former employee can serve as a recruiter, and often do whether they intend to or not. The Container Store's enthusiastic employees do a great job converting the company's customers into employees. However, if in another organization customers consistently hear employees complain of low pay, poor working conditions, and bad supervision, they are not likely to seriously consider the organization as a potential employer. Unhappy employees are not likely to refer friends and family members to an organization in which they do not enjoy working, nor plan for lengthy careers with the organization themselves.

Because any employee can affect a potential applicant's decision to pursue employment with an organization, it is wise for companies to recognize employees' potential recruiting impact and do what they can to ensure that their impact is positive. Giving employees information about how to refer a potential employee to the correct place in the organization and recruiting materials to distribute can facilitate applicants' information search. Hewlett-Packard, for example, invests a considerable amount of time and money training and sending small teams of engineers and managers to recruit their future coworkers. The idea is to give applicants a sense of fit with the organization's culture so that they can make informed decisions about pursuing the firm's job opportunities.[47]

The characteristics of a newly hired person's coworkers can also affect a recruiter's success. If coworkers don't support a new hire's efforts to perform his or her best, the new hire will not live up to his or her potential. Coworkers sometimes pressure each other to maintain certain production levels, and discourage new hires from trying to become "rate busters" by exceeding the group's production norms. Coworkers or team members can also create an unpleasant environment for an unwelcome new hire, increasing the chances that he or she will quit. This sometimes happens if the group's preferred candidate is not chosen. The group might also fail to help a new hire succeed on the job, despite the person's ability and motivation to do so. This can be unintentional, but it underscores why it's important for HR personnel to follow up with new hires. The goal is to ensure that they have the tools, training, and support that they need to succeed. In short, recruiters can help identify high-potential employees, but employees need the resources and opportunity to live up to their potential.

TRAINING AND DEVELOPING RECRUITERS

If different recruiters do not look for the same competencies, values, and experience in potential applicants, many qualified applicants are likely to be overlooked, and many undesirable applicants are likely to be encouraged to apply. Recruiter training and development helps to ensure consistency in terms of what recruiters screen for and the messages they communicate about the job and company.

TABLE 7–2	Recruiter Training Areas

- Recruiting knowledge
- Interpersonal skills
- Presentation skills
- The organization's goals and recruiting objectives
- Legal issues
- Multiple assessments
- Applicant attraction

Not much research exists about the amount of training recruiters receive, but surveys suggest that many recruiters receive very little.[48] When they do receive training, it tends to focus on administrative and procedural (paperwork) issues.[49] However, the research that does exist has made it possible to identify training areas that are likely to make recruiters more effective. Table 7–2 summarizes these key areas. Next, we discuss each in more detail.

Recruiting Knowledge

A recruiter's knowledge can be enhanced in a number of ways. For example, when United Parcel Service (UPS) analyzed the characteristics of all of the workers targeted one of its districts, it found that employees tended to cluster into five distinct groups. By understanding the demographic and psychological characteristics of each group—their ages, career stages, and so forth—and by identifying the type of information each group responded to, UPS was able to train recruiters to tailor their recruitment pitches to appeal to applicants from each group.[50]

Interpersonal Skills

Recruiters can be trained to develop better interpersonal skills and behaviors. Because applicants with limited information about the organization to which they are applying may infer characteristics of the organization from their experience with the recruiter, recruiters should be trained in how to reflect the company's culture and values, how to project warmth and empathy, and how to gain an applicant's trust. Training can also improve a recruiter's listening and communication skills.

Presentation Skills

Presentation skills can be helpful to recruiters attending job fairs, recruiting on college campuses, or making any sort of formal presentation of the organization's job opportunities. Many potential applicants' first exposure to an organizational representative is at a formal presentation. If the presentation is sloppy or doesn't communicate enough meaningful information, they may decide not to apply to the organization. Training can even improve an informal pitch to a potential recruit.

The Organization's Goals and Recruiting Objectives

More important than a recruiter's background or whether the recruiter is internal or external to the organization is that she or he has a strong sense of the organization's goals, business strategy, and recruiting objectives. For example, Canada's Scotiabank Group integrates its diversity goals into all aspects of its staffing program. Diversity objectives are a part of its recruitment, interview, and selection program for both its hiring managers and recruiters. Hiring managers learn appropriate questions to ask in a selection interview as well as recruitment strategies for creating a diverse workforce.[51]

Recruiting quickly at the lowest cost requires different recruiter skills and behaviors than does recruiting for the top talent available in a given profession. In some cases, the recruiter will be expected to evaluate and screen applicants. In other words, he or she will serve the dual purposes of recruiting and selecting. In other cases, the recruiter will be expected to only answer general questions posed by recruits or to focus on stimulating targeted people's interest in the position. Fortunately, both internal and external recruiters can be easily trained with regard to an organization's business strategy and recruiting goals.

Legal Issues

Legal training is critical to establishing and maintaining a consistent, effective recruiting and applicant-screening system. This is important if an organization ever has to defend its recruiting and staffing practices in a court of law. For example, as you learned in Chapter 3, the National Labor Relations Act (NLRA) extends many rights to workers who wish to form, join, or support unions. Employers also cannot discriminate against pro-union applicants. "Salting" occurs when union organizers seek jobs at a nonunion company in order to persuade the workers to join a union.[52] Because an employer violates Section 8(a)(1) of the NLRA by making statements that union applicants will not be hired,[53] interviewers must be trained in how to appropriately respond to salting tactics.

Salting is only one of the many legal situations firms have to deal with. Firms also have to minimize the chances that any illegal discriminatory recruiting is taking place. Training can also help recruiters become aware of any biases they have and give them tools to minimize the likelihood that they will discriminate unintentionally.[54]

Multiple Assessments

Recruiters and hiring managers can also be trained to assess candidates for positions other than the one currently being filled. Even if the company isn't currently looking for a particular candidate's skills and expertise, the company may need these competencies in the future or in a job other than the one being recruited for. In addition to training recruiters about how to profile candidates not currently being hired and assess their fit with multiple positions, recruiters can be trained in the creation and use of a special talent database that might be referenced in the future for other openings. Through relationship marketing, recruiters can keep in contact with candidates in the database and maintain their interest in the company, much as Valero Energy does.

Applicant Attraction

After identifying where good applicants are, recruiters can then be trained to disseminate effective recruiting messages to active job seekers as well as to passive job candidates to attract them. As we have mentioned, passive job candidates often require more active recruiting. Attending trade shows and professional conferences and networking with potential applicants can help a recruiter develop relationships with them that can be tapped in the future. How to start conversations with potential applicants and how to tactfully introduce the idea of considering alternative employment opportunities with the recruiter's organization can be practiced. Training can also enhance recruiters' persuasion skills and ability to sell the job and organization.

RECRUITING METRICS

How does a firm know if it has selected the right recruiters and trained them well? Standard efficiency-oriented recruiting metrics include hiring speed, number of hires achieved per recruiter, and the average cost per hire. Although these metrics can be useful, they are not always tied to a business's strategy and may not be the best recruiting outcomes to track. Take, for example, one major software company that assembled a recruiting team to attract senior software architects—the key employees in its business. Because the cycle for hiring these individuals can exceed five years, the firm does not measure its recruiters on the number of jobs they fill as much as on the number of qualified individuals they identify and the relationships they create with them.[55]

Indeed, because some positions have a greater impact on the company than do others, some firms prioritize or "weight" key positions more heavily in their overall assessment of how well individual recruiters have performed. However, if a firm's resources are limited, the company sometimes assesses only the staffing results of its key positions. Because the performance of even great recruiters can be compromised when they're working with difficult hiring managers, sometimes firms make adjustments for this factor as well as other uncontrollable factors recruiters face.[56]

The following is a list of strategic metrics one HR expert recommends measuring:[57]

- *New hire job performance:* The on-the-job performance ratings for new employees 6 to 12 months after being hired.
- *New hire failure rate:* The percentage of new hires in key jobs who were terminated or asked to leave.
- *Turnover of new hires:* The percentage of employees who voluntarily quit within their first year, or the average tenure of new hires compared to the firm's typical tenure.
- *Manager satisfaction:* The percentage of key managers who are satisfied with the hiring process and the candidates.
- *New hire satisfaction:* The percentage of applicants and new hires in key jobs who are satisfied with the hiring process.
- *New hire time to productivity:* The time it takes for new hires to meet the firm's minimum output standards.
- *Training success:* New hires' scores on any mandatory initial training tests they are given.

Tracking the outcomes recruiters achieve can help a firm to identify areas that can be improved. If the best recruiters can be identified, it can also be possible to identify what makes them successful (profile them) and use this information when hiring and training other recruiters.

Setting Recruiters' Goals

Recruiters' goals must be consistent with the organization's objectives and staffing strategy. An organization usually sets specific goals for their recruiters' activities at job fairs, conferences, interviews, and so forth, including communicating the employer's value proposition, screening candidates, and generating candidates' interest in the position and organization. For a recruiter to pursue the organization's goals, the organization's goals must be known by the recruiter and be consistent with the recruiter's personal goals. Recruiters are likely to have their own goals and motivations, including being liked, hiring people from their alma maters, and enjoying a break from their normal work routines.[58] Monitoring their behavior is usually very difficult for organizations, particularly when the recruiter is working off-site. This makes it even more important that goals of recruiters are aligned with the goals of their firms.

Many recruiters know very little about the success of their recruiting efforts other than the number of positions they have filled, their average time-to-fill for a given position, and so forth. However, an organization's recruiting goals are likely much more complex. Although many possible metrics exist to evaluate recruiters' effectiveness, their performance is not likely to change unless they receive feedback as to how they are doing and how they can improve. Giving them feedback also helps to reinforce what they've learned through training, and helps recruiters identify and self-correct their performance shortcomings. Without this feedback, recruiters cannot know what they should be doing differently.

For the feedback to be most effective, clear goals that are based on the organization's key recruiting objectives should first be set for recruiters. If the organization is interested in hiring customer service representatives to staff a new telephone center as quickly as possible, the company's goals balancing hiring speed with acceptable levels of job performance should be established. If the open position is a "feeder position" for a more important position, recruiter goals linked to new hire promotability may also be included. It is important to think through both the intended and unintended consequences of any goals to ensure that the proper recruiter behaviors and outcomes are being motivated. Giving recruiters feedback on their performance relative to their goals can help them understand what they need to do differently as well as identify recruiters' development needs.

Giving Recruiters the Incentive to Meet Their Goals

One study found that only about one-fourth of in-house recruiters receive incentive pay based on their own, rather than company-wide, performance levels.[59] Too often, however, recruiters are rewarded for short-term goals such as the number of jobs they fill or the total compensation of the people they recruit. If hiring speed is all that is rewarded, the quality of a firm's new hires is likely to be lower than if both new hire quantity and quality are rewarded. At Advanced Technology Services (ATS), a company that maintains complex factory equipment for major manufacturers including Honda and GE, quality of hire is more important than the number of hires or the time to hire. Accordingly, ATS recruiters are evaluated on their hires' one-year retention rates.[60]

Given that the rewarded behaviors and outcomes are the ones recruiters are most likely to pursue, it is imperative that the firm's incentive system be well designed and well tested before being rolled out. This can help eliminate any unintended consequences of the new system. For example, a study of how Navy recruiters reacted to a recruiting incentive plan that included quotas, prizes, and other standards found that recruiting productivity was highest in the period immediately prior to the quota/prize cutoff date and lowest immediately afterward. Additionally, the average quality of the people recruited fell as the cutoff date approached,[61] which was not the intent of the incentive system.

Although recruiting productivity as measured by the total base compensation of new hires and the speed with which they are recruited can be criteria to use to reward recruiters, using them in isolation does not motivate recruiters to hire the best possible talent. An effective incentive system aligns the goals of the organization with the recruiters' goals. Rewarding recruiters for recruiting good employees who remain with the firm and perform well can do a great deal to align the hiring goals of the organization with the recruiter's personal goals. For example, the telecommunications company T-Mobile gives its recruiters quarterly bonuses pegged to their individual performance goals. The goals, which must support the firm's corporate-wide goals, are drafted by recruiters and approved by T-Mobile's managers.[62] If a recruiting function is team based, it is important to link the team's rewards to behaviors that support the effectiveness of the entire team. A balanced incentive plan that considers all the organization's long-term and short-term strategic hiring goals will better motivate recruiters to meet the organization's multiple goals.

DEVELOPING APPLICANT ATTRACTION STRATEGIES

Having a great job opportunity does not always translate into sufficient numbers of quality applicants. Applicants must be attracted to those opportunities before they are willing to apply. One popular model of applicant attraction[63] developed by Professor Sara Rynes suggests that applicants gather information about potential employers to assess the types of rewards the firms offer and to determine whether their skills meet the job's requirements. They also look for signals that help them identify the culture and climate of the organization. This helps potential applicants assess their likely fit with the job and the firm. When applicants are attracted to a firm, they are more likely to apply for jobs, accept job offers, and remain with the company over time. Next, we discuss the role of organizational image, employer brand, and the recruiting message in applicant attraction.

Developing the Organization's Image and Brand

Given the limited amount of information most applicants have early in the job search process, initial application decisions are largely based on general impressions of organizational attractiveness.[64] Every organization has an **image** for itself and its products, whether it is proactive in establishing it or not. The first words or images that come to mind when someone thinks about a particular company generally reflect the company's image. However, the image a person has about an organization is his or her general impression of the organization based on both feelings and facts, and may not be accurate.[65] An organization's image may be positive or negative, weak or strong, clear or vague, and images can vary from person to person and change over time.[66]

Organizational images have been found to differ across subgroups of individuals. In one study, corporate executives and college undergraduates disagreed in their overall corporate image ratings.[67] Executives based their image assessments on economic performance indicators and detailed knowledge of the companies in their industry. College students' image assessments, on the other hand, tended to be influenced more heavily by exposure to, or familiarity with, the organization (using its products, knowing someone who works there, seeing the organization's advertisements, etc.).[68] Not surprisingly, being exposed to a greater amount of positive information about the organization enhanced the organization's image as an employer and increased

image
a general impression based on both feelings and facts

undergraduates' intentions of pursuing employment.[69] College undergraduates' image assessments of organizations as employers were found to be malleable and independent of their assessments of the organization's corporate image, suggesting that organizations that do not have high-profile corporate images may still be able to compete successfully for undergraduate students in the initial stages of their job choice through the use of recruitment messages that establish a positive image for the organization as an employer. Because different subgroups of people base their corporate image assessments on different factors, different methods may meet with differing success in altering an organization's image among different groups, and different information about the organization may need to be provided to appeal to different types of recruits.

brand
a symbolic picture of all the information connected to a company or its products

A **brand** is a symbolic picture of all the information connected to a company or its products, including its image. Organizations often try to link their images and consumer brands with their business strategies. For example, for many people Nieman-Marcus, Goldman Sachs, and Tiffany's probably conjure images of elite, high-quality, and expensive products and services. When you think of Walmart and Dell Computer you probably think of low-cost goods and high-efficiency work processes. These companies created consumer brands for themselves that reflect their business strategies. Brands are often represented by symbols including names, logos, slogans, or designs. Image and brand recognition are created by the accumulation of experiences with the specific product or service, both directly relating to its use, and through the influence of communications, advertising, design, and media exposure.[70]

Developing the Organization's Employer Brand

employer brand
reflects what a company offers as an employer and helps manage internal and external perceptions of what it is like to work there

Firms often craft **employer brands** to reflect what they offer as employers and to manage internal and external perceptions of what it is like to work there. An employer brand answers the question, "Why should I work here?" and influences people's intentions to apply for jobs.[71]

Many factors, including recognition in "best employer" surveys, ethics violations, environmental accidents, and corporate philanthropy, may affect an organization's image positively and negatively. Most people want to be members of an organization that has a favorable image.[72] Research has consistently found that the more favorable a company's image and brand are, the more people are likely to consider the organization attractive as an employer and respond to its recruiting advertisements.[73] This suggests that newer or lesser-known organizations with weak or nonexistent brands will have greater difficulty attracting applicants using passive recruitment sources, such as newspaper advertisements, than organizations that are more widely known and favorably thought of. Companies such as IBM, Johnson & Johnson, and Nike invest a lot of money building and maintaining a certain employer brand. Rich Floersch, McDonald's executive vice president of worldwide human resources, states, "I really believe that the strongest employment brand that you can have is one where employees say they are proud to work for their companies. Our goal is to continue to build that sense of pride."[74]

Attracting the right employees and maintaining their commitment to perform at a high level is an important part of building and supporting a firm's customer brand for its products. Likewise, the strength of the consumer brand plays an important role in attracting the right people to work for the company. Once employed, the pride they share in the company's external reputation helps maintain their loyalty and commitment to deliver on the company's brand promises to its customers.[75]

Yahoo! is one company that has actively tried to create an employer brand based on its corporate mission, brand, and values. Libby Sartain, senior vice president of human resources and chief people officer for Yahoo!, said that the company's employer brand "enabled Yahoo! to do some strong thinking about what we stand for and how we market ourselves to both technical and non-technical talent. The recruitment brand is not tailored to each target audience. However, the brand looks different depending on where it is being used, such as in the college campus, at a technical conference, or for marketing people."[76]

An effective employer brand differentiates a firm from its competitors, and is appealing to targeted applicants. It is also critical that the company deliver on its employer brand promises. In the age of Vault.com and other Internet sites where employees share their experiences with one another, what a firm promises versus delivers to its employees will generally be widely known. If people join an organization expecting that the firm holds certain values and will provide a certain type of employment experience, they are likely to leave if their expectations are not met. The goal of employer branding is not to fool potential applicants but to effectively communicate the firm's message of what it intends to provide as an employer.[77] As one employer branding expert said, "The purpose of the employer brand proposition is not to invent a further set of values, but to help to ensure that the purpose and value statements that currently exist are translated into something relevant and meaningful to employees, and made consistent with the values the organization wishes to project externally."[78]

Jo Pieters, global vice president of recruitment for Philips in the Netherlands, states, "In my view, winning the war for talent means primarily focusing on retention of your current talent and following that, building a strong position in your key labor markets. Therefore, a brand that is only visible in external communications is less valuable than a brand that is truly lived inside. Each and every employee should act as an ambassador of your brand and that requires a strong and recognized internal and external employee value proposition."[79]

Lucy Chang, talent acquisition senior manager for Sun Microsystems, Hong Kong, adds, "I am a strong proponent of employer branding. It is the basic fundamental of any recruitment strategy. You have to know who you are as a company, your messaging, and what is your competitive advantage against other companies. It is a long-term strategy, which I think many companies fail to recognize."[80] Table 7–3 contains some popular companies and their employer brand slogans.

It can be worthwhile for any organization to evaluate its brand among its targeted applicant pools and take steps to make it as strong and positive as possible before launching a recruiting campaign. One study found that the three most effective branding techniques used to appeal to college graduates were building relationships with key faculty, appearing at campus career fairs, and supporting the activities of student organizations on campus.[81]

Many organizations spend a lot of money to try to influence their overall image and their brand as an employer. For example, Hewlett-Packard, Home Depot, and McDonald's have all run television advertisements designed solely to promote their brands as employers. Merrill Lynch spent around $150 million in a single year in image ads to reinforce its new brand as a tech-savvy company.[82] Even as early as 1990, U.S. companies spent over $1.4 billion on advertising intended just to create a favorable impression of themselves.[83]

If an organization wants to distinguish itself as an employer, focusing on influencing its symbolic meaning as an employer can be an effective strategy[84]—for example, whether the company is thought of by applicants as trendy, prestigious, or innovative and its jobs thought of positively in terms of their location, pay, and benefits. Given the power repetitive marketing messages have, recruiters and employees should be trained in how to consistently and clearly promote the employer's brand at every opportunity. One expert believes that managers should market their companies to applicants the same way they would market their products to customers. He suggests that managers arm themselves with a brief pitch designed to attract talent at the drop of a hat. Like an entrepreneur's pitch, this speech should be concise and compelling, and should answer the questions: How is the company different? What is its vision? What is its competitive advantage? Why should a talented person join? What benefits does the company offer?[85]

Proactively establishing a positive employer brand takes time to do well, and can be expensive.[86] In addition to developing the image and the branding strategy, print advertising campaigns, a Web site, radio and television commercials, and even articles in targeted magazines may be created. The Boston Consulting Group's (www.bcg.com) site for new consultants and Federated Department Stores's Retailology (www.retailology.com) site for college recruiting are good examples of how to promote a desirable employer brand online. The "working at Google" videos on YouTube promote Google as a unique experience where you "enjoy what you do,

TABLE 7–3	Employer Brand Slogans

Johnson & Johnson: "Small Company Environment, Big Company Impact"
Eli Lilly: "Innovation Has a Face: Our People"
Medtronic: "Careers with a Passion for Life"
Abbott Labs: "Inspired to Achieve. Make a Difference in Your World"
Sharp: "From Sharp Minds Come Sharp Products"

where you do it, and the people you do it with." Some organizations' product advertisements, including Microsoft and Siemens, are designed clearly to attract talented people to work there. Because they can highlight the organization's facilities, employees, customers, products, and work processes, employer brand advertisements can be effectively shown on television, too. Companies including Verizon and Home Depot have developed TV "commercials" that "sell" their employer brands to viewers. Employer brand advertisements can be particularly helpful for smaller or lesser-known organizations that lack name recognition.

Cleveland-based bank National City Corporation evaluates job candidates by seeing how they perform in a computerized simulation of specific job-related tasks. The simulation also reinforces the company's brand by showing recruits what it's like to be an employee at the company. One company representative states, "We think it creates a unique impression that lets us stand out among our peers in the industry. . . .It gives us a way to share our story and what we're all about."[87]

Magazines and other publications and organizations periodically assess employers in terms of how good they are to work for. This can significantly enhance a firm's employer brand. *Fortune* magazine's annual lists of the "100 Best Companies to Work For" and the "Best Companies for Minorities," *Working Mother* magazine's annual list of the "100 Best Companies for Working Mothers," and the American Association of Retired Persons' list of the "Best Employers for Workers over 50" are good examples of such assessments. How an organization is reputed to treat its employees is likely to have a particularly strong effect on how likely it is to attract applicants. This explains why many organizations are eager to appear on lists such as these.

But being an employer of choice can create challenges as well as opportunities. Many organizations are not prepared to handle the increased volume of job applicants resulting from being named an employer of choice. In the month following the announcement that Edward Jones was number one on *Fortune* magazine's annual "100 Best Companies to Work For" list, the number of job inquiries jumped by nearly 63 percent. The company claims that it was all because of the *Fortune* story and that it did nothing different in its outreach activities.[88]

The increased job seeker interest resulting from a positive brand is not necessarily a negative, but it does increase the burden on the organization's selection system. There is no guarantee that more applicants mean higher applicant quality. However, engaging in a targeted recruiting effort to fill a particular opening can help a firm manage the number of applications it receives and increase the quality of its applicant pools. Meanwhile, the organization's positive employer brand should allow it to improve its interview and job offer acceptance rates. Another downside of such lists is that once a company is on a "best companies to work for" list it risks negative publicity and negative reactions from existing employees if it later falls off the list. Although many employers actively try to be named to these lists, the competition for developing ever-creative and ever-increasing employee benefits might not be something the organization wants to commit to.

This chapter's Develop Your Skills feature describes how to develop an employer brand.

Developing the Recruiting Message

Like a firm's recruiters, image, and employer brand, the recruiting message communicated to potential applicants will affect the number and types of them that will apply. In addition to communicating the nature of the job opportunity that the company is offering, the message can create or reflect the company's brand as well.

Rather than simply stating the core requirements of the open position, it can be more effective to craft the recruiting message in the most appealing and effective way. Even the physical design of the recruiting message or ad can affect the success of a campaign.

Companies that develop recruiting campaigns and ads for organizations have conducted research on how well different recruiting materials attract the attention of potential applicants—including the different styles of the ads, colors, fonts, and sizes as well as how they're positioned on pages (in the case of print ads).[89] More rigorous, scientifically grounded research on recruitment materials is lacking, though.

In any case, the factors that affect what does and does not get the attention of applicants can change rapidly. What was novel and effective a year ago may be obsolete today. Therefore, any conclusions researchers draw from research such as this are likely to have a short lifespan.[90] Moreover, because competitors can copy an organization's recruiting programs, a firm constantly needs to be innovative when it comes to its recruiting campaigns.

DEVELOP YOUR SKILLS
How to Develop an Employer Brand?

A positive employer brand differentiates you as an employer. An employer brand should capture the essence of what it is like to work for your company and appeal to prospective employees. Here are four steps in developing a positive employer brand:[91]

1. *Analyze* the current perceptions of your target audience. Answering questions such as "Why should I want to work for us?" or "Why are we different or unique as a place to work?" can help you understand your strengths as an employer and identify the characteristics you want to play up in your brand. Because people often stay at an organization for the same reasons they joined it in the first place, understanding why employees stay can also help an organization identify its competitive advantage as an employer.
2. *Align* your employer brand with your firm's policies, practices, culture, and values. Use aspects of the corpora-

tion's values, culture, and image to appeal to potential applicants as well as current employees.

3. *Communicate* your story clearly and consistently. Generate favorable publicity such as news stories about your organization featured in various media. Incorporate employer brand elements into the firm's job advertisements and product packaging, and encourage employees to spread the brand via word of mouth. Consider sponsoring scholarships, events, or donating products or equipment to universities at which you would like to portray a strong employer brand.
4. *Measure* and improve your branding effort by periodically repeating step 1 to see whether people's perceptions of the company have changed. Establishing metrics up front can help you assess whether or not your efforts are working.

In terms of the message itself, understanding the goals and values of the targeted applicants and crafting a recruitment message that appeals to them is especially critical in a competitive hiring market. Successful companies are increasingly adapting their employer brands to target different targeted recruits with different values, needs, and ambitions.[92] For example, older workers' lifestyle goals often differ from Generation Y's lifestyle goals, and higher-achieving college students place greater importance on interesting and challenging work than do other students.[93] Stressing the most appealing features of the job being recruited for should improve the organization's ability to attract each subgroup of potential applicants. Recruiting brochures that highlight how important teamwork and diversity are to the firm can have the effect of attracting more women and minorities.[94] Statements in a newspaper ad about company policies, scheduling flexibility, and a targeted equal opportunity statement can similarly influence older workers' attraction to an organization.[95]

UK retailer Tesco explicitly divides its potential frontline recruits into three segments: those joining straight from school, students looking for part-time work, and graduates. A separate section of the company's Web site is devoted to each group and presents recruiting materials tailored to that group.[96] Oil services company Schlumberger became one of the industry's leading recruiters of female engineers by introducing flexible work practices and communicating them during its recruitment efforts.[97]

Although there are relatively few studies on the best types of information to include in a recruiting message, taken as a whole the research suggests that recruiting materials should be informative, address a range of job or organization characteristics, and provide specific information about those characteristics.[98] More detailed job postings have been found to be useful in "weeding out" unqualified applicants through self-selection, increasing the efficiency of the recruitment and hiring process.[99] Providing specific information about a job's location, the type of job, and salary levels in the firm's recruiting materials can thus save organizations time.

Also, as we mentioned earlier, providing more or less information in the recruiting message and/or job listing has been found to have an effect on whether or not applicants will apply to an organization.[100] General ads that include limited job attributes have the potential to appeal to a wide variety of job applicants and generate a lot of applicants, but they also tend to increase the number of unqualified or inappropriate applicants. Ads such as these can also be unappealing to job seekers who are highly focused in their job search strategies.

Information that is particularly unusual or extreme compared to the other job alternatives tends to receive greater attention than attributes set nearer to average levels.[101] Preliminary research evidence also suggests that job seekers use a subset of the total number of organizational or job characteristics as noncompensatory screening factors, rejecting all employment opportunities that do not meet their minimum standards on these characteristics, and are willing to make trade-offs among other characteristics. In particular, salary levels,[102] location,[103] and type of job[104] are common noncompensatory screening variables for which other job and organizational factors cannot make up. Although no job factor is a noncompensatory screening variable for all job seekers, research has found that jobs tend to be rejected more frequently if they fail to meet minimum requirements on these factors regardless of other job characteristics. It also seems that some job factors, particularly high compensation levels, can offset less desirable features of a job and organization. For example, high compensation levels have been found to offset the negative effect of employment-at-will statements,[105] and having an explicit EEO policy has been found to help offset the negative effect of application questions that could appear discriminatory.[106]

Providing specific information about a job's location, the type of job, and salary levels in recruitment materials can save organizations the time and expense of processing and screening candidates who are ultimately not likely to accept job offers once they learn this information. Providing more information and providing more specific information (e.g., the exact starting salary rather than "competitive salary") have been found to influence the decision to apply to an organization.[107] It is important to remember that if some potential applicants are not likely to ultimately accept job offers or to stay with the organization as long as the organization would like, it is not necessarily a limitation for recruiting practices to dissuade these people from ever applying.

Table 7–4 summarizes the practical implications of recruitment research findings.[108]

Developing Realistic Job Previews

When communicating the nature of the work and the organization, organizations have a choice of how objective to be. Some organizations embellish the nature of the work and the reality of working in the organization, making the job seem far more positive and enjoyable than it necessarily is. As we have mentioned, research has found that slanting recruiting information can be detrimental to an organization.[109] Particularly in a strong labor market when other job opportunities exist if the job is not what they expected, "conned" employees are likely to perform poorly and leave the organization.

Other organizations opt to disclose to applicants as little potentially undesirable information as possible to reduce the chance that the applicants will lose interest in the position. The feeling is generally that if the organization told applicants what it was really like to work there, they would not want the job. This focus on getting candidates to accept job offers without their thoroughly understanding what they are getting themselves into can be misguided.

TABLE 7–4	Practical Implications of Recruiting Research Findings[110]

The following is a summary of the practical steps firms should take to improve their recruiting efforts:

• Hire recruiters who are personable, informative, and trustworthy.

• Make a firm's initial recruiting activities (brochures, on-campus recruiting efforts, and so forth) as attractive to candidates as the firm's later recruiting activities.

• Provide applicants with enough accurate information about the job and organization so that they can assess their fit.

• Ensure that all the firm's communications send a positive message about the company's image and attractiveness as an employer.

• Provide clear, specific, and complete information in recruitment materials and messages to prevent candidates from making erroneous inferences.

• Create a positive organizational image in the minds of applicants, both before and during the recruiting effort.

• Respond quickly to applications and inquiries.

• Treat candidates fairly and considerately throughout the recruiting process.

• Enhance applicants' perceptions of fairness, train recruiters to explain the company's selection procedures, keep candidates informed, and avoid communication delays.

• Communicate values of the firm that are consistent with the values and needs of each applicant.

Other companies try to help candidates understand the organization and job. Companies, like the restaurant chain Cracker Barrel (http://careers.crackerbarrel.com), have put interactive features on their Web sites to expose potential applicants to their culture and give them insight into what it is like to work there.

Realistic job previews (RJPs) involve the presentation of both positive and potentially negative information to job candidates. Rather than trying to sell them on the job and company by presenting the job opportunity in the most positive light, realistic job previews strive to present an honest and accurate picture.

realistic job previews (RJPs)
provide both positive and potentially negative information to job candidates

The most common mistake made when initially developing a realistic recruiting message is a tendency to emphasize only the potentially negative features of a job. The purpose, however, is not to present a negative picture but to present a *realistic* picture of the job, presenting both potentially positive and potentially negative aspects in as objective a way as possible to allow prospective applicants to self-select into or out of consideration for the position. Aspects and attributes of a job are, by nature, objective, and any positive or negative interpretation of them should be left to the applicant. For example, rather than stating that the job is high pressure, communicating that the organization is particularly seeking detail-oriented people with a sense of time urgency would be more appropriate.

There is no such thing as a "bad job," only a bad job for a particular individual given his or her interests, competencies, and values. Presenting objective information about a position and letting people self-select into it knowing what the job will really be like helps get them into the right jobs and increases the likelihood that once employed they will stay in those jobs and perform well. The goal is not to deter candidates by focusing on factors that might be perceived negatively, but to provide accurate information about the job and organization.[111] IBM's careers Web site has highly interactive multimedia including "day in the life" videos, Digg, live chat, business-unit specific information, and flash video.[112] Some companies even provide online video tours of their facilities.

If a common reason for employees leaving the organization is that the job isn't what they expected, this is a good sign that the recruiting message could be improved. Firms that experience such a situation can often use an RJP to try to reduce their turnover rates.

John Wanous,[113] a professor of management and human resources, has identified three functions that are served by an RJP:

1. *Self-selection:* Giving applicants a more balanced picture of the job and organization allows them to opt out of the application process if the opportunity is not a good match for them. RJPs do not necessarily make large numbers of applicants more likely to drop out of the application process, and the applicants likely to be lost after communicating realistic information about the job and company are not likely to have been successful hires anyway.[114]
2. *Vaccination:* RJPs may work by "vaccinating" employees' expectations and allowing them to develop coping mechanisms to deal with unpleasant or unexpected aspects of the position. When encountering these aspects on the job, the employee is prepared for them and is less negatively affected by them.
3. *A commitment to the choice:* If employees are informed about the negative aspects of a job before they accept employment, they cannot claim that they did not know about them.[115] Thus, they may be more committed to the choice they have made—that is, they may be more inclined to stay in their positions because they realize they willingly accepted the job despite knowing its realities.[116]

Walt Disney World in Lake Buena Vista, Florida, which employs more than 55,000 people and hires an average of 200 people a day, actively uses realistic job previews in its recruiting practices. Before completing an application or being interviewed, candidates view a film depicting what working at Disney is like. After viewing it, about 10 percent of candidates self-select out of the hiring process. Disney views this as a good thing because those self-selecting themselves out probably wouldn't have been a good fit with the organization.[117] Cisco Systems' Make Friends @ Cisco program uses employee volunteers to answer phone or e-mail queries from job seekers who would like more information about working at Cisco.

Giving applicants the opportunity to self-select out of the hiring process if they do not perceive themselves to be good fits with the position or organization increases the likelihood that the applicants ultimately hired will be good fits and will be better employees as a result.

Given the relatively low cost associated with the development of an RJP, they may be useful for organizations trying to reduce turnover rates for jobs which departing employees say were not what they expected when they accepted job offers.

Some companies have used RJPs to counter inaccurate employer images. Fast food giant McDonald's has responded to critics in the United Kingdom who claim it is a poor employer by launching a poster campaign using the slogan "Not bad for a McJob," which details the benefits and flexible hours the company offers. It is the first time the company has tried to combat the negative misconceptions that have been associated with the title "McJob" ever since the term was used by Douglas Copeland in his best-selling novel *Generation X: Tales for an Accelerated Culture*. A McDonald's executive believes that a huge gap exists between the external perception and the internal reality of working at McDonald's and states, "Our employer reputation isn't justified; we have to accept that this association exists and correct it."[118]

Communicating a realistic picture of the job does not have to be expensive or difficult. The focus is not on aspects of the work that are already visible, or obvious, to applicants, but on aspects of the work not likely to be known by an outsider—say, the fast pace of work, high performance expectations, pay, and benefits. The process of compiling information about the job or organization that candidates will find more and less attractive begins with understanding what the firm's current employees like and dislike about the job. Surveying them might indicate that they like, say, the above-average pay, relatively low educational requirements, generous benefits, and the fact that they are done with work by 2 P.M., which allows them time to spend with their families or to work at second jobs. Information collected from employees who recently resigned can help a firm understand what they did and didn't like. All this information can then be synthesized into a realistic recruiting message that is not so lengthy that it overwhelms applicants.

Of course, the best thing to do with a job that has potentially undesirable characteristics is to take the necessary steps to improve it before recruiting candidates. Perhaps poor supervisors can be trained, pay and benefit levels can be raised, or safety and working conditions can be improved. In other words, providing realistic job information about a bad job is no substitute for providing a better, more appealing job opportunity.

Developing Self-Assessment Tools

In addition to trying to recruit candidates with a particular profile of characteristics, organizations can take steps to make it easier for applicants to self-assess their fit with the job and organization. Because believing that they are a good fit with a company's culture and job opportunities improves a job seeker's attraction to the organization, many organizations try to enable applicants' self-evaluation of their fit with the company. Companies including McDonald's, Walmart, and Home Depot provide information about the organization's culture and values and have created interactive self-assessment tools to help candidates make this assessment.

Some organizations provide an online questionnaire that gives users feedback about their degree of fit with the job and organization.[119] Prospective employees can also use on-site computers to learn about an organization and its job opportunities, take self-assessments to identify their fit with the company's culture, read job descriptions, review current job openings, and immediately apply for jobs.

To ensure an honest self-assessment on the part of the potential applicant, self-assessments should be anonymous. Moreover, the company should not use this information to screen applicants. The best use of such a tool is to help potential applicants determine whether the company is a place where they are likely to enjoy working. If a potential applicant perceives herself as a poor fit and decides not to apply, she and the organization can save time and resources by not pursuing what is ultimately likely to be a poor match.

TIMING THE DISCLOSURE OF INFORMATION

After the firm has identified the more- and less-attractive aspects of the job and the organization, a decision needs to be made about when to communicate this information to applicants. The content of the recruiting message is likely to change over time, focusing initially on broader issues, such as the job title, the general nature and responsibilities of the job, and the job's location. At the initial stage of making contact with a potential recruit, the communication is intended to allow each party

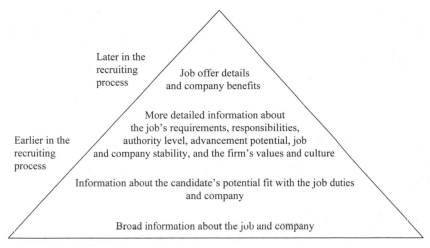

FIGURE 7–2   Information Sought at Different Times in the Recruiting Process

to quickly and cost-effectively assess the general likelihood of a fit between the applicant's competencies, values, and experiences and the organization's particular job openings. If the organization has an opening for an accountant but the potential applicant has a background and an interest in marketing, the recruiting effort is not likely to be pursued further by either party.

As the fit between the recruit and the job begins to look better, information that is more detailed is provided about the job's requirements, responsibilities, authority level, and advancement potential. Job candidates are typically interested in learning all they can about the organization's strategy and position in its market, the firm's available training programs, travel requirements, and the stability of the job and company. Candidates may also be interested in learning what they can about the organization's values and culture, and the recruitment messages from the company can be designed to inform the candidate about these issues both directly and indirectly. Compensation issues can be discussed at any time but are often reserved for late in the recruitment and hiring process. Figure 7–2 summarizes the type of information candidates generally look for earlier versus later in the recruiting process.

We have discussed how applicants interpret recruitment experiences, including perceived recruiter competence and recruitment delays, as symbolic of broader organizational characteristics. An organization that does not keep its word regarding when it will be communicating with applicants or whose interviewers are unprepared and overscheduled is sending a different message to recruits than an organization that is organized, professional, and keeps its word in its interactions with job candidates. It is important that recruiters be trained in what to tell recruits and how to identify issues of importance to each candidate. Some candidates will be focused on the organization's compensation and incentive system, while others will attend more to the opportunities for training and development and job advancement. It is difficult to anticipate all the issues candidates may want to hear about. Providing a communication channel through which candidates can learn more information and ask questions, perhaps via a Web site or phone number, can help balance the need to provide enough information with the need to not provide too much information, which can be both expensive and generally unnecessary at the early stage of the recruiting process.

ACHIEVING RECRUITMENT CONSISTENCY

Recruitment activities lay the foundation for a consistently administered, efficient, and legally defensible staffing effort. Developing a recruiting guide and following the EEOC's best practices related to recruiting are part of this foundation.

Developing a Recruiting Guide

A **recruiting guide** is a formal document that details the process to be followed when a firm recruits for an open position. It should address both internal and external recruiting processes. A recruitment guide clarifies company policies and procedures relating to the budgets, activities, timelines, staff members responsible for recruiting, legal issues, and the specific steps to be taken

recruiting guide
a formal document that details the process to be followed when a firm recruits for an open position

to fill positions. By standardizing the recruiting procedures used by the organization, the guide helps clarify which employees are expected to perform what roles during the recruitment process and helps to ensure that all the relevant recruiting policies and procedures are followed during the process. This can help the organization recruit in the most effective, legal manner by detailing what is and is not acceptable recruiting behavior. The policies and procedures described in the guide also help coordinate the efforts of a firm's internal and external recruiters to ensure they are not at cross-purposes with one another.

Following the EEOC's Best Recruiting Practices

As we discussed in Chapter 3, many legal issues are involved in recruiting and staffing. Table 7–5 summarizes an EEOC task force's best practice ideas in the area of recruitment.[120]

RECRUITING AT THE CONTAINER STORE

The Container Store needs to recruit self-motivated, team-oriented people with the passion for customer service that the firm needs to succeed. Rather than being an obscure function buried within an HR bureaucracy, recruiting is a primary driver of business success at The Container Store. Under the recruiting department's leadership, every individual and department in the organization has a prominent recruiting role.[121] Nearly a third of the company's 2,500 workers were hired via referrals.[122]

The company's most enthusiastic customers often inquire about opportunities and become their best employees.[123] The Container Store's employees also actively recruit customers they think will make great employees. One company executive says, "An employee will say something

TABLE 7–5	EEOC Best Recruiting Practices

Firms acting consistently with EEOC best practices do the following:[124]

- Establish a policy for recruiting and hiring, including the criteria, procedures, responsible individuals, and applicability of diversity and affirmative action initiatives.
- Engage in short-term and long-term strategic planning.
- Identify the applicable barriers to equal employment opportunity.
- Specify the firm's recruiting goals.
- Make a road map for implementing the plan.
- Ensure that there is a communication network that can be used to notify interested persons about the firm's job opportunities. The communication network should include advertising within the organization, within the general media, and media that focus on minorities, people with disabilities, older people, and women.
- Communicate the competencies, skills, and abilities required for available positions.
- Communicate about family-friendly and work-friendly programs.
- Where transportation is an issue, consider arrangements with the local transit authority.
- Participate in career and job fairs and open houses.
- Work with professional associations, civic associations, and educational institutions to attract minorities, women, people with disabilities, and/or older people.
- Provide recruiters, employees, and search firms with instructions to recruit diverse candidate pools and expand the company's search networks.
- Partner with organizations dedicated to serving diverse groups.
- Use internships, work-study, co-op, and scholarship programs to attract and pursue interested and qualified candidates.
- Develop and support educational programs; become more involved with educational institutions that can provide the company with leads used to recruit a more diverse talent pool.
- Ensure that personnel involved in the recruiting and hiring process are well trained in terms of their equal employment opportunity responsibilities.
- Become more involved in the community to improve the company's image and attract diverse candidates.
- Eliminate practices that exclude diverse candidates or create barriers for them.
- Evaluate the firm's managers on the progress they make toward the company's equal employment opportunity goals.

ratio-level measures. If one person can lift 200 pounds and another 100 pounds, then the first person can lift twice as much as the second person whether the weight is in grams or pounds. Thus, the ratio holds because there is a true zero point. In a selection context, years of experience is a ratio measure because ratios will hold whether time is measured in years, minutes, or seconds.

The distinctions among the different types of measures are important because they influence how you can describe and interpret data. For example, it is generally not useful to compute an average of ordinal scores.

Scores

The process of assigning numerical values during measurement is scoring. In order to interpret scores properly, we need to understand the scoring system used. Data is often presented in terms of numerical scores, such as raw scores, standard scores, and percentile scores, which we discuss next.

RAW SCORES **Raw scores** are the unadjusted scores on a measure. On a job knowledge test, the raw score might represent the number of items answered correctly. For measures such as personality inventories that have no "right" or "wrong" answers, the raw score may represent the number of positive responses for a particular trait. Raw scores do not provide much useful information by themselves. Consider your score on a midterm. If you get 30 out of 50 questions correct, it is hard to know whether this is a good or a poor score. You may believe 30 is a poor score, but if you compare the results to the results of other people who took the same test, you may discover that 30 is the highest score. For **criterion-referenced measures**, or standards-based assessments, the scores have meaning in and of themselves. For example, candidates might be expected to exceed a certain level on a criterion measure, such as typing at least 90 words per minute, before they can advance to the next stage of the hiring process.

On criterion-referenced measures it is easy to see what a particular score indicates about proficiency or competence. In general, scores on **norm-referenced measures** have meaning only when compared to the scores of others. For example, candidates who reach a certain norm-referenced measure—for example, who score in the top third of their applicant group on a typing test—would advance to the next stage of the hiring process. Converting raw scores into standard scores (or percentiles), as we describe next, provides you with the kind of comparative information you need to use a norm-referenced measure.

NORMAL CURVE Many human characteristics, such as height, weight, math ability, and typing skill, are distributed in the population in a typical pattern known as the **normal curve**. In other words, the characteristics display a symmetrical bell-shaped appearance like the one shown in Figure 8–1. The distribution of scores under the normal curve is called the **normal distribution**. As you can see, a large number of individual cases cluster in the middle of the curve. The farther from the middle (or average) you go, the fewer the cases. Many distributions of scores follow the same normal curve pattern. Most individuals get scores in the middle range, near average. As score extremes are approached, fewer and fewer cases exist, indicating that progressively fewer individuals get lower scores (represented by the left tail of the curve) or higher scores

raw scores
the unadjusted scores on a measure

criterion-referenced measures
measures in which the scores have meaning in and of themselves

norm-referenced measures
measures in which the scores have meaning only when compared to the scores of others

normal curve
a curve representing the bell-shaped symmetrical distribution of some factor

normal distribution
the distribution of scores under the normal curve

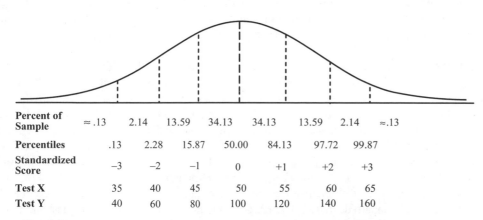

Percent of Sample	≈.13	2.14	13.59	34.13	34.13	13.59	2.14	≈.13
Percentiles		.13	2.28	15.87	50.00	84.13	97.72	99.87
Standardized Score		−3	−2	−1	0	+1	+2	+3
Test X		35	40	45	50	55	60	65
Test Y		40	60	80	100	120	140	160

FIGURE 8–1 The Normal Curve Illustrating Standard Scores and Percentiles

(represented by the right tail of the curve). Other distributions are possible but we will focus on the normal distribution because it is one of the most commonly used.

percentile score
a raw score that has been converted into an expression of the percentage of people who score at or below that score

PERCENTILE SCORE   A **percentile score** is a raw score that has been converted into an expression of the percentage of people who score at or below that score. For example, in Figure 8–1 a score of 55 on Test X or 120 on Test Y would place a person at about the 84th percentile. This means that 84 percent of the people taking the test scored at or below this individual's score.

The second horizontal line below the curve in Figure 8–1 labeled "Percentiles" represents the distribution of scores in percentile units. By knowing the percentile score of an individual, you already know how that individual compares with others in the group. An individual at the 98th percentile scored the same as or better than 98 percent of the individuals in the group. This is approximately equivalent to getting a raw score of 60 on Test X or 140 on Test Y.

Percentiles can yield useful information. Assume you want to make highly competitive job offers. You can use data sources such as the Bureau of Labor and Statistics (BLS), which typically report the 10th, 25th, 50th, 75th, and 90th percentiles in the distribution of salaries for a given occupation. If you wish to pay salaries at the top 10 percent of the distribution, then you can use the BLS's percentiles to figure out how much you should pay.

You can also collect salary information from within your firm to determine what might be a competitive job offer. Assume you collected data from all your employees on their current salary levels. How might you describe the data? We discuss this next.

central tendency
the midpoint, or center, of the data

mean
a measure of central tendency reflecting the average score

median
the middle score, or the point below which 50 percent of the scores fall

mode
the most commonly observed score

CENTRAL TENDENCY   **Central tendency** describes the midpoint, or center, of the data. Typical measures of central tendency include the mean, median, and mode. The **mean** is a measure of central tendency reflecting the average score. For example, you could compute the average salary and then pay at or above this level to be competitive. The **median** is the middle score, or the 50th percentile, which is the point below which 50 percent of the scores fall below. The **mode** is the most commonly observed score.

If scores are normally distributed, as they are in Figure 8–1, then the mean, median, and mode are in the same position. This is not always the case if scores are not normally distributed. In the case of data on annual pay, a distribution could have most employees at the left (lower end) of the range and relatively few employees at the high end. This is not a normal distribution. This is regularly observed in organizations, and it is called *positive skew*. In this case, the mode would be to the left, near the bulk of the distribution, because it is the most commonly observed score. The mean would be shifted to the right due to the high annual pay for a limited number of employees. The median would be somewhere in between. In this case, the firm might extend different job offers depending on which measure it used to describe the data. In labor disputes, it is not uncommon for managers to use average pay as a reference point (indicating higher pay across employees) whereas unions use the mode or median as a reference point (indicating lower pay across employees).

Alternatively, you might see a *bimodal distribution,* or a distribution with two modes, for annual pay. The mean and median would fall between the two modes but neither would be representative of true compensation levels because there are probably two separate employee groups represented in the data. Perhaps the two modes represent some employees who are paid on a salary basis and other employees who are paid on an hourly basis. In this case, you might use one of the two modes to determine your competitive offer for compensation, or you could compute the mean, median, and mode separately for the two groups.

variability
a measure that describes the "spread" of the data around the midpoint

range
the difference between the highest and lowest observed score

outlier
a score that is much higher or lower than most of the scores in a distribution

VARIABILITY   **Variability** describes the "spread" of the data around the midpoint. If you were told that an applicant scored 76 out of 100 points on a work sample test, what would you think? It's hard to know what to conclude without more information. What if you were told the mean was 70? This additional information helps because you can tell that the applicant did better than average, but you are still missing important information. How much better or worse did the applicant actually fare? To answer this, you need to know the variability of scores. What would you think if the lowest score was 64 and the highest was 76? What if you were told the lowest score was 40 and the highest 100? Knowing the variability of a distribution changes your interpretation of scores.

There are a number of alternative measures of variability but typical measures include the range, variance, and standard deviation. The **range** is the difference between the highest and lowest observed scores. The range is highly influenced by any single extreme score (an **outlier**) so it may not effectively represent the true variability in the data. Other measures of variability such as the variance and standard deviation are less affected by outliers. The **variance** is a mathematical measure of the spread based on squared deviations of scores from the mean. You can find the formula for variance in the supplement at the end of this chapter. The **standard deviation** is conceptually similar to the average distance from the mean of a set of scores. It is the positive square root of the variance. A data set with a larger standard deviation has scores with more variance and a larger range. For example, if the average score on a measure was 70, and the standard deviation was 3, the scores would be more tightly clustered around the mean than if the standard deviation was 15. If all the scores were the same, the standard deviation would be 0. If everyone scores the same on a measure, the measure isn't useful in predicting job performance or deciding who to hire. You can see in Figure 8–1 that the range and standard deviation are smaller for Test X than they are for Test Y.

STANDARD SCORES   **Standard scores** are converted raw scores that indicate where a person's score lies in comparison to a referent group. A common standard score is a z score, which measures the distance of a score from the mean in standard deviation units. There are three determinants of a z score: the raw score and the mean and standard deviation of the entire set of scores.

Look at Figure 8–1. Test X and Test Y have different raw score means. Notice that Test X has a mean of 50 and Test Y has a mean of 100. If an individual got a score of 65 on Test X, that person did very well. However, a score of 65 on Test Y would be a poor score. Raw scores often carry limited information by themselves.

Figure 8–1 shows the percent of cases 1, 2, and 3 standard deviations above the mean and 1, 2, and 3 standard deviations below the mean. As you can see, 34 percent of the cases lie between the mean and +1 standard deviation, and 34 percent of the cases lie between the mean and −1 standard deviation. Thus, approximately 68 percent of the cases lie between −1 and +1 standard deviations. Notice that for Test X, the standard deviation is 5, and 68 percent of the test takers scored between 45 and 55. For Test Y the standard deviation is 20, and 68 percent of the test takers scored between 80 and 120.

A z score is calculated by subtracting the referent group's mean from the target individual's raw score, and dividing the difference by the measure's standard deviation in the referent group. The resulting standard z score indicates how many standard deviations the individual's score is above or below the mean of the referent group. It can be seen in Figure 8–1 that approximately 84 percent of scores fall below a z score of +1, whereas nearly 100 percent of people fall below a z score of +3. The simple formula for a z score is:

$$z_{\text{score}} = (\text{Individual's raw score} - \text{Referent group mean})/\text{Referent group standard deviation}$$

A z score is negative when the target individual's raw score is below the referent group's mean, and positive when the target individual's raw score is above the referent group's mean.

To compare candidates, we often need a single overall score that represents each candidate's combined performance on all of the assessment methods used to evaluate them. Combining a candidate's raw scores on two or more measures that use different scoring systems is difficult. Imagine an assessment system that evaluates candidates using an interview scored on a 1-to-10 scale and a job knowledge test that is scored on a 0-to-100 scale. Simply averaging the two scores would give disproportionate weight to one of the tests, depending on the mean and standard deviation. Standardizing both scores by converting them to z scores allows them to be easily combined, as shown in Table 8–1.

variance
a mathematical measure of the spread based on squared deviations of scores from the mean

standard deviation
the positive square root of the variance; it is conceptually similar to the average distance from the mean of a set of scores

standard scores
converted raw scores that indicate where a person's score lies in comparison to a referent group

TABLE 8–1	**Converting Raw Scores to Standard Scores**				
Candidate	**Interview Score**		**Job Knowledge Test Score**		**Overall Score**
	Raw	**Standard**	**Raw**	**Standard**	**Standard Units**
Felix	15	−1.1	87	1.2	(−1.1 + 1.2) = 0.1
Sue	22	1.3	77	−0.2	(1.3 − 0.2) = 1.1
Lin	19	0.3	69	−1.2	(0.3 − 1.2) = −0.9
Pierre	17	−0.4	80	0.2	(−0.4 + 0.2) = −0.2

In Table 8–1, the interview scores have a range of 15 to 22, a mean of 18.25, and a standard deviation of 3. The job knowledge test has a range of 69 to 87, a mean of 78.25, and a standard deviation of 7.46. If you subtract the mean from each raw score and divide by the standard deviation, you will obtain the standard score. For Felix, the calculations would be $(15 - 18.25)/3 = -1.1$ and $(87 - 78.25)/7.46 = 1.2$ (after rounding).

Although meaningfully combining the raw scores would be difficult, combining the z scores is easy and results in a single number reflecting how each candidate did on both of the assessment methods relative to the other candidates. In this case, Sue's outstanding interview score allowed her to overcome her slightly below-average job knowledge test score to be the candidate with the highest overall score. If a company wants to weight multiple assessment methods differently, each standard score can be multiplied by the desired weighting percentage. For example, the formula for weighting the interview score 60 percent and the job knowledge test score 40 percent would be:

$$\text{Overall score} = (.6 \times z_{\text{interview}}) + (.4 \times z_{\text{job knowledge test}})$$

For Felix, this would be $(.6 \times -1.1) + (.4 \times 1.2) = -.18$ rather than the .1 he received when the interview and knowledge test were equally weighted.

Shifting the Normal Curve

When making candidate selection decisions, it is often assumed that the distribution of applicants' fit with the job reflects the normal curve as depicted by the current talent pool shown in Figure 8–2. If this is true, then a large burden is placed on the selection system to accurately identify which candidates fall to the far right of the curve (the best hires). In practice, however, many of the most desirable people for a position are not in the applicant pool at all. The most talented and competent people are often successfully employed because they are usually being promoted and rewarded for the work they do. As a result, most of these people are semi-passive job seekers at best. Without an effective sourcing and recruiting process, they will not apply to your firm. For example, during the 2008 economic downturn, it was difficult to get passive job seekers with deep experience and a proven track record in advertising to apply for positions at other companies.[8]

A passive sourcing approach can result in a distribution of applicants that is shifted to the left, or lower end, as depicted by distribution A. An alternative way of looking at this is to think about the role that sourcing and recruiting play in terms of shaping the qualifications of the applicant pool. If done strategically, sourcing and recruiting can discourage applicants who are a poor fit from applying, and increase the number of high-quality passive and semi-passive candidates who do apply. In this case, the distribution would be shifted to the right, as depicted by distribution B. This recruiting and sourcing approach would yield candidates of higher quality, clearly reducing the burden on the selection system to identify the best candidates. This can significantly increase the likelihood of hiring excellent employees.

Describing and interpreting data is part of the process of using data strategically. Strategic staffing is further enhanced when you can use data to understand relationships between measures and variables. In particular, if you can identify predictors of desired staffing outcomes, then this can lead to new selection tools and interventions, such as recruiter training.

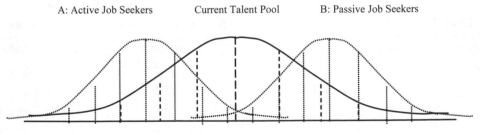

A: Active Job Seekers   Current Talent Pool   B: Passive Job Seekers

FIGURE 8–2 Shifting the Normal Curve

USING DATA STRATEGICALLY

Correlations

A **correlation** indicates the strength of a linear relationship between two variables. If people who score higher on a measure tend to perform better on the job, or if people who score higher on a measure perform lower on the job, scores and job performance are said to be correlated. A **correlation coefficient**, also called "Pearson's r" or the "bivariate correlation," is a single number that ranges from -1 to $+1$; it reflects the *direction* (positive or negative) and *magnitude* (the strength) of the relationship between two variables. A value of $r = 0$ indicates that the values of one measure are unrelated to the values of the other measure. A value of $r = +1$ means that there is a perfectly linear, positive relationship between the two measures. In other words, as the value of one of the measures increases, the value of the other measure increases by an exactly determined amount. By contrast, a value of $r = -1$ means that there is a perfectly negative (inverse) relationship between the two measures. In other words, as the value of one of the measures increases, the value of the other variable decreases by an exactly determined amount. The information provided by correlations is useful for making staffing decisions. The health care literature is full of studies that document the positive correlation between patient outcomes and proper staffing in health care organizations, for example.[9] You can find the formula for correlation in the supplement to this chapter along with the formula for Excel. Correlations can be easily computed using spreadsheets or software such as Microsoft Excel, SAS, or SPSS. In most circumstances, we rarely see correlations remotely approaching $+1$ or -1. Even the correlation between people's height and weight is typically less than .80. In staffing contexts, we rarely have such precisely measured and highly correlated data. Measurement error, to be discussed later, also reduces the magnitude of the correlations we observe. In addition, restricting the variability of our applicant and hired pools can also reduce the size of the correlations we observe.

The typical values we might see in staffing contexts are $+.30$ or $-.30$. Although much lower than the theoretical maximum and minimum, these values can result in significant improvements in the quality of hires. Unstructured interviews, one of the most commonly used selection techniques, often have a correlation of $+.20$ or less with job performance. A well-structured personality test can have a correlation of $+.30$ with job performance. Thus, using such a test can have a significant positive economic impact on an organization by significantly improving the hiring process.

One way of thinking about correlations is depicted in the diagram[10] shown in Figure 8–3. Think of the variance of a given variable as depicted by a circle. If the circles of two different variables are perfectly overlapping, then the variance of one variable is perfectly correlated with the other. In the first example, the two circles are nearly overlapping, suggesting the correlation between X and Y is approximately either $+.90$ or $+.90$. Why either positive or negative? Because the variance is shared regardless of direction of the sign. In the second example, the two circles do not overlap at all, indicating that the correlation between X and Y is 0. In the third example, the two circles overlap nearly half, suggesting the correlation is about $+.70$ or $-.70$. Why a correlation of $\pm.70$ for a nearly 50 percent overlap? As it turns out, the amount of variance shared by two variables is equal to the square of the correlation, or r^2, and $.7^2$ is .49 or about 49 percent overlap. Another good way to understand the correlational relationship between two variables is to graph them. Figure 8–4 illustrates the correlations corresponding to several different patterns of data in **scatter plots**, or graphical illustrations of the relationship between two variables. Each point on the chart corresponds to how a particular person scored on a test and a measure of how he or she performed on the job.

From the scatter plots in Figure 8–4, you can see that a correlation of $+1$ occurs when the data points are in a perfect line. A correlation of $+1$ means that higher test scores on the measure correspond with an exact improvement in performance scores. The test score is called a predictor variable. A **predictor variable** is a variable used to predict the value of an outcome. In this case, the predictor variable (test score) perfectly predicts the outcome (performance). Now notice the lack of a relationship between scores and performance in the graph showing a correlation of $r = -.05$. In this case, the scores are almost completely independent of job performance ratings, and these scores are a poor predictor of performance.

correlation
the strength of a linear relationship between two variables

correlation coefficient
a single number that ranges from -1 to $+1$; it reflects the direction (positive or negative) and magnitude (the strength) of the relationship between two variables

scatter plot
graphical illustration of the relationship between two variables

predictor variable
a variable used to predict the value of an outcome

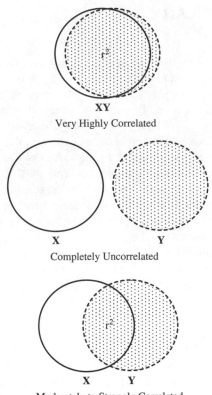

FIGURE 8–3 Diagrams for Correlations

When the relationship is perfect, as it is in the "+1" graph, it is easy to see how the trend line should be drawn. However, when the data do not depict a perfect relationship, it's harder to figure out how to draw the line. In this case, you will need to draw the line in such a way that it minimizes the distance of all the points from the line (i.e., minimizes errors of prediction). This is called a regression line, which will be discussed in the next section. When there is almost no relationship, the regression line will be nearly flat. When there is a negative relationship, the regression line will slope downward.

If you found a correlation of $r = -.43$ between a measure and job performance, would the measure be useful in predicting which candidates are likely to do better on the job? Absolutely—just hire people who perform lower on the measure. The correlation of $r = -.43$ is of a reasonably high magnitude. Thus, it reflects a fairly strong relationship between the measure and on-the-job performance. The direction of the correlation isn't important. To make this easier to understand, imagine that the measure was assessing typing errors on a test and the job performance dimension was typing performance. Candidates scoring lower on the measure made fewer errors, and thus are likely to be better typists. In other words, negative correlations are just as useful as positive correlations—negative correlations involving a desirable staffing outcome just mean that lower-scoring candidates are preferable to those with higher scores.

An additional type of relationship between two variables is a *curvilinear relationship* in which scores are related to outcomes in a nonlinear fashion. This can occur when higher scores are related to higher performance to a point, after which higher scores relate to lower performance. Curvilinear relationships are sometimes found between the personality trait of conscientiousness and job performance.[11] Conscientiousness[12] refers to being self-disciplined, striving to achieve, and tending to think carefully before acting. If you have ever worked with someone who was extremely detail oriented, strove for perfection, and had a hard time making decisions, you probably understand how too much conscientiousness can sometimes be a detriment to performance.

If you were to rely solely on the correlation coefficient to evaluate whether or not being conscientious is a predictor of people's job performance, you might underestimate the measure's usefulness. If a curvilinear relationship exists, rather than selecting candidates with the highest conscientiousness scores, it would be better to select candidates who score closer to the middle range on the measure. There are specialized statistical techniques for testing for curvilinearity,

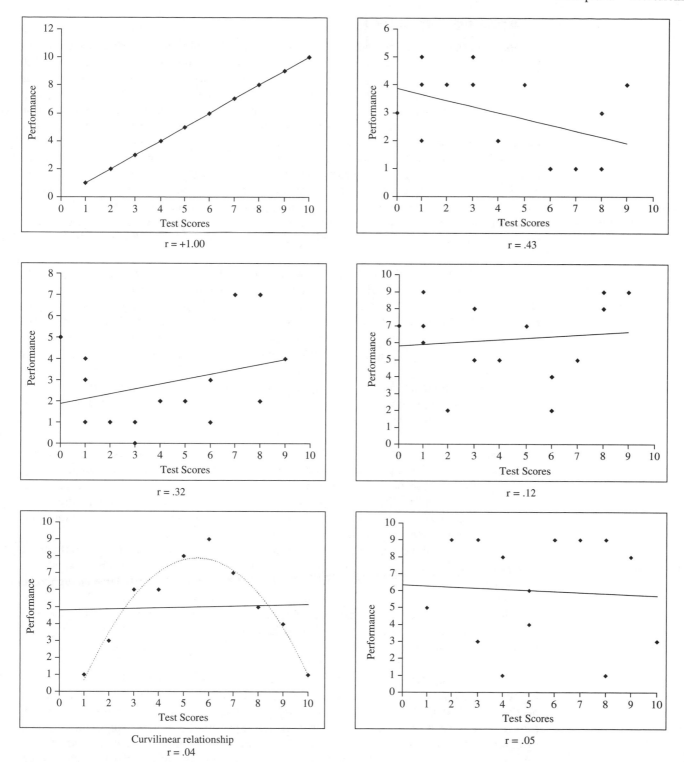

FIGURE 8–4 Correlations Expressed as Scatter Plots

and it is important to collect data to determine whether a linear or curvilinear relationship exists for the position you're filling.

Other uses of the correlation coefficient include:

- Relating store sizes with staffing levels
- Relating seniority in a firm with how well employees perform on the job
- Relating the time to fill a job with new-hire quality
- Relating the quality of new hires with a business's performance and the satisfaction of its customers

Interpreting Correlations

Suppose you find a correlation between a job knowledge test and a measure of job success equal to .15. Should you use the measure? Answering this question requires assessing the likelihood that the observed relationship really exists, and then evaluating whether the relationship is strong enough to make the measure useful given its cost. Whenever two variables are correlated using a subset of the total population, there is always the chance that the sample used does not represent the total population. If you had a group of twenty employees, ten women and ten men, and randomly chose four of them, would you always choose two women and two men? On average, you would. But there would be some instances in which you would end up choosing four women. At other times, you would end up choosing four men. Similarly, when computing a correlation coefficient from a sample of people, the correlation might not accurately represent the correlation that exists in the general population or your applicant pool. **Sampling error** is simply the variability of sample correlations due to chance. The usefulness of a correlation can be evaluated by considering statistical significance and practical significance. Next, we discuss each.

sampling error
the variability of sample correlations due to chance

THE STATISTICAL SIGNIFICANCE OF A CORRELATION Statistical significance is the degree to which the observed relationship is not likely due to sampling error. A correlation is said to be statistically significant if it has less than a certain probability of being due to sampling error—usually 5 percent. If the probability of a correlation due to chance is .03 (versus, say, .30), then the correlation is said to be "statistically significant." In other words, the observed correlation is far enough from zero that it is unlikely to be due to sampling error. The larger a sample, the more likely observed relationships capture the "true" relationship, and even small effect sizes will be statistically significant. In a small sample, the observed relationship must be larger for the relationship to reach statistical significance because there is a greater probability that the observed relationship is due to sampling error.

statistical significance
the degree to which the observed relationship is not likely due to sampling error

THE PRACTICAL SIGNIFICANCE OF A CORRELATION Unfortunately, statistical significance does not guarantee that a predictor is useful. If a sample size is large enough, then even very small correlations can be statistically significant because large samples tend to result in correlation estimates with little sampling error. For example, when the military studies predictors of troop performance, because they have a sample in the tens of thousands, even predictors with a very small correlation with the outcome are statistically significant.

After establishing statistical significance, the focus shifts to practical significance. **Practical significance** means that the observed relationship is large enough to be of value in a practical sense. A correlation that is statistically significant is not necessarily large enough to be of practical significance. Whether or not a correlation is large enough to be practically significant is in the eyes of the measurer. For example, if hiring errors for a particular job are not costly, then a correlation of .2 might be acceptable to an organization. However, a correlation of .2 might be too low for critical jobs in which hiring errors are costly. In yet other situations, a correlation as low as .15 can still be practically significant.

practical significance
an observed relationship that is large enough to be of value in a practical sense

Practical significance is irrelevant unless the relationship is also statistically significant because otherwise the observed correlation could be due to chance. To be useful, a relationship needs to have both practical and statistical significance. Other factors will determine whether or not a correlation is useful: An assessment system that is inexpensive, for example, might still be useful even if the correlation is not large. Alternatively, if an assessment method that correlated .15 with job success was expensive, took a long time to administer, and was only moderately liked by job candidates, it might not be worth using even if it was a statistically significant predictor of a person's job success. It depends on the degree to which the assessment yields a return on the money a firm has invested in its use. For example, even if an organization used an assessment method with a low correlation with job success, the company might still earn a good return on the method. Consequently, it is important to look beyond the magnitude of the correlation.

Identifying statistically and practically significant relationships can help organizations execute their business strategies more effectively. The food wholesaler Sysco is a good example. Sysco, headquartered in Houston, Texas, periodically assesses the correlation between its customers' satisfaction and its employees' satisfaction. The company has found that customer loyalty and operational excellence are affected by a satisfied, productive, and committed workforce. Retaining its employees has also helped Sysco cut its operating costs. After discovering the correlation, Sysco implemented a rigorous set of programs to enhance the retention and satisfaction of its employees.[13]

Regressions

Generally, staffing professionals use more than one measure to assess job applicants because it improves the overall validity of a firm's selection process. However, with a correlation analysis, only two variables can be related to one another so only one predictor variable can be used. **Multiple regression** is a statistical technique that predicts outcomes using one or more predictor variables. Assume the predictors and outcomes are measured on an interval or ratio level. Specialized techniques exist for variables that are measured on a nominal or ordinal level but such approaches are beyond the coverage of this chapter. A human resource professional can do a multiple regression analysis to identify the ideal weights to assign to each assessment score (each predictor) to maximize the validity of a set of assessment methods. The analysis is based on each assessment method's correlation with job success (the outcome) and the degree to which the assessment methods are *intercorrelated*. For an example of what we mean by intercorrelated, suppose that cognitive ability is highly correlated with interview performance. In this case, it might not make sense to use both variables to predict job success because it would be redundant to do so. If the redundancy is too great, the regression analysis will retain only one of the predictors to use in the final prediction equation. In other words, the redundant predictor would be assigned a near-zero weight.

One way of visualizing relationships among the variables in multiple regression is depicted in the diagram[14] shown in Figure 8–5. Assume Y is the criterion, or outcome being predicted, and X and Z are the predictor variables. In the first example you can see by the overlap that both X and Z predict Y, and both X and Z are uncorrelated with each other. In the second example, both X and Z predict Y but X and Z are highly correlated. You can easily see in this second case that X and Z contribute little unique prediction beyond the other. This is similar to a case in which you measure the same concept (e.g., intelligence) using two different but highly related assessments. The redundancy doesn't add new information so you can either eliminate one of the assessments or combine them (depending on cost). In the third example, you see a more typical situation. Here X and Z are moderately correlated with Y and with each other. Both X and Z add unique information to the prediction of Y but they are related to each other. As an illustration, a firm might use a cognitive ability test and structured interview scores to predict job performance and cognitive ability and interview scores might be related.

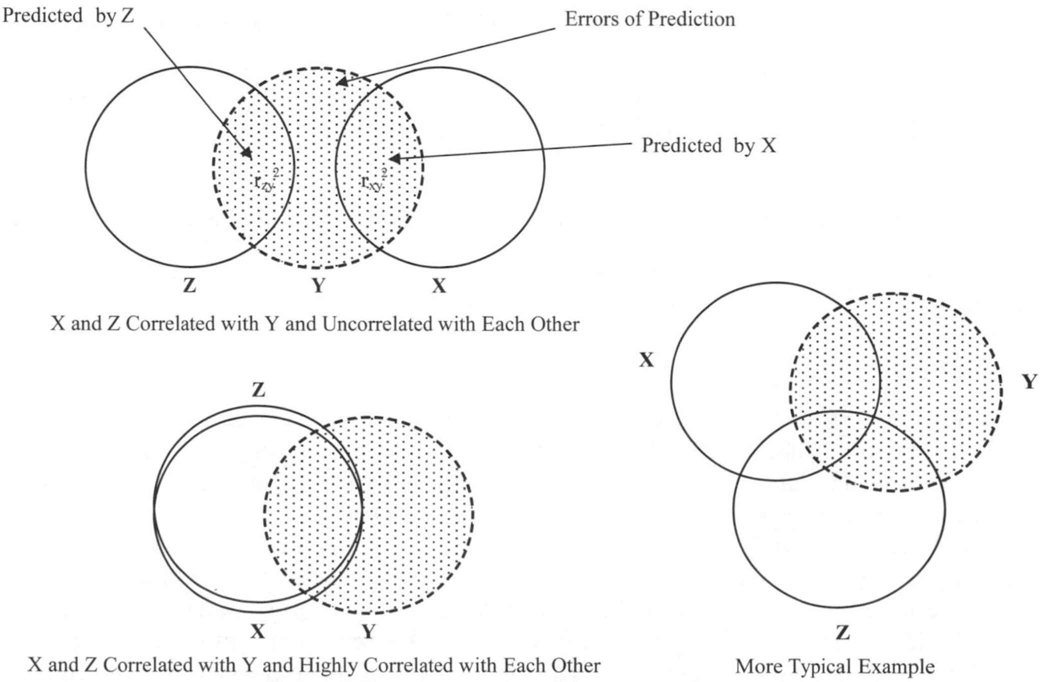

multiple regression
a statistical technique that predicts an outcome using one or more predictor variables; it identifies the ideal weights to assign each predictor so as to maximize the validity of a set of predictors; the analysis is based on each predictor's correlation with the outcome and the degree to which the predictors are themselves intercorrelated

FIGURE 8–5 Diagrams of Multiple Regression

The equations used to do a regression analysis can be computed by hand, but this is a cumbersome process if there are more than two predictor variables. The equation for two predictor variables (a multiple regression) can be found in the supplement at the end of this chapter. A variety of software packages, including Excel, SPSS, SAS, and Stata, can be used to easily perform an analysis using three or more variables and we provide the instructions for using Excel to conduct a multiple regression analysis in the supplement.

Each variable is examined for its statistical relationship to the predicted outcome and a regression (or multiple regression) equation is derived. The regression equation is of the format:

$$\text{Job success}_{predicted} = \text{Constant} + (b_1 \times \text{Test score}_1)$$
$$+ (b_2 \times \text{Test score}_2) + (b_3 \times \text{Test score}_3)\ldots$$

The constant, or intercept, is a number added to everyone's predicted job success score, and the b's are the regression weights that are multiplied by each test score. An applicant's scores on the test(s) are entered into the resulting model and used to calculate the test taker's predicted job success. Because the regression analysis operates on raw scores, these scores do not need to be standardized because the weights take into account the differences in means and standard deviations. For example, if Miguel scored 50 on an interview, 27 on a personality measure, and 20 on a job knowledge test, his predicted job success would be 141 based on the following equation:

$$\text{Job success}_{predicted} = 10 + (2 \times \text{Interview}) + (1 \times \text{Personality}) + (.2 \times \text{Job knowledge})$$

The intercept (10) and weights (2, 1, and .2) come from the results of the statistical analysis. Miguel's score of 141 would then be compared with the other candidates to determine if he should be hired. In general, only equations with variables found to be statistically significant should be used to make staffing decisions.

Regression analysis is also used to predict future headcount requirements. Consider the regression equation that uses projected sales per month and the number of expected customers to determine a firm's headcount requirements:

$$\text{Full-time employees} = 60 + (.00015 \times \text{Sales}) + (.3 \times \text{Expected customers})$$

If the firm's projected sales are $1,000,000, and the company projects that it will acquire 250 new customers, then it will need 285 full-time employees:

$$\text{Full-time employees} = 60 + (.00015 \times 1,000,000) + (.3 \times 250)$$
$$= 60 + 150 + 75 = 285$$

To prevent giving different variables credit for predicting the same part of the criterion, multiple regression analysis examines the effect of each variable (e.g., each test score) on the criterion (e.g., job success) after controlling for other variables.

WHAT ARE THE CHARACTERISTICS OF USEFUL MEASURES?

Two properties of a good measure are its reliability and validity. We discuss each next as well as the importance of a measure's standard error of measurement.

Reliability

reliability
how dependably, or consistently, a measure assesses a particular characteristic

Reliability refers to how dependably, or consistently, a measure assesses a particular characteristic. If you obtained wildly different weights each time you stepped on a scale, would you find the scale useful? Probably not. The same principle applies to measures relevant to staffing, such as job knowledge, personality, intelligence, and leadership skills.

A measure that yields similar scores for a given person when it is administered multiple times is reliable. Reliability sets boundaries around the usefulness of a measure. A measure cannot be useful if it is not reliable, but even if it is reliable, it still might not be useful—for example, if it doesn't measure what you're seeking to determine but something else instead. Reliability is a critical component of any staffing measure, including candidate assessment. If a person completes a personality test twice, will he or she get a similar score or a much different score? If the scores radically change, then perhaps the test isn't reliable. Why would a job candidate score differently when completing a personality test again, you might wonder? Think of why you might score differently on a midterm given on Monday and one given on Friday, and you should have some insights. Some possible reasons are the following:[15]

- *The respondent's temporary psychological or physical state.* For example, differing levels of anxiety, fatigue, or motivation can affect test results. If you are stressed the first time you are tested but are relaxed the second time, you might respond differently.
- *Environmental factors.* Differences in the environment, such as room temperature, lighting, noise, or even the test administrator, can influence an individual's performance. If it is quiet on one occasion, and you hear distracting construction equipment on the other, you might obtain different scores.
- *The version, or form, of the measure.* Many measures have more than one version, or form. For example, the ACT and SAT college entrance examinations have multiple forms. The items differ on each form, but each form is supposed to measure the same thing. Because the forms are not exactly the same, a respondent might do better on one form than on another. If one version happened to be harder, or it was equally challenging but tapped into material you knew less well, then you would perform more poorly. In the case of the ACT and SAT, scores can be adjusted to reflect the difficulty of each form.
- *Different evaluators.* Certain measures are scored subjectively—that is, they are determined by an evaluator's judgments of the respondent's performance or responses. Differences in the training, experience, and frame of reference among the evaluators can result in different scores for a respondent. This is why two interviewers evaluating the same job candidate might come to completely different conclusions about the quality of that job candidate.

These factors are sources of *measurement error* in the assessment process. Measurement error can be systematic or random. In some cases, the measurement error can be random, as in the flip of a coin. You don't always get 50 heads and 50 tails in 100 flips. This is an example of a **random error**. Similar things can happen in a staffing context. Running into traffic on the way to work or experiencing bad weather can cause employee productivity to randomly fluctuate in unpredictable ways. **Systematic errors** are errors that occur because of consistent and predictable factors. For example, an employee's productivity may go down every Tuesday because he or she works late at a second job Monday night.

The sources of systematic errors can include factors such as the time of day or day of the week. Administering a difficult work sample test in the morning might, for example, lead to different results than if the test was administered in the afternoon or late at night. Systematic errors can also result when there are systematic differences across evaluators. For example, some interviewers might regularly tend to rate most interviewees near the middle of a 1-to-10 scale, whereas other interviewers might tend to regularly rate most interviewees on the high end of the scale. In this example, the differences among the evaluators are a source of systematic error. Another source may be due to the measurement items themselves. Items that are reverse-worded, confusing, or overly complex can lead to systematic errors. The following question is a good example:

Using a 1-to-5 scale where 1 is very true and 5 is very untrue, answer this question: "In previous leadership roles you rarely failed to set goals on a timely and consistent basis while providing good feedback to your team."

If you reflect for a moment on this item, you can see how difficult it is to understand and how it could lead to systematic error due to wording. People may systematically vary in the accuracy of their responses, depending on their verbal ability, motivation to complete the survey quickly, or simple attention to detail. This is not random error because it is attached to specific and identifiable personal characteristics.

If there were no systematic or random errors of measurement, then the respondent would get the same score each time. If you step on a scale then you will get a reading. If the scale is perfectly reliable and you step on it again 10 seconds later, you would see the same reading. This is your true score. If in real life, your scale, like ours, slightly fluctuates, then you might see a slightly different reading 10 seconds later. This is random measurement error because it is due to

random error
error that is not due to any consistent cause

systematic errors
error that occurs because of consistent and predictable factors

a variety of factors unrelated to your actual weight. However, if you measure yourself every day in the morning when you wake up and after lunch, you might find you systematically weigh more due to having eaten lunch. In a staffing context, test and performance scores also contain a true score plus some variation due to random and systematic errors. An applicant is unlikely to obtain exactly the same score on a knowledge test every time. Part of this could be due to random factors, or the error could be systematic.

The distinction between random and systematic errors is important: Systematic errors can be controlled or eliminated. For example, you can weigh yourself at the same time each day while wearing the same clothes. Random errors, however, cannot be controlled but still affect the quality of measurement. Some measures are subject to more random errors than others, just as some scales provide more reliable measures of weight than do others.

A **deficiency error** is yet another type of error. It occurs when you fail to measure important aspects of the attribute you would like to measure. The underlying attribute being measured is called a *construct*. If you wanted to measure an applicant's ability to use calculus for an engineering job, then this ability is your construct of interest. However, if the test you were using focused only on algebra, a deficiency error would result. A **contamination error** occurs when other factors unrelated to one's advanced math skills (in this case) affect the observed scores. For example, if the calculus test had many complex word problems, then language could influence the results. If the test was administered under varying conditions (a loud versus a quiet setting, early morning versus late at night, using calm and helpful administrators versus loud and anxious administrators), then these factors could affect scores.

The diagram shown in Figure 8–6 illustrates deficiency, contamination, and relevance. Assume you used supervisory ratings to measure job performance. In what ways might supervisory ratings be deficient? It is possible that supervisors focus on productivity and meeting deadlines more than teamwork, quality, and safety. Or supervisors may not know about the quality of customer service provided and only attend to quantity of sales. In each case, the supervisor may overlook important aspects of job performance and using their ratings alone may result in deficiency. Supervisory ratings can be contaminated, too. What might affect supervisory ratings other than actual job performance? The research literature is filled with information about sources of rater contamination, including stereotypes, halo effects, and similar-to-me bias, among many other sources.[16] This is contamination. The overlapping area between the construct and the measure indicates relevance, or the degree to which the measure captures the intended concept to be measured.

It is impossible to eliminate all sources of error, but measures can be made more reliable by standardizing the measurement process as much as possible. For example, you can pretest the items on a test to ensure they are clear and they statistically correlate with each other consistently. Interviewers can be trained to ask the same questions, avoid bias, and use the same behaviorally based scoring key to make their ratings. Test administrators can give tests at consistent times, under similar conditions, and so forth.

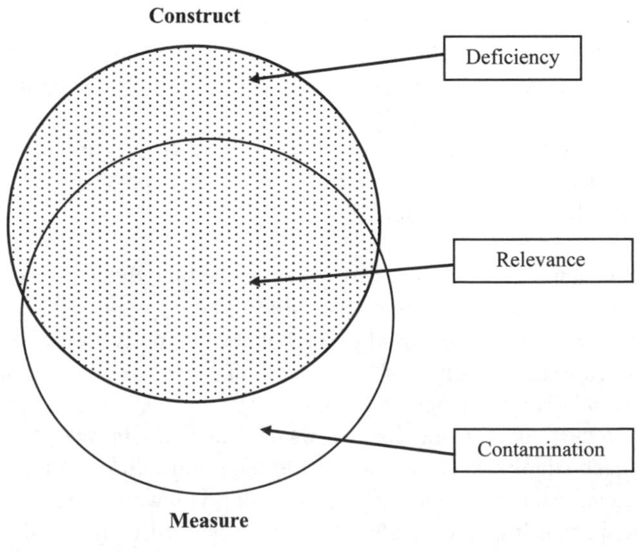

deficiency error
occurs when you fail to measure important aspects of the attribute you would like to measure

contamination error
occurs when other factors unrelated to whatever is being assessed affect the observed scores

FIGURE 8–6 Deficiency, Contamination, and Relevance

| TABLE 8–2 | General Guidelines for Interpreting Reliability Coefficients[17] |

Reliability	
Coefficient	**Interpretation**
.90 and up	Superior
.80–.89	Good
.70–.79	Adequate for most needs
.50–.69	Limited applicability
.00–.49	Not useful at all

Conceptually, reliability is the correlation of an item, scale, or measurement instrument with a hypothetical set of true scores. However, in practice, true scores are not available for the computation of a correlation. Instead, reliability must be estimated by correlating different types of observations. This will be elaborated upon later.

The reliability of a measure is indicated by the *reliability coefficient*, which is expressed as a number ranging between 0 and 1, with 0 indicating no reliability (no correlation between the measure and the true score) and 1 indicating perfect reliability (perfect correlation between the measure and the true score). Like a correlation, we express reliability as a decimal—for example, .70 or .91. The closer the reliability coefficient is to 1.0, the more repeatable or reliable the scores are. Near-perfect reliability is extremely rare. The reason that reliability coefficients are only positive (as opposed to correlations, which can range from -1 to $+1$) is that observed scores and true scores should relate to each other in a consistently positive manner. Table 8–2 presents some general guidelines for interpreting the reliability of a measure.

The reliability coefficient is not the only thing to consider in selecting or rejecting an assessment method. To evaluate a measure's reliability, you should consider the type of measure, the type of reliability estimate reported, and the context in which the measure will be used. There are several types of reliability estimates. Before deciding to use a measure, such as a personality evaluation or cognitive ability test, it is important to learn about the reliability of the measure. Organizations sometimes purchase tests or assessment tools, and information about reliability is often provided by the creator and publisher of these tests and tools. You should be familiar with the different kinds of reliability estimates reported. Next, we discuss several different types of reliability. Reliability can be estimated in one of four ways.

TEST-RETEST RELIABILITY   Test-retest reliability reflects the repeatability of scores over time and the stability of the underlying construct being measured (e.g., a person's math skills, personality, intelligence, honesty, and other relevant characteristics). Test-retest reliability is estimated by the correlation between two (or more) administrations of the same measure across different times or locations on the same sample. This assesses stability over time. Some constructs are more stable than others. For example, mechanical ability is more stable over time than is mood or anxiety. Therefore, we would expect a higher test-retest reliability coefficient on a mechanical aptitude test than on a measure of anxiety. For constructs like mood, which vary over time, an acceptable test-retest reliability coefficient may be lower than is suggested in Table 8–2.

test-retest reliability
reflects the repeatability of scores over time and the stability of the underlying construct being measured

ALTERNATE OR PARALLEL FORM RELIABILITY   Developers often make multiple forms or versions of a measure that are intended to assess the same thing and be of the same difficulty level. **Alternate or parallel form reliability** indicates how consistent scores are likely to be if a person completes two or more forms of the same measure. This reliability is estimated by the correlation between two (or more) administrations of different forms that are supposed to measure the same construct to the same population. A high parallel form reliability coefficient indicates that the different forms are very similar, which means that it makes virtually no difference which version of the measure is used. On the other hand, a low parallel form reliability coefficient suggests that the different forms are probably not comparable and may be measuring different things. In this case, the multiple forms cannot be used interchangeably and scores on each form cannot be directly compared.

alternate or parallel form reliability
indicates how consistent scores are likely to be if a person completes two or more forms of the same measure

internal consistency reliability
indicates the extent to which items on a given measure assess the same construct

INTERNAL CONSISTENCY RELIABILITY   **Internal consistency reliability** indicates the extent to which items on a given measure assess the same construct. A high internal consistency reliability coefficient indicates that the items on a measure function in a similar manner. Internal consistency is based on the correlation among the items comprising a measure. For example, you might have 10 items measuring math skill. If all the items measure math skill reliably, and they are internally consistent, then scores on one item should correlate highly with scores on another. Items in the measure can be split into even and odd items or first half and second half items. Scores on these halves can then be correlated with each other. This is called *split-half reliability,* which is one indicator of internal consistency. The most commonly used indicator of internal consistency is *Cronbach's alpha.* It is an estimate of the average of all possible split-half reliabilities.

If finance and history questions were included on an exam for a staffing class, the test would have lower internal consistency reliability than if the test contained only staffing-related questions because the different types of items would yield varying patterns of scores. Measures that assess multiple characteristics are usually divided into distinct sections, and a separate internal consistency reliability coefficient is reported for each section in addition to one for the whole measure.

inter-rater reliability
indicates how consistent scores are likely to be if the responses are scored by two or more raters using the same item, scale, or instrument

INTER-RATER RELIABILITY   **Inter-rater reliability** indicates how consistent scores are likely to be if the responses are scored by two or more raters using the same item, scale, or instrument. On some measures, like during Olympic gymnastic events, different raters evaluate responses or behaviors and subjectively determine a score. Often in business contexts different people evaluate the same job applicant (e.g., the HR recruiter and the hiring manager). Differences in raters' judgments create variations in a person's scores for the same measure or event.

Inter-rater reliability is based on the correlation of scores between or among two or more raters who rate people or objects using the same item, scale, or instrument. A high inter-rater reliability coefficient indicates that the judgment process is consistent and that the resulting scores are reliable. Although inter-rater reliability coefficients are typically lower than other types of reliability estimates, rater training can increase inter-rater reliabilities. This type of reliability is particularly important for understanding the usefulness of interview evaluations.

These four reliability estimation methods are not necessarily mutually exclusive, nor do they need to yield the same results. A measure of job knowledge that has many different dimensions within the test might show low internal consistency reliability. However, people's job knowledge characteristics might be relatively stable, in which case the test scores will be similar across administrations (high test-retest reliability). In this case, you should compute separate internal consistency reliabilities for each dimension. As another illustration, two distinct measures of leadership capability might yield high parallel forms reliability. Additionally, the items within each of the measures might be internally consistent. However, the test-retest reliability could be low if leadership training occurred between the administration of the two tests. In this case, you would expect to see low test-retest reliability because the training ought to change or improve people's leadership capabilities.

Clearly, the acceptable level of reliability will differ depending on the type of measure and the reliability estimate used. A measure of mood may exhibit low reliability across administrations because, as we explained, moods fluctuate over time. However, the measure might still be useful for predicting how applicants will react during interviews. In this case, the items measuring mood must yield consistent scores among themselves, even if they vary over time as an overall score.

Standard Error of Measurement

standard error of measurement (SEM)
the margin of error that you should expect in an individual score because of the imperfect reliability of the measure

As we have explained, the measurement process always contains some type of error. The problem is that we wish to use imperfect scores to make decisions despite the presence of error. It is helpful to know how much error exists when we use a given score. The **standard error of measurement (SEM)** is the margin of error that you should expect in an individual score because of the imperfect reliability of the measure. (The formula for SEM is given in this chapter's supplement.) SEM represents the spread of scores you might have observed had you tested the same person repeatedly. The lower the standard error, the more accurate the measurements. If the SEM is zero, then the observed score is the true score. However, we know that error exists so we can compute a range of possibilities around the observed score. This is a *confidence interval.* Although not technically precise, you can think of it in this manner. If you score 85 out of a possible 100 on a measure that has an SEM of 2, there is a 68 percent chance that the "true" score lies between 83 and 87, and about a 95 percent chance that the true score lies between 81 and 89.

In a normal distribution, 68 percent of cases fall between $+1$ and -1 standard deviations from the mean, and approximately 95 percent of cases in a population fall between $+2$ and -2 standard deviations from the mean. The SEM tells us the standard deviation of errors. If we center our mean around 85 (the observed score), then we can use the SEM to determine the chance that the true score will fall within a given range. With an SEM of 2, one standard deviation of error below the mean is $83(85 - 2)$ and one standard deviation above the mean is $87(85 + 2)$. This gives us a 68 percent confidence interval. A similar computation can be made for the 95 percent confidence interval.

The SEM is a useful measure of the accuracy of individual scores. If you have received a manual with a test or assessment tool, then when you're evaluating the reliability coefficients of a measure, it is important to review the explanations provided for the following:

- ***The types of reliability used.*** The manual should explain why a certain type of reliability coefficient was reported and discuss any known sources of random measurement error.
- ***How the reliability studies were conducted.*** The manual should describe the conditions under which the data was obtained, including the length of time that passed between the administrations of a measure in a test-retest reliability study. In general, reliabilities tend to drop as the time between administrations increases.
- ***The characteristics of the sample group.*** The manual should indicate the important characteristics of the sample group used to gather the reliability information, such as the education levels, ages, occupations, and other relevant characteristics of the people in the group. This will allow you to compare the characteristics of the people you want to measure with the sample group. If they are sufficiently similar, then the reported reliability estimates will probably hold true for your population as well.

The important thing to remember is that high reliability measures will have lower SEMs, which means that observed scores are more likely to reflect true scores. Additionally, reliabilities can drift over time. With longer periods between administrations, test-retest correlations are likely to go down, and the SEMs will then go up. Moreover, as we have explained, even if a measure is reliable, it doesn't mean it's useful. Reliable measures may or may not measure what you intend to measure, and they may or may not predict desired staffing outcomes. This is where the issue of validity comes into play, which we discuss next.

Validity

Validity is the most important issue in selecting a measure. It refers to how well a measure assesses a given construct and the degree to which you can make specific conclusions or predictions based on observed scores. Validity is the cornerstone of strategic staffing. If you wish to use data to make decisions, then the data must relate in meaningful ways to desired outcomes. If you can predict high-quality talent using various kinds of tests, then they will give you a competitive edge over firms that do not use valid tests for selection.

validity
how well a measure assesses a given construct and the degree to which you can make specific conclusions or predictions based on observed scores

It is important to understand the differences between reliability and validity. Validity will tell you how useful a measure is for a particular situation; reliability will tell you how consistent scores from that measure will be. You cannot draw valid conclusions unless the measure is reliable. But even when a measure is reliable, it might not be valid. For example, you might be able to measure a person's shoe size reliably, but it probably won't be useful as a predictor of the person's job performance. Any measure used in staffing needs to be both reliable and valid for the situation.

Figure 8–7 shows a popular bull's-eye illustration of the relationship between reliability and validity. The center of the target is whatever construct you are trying to measure, usually some aspect of job success. Each "shot" at the bull's-eye is a measurement for a single person. A bull's-eye means that your measure is perfectly assessing the person on that construct. The further you are from the center, the more your measurement is off for that person.

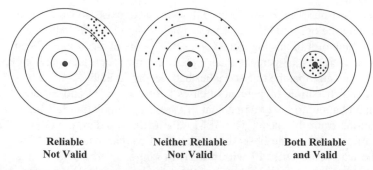

| Reliable
Not Valid | Neither Reliable
Nor Valid | Both Reliable
and Valid |

FIGURE 8–7   Illustration of Reliability and Validity

The dots close together in Figure 8–7 reflect higher reliability than the dots more spread out. Dots centered on the bull's-eye reflect higher validity than dots clustered away from the bull's-eye. You can easily see that if the measure is not reliable (the dots are widely scattered), it is not possible for them to be valid (on target).

Figure 8–7 shows three possible situations. In the first one, we hit the target consistently, but miss the center of the target—we are consistently measuring the wrong value for all observations. This measure is thus reliable (consistent), but not valid (not accurate). An everyday example might be a scale that consistently registers a weight that is 20 pounds too heavy. A staffing example might be a math test that gives consistent results but that is too easy. In the second bull's-eye, hits are spread across the target, and we are consistently missing the center, reflecting a measure that is neither reliable nor valid. This is like a scale that gives random readings and is on average 20 pounds off. A math test that does a poor job of measuring math and is plagued by error (it is both contaminated and deficient) might yield the second pattern. The third bull's-eye shows hits that are consistently in the center of the target, reflecting a measure that is both reliable and valid. This is like a scale that gives the same weight each time, and the weight is accurate. In staffing, this pattern might be exhibited by a high-quality math test that is consistent in results and neither deficient nor contaminated. This is our goal in measurement and assessment.

A measure's validity is established in reference to a specific purpose. Thus, the measure might be valid for some purposes but not be valid for others. For example, a measure you use to make valid predictions about someone's technical proficiency on the job may not be valid for predicting his or her leadership skills, job commitment, or teamwork effectiveness.

Similarly, a measure's validity is established in reference to specific groups called *reference groups.* Thus, the same measure might not be valid for different groups. For example, a problem-solving skills measure designed to predict the performance of sales representatives might not be valid or useful for predicting the performance of clerical employees.

As we have explained, the manuals that accompany assessment tools, or tests, should describe the reference groups used to develop the measures. The manuals should also describe the groups for whom the measure is valid and how the scores for the individuals belonging to each of the groups were interpreted. You, then, must determine if the measure is appropriate for the particular type of people you want to assess. This group of people is called your *target population,* or *target group.*

Although your target group and the reference group might not have to match perfectly, they must be sufficiently similar so that the measure will yield meaningful scores for your group. For example, you will want to consider factors such as the occupations, reading levels, and cultural and language differences of the people in your target group. Use only assessment procedures and instruments demonstrated to be valid for your target group(s) and for your specific purpose. This is important because the Uniform Guidelines on Employee Selection Procedures require assessment tools to have adequate supporting evidence for the conclusions reached with them in the event adverse impact occurs. Although all employee selection procedures—for example, interviews—do not have to be validated, scored assessments that have an adverse impact should be validated if technically feasible.

The user of an assessment tool is ultimately responsibility for making sure that validity evidence exists for the conclusions reached using the measures. This applies to all measures and procedures used (including interviews), whether the measures have been bought off-the-shelf, developed externally, or developed in-house. This means that if you develop your own measures or procedures, you should conduct your own validation studies. If validation is not possible, the scored assessment should be eliminated. If informal or nonscored assessments have an adverse impact, the employer should either eliminate the tool or use a more formal one that can be validated.

Although the Uniform Guidelines focus on adverse impact and legal liability, validation is even more important from a strategic perspective. Strategically, it makes sense to use only those measures that reliably and validly assess what is important to job success and that predict desired outcomes. Anything else is potentially an expensive waste of time. Invalid measures can lead to missed opportunities for selecting high-quality talent, or worse yet, the selection of people who will perform poorly. The cost of selection-related errors is high. However, they can be dramatically reduced by using valid measures for selection. There are many types of validity, all of which address the usefulness and appropriateness of using a given measure. We discuss them next.

FACE VALIDITY   One aspect of validity is whether the measure *seems* to measure what it is supposed to measure. This is **face validity**. It is a subjective assessment of how well items or measures seem to be related to the requirements of the job. Face validity is often important to job applicants who tend to react negatively to assessment methods if they perceive them to be unrelated to the job (or not face valid). Even if a measure seems face valid, if it does not predict job performance, then it should not be used. Hypothetically, a measure of extroversion might look like an acceptable way to measure job candidates applying for a sales position. Nonetheless, it might still fail to predict whether or not an extroverted person performs well as a sales representative. Perhaps outgoing salespeople talk too much and sell too little, for example.

> **face validity**
> *a subjective assessment of how well items seem to be related to the requirements of the job*

VALIDATION   In order to be certain an employment measure is useful and valid, you must collect evidence relating the measure to a job. The process of establishing the job relatedness of a measure is called **validation**. Validation is the cumulative and ongoing process of establishing the job relatedness of a measure.

The Uniform Guidelines on Employee Selection Procedures discuss the following three methods of conducting validation studies and describe conditions under which each type of validation method is appropriate:

> **validation**
> *the cumulative and ongoing process of establishing the job relatedness of a measure*

- **Content-related validation** is the process of demonstrating that the content of a measure assesses important job-related behaviors. For example, a mathematical skills test would have high content validity for an engineering position, but a typing skills test might have low content validity if the job required only minimal typing. However, the same typing test might have strong content validity for a clerical position.[18] Content validity also applies to the items making up a measure. A math test might have low content validity if it includes items focusing on, for example, psychology or biology, or other facets unrelated to the position being hired for.

> **content-related validation**
> *the process of demonstrating that the content of a measure assesses important job-related behaviors*

- **Construct-related validation** is the process of demonstrating that a measure assesses the construct, or characteristic, it claims to measure. This method often applies to measures that attempt to assess the abstract traits of candidates, such as their personalities, honesty, or aptitudes. A construct-related validation would need to be done if, for example, a bank wanted to test its tellers for a trait such as "numerical aptitude." In this case, the aptitude is not an observable behavior, but a concept created to explain possible future behaviors. To demonstrate that the measure possesses construct validity, the bank would need to show (1) that the measure did indeed assess the desired trait (numerical aptitude) and (2) that this trait corresponded to success on the job.[19] Construct validity is established by the pattern of correlations among items within a measure and the pattern of correlations of the scores from that measure with other relevant outcomes. Content validity can also be used to help establish construct validity.

> **construct-related validation**
> *the process of demonstrating that a measure assesses the construct, or characteristic, it claims to measure*

- **Criterion-related validation** is the process of demonstrating that there is a statistical relationship between scores from a measure (the predictor) and the criterion (the outcome), usually some aspect of job success such as job performance, training performance, or job tenure. This form of validation uses either correlational or regression-based procedures. In other words, in the case of a positive relationship, individuals who score high on the measure should tend to perform better on the job

> **criterion-related validation**
> *the process of demonstrating that there is a statistical relationship between scores from a measure (the predictor) and the criterion (the outcome)*

success criterion than those who score low. If the criterion is obtained at the same time the predictor measure is collected, it is called *concurrent validity;* if the criterion is obtained after the initial measure (the predictor) is collected, then it is called *predictive validity.* Consider the position of a millwright, who installs, repairs, replaces, and dismantles machinery and heavy equipment. A measure might be designed to assess how employees' mechanical skills are related to their performance when it comes to servicing machines (criterion). A strong relationship would validate using the measure.[20] Predictive validity would be estimated if you measured employees' mechanical skills before they were hired and then correlated those skills with their subsequent performance. Concurrent validity would be estimated if at a single point in time you measured the mechanical skills of a company's current employees as well as correlated their scores with their performance. The criterion-related validity of a measure is measured by the validity coefficient, which we discuss in more detail in the next section of this chapter.

All types of validity are important. You can establish content validity for a math skills test using job analysis techniques to determine the level, type, and difficulty of math required for a position and the importance of math to job performance. You can then construct a large number of items that would potentially measure math skills and establish that job experts agree that the items are related to the math skills. You can also use job expert ratings to establish that each math test item is essential by computing a content validity ratio (the formula is available in the chapter supplement). You can also ask job incumbents and supervisors to determine if any important math skills are missing from the measure. This would help to establish the content and face validity of the measure. Then you could correlate the math skills test with the performance of engineers to see if they predict job performance. This establishes criterion-related validity. All these forms of validity, combined with reliability information and information about how the items within the math skill test relate to each other can then establish the construct validity of the measure.

validity coefficient

a number between 0 and +1 that indicates the magnitude of the relationship between a predictor (such as test scores) and the criterion (such as a measure of actual job success)

THE VALIDITY COEFFICIENT   The **validity coefficient** is a number between 0 and +1 that indicates the magnitude of the relationship between a predictor (such as test scores) and the criterion (such as a measure of actual job success). The validity coefficient is the absolute value of the correlation between the predictor and criterion. The larger the validity coefficient, the more confidence you can have in predictions made from the scores. Because jobs and people are complex, a single measure can never fully predict what a person's job performance will be because success on the job depends on so many factors. Therefore, validity coefficients rarely exceed .40 in staffing contexts.[21]

As a general rule, the higher the validity coefficient, the more beneficial it is to use the measure. Validity coefficients of .21 to .35 are typical for a single measure. The validities of selection systems that use multiple measures will probably be higher because you are using different tools to measure and predict different aspects of performance. By contrast, a single measure is more likely to measure or predict fewer aspects of total performance. Table 8–3 shows some general guidelines for interpreting a single measure's validity. It is difficult to obtain validity coefficients above .50 even if multiple measures are used.

TABLE 8–3   General Guidelines for Interpreting Validity Coefficients[22]

Validity

Coefficient Value	Interpretation
Above .35	Very beneficial
.21–.35	Potential to be useful
.11–.20	Useful in certain circumstances
Below .11	Unlikely to be useful

EVALUATING VALIDITY   Evaluating a measure's validity is a complex task. In addition to the magnitude of the validity coefficient, you should also consider at a minimum the following factors:

- The level of adverse impact associated with your assessment tool
- The number of applicants compared to the number of openings
- The number of currently successful employees
- The cost of a hiring error
- The cost of the selection tool
- The probability of hiring a qualified applicant without using a scored assessment tool.

Here are three scenarios illustrating why you should consider these factors, individually and in combination with one another, when evaluating validity coefficients:[23]

Scenario One: You have few applicants for each open position. Most of the applicants will be hired because the positions do not require a great deal of skill. In this situation, you might be willing to accept a selection tool that has a validity in the range of "potential to be useful" or "useful in certain circumstances" if the assessment method is cheap, you need to fill the positions quickly, you do not have many applicants to choose from, and the level of skill required is not that high.

Scenario Two: You are recruiting for jobs that require a high level of accuracy, and mistakes could be dangerous or costly. In this case, a slightly lower validity coefficient would probably not be acceptable to you because hiring an unqualified worker would be too much of a risk. Instead, you would need to use a selection tool that reported validities considered to be "very beneficial."

Scenario Three: The company you are working for is considering a very expensive assessment system that results in fairly high levels of adverse impact. There are other assessment tools on the market associated with lower adverse impact, but they are less valid and just as costly. Additionally, making a hiring mistake would put your company at too much risk. Consequently, your company decides to implement the assessment given the difficulty in hiring for the particular positions, the "very beneficial" validity of the assessment, and your failed attempts to find alternative instruments with less adverse impact. However, your company will continue to try to find ways to reduce the adverse impact of the system.

Clearly, most situations require you to consider multiple factors. For example, the recruiting and selection context must be considered along with validity. Even if a staffing system is valid and predicts job success well, unintended consequences may result from the use of the system. For example, the following might be adversely affected:

- *Applicants.* A valid assessment system can result in adverse impact by differentially selecting people from various protected groups, have low face validity, and result in lawsuits. As we discussed in Chapter 3, fair employment legislation prohibits the use of tests to discriminate against job applicants because of their race, color, religion, sex, or national origin. In some cases, job candidates may perceive valid measures as irrelevant to the job in question.
- *The organization's time and cost.* A valid assessment system can have an unacceptably long time to fill or cost per hire; result in the identification of high-quality candidates who demand high salaries, resulting in increasing payroll costs; and be cumbersome, difficult, or complex to use.
- *Future recruits.* A system can be valid but if it is too long or onerous then applicants, particularly high-quality applicants, are more likely to drop out of consideration; word that a firm is using time-consuming selection practices could reduce the number of applications; a valid system could result in differential selection rates and reduce the number of applicants from a particular gender, ethnicity, or background; and valid systems can still be viewed as unfair, resulting in fewer future applicants.
- *Current employees.* The assessment system may favor external applicants or not give all qualified employees an equal chance of applying for an internal position; employees might therefore question its fairness.

The point here is not to ignore validity. Rather, it is to highlight the need to address these factors so that highly valid measures can be used for selection while minimizing the downsides of using them.

Validity is typically evaluated using single samples for specific jobs. There are limitations, both practical and statistical, to conducting validity studies in cases in which there are relatively few people in a given position. Computing validities with small samples can lead to large sampling errors and reduce the likelihood that your findings will be statistically significant. One method of dealing with this problem is to use validity generalization.

validity generalization
the degree to which evidence of validity obtained in one situation can be generalized to another situation without further study

VALIDITY GENERALIZATION   **Validity generalization** refers to the degree to which evidence of a measure's validity obtained in one situation can be generalized to another situation without further study.[24] A statistical technique called *meta-analysis* is used to combine the results of validation studies done for a single measure on many different target groups and for a variety of jobs. The goal of the meta-analysis is to estimate a measure's "true validity" and to identify whether we can generalize the results to all situations or determine if the same measure works differently in different situations.

Validity generalization studies can often give staffing professionals insight about the strength of the relationship between a measure and a person's job performance. However, there is no guarantee that all employers would find the same level of validity of a study when it comes to their own workforces. Every organization has different situational factors that can drastically impact the validity of a measure. Although the legal acceptability of validity generalization has yet to be thoroughly considered in the courts, online assessment companies, such as preVisor (www.previsor.com), are increasingly using validity generalization as part of their validation of their collection of products.

Using Existing Assessment Methods

Conducting your own validation study is expensive. Moreover, as we have explained, many smaller firms do not have enough employees in a relevant job category to make it feasible to conduct a study. One alternative is to conduct cooperative studies across firms within an association to collect more validation data more quickly. For example, insurance companies can share data to obtain large amounts of validation data on specific positions. Another alternative is that it can be advantageous to use professionally developed assessment tools and procedures for which documentation on validity already exists. However, you must ensure that the validity evidence obtained from an "outside" study can be suitably "transported" to your particular situation. In fact, the Uniform Guidelines require as much. To determine if a particular measure is valid for your intended use, consult the manual and available independent reviews such as those in Buros Institute's *Mental Measurements Yearbook*[25] and *Test Critiques*.[26]

When evaluating validity information purchased from a vendor, you should consider the following:

- *Available validation evidence supporting the use of the measure for specific purposes.* The manual should include a thorough description of the procedures used in the validation studies and the results of those studies. Also consider the definition of job success used in the validation study.
- *The possible valid uses of the measure.* The purposes for which the measure can legitimately be used should be described, as well as the performance criteria that can validly be predicted.
- *The similarity of the sample group(s) on which the measure was developed with the group(s) with which you would like to use the measure.* For example, was the measure developed on a sample of high school graduates, managers, or clerical workers? What was the racial, ethnic, age, and gender mix of the sample?
- *Job similarity.* A job analysis should be performed to verify that your job and the original job are substantially similar in terms of ability requirements and work behavior.
- *Adverse impact evidence.* Consider the adverse impact reports from outside studies for each protected group that is part of your labor market. If this information is not available for an otherwise qualified measure, conduct your own study of adverse impact, if feasible.

This chapter's Develop Your Skills feature provides some advice on measuring the characteristics of job applicants.

DEVELOP YOUR SKILLS
Assessment Tips[27]

To effectively assess job candidates, employers must be aware of the inherent limitations of any assessment procedure as well as how to properly use their chosen assessment methods. Here are 10 tips on conducting an effective assessment program:

1. The measures should be used in a purposeful manner—have a clear understanding of what you want to measure and why you want to measure it.
2. Use a variety of tools—because no single measurement tool is 100 percent reliable or valid, use a variety of tools to measure job-relevant characteristics.
3. Use measures that are unbiased and fair to all groups—this will allow you to identify a qualified and diverse set of finalists.
4. Use measures that are reliable and valid.
5. Use measures that are appropriate for the target population—a measure developed for use with one group might not be valid for other groups.
6. Ensure that your administration staff is properly trained—the training should include how to administer the measure as well as how to handle special situations with sensitivity—for example, how and when to provide reasonable accommodations for people with disabilities.
7. Ensure suitable and uniform assessment conditions—noise, poor lighting, inaccurate timing, and damaged equipment can adversely affect respondents.
8. Keep your assessment instruments secure—developers and administrators should restrict access to the instrument's questions, and the measures should be periodically revised.
9. Maintain the confidentiality of the results—the results should be shared only with those who have a legitimate need to know. Personal information should not be released to other organizations or individuals without the informed consent of the respondent.
10. Interpret the scores properly—the inferences made from the results should be reasonable, well founded, and not based on superficial interpretation; careful attention should be paid to contamination and deficiency errors; the manual for the tools should also provide instructions on how to properly interpret the results.

Selection Errors

Professionally developed measures and procedures that are used as part of a planned assessment program can help you select and hire more qualified and productive employees even if the measures are not perfect. It is essential to understand that *all assessment tools are subject to errors*, both in measuring a characteristic, such as verbal ability, and in predicting job success criteria, such as job performance. This is true for all measures and procedures.

- Do not expect any measure or procedure to measure a personal trait or ability with perfect accuracy for every single person.
- Do not expect any measure or procedure to be completely accurate in terms of predicting a candidate's job success.

Certainly, selecting employees who are highly able is important. However, there are many factors that affect a person's performance. You also need a motivated employee who clearly understands the job to be performed, for example. The employee also needs the time and resources necessary to succeed in the job. Several of these factors can be predicted using good measurement tools. This is why selection procedures typically involve three to five distinct selection measures (at a minimum) that are combined in some fashion to make a final hiring decision.

Despite these efforts, there always will be cases in which a score or procedure will predict someone to be a good worker, who, in fact, is not. There will also be cases in which an individual receiving a low score will be rejected when he or she would actually be a capable and good worker. In the staffing profession, these errors are called **selection errors**. False positives and false negatives are two types of selection errors. False positives occur when you erroneously classify a weak applicant as being a good hire. False negatives occur when you erroneously classify a strong applicant as being a weak hire. As you try to reduce one type of error you may increase the other so there are trade-offs in how you make your hiring decision. These issues will be covered more in the following chapters.

Selection errors cannot be completely avoided, but they can be reduced, for example, by using a variety of measures. Using a variety of measures and procedures to more fully assess people is referred to as the **whole-person approach** to assessment. This approach will help reduce the number of selection errors and boost the effectiveness of your overall decision making.[28]

selection errors
not hiring someone who would have been successful at the job or hiring someone who is not successful at the job

whole-person approach
the practice of using a variety of measures and procedures to more fully assess people

Standardization and Objectivity

standardization
the consistent administration and use of a measure

Standardization is the consistent administration and use of a measure. Standardization reflects the consistency and uniformity of the conditions as well as the procedures for administering an assessment method. Computerization helps to ensure that all respondents receive the same instructions and the same amount of time to complete the assessment. Because maintaining standardized conditions is the responsibility of the people administering the assessment, training all administrators in proper procedures and control of conditions is critical. This is true for interviewing as well as any other assessment approach. In addition to being legally important, standardization is also valuable because recruiters should consistently evaluate candidates on their competencies, styles, and traits.

Norms reflect the distribution of scores of a large number of people whose scores on an assessment method are to be compared. The standardization sample is the group of respondents whose scores are used to establish norms. These norms become the comparison scores for determining the relative performance of future respondents.

objectivity
the amount of judgment or bias involved in scoring an assessment measure

Objectivity refers to the amount of judgment or bias involved in scoring an assessment measure. The scoring process for *objective measures* is free of personal judgment or bias. The number of words typed in a minute is an objective measure, as is the amount of weight a firefighter candidate can lift. *Subjective measures*, on the other hand, contain items (such as essay or interview questions) for which the score can be influenced by the attitudes, biases, and personal characteristics of the person doing the scoring. Whenever hiring decisions are subjective, it is also a good idea to involve multiple people in the hiring process, preferably of diverse gender and race, to generate a more defensible decision.[29] Because they produce the most accurate measurements, it is best to use standardized, objective measures whenever possible.

CREATING AND VALIDATING AN ASSESSMENT SYSTEM

Creating an effective assessment and selection system for any position in any organization begins with a job analysis. As you learned in Chapter 4, after understanding the requirements of job success, you identify the important KSAOs and competencies required of a successful employee. You then identify reliable and valid methods of measuring these KSAOs and competencies, and create a system for measuring and collecting the resulting data. The integrity and usefulness of the data generated by each measure needs to be considered when deciding which measures to use. The data collected from each measure is then examined to ensure that it has an appropriate mean and standard deviation. Remember, a measure on which everyone scores the same or nearly the same is not as useful as a measure that produces a wide range of scores. Candidates' scores on each assessment method are then correlated or entered into a regression equation to evaluate any redundancies among the measures and to assess how well the group of measures predicts job success. Adverse impact and the cost of the measures are also considered in evaluating each measure. After the final set of measures is identified, selection rules are developed to determine which scores are passing. The usefulness and effectiveness of the system is then periodically reevaluated to ensure that it is still predicting job success without adverse impact.

Benchmarking

It is sometimes useful to compare an organization's staffing data with those of other organizations to understand better whether the organization is doing well or poorly on a particular dimension. For example, is a voluntary turnover rate of 30 percent good or bad? In some positions, such as the positions held by retail employees, this would be a good turnover level compared to the industry average. In other positions, a 30 percent turnover rate would be unusually high. Benchmarking other firms can give a company comparative information about dimensions including:

- Application rates
- Average starting salaries
- Average time to fill
- Average cost per hire

There are numerous sources of relatively high-quality benchmark information, but it can be expensive. Some sources of benchmarking data include:

- Corporate Leadership Council
- Watson Wyatt and other staffing consulting firms
- Hackett Group
- The Saratoga Institute (now part of PricewaterhouseCoopers)
- Staffing.org
- Many industry associations, such as the Society for Human Resource Management, track benchmark information and make it available to their members.

Evaluating Assessment Methods

The determinants of the effectiveness of any internally or externally developed assessment method include:

1. *Validity*—whether the assessment method predicts the relevant components of job success
2. *Return on investment*—whether the assessment method generates a financial return that exceeds the cost associated with using it
3. *Applicant reactions*—including the perceived job relatedness and fairness of the assessment method
4. *Usability*—the willingness and ability of people in the organization to use the method consistently and correctly
5. *Adverse impact*—whether the method can be used without discriminating against members of a protected class
6. *The selection ratio*—whether the method has a low selection ratio

The importance of a firm's selection ratio and base rate to the effectiveness of an assessment method deserve further elaboration. Taylor and Russell[30] were among the first to demonstrate that validity alone will not determine the usefulness of an assessment. The tables they generated, taking into account selection ratio and base rate, demonstrated that assessments with high validity may not prove useful if a high number of those assessed are hired and that assessments with relatively low validity can still have a substantial impact on the improvement of job success rates if only a few of those assessed are hired. This work laid the foundation for utility analysis, which is discussed in a later chapter.

A **selection ratio** is the number of people hired divided by the number of applicants. Lower selection ratios mean that a lower percentage of applicants are hired, and higher selection ratios mean that a greater percentage of applicants are hired. Lower selection ratios mean that the company is being more selective, and can reflect either hiring a low number of people or receiving a large number of applications. For example, a selection ratio of 75 percent means that the company is hiring 75 of every 100 applicants, which doesn't give the assessment method as good of a chance to weed out the applicants who are less likely to do the job well. Imagine if your selection ratio is 1.00 (100%), in which case you are hiring everyone who applies—no assessment tool can be useful in that circumstance.

selection ratio
the number of people hired divided by the number of applicants

The **base rate** is the percent of employees who are defined as currently successful performers. Clearly, organizations desire a base rate of 100 percent as this reflects a situation in which all employees are performing satisfactorily. The firm's system of HR practices, including staffing, training, compensation, and performance management, work together to affect a firm's base rate. If your base rate is 100 percent, then everyone who gets hired is already successful, and using an additional assessment tool will not improve your success rate.

base rate
the percent of employees who are defined as currently successful performers

The potential to improve the effectiveness of a new assessment system in terms of improving the base rate of a firm depends on the percent of its currently successful employees (the current base rate), the selection ratio, and the new assessment method's validity.[31] If the current base rate is high, and most employees are successful in their jobs, the potential impact of the new assessment method will be lower than if the base rate is lower and more of the firm's employees are performing poorly. A high-performing system (as evidenced by a high base rate) simply has less room for improvement than a lower-performing system.

Lowering the selection ratio can also improve the impact of the selection system. A selection ratio of 80 percent means that the company is only screening out 20 percent of its applicants and is possibly hiring many candidates who its assessment system has identified as lower potential performers. Of course, if the sourcing and recruiting processes resulted in a high-quality candidate pool that contains many potential high performers, a lower selection ratio might not improve the firm's selection process as much.

The validity of a new assessment method can also affect the impact of the selection system. As we have discussed, assessment methods with higher validities are better able to improve the selection process than those with low validities. If the current base rate is high, the current selection ratio is high, and the validity of the new assessment method is moderate or low, it may not be worthwhile to use it.

ASSESSMENT DEVELOPMENT AT VALTERA[32]

Valtera's retail merchandising client wanted to hire better employees to enhance the execution of its low-cost and high-service strategy. The Valtera team conducted a job analysis by visiting the retailer's various sites, observing employees on the job, and interviewing them, their supervisors, and the company's executives. This process resulted in a detailed list of the tasks performed on the job and a list of the KSAOs required to perform the tasks. Job experts (employees) provided ratings on the frequency of the tasks they performed and their relative importance. They also rated the importance of the KSAOs and the degree to which new hires need to have them. The job experts also linked the KSAOs back to the job's tasks and work behaviors to ensure that the important KSAOs were related to actual job performance. These steps provided content validity evidence.

After collecting job analysis information, the Valtera team analyzed the data. The group checked the means and standard deviations of the KSAO ratings to determine which KSAOs were the most important for the job. The team then developed computerized measures to assess the most critical KSAOs. The format also had to fit the company's strategy and culture. Because the company wanted Valtera to focus on identifying measures, not interviews, the team created six different measures including arithmetic, math word problems, situational judgment, personality, and a coding test, in which each applicant was asked to look up the code for an item. The Valtera team also developed a job performance measure based on the job analysis results.

Next, the team conducted a concurrent validation study using its current employees to determine if the measures predicted job performance. The team administered the measures to employees and asked their supervisors to rate them using the performance measures the group had developed.

Each measure was examined to identify which items worked best, and the team confirmed that the reliability of each measure was acceptable. Next, the team analyzed the relationships between employees' scores on the six measures and job performance using correlation and regression analyses. As a result of these analyses, the six measures were reduced to four.

The scores on the reading, math word problems, situational judgment, and personality measures were put into a regression analysis to see how they worked together and to determine an optimal predicting equation to compute an overall battery score. The overall battery score was significantly related to performance. Valtera conducted analyses to assess if the measurement battery was biased against members of protected groups and found no evidence of bias. A cut score was identified by looking at any adverse impact results, passing rates, and the business needs of the company.

Valtera's results convinced the client that adopting the selection system would result in a positive financial return for the retail company by improving how well its new employees performed. The client continues to use the selection system to hire new employees.

Summary

Sound measurement lays the foundation for effective staffing. If job characteristics are poorly measured during a job analysis and if applicant characteristics are poorly assessed, it will be difficult to impossible to identify and hire the applicants who would be the best hires. Although measurement perfection is unlikely, using measures with appropriate reliability and validity will improve the accuracy of the predictions we make. Understanding different ways of describing data and knowing the appropriate use and interpretation of correlation and regression analysis help the staffing specialist best use data to make decisions, and evaluate the performance of outside consultants as well.

Acquiring and utilizing relevant information is an important part of making good decisions, and staffing decisions are no exception. Decision makers best use and improve the staffing system by understanding historical relationships among attributes of the staffing system, such as the recruiting source, recruiting message, and assessment methods used, and desired organizational outcomes. Outcomes of staffing system performance include performance, customer satisfaction, and the retention of top performers. The staffing improvements made possible by analyzing staffing data include reduced time to productivity for new hires, increased retention of high performers and high-potential employees, increased new hire quality, and greater hiring manager satisfaction. As you will learn in Chapter 13, the match between new hires and organizations can be enhanced and staffing practices and strategies can be better connected to the company's business strategy by analyzing data to improve a staffing system.

Takeaway Points

1. Measurement is essential to making good hiring decisions. Improperly assessing and measuring candidates' characteristics can lead to systematically hiring the wrong people, offending and losing good candidates, and even exposing your company to legal action. By contrast, properly assessing and measuring candidates' characteristics can give your organization a competitive advantage.

2. Measures of central tendency such as the mean, median, and mode and measures of variability such as range, variance, and standard deviation are useful for describing distributions of scores. This information can be used to compute standard scores, which can tell you how any individual performed relative to others and which can be used to easily combine scores that have different means and standard deviations.

3. Correlation is the strength of a relationship between two variables. Multiple regression is a statistical technique based on correlation analysis. The technique identifies the ideal weights to assign each test so as to maximize the validity of a set of assessment methods; the analysis is based on each assessment method's correlation with job success and the degree to which the assessment methods are intercorrelated. Correlation and regression analyses are used to evaluate how well an assessment method predicts job success and to evaluate the effectiveness of a firm's overall staffing system.

4. Practical significance occurs when the correlation is large enough to be of value in a practical sense. Statistical significance is the degree to which the relationship is not likely due to sampling error. To be useful, a correlation needs to have both practical and statistical significance.

5. Reliability is how dependably or consistently a measure assesses a particular characteristic. Validity is how well a measure assesses a given construct and the degree to which you can make specific conclusions or predictions based on a measure's scores. A measure must be reliable in order to be valid. In order to be useful, a measure must be both reliable and valid.

6. Standardization is the consistent administration and use of a measure. Objectivity is the amount of judgment or bias involved in scoring an assessment measure. Because they produce the most accurate measurements, it is best to use standardized, objective measures whenever possible.

Discussion Questions

1. What types of measures of job candidates are most likely to be high in terms of their reliability and validity? Does this make them more useful? Why or why not?

2. How would you explain to your supervisor that the correlation between interview scores and new hire quality is low and persuade him or her to consider a new job applicant evaluation method?

3. What correlation would you need to see before you were willing to use an expensive assessment test?

4. When would it be acceptable to use a measure that predicts job success but that has adverse impact?

5. What do staffing professionals need to know about measurement?

Exercises

1. *Strategy Exercise:* Teddy bear maker Fuzzy Hugs pursues a high-quality, low-cost strategy and can't afford to hire underperforming manufacturing employees given its lean staffing model. Fuzzy Hugs has identified an assessment system that has high validity and predicts job success well but that is also very expensive and results in fairly high levels of adverse impact. The company is concerned about maintaining a diverse workforce, and wants to avoid legal trouble. The assessment tools it identified that had lower adverse impact had substantially lower validity as well, and were almost as expensive.

   The company asks your professional advice about whether it should use the new assessment system. What advice do you give?

2. *Develop Your Skills Exercise:* This chapter's Develop Your Skills feature gave you some tips on assessing job candidates. Based on what you read in this chapter, what are three additional tips that you would add to the list?

(Additional exercises are available at the end of this chapter's supplement that will enable you to build additional computational and decision-making skills when using data.)

3. *Opening Vignette Exercise:* The opening vignette described how Valtera developed an assessment system to enable its retail merchandising client to hire better employees to enhance the execution of its low-cost and high-service strategy. Reread the vignette and answer the following questions:

   a. What other measures do you think could be considered for the job given the company's high–service quality goal? Why?

   b. If you applied to this company and were tested on reading, math word problems, situational judgment, and personality measures for a retail sales position, how would you respond? Would you think that these methods were fair?

CASE STUDY

You just became the head of staffing for BabyBots, a manufacturer of small robots. You were surprised to learn that the company had never validated the manual dexterity test it uses to assess job candidates for its manufacturing jobs. You decided to do a concurrent validation study and administered the test to thirty manufacturing workers. Their scores are reported in Table A, along with their ages, sex, race, and job performance ratings. You also calculated the correlation between the manual dexterity test and job performance to assess the test's validity. You then examined the relationship between employees' test scores and their performance ratings. The results of this analysis are shown in Table B.

TABLE A	Validation Data for the Manual Dexterity Test				
Employee	Sex	Race	Age	Test Score	Performance Rating
1	0	0	35	36	90
2	0	1	32	44	95
3	1	0	44	50	95
4	0	2	42	49	93
5	1	2	36	46	89
6	0	1	33	52	94
7	0	1	45	50	92
8	0	0	48	50	93
9	1	2	34	42	83
10	1	2	46	44	89
11	1	0	30	40	87
12	1	0	39	48	95
13	1	2	31	47	90
14	0	1	49	39	80
15	1	0	47	48	92
16	1	1	40	38	79
17	0	0	44	38	80
18	0	1	33	36	72
19	1	0	43	46	89
20	1	0	36	48	92
21	1	1	22	46	89
22	0	2	28	32	70
23	1	2	19	48	94
24	0	2	23	48	94
25	0	2	27	36	74
26	1	1	18	46	85
27	1	1	26	44	79
28	0	1	21	50	95
29	0	2	23	34	70
30	1	1	28	44	83
Mean			34.07	43.97	86.73
SD			9.33	5.54	7.91
Min			18.00	32.00	70.00
Max			49.00	52.00	95.00
Range			31.00	20.00	25.00

Performance rating: 0 = 0% efficiency, 100 = 100% efficiency
Sex: 0 = male; 1 = female
Race: 0 = Hispanic; 1 = White; 2 = Black

TABLE B	Correlation Table		
	Age	Test	Job Performance
Age	1.00		
Test	0.12	1.00	
Job Performance	0.18	**0.86**	1.00

Note: Correlations underlined and in bold indicate statistical significance at a level of $p < .05$.

Above a Cutoff of 43

Sex	Above 43	Total Count	Percent
Males (0)	7	14	50.00 .
Females (1)	13	16	81.25
Total	20	30	66.67

Above a Cutoff of 43

Race	Above 43	Total Count	Percent
Hispanic (0)	6	9	66.67
White (1)	8	11	72.73
Black (2)	6	10	60.00
Total	20	30	66.67

QUESTIONS

1. What kind of relationship exists between employees' scores on the manual dexterity test and their performance ratings?
2. Suppose a candidate scored 44 on the manual dexterity test. The regression equation predicting job performance using the manual dexterity test is:
   32.465 + (1.234 × Manual dexterity test score)
   What is the candidate's predicted job performance?
3. Assume that only candidates with predicted performance above 85 are to be hired. This translates to a score of at least 43 on the manual dexterity test. Assume only those with scores above 43 were hired (20 of the 30 people in this sample). Would the use of this test have led to evidence of adverse impact based on sex or race? The relevant data on the 20 people exceeding the cutoff are presented above.
4. Given the validity results you found, would you recommend use of this test as a selection device? If so, how would you use it?

Semester-Long Active Learning Project

Finish the assignment for Chapter 7 and begin researching, describing, and critically analyzing the alignment between the position you chose and the firm's existing assessment practices. Devise a series of assessment methods (interviews, assessment centers, work samples, and so forth) for evaluating job candidates. Using what you learned in Chapter 4, identify how your assessment plan will enable the company to be compliant with EEO laws and other legal requirements.

Case Study Assignment: Strategic Staffing at Chern's

See the appendix at the back of the book for this chapter's Case Study Assignment.

Chapter Supplement

Attenuation Due to Unreliability

Because correlations are an important tool for determining the strategic usefulness of a particular assessment tool and for legal defensibility, it is important to recognize that observed correlations can be influenced by some important factors that may exist in organizational contexts. Attenuation is the weakening of observed correlations. No measure is perfect, and unreliability of measures can attenuate correlations.[33]

Consider Figure 8–8. In the first scatter plot we have depicted a perfect correlation along with arrows indicating the addition of random error. In the second scatter plot you can see the impact of the added measurement error (unreliability). You can easily see how unreliability adds "noise" or error to the system, attenuating the correlation. The observed correlation has moved from being perfect, +1.0, to about +.67. In the most extreme case, a correlation with a random variable (a completely unreliable measure) will hover around zero. The impact of error is another illustration of why it is important to be systematic in your staffing system and procedures. If different interviewers are affected by noninterview factors then they cannot be reliable and their scores will not be as strongly correlated with later job performance. Observed correlations can be corrected for attenuation if you know the reliability of the measure(s). The formula is:

$$\text{Corrected } r_{XY} = \frac{\text{Observed } r_{XY}}{\sqrt{r_{XX} \times r_{YY}}}$$

Where r_{XY} represents the correlation between X and Y and r_{XX} and r_{YY} represent the reliability of measures of X and Y, respectively.

Correction for Range Restriction

Another factor that can influence correlations in organizations is range restriction. Organizations do not hire randomly and they keep only the best performing employees. This reduces the variability of employees within the organization. Range restriction refers to the reduction of variability in observed scores, often due to some management practice or use of a selection device. Range restriction tends to attenuate observed correlations.

For example, we downloaded data from the Bureau of Labor and Statistics and correlated the relationship between educational level and income. Below you will find the table of correlations using actual data with varying levels of range restriction:

You can see that you would conclude education is strongly related to income using the full sample but you might conclude education is unimportant if you included only those with advanced degrees. Why the difference? As education is increasingly restricted in range, it can have less and less rela-

TABLE C	Restriction of Range	
Cases Selected	**Correlation**
All possible cases:	.838
Only people with some income:	.452
Only people who graduate from high school:	.410
Only people who graduate with some college:	.293
Only people with a Master's or Ph.D. or M.D. degree	.001

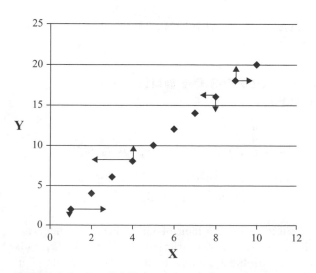

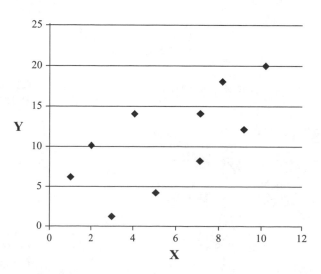

FIGURE 8–8 Unreliability and Correlation

tionship with income. Imagine if everyone had exactly the same level of education—education could not influence income.

As a staffing example, assume you selected only those who scored in the top quarter of a personality test. You would restrict the range of variability in the scores on the personality test. This is a problem when establishing criterion-related validity in organizations. If you use a selection tool, or any process correlated with a selection tool, to make staffing decisions, then you will necessarily restrict the range of scores. Even retaining only the best employees will restrict variability in important ways. You can correct an observed correlation for range restriction if you know the unrestricted variability (or standard deviation). The formula is:

$$\text{Corrected } r_{XY} = \frac{r_{XY}(S_U/S_R)}{\sqrt{1 - r_{XY}^2 + r_{XY}^2(S_U^2/S_R^2)}}$$

Where r_{XY} represents the correlation between X and Y, and s_U and s_R refer to the unrestricted and restricted standard deviations, respectively. You can use this formula to correct for range restriction on either the predictor or criterion as long as you have the restricted and unrestricted standard deviations. More sophisticated formulae exist for indirect range restriction or simultaneous correction for more than one variable.[34]

Measurement Formulas

Unless indicated otherwise, Xs are the observed scores, Ys are outcome scores, and ns are the number of observations in the sample. Sample Excel formulas assume data exist in columns of cells ranging from A1 to A30, continuing with B1 to B30 and so forth.

MEAN

$$\overline{X} = \frac{\sum X}{n}$$

In Excel: @average(A1:A30)

RANGE

$$X_{max} - X_{min}$$

In Excel: @Max(A1:A30)–@Min(A1:A30)

SAMPLE VARIANCE

$$var_x = \frac{\sum X^2 - \frac{(\sum X^2)}{n}}{n - 1}$$

OR

$$var_x = \frac{\sum(X - \overline{X})^2}{n - 1}$$

In Excel: @Var(A1:A30)

SAMPLE STANDARD DEVIATION

$$s_X = \sqrt{\frac{\sum(X - \overline{X})^2}{n - 1}}$$

OR

$$s_X = \text{positive square root of the variance}$$

In Excel: @stdev(A1:A30)

z score
a standard score that indicates the distance of a score from the mean in standard deviation units

z SCORE

$$z = \frac{(X - \overline{X})}{s_X}$$

SAMPLE COVARIANCE

$$\text{cov}_{XY} = \frac{\sum XY - \frac{(\sum X)(\sum Y)}{n}}{n - 1}$$

In Excel: @covar(A1:A30,B1:B30)

CORRELATION COEFFICIENT

$$r_{XY} = \frac{\text{cov}_{XY}}{S_X S_Y}$$

In Excel: correl(A1:A30,B1:B30)

SIMPLE REGRESSION

$$y = bx + a$$
$$b = \text{cov}_{xy}/S_x^2 \quad \text{OR} \quad b = r_{xy}(s_y/s_x)$$
$$a = \overline{y} - b\overline{x}$$

Where y' is the outcome variable being predicted, x is the predictor, b is the slope of the regression line, and a is the constant or intercept.

In Excel: @slope(A1:A30,B1:B30) and @intercept(A1:A30,B1:B30)

MULTIPLE REGRESSION WITH TWO VARIABLES

$$y' = b_1 x_1 + b_2 x_2 + a$$
$$b_1 = (r_{y1} - r_{y2} r_{12})/(1 - r_{12}^2) \times (s_y/s_1)$$
$$b_2 = (r_{y2} - r_{y1} r_{12})/(1 - r_{12}^2) \times (s_y/s_2)$$
$$A = \overline{Y} - (b_1 \times \overline{x}_1) - (b_2 \times \overline{x}_2)$$

Where y' is the outcome variable being predicted, x_1 and x_2 are the two predictor variables, b_1 is the slope for variable x_1, b_2 is the slope for variable x_2, and a is the constant or intercept. Also, r_{y1}, r_{y2}, and r_{12} denote the correlations between the outcome and x_1, the outcome and x_2, and the two predictors x_1 and , respectively. Additionally, s_y, s_1, and s_2 are the standard deviations of y, x_1, and x_2, respectively.

In Excel 2007 it is relatively easy to compute a multiple regression for multiple predictors.

1. Make sure the Analysis ToolPak is installed (other versions of Excel will require slightly different instructions). This is a Microsoft Office Excel add-in that adds custom commands or custom features to Microsoft Office.
   a. Click the Microsoft Office Button image, and then locate "Excel Options" at the bottom of the dialog box and click on it.
   b. Click "Add-Ins" then at the bottom of the dialog box look for "Manage:" and ensure it shows "Excel Add-ins." Click "Go".
   c. In the "Add-Ins available:" box, select the "Analysis ToolPak" check box, and then click "OK". If you already have a check mark in "Analysis ToolPak" then it is already installed. Do not uncheck it and click the red X in the corner of the box to cancel. Otherwise, continue.
   d. If you are prompted that the Analysis ToolPak is not currently installed on your computer, click "Yes" to install it. Once loaded, the Data Analysis command is available in the Analysis group on the Data tab.
2. Ensure each column is labeled and there are no missing data points in your data set.
3. Click "Data" then go to the "Analysis" box and click "Data Analysis".
   a. Scroll down and click on "Regression" then "OK".
   b. Click on "Input Y Range" and type in the range for the outcome for Y or highlight it using your mouse, including the label for the column (e.g., K1:K49, if your outcome is in column K, you have 48 cases, and a column label).
   c. Click on "Input X Range:" and type in the range for all of the predictors or highlight it using your mouse, including the label for the columns (e.g., B1:F49, if you have 48 cases, 5 predictors, and column labels).
   d. Click "Labels" if you have included them as suggested.
   e. Click "OK". You just ran a multiple regression. You can follow a similar process for computing a correlation matrix by selecting "Correlation" in the "Data Analysis" option.

SPLIT-HALF RELIABILITY (SPEARMAN–BROWN)

$$r_{xx} = 2r_{1/2\,1/2}/(1 + r_{1/2\,1/2})$$

Where $r_{1/2\,1/2}$ is the correlation between scores on each half of the measure.

COEFFICIENT ALPHA

$$\alpha = \frac{k}{k - 1}\left[1 - \frac{\Sigma\sigma_i^2}{\Sigma\sigma_T^2}\right]$$

Where k is the number of items, σ_T^2 is the variance of each item, and α σ_T^2 is the variance of total scores on the measure.

STANDARD ERROR OF MEASUREMENT

$$\text{SEM} = s_X\sqrt{1 - r_{XX}}$$

SEM = standard error of measurement also known as the standard deviation of observed scores for a given true score
r_{xx} = reliability
s_x = standard deviation of observed scores

CONTENT VALIDITY RATIO (CVR)

$$CVR = \frac{\left(n_e - \dfrac{N}{2}\right)}{\dfrac{N}{2}}$$

Where n_e = number of judges stating that the knowledge, ability, skill, competency, or other characteristics measured by the item is essential to job performance, and N = the total number of judges rating the items.

Supplementary Computations

You can access the data for this section online at the Pearson Web site (UniversalToys.xls).

You work at a manufacturing plant called Universal Toys and you were just put in charge of a project to evaluate the validity of the current selection system. Your job is to evaluate the usefulness of two conscientiousness measures using the same test taken 2 weeks apart, a cognitive ability test, and two interview scores. The conscientiousness measure is a standard personality measure for work environments with scores ranging from 1 to 10 (ConscT1 = time 1, ConscT2 = time 2, two weeks later). The cognitive ability measure is a standard measure of intelligence, with typical scores ranging from 80 to 130 (CogAbil). The first interview score is from an unstructured interview with the hiring manager and it ranges from 1 to 7 (HiringMgr). The second interview score is from a structured interview with the HR manager assessing key capabilities and experience and it ranges from 1 to 7 (HR Mgr). All of these assessments have been used for the past 3 years to hire employees and you have data on 48 current manufacturing employees with their scores on the predictors recorded in your Human Resource Information System (HRIS). Scores for these 48 employees are reported in the spreadsheet, along with their age, sex, race, position code, and managerial job performance ratings. You are also asked to conduct an adverse impact analysis. Race is coded as "0" for white, "1" for African American, and "2" for Hispanic/Latino. Males are coded as "0", females as "1". Position 1 refers to assembly, 2 to equipment setup, and 3 to quality control. Performance is measured as a rating from the Team Production Leader and it ranges from 10 to 50. Attach printouts or cut and paste into a document and perform the following analyses on the data:

1. Using Excel or counting by hand, plot the distribution of HR manager interview scores for employees numbered 1 through 16 with scores on the X axis and frequency of scores on the Y axis. Describe the pattern.

2. By hand calculate the mean, median, mode, range, variance, and standard deviation for the cognitive ability test for employees numbered 1 through 16. If you wish, you can repeat this for practice on numbers 33–48.

3. Using Excel, repeat the calculations you just did by hand to check your work.

4. Using Excel, calculate the mean, median, mode, variance, and standard deviation for all interval or ratio level variables, including performance, across all employees (1 through 48).

5. By hand create a scatter plot of cognitive ability and performance for employees numbered 33 through 48. By hand compute a correlation of these same data points. Confirm your findings using Excel.

6. By hand compute a simple regression of the relationship between cognitive ability and performance for employees numbered 33 through 48. Use Excel to confirm the slope and intercept. Compute a predicted score for someone with an ability score of 118.

7. Use the correlation function to correlate the two sets of conscientiousness scores. What does this correlation tell you? Use the correlation function to correlate each of the conscientiousness scores with performance. With a sample size of 48 and a *p*-value of .05, any correlation over .285 (ignoring the sign) is statistically significant. What did you find?

8. Now use the Regression function in the Data Analysis option to predict job performance using the two conscientiousness scores. What did you find? Why?

9. Insert a column after the two conscientiousness scores. Compute an average score for conscientiousness using the two conscientiousness scores. Correlate average conscientiousness score with job performance. Assume job performance has a reliability of .90. Use the reliability of the conscientiousness measure and the reliability of job performance to correct the observed correlation for attenuation.

10. Use the correlation function to correlate the two sets of interview scores. What is the value and what does this correlation tell you? Why do you think you observed this value?

11. Use the Regression function in the Data Analysis option to predict job performance using the two interview scores. What did you find and what would you recommend?

12. Use the correlation function to correlate ability with job performance. Correct this correlation for range restriction, assuming the unrestricted population has a standard deviation of 15 for ability.

13. Use the Regression function in the Data Analysis option to predict job performance using the average conscientiousness measure you created, cognitive ability, and interview scores from the hiring and HR managers. Look at the *p*-value for each predictor. Any value less than .05 is significant. What do you see and what would you conclude? Are there any variables you can drop? Why or why not?

14. Write out the multiple regression equation from your results including all variables. What is the predicted score for someone with scores of 6, 120, 5, and 7 for average conscientiousness, cognitive ability, hiring manager interview score, and HR manager interview score, respectively?

15. What do you conclude overall about the validity of the current system? Write a short paragraph. Rerun the regression analysis dropping variables if you deem it appropriate to do so. Write out the final multiple regression equation you would recommend using.

16. Look at the Applicant Data in the Applicant tab of the Excel spreadsheet. Use Excel and your multiple regression equation to compute predicted scores on all of the applicants. Assume you wanted to hire only the top 50 percent of these applicants based on their predicted performance. Evaluate the implications of hiring only the top 50 percent of applicants for adverse impact by sex and race. Write a short paragraph and include computations for adverse impact.

17. Given the validity and adverse impact analysis results you found, what would you recommend? Is there adverse impact? Is this a legally defensible staffing system? Do the assessments have reliability and validity?

Endnotes

1. Based on an interview with Mary Doherty of Valtera on December 14, 2006.

2. Pearson, N., Lesser, E., and Sapp, J., "A New Way of Working," Executive Report, IBM Global Services, NY, 2010, ftp://ftp.-software.ibm.com/software/solutions/soa/pdfs/GBE03295-USEN-00.pdf. Accessed June 1, 2010. LaValle, S. "Business Analytics and Optimization for the Intelligent Enterprise," IBM Global Services, NY, 2009, http://www-03. ibm.com/innovation/us/smarterplanet/assets/smarterBusiness/business_analytics/gbe03211-usen-00.pdf. Accessed June 1, 2010.

3. Kelly, J. "Human Resources Data Analytics Brings Metrics to Workforce Management," 11 December 2008, SearchBusiness Analytics.com, http://searchbusinessanalytics. techtarget.com/news/1507118/Human-resources-data-analytics-brings-metrics-to-workforce-management. Accessed June 1, 2010. Neumann, D. "The Power of Analytics in Human Capital Management," *Talent Management*, April 2008, http://www.personneldecisions .com/uploadedFiles/Articles/PowerofAnalyticsHCMgmt.pdf, Accessed June 1, 2010.

4. "Case Study: TEKsystems," *Brainbench.com Skills Measurement Report*, October 2003, www.brainbench.com/ pdf/CS_TEKsystems.pdf. Accessed February 8, 2007.

5. "How Did a Large Provider of Business Services Reduce Turnover by Nearly 50%?," *PeopleAnswers Newsletter*, Spring 2009, http://www.peopleanswers.com/ site/app?reqPage=abou- tus_news_newsletters_detail&reqItemId=9#Article1. Accessed June 1, 2010; "Testimonials" Curt Gray of AmeriPride, http://www.peopleanswers.com/site/app?reqPage=results_testim onials&sortBy=0. Accessed June 1, 2010; "About AmeriPride," http://www.ameripride.com/US_Info/ About AmeriPride/ Our History.jsp?bmUID=1275448271107. Accessed June 1, 2010.

6. Adapted from Stevens, S. S., "Measurement, Statistics, and the Schemapiric View," *Science,* 161 (1968): 850.

7. Singh, R., "The Emperor's New Metrics, Part 2," Electronic Recruiting Exchange, September 8, 2005, www.ere.net/articles/ db/001D8B71AF754FA 18E074813EB6ADD8A.asp. Accessed January 24, 2007.

8. Hansen, F. "Ad Firm Finds Recruiting Passive Candidates in a Downturn Is No Easy Sell," *Workforce Management Online,* January 2009, http://www.workforce.com/archive/feature/26/ 13/05/index.php. Accessed June 1, 2010.

9. Joint Commission Resources, "Looking at Staffing Effectiveness Data," February 2003, www.jcrinc.com/4016. Accessed February 8, 2007.

10. These are often called Venn diagrams but this term is not technically correct. Venn diagrams represent all hypothetically possible relations among sets or collections of sets. Ballantines are much less precise and do not represent relationships among sets. However, many people still call these overlapping circles Venn diagrams because of their similarity to them. Cohen, J., Cohen, P., West, S. G., and Aiken, L. S. *Applied Multiple Regression/Correlation Analysis for the Behavioral Sciences* (3rd ed.), Mahwah, NJ: Lawrence Erlbaum Associates, 2003.

11. LaHuis, D. M., Martin, N. R., and Avis, J. M., "Investigating Nonlinear Conscientiousness—Job Performance Relations for Clerical Employees," *Human Performance,* 18, 3 (2005): 199–212 and Vasilopoulos, N. L., Cucina, J. M., and Hunter, A. E., "Personality and Training Proficiency: Issues of Bandwidth-Fidelity and Curvilinearity," *Journal of Occupational and Organizational Psychology,* 80, 1 (2007): 109–131.

12. See Digman, J. M., "Personality Structure: Emergence of the Five-Factor Model," *Annual Review of Psychology,* 41 (1990): 417–440.

13. Carrig, K., and Wright, P. M., "Building Profit Through Building People," *Workforce Management Online,* January 2007, www.workforce.com/section/09/feature/24/65/90/ index. html. Accessed February 9, 2007.

14. Cohen, J., Cohen, P., West, S. G., and Aiken, L. S. *Applied Multiple Regression/Correlation Analysis for the Behavioral Sciences* (3rd ed.), Mahwah, NJ: Lawrence Erlbaum Associates,

2003, 38; Cohen, J., and Cohen, P. *Applied Multiple Regression/Correlation Analysis for the Behavioral Sciences,* Hillside, NJ: Lawrence Erlbaum Associates, 1975. Cohen and Cohen were among the first to use a diagram of three intersecting circles to illustrate 3 variable regression relationships. They called it a ballantine because of its similarity to the logo for a particular brand of beer. The authors of this text are proud owners of a serving tray with a Ballantine logo.

15. Based on *Testing and Assessment: An Employer's Guide to Good Practices,* U.S. Department of Labor Employment and Training Administration, 2000, www.onetcenter.org/dl_files/ empTestAsse.pdf. Accessed January 19, 2007.

16. Bretz, R. D., Jr., Milkovich, G. T., and Read, W. The Current State of Performance Appraisal Research and Practice: Concerns, Directions, and Implications. *Journal of Management,* 18, 2 (1992): 321–352.

17. From *Testing and Assessment*, 3–3.

18. French, W. L., *Human Resources Management* (2nd ed.), Boston, MA: Houghton Mifflin Co., 1990.

19. Ibid, 260.

20. Ibid.

21. *Testing and Assessment.*

22. Ibid.

23. Ibid.

24. Rafilson, F., "The Case for Validity Generalization," *ERIC/TM Digest,* 1991, http://ericae.net/db/edo/ED338699.htm. Accessed January 26, 2007.

25. Spies, R.A., Plake, B.S. (eds.), Geisinger, K.F., and Carlson, J.F., *The Eighteenth Mental Measurements Yearbook,* Lincoln, NE: Department of Educational Psychology at the University of Nebraska, 2010. See www.unl.edu/buros. Accessed September 17, 2010.

26. Keyser, D. J., and Sweetland, R. C., *Test critiques* (Vols. 1–10). Austin, TX: PRO-ED, 1984–1994.

27. Adapted from *Testing and Assessment.*

28. Ibid.

29. Hansen, F., "Recruiting on the Right Side of the Law," *Workforce Management Online*, May 2006, www.workforce. com/section/06/feature/24/38/12/. Accessed June 30, 2006.

30. Taylor, H. C., and Russell, J. T., "The Relationship of Validity Coefficients to the Practical Effectiveness of Tests in Selection," *Journal of Applied Psychology,* 23 (1939): 565–578.

31. Ibid.

32. Based on an interview with Mary Doherty of Valtera on December 14, 2006.

33. Charles, E. P., "The Correction for Attenuation Due to Measurement Error: Clarifying Concepts and Creating Confidence Sets," *Psychological Methods,* 10, 2 (2005): 206–226.

34. Sackett, P. R., Lievens, F., Berry, C. M., and Landers, R. N., "A Cautionary Note on the Effects of Range Restriction on Predictor Intercorrelations," *Journal of Appliede Psychology,* 92, 2 (2007): 538–544.

Assessing External Candidates

LEARNING OBJECTIVES
After studying this chapter, you should be able to:

- Identify different external assessment goals.

- Describe what is meant by an assessment plan.

- Describe different assessment methods and how each is best used.

- Discuss how to evaluate external assessment methods.

- Identify ways to reduce the adverse impact of an assessment method.

Selecting Flight Attendants at Southwest Airlines

Because fun and friendly customer service is essential to the success of Southwest Airlines's differentiation strategy, it takes flight attendant candidate assessment and selection very seriously.[1] Southwest's vice president of people (the people department is Southwest's equivalent of a human resources department) feels that fun counterbalances the stress of hard work. Because it believes that fun is about attitude, Southwest hires for attitude and trains for skills. The former chairman of Southwest, Herb Kelleher, believed that the company can train new hires to do whatever they need to, but that it could not change people's inherent attitudes.[2] Accordingly, Southwest Airlines looks for leadership and a sense of humor in its flight attendants.

Southwest Airlines's mission statement includes the following language: "Creativity and innovation are encouraged for improving the effectiveness of Southwest Airlines."[3] Although each department has a unique hiring process, the principle of hiring fun people with a creative spirit is central to each department.[4] Southwest asks your advice about how it can evaluate flight attendant candidates for their attitudes, leadership, and fit with the company's unique culture. After reading this chapter, you should have some good ideas to share with the company.

After strategic planning, writing a job description and person specification, sourcing candidates, and recruiting, the next step in the staffing process is assessing the degree to which job candidates possess the required qualifications and characteristics to perform the job well. The focus of this chapter is on the assessment of external job candidates—the next chapter covers the assessment of internal job candidates.

Why is assessment so important? Even if a firm's applicant pool contains some people who would make great hires, if the firm's assessment system can't identify them, they will not become employees. The goal of assessment is to identify the job candidates who would make good hires, and to screen out people who would make poor hires.

A poor assessment system is little better than picking job applicants at random and giving them job offers. By contrast, a well-designed assessment system can increase the number of good hires and reduce the number of bad hires an organization makes. What difference does this make to organizations? For jobs in which there is a meaningful performance difference between high and low performers, identifying and hiring the best candidates can dramatically increase productivity and performance. Consider computer programmers—the performance of star programmers can be eight to ten times greater than the performance of average programmers.[5]

Eyeglass company Luxottica Group gives all of its retail associate job candidates a 20-minute prehire assessment test that costs about $10. New hires scoring in the top quartile on the test sell an average of $14 more per hour than those scoring in the bottom quartile, returning the company's investment in the test in the associates' first hours on the job.[6]

In addition to identifying the job candidates who fit the person specification for the job, the assessment system should also evaluate candidates' fit with the organization's culture and business strategy. This allows a firm to identify those people best able to do the job and help the company execute its business strategy. For example, a candidate who meets a job's technical requirements will likely be a bad hire for a company pursuing an innovation strategy if she or he is risk averse and not creative.

Sunglass Hut was facing high turnover due to its use of kiosk stores, where an associate often works alone. To try to reduce turnover, it added assessment questions about whether candidates like to work on their own and their fit with the company's culture. New hires now stay on the job twice as long and turnover fell from 110 to 73 percent.[7]

Depending on their business strategy and competitive advantage, as well as their talent philosophy and culture, different companies value different characteristics for similar jobs. For example, a retail store such as Wal-Mart that relies on low cost and high efficiency may look for efficiency-oriented candidates whom it can hire at a relatively low cost. A high-end retail store, such as Tiffany's that pursues a differentiation strategy based on high-quality customer service, may prefer to hire candidates who excel at customer relations and interpersonal skills, even if a higher salary is required to hire them. The choice of which candidates to hire should be based on who is likely to experience the greatest job success and who can best meet the overall hiring goals for the position, including job performance, promotability, and the cost of the total rewards package.

Apache Corporation, an independent oil company, has outperformed its peers by cultivating a culture supporting fast decision making and risk taking. Because new hires are important in maintaining this culture, Apache looks for external candidates who have shown initiative in getting projects done at other companies.[8] The core competencies that telecommunications giant AT&T considers most important to success and evaluates in applicants include planning, organization, interpersonal effectiveness, decision making, and problem analysis.[9] Internet company Yahoo! looks for really smart, passionate people who have conviction, courage, and a willingness to take some risk.[10] And Microsoft, which receives over 40,000 résumés a month, is only interested in hiring top talent with the core competencies needed for the position being filled and who have long-term potential as well.[11]

If a company wants to give employees a lot of independence and discretion once they're hired, it is only by designing rigorous assessment processes that employees can later have this freedom.[12] Although companies' primary hiring goal is usually job performance, some companies, including Southwest Airlines, subscribe to the philosophy that what people know is less important than who they are. These firms believe that the primary goal of assessment is to find people with the right mind-set, attitude, and personal attributes.

The real estate services company Planned Cos., a provider of janitors, maintenance workers, doormen, concierges, and security guards, believes its hire-for-attitude approach has minimized turnover and improved client retention rates. As CEO Robert Francis said, "You take inherently positive individuals and then provide the necessary training. In our work, employees need to be 'on' day in and day out."[13]

Assessment methods tend to become more complex the more critical a job is to the firm and the more complex the required competencies are. If a job is difficult to do well, then it is even more important to recruit strategically, assess job candidates carefully, and choose new hires wisely.

Different assessment methods are useful for assessing different job candidate characteristics. In this chapter, first we discuss the different types of goals that exist for external candidate assessment and then describe a variety of commonly used assessment methods and their strengths and weaknesses. Finally, we discuss ways of evaluating external assessment methods. After reading this chapter, you should have a good understanding of the external assessment process and how to best use different external assessment methods.

THE FIRM'S EXTERNAL ASSESSMENT GOALS

As we have explained, the primary goal of job candidate assessment is to identify the job candidates who will be the best hires in terms of meeting the organization's staffing goals, which usually includes performing at a high level and enhancing strategy execution. Identifying the job candidates who would be the worst hires is also important, as not hiring poor performers can be even more important and valuable than hiring good performers. There are a variety of other important goals organizations have when assessing external job candidates, and we discuss several of them next.

Maximizing Fit

Why are some very talented people considered undesirable hires despite their high level of skill? The answer lies in the many ways in which people need to fit with an employment opportunity to be a successful match. One goal of assessment is to maximize the degree to which the person fits the organization, work group, and job. Next, we describe each of these dimensions of fit in greater detail.[14]

person-job fit

the fit between a person's abilities and the demands of the job and the fit between a person's desires and motivations and the attributes and rewards of a job

THE PERSON-JOB FIT **Person-job fit** is the fit between a person's abilities and the demands of the job and the fit between a person's desires and motivations and the attributes and rewards of a job.[15] Effective staffing enhances the degree to which an employee meets a job's requirements and the degree to which the job meets the individual's needs.[16] Because the most important staffing outcome is usually the new hire's job performance, person-job fit is the primary focus of most staffing efforts. From the organization's perspective, if it has an opening for an accountant, if the new hire is not an effective accountant, then the staffing effort cannot be considered successful, regardless of how many other positive staffing outcomes are achieved. In organizations that are growing rapidly, the scope of any job expands quickly. To prepare for this, Google tries to hire people who are "overqualified" for the position they are being recruited for, who can handle the expanding job duties, and who are likely to be promoted multiple times.[17]

From the applicant's perspective, if the job does not meet his or her financial, career, lifestyle, and other needs, then the match also is not ideal. An individual motivated by commissions and individually based merit pay is not likely to be a good fit with a job based on teamwork and group rewards. Similarly, an individual who does not enjoy working with people should not be placed in a customer service position. Research suggests that person-job fit leads to higher job performance, satisfaction, organizational commitment, and intent to stay with the company.[18]

THE PERSON-GROUP FIT   In addition to the fit between the recruit and the nature of the work, the fit between the recruit and his or her potential work team and supervisor is also important. **Person-group fit** (or person-team fit) is the match between an individual and his or her work group, including the supervisor. Good person-group fit means that an individual fits with the goals, work styles, and skills of coworkers. Person-group fit recognizes that in many jobs, interpersonal interactions with group members and teammates are important in getting the work done. Employees must also be able to work effectively with their supervisor. Person-group fit leads to improved job satisfaction, organizational commitment, and intent to stay with the company.[19]

person-group fit
the match between an individual and his or her work group, including the supervisor

Because teamwork, communication, and interpersonal competencies can be as critical to team performance as team members' ability to perform core job duties, person-group fit can be particularly important when hiring for team-oriented work environments.[20] At Men's Wearhouse, CEO George Zimmer rewards team selling because shoppers want to have a positive total store experience. The company takes team selling so seriously that it even terminated one of its most successful salespeople because he focused only on his own sales figures. After firing the salesperson, the store's total sales volume increased significantly.[21] Individual characteristics such as personal goals that are consistent with those of the group, and skills that complement those of the rest of the group's members are particularly important to assess.

THE PERSON-ORGANIZATION FIT   **Person-organization fit** is the fit between an individual's values, beliefs, and personality and the values, norms, and culture of the organization.[22] Research has found that a good fit has a strong positive relationship with an employee's job satisfaction, organizational commitment, and intent to stay with the company. It also has a moderate impact on employees' attitudes and "citizenship behaviors"—behaviors people engage in that go beyond their job requirements, such as helping others or talking positively about the firm.[23] Some organizational values and norms important for person-organization fit include integrity, fairness, work ethic, competitiveness, cooperativeness, and compassion for one's customers and fellow employees. Despite the potential overlap between person-job and person-organization fit, research suggests that people can experience differing degrees of fit with their jobs versus the organizations for whom they work.[24]

person-organization fit
fit between an individual's values, beliefs, attitudes, and personality and the values, norms, and culture of the organization

How can person-organization fit be maximized? One good way is to identify those applicant qualifications, competencies, and traits that relate to the organization's strategy, values, and work processes. Individuals whose work styles are inconsistent with the organization's culture, business strategy, and work processes are not likely to be as successful as individuals who are good fits in these ways. For example, even if Juan is technically well qualified as a biomedical researcher, if he avoids risk, is indecisive, and tends to ruminate over a decision, he may be unsuccessful in an innovative, fast-paced, and forward-looking organization.

Adobe Systems President and CEO Shantanu Narayen tries to hire people who share the company's fundamental values. He states, "Unless people really internalize and believe in the core values of the company, they're unlikely to be successful."[25] Deloitte Consulting constantly pays attention to hiring the right fit because it is very expensive to recruit and because it is even more costly to train new employees. To identify fit, Deloitte uses behavioral interviews and case questions to assess integrity, collaboration skills, and the ability to think logically and solve problems.

A new hire must be able and willing to adapt to the company by learning, negotiating, enacting, and maintaining the behaviors appropriate to the company's environment.[26] To successfully adapt, new hires must be open minded, have sufficient information about the organization's expectations and standards—and their own performance in light of those standards—and the ability to learn new behaviors and habits.

It is important to note that hiring for any type of fit does not mean hiring those whom we are most comfortable with, which can lead to dysfunctional stereotyping and discriminating against those different from ourselves who may offer a great deal to the success of the firm. One company that assesses and selects employees based on their fit with the organization and its core values is Johnson & Johnson (J&J). J&J's credo[27] clearly spells out its values: customer well-being, employee well-being, community well-being, and shareholder well-being, in that order. J&J recruits, hires, and evaluates employees against their credo, which is central to J&J's organizational culture. Ralph Larsen, J&J's chairman and CEO, attributes the majority of J&J's success to its core values.[28]

person-vocation fit

the fit between a person's interests, abilities, values, and personality and his or her chosen occupation, regardless of the person's employer

THE PERSON-VOCATION FIT **Person-vocation fit** is the fit between a person's interests, abilities, values, and personality and his or her chosen occupation, regardless of the person's employer.[29] For example, a social individual who dislikes detail work and working with numbers would be a poor fit with the accounting vocation.

Although individuals usually choose a vocation long before applying to an organization, understanding person-vocation fit can still be useful in staffing. Companies that would like to develop their own future leaders, or smaller organizations that need employees to fill more than one role, may be able to use applicants' vocational interests to determine whether they would be a good fit. Retaining valued employees might be easier if an organization can match their interests with a variety of career opportunities within the company. Some people pursue two or more different vocations over the course of their careers because they have diverse interests or because they become bored working in the same vocation for a long period of time. Organizations may better retain these valued career changers by understanding their vocational preferences and designing career tracks or career changes. If the measure is successful, valued employees who would otherwise be likely to leave the organization to pursue a different type of vocation may be able to pursue multiple vocations without leaving the company.

Table 9-1 summarizes these four different types of fit.

TABLE 9-1	Dimensions of Fit
Type of Fit	**Possible Dimensions of Fit**
Person-Job Fit: the potential of an individual to meet the needs of a particular job and the potential of the job to meet the needs of the individual	Intelligence Job-related skills and competencies Job knowledge Previous experience Personality related to performing job tasks
Person-Group Fit: the match between individuals and their work groups, including their supervisors	Teamwork skills Expertise relative to other team members Conflict management style Preference for team-based work Communication skills Personality related to working well with others
Person-Organization Fit: the fit between an individual's values, beliefs, and personality and the values, norms, and culture of the organization	Alignment between one's personal motivations and the organization's purpose Values Goals
Person-Vocation Fit: the fit between an individual's interests, abilities, values, and personality and his or her occupation	Aptitudes Interests Personal values Long-term goals

COMPLEMENTARY AND SUPPLEMENTARY FIT   There are two ways people can fit in to an organization or work group.[30] **Complementary fit** is when a person adds something that is missing in the organization or work group by being different from the others, typically by having different skills or expertise.[31] A research and development organization looks for a complementary fit when, for example, it seeks scientists with new backgrounds and skills to work with existing scientists to develop a new line of products. As J. J. Allaire, founder, chairman, and executive vice president of products at Allaire Corporation, said, "It's tempting not to hire people who compensate for your weaknesses—because you don't want to admit that you have any. But ... you've got to understand the strengths and weaknesses of your entire group and hire accordingly."[32]

Supplementary fit occurs when a person has characteristics that are similar to those that already exist in the organization.[33] Supplementary fit can be important when a firm needs to replace a departing customer service representative with another person who can perform the job similarly to the other customer service representatives. In this case, the organization wants to hire customer service representatives with similar skills and characteristics.

Both complementary and supplementary fit are important as together they help to ensure that new hires will not only fit in with the work group and organization but also bring new skills and perspectives that will enhance the work group's and organization's performance.

complementary fit
when a person adds something that is missing in the organization or work group by being different from the others

supplementary fit
when a person has characteristics that are similar to those that already exist in the organization

Assessing Accurately

Another goal of external assessment systems is that they be valid, or that they accurately identify the candidates who would be the best or worst employees. The wider the spread of talent in an applicant pool, the greater the pressure on the assessment system to weed out the bad fits and identify the good ones.

Another way to express this idea is to think about the possible outcomes of an assessment effort. Candidates are either hired or not hired, and will be either good performers or poor performers on the job. As shown in Figure 9-1, hiring people who become good performers generates *true positives*. Not hiring people who would have been poor performers produces *true negatives*. Both of these outcomes are desirable and are goals of the staffing effort. The two possible undesirable outcomes are not hiring people who would have been good performers, generating *false negatives,* or hiring people who perform poorly, generating *false positives*. (Recall that we first discussed false negatives and positives in Chapter 8.) No assessment system is perfect, but more valid assessment systems do a better job than less valid ones of identifying both the most and least desirable hires from the pool of job candidates and generating high numbers of true positive and true negative hiring outcomes.

In some jobs, one type of error can be more important than the other type. For example, false positives are particularly expensive for high-risk jobs like pilots or surgeons. False negatives, on the other hand, are particularly costly in highly competitive jobs or markets in which losing someone good to a competitor not only weakens a firm's market position but considerably strengthens its competition's. When a top scientist chooses to join a competitor, not only does the company not acquire the top talent, its competitor is strengthened as well. After international soccer star David Beckham came to the United States to play for the L.A. Galaxy, his former Real Madrid soccer club

	Poor Performer	Good Performer
Hired	False Positive ☹	True Positive ☺
Not Hired	True Negative ☺	False Negative ☹

FIGURE 9-1   Possible Assessment Outcomes

lost a substantial amount of revenue from his jersey sales alone.[34] False negatives can also be expensive when a member of a protected class is not hired, sues, and wins a big settlement.

Accurate assessments are also affected by job candidates' motivation.[35] Due to minority subgroup members' awareness of subgroup differences on standardized tests, the administration of employment tests can produce a **stereotype threat** that creates frustration among minority test takers and ultimately lower test scores due to lowered expectations and effort.[36] Together, these factors can lead to differences in subgroup test performance that are not due to differences in knowledge or ability.[37] One study found that greater anxiety and lower motivation predicted African Americans' increased likelihood of withdrawing from a job selection process.[38]

stereotype threat
awareness of subgroup differences on standardized tests creates frustration among minority test takers and ultimately lower test scores

Maximizing the Firm's Return on Its Investment in Its Assessment System

Another important goal is maximizing the firm's return on its investment in its assessment system. The greater the return on the investment in an assessment method, the greater the assessment method's value. One assessment method may be slightly superior to another in identifying the best candidates, but if its cost exceeds the gain to the organization of hiring these slightly better candidates, then the other method may be the better choice. Although some managers are more influenced by the simple correlation between predictor and criterion, Table 9-2 presents a basic formula for calculating the return on investment of an assessment method compared to hiring randomly.

The return on investment formula presented in Table 9-2 reflects both the economic gain of hiring better employees and the economic gain of not hiring lower-performing employees that can result from using an assessment method versus hiring randomly. The economic value of improved performance formula presented in Table 9-2 subtracts the costs of using a predictor from the economic gain derived from using the predictor compared to randomly selecting candidates. The economic value of improved job performance resulting from using an assessment method rather than randomly selecting job candidates depends on the number of people hired, how long they stay with the company, their job performance improvements resulting from using the assessment method, and the value of the performance improvements. The cost of the assessment method multiplied by the number of people assessed is the cost of using the predictor.

The value of retaining top performers should be evident from the previously mentioned formula. The longer good performers stay with your company, the greater the return on the company's investment in them. Because research has shown that people who have frequently changed jobs in the past are more likely to do so in the future,[39] some companies consider frequent job changes without evidence of professional advancement as a negative factor in their hiring decision. One survey of more than 1,400 chief financial officers found that for 87 percent of them, the length of time a job candidate has spent with previous employers was an important

---

TABLE 9-2 Return on Investment Formulas[40]

Economic value of improved performance = $(N_h \times T \times r_{xy} \times Z_y) - (N_a \times C_a \times SR)$

Savings from avoiding bad hires = $(N_h \times HA \times CBH) - (N_a \times C_a)$

   ROI = Economic value of improved performance + Savings from avoiding bad hires

Where:

N_h =	Number of people hired
T =	Average number of years employees stay in the position
r_{xy} =	Correlation between assessment method and job performance (the amount of improvement in job performance from using the assessment method)
Z_y =	Dollar value of improved job performance using the new assessment method (default value = 40 percent of average base salary)
N_a =	Number of job candidates assessed
C_a =	Cost per assessment
SR =	Selection ratio (the number of candidates assessed before making a hiring decision)
HA =	Percentage of bad hires avoided (default value 5 percent)
CBH =	Average cost of a bad hire (default value $7,500)
ROI =	Dollar return on the assessment method investment

factor in making hiring decisions.[41] Because so many factors influence job tenure, we advise caution when using candidates' previous job tenure to predict their likely future job tenure.

The savings from avoiding bad hires reflects the fact that bad hires can actually cost the organization money. The return on investment from a new assessment method is the sum of the economic value of improved performance and the savings from avoiding bad hires.

Although staffing should be seen as an investment rather than a cost, cost is still important for many companies that simply don't have the money to invest in more expensive systems even if they are more accurate at identifying the best new hires. Nonetheless, the formula provides a way to estimate the ROI of any new assessment method. We would like to note that some managers are less convinced by ROI formulas and are more strongly influenced by the correlation between the assessment methods and the criterion (turnover, job performance, and so on).

Generating Positive Stakeholder Reactions

Meeting the needs of different stakeholders in the staffing process is another assessment goal. Recruits, hiring managers, and recruiters should all be satisfied with the processes and outcomes involved in using an assessment method. For example, requiring hiring managers to take three hours out of their busy day to interview each job candidate might not be practical or even possible. Recruiters may feel that doing 20-minute phone interviews to prescreen each job applicant is too burdensome, and applicants may feel that three separate visits for different assessments are excessive. So, although an assessment method might be valid and identify the best and worst job candidates, if it does not also meet the needs of the firm's stakeholders, it is not as effective as it could be.

An assessment method's speed, usability, and ability to predict job success all influence the ease of getting people in the organization to use it correctly and consistently. Training recruiters and hiring managers in the use of the technique and its benefits, assessing and rewarding them for using it correctly and consistently, and having an assessment system expert perceived as credible and competent available to help when needed can increase the adoption and the correct and consistent use of new assessment methods.

Supporting the Firm's Talent Philosophy and Human Resource Strategy

Another goal of an assessment system is to support the organization's talent philosophy and HR strategy. Viewing applicants and employees as investors might stimulate a company to incorporate more interviews into the assessment process and develop a comprehensive careers section on its Web site to allow candidates ample opportunity to learn as much as possible about the company before joining it. A firm viewing employees as assets will tend to focus on efficient candidate assessment and minimize candidates' opportunities to meet with a variety of the firm's representatives to learn about different jobs. An organization that wants people to contribute over long-term careers should evaluate job candidates in terms of their long-term career potential within the company, rather than evaluate them just for the current open position. In this case, identifying the competencies, styles, and traits required for career advancement within the company is also relevant. If an organization does not plan to promote from within, its recruitment profile and screening criteria should focus only on the open position.

Establishing and Reinforcing the Firm's Employer Image

Another goal of external assessment can be to establish and maintain an organization's employer image. A company that wants to be known as an innovative and engaging place to work might reinforce that image during the assessment process by asking applicants challenging interview questions that require creativity. Every interaction job applicants have with a firm establishes and reinforces the firm's employer image. Consequently, one of the goals of the assessment process should be to consistently reinforce the firm's desired image.

Identifying New Hires' Developmental Needs

Assessment tests can also identify new hires' developmental needs. If a top candidate's assessment scores show that her organization and time management skills are good but her customer service skills need further development, posthire training can improve these skills. Some assessment methods even identify applicants' preferred learning styles, which can decrease their training time, improve the effectiveness of their training, and increase their retention.[42]

Assessing Ethically

Ethics is an important issue in staffing, and particularly in assessment. The entire selection process needs to be managed ethically. The people administering an assessment need to be properly trained and appropriately qualified, and applicants' privacy needs to be protected at all times. For example, firms need to think through the ethics of using assessment methods applicants find invasive, including integrity tests and genetic tests. Managing the process ethically also involves explaining to candidates how any test results will be used and how their privacy will be protected, and communicating with them when you promise you will.

Complying with the Law

Legal issues loom large when it comes to assessment. Thus, companies have good reason to protect themselves against potential charges of hiring discrimination. In addition to the negative publicity generated by a lawsuit, plaintiffs are often successful and court awards regularly run into the hundreds of thousands of dollars. One landmark case in this area is *Griggs v. Duke Power Company*.[43] In this case, the Supreme Court found that under Title VII of the Civil Rights Act of 1964, if an employment test disparately impacts ethnic minority groups, the firm must demonstrate that the test is "reasonably related" to the job for which the test is required. Credit checks, background checks, and cognitive ability tests are among the most likely assessment methods to result in disparate impact.

Following the Uniform Guidelines on Employee Selection Procedures (UGESP),[44] which we introduced in Chapter 3, and conducting fair, consistent, and objective assessments are important to legal compliance. We discuss these next.

UNIFORM GUIDELINES ON EMPLOYEE SELECTION PROCEDURES As you learned in Chapter 3, the UGESP assist organizations in complying with requirements of federal law prohibiting race, color, religion, sex, and national origin discrimination in hiring practices by providing a framework for determining the proper use of tests and other assessment procedures. Under Title VII, the UGESP apply to the federal government with regard to federal employment; to most private employers with at least 15 employees for 20 weeks or more a calendar year; to most labor organizations, apprenticeship committees, and employment agencies; and to state and local governments with at least 15 employees. Through Executive Order 11246, they also apply to federal government contractors and subcontractors.[45]

Here are some sample UGESP guidelines that pertain to candidate assessment:[46]

- A test of knowledge and abilities may be used if it measures a representative sample of knowledge, skills, or abilities that are necessary to performance of the job and are operationally defined.
- Knowledge must be defined in terms of behavior and must be part of a body of learned information that is actually used in and necessary for required, observable job behaviors.
- Abilities must be defined in terms of observable aspects of job behavior and should be necessary for the performance of important work behaviors. Any selection procedure measuring an ability should closely approximate an observable work behavior.
- To the extent that the setting and manner of the administration of the selection procedure fail to resemble the work situation, the less likely it is that the selection procedure is content valid, and the greater the need for other validity evidence.

The entire UGESP are available online,[47] and staffing specialists should develop a thorough knowledge of this document. The *Principles for the Validation and Use of Personnel Selection Procedures*[48] and the *Standards for Educational and Psychological Testing*[49] are also important documents that provide standards and guidelines for developing and using various assessment methods.

FAIR, CONSISTENT, AND OBJECTIVE ASSESSMENTS Good hiring practices compare all applicants using the same fair, consistent, and objective information predictive of job success. A false or contradictory reason given for not hiring someone can be considered a pretext for discrimination. For example, if an employer states that an applicant was not hired because of insufficient experience, but the successful candidate has less experience, the contradiction can be interpreted as a pretext for discrimination.

One employment law expert goes so far as to advise companies to drop the use of vague terms such as *best fit* when documenting why someone was hired because the ambiguity makes it more difficult to reconstruct the selection process and explain why the candidate was chosen.[50] Recruiters and hiring managers should be able to articulate objective, neutral reasons for rejecting or hiring any applicant. The required qualifications must make sense to the EEOC and its state-level equivalents who are looking for a simple, fair process that treats all applicants the same.

Consistently applied, objective assessment methods based on bona fide occupational qualifications (BFOQ) derived from a job analysis are best for legal compliance. Subjective assessment criteria that involve speculation about the types of employees customers prefer to deal with or how a candidate is likely to perform on the job are not advisable. Although it is not illegal to reject someone based on subjective evaluations and speculation, subjective evaluations and speculation are precursors to stereotyping. Of course, this can quickly get employers into legal trouble.[51]

EXTERNAL ASSESSMENT METHODS

Typically, job candidates are assessed in waves. When people first apply for a job, they are *job applicants* and are evaluated against the minimum acceptable criteria for the job, such as relevant education and skills. The purpose of these **screening assessment methods** is to narrow a pool of job applicants down to a smaller group of *job candidates*. The job candidates are then assessed in more depth using **evaluative assessment methods** that evaluate the pool of job candidates to determine whom to hire. Job offers may be made contingent on passing **contingent assessment methods**. Contingent assessments are used when the firm has identified whom it wants to hire. If the finalist passes the contingent assessment (typically a background check, drug screen, proof of employment eligibility, and so forth) their contingent job offer becomes a formal job offer. Assessments tend to get more detailed and rigorous as people move from being job applicants to receiving job offers.

Table 9-3 summarizes the general effectiveness of many possible assessment methods used to predict on-the-job performance (validity), applicant reactions, the relative cost of the methods compared to other assessment methods, adverse impact, and ease of use. The values presented are typical of those found in organizations, but the exact validity, cost, and adverse impact will vary from job to job and from company to company. Thus, we advise you to exercise caution when using these values. Differences in the quality of an assessment

screening assessment methods
methods that narrow a pool of job applicants down to a smaller group of job candidates

evaluative assessment methods
methods that evaluate the pool of job candidates to determine who will be hired

contingent assessment methods
methods whereby a job offer is made contingent upon a candidate passing the assessment

TABLE 9-3	A Comparison of Some Commonly Used External Assessment Methods

Assessment Method	Average Validity[52]*	Applicant Reactions[53]	Relative Costs[54] (Development/ Administration)	Adverse Impact	Usability
Assessment centers	.37	Good	High/High	Low	Difficult
Cognitive ability tests	.51	OK	Low/Low	High	Easy
Integrity tests	.41	OK	Low/Low	Low	Easy
Job knowledge tests	.48	OK	High/Low	Low	Easy
Reference checks	.26	OK	Low/Low	Low	Easy
Situational judgment tests	.34	Good	High/Low	Low	Moderate
Structured interviews	.51–.63	Good	High/High	Mixed	Moderate
Unstructured interviews	.20–.38	OK	Low/High	Mixed	Easy
Personality testing	−.13–.33	OK	High/Low	Low	Easy
Biodata	.35	OK	High/Low	Low	Easy
Weighted application forms	.50	Good	High/Low	Low	Easy
Simulations	.54	Good	High/High	Low	Difficult
Work samples	.33	Good	High/High	Low	Difficult

*Validity values range from −1 to 1, with numbers closer to −1 or +1 reflecting better prediction of job performance.

method's development, the degree of training users receive, and how consistently the tools are used can all influence the costs and validity of any assessment method as well as its adverse impact and applicant reactions to it.

Although we group the following external assessment methods into screening, evaluative, and contingent categories based on how they are typically used, it is possible to use any screening or evaluative assessment method at any time during the hiring process. Contingent assessment methods, of course, must be administered after a contingent job offer is extended.

Screening Assessment Methods

RÉSUMÉS AND COVER LETTERS   Although little research exists on the validity or adverse impact of using résumés as an assessment method, résumés and cover letters have historically been a core part of the hiring process. Applicants volunteer information about themselves and their interest in the position in a cover letter, and provide a résumé summarizing their relevant education and work and nonwork experiences. As we have explained, technology has facilitated the management of the large number of résumés companies often receive, and software tools have made it possible for firms to do a better job searching them for relevant information. One of the biggest drawbacks of résumés and cover letters is that applicants do not use the same format or include the same information in their résumés, which can make it difficult to compare them.

Because the information put on résumés may not be accurate, it is important to confirm the accuracy of any résumé information a firm relies on when making a hiring decision. Experts estimate that 10 to 30 percent of job seekers shade the truth or flat-out lie on their résumés, particularly in the areas of education, previous compensation, reason for leaving previous jobs, and previous job titles and accomplishments.[55] The fact that firms have even fired CEOs after discovering that they have inflated their educational credentials illustrates how important it is to confirm the accuracy of all self-reported information used to make hiring decisions.[56] False information can be reduced by requiring applicants to sign a statement when submitting an application or résumé that knowingly falsifying this information can result in immediate termination.

Because many firms now use automated résumé scanning and screening software, it is important to proofread your own résumé and cover letter for accuracy and to correct any typographical or spelling errors. If a word the firm uses to screen candidates is misspelled, the computer system won't identify your résumé as a good match. Just for fun, Table 9-4 contains some actual résumé and cover letter blunders.

This chapter's Develop Your Skills feature will help you maximize the effectiveness of your own online résumé.

job applications

forms that require applicants to provide written information about their skills and education, job experiences, and other job-relevant information

JOB APPLICATIONS   **Job applications** require applicants to provide written information about their skills and education, job experiences, and other job-relevant information. Although the information on an application may replicate information already contained on a résumé, applications help to ensure that consistent information is collected. They also help HR professionals check the accuracy of the information provided. Many employers require all applicants, regardless of the job they're applying for, to complete a job application form. Although job applications often contain a statement that providing inaccurate information is grounds for dismissal, it is still best to verify any information used to screen candidates. Figure 9-2 shows a typical job application form.

TABLE 9-4 Actual Résumé Blunders

These are from actual résumés:[57]
- "You are privileged to receive my résumé."
- "Able to say the ABCs backward in under five seconds."
- "I often use a laptap."
- "I will accept nothing less than $18 annually."
- Reason for leaving last job: "Pushed aside so the vice president's girlfriend could steal my job."
- Accomplishments: "Completed 11 years of high school."
- "I am relatively intelligent, obedient, and as loyal as a puppy."
- Specified that his availability to work Fridays, Saturdays, or Sundays "is limited because the weekends are 'drinking time.' "
- Explained a three-month gap in employment by saying that he was getting over the death of his cat.
- Explained an arrest record by stating, "We stole a pig, but it was a really small pig."

Instructions: Print clearly in black or blue ink. Answer all questions. Sign and date the form.

Position Applied For: _____ **Today's Date:** _____

PERSONAL INFORMATION

Full Name: _____

Street Address: _____

City, State, Zip Code: _____

Phone Number: (_____)_____

Are you eligible to work in the United States? Yes _____ No_____

If you are under age 18, do you have an employment/age certificates? Yes _____ No_____

Have you been convicted of or pleaded no contest to a felony within the last five years?

Yes _____ No_____

If yes, please explain: _____

_____

AVAILABILITY

Days/Hours Available:

Monday from _____ to _____

Tuesday _____ to _____

Wednesday _____ to _____

Thursday _____ to _____

Friday _____ to _____

Saturday _____ to _____

Sunday _____ to _____

What date are you available to start work? _____

EDUCATION

Name and Address of School	Degree/Diploma	Graduation Date

_____

_____

_____

_____

Skills and Qualifications: Licenses, Skills, Training, Awards

_____

_____

EMPLOYMENT HISTORY

Present or Last Position:

Employer: _____

FIGURE 9-2 An Example of a Job Application Form

Address: _____

Supervisor: _____

Phone: _____

E-mail: _____

Position Title: _____

From: _____ To: _____

Responsibilities: _____

_____

Salary: _____

Reason for Leaving: _____

May We Contact This Employer?

Yes _____ No _____

THREE REFERENCES (required)

Name/Title   Address   Phone

_____

_____

_____

I certify that information contained in this application is true and complete.

I understand that providing false information may be grounds for not hiring me or for immediate termination of employment at any point in the future, if I am hired. I authorize the verification of any or all information listed above.

Signature_____

Date_____

FIGURE 9-2 (Continued)

To standardize the information collected from job applicants, some organizations have begun using online applications. For example, when job seekers apply at any The Fresh Market gourmet grocer location, they first complete an online employment application. Within minutes of finishing the less-than-30-minute application, the hiring manger receives a three-page report via e-mail that summarizes the biographical information provided by the individual, answers to the application questions and an analysis of the answers, and a page of follow-up interview questions if the applicant passes the online screening.[58]

To take the subjectivity out of the store manager's interview process, McDonald's developed an online application for job candidates in the United States that asks them questions about their work experiences, preferences, and how they would respond to certain situations. Based on the results, the questionnaire prompts a green light to the hiring manager, signaling that the candidate would be a good hire; a yellow light, meaning that the manager should ask more questions; or a red light, meaning do not hire the person.[59]

Online applications cannot only be fast and cost-efficient, they can also greatly reduce the initial assessment burden placed on recruiters or hiring managers. For example, using Web-based assessment tools for screening applicants applying for hourly positions decreased the number of employment interviews Sherwin-Williams conducts each year by more than 5,000. Using online candidate assessment tools also reduced the turnover among hourly workers at Kroger grocery stores by 25 percent, meaning that the company now spends 25 percent less time recruiting and hiring candidates.[60]

In addition to providing in-store kiosks at which online applications can be completed, employers including American Express now direct job seekers to their corporate Web sites to answer a series of preliminary screening questions, such as the degrees they obtained and their willingness to relocate, and then apply for jobs. American Express uses its questionnaire to weed out the bottom half of candidates, which allows its recruiters to focus their time and attention on more promising applicants.[61]

WEIGHTED APPLICATION BLANKS   The information collected on a job application can be weighted according to its importance. Having job experts participating in a job analysis rate the relative importance of and the relative time spent on each job duty can inform these weights.[62] The degree to which different application-blank information differentiates high and low performers can also inform the weights to use for each item. When information receives different weights, the assessment method is a **weighted application blank**. As shown in Table 9-3, weighted application blanks are received well by applicants, relatively inexpensive, easy to use, and have an average validity of .50.

weighted application blank
a job application on which different information receives different weights

---

DEVELOP YOUR SKILLS
Online Résumé Tips[63]

When you apply to an organization, your résumé is likely one of the first things a prospective employer will look at. Employers routinely mine the some 70 million résumés on job site Monster.com, for example. Now that many employers receive résumés only through the Internet and process résumés electronically using search terms, it is important to ensure that your résumé makes the cut. Here are some tips to help your résumé rise to the top of the stack.

1. State your experience as achievements rather than stating the requirements of past jobs. For example, instead of writing, "Supervised the completion of strategic marketing agreements," write, "Successfully met strategic marketing agreements on schedule and under budget."

2. Use your résumé to highlight areas not covered in the company's online application, including your language skills, technical skills, volunteer work, and professional organization involvement relevant to your ability to perform the job.

3. Add a section near the top of your résumé named "skills" or, even, "keywords," where you list as many keywords as possible to describe yourself. When developing your list, be creative, but be accurate. Include the standard job titles for your current and previous jobs, particularly if a previous employer used nonstandard titles. List any job-specific, profession-specific, and industry-specific tools including software or hardware that you use or are qualified to use. Include any industry and professional organizations of which you are a member. Include any common professional or technical acronyms as well as the words that

explain them. The phrase explaining the acronym does not have to be in the same sentence or paragraph, but including both versions will increase the probability that your résumé will appear in the search results whether the recruiter searches on the acronym or the phrase that it represents. Also, be as creatively inconsistent as you can—for example including *M.B.A, MBA, Master of Business Administration, Masters in Bus. Admin,* and so forth, will ensure that your résumé will appear in the search results regardless of the exact words input by the recruiter.

4. Be sure to include the word *resume* in your résumé as recruiters frequently use it when searching for résumés. Put it in the top line (e.g., "J. Cortina's Resume") as well as in the file name (J. Cortina-resume.html). Using the word *résumé,* which is technically the correct form of the word, replaces the letter *e* with a character code to create the é. Some search software does not recognize this character as an *e* and will not find your résumé.

5. Attend to the security of your online résumé. Remove your standard contact information, including your address, phone number, business e-mail address, and personal address if it is associated with a detailed profile on you (as in AOL). Replace this information with a Web-based e-mail address that is harder to trace to you personally, like hotmail.com, Gmail, and MSN.

6. Don't use a goofy e-mail address (e.g., hotstuff@aol.com) or your messages will probably be deleted unread. Use the e-mail address as an opportunity to market and differentiate yourself—like kbell-web-pro@aol.com or kbell-MIT-PhD@aol.com.

Developing a weighted application blank involves:

1. Selecting an employee characteristic to be measured;
2. Identifying which job application questions predict the desired employee behaviors and outcomes;
3. Evaluating the questions' relative predictive power;
4. Assigning weighted values to each relevant question; and
5. Scoring each applicant's completed job-application form using the scoring key.

Candidate advancement decisions are made according to applicants' weighted scores. It can even be possible to determine the total score below which a prospective employee might be a bad risk for the company and above which the applicant is likely to be a successful employee.[64] Weighted application blanks look like regular application blanks, and applicants typically do not know that a weighted scoring system will be used to evaluate their answers. Although this encourages honest answers, any applicant-provided information should be verified if it is to be used in making a hiring decision. Figure 9-3 shows a sample (fictitious) weighted application blank scoring key for a sales associate position.

One criticism of the weighted application blank is that it doesn't matter why an item differentiates successful from unsuccessful performers, only that it does. To maximize the chances that an item will work over time, it is best to know or at least have an idea why the question predicts job success. For example, asking whether someone was ever the captain of a sports team is a clear indicator of leadership. Weighted application blanks have been used successfully with occupations including production workers,[65] scientists,[66] and life insurance salespeople.[67]

biodata

information about candidates' interests, work experiences, training, and education

BIOGRAPHICAL INFORMATION (BIODATA) Biographical information, also referred to as **biodata**, is collected via questions about candidates' interests, work experiences, training, and education, assessing a variety of personal characteristics such as achievement orientation and preferences for group versus individual work. Biodata questionnaires allow people to describe more personal aspects about themselves and their experiences and successes in social, educational, or occupational pursuits.[68] Biodata can be collected as part of a job application or via a separate questionnaire.

Biodata, when properly done, can be both valid[69] and low in adverse impact[70] although adverse impact is a possible issue. Adverse impact may depend on the degree to which items directly or indirectly reflect cultural differences in people's social, educational, or economic advancement opportunities. Thus, when developing a biodata questionnaire, you should include items with the potential for reducing adverse impact, and validate and check the biodata for adverse impact before using it in making hiring decisions. Guidelines, regulations, and statutes

---

Previous Occupation

Social +1

Not social −1

Education

8 years 0

9–10 years + 1

11–12 years + 2

12–13 years + 3

Over 13 years + 2

Personal Sales Experience

Previous sales experience + 2

Full- or Part-Time Preference

Full time + 2

Part time −1

Confidence

Replies to question, "What amount are you confident of selling each month" + 1

Does not reply to question − 1

Family Sales Industry

Has anyone in your family ever worked in sales?

Yes + 2

No 0

FIGURE 9-3 A Weighted Application Blank Scoring Key for a Sales Associate Position

TABLE 9-5	Sample Biodata Items

Choose the best response to each question.

1. How many different paying jobs have you held for more than two weeks in the past year?
   (a) 5–6
   (b) 3–4
   (c) 1–2
   (d) None

2. In my leisure time, the activities I most enjoy doing are:
   (a) Team sports
   (b) Individual sports
   (c) Constructing things
   (d) Reading
   (e) Social activities
   (f) None of the above

3. Have any of your family ever worked in this industry?_____ Yes_____ No

4. Have you ever repaired small motors at home?_____ Yes_____ No

restrict certain types of information from being included on biodata questionnaires to protect applicants from being denied employment based on factors unrelated to jobs. Unless demonstrated to be job relevant, items addressing race, gender, marital status, number of dependents, birth order, and spouse's occupation are clearly not appropriate as a basis for making selection decisions. As long as they are correlated with job success or related to "business necessity," other personal items, such as a person's grade point average or level of education, can be used for personnel decisions although their tendency to cause adverse impact needs to be checked. Table 9-5 contains some sample biodata items.

For moral, ethical, and legal reasons, biodata items should not be intrusive or make the respondent uncomfortable. In general, a biodata item should not inquire about activities to which not everyone has equal access or about events over which the individual has no control.[71] Nonetheless, just because one respondent was a captain on a sports team and another respondent went to a small school without sports teams does not diminish the first respondent's accomplishments. This highlights the balance we must strike when using biodata items.[72]

As shown in Table 9-3, well-developed biodata items can have acceptable predictive validity (average validity of .35) for a variety of criteria including training, job performance, tenure, and promotions.[73] When properly done, biodata is also among the best assessment techniques in terms of minimizing adverse impact although applicants may perceive them as invasive[74] and different keys may be needed for males and females.[75] Biodata have been used to predict many aspects of job success with many different jobs, including research competence and creativity.[76]

Creating a biodata assessment involves:

1. defining job performance;
2. identifying employees who have done the job successfully;
3. collecting biographical data;
4. correlating the biographical data with the performance scores;
5. creating the final biodata form; and
6. testing, using, and continually checking the accuracy of the biodata.

An example of a biodata formula to predict the tenure of secretaries is as follows:

Tenure = (3.1 × years of education) + (4.2 × years of related job experience)

− (1.4 × miles from office).

Biodata has been used successfully to predict success with electricians,[77] blue-collar workers,[78] and managers.[79] Internet search company Google asks job applicants to complete an elaborate online survey that explores their attitudes, behavior, personality and biographical details going back to high school. The questions range from the age when applicants first got excited about computers to whether they have ever tutored or established a nonprofit organization and are used to predict how well a person will fit into Google's culture. To create the biodata formulas, Google asked every employee who had been working at the company for at least five months to fill out a 300-question survey. It then compared this data with 25 separate measures of each employee's performance, including the employee's supervisor and peer performance reviews, and their compensation to identify which biodata items predicted performance.[80]

The difference between job applications, weighted application blanks, and biodata can be confusing. Job applications are the forms job applicants expect to complete to provide information about themselves when they are applying for a job. Weighted application blanks look like regular job application forms, but unlike regular job applications, applicants' responses are scored and combined to determine the individual's likely fit with the job and the organization. Job applications may contain biodata items but do not have to. Weighted application blanks are designed to assess different types of biodata. When items on a job application are evaluated to determine how well they predict job success, these items become biodata. For example, asking applicants to state their years of experience in an industry could be a minimum-qualifications question on a job application, but when people's responses to that question are correlated with their subsequent job performance, then it becomes biodata. As with any assessment, job applications, weighted application blanks, and biodata should not be used alone. They should be a part of a system that uses several types of assessments to evaluate different aspects of likely job performance. Job applications, weighted application blanks, and biodata are most commonly used early on in the hiring process as screening assessment methods.

TELEPHONE SCREENS   As we have explained, many firms use quick telephone interviews as a screening assessment method to assess applicants' availability, interest, and preliminary qualifications for a job. Some recruiters use the phone interview to assess an applicant's on-the-job critical screening factors to prevent both parties from wasting time. Other recruiters use the telephone screen as a way to develop a more thorough picture of the individual and/or to give them a good impression of the company. The phone screen can also help to identify other positions with which the applicant might be a good fit.[81]

In an earlier chapter, we noted that one common assessment mistake companies make is to assume that highly qualified and experienced applicants wouldn't be happy in a job with less responsibility than positions they've held in the past. There are many reasons people may want to move to lower-stress and lower-responsibility positions including the opportunity to work for a stable and growing company, a positive work environment, and the challenge of learning new things. Highly qualified people are likely to get up to speed faster (saving training costs), help mentor other employees, and can be a good value. A quick telephone screen can allow a seemingly overqualified applicant to elaborate on his or her interest in the position and receptiveness to accepting a lower salary.[82]

Evaluative Assessment Methods

COGNITIVE ABILITY TESTS   Research shows that individuals with higher levels of general mental ability acquire new information more easily and more quickly, and are able to use that information more effectively. Frank Schmidt and Jack Hunter's[83] research suggests that general cognitive ability influences job performance largely through its role in the acquisition and use of information about how to do one's job. Research supports the idea that cognitive ability is more important in complex jobs, when individuals are new to the job, and when there are changes in the workplace that require workers to learn new ways of performing their jobs.[84] Some companies, including Internet search firm Google, prefer to hire for intelligence rather than experience.[85]

Many organizations, including the National Football League,[86] use cognitive ability tests. **Cognitive ability tests** are computerized or paper-and-pencil tests that assess candidates' general mental abilities, including their verbal and mathematical reasoning, logic, and perceptual abilities. Because the scores on these tests can predict a person's ability to learn via training or on the job,[87] be adaptable and solve problems, and tolerate routine, their predictive value may rise, given the increasing trend toward jobs requiring innovation, continual training, and nonroutine problem solving. There are many different types of cognitive ability tests, including the Wonderlic Personnel Test, Raven's Progressive Matrices, the Kaufman Brief Intelligence Test, and the Wechsler Abbreviated Scale of Intelligence. Table 9-6 contains some questions like those found on the Wonderlic Personnel Test.

Despite being easy to use and one of the most valid selection methods for all jobs, with an average validity of .51, cognitive ability tests produce racial differences that are three to five

cognitive ability tests
tests that assess a person's general mental abilities, including their verbal and mathematical reasoning, logic, and perceptual abilities

TABLE 9-6	Cognitive Ability Test Items

The following questions are like those found on the Wonderlic Personnel Test measuring cognitive ability. The answers are at the bottom of the table.

1. Assume the first two statements are true. Is the final one (1) True, (2) False, (3) Not certain
   - The girl plays basketball.
   - All basketball players wear hats.
   - The girl wears a hat.

2. Pencils sell for $0.17 each. What will four pencils cost?

3. How many of the five pairs of items listed below are exact duplicates?
   Smith, T. J.   Smith, J. T.
   Liao, G. K.   Liao, G. K.
   Barry, P. P.   Barry, J. P.
   Kovich, L. E.   Kovich, E. E.
   Garcia, T. S.   Garcia, T. S.

4. DEMAND DEFILE—Do these words
   1. Have similar meanings?
   2. Have contradictory meanings?
   3. Mean neither the same nor opposite?

Answers: (1) True, (2) 68 cents, (3) 2, (4) 3

---

times larger than other predictors, such as biodata, personality inventories, and structured interviews.[88] Although the reasons for the disparate impact are not fully understood, it is thought that factors including culture, the different access people have to test coaching and preparation programs, and the different test motivation levels due to different perceptions of the test's validity among people in different subgroups might have an impact.[89] Applicants also often dislike cognitive ability tests because they don't seem job related.[90]

Because disparate impact can be problematic when using cognitive ability tests,[91] employers should evaluate the effect a test has on protected groups before using the test. We stress that no assessment method is best used alone, but this is particularly true in the case of cognitive ability tests. However, they can often be combined with other predictors to reverse the adverse impact they have while increasing the overall validity of the testing process.[92]

NONCOGNITIVE ABILITY TESTS   Tests can also measure psychomotor, sensory, and physical abilities. **Psychomotor tests** assess a person's capacity to manipulate and control objects. Reaction times, manual dexterity, and arm-hand steadiness are examples of psychomotor abilities. **Sensory tests** assess candidates' visual, auditory, and speech perception. The ability to speak clearly, discriminate colors, and see in low light conditions are examples of sensory abilities. **Physical ability tests** assess a person's strength, flexibility, endurance, and coordination. The ability to lift certain amounts of weight, exert yourself physically over extended periods, and keep your balance when in an unstable position are examples of physical abilities. Physical ability tests can reduce injuries by ensuring that employees can do necessary, job-related tasks. For example, firefighters must be able to carry heavy hoses up stairs, delivery people must be able to safely lift and move heavy boxes, and so forth. Because physical ability tests can result in adverse impact against women, it is important that all applicants have a fair chance to perform and show that they meet the job's BFOQs. As shown in Table 9-3, when carefully developed to assess a job's requirements, noncognitive tests can be highly valid, well received by applicants, and relatively easy to use.

psychomotor tests
tests that assess the capacity of a person to manipulate and control objects

sensory tests
assess visual, auditory, and speech perception

physical ability tests
tests that assess a person's physical abilities including strength, flexibility, endurance, and coordination

VALUES ASSESSMENTS   Businesses often have key values and core competencies tied to their business strategies. As we have discussed, it is important to make sure new employees appreciate and share these values. Some companies, including J&J, which we mentioned at the beginning of the chapter, have improved their corporate effectiveness by actively matching their candidates' values to their corporate cultures.[93] Computerized or paper-and-pencil assessments of candidates' values exist. Some firms try to evaluate them by watching groups of candidates interact with one another on structured tasks and exercises. The vignette at the end of the chapter explains how Southwest Airlines accomplishes this.

PERSONALITY ASSESSMENTS   Personality has had a spotty reputation as a predictor of work outcomes. Until the 1990s, personality assessments were a poor predictor of performance.[94] Some of the early tests that were tried were designed for employment screening, but others were tests originally intended for diagnosing mental illness. The Minnesota Multiphasic Personality Inventory (MMPI) and the California Psychological Inventories presented applicants with true/false questions including:[95]

- I believe my sins are unpardonable.
- I would like to be a florist.
- Evil spirits possess me sometimes.
- I have no difficulty starting or holding my bowel movement.
- I go to church almost every week.

Given questions like these, it is not surprising that their ability to predict job success was among the lowest of any assessment method! Fortunately, research on the use of personality in predicting job success continued. As shown in Table 9-3, personality tests can have low to moderate validity (ranging from −.13 to .33), which improves when the personality assessment is well matched to specific job criteria.[96] Because hundreds of different personality traits exist, researchers combined related personality traits and reduced this list into a few broad behavioral (rather than emotional or cognitive) traits that each encompasses many more specific traits. As a group, these Big Five factors of personality capture up to 75 percent of an individual's personality.[97] The Big Five factors are:

- *Extraversion:* outgoing, assertive, upbeat, and talkative; predicts salesperson performance.[98]
- *Conscientiousness:* attentive to detail, willing to follow rules and exert effort; predicts performance across all occupations.[99]
- *Emotional Stability:* calm, optimistic, well adjusted, able to allocate resources to accomplish tasks; predicts job performance in most occupations, particularly those involving interpersonal interactions and teamwork such as occupations in management, sales,[100] and teaching.[101]
- *Agreeableness:* sympathetic, friendly, cooperative; predicts performance in jobs involving teamwork and interpersonal interactions.[102]
- *Openness to Experience:* imaginative, intellectually curious, open to new ideas and change; predicts creativity and expatriate performance.[103]

Conscientiousness and emotional stability seem to predict overall performance for a wide range of jobs.[104] These two "generalizable" traits seem to affect performance through "will do" motivational components. On the other hand, general mental ability affects performance in all jobs primarily through "can do" capabilities.[105] Extraversion, agreeableness, and openness to experience are valid predictors of performance only in specific occupations or for some criteria.[106] Extraversion predicts performance in occupations where a significant portion of the job involves interacting with others, particularly when influencing others and obtaining status and power is required, such as in managerial and sales jobs.[107] Agreeableness is a valid predictor when it comes to jobs involving a significant amount of interpersonal interaction, such as helping, nurturing, and cooperating with others. The trait might also be the single best personality predictor of who will and will not work well in a team.[108] Employees who are argumentative, inflexible, uncooperative, uncaring, intolerant, and disagreeable are likely to be less effective working in teams and also engage in more counterproductive behaviors, such as theft. One's openness to new experiences is a predictor of a person's creativity and ability to adapt to change.[109] Employees who are artistically sensitive, intellectual, curious, polished, original, and independent are likely to deal better with change and be innovative on the job.[110]

The Big Five are very stable over time, and seem to be determined in part by genetics.[111] Like all personality tests, the validity of the Big Five is not high enough to warrant the selection of applicants based solely on their personality test scores. Personality tests including the Big Five tend to have low adverse impact and may be able to alleviate the adverse impact caused by other assessment methods, such as cognitive ability.

Because job performance reflects many different behaviors, some scholars feel that broad dispositions such as the Big Five might best predict it. Some research has supported this proposition[112] although the validities of the five traits are relatively low compared to other assessment methods. Conscientiousness is the most consistent predictor of performance across all occupations, with an average validity of .31,[113] suggesting that conscientiousness may be a useful assessment method for all jobs.

Some prominent scholars argue that the best criterion-related validities will result from matching specific traits (traits narrower than the Big Five) to specific job-relevant performance dimensions.[114] When choosing a personality assessment, it is critical to match the trait to some aspect of job success in terms of both content and specificity. If a firm wants to predict broadly defined job success, broad traits, such as the Big Five, may be better predictors than narrower traits. If the firm wants to predict more specific job success dimensions and work behaviors, such as customer service skills, then narrower traits such as a person's customer service orientation, sales drive, and social interests[115] might have higher validity.

Faking can also be an issue with personality assessments,[116] although there is some evidence that applicants who try to enhance their personality test responses also try to manage other's impressions of them on the job, which can actually help them perform the job better.[117] When considering using any personality or values assessment, it is important to assess the test's validity and adverse impact. No personality test will work for all jobs or for every company. How the assessment has held up to any legal challenges is also important, as are applicant reactions to its use. Buros Institute of Mental Measurements publishes a *Mental Measurements Yearbook*[118] that reviews a variety of commercially available cognitive ability tests as well as personality and other types of assessment tests.

Personality tests are easy to use, but applicants often react to poorly to them. Drug users, in particular, have been found to react negatively to them.[119] The biggest legal problem with personality tests is based on privacy issues. For example, if the tests ask about invasive topics, such as a person's religious beliefs and sexual preferences, that are not shown to be related to job success or to the job requirement being predicted, this can get firms into trouble.[120]

Psychological assessments designed for clinical or diagnostic use, such as the MMPI and California Psychological Inventories, should not be used to assess the personality of candidates except when jobs they are applying for could endanger the public safety, such as police officers, firefighters, and airline pilots. The courts have consistently ruled against the use of clinical psychological assessments in the general business environment.[121] The use of clinical personality instruments is also inconsistent with the ADA because the tests are designed to diagnose abnormal behavioral patterns. The ADA states that an employer "shall not conduct a medical examination or make inquiries as to whether such applicant is an individual with a disability or as to the nature and severity of such disability." Discuss the use of any psychological test with a qualified lawyer and assess its compliance with the ADA and other laws.[122] Except in certain situations, if an assessment reveals anything about an employee's mental impairment or a psychological condition, even if it is unintentional, the ADA has been violated.[123]

INTEGRITY TESTS Why is integrity important? U.S. stores lose tens of billions of dollars each year to shoplifting and employee theft.[124] Hiring employees less likely to steal or engage in other illegal or counterproductive behaviors can be particularly important for jobs requiring money handling (such as the jobs held by clerks, tellers, or cashiers) or handling controlled substances (such as the jobs held by police officers and security people). **Integrity tests** are typically written tests that use multiple-choice or true/false questions to measure candidates' attitudes about their trustworthiness, honesty, moral character, and reliability. Integrity tests can be *clear purpose*— that is, they can openly assess integrity. The following is an example of a clear purpose question: "Did you ever write a check knowing you did not have enough money in the bank to cover it?" Alternatively, an integrity test can be *general purpose* and indirectly assess people's integrity. The following is a general purpose question: "Do you like to take chances?"[125]

integrity tests
tests that measure people's trustworthiness, honesty, moral character, and reliability

Integrity tests do not tend to result in adverse impact and appear to be unrelated to cognitive ability. Accordingly, when used with cognitive ability tests, integrity tests can add validity to the selection process and reduce adverse impact. Faking also does not appear to be a problem with integrity tests. Perhaps dishonest applicants choose not to lie more than do honest applicants because they feel that *everyone* is like themselves—dishonest. In other words, they might not think that they need to fake their answers because they believe that everyone is dishonest to some extent.[126] It is also possible to embed items on an integrity test that detect faking. For example, although some people are consistently honest in all areas of their lives, respondents agreeing with items asking if they "always" engage in good behavior or "never" engage in bad behavior are often being dishonest.

As shown in Table 9-3, the validity of integrity tests averages .41. In terms of detecting counterproductive work behaviors, clear purpose integrity tests are more valid (.55) than general purpose tests (.32).[127] Both tests predict more generally counterproductive behaviors, including absenteeism and disciplinary problems, better than they predict employee theft.[128] Applicants also tend to react somewhat unfavorably to integrity tests,[129] although, nondrug users have been found to react more favorably to the tests than drug users.[130] Another issue with integrity tests that applies to all assessment methods is ethical in nature. Some of the people who score poorly on integrity tests are misclassified and wouldn't have stolen from the company. Managers must decide if it is fair or ethical to use a test that incorrectly screens out good applicants.

Integrity tests are relatively inexpensive and can be administered any time during the hiring process. Some companies screen all prospective applicants with integrity tests, and others only screen finalists.[131] As with any assessment method, check that the test truly predicts counterproductive work outcomes, including absenteeism, theft, and disciplinary problems before making the test part of the assessment process. Not all commercially available tests have been properly validated—that is, not all of them follow the American Psychological Association's guidelines for using integrity tests.[132] In addition, because theft is not a problem for all companies, sometimes the cost of integrity testing outweighs the gains a company achieves by reducing its employee-related theft.[133] As with any assessment test, applicants' privacy rights need to be protected. Integrity tests also have legal issues. Some states, including California and Massachusetts, limit the use of honesty and integrity testing in making hiring decisions.[134]

POLYGRAPH TESTS   A **polygraph test** measures and records physiological factors thought to be indicators of anxiety, including a candidates' blood pressure, respiration, pulse, and skin conductivity, while the person answers a series of questions. Because anxiety often accompanies the telling of lies, polygraphs are thought to assess lying and honesty. However, if the person is anxious for other reasons, or can voluntarily control his or her anxiety level, the conclusions can be unreliable.

The Polygraph Protection Act prohibits employers from requiring applicants or employees to take a polygraph test, using polygraph results for any employment decision, and discharging or disciplining anyone who refuses to take a polygraph. The only exceptions are for the military, police, private security firms, and controlled substance manufacturers. During theft, embezzlement, or sabotage investigations that resulted in economic loss or injury to an employer, employees can be tested.[135]

JOB KNOWLEDGE TESTS   **Job knowledge tests** measure a candidates' knowledge (often technical) required by a job. These tests are often in multiple-choice, essay, or checklist format and can assess either the candidate's knowledge of a job's duties or experience level with regard to the job's tasks, tools, and processes. An example is a test assessing an HR job applicant's knowledge of human resources. As shown in Table 9-3, job knowledge tests generally result in minimal adverse impact and can be highly valid (average validity of .48), particularly for complex jobs.[136] Many firms use job knowledge tests.

INTERVIEWS   Research has shown that organizations that use more quality staffing practices show higher levels of profitability and sales growth[137] and lower turnover[138] than organizations that use fewer of them. Interviews are perhaps the most commonly used selection tool.[139] When interview processes are effectively implemented they can enhance the selection process, resulting in the selection of higher-performing and better-fitting employees who will remain with a firm over a longer period of time.[140]

Interviews can assess a variety of skills, abilities, and styles, including people's communication skills, interpersonal skills, and leadership style. Applicants react very well to interviews, and job seekers often rate interviews as the most job-related selection procedure.[141] Doubletree Hotels used the results of interviews with 300 high- and low-performing employees and began screening candidates on the "dimensions of success" it identified. Based on interviews with reservation agents, Doubletree identified seven dimensions for success on the job: practical

polygraph test
measures and records physiological factors thought to be indicators of anxiety, including a candidates' blood pressure, respiration, pulse, and skin conductivity while the person answers a series of questions

job knowledge tests
tests that measure candidates' knowledge (often technical) required by a job

learning, teamwork, tolerance for stress, sales ability, attention to detail, adaptability/flexibility, and motivation. Doubletree then designed specific interview questions to probe for these and other attributes.[142]

In addition to evaluating job applicants, interviews can also serve an important recruiting purpose and communicate information about the job and organization to applicants. Remember, applicants choose organizations as much as organizations choose applicants. However, it can be difficult for a single interview to serve both purposes. Often applicants being assessed are too distracted to focus on the recruiting information being conveyed to them. They are likely to learn more about a job and organization during interviews focused solely on recruitment.[143] Thus, if a company decides to use interviews for recruiting purposes, the interviews should ideally focus exclusively on recruiting.

There are several types of interviews used for candidate assessment, and next, we discuss some of the most common: unstructured interviews, structured interviews, behavioral interviews, and situational interviews.

Unstructured interviews ask questions that vary from candidate to candidate and that differ across interviewers. There are typically no standards for scoring or evaluating candidates' answers, and they are not always highly job related. The interview questions are often casual and open ended (e.g., "tell me about yourself") and can be highly speculative (e.g., "What do you see yourself doing in five to ten years?"). The interviewer often relies on his or her personal theories about what makes someone a good hire, such as personal appearance and nonverbal cues (whether or not the candidate fidgets or makes eye contact, for example), and makes a quick global evaluation of the candidate when the interview has finished. As shown in Table 9-3, the reliability of unstructured interviews can be low (averaging .20 to .38) due to their lack of consistency, which reduces their validity. Many managers nonetheless like using unstructured interviews because they feel that they are good judges of others, or believe that they have devised clever (although unvalidated) ways of verbally evaluating candidates. Given their expense and the legal risks associated with asking nonstandardized questions that have not been validated or shown to be related to job success, it is hard to recommend unstructured interviews over structured ones.

unstructured interview
questions that vary from candidate to candidate and that differ across interviewers

Structured interviews are interviews in which candidates are asked a series of standardized, job-related questions with predetermined scores for different answers.[144] Because the same questions are asked in the same way for all applicants, and because raters are trained to consistently use the same rating scales to evaluate answers, structured interviews tend to be quite reliable and valid. As shown in Table 9-3, they have an average validity of as high as .63, and are liked by applicants.

structured interviews
interviews in which candidates are asked a series of standardized, job-related questions with predetermined scores for different answers

They can be moderately expensive to develop. Nonetheless, research consistently demonstrates that well-executed structured interviews result in good prediction of high-performing employees.[145] One study determined that the use of structured interviews for a sales force reduced annualized turnover from 38.7 percent to 13.6 percent.[146] Research has shown that properly implemented structured interviews used as part of a selection system can also reduce adverse impact[147] and decrease related legal risks.[148] A review of litigation outcomes shows that organizational defendants are much more likely to prevail in courts of law when using job-related structured interview formats.[149] This is because structured interviews help to reduce distortions caused by interviewer bias, differences in the questions asked to applicants, and factors unrelated to the job, such as a candidate's physical attractiveness, sex or race, and style of dress. Table 9-7 outlines the steps involved in crafting a structured interview.

Interviewer training in consistently asking and scoring the interview questions, body language, note taking, and asking follow-up questions is key to the improved performance of structured interviews compared to unstructured interviews because of the importance of their consistent administration and scoring.[150] As the U. S. Office of Personnel Management states, "It is essential to train the person who will administer the structured interview. Interviewer training increases the accuracy of the interview."[151]

There are two types of structured interviews: behavioral and situational. The choice of behavioral or situational interview questions depends on the level of the prior work experience of candidates. When interviewing people with limited work experience, situational questions (e.g., "what would you do if...") are likely to generate more insightful answers than behavioral questions (e.g., "what did you do when..."). We discuss behavioral and situational interviews in more detail next.

TABLE 9-7	Steps to Crafting a Structured Interview

1. For the job requirements to be measured by a structured interview, identify the actions and behaviors that illustrate each qualification. For example, what does *leadership skills* mean in the context of the job being filled? What do people with good and bad leadership skills do? What is the impact of different leadership strategies? Are different leadership approaches equally effective?
2. Write questions that will generate relevant information about the degree to which candidates possess each job requirement.
3. Create an answer key with benchmark responses for at least the high, middle, and low scores on the scale.
4. Weight the benchmark responses based on the importance of each question relative to the others. Give more important questions greater weight relative to the other questions.
5. Select and train interviewers to increase the interview's standardization, reliability, and validity.
6. Evaluate the effectiveness of the structured interview in terms of its validity and the reactions of stakeholders, including how fair and job related they perceive it to be.

behavioral interviews

interviews that use information about what the applicants have done in the past to predict their future behaviors

Behavioral interviews are based on the idea that what applicants have *done* in the past is a better indicator of their future job success than what they believe, feel, think, or know.[152] In a behavioral interview, the interviewer first asks a candidate to describe a problem or situation the person faced while working or any other relevant situation that highlights a particular skill, trait, or core competency. Then the candidate describes the action he or she took and the results it generated. For example, to assess leadership skills, a candidate can be asked to describe an ineffective team she was on, what action she took, and what results she obtained. Factors such as a candidate's work ethic, temperament, values, and general compatibility with the organization can often be assessed in behavioral interviews. Table 9-8 shows an example of a behavioral interview question and scoring key.

Candidates rarely give the exact answers suggested in the benchmark responses. However, training can help interviewers determine how to score an applicant's actual answer. Also, if a candidate has a limited work history or is unable to come up with an appropriate situation or problem, it can take skilled probing to obtain a scorable response. Behavioral interviews are most useful when it comes to evaluating job candidates who have employment experience. However, they can also be effectively used to assess candidates with little or no work experience. For example, McDonald's believes that a well-run interview can identify an applicant's potential to be a successful employee committed to delivering outstanding service. McDonald's uses an interview guide that helps to predict how an applicant's past behavior is likely to influence his or her future performance. The questions probe actual events or situations the candidate faced rather than allowing applicants to give a general or theoretical response. The interviewer rates candidates on their responses and offers jobs to those who earn the highest ratings.[153]

As a job candidate, when preparing for behavioral interviews it can be useful to learn to use the STAR technique to help the recruiter effectively evaluate your response:

- **S**ituation or **T**ask: Describe a specific event or situation, giving enough detail for the interviewer to understand the situation and what you needed to accomplish. The situation can be from a previous job, volunteer activity, or any relevant event. For example, "Advertising revenue was falling and clients were not renewing contracts."

TABLE 9-8	A Behavioral Interview Question Assessing a Candidate's Persistence

Question: Tell me about a time when you were working on a project that you felt was important but that others thought was a waste of time. What did you do, and what was the result?

5—*Excellent:* I pursued the project despite the obstacles because I really believed in it. I wanted the project to succeed and I tried to find ways around problems.

4

3—*Marginal:* I continued working on the project but shifted my focus to other projects that had higher probabilities of success.

2

1—*Poor:* Once I felt that the project had low support, I stopped working on it.

- **A**ction that you took: Describe the actual action that you took. For example, "I designed a new Web site and promotional campaign. I also designed and delivered a customer service training session for our sales agents to develop selling and retention skills."
- **R**esults that you achieved: Describe what happened, how the event ended, what you accomplished, and what you learned. For example, "New advertisers increased 25 percent over the next three months and our retention rate decreased by half. We also regained 40 percent of our former clients."

Behavioral interviews are more reliable and substantially better at predicting job performance than are unstructured interviews.[154] Compared to unstructured interviews, behavioral interviews have been shown to improve the average job performance of new hires[155] and reduce subsequent employee turnover.[156]

Behavioral interviews also reduce the effects of interviewer biases.[157] Research has found that interviewers are more influenced by the attractiveness of applicants and applicants' attempts to create a positive impression of them in unstructured interviews than in structured ones.[158]

Companies, including Southwest Airlines, use **situational interviews**, asking people not about their past behaviors but about how they might react to hypothetical situations and how they exemplify the firm's core.[159] Situational interviews have fairly high validities but are often slightly less valid than behavioral interviews.[160]

situational interviews
asking people how they might react to hypothetical situations

As they do with behavioral interviews, job experts create a rating scale for a continuum of possible answers given during situational interviews. The answers range from excellent to poor and link directly to the behavioral objectives determined by the job analysis. Excellent answers indicate probable success, marginal answers reflect probable difficulty, and poor answers indicate probable failure in performing the related job task. Although the exact expert-generated answers are rarely given, interviewers are trained to score their responses meaningfully at some point on the continuum marked by these anchors. Table 9-9 illustrates a behavioral interview rating scale that can be adapted for any type of structured interview.

One caution about behavioral and situational interviews is warranted. Web sites including Vault.com and WetFeet.com provide extensive information about companies' recruiting and hiring processes, actual interview questions, and summaries of the firms and their cultures. Companies' own Web sites often describe the qualities they are looking for in new hires and what it takes to fit into their cultures. These resources make it possible for some job seekers to fabricate answers to interview questions they've anticipated.

How can an employer spot false stories and improve the validity of their behavioral interviews? They can do so by asking follow-up questions, curiously requesting more specific information about the story, asking the candidate what he or she was thinking or feeling at the time, and asking what the candidate learned from the experience. This can make it more difficult for the candidate to fabricate a consistent story.[161]

TABLE 9-9 A Situational Interview Question Assessing a Candidate's Communication Skills

Question: Imagine that you are currently very busy working on several important projects with firm deadlines, but your supervisor brings you a stack of unrelated paperwork to complete that you feel is unrelated to any of your projects. In addition, you are certain that attending to this new paperwork will cause you to miss several project deadlines. What would you do?

5—*Excellent:* Explain the conflict to my supervisor and try to identify and discuss alternatives. It would be important to me to ensure that any changes were acceptable to both my manager and myself.

4

3—*Marginal:* Tell my supervisor about the conflict.

2

1—*Poor:* Accept the conflict as part of the job and do the best I can.

---

situational judgment tests

measures of noncognitive skills; short scenarios are presented verbally, in writing, or in videos, and candidates are asked what they believe is the most effective response, or to choose the best response from a list of alternatives

SITUATIONAL JUDGMENT TESTS Like situational interviews, **situational judgment tests** measure job candidates' noncognitive skills. Short scenarios are presented verbally, in writing, or in videos, and candidates are asked what they believe is the most effective response, or to choose the best response from a list of alternatives. The tests have a moderate validity of about .34. The FBI uses situational judgment tests to measure candidates' integrity, and their ability to organize, plan, prioritize, relate effectively to others, maintain a positive image, evaluate information and make decisions, and adapt to changing situations.[162]

graphology

any practice that involves determining personality traits or abilities from a person's handwriting

GRAPHOLOGY Some employers use handwriting analysis in staffing decisions. **Graphology** includes any practice that involves determining personality traits or abilities from a person's handwriting. In 1996, about 6,000 American companies reported using graphology. The real number may be higher because many companies use, but do not admit to using, the technique.[163] We do not recommend graphology as an assessment method because it has been found to have little or no validity.[164] Applicants tend to be skeptical about it and find it invasive if they're not being told their handwriting is being used to assess them.[165] Courts also tend not to like graphology[166] because it can result in people with physical and emotional handicaps being discriminated against, violating the ADA.[167] A good rule of thumb is that if an individual who has an ADA-defined disability cannot take a test, then it should not be used unless it can be adapted for use by those individuals. Handwriting analysis clearly falls into the group of tests that cannot be adapted to be administered to individuals who fall within one or more ADA-defined disabilities.

job simulations

simulations that measure people's job skills by having them perform tasks similar to those performed on the job

JOB SIMULATIONS Many job candidates look good on paper or during interviews. The question is, can they really do the job successfully? **Job simulations** measure people's job skills by having them perform tasks similar to those performed on the job. Simulations can be *verbal*, requiring interpersonal interaction and language skills, such as a role-playing test for a call center worker. *Motor* simulations involve the physical manipulation of things, such as an assembly task or a test to see if a candidate can properly operate a machine. Multiple, trained raters and detailed rating systems are typically used to evaluate and score candidates.

Simulations also differ in their degree of *fidelity,* or the similarity between the scenario and the actual job tasks. In high-fidelity tests very realistic scenarios and often expensive equipment, such as flight simulators, are used. Cleveland-based bank National City Corporation's dynamic simulation uses interactive experiences with both video and audio.[168] Low-fidelity tests simulate the task via a written or verbal statement, to which candidates respond verbally or in writing. (Behavioral interviews can be a type of verbal, low-fidelity simulation.)

Simulations can be highly valid (averaging .54) and generally result in minimal adverse impact. Job candidates also tend to like them because they are highly job related. Because of their expense, particularly for high-fidelity simulations, some firms choose to use simulations later in the assessment process after the pool of applicants has been reduced. If a company plans to train new employees, then using simulations will probably be less appropriate. The use of simulations is rising, particularly for jobs in manufacturing, sales, health care, and call centers.[169]

L'Oréal uses an online simulation that simulates real-world market conditions. Student teams log on to the Internet and "become" general managers of a cosmetics company. They decide how much to invest in research and development, how much to spend on marketing, and find ways to cut production costs without compromising quality. The game responds to every move by showing players how their decisions affect their simulated company's virtual share price. In the first four years it used the simulation, L'Oréal hired 186 executives and employees from 28 countries.[170]

Prudential Realty uses a simulation that shows videos of actors posing as homebuyers. The actors "talk" to the aspiring realtors, who then choose from a list of what they consider the best response to the situation. Prudential feels that it can teach new real estate agents sales skills, but they still need certain personality traits to succeed in the business. The simulation reveals whether job applicants have those traits or not. In their first year, high scoring agents earned over 300 percent more than those who scored low.[171] Simulations can also serve as a recruiting tool—one real estate firm places a monthly newspaper ad that states, "Test Drive a Career in Real Estate Today" and directs readers to the company's Web site to do a simulation.[172]

Because they seem so job relevant, it can be tempting to overweight simulations in making screening decisions and ignore other components of the recruitment process. Experts recommend balancing simulation results with interviews, written assessment tests, and reference and background checks. No matter how well Prudential job applicants perform on the realtor simulation, they must still do well at an interview. At L'Oréal, the top-performing teams make a presentation to a panel of judges during which they explain their business strategy and try to convince L'Oréal to invest in their fictitious companies. The presentation helps L'Oréal assess candidates' personalities and communication skills.[173] Depending on their cost, simulations can be used earlier in the assessment process. More expensive simulations can be reserved for use later in the process to assess a smaller group of candidates.

WORK SAMPLES **Work samples** require a candidate to perform observable work tasks or job-related behaviors to predict future job success. Work samples can include simulations, giving candidates an actual job task to perform, or even probationary hiring. The samples can also simulate critical events that might occur on the job to assess how well a candidate handles them. A candidate for a 911 dispatch center might be asked to handle calls from distraught people and handle a high volume of calls to assess how they respond. Work samples can also take the form of a picture or description of an incident. A candidate then responds to a series of questions and indicates the decisions he or she would make and actions he or she would take. Job experts then score the test. Although they can be expensive to develop and administer, particularly in the case of probationary hiring, work samples tend to be highly reliable and can have high validity and low adverse impact if done well.

work samples
require a candidate to perform observable work tasks or job-related behaviors to predict future job success

Work samples do not measure applicants' aptitudes, only what they are able to do at the current time. Work-sample trainability tests provide candidates with a period of training prior to being tested. They are then evaluated while completing the work sample. Work sample trainability tests are useful when the company intends to extensively train new hires.

As shown in Table 9-3, work samples have an average validity of .33, low adverse impact, and are generally received well by applicants. The difficulty of faking on-the-job proficiency helps to increase the validity of work samples. They are most useful for jobs and work tasks that can be completed in a short period of time. The tests are less able to predict a person's performance on tasks that take days or weeks to complete. A person's portfolio is a type of work sample. However, it can be faked if not done while a company representative is watching. Someone else could have created the "great" samples a candidate brings in as representative of his or her work.

Assessment centers that put candidates through a variety of simulations and assessments to evaluate their potential fit with and ability to do the job are one type of work sample. As shown in Table 9-3, assessment centers have an average validity of .37 and low adverse impact, although they tend to be expensive and are one of the more difficult assessment methods to use. We discuss assessment centers in more detail in Chapter 10.

REFERENCE CHECKS As you learned in Chapter 3, reference checks can reveal information about a candidate's past performance or measure the accuracy of the statements a candidate makes in an interview or on his or her résumé. Individuals familiar with the person—usually people referred by the job candidate—are asked to provide confirmation of a candidate's statements or an evaluation of the job candidate. Applicants generally expect reference checks as a part of the hiring process. Although many previous employers are unwilling to provide extensive information about a candidate due to the risks of a defamation lawsuit, references should still be contacted because not checking them increases the risk that an organization will be accused of negligent hiring. Sometimes employees who have relocated but who have worked with the candidate in the past can provide useful information. Reference checks have low adverse impact but have a relatively low average validity of .26. The validity might be greater if candidates' references were more candid.

Rather than asking general questions about the candidate, asking references for relevant information about the indicators of success that you have established for the job can generate more useful information, as can asking questions about the types of situations and work environments in which the candidate would excel. Sometimes more detailed questions can get a better response from reluctant references. One expert suggests setting up scenarios so the supervisor can better understand the context of your question, such as:[174]

- I'm wondering what kind of environment would be the best fit for Kim. Do you recommend a more structured environment, with clear guidelines and close supervision, or would she excel in a more self-directed culture?

- Some people constantly reinvent their jobs and willingly assume responsibilities beyond their job description. Other people are only interested in performing their job duties and little else. Can you tell me where Manuel fits on that continuum?
- We often struggle to find the ideal balance between quality and production. If John leaned in one direction more than the other, would you say it was toward quality or quantity?

The laws related to doing reference checks differ by state. Some states, including Wisconsin, broadly protect employers giving factual information as part of reference checks. Because other states are less employer-friendly, it is wise to become familiar with your local and state laws.

Although many companies use reference checks as a contingent assessment method, it can be helpful to contact a person's references earlier in the assessment process. Reference checks can generate valuable information about a candidate's previous work responsibilities and performance, help rank candidates, and assist in making your final decision. It is a good idea to check at least three references for each candidate, with one of those three being a direct supervisor.

A growing trend related to reference checks is recruiters' use of social networking sites like Facebook or MySpace to screen job candidates. Recruiters look for anything from unprofessional screen names, discriminatory remarks, communication skills, and qualifications.[175] It is important to remember that information posted on these sites can often be found years later, highlighting the importance of using your profile to consistently communicate a professional image to professional employers. Another trend to be aware of is the presence of Web-based services that offer fake work histories and references to job seekers.[176]

Contingent Assessment Methods

MEDICAL AND DRUG TESTS Because of the potential to violate applicants' privacy and the importance of legal compliance, medical tests, including drug tests, should be used with great care. Medical exams are usually used to identify a job candidate's potential health risks and must assess only job-related factors consistent with a business necessity.[177] The ADA regulates the use of medical exams to prevent employers from screening out individuals with disabilities for reasons unrelated to job performance. Nonetheless, the medical information for all employees hired in the same job category should be assessed, regardless of whether or not the employee has a disability.[178] A survey investigating new hire medical testing found that 60 percent of the U.S. firms surveyed required medical exams for at least some jobs.[179] The most common medical test used is drug testing, and the most frequently given reason for drug testing is to establish an applicant's ability to perform the job tasks he or she would be assigned.[180]

Genetic testing is a type of testing that can identify people genetically susceptible to certain diseases that could result from exposure to toxic substances in the workplace, such as chemicals or radiation. Although some companies have experimented with genetic screening, with the passage of the Genetic Information Nondiscrimination Act of 2008 (GINA), it is now illegal to deny U.S. citizens jobs simply because they have an inherited illness, or a genetic predisposition to a particular disease.[181]

Any medical information obtained should be kept confidential and stored separately from other applicant and employee files.[182] Medical tests can be administered only after all other application components have been cleared and a job offer has been extended. Only by making the job offer contingent upon passing the drug or other medical test is it possible for an applicant to tell whether he or she was rejected on the basis of a disability and not because of insufficient skills or experience.

The timing of a medical test is also critical. The courts have made it clear that an applicant's medical information should be the last information collected after making a contingent job offer. Some companies find themselves in legal trouble just for failing to follow the required legal sequence. One company had not completed the background checks on some of its applicants before asking them to take medical and blood tests. When some of these individuals were found to be HIV-positive but had not revealed it prior to the medical exam, the company rescinded the offers made to them, citing that the applicants had not been forthright about their condition. Three candidates sued the company, and the court determined that it did not matter whether the candidates had been forthright about their health condition. The court concluded that administering the medical tests before the background check was complete made it difficult for the applicants to determine whether they had been denied employment because of issues with their background checks or with their physical exam.[183]

Drug tests are an assessment method that has generated great debate. Opponents of drug testing often cite privacy concerns, the fact that drug tests sometimes are wrong, and numerous studies questioning the cost-effectiveness of drug tests. On the other hand, the cost of drug and alcohol abuse costs employers billions of dollars every year. Some of the costs of employee drug and alcohol abuse are obvious (e.g., increased absences, accidents, and errors). Less obvious costs, including low employee morale, increased health care costs, increased workers' compensation claims, and higher turnover, can be equally harmful.[184]

Drug testing is not required under the Drug-Free Workplace Act of 1988. Although many state and local governments have statutes that limit or prohibit workplace testing unless required by state or federal regulations for certain jobs, most private employers have the right to test for a wide variety of illegal substances. Familiarizing yourself with all relevant state and federal regulations that apply to your organization is essential before designing a drug testing program.[185] Some collective bargaining agreements also affect firms' drug testing policies.

An organization should have a clear drug testing policy in place before conducting drug tests. The policy should address issues such as who will be tested, the consequences of a positive test, what substances will be tested for, when the testing will be conducted, cutoff levels, safeguards, and confirmation procedures. Candidates should be informed of the policy and its details. The Department of Labor has online tools and information to help employers develop sound drug testing policies and effective, balanced drug-free workplace programs that go beyond drug testing.[186]

BACKGROUND CHECKS   A **background check** assesses factors such as a person's personal and credit information, character, lifestyle, criminal history, and general reputation. Unless a business is involved in national defense or security, background checks must be relevant to the nature of the job and job requirements. Employers must tell people when they apply for a job that background checks will be conducted, and the applicants must first give their written consent.[187] Staffing professionals need to fully document all background checking efforts and any contact they have had with candidates' former employers, supervisors, and references.

Preemployment background checks for misdemeanor and felony convictions or other offenses are routine in many industries, including the financial services, health care, childcare, and eldercare industries. In the United States, criminal records are archived at the county level. Consequently, to do a background check, you must search the criminal records in each county where the job candidate has lived. Because this is burdensome, many companies prefer to outsource background checks to qualified firms. Because crimes committed posthire could contribute to a negligent retention charge, at least one such background-checking firm, Verified Person, sends its clients automated biweekly updates that alert them to any new misdemeanor or felony convictions committed by their employees.[188]

Organizations are also using online searches to learn about job candidates. Using a search engine like Google to find information about a candidate can uncover additional information about them. Job candidates have even been denied job offers due to unprofessional content placed on social networking sites, such as Facebook and MySpace.[189] Because so much Internet content is archived, employers can access information about a candidate that goes back many years.

A consumer report (credit check) contains information about an individual's personal and credit information that can give you insight, or clues, about a person's character.[190] If the reports comply with the Fair Credit Reporting Act (FCRA), employers can use them when hiring new employees and when evaluating employees for promotion, reassignment, and retention. The FCRA protects the privacy of consumer report information and guarantees that the information supplied by consumer reporting agencies is as accurate as possible. A job applicant must give written consent before a background check of his or her credit can be conducted. Even if a candidate has had poor credit in the past, employers cannot use this information in their hiring decisions if it is more than seven years old unless it applies to the hiring of high-profile job candidates who earn $75,000 or more.[191] Any credit data from consumer credit reports must be destroyed after they have fulfilled the "business purpose."[192] The FTC's Web site (www.ftc.gov) provides more information on the requirements of the Fair and Accurate Credit Transactions Act. State requirements generally supersede federal requirements and can be even stricter.

background check
an employee screening method that assesses factors such as a person's personal and credit information, degrees held, character, lifestyle, criminal history, and general reputation

Amendments to the FCRA that went into effect September 30, 1997, significantly increase the legal obligations of employers who use credit checks. Congress expanded employers' responsibilities because it was concerned that inaccurate or incomplete consumer reports could cause applicants to be denied jobs or employees to be denied promotions unjustly. The amendments ensure (1) that individuals are aware that consumer reports may be used for employment purposes and agree to such use, and (2) that an individual be notified promptly if information in the person's consumer report results in a negative employment decision.[193] To be covered by the FCRA, a report must be prepared by a consumer reporting agency (CRA) that assembles such reports for other businesses. For sensitive positions, employers often order investigative consumer reports that include interviews with an applicant's or employee's friends, neighbors, and associates. All these types of reports are consumer reports if they are obtained from a CRA.

If negative information is found, the employer must give the job applicant an "adverse action notice" that includes the screening company's name and contact information and explains that the applicant can dispute the information for either accuracy or completeness. Applicants must also be given a fair amount of time to contest the findings.[194] Job seekers can check the accuracy of and correct errors in their background reports and credit histories by researching them themselves. MyBackgroundCheck.com and MyJobHistory.com both allow individuals to perform background checks on themselves and provide their potential employers with certificates that verify their degrees, and their credit, employment, and criminal history.

Improperly documenting information gathered as part of a background check can expose an employer to potential lawsuits. A case in point: When Interim Healthcare of Fort Wayne, Indiana, was accused of negligently hiring and retaining a home nursing aid, it could not show evidence of having conducted a proper background check on its employee.[195] Fully documenting its background-checking efforts may have absolved Interim Healthcare of the accusations.[196]

It should be noted that an employer does not have to prove that allegations of misconduct leading to an adverse employment decision are true as long as it conducts a proper investigation and acts in good faith on the information that it obtains. Thus, an employer can greatly reduce its potential liability for negligent hiring just by conducting a reasonable background check. Even if an employer is not able to actually obtain any information about a candidate from a previous place of work, going through the investigative process and documenting it well will go a long way toward reducing the firm's liability.[197]

USING MULTIPLE METHODS

As we explained in the last chapter, most organizations use multiple tools to assess candidates—perhaps a résumé screen, an interview, personality or skills assessments, reference and background checks, and some form of simulation. Renda Broadcasting in Pittsburgh, Pennsylvania, regularly hires advertising sales representatives to work in the firm's 25 radio stations. In addition to a three- or four-stage structured interviewing process, candidates make a final presentation to the sales manager and general manager of the station to assess their communication skills before a job offer contingent on background checks and drug screens is made.[198]

Obviously, few assessment methods are appropriate for all purposes. For example, job knowledge tests and assessment centers probably wouldn't be appropriate for low-level jobs or jobs for which extensive training will be provided to candidates after they are hired. Similarly, personality tests will differ in terms of their usefulness for different jobs. Also, as we have indicated, firms should consider how applicants will react to the assessment methods used—applicants who have positive perceptions about a company's selection processes and view them as fair are more likely to view the company favorably, accept its offers, and recommend the employer to others.[199]

Like Southwest Airlines, Nucor Steel uses written tests and in-depth interviews to evaluate job candidates. It also relies on the expertise of industrial psychologists, who frequently visit the company's plants to screen applicants and evaluate employees. Nucor's highly entrepreneurial, extremely performance-oriented, tough culture means that smart minds are more important than big muscles. Because this environment is not for everybody, Nucor works extra hard to find the right people.[200]

Can you imagine receiving a job offer after only a 15-minute interview? What would you think of a company that did this? Obviously, more extensive assessment procedures reflect a concerted effort on the part of the company to match candidates with the right jobs. Thus, more rigorous assessment procedures tend to impress good candidates, rather than turn them off. The methods of combining the scores from multiple assessments are discussed in Chapter 11.

REDUCING ADVERSE IMPACT

Some of the most useful assessment methods for predicting job performance often result in adverse impact. (As we explained, cognitive ability tests are one such method.) U.S. courts have ruled that it is not permissible to adjust members of a protected group's scores to reduce the assessment method's adverse impact. For example, **race norming**, or adjusting scores on a standardized test by using separate curves for different racial groups, is illegal. Race norming could award a minority applicant for a job with a test percentile score of 48 the same score on a test as a white applicant scoring in the 75th percentile. The Civil Rights Act of 1991 prohibits score adjustments, the use of different score requirements for different groups of test takers, or alteration of employment-related test results based on the demographics of the test takers. That said, there are some strategies you can use to try to reduce adverse impact (although not all of them will necessarily be successful):

race norming
adjusting scores on a standardized test by using separate curves for different racial groups

- Target applicants to increase the numbers of qualified minority applicants who apply with your firm.
- Expand the definition of what constitutes a good job performance to include other performance characteristics, such as people's commitment and reliability, in addition to their task performance.
- Combine predictors to reduce adverse impact, although this does not always work. Suppose, for example, a cognitive ability test predicts on-the-job performance but discriminates against women. In this case, using the test in conjunction with another valid assessment method that either does not have any adverse impact based on sex or that discriminates against men can reduce or eliminate the adverse impact of the cognitive ability test when the two predictors are used together.[201]
- Use well-developed simulations rather than cognitive ability tests.
- Use assessment methods with less adverse impact early in the selection process and those with greater adverse impact later in the process, if only a few applicants will be ultimately hired (the selection ratio will be low).
- Use **banding**—that is, assign the same score to applicants who score in the same range on an assessment. For example, candidates that score in the 93 to 100 percent range would be placed in the "A" band; those that score in the 85 to 95 percent range would be placed in the "B" band, and so forth. You could then use only the banded score to compare applicants—this technique can reduce an assessment's adverse impact but will also reduce the validity of the test.

banding
assigning the same score to applicants who score in a range on the assessment

ASSESSMENT PLANS

Companies use many different methods to assess job candidates. How should a firm choose which to use? An **assessment plan** describes which assessment method(s) will be used to assess each of the important characteristics on which applicants will be evaluated, in what sequence the assessments will take place, and what weight each assessment will receive in determining an overall score for that characteristic based on the importance of each characteristic to a person's job performance. The characteristics that candidates will be trained to develop after being hired won't be assessed nor listed in the plan. However, any existing qualifications required to qualify for the training program should be assessed. Table 9-10 shows an example of an assessment plan for an accountant. The weights for each assessment method are based on the job analysis ratings of the relative importance and relative time spent on each dimension.

assessment plan
describes which assessment method(s) will be used to assess each of the important characteristics on which applicants will be evaluated, in what sequence the assessments will take place, and what weight each assessment will receive in determining an overall score for that characteristic based on the importance of each characteristic to job performance

Which assessment methods are used and when is up to the company depending on its goals. Sometimes firms use cheaper assessment methods first and more expensive methods later when fewer candidates remain under consideration. To quickly reduce very large candidate pools

| TABLE 9-10 | Example of an Assessment Plan for an Accountant |

		Assessment Method and Its Sequence in the Assessment Process						
Characteristic	**Importance of Characteristic to Job Performance (1 = most important)**	**Select (S) Train (T)**	**Résumé**	**Phone Screen**	**Accounting and Budgeting Test**	**Recruiter Interview**	**Simulation**	**Hiring Manager Interview**
Customer focus	1	S	1 (.15)	2 (.15)		3 (.20)	4 (.25)	5 (.25)
Accounting skills	1	S	1 (.15)	2 (.15)	3 (.40)		4 (.30)	
Budgeting skills	1	S	1 (.20)	2 (.20)	3 (.25)		4 (.35)	
Time management skills	2	S				1 (.30)	2 (.40)	3 (.30)
Delegating skills	2	S		1 (.20)		2 (.40)	3 (.40)	
Ability to use company's accounting software	3	T						
Attention to detail	3	S		1 (.25)		2 (.25)	3 (.50)	

to a more manageable size, it can make sense to use the lowest cost assessment methods first, or those assessing candidates' abilities to perform essential job functions. It can also be a good idea to use the most valid assessment methods first, or methods that encourage candidates to self-select—that is, prompt those people who would likely drop out of the hiring process later on to drop out earlier. Some companies require candidates to visit the careers sections of their Web sites for this very purpose.

The weights to be given each assessment score are in parentheses next to each number and total 100 percent across each row.

Referring to Table 9-10, the numbers under each assessment method indicate the order in which the various assessment methods will be used to assess each characteristic. Reading across the first row, consumer focus is one of the top three characteristics relevant to internal accountants' job performance, and it will be assessed rather than trained posthire. Consumer focus is first assessed via a résumé scan, then through a phone screen. A recruiter interview, simulation performance, and hiring manager interview then further assess each candidate's customer focus. In terms of combining each of the assessment scores into one rating for each characteristic, weights are given to each assessment score (shown in parentheses next to each number) that total 100 percent for each characteristic being assessed. In this case, customer focus assessed via the résumé and phone screen will each be weighted .15, via the recruiter interview .20, via the simulation .25, and via the manager interview .25. In determining an overall candidate score that can be used to compare candidates, each characteristic is weighted based on its importance to job performance (based on the relative importance and relative time spent information about each job duty collected during the job analysis). In this case, the characteristics rated 1 in importance might each be weighted .20, those rated 2 might each be weighted .15, and the one rated 3 might be weighted .10.

SELECTING FLIGHT ATTENDANTS AT SOUTHWEST AIRLINES

Southwest Airlines wants to evaluate its flight attendant candidates for their attitudes, leadership, and fit with the company's unique culture. Rather than evaluating flight attendant candidates for a fixed set of skills or experiences, Southwest Airlines looks for the energy, humor, team spirit, and self-confidence that matches its offbeat, creative, customer-focused culture.[202] Job candidates don't just interview for a job, they audition—and the audition starts the moment they call for an application. In fact, they are being evaluated even when they think that they're not being assessed: When a recruit calls, managers jot down anything memorable about the conversation, good or bad. Recruits flown out for interviews receive special tickets that alert gate agents, flight attendants, and others to pay special attention. Employees observe whether recruits are consistently friendly to others or complaining and drinking cocktails at 9 A.M., and pass their observations on to the people department.[203] When flight attendant candidates give five-minute speeches about themselves in front of as many as 50 other recruits, managers watch the audience as closely as the speaker to see who is enthusiastically supporting their potential coworkers. Unselfish people who will support their teammates are the ones who catch Southwest's eye, not the applicants who seem bored or distracted or use the time to polish their own presentations.[204]

Southwest also applies the general principles of behavioral interviewing to identify people with the Southwest spirit. Prospective employees are often asked during an interview how they recently used their sense of humor in a work environment and how they have used humor to defuse a difficult situation. Southwest also looks for humor in the interaction people have with each other during group interviews.[205]

To assess the leadership skills of would-be flight attendants, Southwest Airlines has used a group assessment exercise called "Fallout Shelter," in which the candidates imagine they are a committee charged with rebuilding civilization after a just-declared nuclear war. The groups are given a list of 15 people from different occupations including a nurse, teacher, all-sport athlete, biochemist, and pop singer and have 10 minutes to make a unanimous decision about which seven people can remain in the only available fallout shelter. As the candidates discuss, and debate one another, each is graded on a scale ranging from "passive" to "active" to "leader."[206]

Southwest's flight attendant assessment methods not only keep turnover low but also help it execute its customer service strategy. Southwest also consistently receives the lowest number of passenger complaints in the industry.[207]

Summary

The primary goal of external candidate assessment is typically identifying the job candidates who fit the person specification for the job being filled, and to identify people who would likely be poor performers and screen them out. The assessment system should also evaluate candidates' fit with the organization, group, and supervisor and their ability to contribute to business strategy execution. This allows a firm to identify the job candidates best able to perform the open job and best able to help the company execute its business strategy and enhance its competitive advantage.

There are a variety of important goals organizations have when assessing external job candidates, including return on investment, shareholder reactions, establishing and reinforcing the firm's employer image, and complying with legal requirements by using valid assessment methods in a fair, consistent, and objective manner.

Companies can choose from many different assessment methods to assess job candidates. The choice should be based on which methods best assess the applicant characteristics or competencies identified as important during the job analysis as well as the ability of the assessment method to meet other important goals of the external assessment process. Because different methods are good at assessing different things, and differ in their cost, validity, applicant reactions, and adverse impact, it is often necessary to use more than one assessment method. Just because an assessment method results in adverse impact, if it does a good job predicting job success it may be worthwhile to investigate the usefulness of various strategies to reduce its adverse impact so that it can continue to be used.

Takeaway Points

1. A firm's external assessment goals include person-job, person-group, and person-organization fit as well as validity, return on investment, stakeholder reactions, consistency with the firm's talent philosophy and HR strategy, and establishing and reinforcing the company's employer image.
2. A wide variety of assessment methods exist, including résumés, medical tests, cognitive ability tests, job knowledge tests, simulations, and interviews. Assessment methods differ in terms of their cost, validity, how applicants react to them, usability, speed, and adverse impact.
3. The adverse impact associated with an assessment method can sometimes be reduced by targeting applicants to increase the numbers of qualified minority applicants who apply and by expanding the definition of what constitutes good job performance to

include other performance characteristics, such as people's commitment and reliability, in addition to their task performance. Also, using well-developed simulations rather than cognitive ability tests and using assessment methods with less adverse impact early in the selection process and those with greater adverse impact later in the process can also help as can banding applicants as they're assessed.
4. The assessment plan describes which assessment methods will be used to assess each of the characteristics upon which applicants will be evaluated, in what sequence the assessments will take place, and what weight each assessment will receive in determining a candidate's overall score. The importance of each characteristic to job performance is also identified, as is whether each characteristic will be evaluated or trained for after a candidate is hired.

Discussion Questions

1. When should employers reassess the assessment methods they use in hiring?
2. Discuss the advantages and disadvantages of both structured and unstructured interviews. Which would you prefer to use? Why?
3. Why go to all the trouble of sometimes costly and time-consuming assessments when there are no guarantees they will result in a successful hire?
4. What do you feel are the least effective external assessment methods? Why?
5. Do you think that it is appropriate for employers to research applicants' backgrounds? What about credit histories? Substantiate your answer.

Exercises

1. *Strategy Exercise:* There are many consulting firms that specialize in candidate assessment and selection.

   Johnson & Johnson is the world's most comprehensive and broadly based manufacturer of health care products. J&J pursues a business strategy of serving the consumer, pharmaceutical, and medical devices and diagnostics markets with a focus on research-based, technology-driven products.[208] The company's credo prioritizes its responsibilities to its customers, employees, the community, and its stockholders in that order. Go to www.jnj.com and learn more about Johnson & Johnson's credo. Then answer the following questions.

   a. In what ways does J&J's focus on its credo and hiring people who fit its credo help the company perform well?
   b. Use the Internet to identify at least five assessment tools that could help J&J identify applicants who fit its credo. Identify which ones you would recommend to J&J and describe why.

2. *Develop Your Skills Exercise:* This chapter's Develop Your Skills feature gave you some tips for writing an online résumé.

   Using this information, write your own résumé that could be posted online. Exchange résumés with two classmates and give each other feedback on how to improve each other's résumés.

3. *Opening Vignette Exercise:* Southwest Airlines believes that it needs employees with creativity, humor, and the ability to work well with others to successfully execute its differentiation strategy. This chapter's opening vignette provided some information about how the company currently assesses job candidates on these dimensions. Reread the opening vignette and its conclusion, and answer the following questions in a group of three to five students. Be prepared to share your answers with the class.

   a. Do you think it's appropriate for Southwest Airlines to assess creativity and humor during its assessment process?
   b. How would you react if you went through Southwest's assessment process? Identify some things that you would both like and dislike and explain why.
   c. Identify two other assessment methods you think Southwest could use to assess applicants' humor and creativity.

CASE STUDY

World War II Spy Assessment for the Office of Strategic Services (OSS)

Thank you to Joe McCune of Rutgers University for allowing us to provide this exercise.

ROLE

It is 1940, and you are a selection specialist assigned to the Office of Strategic Services (OSS). Your assignment is to work as a team with three to four other classmates to develop a selection system to "identify operatives who could successfully undertake hazardous intelligence-gathering missions behind enemy lines." In other words, you are to select spies who will work in Japan, Italy, or Germany.

CHALLENGES

1. You have been given limited job information, no job description, KSAOs, competencies, or performance criteria related to the position.
2. Since the advertisements for the job must be vague to maintain secrecy, they will attract undesirable candidates, including people who are chronically bored, pathologically adventuresome, neurotically attracted to danger, and so forth. Therefore, you will need to include a process to weed out such individuals.

3. You have no time to validate your assessment methods—they need to be implemented immediately.

TASK

In the time allowed, identify the important characteristics (aptitudes, competencies, and so forth) a person needs to be a spy and develop three tests and simulations that will help you identify successful spies. The selection procedure will occur over a three-day period in a private facility (Station S in Virginia).

ASSIGNMENT

1. Create a list of important characteristics discussed previously. Remember, in 1940, there were no computers, video phones, or satellites. Spies needed to do things like access locked buildings, identify possible informants, and persuade them to provide useful information about enemy actions.
2. Determine the *three* most important qualities that an applicant must possess.
3. Develop procedures to test for each of those characteristics during the three-day procedure at Station S.
4. Describe how you will evaluate the effectiveness of your selection system.

Semester-Long Active Learning Project

Finish the assignment for Chapter 8. Be sure to justify your recommendations and use concrete examples along with scoring keys to highlight the specific methods for selecting employees. Create a formal assessment plan linking your assessment methods to the characteristics being assessed.

Case Study Assignment: Strategic Staffing at Chern's

See the appendix at the book of the book for this chapter's Case Study Assignment.

Endnotes

1. Pfeffer, J., *The Human Equation: Building Profits by Putting People First*, Boston, MA: Harvard Business School Press, 1998.
2. Freiberg, K., and Freiberg, J., *Nuts! Southwest Airlines' Crazy Recipe for Business and Personal Success*, Austin, TX: Bard Press, 1996.
3. "The Mission of Southwest Airlines," www.southwest.com/about_swa/mission.html. Accessed September 29, 2006.
4. Freiberg and Freiberg, *Nuts! Southwest Airlines' Crazy Recipe for Business and Personal Success.*
5. Kelley, R., and Caplan, J., "How Bell Labs Create Star Performers," *Harvard Business Review* (July–August 1993): 128–139; DeMarco, T., and Lister, T., *Peopleware: Productive Projects and Teams*, New York: Dorset House Publishing Company, 1987: 44.
6. Hansen, F., "Tiny Tweaks Improve Testing Results," *Workforce Management Online*, February 2010, http://www.workforce.com/archive/feature/27/01/93/index.php. Accessed March 24, 2010.
7. Ibid.
8. Palmeri, C., "The Fastest Drill in the West," *BusinessWeek*, October 24, 2005: 86–88.
9. Poe, A. C., "Graduate Work: Behavioral Interviewing Can Tell You If an Applicant Just out of College Has Traits Needed for the Job," *HR Magazine*, 48, 10 (October 2003), www.shrm.org/hrmagazine/articles/1003/1003poe.asp. Accessed October 3, 2006.
10. Rosensweig, D., "What I Know Now," *Fast Company*, February 2005: 96.
11. Overman, S., "With Economic Recovery Predicted, Companies Should Sharpen Recruiting Skills Now," *Society for Human Resource Management*, November 24, 2003, www.shrm.org/hrnews_ published/archives/CMS_006419. Accessed November 15, 2004.
12. Carbonara, P., "Hire for Attitude, Train for Skill," *Fast Company*, August 1996, 4: 73.
13. Hansen, F., "Company's Customized Test Goes Beyond Job Skills," *Workforce Management Online*, March 2010. Available online at: http://www.workforce.com/archive/feature/27/08/35/index.php. Accessed March 26, 2010.
14. For a more extensive discussion see Kristof-Brown, A. L., Zimmerman, R. D., and Johnson, E. C., "Consequences of Individuals' Fit at Work: A Meta-Analysis of Person-Job, Person-Organization, Person-Group, and Person-Supervisor Fit," *Personnel Psychology*, 58 (2005): 281–342.
15. Adapted from Edwards, J. R., "Person-Job Fit: A Conceptual Integration, Literature Review, and Methodological Critique," In C. L. Cooper and I. T. Robertson (eds.), *International Review of Industrial and Organizational Psychology*, 6, New York: Wiley, 1991: 283–357.
16. Caldwell, D. F., and O'Reilly, C.A., "Measuring Person-Job Fit Within a Profile Comparison Process," *Journal of Applied Psychology*, 75 (1990): 648–657; Edwards, "Person-Job Fit."
17. Delaney, K. J., "Google Adjusts Hiring Process as Needs Grow," *Wall Street Journal*, October 23, 2006: B1.
18. Kristof-Brown, Zimmerman, and Johnson, "Consequences of Individuals' Fit at Work."
19. Ibid.
20. Werbel, J. D., and Gilliland, S. W., "Person-Environment Fit in the Selection Process," In G. R. Ferris (ed.), *Research in Personnel and Human Resource Management*, 17, Stamford, CT: JAI Press, 1999: 209-243.
21. Sinton, P., "Teamwork the Name of the Game for Ideo," *San Francisco Chronicle*, February 23, 2000, www.sfgate.com/cgi-bin/article.cgi?file=/chronicle/archive/2000/02/23/BU3 9355.DTL.
22. Kristof, A. L., "Person-Organization Fit: An Integrative Review of its Conceptualizations, Measurement, and Implications," *Personnel Psychology*, 49 (1996): 1–50; Kristof, A. L., "Perceived Applicant Fit: Distinguishing Between Recruiters' Perceptions of Person-Job and Person-Organization Fit," *Personnel Psychology*, 53 (2000): 643–671.
23. Kristof-Brown, Zimmerman, and Johnson, "Consequences of Individuals' Fit at Work."
24. O'Reilly, C. A. III, Chatman, J., and Caldwell, D. V., "People and Organizational Culture: A Profile Comparison Approach to Assessing Person-Organization Fit," *Academy of Management Journal*, 34 (1991): 487–516.
25. Bryant, A., "Connecting the Dots Isn't Enough," *The New York Times*, July 18, 2009, http://www.nytimes.com/ 2009/07/19/business/19corner.html?_r=1. Accessed March 10, 2010.
26. Ashford, S. J., and Taylor, M. S., "Adaptations to Work Transitions: An Integrative Approach," In G. Ferris and K. Rowland (eds.), *Research in Personnel and Human Resources Management*, 8 (1990): 1–39.
27. www.jnj.com.
28. Michaels, L., "The HR Side of Competitive Advantage," *Thunderbird Magazine*, 2002.
29. Holland, J. L., *Making Vocational Choices: A Theory of Vocation Personalities and Work Environments*, Upper Saddle River, NJ: Prentice-Hall, 1985.
30. Muchinsky, P. M., and Monahan, C. J., "What Is Person-Environment Congruence? Supplementary Versus Complementary

Models of Fit," *Journal of Vocational Behavior*, 31 (1987): 268–277.

31. Ibid.

32. Anders, G., "Talent Bank," *Fast Company*, June 2000: 94.

33. Muchinsky and Monahan, "What Is Person-Environment Congruence?"

34. Scott, M., "Beckham Drives Madrid to Top of Money League," *The Guardian*, February 16, 2006, football. guardian. co.uk/News_Story/0,,1710792,00.html. Accessed April 27, 2007; Eichelberger, C., "Beckham Sparks $13.3 Million in Sales for Galaxy, Covers Salary," April 19, 2007, Bloomberg, www.bloomberg.com/apps/news?pid=20601079&refer=amsports&sid=a1Z1CV_s_BdI. Accessed April 27, 2007.

35. McCarthy, J., Crabluik, C., and Blake, J.,"Progression through the Ranks: Assessing Employee Reactions to High-Stakes Employment Testing," *Personnel Psychology*, 62 (2009): 793–832.

36. Steele, C. M., and Aronson, J., "Stereotype Threat and the Intellectual Test Performance of African Americans," *Journal of Personality and Social Psychology*, 69 (1995): 797–811.

37. Arvey, R. D., Strickland, W., Drauden, G., and Martin, C., "Motivational Components of Test Taking," *Personnel Psychology*, 43 (1990): 695–716; Chan, D., Schmitt, N., DeShon, R. P., Clause, C. S., and Delbridge, K., "Reactions to Cognitive Ability Tests: The Relationships between Race, Test Performance, Face Validity Perceptions, and Test-Taking Motivation," *Journal of Applied Psychology*, 82 (1997): 300–310; Ployhart, R. E., Ziegert, J. C., McFarland, L. A., "Understanding Racial Differences on Cognitive Ability Tests in Selection Contexts: An Integration of Stereotype Threat and Applicant Reactions Research," *Human Performance*, 16, 3 (2003): 231–259.

38. Schmit, M. J., and Ryan, A. M., "Applicant Withdrawal: The Role of Test-Taking Attitudes and Racial Differences," *Personnel Psychology*, 50, 4 (1997): 855–876.

39. Judge, T. A., and Watanabe, S., "Is the Past Prologue? A Test of Ghiselli's Hobo Syndrome," *Journal of Management*, 21 (1995): 211–229.

40. Adapted from Handler, C., and Hunt, S., "Estimating the Financial Value of Staffing Assessment Tools," *Workforce Online*, March 2003, www.workforce.com/archive/article/23/40/88.ph. Accessed October 2, 2006.

41. Minton-Eversole, T., "Number of Employers Doesn't Always Equate to Hiring Advantage," *Society for Human Resource Management Online*, December 2006, www.shrm.org/ema/news_published/CMS_019470.as. Accessed January 22, 2007.

42. Tyler, K., "Put Applicants' Skills to the Test," *HR Magazine*, January 2000: 75–77.

43. *Griggs v. Duke Power Co.*, 401 U.S. 424 (1971).

44. See www.dol.gov/dol/allcfr/Title_41/Part_60-3/toc.htm. Accessed February 7, 2007.

45. Equal Employment Opportunity Commission, "Uniform Employee Selection Guidelines Interpretation and Clarification (Questions and Answers)," www.uniformguidelines.com/questionandanswers.html. Accessed October 24, 2006.

46. Uniform Guideline 14C(4), 43 Fed. Reg. 38, 302 (1978).

47. www.dol.gov/dol/allcfr/Title_41/Part_60-3/toc.htm.

48. http://sioorg/_Principles/principlesdefault.aspx.

49. www.apa.org/science/standards.html.

50. Hansen, F., "Recruiting on the Right Side of the Law," *Workforce Management Online*, May 2006, www.workforce.com/section/06/feature/24/38/12/. Accessed June 30, 2006.

51. Ibid.

52. Source for validity coefficients: Schmidt, F. L., and Hunter, J. E., "The Validity and Utility of Selection Methods in Personnel Psychology: Practical and Theoretical Implications of 85 Years of Research Findings," *Psychological Bulletin*, 124 (1998): 262–274; Situational judgment test validity is from McDaniel, M. A., Morgeson, F. P., Finnegan, E. B., Campion, M. A., and Braverman, E. P., "Use of Situational Judgment Tests to Predict Job Performance: A Clarification of the Literature," *Journal of Applied Psychology*, 86 (2001): 730–740; Biodata validity is from Reilly, R. R., and Chao, G. T., "Validity and Fairness of Some Alternative Employee Selection Procedures," *Personnel Psychology*, 35 (1982): 1–62; work sample validity is from Roth, P. L., Bobko, P., McFarland, L. A., "A Meta-Analytic Analysis of Work Sample Test Validity: Updating and Integrating Some Classic Literature," *Personnel Psychology*, 58, 4 (2005): 1009-1037; for structured and unstructured interviews also from McDaniel, M. A., Whetzel, D. L., Schmidt, F. L., and Maurer, S. D., "The Validity of Employment Interviews: A Comprehensive Review and Meta-Analysis," *Journal of Applied Psychology*, 79 (1994): 599-616; Weisner, W. H., and Cronshaw, S. F., "A Meta-Analytic Investigation of the Impact of Interview Format and Degree of Structure on the Validity of the Employment Interview," *Journal of Occupational Psychology*, 61 (1988): 275–290.

53. Based in part on Hausknecht, J. P., Day, D. V., and Thomas, S. C., "Applicant Reactions to Selection Procedures: An Updated Model and Meta-Analysis," *Personnel Psychology*, 57, 3 (2004): 639-683; Coyne, I., and Bartram, D., "Assessing the Effectiveness of Integrity Tests: A Review," *International Journal of Testing*, 2 (2002): 15–34.

54. From Ryan, A. M., and Tippins, N. T., "Attracting and Selecting: What Psychological Research Tells Us," *Human Resource Management,* 43 (2004): 305–318.

55. Sahadi, J., "Top 5 Résumé Lies," CNN/Money, December 9, 2004, http://money.cnn.com/2004/11/22/pf/resume_lies/index.htm. Accessed April 27, 2007.

56. See, e.g., Marquez, J., "RadioShack Gaffe Show Need to Screen Current Employees," *Workforce Management Online*, March 14, 2006, www.workforce.com/section/00/article/24/29/52.html. Accessed October 4, 2006.

57. Fisher, A., "10 Dumbest Résumé Blunders," *Fortune*, April 25, 2007, http://money.cnn.com/ 2007/04/25/news/economy/resume.blunders.fortune/index.htm?postversion=2007042510. Accessed April 25, 2007; "Résumé Quotations," Offshore-environment.com, 2007, www.offshore-environment.com/takebreak.html. Accessed April 25, 2007; Robert Half International, "Real-Life Blunders to Avoid," Yahoo! Hotjobs, 2007, http://hotjobs.yahoo.com/jobseeker/tools/ept/careerArticles Post.html?post=57. Accessed April 25, 2007.

58. Martinez, M., "Screening for Quality on the Web," *Employment Management Today*, 9, 1 (Winter 2004), www.shrm.org/ema/emt/articles/2004/winter04cover.as. Accessed October 4, 2006.

59. Marquez, J., "When Brand Alone Isn't Enough," *Workforce Management*, March 13, 2006: 1, 39-41, www.workforce.com/archive/feature/24/29/58/index.php?ht=mcdonald%20s%20 mcdonald%20s. Accessed July 10, 2006.

60. Martinez, "Screening for Quality on the Web."

61. Ibid.

62. England, G. W., *Development and Use of Weighted Application Blanks*, Dubuque, Iowa: W.M.C. Brown, 1961.

63. MacMillan, D., "The Art of the Online Résumé," *BusinessWeek*, May 7, 2007: 86; Jobweb.com, "More Tips for Navigating the Online Application Process," www.jobweb.com /resources/ library/Interviews/More_Tips_for_N_280_1.htm. Accessed May 2, 2007; Job-hunt.org, "Your CyberSafe Résumé," www. job-hunt.org/resumecybersafe.shtml. Accessed May 2, 2007; Job-hunt.org, "Developing Key Words," www. job-hunt.org/ resumekeywords.shtml. Accessed May 2, 2007.

64. Kaak, S. R., "The Weighted Application Blank," *Cornell Hotel and Restaurant Administration Quarterly*, 39, 2 (1998): 18–24.

65. Dunnette, M. D., and Maetzold, J., "Use of a Weighted Application Blank in Hiring Seasoned Employees," *Journal of Applied Psychology*, 35 (1955): 308–310.

66. Segal, S. M., Busse, T. V., and Mansfield, R. S., "The Relationship of Scientific Creativity in the Biological Sciences to Predoctoral Accomplishments and Experiences," *American Educational Research Journal*, 17, 4 (Winter 1980): 491–502.

67. Goldsmith, D. B, "The Use of the Personal History Blank as a Salesmanship Test," *Journal of Applied Psychology*, 6 (1922): 149–155.

68. For more information about biodata, see Eberhardt, B. J., and Muchinsky, P. M., "Biodata Determinants of Vocational Typology: An Integration of Two Paradigms," *Journal of Applied Psychology*, 67 (1982): 714–727.

69. Mount, M. K., Witt, L. A., and Barrick, M. R., "Incremental Validity of Empirically Keyed Biodata Scales over GMA and the Five Factor Personality Constructs," *Personnel Psychology*, 53, 2 (2000): 299–323.

70. See West, J., and Karas, M., "Biodata: Meeting Clients' Needs for a Better Way of Recruiting Entry-Level Staff," *International Journal of Selection and Assessment*, 7, 2 (1999): 126–131.

71. Stricker, L. J., and Rock, D. A., "Assessing Leadership Potential with a Biographical Measure of Personality Traits," *International Journal of Selection and Assessment*, 6, 3 (1998): 164–184.

72. Mael, F. A., "A Conceptual Rationale for the Domain and Attributes of Biodata Items," *Personnel Psychology*, 44 (1991): 763–927.

73. Reilly, R.R., and Chao, G.T., "Validity and Fairness of Some Alternative Employee Selection Procedures."; Schmitt et al., "Meta-Analyses of Validity Studies Published Between 1964 and 1982 and the Investigation of Study Differences."; Hunter and Hunter, "Validity and Utility of Alternative Predictors of Job Performance."; Snell et al., "Adolescent Life Experiences as Predictors of Occupational Attainment."

74. Phillips and Gully, "Fairness Reactions to Personnel Selection Techniques in Singapore and the United States."

75. Reilly, R. R. ,and Chao, G. T., "Validity and Fairness of Some Alternative Employee Selection Procedures."

76. Eberhardt and Muchinsky, "Biodata Determinants of Vocational Typology."

77. Pannone, R. D., "Predicting Test Performance: A Content Valid Approach to Screening Applicants," *Personnel Psychology*, 37 (1984): 507–514.

78. Pannone, R. D., "Blue Collar Selection," In G. S. Stokes, M. D. Mumford, and W. A. Owens (eds.), *Biodata Handbook*, Palo Alto, CA: CPP Books, 1994: 261–274.

79. Wilkinson, L. J., "Generalizable Biodata? An Application to the Vocational Interests of Managers," *Journal of Occupational and Organizational Psychology*, 70 (1997): 49-60.

80. Hansell, S., "Google Answer to Filling Jobs Is an Algorithm," *New York Times*, January 3, 2007, http://query.nytimes.com/gst/ fullpage.html?res=9F06E7DA1730F930A35752C0A9619C8B 63&sec=&spon=&pagewanted=1. Accessed May 1, 2007.

81. Frase-Blunt, M., "Dialing for Candidates," *HR Magazine*, April 2005: 78–82.

82. Wells, S. J., "Too Good to Hire?" *HR Magazine*, October 2004: 48–54.

83. Schmidt, F. L., and Hunter, J. E., "Employment Testing: Old Theories and New Research Findings," *American Psychologist*, 36 (1981): 1128–1137; Schmidt and Hunter, "The Validity and Utility of Selection Methods in Personnel Psychology."

84. Hunter, J. E., "Cognitive Ability, Cognitive Aptitudes, Job Knowledge, and Job Performance," *Journal of Vocational Behavior*, 29, 3 (1986): 340–362; Murphy, K., "Is the Relationship Between Cognitive Ability and Job Performance Stable Over Time?" *Human Performance*, 2 (1989): 183–200; Ree, M. J., and Earles, J. A., "Intelligence Is the Best Predictor of Job Performance," *Current Directions in Psychological Science*, 1 (1992): 86–89.

85. Conlin, M., "Champions of Innovation," *IN*, June 2006: 18–26.

86. Walker, S., "The NFL's Smartest Team," *Wall Street Journal Online*, September 30, 2005, http://online.wsj.com/article_ email/ SB112804210724556355-IRjf4NjlaZ 4n56rZH2JaqWHm4 .html. Accessed May 4, 2007.

87. Gully, S. M., Payne, S. C., and Koles, K. L. K, "The Impact of Error Training and Individual Differences on Training Outcomes: An Attribute-Treatment Interaction Perspective," *Journal of Applied Psychology*, 87 (2002): 143–155.

88. Outtz, J. L., "The Role of Cognitive Ability Tests in Employment Selection," *Human Performance*, 15 (2002): 161–171.

89. Hough, L., Oswald, F. L., and Ployhart, R. E., "Determinants, Detection and Amelioration of Adverse Impact in Personnel Selection Procedures: Issues, Evidence and Lessons Learnt," *International Journal of Selection and Assessment*, 9, 1/2 (2001): 152–194.

90. Smither, J. W., Reilly, R. R., Millsap, R. E., Pearlman, K., and Stoffey, R. W., "Applicant Reactions to Selection Procedures," *Personnel Psychology*, 46 (1993): 49-76.

91. Roth, P. L., Bevier, C. A., Bobko, P., Switzer, F. S., and Tyler, P., "Ethnic Group Differences in Cognitive Ability in Employment and Educational Settings: A Meta-Analysis," *Personnel Psychology*, 54, 2 (2001): 297–330; Murphy, K. R., "Can Conflicting Perspectives on the Role of 'g' in Personnel Selection Be Resolved?" *Human Performance*, 15 (2002): 173–186; Murphy, K. R., Cronin, B. E., and Tam, A. P., "Controversy and Consensus Regarding Use of Cognitive Ability Testing in Organizations," *Journal of Applied Psychology*, 88 (2003): 660–671.

92. Outtz, "The Role of Cognitive Ability Tests in Employment Selection."

93. Pfeffer, J., "Why Résumés are Just One Piece of the Puzzle," *Business 2.0*, December 1, 2005, http://money.cnn.com/ magazines/business2/business2_archive/2005/12/01/8364603/ index.htm. Accessed June 27, 2006.

94. Guion, R. M., and Gottier, R. F., "Validity of Personality Measures in Personnel Selection," *Personnel Psychology*, 18 (1965): 135–164; Mischel, W., *Personality and Assessment*, New York: Wiley, 1968; Davis-Blake, A., and Pfeffer, J., "Just a Mirage—The Search for Dispositional Effects in Organizational Research," *Academy of Management Review*, 14 (1989): 385–400.

95. O'Meara, D. P., "Personality Tests Raise Questions of Legality and Effectiveness," *HR Magazine*, January 1994, http://findarticles.com/p/articles/mi_m3495/is_n1_v39/ai_15162186/pg_1. Accessed May 4, 2007.

96. See Morgeson, F. P., Campion, M. A., Dipboye, R. L., Hollenbeck, J. R., Murphy, K., and Schmit, N., "Reconsidering the Use of Personality Tests in Personnel Selection Contexts," *Personnel Psychology*, 60 (2007): 683–729.

97. Mount, M. K., and Barrick, M. R., "The Big Five Personality Dimensions: Implications for Research and Practice in Human Resources Management," In G. R. Ferris (ed.), *Research in Personnel and Human Resources Management*, 13 (1995), Greenwich, CT: JAI Press: 153–200.

98. Vinchur, A. J., Schippmann, J. S., Switzer, F. A., and Roth, P. L., "A Meta-Analysis of the Predictors of Job Performance for Salespeople," *Journal of Applied Psychology*, 83 (1998): 586–597.

99. Barrick, M. R., and Mount, M. K., "The Big Five Personality Dimensions and Job Performance: A Meta-Analysis," *Personnel Psychology*, 44 (1991): 1–26.

100. Vinchur, A. J., Schippmann, J. S., and Switzer, F. S. III., "A Meta-Analysis of the Predictors of Job Performance for Salespeople," *Journal of Applied Psychology*, 83: 586–597; Judge, T. A., and Bono, J. E., "Relationship of Core Self-Evaluation Traits—Self-Esteem, Generalized Self-Efficacy, Locus of Control, and Emotional Stability—With Job Satisfaction and Job Performance: A Meta-Analysis," *Journal of Applied Psychology*, 86 (2001): 80–92.

101. Mount, M. K., Barrick, M. R., and Stewart, G. L., "Five-Factor Model of Personality and Performance in Jobs Involving Interpersonal Interactions," *Human Performance*, 11 (1998): 145–165.

102. Ibid.

103. Jordan, J., and Cartwright, S., "Selecting Expatriate Managers: Key Traits and Competencies," *Leadership and Organization Development Journal*, 19 (April 1998): 89-96.

104. Barrick, M. R., and Mount, M. K., "Yes, Personality Matters: Moving on to More Important Matters," *Human Performance*, 18, 4 (2005): 359-372.

105. Schmidt and Hunter, "The Validity and Utility of Selection Methods in Personnel Psychology."

106. Barrick, M. R., Mount, M. K., and Judge, T. A., "The FFM Personality Dimensions and Job Performance: Meta-Analysis of Meta-Analyses," *International Journal of Selection and Assessment*, 9 (2001): 9-30.

107. Ibid.

108. Mount, M. K., Barrick, M. R., and Stewart, G. L., "Personality Predictors of Performance in Jobs Involving Interaction with Others," *Human Performance*, 11 (1998): 145–166.

109. George, J. M., and Zhou, J., "When Openness to Experience and Conscientiousness Are Related to Creative Behavior: An Interactional Approach," *Journal of Applied Psychology*, 86 (2001): 513–524; LePine, J. A., Colquitt, J. A., and Erez, A., "Adaptability to Changing Task Contexts: Effects of General Cognitive Ability, Conscientiousness, and Openness to Experience," *Personnel Psychology*, 53 (2000): 563–593.

110. Barrick and Mount, "Yes, Personality Matters."

111. Costa, P. T., Jr., and McCrae, R. R., "Four Ways Five Factors Are Basic," *Personality and Individual Differences*, 13 (1992): 653–665.

112. Ones, D. S., and Viswesvaran, C., "Bandwidth-Fidelity Dilemma in Personality Measurement for Personnel Selection," *Journal of Organizational Behavior*, 17 (1996): 609-626.

113. Mount and Barrick, "The Big Five Personality Dimensions."

114. Schneider, R. J., Hough, L. M., and Dunnette, M. D., "Broadsided by Broda Traits: How to Sink Science in Five Dimensions or Less," *Journal of Organizational Behavior*, 17, 6 (1996): 639-655.

115. Frei, R. L., and McDaniel, M. A., "Validity of Customer Service Measures in Personnel Selection: A Review of Criterion and Construct Evidence," *Human Performance*, 11, 1 (1998): 1–27.

116. Morgeson, F. P., Campion, M. A., Dipboye, R. L., Hollenbeck, J. R., Murphy, K., and Schmitt, N., "Reconsidering the Use of Personality Tests in Personnel Selection Contexts," *Personnel Psychology*, 60 (2007): 683–729.

117. Ellingson, J. E., Smith, D. B., and Sackett, P. R., "Investigating the Influence of Social Desirability on Personality Factor Structure," *Journal of Applied Psychology*, 86 (2001): 122–133; Smith, D. B., and Ellingson, J. E., "Substance Versus Style: A New Look at Social Desirability in Motivating Contexts," *Journal of Applied Psychology*, 87 (2002): 211–219.

118. See www.unl.edu/buros.

119. Rosse, J. G., Miller, J. L., and Ringer, R. C., "The Deterrent Value of Drug and Integrity Testing," *Journal of Business and Psychology*, 10, 4 (1996): 477–485.

120. See *Saroka v. Dayton Hudson*, 235 Cal. A 3d 654 (1991).

121. See "Another Defeat for MMPI Psychological Test," *FairTest Examiner*, Summer 2000, www.fairtest.org/examarts/Summer%2000/Defeat%20for%20 MMPI %20Psych%20Test.html. Accessed May 2, 2007.

122. Canoni, J. D., "Widely Used Psychological Test Found to Violate ADA," *Nixon Peabody LLP Employment Law Alert*, June 16, 2005, www.nixonpeabody.com/linked_media/publications/ELA_06162005.pdf#search=%22psychological%20testing%20ada%22. Accessed October 11, 2006.

123. See Ruiz, G., "Staying Out of Legal Hot Water While Conducting Background Checks," *Workforce Management Online*, June 2006, www.workforce.com/section/06/feature/24/39/38/. Accessed April 30, 2007.

124. Woyke, E., "Attention, Shoplifters," *BusinessWeek Online*, September 11, 2006, www.businessweek.com/magazine/content/06_37/b4000401.htm?chan=tc&campaign_id=bier_tcst0. Accessed October 6, 2006.

125. See Sackett, P. R., and Wanek, J. E., "New Developments in the Use of Measures of Honesty, Integrity, Conscientiousness, Dependability, Trustworthiness, and Reliability for Personnel Selection," *Personnel Psychology*, 49 (1996): 787–829; Goldberg, J. R., Grenier, R. M., Guion, L. B., Sechrest, L. B., and Wing, H., *Questionnaires Used in the Prediction of Trustworthiness in Pre-Employment Selection Decisions: An APA Task Force Report*, Washington, DC: American Psychological Association, 1991.

126. See Ryan, A. M., and Sackett, P. R., "Preemployment Honesty Testing: Fakability, Reactions of Test Takers, and Company Image," *Journal of Business and Psychology*, 1 (1987): 248–256; Cunningham, M. R., Wong, D.T., and Barbee, A. P., "Self-Presentation Dynamics on Overt Integrity Tests: Experimental Studies of the Reid Report," *Journal of Applied Psychology*, 79 (1994): 643–658.

127. Ones, D. S., Viswesvaran, C., and Schmidt, F. L., "Comprehensive Meta-Analysis of Integrity Test Validities: Findings and Implications for Personnel Selection and Theories of Job Performance," *Journal of Applied Psychology*, 78 (1993): 679-703.

128. Ibid.

129. Phillips and Gully, "Fairness Reactions to Personnel Selection Techniques in Singapore and the United States."; Steiner, D. D.,

and Gilliland, S. W., "Fairness Reactions to Personnel Selection Techniques in France and the United States," *Journal of Applied Psychology*, 81 (1996): 134–141.

130. Rosse, Miller, and Ringer, "The Deterrent Value of Drug and Integrity Testing."

131. Arnold, D. W., and Jones, J. W., "Who the Devil's Applying Now?" Crimcheck.com, www.crimcheck.com/employment_testing.htm. Accessed May 3, 2007.

132. Goldberg, L. R., Grenier, J. R., Guion, R. M., Sechrest, L. B., and Wing, H., *Questionnaires Used in the Prediction of Trustworthiness in Pre-Employment Selection Decisions: An APA Task Force Report*. Available online at: http://www.egad connection .org/Questionnaire%20used%20in%20the%20prediction%20of 20trustworthiness%20in%20preemployment%20selection%20 decisons.pdf. Accessed September 23, 2010.

133. Townsend, I W., "Is Integrity Testing Useful. The Value of Integrity Tests in the Employment Process," *HR Magazine*, July 1992, http://findarticles.com/p/articles/mi_m3495/is_n7_v37/ ai_12787161. Accessed May 3, 2007.

134. Hansen, F., "Company's Customized Test Goes Beyond Job Skills," *Workforce Management Online*, March 2010. Available online at: http://www.workforce.com/archive/feature/27/08/35/ index.php. Accessed March 26, 2010.

135. U.S. Department of Labor, "Employee Polygraph Protection Act of 1988 (EPPA)," *Employment Law Guide*, www.dol.gov/ compliance/guide/eppa.htm. Accessed October 9, 2006.

136. Dye, D. M., Reck. M., and McDaniel, M. A., "The Validity of Job Knowledge Measures," *International Journal of Selection and Assessment*, 1 (1993): 153–157.

137. Terpstra, D. E., and Rozell, E. J., "The Relationship of Staffing Practices to Organizational Level Measures of Performance," *Personnel Psychology*, 46, 1 (1993): 27–48.

138. Shaw, J. D., Delery, J. E., Jenkins, G. D. Jr., and Gupta, N., "An Organization-level Analysis of Voluntary and Involuntary Turnover," *Academy of Management Journal*, 41, 5 (1998): 511–525.

139. Ployhart, R. E., Schneider, B., and Schmitt, N., *Staffing Organizations: Contemporary Practice and Theory* (3rd ed.), Mahwah, NJ: Lawrence Erlbaum, 2006.

140. Christian, M. S., Edwards, B. D., and Bradley, J. C., "Situational Judgment Tests: Constructs Assessed and a Meta-analysis of Their Criterion-related Validities," *Personnel Psychology*, 63, 1 (2010): 83–117; Kristof-Brown, A. L., Zimmerman, R. D., and Johnson, E. C., "Consequences of Individual's Fit at Work: A Meta-analysis of Person-job, Person-organization, Person-group, and Person-supervisor Fit," *Personnel Psychology*, 58 (2005): 281–342; McDaniel, M. A., Whetzel, D. L., Schmidt, F. L., and Maurer, S. D.,"The Validity of Employment Interviews: A Comprehensive Review and Meta-analysis," *Journal of Applied Psychology*, 79 (1994): 599-616.

141. Steiner and Gilliland, "Fairness Reactions to Personnel Selection Techniques in France and the United States."; Phillips and Gully, "Fairness Reactions to Personnel Selection Techniques in Singapore and the United States."

142. Carbonara, "Hire for Attitude, Train for Skill."

143. Barber, A. E., Hollenbeck, J. R., Tower, S. L., and Phillips, J. M., "The Effects of Interview Focus on Recruitment Effectiveness: A Field Experiment," *Journal of Applied Psychology*, 79 (1994): 886–896.

144. Pursell, E. D., Campion, M. A., and Gaylord, S. R., "Structured Interviewing: Avoiding Selection Problems," *Personnel Journal*, 59, 11 (1980): 907–912.

145. Christian, M. S., Edwards, B. D., and Bradley, J. C., "Situational Judgment Tests: Constructs Assessed and a Meta-analysis of Their Criterion-related Validities," *Personnel Psychology*, 63, 1 (2010): 83–117.

146. Oliphant, G. C., Hansen, K., and Oliphant, B. J., "Predictive Validity of a Behavioral Interview Technique," *Marketing Management Journal*, 18, 2 (2008): 93–105.

147. Pulakos, E. D., and Schmitt, N., "An Evaluation of Two Strategies for Reducing Adverse Impact and Their Effects on Criterion-related Validity," *Human Performance*, 9, 3 (1996), 241–258.

148. Pettersen, N. and Durivage, A., *The Structured Interview*, Quebec, CA: Presses de l'Universite du Quebec, 2008; Campion, M. A., Palmer, D. K., and Campion, J. E., "A Review of Structure in the Selection Interview," *Personnel Psychology*, 50, 3 (1997): 655–702.

149. Williamson, L. G., Campion, J. E., Malos, S. B., Roehling, M. V., and Campion, M. A., "Employment Interview on Trial: Linking Interview Structure with Litigation Outcomes," *Journal of Applied Psychology*, 82, 6 (1997): 900–912.

150. Cesare, S. J., "Subjective Judgement and the Selection Interview: A Methodological Review," *Public Personal Management*, 25 (1996): 291–306; Campion, M. A., Palmer, D. K., and Campion, J. E., "A Review of Structure in the Selection Interview," *Personnel Psychology*, 50, 3 (1997): 655–702.

151. United States Office of Personnel Management., *Structured Interviews: A Practical Guide*, Washington, D. C.: U.S. Office of Personnel Management, 2008, 15.

152. Fitzwater, T. L., *Behavior-Based Interviewing: Selecting the Right Person for the Job*, Menlo Park, CA: Crisp Learning, 2000.

153. "Recruiting, Selecting and Training for Success," *The Times 100*, www.thetimes100.co.uk/case_study.php?cID=28&csID= 194&pID=1. Accessed July 10, 2006.

154. Campion, M. A., Palmer, D. K., and Campion, J. E., "A Review of Structure in the Selection Interview," *Personnel Psychology*, 50, 3 (1997): 655–702; McDaniel, M. A., Whetzel, D. L., Schmidt, F. L., and Maurer, S. D., "The Validity of Employment Interviews: A Comprehensive Review and Meta-analysis," *Journal of Applied Psychology*, 79 (1994): 599-616; Salgado, J. F., and Moscoso, S., "Comprehensive Meta-analysis of the Construct Validity of the Employment Interview,"*European Journal of Work and Organizational Psychology*, 11 (2002):299-324; Wiesner, W. H., and Cronshaw, S. F., "A Meta-analytic Investigation of the Impact of Interview Format and Degree of Structure on the Validity of the Employment Interview," *Journal of Applied Psychology*, 61 (1988): 275–290.

155. Kreitner, R., and Kinicki, A., *Organizational Behavior* (8th ed.), Burr Ridge, ILL: McGraw-Hill/Irwin, 2007.

156. Oliphant, G. C., Hansen, K., and Oliphant, B. J., "Predictive Validity of a Behavioral Interview Technique," *Marketing Management Journal*, 18, 2 (2008): 93–105.

157. Bragger, J. D., Jutcher, E., Morgan, J., and Firth, P., "The Effects of the Structured Interview on Reducing Biases Against Pregnant Job Applicants," *Sex Roles*, 46 (2002): 215–226; Brecher, E., Bragger, J., and Kutcher, E., "The Structured Interview: Reducing Biases toward Job Applicants with Physical Disabilities," *Employee Responsibilities and Rights Journal*, 18 (2006): 155–170.

158. Barrick, M. R., Shaffer, J. A., and DeGrassi, S. W., "What You See May Not Be What You Get: Relationships among Self-Presentation Tactics and Ratings of Interview and Job Performance," *Journal of Applied Psychology*, 94, 6 (2009): 1394–1411.

159. Pfeffer, "Why Résumés Are Just One Piece of the Puzzle."

160. Taylor, P. J., and Small, B., "Asking Applicants What They *Would Do* Versus What They *Did Do*: A Meta-Analytic

Comparison of Situational and Past Behavior Employment Interview Questions," *Journal of Occupational and Organizational Psychology*, 75, 3 (2002): 277–294.

161. Kennedy, J., "What To Do When Job Applicants Tell ... Tales of Invented Lives," *Training*, October 1999: 110–114.

162. "FBI Special Agent Selection Process: Applicant Information Booklet," September 1997, www.fbi.gov/employment/booklet/phase1.htm. Accessed October 9, 2006.

163. Bianchi, A., "The Character-Revealing Handwriting Analysis," *Inc.*, February 1996, www.inc.com/magazine/19960201/1549.html. Accessed May 3, 2007.

164. Ben-Shakar, G., Bar-Hillel, M., Blum, Y., Ben-Abba, E., and Flug, A., "Can Graphology Predict Occupational Success? Two Empirical Studies and Some Methodological Ruminations," *Journal of Applied Psychology*, 71 (1986): 645–653.

165. Phillips and Gully, "Fairness Reactions to Personnel Selection Techniques in Singapore and the United States."

166. See Spohn, J., "The Legal Implications of Graphology," *Washington University Law Quarterly*, 75, 3 (Fall 1997), www.wulaw.wustl.edu/WULQ/75-3/753-6.html#fn4. Accessed May 3, 2007.

167. Ibid.

168. Ruiz, G., "Job Candidate Assessment Tests go Virtual," *Workforce Management Online*, January 2008, http://www.workforce.com/section/06/feature/25/31/79/index.html. Accessed March 12, 2010.

169. Zimmerman, E., "Use of Job Simulations Rising Steadily," *Workforce Management Online*, October 10, 2005, www.workforce.com/section/06/feature/24/18/59. Accessed October 4, 2006.

170. Johne, M., "Prize for Playing the Game: A Career," *Queen's School of Business Media and News*, http://business.queensu.ca/news/a_career.htm. Accessed June 21, 2006.

171. Ibid.

172. Martinez, "Screening for Quality on the Web."

173. Johne, "Prize for Playing the Game."

174. Falcone, P., "Getting Employers to Open Up on a Reference Check," *HR Magazine*, July 1995, http://findarticles.com/p/articles/mi_m3495/is_n7_v40/ai_17152485. Accessed April 27, 2007.

175. "One in Five Bosses Screen Applicants' Web Lives: Poll," *Reuters*, September 11, 2008, http://www.reuters.com/article/idUSPAR15282420080911. Accessed January 22, 2010.

176. Leonard, B., "Fake Job Reference Services Add New Wrinkle to Screening," *HR Magazine*, January 2010: 9.

177. 42 U.S.C. § 12112(d) (4) (1994); 29 C.F.R. § 1630.14(c) (2000).

178. 42 U.S.C. § 12112(d) (1994); 29 C.F.R. § 1630.14 (1998).

179. American Management Association, *AMA 2004 Workplace Testing Survey: Medical Testing*, New York: American Management Association, 2004, 1.

180. American Management Association, *2001 AMA Survey on Workplace Testing: Medical Testing: Summary of Key Findings*, New York: American Management Association, 2001, 1; "The Genetic Information Nondiscrimination Act (GINA) of 2008," available at http://www.shrm.org/LegalIssues/FederalResources/FederalStatutesRegulationsandGuidanc/Pages/TheGeneticInformationNondiscriminationActof2007.aspx.

181. "US to Outlaw Corporate Prejudice Based on Genes," *New Scientist*, May 5, 2007, www.newscientist.com/channel/life/genetics/mg19426023.300-us-to-outlaw-corporate-prejudice-based-on-genes.html. Accessed May 9, 2007.

182. 42 U.S.C. § 12112(d) (3) (1994); 29 C.F.R. § 1630.14(b) (1)-(2) (2000).

183. *Leonel v. American Airlines Inc.*, (9th Cir. 2005), No. 03-15890. See also, Ruiz, G., "Use Care When Conducting Pre-Employment Tests," *Workforce Management Online*, June 2006, www.workforce.com/archive/article/24/41/15.php?ht=care%20when%20conducting%20pre%20employment%20tests%20care%20when%20conducting%20pre%20employment%20tests. Accessed October 6, 2006.

184. U.S. Department of Labor, "Working Partners News Room," www.dol.gov/asp/programs/drugs/workingpartners/newsroom.as. Accessed October 19, 2006.

185. U.S. Department of Labor, "Drug Testing," *ELaws—Drug-Free Workplace Advisor*, http://www.dol.gov/elaws/drugfree.htm. Accessed September 23, 2010.

186. Carr, E., "Current Issues in Employee Substance Abuse Testing," *The Synergist*, May–June 2004, http://www.dol.gov/asp/programs/drugs/workingpartners/materials/abuse_testing.asp. Accessed October 19, 2006.

187. Frieswick, K., "Background Checks," *CFO Magazine*, August 1, 2005, www.cfo.com/article.cfm/4220232/1/c_4221579?f=insidecfo. Accessed October 9, 2006.

188. McGregor, J., "Background Checks That Never End," *BusinessWeek*, March 20, 2006: 40.

189. Conlin, M., "You Are What You Post," *BusinessWeek*, March 27, 2006: 52–53.

190. Federal Trade Commission, "Using Consumer Reports: What Employers Need to Know," March 1999, http://www.ftc.gov/bcp/edu/pubs/business/credit/bus08.shtm. Accessed May 3, 2007.

191. Ruiz, "Staying Out of Legal Hot Water While Conducting Background Checks."

192. Frieswick, "Background Checks."

193. Federal Trade Commission, "Using Consumer Reports."

194. Crane, A. B., "The ABCs of Pre-Employment Background Checks," Bankrate.com, February 16, 2005, www.bankrate.com/brm/news/advice/20050216a1. Accessed October 9, 2006.

195. *Interim Healthcare of Fort Wayne, Inc. v. Moyer*, 746 N.E.2d 429, 431 (Ind. App. 2001).

196. Ruiz, "Staying Out of Legal Hot Water While Conducting Background Checks."

197. Ibid.

198. Stevens-Huffman, L., "Hiring Top Sales Performers," *Workforce Management Online*, May 2006, www.workforce.com/archive/feature/24/36/39/index.php?ht=. Accessed June 27, 2006.

199. Hausknecht, Day, and Thomas, "Applicant Reactions to Selection Procedures."

200. Carbonara, P., "How Nucor Hires: Build Yourself a Job," *Fast Company*, August 1996: 76.

201. See Potosky, D., Bobko, P., and Roth, P. L., "Forming Composites of Cognitive Ability and Alternative Measures to Predict Job Performance and Reduce Adverse Impact: Corrected Estimates and Realistic Expectations," *International Journal of Selection and Assessment*, 13, 4 (2005): 304–315.

202. Pfeffer, *The Human Equation*.

203. Kaihla, P., "Best-Kept Secrets of the World's Best Companies," *Business 2.0*, March 23 2006, money.cnn.com/2006/03/23/magazines/business2/business2_bestkeptsecrets/index.htm. Accessed September 28, 2006.

204. Ibid; Freiberg and Freiberg, *Nuts! Southwest Airlines' Crazy Recipe for Business and Personal Success.*

205. Freiberg and Freiberg, *Nuts! Southwest Airlines' Crazy Recipe for Business and Personal Success.*

206. Carbonara, "Hire for Attitude, Train for Skill."

207. Kaihla, "Best-Kept Secrets of the World's Best Companies."; "We Weren't Just Airborne Yesterday," Southwest Airlines, www.southwest.com/about_swa/airborne.html. Accessed September 29, 2006.

208. Johnson & Johnson, "2009 Investor Fact Sheet," Johnson & Johnson, http://www.investor.jnj.com/investor-facts.cfm. Accessed September 23, 2010.

10 Assessing Internal Candidates

Outline

LEARNING OBJECTIVES

After studying this chapter, you should be able to:

- Identify the goals of internal assessment.
- Discuss how internal assessment can enhance a firm's strategic capabilities.
- Describe different internal assessment methods.
- Discuss the importance of integrating succession management and career development.
- Describe two models of internal assessment.

Internal Assessment at WellPoint

WellPoint, a health benefits company employing over 42,000 people across the United States and serving the health care needs of over 34 million members through its subsidiaries,[1] encourages leadership and entrepreneurship at all levels of the company. It holds employees personally responsible for excellence, delivering on the firm's promises, acting with integrity, and always putting customers first. These values have established WellPoint as the leading health insurer in the United States.[2]

WellPoint's talent philosophy includes promoting from within. The company wants to identify and evaluate viable internal candidates for every management position in the company. The company believes that identifying and tracking the development of promising internal talent, and enabling top management to evaluate candidates throughout the corporation's locations, will be critical to its future performance. WellPoint asks for your advice on how it can best assess internal candidates for its management positions. After reading this chapter, you should have some good ideas to share with the company.

Internal assessment is the evaluation of a firm's current employees for training, reassignment, promotion, or dismissal purposes. In addition to evaluating which employee skills are needed to execute their business strategies and assessing their employees to see if they have these skills, firms assess their workers' suitability for other jobs and create development opportunities for them. If done on a continual basis, internal assessment enhances a firm's workforce capabilities and better aligns employees' competencies with the firm's business strategy.

Despite the fact that internal assessment is such a critical staffing function, many companies do internal staffing very poorly. Because employees are "known," their managers and organizations often mistakenly assume the employees do not need to be systematically and deliberately assessed. This can be particularly problematic in smaller firms where most employees regularly work with each other and feel that they know each other's capabilities.

In this chapter, we discuss some of the primary goals of internal assessment followed by a variety of internal assessment methods. Finally, we discuss two internal assessment models and ways of evaluating the effectiveness of an internal assessment system. After reading this chapter, you should have a good understanding of the importance of internal assessment and assessing employees for a variety of staffing-related purposes.

internal assessment
the evaluation of a firm's current employees for training, reassignment, promotion, or dismissal purposes

THE FIRM'S INTERNAL ASSESSMENT GOALS

The assessment goals identified in the previous chapter are relevant to internal assessment as well. These goals are as follows:

- maximizing fit,
- assessing accurately,
- maximizing the company's return on its investment in its assessment system,
- generating positive stakeholder reactions,
- supporting the firm's talent philosophy and HR strategy,
- establishing and reinforcing the firm's human resource strategy,
- establishing and reinforcing the firm's employer image,
- identifying employees' developmental needs,
- assessing ethically, and
- complying with the law.

Internal assessment can serve three additional purposes: evaluating employees' fit with the firm's other jobs, assessing employees to enhance the firm's strategic capabilities, and gathering information with which to make downsizing decisions. We discuss each of these goals next, as well as how the external assessment goals identified in Chapter 9 apply to internal assessment.

Evaluating Employees' Fit with Other Jobs

Assessing employees' competencies to determine their fit with the requirements of other jobs in the company is one of the most common uses of internal assessment. When an employee wants to be considered for another position or for a promotion, he or she is typically evaluated against the company's values and requirements for the position compared to other applicants. For example, when evaluating store employees for promotion opportunities, the discount retailer Costco evaluates employees on their intelligence, people skills, and merchandising savvy.[3] Internal leadership assessments can also be used to identify who a company's potential future leaders should be. PanCanadian Petroleum, for example, actively tries to identify "bright lights" and employees who possess critical skills by scanning the entire organization for high-potential young managers.[4]

Enhancing the Firm's Strategic Capabilities

Aligning a firm's talent with its vision, goals, and business strategy positions the firm to compete effectively and win in the marketplace.[5] To be able to plan and prepare for its future business needs, a company needs to assess its current employees with an eye toward the future. This includes their ability and willingness to learn and adapt to new situations.[6] In addition, a company cannot know what training to offer employees unless it first assesses their strengths and weaknesses. Although this is true for all companies, it is particularly true for firms changing their business strategies or pursuing a different competitive advantage.

When FedEx wanted to adjust its policies-and-procedures-driven organizational culture to focus on leadership and getting the job done, it first needed to assess and develop the leadership skills of its mid-level managers. To do this, it used a Web-based tool to evaluate and develop the seven leadership competencies FedEx considers essential for mid-level managers.[7] When a market leader in the food industry wanted to better execute its growth strategy, it shifted its focus from managing costs to generating top-line growth. The company knew it needed employees with new capabilities, including the ability to innovate, think strategically, and maintain a strong customer focus. To determine who these people would be and to develop their skills, the firm conducted an internal talent assessment by presenting future-oriented simulations in an assessment center. The developmental planning and coaching enhanced participants' capabilities and improved the company's ability to execute its new strategy.[8]

After a firm assesses its employees, underperforming employees with low potential are typically transitioned out of the company. Meanwhile, "blocked" employees—that is, good employees who lack promotional opportunities—are assisted in terms of improving their motivation and performance. High-potential employees are identified for further development and are prepared for advancement opportunities.[9] Some firms prefer to call groups of employees targeted for accelerated development "acceleration pools" rather than "high-potential pools" because the latter term implies that employees not in the pool are not high potential.[10] To avoid alienating employees not labeled "high potential," Yahoo! avoids calling any employees high potential. The firm's executive training program is offered not only to individuals identified as promotion candidates, but other employees as well. Nonetheless, Yahoo! pays special attention to its stars and focuses on the training and career development of select employees to reduce the chances that these key employees will leave. The leadership potential of employees is also identified through their performance reviews and at an annual session held by Yahoo!'s senior executives.

Gathering Information with Which to Make Downsizing Decisions

In addition to bringing in new employees and moving employees into other jobs in the company, staffing sometimes involves transitioning employees out of the company through downsizing. Firms often downsize to reduce their headcount and corresponding labor costs, or to improve their efficiency. As we have indicated, in addition to using internal assessments to identify low performers who should be downsized, employees can also be assessed with an eye toward the competencies and capabilities the firm anticipates needing in the future. Employees who have the competencies the company needs to execute its business strategy or to create or maintain its competitive advantage might be retained, and employees lacking the characteristics and abilities the firm needs to succeed in the future might be the ones let go. The information services department of one particular firm is a case in point. After completing a strategic staffing plan that previously promoted employees based solely on how well they had performed in the past, the department began considering the competencies it would need in the future. As a result, some previously high-performing employees were asked to leave because they were judged unable to learn and apply new technology. Other employees who weren't currently high performers were kept because their skills and experience were consistent with the company's future talent needs.[11] Some companies also assess not only whether employees have the competencies the firm needs to compete successfully in the future, but also whether or not they really want to use those competencies.[12] We discuss downsizing more extensively in Chapter 12.

Gathering Information with Which to Make Restructuring Decisions

Restructuring involves reorganizing work to enhance the firm's strategic execution. This usually requires moving some employees to other positions, changing job requirements, and transitioning some employees out of the company. Both restructuring and downsizing decisions should be based on the firm's business plan and consider the ability of individual employees to contribute to the new plan. Understanding a company's profit-generating processes, services, and products and how a firm's jobs and employees contribute to each of them will make employee reassignments more strategic and effective.

Maximizing Fit

Person-job, person-group, and person-vocation fits, described in Chapter 9, are relevant to internal assessment as well as external assessment. Just as new hires need to be able to perform the jobs for which they are hired, employees need to perform their new jobs and effectively work with their new supervisors and coworkers.

To hire the best managers, the nature of the hiring process is as important as the assessment methods used to evaluate candidates. Due to union contracts or company policies, some organizations promote employees because of seniority rather than because they would be the best fit with the open job. Although experience and seniority tend to be somewhat related to a person's on-the-job performance, the relationship is not always strong. There is no guarantee that the most senior employee will be the most qualified, or the best fit, for the job.[13] It is as important to assess internal candidates on the characteristics required in the open position as it is to assess external candidates.

For example, many public institutions use a complicated system of job bidding for state jobs which is based on both seniority and job qualifications. If a department's administrative assistant position is vacated at the state university, employees in the same job classification from across all state agencies can bid on the position. The department may ultimately have to select, not from an ideal pool of candidates with university experiences, but rather from a pool of employees with similar jobs from correctional institutions, state government agencies, etc.[14]

To maximize the person-organization fit, a firm should assess its employees' qualifications, styles, and values that relate to the organization's strategy, values, and processes. As people move up the company's hierarchy, they are increasingly responsible for shaping and reinforcing the company's culture. Ensuring that the people who are promoted will reinforce rather than undermine the organization's values can be an important internal assessment goal. At the same time, it is not always best for the next generation of managers to maintain the status quo. Leadership, innovation, and competitive reassessment all determine what a firm will need in the future.

Complementary and supplementary fits are also relevant internal assessment goals. An employee being transferred or promoted needs to complement or extend the competencies of his or her new work group. Together, complementary and supplementary fit help to ensure that promoted or transferred employees will work well in their new work groups and bring new, helpful skills to the table.

Assessing Accurately

Internal assessment systems must also be valid and accurately identify the candidates who would be the most and least successful in open jobs. No assessment system is perfect. Obviously, however, more valid assessment systems do a better job than less valid ones. High validity, or accurately predicting job performance and other important criteria, such as tenure and promotability, is a critical function of both internal and external assessment systems. As you learned in Chapter 9, the goal is to generate high numbers of true positive and true negative hiring outcomes, and minimize the numbers of false positive and false negative outcomes.

Maximizing the Firm's Return on Its Investment in Its Assessment System

Another important internal assessment goal is to maximize the firm's return on its investment in its internal assessment system. As we explained in Chapter 9, some companies simply do not have the money to invest in expensive assessment systems, even if they more accurately identify the best talent. Sometimes less costly selection procedures—for example, using better performance reviews and assessing employees while they rotate through job assignments—can yield comparable, valid results. The equations provided in Chapter 9 provide a way to estimate a company's return on its investment in a new assessment system.

Generating Positive Stakeholder Reactions

Meeting the needs of different stakeholders in the staffing process is another assessment goal. As with external assessment methods, if an internal assessment method does not also meet the needs of the firm's employees, hiring managers, and recruiters, it is not as effective as it could be. For example, a firm's managers might not want to regularly assess each of their employees' promotion potential and developmental needs because of the sheer time involved. Employees might react negatively to the processes used to determine who gets a promotion if they perceive them to be unfair. An assessment method's fairness, ease of use, speed, and ability to predict important job success outcomes all influence whether recruiters, supervisors, and managers use it correctly and consistently. Training people about the benefits of assessment techniques and their use and rewarding people for doing so correctly and consistently can help. So can having a reliable and competent assessment system expert available to assist them.

Another negative stakeholder reaction can occur when employees are turned down for the promotions or lateral moves for which they were considered. These employees might potentially be less motivated or even try to leave the organization. The potential for this to occur is even greater when an employee has been turned down multiple times. It is important to treat these employees with a great deal of respect and maximize their procedural and interactional justice perceptions. Honest communication about what they could do to be more competitive for the positions they are interested in, and developing an action plan to give them training or developmental experiences that would better prepare them for the position can enhance their motivation. If an employee is interested in a position that the firm feels he or she will not likely ever get, it is important to communicate this honestly but sensitively to the employee and to try to find another career path for the person. If a talented employee who has been passed over for promotion or transfer in the past is a finalist for a current position, it can be a good idea to consider this when choosing whom to promote or transfer. The choice may be between promoting the person or losing him or her.

After spending the time and money to hire, train, and develop subordinates, some managers do not want their best employees transferred out of their unit. This can reduce their willingness to participate in internal assessment programs. If managers fear their resources could be poached from within, policies and procedures such as a minimum period of time an employee must stay in a job before being promoted can be implemented.[15] Other managers naturally feel rewarded by developing and mentoring their employees to move up in an organization. Indeed, managers who are known for developing their direct reports and who are more rapidly promoted within the firm are also likely to be managers who have little difficulty recruiting talented employees who want to work for them.

Managers should be assessed and rewarded for their ability to develop promotable talent. They need to believe the rewards of participating honestly in the process are greater than the rewards of not doing so. One way to do this is by tying their performance appraisals and pay to their participating in internal assessment programs. Communicating and reinforcing strong, clear statements of this nature to managers can help get their buy-in to the idea that talent belongs to the company rather than themselves. For example, when Warner-Lambert's human resources team prepared a set of principles as part of a redesign of its practices, the first principle stated, "Talent across the company is managed for the larger interests of the company. Our divisions are the stewards of that talent, and company-wide interests prevail."[16]

Supporting the Firm's Talent Philosophy and Human Resource Strategy

Another goal of an assessment system is to support the organization's talent philosophy and human resource strategy. Viewing employees as investors might stimulate a company to incorporate more developmental feedback into the assessment process to improve the promotability of employees. By contrast, a firm that views its employees merely as assets is less likely to do this. An organization that wants people to contribute over long-term careers needs to view employees in terms of their long-term career potential within the company, and to help employees identify and pursue career paths that interest them. In this case, identifying the competencies, styles, and traits required for career advancement within the company is also relevant.

Reinforcing the Organization's Employer Image

Maintaining an organization's employer image is an important staffing goal. To establish and maintain its image as an employer, a company must "walk the walk" and genuinely be what it claims to be. An organization claiming to provide an environment in which employees can grow their careers will not be successful in establishing or maintaining that image if it does not give them performance feedback and development opportunities. One of the goals of the internal assessment process should be to reinforce the organization's desired image among employees. This can also help improve employee retention by reminding them that the company values them and by clarifying how they fit into the company's strategy and future direction.

Identifying Employees' Developmental Needs

As we have discussed, if an employee's assessment shows that he or she lacks critical skills that will be needed in the future, training and development can be provided to correct the situation. For example, Wyeth Pharmaceuticals regularly assesses its employees' skills. Employees who fail to obtain scores of at least 90 percent must immediately improve their skills and then later undergo another round of testing of them.[17]

Assessing Ethically

As we discussed in Chapter 9, the entire selection process needs to be managed ethically. The process needs to be honest. Employees need to understand how it works, including how their test results will be used and ensured that their privacy will be protected. The firm also needs to communicate with candidates when it promises to. As we explained in Chapter 9, test administrators should be properly qualified and trained, and the firm should carefully consider the ethics of using any assessment methods applicants find invasive.

An additional ethical issue involves the confidentiality of an employee's application for another position in the company. If a supervisor or work group thinks that an employee is likely to leave, they may treat the employee differently and invest less in the person's future development. Some employees do not want their supervisors or coworkers to know that they are considering other opportunities. Consequently, it can be important for the firm to have confidentiality policies and procedures in place to respect the wishes of these employees.

Complying with the Law

The Uniform Guidelines on Employee Selection Procedures discussed in Chapter 9 apply to all selection procedures used to make employment decisions, including performance evaluations and other internal assessment methods.[18] The Principles for the Validation and Use of Personnel Selection Procedures and the Standards for Educational and Psychological Testing discussed in Chapter 9 are also relevant for internal as well as external assessment. Fair, consistent, and objective assessments are key to assessment systems being legally compliant.

Monitoring equal employment opportunity (EEO) statistics based on positions and levels in the company is an important part of EEO compliance, too. In fact, the liability risk is often greater with internal versus external assessment and staffing efforts. This is particularly true when it comes to employee termination decisions and "glass ceiling" problems, which limit the advancement of women and minorities. Companies including Texaco and Coca-Cola have found themselves in legal trouble for promoting minorities at lower rates than Caucasians. *Roberts v. Texaco*[19] found that African Americans were significantly underrepresented in high-level management jobs, and that Caucasian employees were promoted more frequently and at far higher rates for comparable positions within Texaco.

The plaintiffs in a lawsuit lost by Coca-Cola[20] alleged that the company's written and unwritten policies and practices allowed supervisors to essentially handpick candidates via word of mouth based on subjective criteria. Jobs were filled without being posted, candidates were chosen in advance, and supervisors disregarded the results of panel interviews and manipulated scores in order to ensure that their favorites were chosen. Because this system prevented qualified African Americans from competing equally for positions or from even knowing that they were available, they were denied the opportunity to advance to the same level and at the same rate as equally qualified Caucasian employees.

To open up the promotion process and relieve the concerns of women and minorities who often feel shut out of promotion opportunities, Kodak's Leadership Assessment and Development Center began an open-door program to develop anyone interested in being considered for a supervisory position. This approach enhanced the perceived fairness of the promotion process, and the experience helps many employees realize that they are not interested in higher-level jobs after all. After attending the introductory course, "So You Want to Be a Leader?" about 25 percent of participants "deselect" themselves, and after the second course giving instruction on handling supervisory duties including budgeting, staffing, and production, another 25 percent drop out.[21]

A firm's internal selection processes can be heavily influenced by union contracts as well. Unions generally negotiate for promotions to be based on seniority, and any internal assessment or internal staffing terms included in a union contract must be complied with. The National Labor Relations Act of 1935 protects employees from discrimination based on their involvement in a union, and prohibits employers from making staffing decisions to discourage union membership. Employees also may not be discriminated against because they filed charges or gave testimony under the National Labor Relations Act. Although America is losing its manufacturing companies, unions remain strong in academia, hospitals, and the public sector.

INTERNAL ASSESSMENT METHODS

The assessment methods described in Chapter 9, including biographical information, structured interviews, simulations, assessment centers, and clinical assessments, can be as useful for assessing internal candidates as they are for external candidates. When an international medical products supply company redefined its field sales managers' roles to better address the company's business challenges, it identified new competencies, behaviors, and performance standards. It then immersed its current and potential field sales managers in simulations that reflected the changing nature and demands of the new roles. The idea was to assess the employees' fit with the job skills they would need. It also provided a realistic preview of the position's new requirements and identified the strengths and weaknesses of employees and the development they would need.[22]

In addition to all the assessment methods used with external applicants, there are a variety of additional assessment methods that can be used with internal job candidates. Because internal job candidates already work for the company, more and richer information is usually available to recruiters. Although employees can be assessed by an outside contractor, informal assessment methods conducted by the employee and supervisors can be equally effective and less costly.[23]

Skills Inventories

skills inventory
a company-maintained list outlining which employees have certain skills, competencies, and other relevant job characteristics

As John Walker, the global leader of Dow Chemical Company's human resource department, states, "A lot of organizations talk about their core competencies, but unless they measure them it can be difficult to know what they really are."[24] A **skills inventory** (or skills databases) allows a company to maintain a list outlining which employees have certain skills, competencies, and other relevant job characteristics. For example, if a firm were to need a sales associate who speaks French, the company could simply query its skills inventory database. The skills required for each job can also be used to create training and development plans for employees who want to eventually apply for those jobs.

Some companies use sophisticated software systems to manage the process, whereas others rely on paper or spreadsheets. Technology can assist in the effective compilation and presentation of this information, including modules from SAP, PeopleSoft, Oracle, and Saba Software. When kept in a database, the information can be quickly searched to assign employees to new projects or to help identify employees to consider for other positions. Some organizations hold employees responsible for keeping their skills inventories updated and accurate via the company's intranet. Once an employee possesses all of the qualifications necessary to be considered for another position, the software identifies the employee as ready to be considered when a vacancy arises.

The organization and its budget determine the number and types of skills tracked and at what level of detail each is evaluated. Skills inventories can be limited to basic information, such as the education, work experience, or training and certifications completed by employees when they initially begin working for the company. Alternatively, the inventories can be continually updated as employees acquire additional skills and qualifications. The latter is preferred—the better and more current the information in a skills inventory is, the more useful it will be in terms of predicting who will do the best job and where. IBM considers skills to be a company asset, and keeps its skills inventory open to managers and employees. Managers can view and update their employees' files, and employees can view and update their own files. When forming teams, staff members query the inventory to find out which employees have complementary skills.[25]

Mentoring Programs

Mentoring is a dynamic, reciprocal relationship between a more-experienced employee (mentor) and a more junior employee (protégé) aimed at promoting the career development of both.[26] Mentoring relationships can be established through formal mentoring programs in which a mentor is assigned to an employee, or they can be informal and develop on their own.

mentoring
a dynamic, reciprocal relationship between a more-experienced employee (mentor) and a more junior employee (protégé) aimed at promoting the career development of both

Mentoring people can be a good way to initially assess employees as well as enhance their careers and improve their chances of being promoted. Mentors can be asked to nominate their protégés for positions they feel they are ready for or vice versa. Mentoring can also be an effective training tool for smaller companies that can't afford formal training programs.

Via its Executive Coaching Practice program, Wachovia Corporation developed over 70 internal coaches who mentor and support 189 leaders across the bank. The coaches evaluate participants' leadership competencies, create individual development plans for them, and provide them with ongoing support. In 2006, Wachovia estimated that the program reaped the firm over $360,000 per coaching engagement.[27]

Performance Reviews

An employee's supervisor usually conducts performance reviews (also called performance appraisals). An employee's supervisor is often the person not only most familiar with the employee's performance, but also responsible for it. Thus, employees generally expect performance appraisals from their supervisors and prefer it to be their main source of feedback.[28] Nevertheless, this doesn't mean the appraisal process has to be limited to supervisors only. For example, an employee's peers and subordinates see different aspects of the person's work behaviors and performance.[29] Moreover, in some situations, an employee's supervisor is actually *less* able to observe him or her than other people. Traveling salespeople are a good example. Many of these people spend most of their time working alone—not under the eye of their supervisors. In this case, people other than the supervisor might be better qualified to evaluate the salespeople.[30]

Multisource Assessments

Multisource assessments (sometimes called 360-degree assessments) involve an employee's supervisor as well as other people familiar with the employee's job performance. These raters typically include the employee, his or her subordinates, peers, and even the company's internal and external customers.[31] The sources can be used alone or together, as shown in Figure 10-1,

multisource assessments
performance reviews that involve an employee's supervisor as well as other people familiar with the employee's job performance

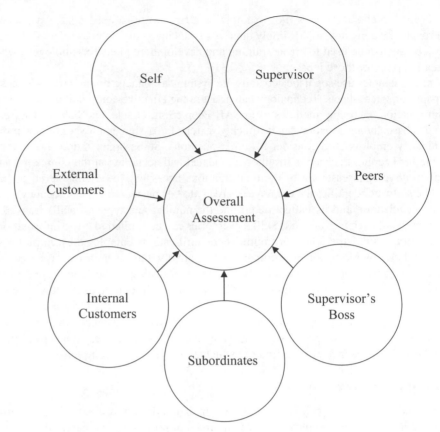

FIGURE 10-1 Multisource Assessments

and should be weighted based on their credibility. A source's ability to actually observe and accurately rate the employee should also be considered. Table 10-1 summarizes the frequency with which each rating source is able to observe an employee's task and interpersonal behaviors. Next, we discuss each of the sources in more detail.

Asking an employee to assess his or her own performance and capabilities can be useful. Self-assessments help identify areas in which employees feel they could benefit from additional coaching or development. The problem is that people aren't always good judges of their own talents. Some high performers tend to rate themselves lower than do other raters, and others rate themselves too high.[32] The key reasons to include self-evaluations are to allow employees to provide performance documentation that their supervisors or others don't have and convey their developmental goals and desired career tracks to the firm.

Peers tend to get a good look at each other's task and interpersonal behaviors. This is especially the case when work is done in teams. At the consulting firm Booz Allen Hamilton, for example, employees receive 360-degree competency assessments annually, involving as many as 15 of their colleagues.[33] For peer ratings to work well, employees must believe the process is fair.[34]

To reduce the influence of politics and friendships, peers need to understand the characteristics required for success and be familiar with the job requirements matrix for the position. As is done with Olympic judges, some companies eliminate the lowest and highest peer ratings and average the rest.[35] Employees can be asked to assess each peer's promotion readiness or to rank

TABLE 10-1	The Frequency with Which Different Raters Are Able to Observe an Employee's Task and Interpersonal Behaviors					
	Self	**Supervisor**	**Subordinates**	**Peers**	**Internal Customers**	**External Customers**
Task Behaviors	High Frequency	Medium Frequency	Low Frequency	Medium-to-High Frequency	Medium Frequency	Low Frequency
Interpersonal Behaviors	High Frequency	Low Frequency	Medium-to-High Frequency	Medium-to-High Frequency	Medium Frequency	Medium Frequency

order or vote for their most promotable peers. Some firms ask employees to nominate peers they feel would be good candidates for openings. Peer ratings have been found to have an average validity of .51 when it comes to predicting promotion criteria.[36]

Asking subordinates to appraise their managers is often the most controversial feature of a multisource assessment program. Although subordinates may not see all their supervisors' task behaviors, they very often see their interpersonal and leadership behaviors. Thus, subordinates have a unique and important perspective on their managers' behaviors, strengths, and limitations. One shortcoming of subordinate feedback is that subordinates are often reluctant or even afraid to give their supervisors negative feedback. Rater anonymity is critical. If subordinates feel that their responses might be identifiable (e.g., if the supervisor has only a few subordinates and can discern "who said what") or if they fear reprisal, then subordinate ratings are not likely to be accurate, if subordinates agree to participate at all.

Internal customers are users of any products or services supplied by another employee or group within the same organization. *External customers* are those outside the firm, including other companies and the general public. Both internal and external customers have a moderate opportunity to observe employees' task and interpersonal behaviors. Their feedback helps to incorporate the perspective of the company's stakeholders beyond the typical chain of command. Because employees are often rewarded only for satisfying the expectations of the people who control their compensation, incorporating customer feedback into the rewards process expands the range of stakeholders employees will seek to please.

Because external customers do not see or understand the work processes and rules that influence employees' task behaviors, they often cannot easily separate an employee's task behaviors from the regulations, policies, and resources that affect and constrain the employee's options. As a result, some experts believe that it can be best to ask external customers to only evaluate an employee's interpersonal behaviors.[37]

Often the ratings provided by people who do not supervise the worker are used only for employee development and performance evaluations. By contrast, promotion and transfer decisions are usually based on supervisors' ratings. In addition, most firms require a supervisor's manager to ensure that he or she has been diligent in conducting an employee's performance assessment as well as confirm the results of it. To spot good promotion candidates who might have been overlooked or underestimated by their supervisors and their supervisors' bosses, WellPoint sets up "challenge sessions" in which supervisors in a group scrutinize one another's evaluations.[38]

Job Knowledge Tests

Job knowledge tests can be as useful for internal assessment as they are for external assessment. Because well-developed and validated job knowledge tests can measure a person's knowledge, experience, cognitive ability, and motivation to learn, they can help to predict which employees will perform the best in an open position. Many organizations, including police departments, use job knowledge tests to assess promotion candidates. At the U.S. Customs Service, evaluating employees for promotion to special-agent positions involves a five-hour battery of tests that includes a job knowledge test assessing a candidate's technical skills; a critical thinking test; and an in-basket exercise that measures the candidate's leadership competencies, including how well they plan, prioritize, schedule, and delegate work. Applicants who pass the battery then take a writing-skills assessment test and participate in a structured interview.[39]

Assessment Center Methods

As you have learned, assessment centers measure job candidates' knowledge, skills, abilities, and competencies by putting them through a series of simulations and exercises that reflect the typical challenges of the job they're applying for. Assessment centers can very effectively identify a person's strengths and weaknesses. The centers also can do a good job of predicting how successful candidates are likely to be in particular positions.[40] The degree to which the centers result in adverse impact, or disproportionate hiring rates for different ethnic or gender subgroups, varies depending on the exercises used.

Because Cessna Aircraft Company has fewer people doing more work than it used to, it feels that it can't afford to make a bad hiring decision. Thus, the company wants to have a good look at how people will do their jobs before they hire them. Cessna's Independence, Missouri, plant uses an elaborate role-playing exercise for managers that simulates a "day in the life" experience of a busy executive. A job candidate spends up to 12 hours in an office with a phone, fax, and in-basket stuffed with files and letters. Throughout the day, the job candidate works through memos and handles problems, such as a phone call from an angry customer. This type of exercise is typical of the type of assessment that an outside assessment center would conduct.[41]

As we have explained, because of their high cost relative to other assessment methods, assessment centers are used more for managerial and higher-level jobs. Many of the skills and competencies assessment centers evaluate can also be assessed by giving employees the opportunity to demonstrate their managerial talent by becoming a project team leader or committee chair. Assessment centers seem to work in a variety of organizational settings, and can be useful for making selection and promotion decisions as well as training, career planning, and improving a person's managerial skills.

Clinical Assessments

clinical assessments
assessments that rely on trained psychologists to subjectively analyze a candidate's attributes, values, and styles in the context of a particular job

Clinical assessments rely on trained psychologists to subjectively analyze a candidate's attributes, values, and styles in the context of a particular job. Ability and personality tests, interviews, and direct observations of the behavior of employees are different types of activities done during clinical assessments. The clinical assessment is usually presented as a written description of the candidate, and may or may not contain a "clear hire" or "don't hire" recommendation.[42] Like the tests conducted at assessment centers, clinical assessments are expensive. Consequently, they tend to be used for higher-level positions, such as executive and CEO positions—that is, positions associated with greater power and influence and for whom the job descriptions may be more flexible. In cases such as these, companies sometimes use a psychologist to try to evaluate a candidate's strengths and weaknesses and determine the broad impact a candidate would likely have on the organization if the person were hired.

The Nine Box Matrix

nine box matrix
a combined assessment of an employee's performance and potential

A **nine box matrix** is a combined assessment of an employee's performance and potential. Many *Fortune* 500 companies including Bank of America, GE, and Medco Health Solutions use some variety of the nine box matrix for classifying their managers' current job performance and potential for advancement. For example, using the nine box matrix, an individual who is performing well might not be judged as highly as someone who has not gotten comparable results but has persevered in a stretch assignment.[43] Table 10-2 illustrates the nine box matrix.

The value of the nine box matrix depends on the quality of the assessment methodology that determines the box in which each individual is placed. The nine box matrix is a method for displaying judgments made about employees, not for making those judgments. It can help companies understand the overall strength of their workforces, but only if the employees are accurately evaluated in the first place.[44]

Career Crossroads Model

When Walt Mahler, a human resource consultant and teacher, got involved in the design of General Electric's succession management process in the early 1970s, he found that different leadership levels in an organization require different sets of competencies and values.[45] Mahler concluded that the most successful leaders change their perspective on what is important as they move to higher levels of leadership. For example, a finance manager has to see his or her role differently when managing the finance function than when managing an entire business unit. If the business-unit leader failed to broaden his or her view of finance as the most critical aspect of his or her job, the leader would not master the additional nonfinance aspects of the business. It can be very difficult for individuals to change their perspective about what is important after years of schooling and work experience. That said, a leader's values and priorities *must* change to fit the enhanced breadth of each new position he or she holds.

The career crossroads model focuses on managerial and leadership positions rather than technical or professional work. The natural hierarchy of work that exists in most large, decentralized

TABLE 10-2	The Nine Box Matrix[46]		

		Current Job Performance		
		Exceptional	**Fully Performing**	**Not Yet Fully Performing**
Likely Future Potential	Eligible for Promotion	1 Exceptional performer ready to be promoted; should be promoted quickly as the person is also at risk of leaving	3 Full performer capable of being promoted but with room to improve in current job; focus on improving the employee's current performance to enable the person to be promoted in the future	6 Employee is new to the job but may eventually be a good candidate for promotion
	Room for Growth in Current Position	2 Exceptional performer not yet ready for promotion; should be developed further to prepare the employee for future promotion	5 Full performer with room to grow in current position; focus on employee's performance improvement	8 Performs some parts of job poorly but should continue to grow in current position; identify reasons for underperformance and further develop employee's skills
	Not Likely to Grow Beyond Current Position	4 Exceptional performer not likely to grow beyond scope of current position; consider involving the employee in the training of others	7 Full performer not likely to grow beyond scope of current position; coach and develop to improve both the employee's performance and potential	9 Underperformer not likely to grow beyond scope of current position; identify reasons for low performance and consider reassigning the employee to a lower level or transitioning the person out of the company

business organizations consists of six career passages—from the entry level to the top job, with each passage representing increased complexity. The six passages are:

- Starting Point: Managing yourself
- Passage 1: Managing others
- Passage 2: Managing managers
- Passage 3: Managing a function
- Passage 4: Managing a business
- Passage 5: Managing multiple businesses
- Passage 6: Managing the enterprise

Each passage requires that a person learn new values and skills and unlearn old ones. One of the biggest talent mistakes organizations can make is to promote people based solely on their mastery of their current positions rather than on their potential and readiness to assume the responsibilities and adopt the values of their new positions as leaders (although some continued development and coaching is generally required for this to occur). Effective succession management should produce an abundance of high-performing, high-potential talent to draw from for each leadership level. Because the career crossroads model takes a long-term perspective, it enhances the organization's ability to create its own leadership talent from a broad talent base rather than relying on identifying and hiring external star performers to become the firm's leaders.

In smaller organizations, the number of leadership layers is reduced, but the skills required of leaders are similar. Managing others rather than solely managing oneself is the most common transition, and one that many people find difficult. In very small organizations, the owner typically manages everyone else in the company. However, in medium-sized companies, there may be a middle layer of management in which managers or supervisors are themselves managed. Depending on the organization's needs and structure, functional managers may exist, and the owner acts as the CEO. Smaller organizations are also unlikely to have the luxury of having a large number of employees to choose from when a leadership position opens. The situation can be even more critical for the survival of smaller organizations because the departure of even one key person can cripple the organization if a successor is not found quickly.

MANAGING SUCCESSION

succession management

an ongoing process of systematically identifying, assessing, and developing an organization's leadership capabilities to enhance its performance

Succession management is an ongoing process of systematically identifying, assessing, and developing an organization's leadership capabilities to enhance its performance.[47] Succession management involves ongoing strategic talent planning, retirement and retention planning, and talent assessment and development.[48] As we explained in earlier chapters, succession management can ensure the continuity of a firm's leadership, prevent key positions from remaining vacant, and prevent employees from being promoted prematurely.

Succession management requires much more than simply identifying which employees should be promoted. It should integrate the management of a firm's talent with the organization's strategic plan. If done far enough in advance, succession management can sometimes affect the choice of which business strategy to pursue. For example, if a regional clothing store is planning to expand nationally, having a substantial amount of managerial talent in the firm's pipeline can be a prerequisite for opening the new stores. If the firm's succession planning indicates that managerial talent is in short supply, the organization can make hiring employees with the potential to become store managers a key goal of its recruiting and hiring process. Alternatively, the company can plan to hire store managers from outside of the company to staff its new locations. Or, it can scale back its expansion plans altogether.

In short, succession management affects the organization's long-term direction and growth. This is particularly important when you consider the fact that so many baby boomers are retiring. The increased demand for diverse employees is also becoming more important. As a result, many organizations are integrating workforce diversity into their succession management.[49] Allstate, for example, has successfully used succession management to ensure that it identifies and develops diverse slates of qualified candidates for all its key positions. The insurance company assesses all employees' current job skills and creates road maps for them outlining the competencies they need to advance within the company. The company then makes sure they get the training they need, including coaching and mentoring, classroom training, and a variety of career experiences.[50]

Although succession management can expedite the process of replacing a departing employee, employees identified by succession management as candidates for an open position should not be the only employees considered for the job. Ideally, information about an opening should be disseminated to all employees to give them the opportunity to apply for the position in case some talent is being overlooked. As you learned earlier in the chapter, it is also important to ensure that information about position openings does not become a secretive, employee-alienating situation. It is obviously not ideal for a qualified employee who would have been interested in a job opportunity to not learn about the vacancy and miss the opportunity. Moreover, sometimes it can create legal problems for companies, as the Coca-Cola discrimination example presented earlier in the chapter illustrated. When done well, succession planning reinforces a company's philosophy of treating its employees as investors rather than assets. It is a key driver of employee retention and sends a signal to the firm's stakeholders that the company's leaders are preparing for the future.[51]

succession management plans

written policies that guide the succession management process

Succession management plans are written policies that guide the succession management process. Succession management plans should be put in place before they are needed, and can be very good investments. One study found that chief executives hired from outside the company are paid almost three times more than those promoted from within.[52]

When McDonald's CEO, Jim Cantalupo, died unexpectedly in 2004, he was replaced six hours later. A few weeks later, his replacement, Charlie Bell, was diagnosed with cancer, and the company's board of directors again made an orderly replacement, in part because McDonald's had a good succession management plan.[53] By contrast, when Frank Lanza, chairman and CEO of defense contractor L-3 Communications, died suddenly and unexpectedly at age 74, the company hadn't prepared for it. The firm's board of directors took three days just to name an interim chief executive, and the company was widely speculated to be a takeover target because of the leadership crisis.[54]

It should be noted that succession management not only helps a firm's future managers and top executives prepare for their positions, it also results in the creation of a series of "feeder groups" up and down a firm's leadership talent pipeline.[55] By contrast, **replacement planning** is narrowly focused on creating backup candidates for specific senior management positions. Replacement planning is helpful for quickly identifying a possible successor when a position unexpectedly opens. However, it does little to improve a firm's long-term leadership readiness.

replacement planning
the process of creating backup candidates for specific senior management positions

Developing a Succession Management System

After choosing the position on which to focus, the first general step in a succession management project is to check that the job description outlines the current and future competencies, behaviors, and values a person needs to perform at a high level in the key position. For example, if the organization is planning to change its culture to become more service oriented, new customer service competencies will probably need to be added to the job requirements matrix and job specification. If technology will become more integrated with the position, technology skills should be added. As people move up in an organization, new ways of managing and leading are needed in terms of: (1) the capabilities required to execute the new responsibilities; (2) new time frames governing how one works; and (3) new work values, or what is believed to be important and the focus of one's effort.[56]

The second general step is to identify each interested candidate's strengths, weaknesses, and succession readiness through formal assessment centers and skills testing, or more informally via supervisory assessments. Maintaining skills inventory records can seem burdensome, but it is a critical task. One of the barriers to successfully maintaining these records is the volume of information that is sometimes requested from managers responsible for updating the system. If the system is user-friendly and only data relevant to making advancement decisions is collected, then the burden will be reduced.

The third step is to create a plan to continually and systematically improve the capabilities of all identified succession candidates. This requires that succession management be thought of as a continuous process, not something that is done only once or twice a year. Using the assessment of candidates' competencies, training programs and development opportunities can be identified to increase candidates' readiness for the key positions. If candidates are given information about the areas in which further development would help prepare them for their targeted positions, they can be active partners in systematically building the competencies they need to move to those positions. As we explained earlier in the chapter, some companies enable employees to access their own profiles to ensure that the information about them is updated and accurate. This also tends to make employees active partners in the succession management process.

The fourth step is to create a plan to identify qualified and interested internal candidates for open positions. A thorough and updated database of skill profiles can greatly facilitate this step. In addition, work assignments and other developmental activities need to be regularly assigned to candidates who are likely to be promoted or who want to be promoted.

Figure 10-2 shows a database used to track succession candidates. The succession pool for Customer Service Manager Peter Fry is shown, as well as the time frame in which each successor is expected to be ready to assume Fry's position. Clicking on each succession candidate's name brings up additional information about that candidate's strengths and development needs.

Job	Incumbent	Turnover Risk	Possible Successors	Successor Readiness
Customer Service Manager	Peter Fry	Moderate	Amy Finn	3–6 months
			John McCarthy	6–12 months
			Sara Menendez	3–6 months

Strengths: leadership, customer service skills
Needs: budgeting experience

FIGURE 10-2 Succession Management Database

TABLE 10-3	Steps in Developing a Succession Management System

1. Assess current and future competencies, behaviors, values, etc., needed for future job performance in the chosen position
2. Assess each identified and interested candidate's strengths, weaknesses, and readiness to move into other positions
3. Create a plan to continually and systematically improve the capabilities of all identified succession candidates
4. Create a plan to identify qualified and interested internal candidates for open positions
5. Evaluate the system on relevant criteria including the number of positions filled with candidates who have been the target of succession management activities
6. Continually improve the system

The fifth step involves evaluating the company's succession management system. One large organization boasted having a succession management process, but after analyzing the data about the program's success, it realized that virtually no senior managers ever came out of it. Clearly, some other subjective criteria were being used to determine promotions, which risks demoralizing good employees and increasing their turnover.[57] The sixth, and final step, is to continuously improve the succession management system. Succession plans should also be continuously reviewed and modified as an organization changes. The process should be designed to be ongoing, fluid, and adaptable to a firm's shifting business conditions. Table 10-3 summarizes the steps involved in developing an effective succession plan.

What Makes a Succession Management System Effective?

The best succession systems bridge the gap between the individual career development opportunities facing employees and the long-term business conditions facing firms.[58] For example, if the succession management system fails to identify qualified internal candidates for a particular position, action plans need to be developed to remedy the talent gap. The company might look externally for talent, or, it might redesign the work to reduce the need for the talent expected to be in short supply. The system might also reveal that a firm has a larger number of interested and qualified internal candidates for a target position than was expected or than is realistically needed. This knowledge can help an organization plan alternate career paths for the surplus talent, helping to prevent the turnover of these employees when they do not get the promotions for which they are ready.

As with assessment methods, fairness and communication openness are critical components of succession management. The process should be impartial, open, and backed by top management. Employees should be able to express an interest in being considered for positions that appeal to them, and should not be coerced into pursuing positions in which they are not interested. The succession management process also needs to make sense to, and be usable by, different business units. A standardized process can help to focus and guide the development of employees to meet the strategic needs of the organization, and increase employee perceptions of the program's fairness by reducing opportunities for favoritism.

The process should also align with other human resource processes, including recruitment, selection, rewards, training, and performance management. For example, if the current succession plan for a position indicates that the organization lacks depth in a particular talent, adjustments to the recruitment and selection system can bring more of that talent into the organization. Finally, for a succession management program to work well, a firm's managers need to be involved in and committed to the process. Their employee assessments, promotabilty ratings, and employee development activities are crucial. Table 10-4 provides some tips for effective succession management.

CAREER PLANNING

career planning
a continuous process of career-oriented self-assessment and goal setting

Career planning is a continuous process of career-oriented self-assessment and goal setting.[59] When integrated with the organization's succession management and labor forecasting processes, career planning and succession management can help give any organization a snapshot of the talent available to meet its current and future needs.[60]

In the career planning process, the goals, preferences, and capabilities of employees are assessed via interest inventories, interviews, assessment centers, and so forth. The current and

TABLE 10-4	Succession Management Tips

Here are some experts' recommendations for creating and maintaining an effective succession management system:

- *Keep the process simple.* Make the process logical and simple so that busy line managers do not feel that the process is burdensome.[61]
- *Use technology to support the process.* Information technology enables the timely monitoring and updating of developmental needs and activities.[62]
- *Align your succession management plan with your firm's overall business strategy.* Top executives and line managers will be more supportive of a system that clearly reinforces the organization's corporate goals and objectives.[63]
- *Focus on development.* Succession management must be a flexible system oriented toward developmental activities rather than merely a list of high-potential employees and future positions they might fill.[64]
- *Model effective succession management behaviors at the top.* Company executives need to both model effective succession management behaviors and hold line managers responsible for developing their subordinates' skills and knowledge.[65]
- *Approach succession management as a key business activity.* Because it plays a key role in a firm's long-term business strategy execution, succession management should be treated as a key activity for the firm.[66]

future needs of the organization based on the human resource strategy and succession plan of the firm are then compared to the talents and motivations of employees, and the degree of match or mismatch is discussed with each individual employee. Career development opportunities are then identified to help workers build the competencies and talents they need to achieve their future goals. General Mills tailors each employee's career development to his or her professional needs, long-term aspirations, and potential for personal growth.[67]

Organizations can increase employee retention and the depth of talent available for leadership positions by integrating the career planning and succession management processes, and by linking them to organizational goals and strategies. By helping individuals match their career interests with realistic career opportunities in the organization in which they currently work, career planning can reduce employees' perceptions that they need to leave the organization to accomplish their career goals. Kimberly-Clark, for example, provides its employees career paths that are both broad and diverse. By giving its employees cross-functional opportunities (opportunities in different positions in different departments),[68] the company helps them increase their responsibility levels, expertise, and leadership capabilities so they can reach their goals.

Like succession management, career planning needs to complement the expected future talent needs of the organization. For example, if an organization expects to expand in the next 10 years, career planning can help identify current employees who are willing to pursue advancement opportunities in the company and help it execute its expansion goals.

Too often succession management is done without telling employees that the organization recognizes their potential. An organization's high-potential talent should be informed of their status in the company and should know that the organization has its eye on them for advancement in the company. Career planning helps to facilitate this process and coordinate employees' personal goals with the organization's needs. For example, as part of its career planning effort, The Hartford Financial Services Group has a Web site that employees and their managers can search by subject, competency, course title, and so forth to identify developmental opportunities for employees. Employees can also use The Hartford's intranet to look up job families, identify possible advancement paths, and identify the differences in expectations, responsibilities, and competencies required for the paths.[69]

As with succession management, the career planning process should be evaluated and improved as the organization's and employees' needs change. Because employees need to stay with the organization long enough to transition into the other positions for the succession management and career planning processes to be worthwhile, the return on the career planning and succession management investment is obviously greater for organizations with lower levels of employee turnover. Integrated career planning and succession management programs can show employees that their career goals can be reached within the organization.

This chapter's Develop Your Skills feature describes how to create your own career development plan. Many career development tools are available to expand and improve employees' skill sets and prepare them to be competitive for other positions in the organization. These tools increase the probability that future internal recruitment efforts will be successful, and include:

- *Assessment centers* that simulate the position an employee is interested in pursuing so the person can evaluate whether or not he or she will be a good fit for the job.
- *Career counseling and career development workshops* that help individuals understand the jobs that best match their aspirations and talents as well as develop the skills they need to successfully compete for opportunities.
- *Training and continuing education* that can provide employee's with skills training in a more formalized educational setting. Professional associations can also be a source of continuing education.
- *Job rotation, challenging assignments, and mentoring* that can provide skill development less formally.
- *Sabbaticals* that can be used to reenergize employees and give them the opportunity to develop skills and pursue other interests via workshops, formal classes, or travel.
- *Challenging and developmental job assignments* that enhance employees' key competencies and give them on-the-job experience before they assume new positions.

The last item in the list—challenging job assignments—is one of the best career development tools.[70] However, it is common for organizations to try to fill challenging assignments with people able to do the job well right now rather than to consider the assignments opportunities for career development. Sometimes firms are reluctant to use challenging job assignments for career development because their managers believe that moving people around and taking them away from their current job responsibilities is not worth the disruption. There can also be a lack of clarity about what skills should be developed in whom and what learning opportunities the job assignment offers.[71]

DEVELOP YOUR SKILLS
Making a Career Development Plan

A career development plan should be an important part of your career planning process. Specifying your career goals and creating an action plan for your personal and professional growth will better enable you to meet those goals. A career development plan typically contains both short- and long-term career goals as well as the actions, courses, activities, and other types of development that you plan to undertake to meet them. In making a career development plan, follow these three steps:

1. *Assess yourself.* Identify your current skills, knowledge, abilities, and interests. If you don't currently know what career you intend to pursue, books[72] and online career development tools, such as the following, can be of help:
   - *Testing Room* (http://quintcareers.testingroom.com): After you complete a self-assessment, the Web site suggests 20 to 40 careers that fit you.
   - *Career Planner* (www.careerplanner.com): Provides online career tests, one-on-one career counseling sessions, and free career planning information, advice, and ideas.
   - *Bridges Transitions Inc.* (http://access.bridges.com/portal/client/landingPage.do): Helps you identify possible career choices by matching careers with your chosen characteristics.
2. *Set goals.* Identify your short- and long-term career goals based on your personal and career interests. Your career goals might involve being promoted or attaining greater responsibility and variety in your present position. When setting your career goals, consider the following:[73]
   - Looking beyond the current year, what are your goals for future career development?
   - What competencies would you like to develop to position yourself for future success and career growth?
   - Are there any changes taking place in your company that could affect your developmental priorities?
   - Generate a list of goals and then prioritize the top three goals on which to concentrate your efforts.
   - Seek feedback and discuss your options with your supervisor and others familiar with your work performance, interests, and aptitudes to gain additional insight.
3. *Develop an action plan.* Evaluate the gap between your current situation and your goals and clarify what capabilities you need to develop. For each objective, identify the time frame for its completion and how you plan to develop the capability. Your action plan options include on-the-job or formal education or training, mentoring, making a lateral move, changing to a lower job grade for developmental purposes, gaining experience in a different geographical region or culture, or taking a temporary assignment to explore a new area before committing to it.[74] Your action plan can and should be revised as your goals change and as your competencies develop.

Because people learn when they are put in situations that require skills they do not currently have, organizations should consider using challenging job assignments as part of their career development process. Some organizations have formal systems to evaluate the development potential of projects and assign the jobs associated with them to fast-tracked talent. Cox Communications, a cable-TV and telecommunications provider, begins its talent review process by gathering information about its employees' career interests and willingness to relocate. Managers provide feedback to their employees through a series of review meetings, and then work with them to create development plans to match them to projects based on their needs.[75]

Figure 10-3 shows a sample career plan.

After you analyze your talents, interests, and goals and research possible occupations, you are ready to set career goals and plan how to reach them. A career plan helps you identify both short- and long-term goals and activities to help you succeed in your chosen career.

Career Goal:
To become a robotic engineer and ultimately design, plan, and supervise the construction of robots to be used in police work.

Requirements:
Bachelor's or master's degree in engineering.
Teamwork skills.
Creativity.
Analytical skills.
Knowledge of mechanical and electrical engineering.

Related Current Skills and Interests:
Summer worker for Robotronics Inc.
Earned A's in high school and college robotics and engineering courses.
Experience working in a team.
3.8/4.0 high school GPA.
3.9/4.0 college GPA.

Career Plan:
Earn a bachelor's degree from Virginia Tech's College of Engineering.
Gain related job experience by finding a summer robotics internship through the university's career placement center.
Network to develop relationships with five robotic engineers.
Network to develop relationships with three robotic engineering professors in my areas of interest.
Join campus organizations for engineering students.
Join a national robotics association.

Short-Term Goals:
Maintain high current GPA.
Graduate in the top 10 percent of my college class.
Earn good test scores and be accepted to a quality robotics graduate program.
Continue to acquire related work experience at Robotronics Inc.
Improve my creativity and analytical skills by taking courses designed to enhance them.

FIGURE 10-3 A Sample Career Plan

INTEGRATING SUCCESSION MANAGEMENT AND CAREER PLANNING

An organization's succession management and career planning processes should be thoroughly integrated with one another. The two also need to be integrated with the firm's other human resource functions and systems. The goal is to identify human resource management practices that presently encourage or discourage effective succession management and employee development. For example, if employees tend to perceive a particular promotion as unattractive because it requires longer hours, greater responsibility, and very little additional pay, addressing these issues can increase the desirability of the position. Likewise, if an organization's external recruitment and selection systems do not result in talented and promotable new hires, the succession management and career development programs will have very little raw material with which to work. As a result, a firm's talent "bench" is likely to stay weak regardless of the organization's commitment to promotion from within.

Delta Air Lines is an example of a company that has successfully integrated its succession management and career planning processes. Delta Air Lines's human resource planning process integrates employees' career interests, skills, and abilities as well as their perceptions of their own job performance with their managers' assessments of their performance and experiences to assess employees promotability, possible job moves, strengths, and developmental needs. During review meetings, the assessments are examined and validated, and the succession plans for all the company's executive positions are reviewed. Managers then provide feedback to their employees and work with them to create an appropriate development plan. The highest-potential employees receive a year of focused development and special exposure opportunities. The success of Delta's human resource planning process is evaluated by measuring the promotions of employees against the company's succession plans, the diverse mix of those people thought to be promotable, and the retention of high-potential employees.[76] Colgate-Palmolive uses its performance management process and each employee's individual development plan to identify high-potential talent at the company's local, regional, and global levels. When it's considering staffing a position, Colgate-Palmolive doesn't consider only what the business needs but also the development needs of various candidates to round out each candidate's overall experience.[77]

Firms also need to assist and encourage employees to decide for themselves where they want their careers to go. American Greetings interviews all of its high-potential employees to determine what they like and dislike about their jobs and what their individual goals are. Even if an employee claims to have no interest in advancement, American Greetings creates a developmental plan with the primary objective of making him or her more effective in the job he or she already has.[78]

INTERNAL ASSESSMENT AT WELLPOINT

At the beginning the chapter, you learned that WellPoint wanted to do a better job identifying and tracking the development of its promising internal talent. The firm's top managers also wanted to be able to evaluate candidates across the company's locations. To do this, WellPoint combined the performance appraisals of its employees with its succession management system on an annual basis. Each of the 600 participants in the company's succession plan writes a self-evaluation to which his or her supervisor adds a performance appraisal, core competency rating, and an assessment of the employee's potential for promotion. The supervisor also indicates who might be capable of replacing the employee if he or she is promoted. That data is combined with the employee's other characteristics, such as the person's education, language skills, and experience, to create an employee profile that is then assembled into WellPoint's succession charts.[79] WellPoint's managers can also enter detailed queries into the firm's succession-planning database in order to best match employees with different job opportunities that arise.[80]

The company also prepares its future succession candidates with an integrated training and career development program. Because WellPoint fills over 85 percent of its management positions internally, it saves hundreds of thousands of dollars annually on executive search expenses. It has also reduced its time to fill executive positions to 35 days, and reduced its managerial turnover rate by 6 percent. WellPoint estimates that its succession management system has saved over $21 million in recruiting and training expenses alone.[81] The company estimates that it saved $1 million in a single incident when it filled two top-level executive positions internally and then "backfilled" each resulting vacancy with internal candidates going down five management levels.[82]

WellPoint is also able to spot problematic areas in its succession chart. Being able to do so has allowed the firm to develop initiatives to shore up its workforce in those areas. The firm also uses its database to assess its core competencies, determine where it needs to focus its developmental and training resources, and pinpoint lateral opportunities for employees.[83]

Summary

The success of an internal staffing strategy depends in large part on the retention and development of internal talent. A commitment to internal recruitment rather than staffing higher-level positions externally can give organizations a competitive advantage over their competitors by enabling succession planning, reducing the risk top employees will leave for better jobs elsewhere, and minimizing the risk of critical positions in the organization remaining vacant after the departure of an incumbent. Succession management practices help to ensure that successors are developed and ready to assume their new roles when an opening arises. By facilitating the smooth transitioning of talent as people move through the organization and optimally deploying talent across the organization, succession management and internal recruiting help an organization execute its business strategy and meet its business goals. Career planning is best done in conjunction with succession management to ensure that employees desire the job and career opportunities that the organization would like them to pursue.

Takeaway Points

1. A company's internal assessment goals largely mirror its external assessment goals. These objectives include evaluating the fit of employees with other jobs, enhancing the firm's strategic capabilities, gathering information with which to make downsizing decisions, maximizing fit, making accurate and ethical assessments, generating a high return on the firm's investment in its assessment system, generating positive stakeholder reactions, supporting the firm's talent philosophy and human resource strategy, reinforcing the organization's employer image, identifying development needs, and maintaining legal compliance.

2. By assessing its current capabilities and future talent needs as well as the potential of its employees to learn necessary new skills, a firm can enhance its strategic position. In addition to ensuring that the company has the right amount of the right skills in place when it needs them, the information can be used to develop career paths for employees and provide them with the training they need to reach their goals, as well as the firm's goals.

3. The methods used to conduct an internal assessment include skills inventories, mentoring, job knowledge tests, performance reviews, tests conducted at assessment centers, and clinical assessments.

4. The nine box matrix and the career crossroads model are two types of internal assessment models that have been developed.

5. Integrating its succession management system with the career development plans of its employees helps a company align its career goals with the firm's leadership succession needs. The career planning process assesses the goals, preferences, and capabilities of employees, and compares them with the current and future needs of the organization based on the company's human resource strategy and succession plan. Matches or mismatches are then discussed with each individual employee to remedy the gaps and offer the employee potential career development opportunities. A company can also change its recruiting strategies, business strategies, and the way it does its work to remedy a talent gap.

6. Like external assessment systems, internal assessments should be continually reevaluated and changed over time as a firm's business strategies and workforce change.

Discussion Questions

1. How is internal assessment useful for more than just evaluating employees for other positions in the company?

2. Do you feel that multisource feedback is appropriate? Why or why not?

3. Using the nine box matrix, an employee doing a good job might actually be rated lower than a mediocre employee who has been working in a developmental stretch assignment. Do you feel that this is fair? Why or why not?

4. Given how important succession management programs are, how can companies persuade their managers to support and commit to their succession management activities?

5. Why is it important to integrate succession management with career planning?

Exercises

1. *Strategy Exercise:*   Working in groups of three to five students, read the following vignette and develop some suggestions for the company based on the material you read in this chapter. Be prepared to share your ideas with the class.

Twisted is a small company with big dreams. The shopping mall–oriented hot pretzel company has successfully grown its revenues by a rate of 10 percent annually over the last 10 years. Twisted wants to sustain its growth rate in the years ahead.

The company has traditionally hired new store managers from outside of the company. However, in the last few years, it has had a difficult time recruiting enough of these people. The CEO feels that there are probably a large number of employees who might make good managers. However, the company has no good internal assessment systems in place to identify them. The CEO asks your group to help the firm identify internal managerial talent so it can continue to pursue its growth strategy. What methods would you suggest for doing so?

2. *Develop Your Skills Exercise:* This chapter's Develop Your Skills feature describes how to create a career development plan. It is never too soon to identify your short- and long-term career goals and analyze what skills, experiences, and other things you need to do to obtain your goals. Your assignment is to create your own career development plan that focuses on one- and five-year time horizons. Your action plan should include realistic activities that you can undertake to enhance your ability to meet the career goals you identify.

3. *Opening Vignette Exercise:* In this chapter's opening vignette, you learned how WellPoint combines succession management and performance appraisals into one annual process that allows it to quickly identify and assess internal candidates for managerial positions. Working in a group of three to five students, reread the vignette. Be prepared to share with your class your answers to the following questions:
   a. Why do you think that WellPoint's internal assessment and development system is so successful?
   b. What additional ideas do you have that could help WellPoint fill as many managerial positions as possible with its current employees?

CASE STUDY

Succession Management at General Electric[84]

General Electric (GE) is widely recognized and respected for its leadership talent and its succession management system. One of the best examples of succession management is how GE's former CEO, Jack Welch, shaped and elevated the company's philosophy, practice, and reputation for developing leaders. In a 1991 speech, Welch stated, "From now on, choosing my successor is the most important decision I'll make." GE's commitment to developing leaders from within has yielded positive results for both the company's employees and for GE. In fact, the program has been so successful that it's been widely emulated by other global organizations.

Measuring and developing talent lies at the forefront of GE's business strategy discussions. GE's operating system, referred to as its "learning culture in action," entails year-round learning sessions in which leaders from GE and outside companies share best practices with one another and generate ideas for new practices. Harry Elsinga, manager of executive development at GE, notes, "We really have a tight organization around how we combine our leadership meetings and how we approach our business. We have a constant cycle going on throughout the year where we talk about business and people at the same time. How do we develop talent in those businesses, how do we make sure that we have the right people to open a particular plant or to do an acquisition, etc.? Those discussions always go hand in hand. And it's not a one-time kind of conversation; this is a constant, ongoing process."[85]

GE's succession management system is fairly simple. GE managers and executives are moved from job to job every two to three years, and each job change or promotion is a well-thought-out process that provides managers with much-needed experience and exposure to certain elements of the business. This has allowed GE to build a management team that is very knowledgeable and experienced.

QUESTIONS

1. Do you think that GE's approach to succession management would work for all organizations? Why or why not?
2. What are some possible disadvantages of moving people to new jobs every two to three years?
3. Why does GE's succession management approach work so well?

Semester-Long Active Learning Project

Develop an internal assessment strategy for evaluating employees for your chosen position. If the job you chose is not staffed internally, create an employee assessment plan to evaluate employees already in the position in the event downsizing becomes necessary.

Case Study Assignment: Strategic Staffing at Chern's

See the appendix at the back of the book for this chapter's Case Study Assignment.

Endnotes

1. "WellPoint and WellChoice Complete Merger," WellPoint, http://phx.corporateir.net/phoenix.zhtml?c=130104&p=irol-newsArticle_general&t=Regular&id=799275&. Accessed April 27, 2007.
2. "Careers," WellPoint, www.wellpoint.com/careers/default.asp. Accessed October 13, 2006.
3. Boyle, M., "Why Costco Is So Addictive," *Fortune,* October 25, 2006, http://money.cnn.com/magazines/fortune/fortune_archive/2006/10/30/8391725/index.htm?postversion=2006102515. Accessed October 25, 2006.

4. Fulmer, R. M., "Choose Tomorrow's Leaders Today," *Graziado Business Report,* Winter 2002, http://gbr.pepperdine.edu/021/succession.html. Accessed October 16, 2006.

5. Bergeron, C., "Build a Talent Strategy to Achieve Your Desired Business Results," *Handbook of Business Strategy,* 5, 1 (2004): 133–140.

6. Bechet, T. P., and Walker, L. W., "Aligning Staffing with Business Strategy," *Human Resource Planning,* 16 (1993): 1–16.

7. Harris, P., "Case Study: Web-Based Development Delivers for FedEx," Learning Circuits, September 2004, http://www.astd.org/LC/2004/0904_harris.htm. Accessed September 23, 2010.

8. "Creating Leadership Capabilities for Success Within a Rapidly Evolving Industry," Personnel Decisions International, www.personneldecisions.com/results/casestudydetailgeneric.asp?id=28. Accessed October 16, 2006.

9. Bechet and Walker, "Aligning Staffing with Business Strategy."

10. Wells, S. J., "Who's Next?" *HR Magazine,* November 2003: 45–50.

11. Bechet and Walker, "Aligning Staffing with Business Strategy."

12. Inter-Agency Benchmarking and Best Practices Council, *Serving the American Public: Best Practices in Downsizing,* September 1997, http://govinfo.library.unt.edu/npr/library/papers/benchmrk/downsize.html#4. Accessed October 25, 2006.

13. Jacobs, R., Hofmann, D. A., and Kriska, D., "Performance and Seniority," *Human Performance,* 3, 2 (1990): 107–121; Quinones, M. A., Ford, J. K., and Teachout, M. S., "The Relationship Between Work Experience and Job Performance: A Conceptual and Meta-Analytic Review," *Personnel Psychology,* 48, 4 (1995): 887–910.

14. Professor Barbara Rau, University of Wisconsin-Oshkosh, Personal Communication, 2010.

15. Newman, E., "Improving the Internal Recruiting Process: A Strategic Opportunity for HR," Electronic Recruiting Exchange, March 29, 2005, www.ere.net/articles/db/6689570981974CD49F570CC50 B92DA41.asp. Accessed October 13, 2006.

16. In Kesler, G. C., "Why the Leadership Bench Never Gets Deeper: Ten Insights About Executive Talent Development," *HR Planning Society Journal,* 25, 1 (2002): 32–44.

17. "2007 Training Top 125," *Training Magazine,* March 2007, www.trainingmag.com/managesmarter/images/pdfs/2007Top 125.pdf. Accessed May 23, 2007.

18. Equal Employment Opportunity Commission, "Uniform Employee Selection Guidelines Interpretation and Clarification (Questions and Answers)," www.uniformguidelines.com/questionandanswers.html. Accessed October 24, 2006.

19. *Roberts v. Texaco, Inc.,* 94 Civ. 2015 (CLB).

20. *Abdallah v. Coca-Cola,* 133 F.Supp.2d 1364 (N.D. Ga. 2001), No. 1-98-CV-3679.

21. Feeney, S. A., "Irreplaceable You," *Workforce Management,* August 2003: 36–40.

22. Personnel Decisions International, "Aligning Talent with Changing Business Needs," www.personneldecisions.com/results/casestudydetailgeneric.asp?id=24. Accessed October 16, 2006.

23. Kim, S., "Linking Employee Assessments to Succession Planning," *Public Personnel Management,* 32, 4 (Winter 2003): 533–548.

24. McCafferty, J., "A Human Inventory," *CFO Magazine,* April 1, 2005, www.cfo.com/article.cfm/3804634/c_3805512?f=single-page. Accessed May 15, 2007.

25. Treasury Board of Canada Secretariat, *Employee Skills Inventories for the Federal Public Service,* 1994, www.tbs-sct.gc.ca/pubs_pol/hrpubs/TB_85A/dwnld/invent_e.rtf. Accessed May 16, 2007.

26. Healy, C. C., and Welchert, A. J., "Mentoring Relations: A Definition to Advance Research and Practice," *Educational Researcher,* 19, 9 (1990): 17.

27. "2007 Training Top 125," *Training Magazine.*

28. Bernardin, H. J., and Beatty, R. W., *Performance Appraisal: Assessing Human Behavior at Work,* Boston, MA: Kent, 1984.

29. Borman, W. C., "The Rating of Individuals in Organizations: An Alternative Approach," *Organizational Behavior and Human Performance,* 12 (1974): 105–124.

30. Kane, J. S., and Lawler, E. E., "Performance Appraisal Effectiveness: Its Assessment and Determinants," In B. Staw (ed.), *Research in Organizational Behavior* 1, Greenwich, CT: JAI Press, 1979.

31. For a more thorough discussion of performance appraisal see Murphy, K. R., and Cleveland, J., *Understanding Performance Appraisal: Social, Organizational, and Goal-based Perspectives,* Thousand Oaks, CA: Sage, 1995.

32. Yammarino, F., and Atwater, L., "Understanding Self-Perception Accuracy: Implications for Human Resource Management," *Human Resource Management,* 32, 2 (1993): 231–247; John, O. P. and Robins, R. W., "Accuracy and Bias in Self-Perception: Individual Differences in Self-Enhancement and the Role of Narcissism," *Journal of Personality and Social Psychology,* 66, 1 (January 1994): 206–219; Furnham, A., and Stringfield, P., "Congruence in Job-Performance Ratings: A Study of 360 Feedback Examining Self, Manager, Peers, and Consultant Ratings," *Human Relations,* 51, 4 (April 1998): 517–530.

33. "2007 Training Top 125," *Training Magazine.*

34. Reilly, R. R., and Chao, G. T., "Validity and Fairness of Some Alternative Employee Selection Procedures," *Personnel Psychology,* 35 (1982): 1–62.

35. United States Office of Personnel Management, "360-Degree Assessment: An Overview," September 1997, www.opm.gov/perform/wppdf/360asess.pdf. Accessed October 25, 2006.

36. Reilly and Chao, "Validity and Fairness of Some Alternative Employee Selection Procedures."

37. United States Office of Personnel Management, "360-Degree Assessment: An Overview."

38. Kiger, P. J., "Elements of WellPoint's Succession-Planning Program," *Workforce,* April 2002, 51.

39. "Testing Becomes Key Element of Customs' Hiring and Merit Promotion Processes," *U.S. Customs Today,* November 2000, www.cbp.gov/custoday/nov2000/tests.htm. Accessed October 31, 2006.

40. Gaugler, B. B., Rosenthal, D. B., Thornton, G. C., III., and Bentson, C., "Meta-Analysis of Assessment Center Validity," *Journal of Applied Psychology,* 72 (1987): 493–511.

41. Carbonara, P., "Hire for Attitude, Train for Skill," *Fast Company,* August 1996: 73.

42. Ryan, A. M., and Sackett, P. R., "A Survey of Individual Assessment Practices by I/O Psychologists," *Personnel Psychology,* 40 (1987): 455–488.

43. Fulmer, "Choose Tomorrow's Leaders Today."

44. Personal communication with Steve Drotter, October 13, 2006.

45. For a more detailed discussion of this section's material, see Mahler, W. R., and Wrightnour, W. F., *Executive Continuity: How to Build and Retain an Effective Management Team,* Homewood, IL: Dow Jones-Irwin, 1973; Mahler, W., and Drotter, S., *The Succession Planning Handbook for the Chief*

Executive, Midland Park, NJ: Mahler Publishing Co., 1986; and Charan, Drotter, and Noel, *The Leadership Pipeline.*

46. Adapted from Charan, R., Drotter, S., and Noel, J., *The Leadership Pipeline: How to Build the Leadership-Powered Company,* San Francisco, CA: Jossey-Bass, 2001.

47. National Academy of Public Administration, *Paths to Leadership: Executive Succession Planning in the Federal Government,* Washington, D.C.: National Academy of Public Administration, 1997.

48. Metzler, J. C., "Planning for Transition," *American Institute of Certified Public Accountants* 7, August 2005, http://pcps .aicpa.org/NR/rdonlyres/42B0698A-4576-4795-AEDC-DD7E 3DF5E94B/0/SFCvolume7final.pdf. Accessed October 27, 2006.

49. See Beeson, J., "Succession Planning," *Across the Board,* 37, 2 (2000): 38–43; Crockett, J., "Diversity: Winning Competitive Advantage Through a Diverse Workforce," *HR Focus,* 5, 76 (1999): 9–10; Stewart, J. K., "Diversity Efforts Dragging: Women of Color Find Progress Can Be Made, But It's Slow," *Chicago Tribune,* September 1, 1999: 7.

50. Crockett, "Diversity: Winning Competitive Advantage Through a Diverse Workforce."; Stewart, "Diversity Efforts Dragging."

51. Aitchinson, C., "Succession Planning at the Dixons Group," *Strategic HR Review,* 3, 5 (August 2004): 24–27.

52. Nash, J., "A New Boss from Outside Costs More. . . a Lot More," *Workforce Management Online,* March 14, 2007, www.workforce.com/section/00/article/24/80/43.html. Accessed March 21, 2007.

53. Dye, C. F., "Is Anyone Next in Line? Succession Plans Are Critical to Ensuring a Smooth Transition when an Organization Faces an Unexpected—or an Expected—Leadership Vacancy," *Healthcare Financial Management,* February 2005, http:// findarticles.com/p/articles/mi_m3257/is_2_59/ai_n9772397. Accessed May 14, 2007.

54. Clark, H., "To Tell or Not to Tell," *Forbes,* October 18, 2006, www.forbes.com/2006/10/18/leadership-health-cancer-lead-manage-cx_hc_1018succession.html. Accessed May 14, 2007.

55. Charan, Drotter, and Noel, *The Leadership Pipeline.*

56. Ibid, 167.

57. Feeney, "Irreplaceable You."

58. Frauenheim, E., "Firms Walk Fine Line with 'High-Potential' Programs," *Workforce Management,* November 15, 2006, www.workforce.com/section/11/feature/24/54/84/index.html. Accessed November 15, 2006.

59. Kleinknecht, M. K., and Hefferin, E. A., "Assisting Nurses toward Professional Growth: A Career Development Model," *Journal of Nursing Administration,* 12, 4 (1982): 30–36.

60. Pope, B., *Workforce Management: How Today's Companies Are Meeting Business and Employee Needs,* Homewood, IL: Business One Irwin, 1993.

61. Fulmer, "Choose Tomorrow's Leaders Today."

62. Ibid.

63. Ibid.

64. Conger, J. A., and Fulmer, R. M., "Developing Your Leadership Pipeline," *Harvard Business Review* (December 2003): 76–84.

65. Guthridge, M., Komm, A. B., and Lawson, E., "The People Problem in Talent Management," *McKinsey Quarterly,* October 26, 2006, www.mckinseyquarterly.com/article_page.aspx?

ar=1755&L2=18&L3=31&srid=63&gp=1. Accessed October 26, 2006.

66. Metzler, "Planning for Transition."

67. "Career Development in Canada," General Mills, www.general-mills.com/corporate/careers/development_canada.aspx. Accessed October 16, 2006.

68. "Experienced/MBAs," Kimberly-Clark, 2007, www.kimberly-clark.com/careers/na/exp_mba.aspx. Accessed May 16, 2007.

69. Joinson, C., "Employee, Sculpt Thyself...With a Little Help," *HR Magazine,* May 2001, http://findarticles.com/p/articles/ mi_m3495/is_5_46/ai_74829358/pg_2. Accessed October 16, 2006.

70. Brutus, S., Ruderman, M. N., Ohlott, P. J., and McCauley, C. D., "Developing from Job Experiences: The Role of Organization-Based Self-esteem," *Human Resource Development Quarterly* 11, 4 (2001): 367–380.

71. Chambers, E. G., Foulon, M., Handfield-Jones, H., Hankin, S. M., and Michaels, E. G., III, "The War for Talent," *McKinsey Quarterly,* 1998: 44–57.

72. There are many books on the topic of career planning, including: Maltz, S., and Grahn, B., *A Fork in the Road: A Career Planning Guide for Young Adults,* Manassas Park, VA: Impact Publications, 2003; Lore, N., *The Pathfinder: How to Choose or Change Your Career for a Lifetime of Satisfaction and Success,* New York: Fireside Books, 1998; Bolles, R. N., *What Color Is Your Parachute? 2007: A Practical Manual for Job-Hunters and Career Changers,* Berkeley, CA: Ten Speed Press, 2007.

73. Based on "What Should I Consider in Creating My Learning and Development Plan?" Government of Alberta, September 7, 2004, www.pao.gov.ab.ca/toolkit/planguide/what-should-i-consider.htm. Accessed October 16, 2006.

74. U.S. Coast Guard, "Career Development Planning," *A Supervisor's Guide to Career Development and Counseling for Civilian Employees,* www.uscg.mil/hq/cgpc/cpm/home/ sgfch7.htm. Accessed October 16, 2006.

75. "2007 Training Top 125," *Training Magazine.*

76. Ellis, K., "Making Waves," *Training,* 40, 6 (June 2003): 16–21.

77. Ibid.

78. Caudron, S., "Plan Today for an Unexpected Tomorrow," *Personnel Journal,* 75, 9 (September 1996): 40–45.

79. Kiger, P. J., "Succession Planning Keeps WellPoint Competitive," *Workforce,* April 2002: 50–54.

80. Frauenheim, E., "Software Products Aim to Streamline Succession Planning," *Workforce Management Online,* January 2006, www.workforce.com/section/06/feature/24/24/94/242496 .html. Accessed October 13, 2006.

81. Kiger, "Succession Planning Keeps WellPoint Competitive."

82. Frauenheim, E., "Succession Progression," *Workforce Management,* January 16, 2006: 31–34.

83. Kiger, "Succession Planning Keeps WellPoint Competitive."

84. Heiden, S., "Managing Succession Plans and Career Paths," *Chief Learning Officer,* May 2007, http://www.clomedia.com/features/ 2007/April/1780/index.php. Accessed May 16, 2007; Knudson, L., "Generating Leaders GE Style," *HR Management,* 2007, www.hrmreport.com/pastissue/article.asp?art=269158&issue=18 6. Accessed May 16, 2007; Leonard, B., "Turnover at the Top," *HR Magazine,* May 2001, http:// findarticles.com/p/articles/ mi_m3495/is_5_46/ai_74829356/pg_1. Accessed May 16, 2007.

85. Knudson, "Generating Leaders GE Style."

Choosing and Hiring Candidates

LEARNING OBJECTIVES

After studying this chapter, you should be able to:

- Describe different ways of combining candidates' scores on different assessment methods to calculate an overall score.
- Describe three different ways of making a final choice of whom to hire.
- Discuss the factors that influence the content of a company's job offer.
- Describe the four different job offer strategies.
- Describe different types of fairness and explain why candidates' perceptions of fairness are important to staffing.

Hiring Top Performers at MarineMax

Yacht maker MarineMax is a publicly traded, billion-dollar boat broker with over 85 retail locations in 21 states.[1] Focused on premium brands, such as Sea Ray, Boston Whaler, Meridian, Hatteras, Grady White, and the Ferretti Group, MarineMax complements its industry-leading brands with exclusive, value-added services including dedicated delivery captains, classroom and in-water customer training, professionally organized Getaways! cruises, a no-haggle sales approach, and extensive after-sale service.[2]

Despite its size and continued growth, MarineMax works hard to retain the high level of service and personal interaction found at smaller companies. To continue its growth, MarineMax needs enthusiastic, talented, and highly motivated employees with leadership potential for jobs across the company.[3] The company knows that these people are hard to find and looks for ways to present appealing job offers to top talent. The company's managers know these people are interested in intangible benefits, such as challenging work and advancement opportunities, in addition to top pay.[4] MarineMax asks you for advice on how it can best persuade its top finalists to accept its job offers without ratcheting up its labor costs more than necessary.

Up to this point in the book, we have focused on planning the staffing effort, attracting applicants, and evaluating job candidates. The next stage of the staffing process involves choosing and hiring the best finalists. Because the cost of making a bad hiring decision is often many times that person's salary,[5] not to mention the effects of losing a high-potential candidate to a competitor, choosing whom to hire and persuading them to accept your offer is a critical part of the strategic staffing process.

Imagine the following evaluation scores for two finalists for a financial analyst's position: Maria scored 80/100 on a job knowledge test, 35/50 on a structured interview, and 45/50 on a personality and values test designed to assess her fit with the organization's culture and values. Pete scored 70/100 on the job knowledge test, 45/50 on the structured interview, and 35/50 on the personality and values test. Based on these scores, who should be hired? The answer depends on the way the firm weights and combines the scores. If the scores are averaged, Maria would receive the job offer. But if the structured interview scores are given greater weight than the other assessments, Pete might be the preferred candidate. If candidates must score at least 75 on the job knowledge test, however, then Pete would be out of the running.

There are different methods of combining candidates' assessment scores. All the methods are relatively easy to understand, but you need to know how to use them. You also need to understand how to go about persuading the best candidates to join your firm. In this chapter, we discuss the methods used to choose candidates as well as the employment contract and job offer process, negotiation, and closing the deal. After reading this chapter, you should have a good understanding of how best to choose which finalist should receive a job offer, and how to persuade that person to become an employee of your firm.

CHOOSING CANDIDATES

Some candidates are so exemplary that to prevent them from accepting other companies' offers, firms quickly offer to hire them prior to evaluating all their potential candidates. However, this is unusual. It is more common to combine candidates' scores on a variety of assessment methods and compare their overall scores to determine whom to hire. We discuss how this is done next.

Combining Candidates' Scores

There are two ways of combining candidates' assessment scores so that they can be compared with one another: the multiple hurdles approach and the compensatory approach.

THE MULTIPLE HURDLES APPROACH   Requiring candidates to perform at a satisfactory level on one assessment before being allowed to continue in the selection process is called a **multiple hurdles approach**. As we explained in Chapter 8, it is common for firefighter candidates to be required to pass a strength test (e.g., a test requiring them to lift 40 pounds) early in the assessment process. If candidates lack the physical capabilities they need, there is no point in wasting their time as well as the company's time and resources by continuing to evaluate them.

multiple hurdles approach
a scoring approach whereby candidates must receive a passing score on an assessment before being allowed to continue on in the selection process

The FBI uses a multiple hurdles approach when hiring special agents. Because their cognitive abilities, problem-solving, and decision-making skills are so important, the FBI requires special agent applicants to pass a biodata inventory, a cognitive ability test, and a situational judgment test before being allowed to proceed in the hiring process.[6] Because the multiple hurdles approach is costly and takes more time, the approach is generally used when the cost of an employee's poor performance is high—for example, when the person has the potential to put people's safety at risk.

American Express uses a three-part multiple hurdle assessment system in which only people performing well on the current assessment are allowed to advance to the next stage of the assessment process. The first assessment is a questionnaire candidates complete on the company's Web site. The questionnaire assesses their work history, degrees obtained, and willingness to relocate. A summary report is then e-mailed to an American Express HR representative, who decides which applicants become candidates and advance to Level 2. Level 2 involves taking a 45-minute test to assess whether candidates have the necessary characteristics identified by a job analysis. Candidates who do well on the test reach Level 3 and are invited for an interview.[7]

THE COMPENSATORY APPROACH　When you think about the best professors you have had, do you think they are equally talented in every way? Probably not. It's more likely that your favorite professors had different talents as well as different combinations of them. For example, you might have had a professor with outstanding storytelling skills, whereas another one of your professors who lacked those skills could have been equally effective because of his or her ability to inspire and challenge you. The **compensatory approach** takes differences such as these into account. It allows high scores on some assessments to compensate for low scores on other assessments. For example, a company might allow a candidate's successful work experience to compensate for a lower grade point average (GPA).

There are several ways to execute the compensatory approach. Job experts can review each candidate's scores on the different assessments as well as any notes and other information acquired during the assessment process. The overall judgment of the firm's job experts can then be used to integrate the different scores and determine each candidate's total score. Their judgment can also be used to make the final hiring decision or to determine if a candidate advances to the next phase of the hiring process. However, because different experts are likely to use different criteria and weigh it differently, the risk of legal troubles increases when this method is used. Nonetheless, if the job experts have a significant amount of experience when it comes to making selection decisions, and if their acceptance of the selection process is important, relying on their judgment can be appropriate.

Job experts' ratings may or may not produce the same scores as **unit weighting**. Unit weighting involves giving multiple assessments equal weight when computing a candidate's overall score. If all the assessment methods a firm administers are equally useful predictors of job success, then unit weighting is appropriate. However, as we discussed in Chapter 8, when different assessments are made using different scales (e.g., if an interview is scored on a 1 to 10 point scale but intelligence is scored on a 1 to 60 point scale) simply adding them together to produce an overall score does not equally weight the scores. The importance of the intelligence assessment would be overweighted and the importance of the interview would be underweighted. In this case, the raw scores must be standardized before being combined.

Table 11-1 shows an example of converting raw to standardized scores that are combined using a unit weighting approach. Ying's score of 89/100 is 1.5 standard deviations above average

compensatory approach
an approach whereby high scores on some assessments can compensate for low scores on other assessments

unit weighting
giving multiple assessments equal weight when computing a candidate's overall score

TABLE 11-1	Standardizing and Combining Raw Scores Using the Unit Weighted Approach

	Ying		Tony	
	Raw	Standardized	Raw	Standardized
Structured Interview	89	1.5	60	.4
Knowledge Test	25	1.1	35	1.7
Assessment Center	6	.9	7	1.1
Unit Weighted Overall Score		3.5		3.2

on the standardized interview, and Tony's score of 60/100 is .4 standard deviations above average. Ying's knowledge test score of 25/40 is 1.1 standard deviations above average, and Tony's score of 35/40 is 1.7 standard deviations above average. Ying's assessment center score of 6/10 is .9 standard deviation above average, and Tony's assessment center score of 7/10 is 1.1 standard deviations above average. Because the scoring of the assessment methods is so different, using scales ranging from 1 to 10 and 0 to 100 and then adding candidates' raw scores would greatly overweight their structured interview scores and underweight their assessment center scores. Standardizing these scores makes it possible to compute an overall score for each candidate that can be compared with other candidates' overall scores. In this case, although Tony outperformed Ying on the knowledge test and assessment center, Ying's strong performance relative to Tony's in the structured interview resulted in her overall score of 3.5. That's greater than Tony's overall score of 3.2, so Ying is determined to be the stronger candidate.

rational weighting
a weighting method whereby experts assign a different subjective weight to each assessment score

Rational weighting requires experts to assign a different subjective weight to each assessment score. Job experts, including hiring managers, determine the weights based on the extent to which the job experts believe each assessment is important to a person's on-the-job success. A candidate's score on each assessment method is then multiplied by that assessment method's weight, and each assessment's weighted score is then added to produce an overall score. Although this approach has the advantage of recognizing that each score contributes differently to the candidate's overall assessment, it requires the job experts to agree on the weights. In addition, there is no guarantee that the experts' weights will best predict success on the job. Clinical assessments, which we discussed in Chapter 10, utilize the rational weighting approach.

Statistical Weighting
a weighting method using a statistical technique, such as multiple regression, to assign a different weight to each assessment score

Statistical weighting involves the use of a statistical technique, such as multiple regression, to assign a different weight to each assessment score. A multiple regression analysis, a data analysis tool initially discussed in Chapter 8, is a statistical technique that identifies the ideal weights to assign each assessment score based on each assessment method's correlation with job success and the degree to which the different assessment methods are intercorrelated. A multiple regression analysis is the most scientific approach to determining how to weight each assessment. Recall that the output of a multiple regression includes a formula that looks like this:

$$\text{Overall score} = c + (b1 \times a1) + (b2 \times a2) + (b3 \times a3)\ldots$$

Recall also that c is a constant, the b's are the statistical weights applied to each assessment method to maximize the validity of the group of assessment methods, and the a's are a candidate's scores on each of the assessment methods. Any number of assessment methods can be used. For example, if the regression equation for a salesperson looked like this:

$$\text{Overall score} = 24 + (.20 \times \text{Cognitive ability}) + (.25 \times \text{Interview}) + (.15 \times \text{Personality})$$

and the candidate's cognitive ability score was 70, his or her interview score was 75, and personality score was 50, then the candidate's overall score would be 64.25:

$$\text{Overall score} = 24 + (.2 \times 70) + (.25 \times 75) + (.15 \times 50)$$

$$\text{Overall score} = 64.25$$

This overall score is then used to evaluate whether the candidate should advance to the next phase of the assessment process or whether a job offer should be extended. This method can produce better hiring outcomes than can either unit weighting or rational weightings by job experts. However, to be accurate, the multiple regression approach requires HR professionals to collect a sample of several hundred or more candidates. If you don't have a large sample size with which to work, unit weighting or rational weighting may be a better choice.

COMBINING THE MULTIPLE HURDLES AND COMPENSATORY APPROACHES   Often, some job requirements are essential to performing a job, but others can compensate for each other, as we have indicated. For example, a data entry candidate might need to type a certain number of words per minute with a minimum number of errors. These skills might be used as hurdles in an initial assessment. However, his or her cognitive abilities, job knowledge, and personality might be compensatory factors. In this case, after clearing the initial hurdles, the person's cognitive abilities, job knowledge, and personality scores would be weighted and combined in a compensatory manner, and the highest scoring candidate offered the job. The FBI special-agent selection process we mentioned earlier in the chapter is an example of such an approach.[8]

Cut scores, rank ordering, or banding, which we first discussed in Chapter 8, can be used to choose which finalists receive job offers. If a cut score is used, only finalists who exceed a minimum score on some or all of the assessments are hired. Cut scores are often determined by job experts based on the job's requirements or by a regression equation. The level of a cut score is based on what level of predicted performance is minimally acceptable. If a company's talent strategy is to hire only the best, the cut score would be set at a high level. By contrast, if a firm is focused on filling vacancies in the short term rather than hiring people for long-term careers, then a lower cut score might be more appropriate. If a company is pursuing a cost-leadership strategy, a lower cut score might be necessary to hire people at the targeted salary level. One problem with high cut scores is that they increase the number of false negatives because they result in the rejection of higher numbers of qualified candidates. Because this can increase the adverse impact of the selection system, a firm might consider lowering its cut scores to reduce the number of false negatives among women and minorities.

Cut scores can be set in three ways. If job experts can establish a minimally acceptable competency level, then the cut score can be set at this level. If the company needs to hire quickly, the first candidate who exceeds the cut score is sometimes hired. However, by taking this approach, the firm risks losing the opportunity to hire a more desirable candidate who might soon be recruited. If a company's strategy is to hire top talent, it makes more sense to generate a pool of candidates before making a final hiring decision unless an exceptional candidate is identified early on.

Another option is to compare candidates' assessment scores to each other and rank order them from highest to lowest score. One of the primary issues with using rank ordering is that it does not guarantee that any of the candidates meet or exceed minimum hiring standards. Cut scores do a better job of reducing the number of unqualified people being hired. Combining the two methods and making job offers to the highest-ranked candidates who exceed a cut score helps to leverage the strengths of both approaches.

Because rank ordering candidates can result in adverse impact, it is not always a desirable way to choose your employees, despite the fact that it can be highly valid and cost-effective. Sometimes banding can be a better alternative. Recall that with banding, everyone who scores within a certain range of scores is considered to have performed equivalently and assigned the same grade. A student earning 98 percent in a course receives the same A grade as a student earning 93 percent. Hiring within the band is then done randomly or based on other factors, such as the firm's Equal Employment Opportunity (EEO) or affirmative action goals, the company's desire to promote an internal candidate who might otherwise leave the company, the experience and languages spoken by candidates, and so forth. The widths of the bands are generally calculated on the basis of the standard error of measurement[9] described in Chapter 8. Table 11-2 illustrates the use of banding.

Although banding can help reduce adverse impact, it does not always do so.[10] It also cannot remedy deficiencies in the sourcing and recruiting of qualified minorities. However, it can

TABLE 11-2	Banding Candidates	
Candidate	**Overall Score**	**Band**
Amy	87	1
Yu	85	1
Lee	79	2
Pedro	78	2
Amila	78	2
Bill	65	3
Tim	63	3
Lin	61	3

help minimize the impact of measurement errors. After all, is someone with an overall assessment score of 87.3 vastly better than a candidate whose score is 87.1—or even 86? Probably not. No test is perfect—a candidate's true score is likely to be a little higher or lower than the score the person actually receives. Thus, rank ordering candidates won't always produce the most accurate result or best hire. This is particularly true when the differences between candidates' scores are relatively small or when the standard error of measurement is large.

When using cut scores or rank ordering, an additional decision needs to be made about whether to hire from the top of the list down, or to create a pool of finalists from which to make a final choice. This pool of finalists can then be rank ordered based on overall or specific assessments. Alternatively, the candidates can be randomly selected or banded. There is no one best method of choosing the finalists to whom to extend job offers. At the very least, the firm's cutoff scores should be set high enough so the company's new hires at least meet or exceed any minimum standards of success.[11]

Who Makes the Final Hiring Decision?

Industrial-organizational psychologists are experts at candidate assessment and test construction. Human resource professionals are experts in the staffing process. Although these people develop staffing policies and procedures, often make initial applicant screening decisions, and either have or know how to find legal and technical information relevant to the assessment and hiring process, it is hiring managers who are usually responsible for making actual hiring decisions. Because the hiring manager will be supervising the person hired, he or she is also one of the primary stakeholders in the staffing process and should be involved in creating and evaluating staffing policies and procedures. If the work is done in interdependent teams, it is also not uncommon for the teams to be involved in making the final choice.

Legal Issues Related to Hiring Candidates

Legal issues are present throughout the hiring process. The candidate-choosing stage is no exception. In addition to the legal issues discussed in Chapter 3, people involved in the staffing process should be familiar with the Fair Labor Standards Act (FLSA), the Family and Medical Leave Act (FMLA), and the Uniform Guidelines on Employee Selection Procedures (UGESP).

THE FAIR LABOR STANDARDS ACT   The FLSA[12] covers working hours and the payment of overtime or compensatory time off to nonexempt employees. If an applicant is not hired because the person has previously exercised his or her rights under the FLSA (by requesting earned overtime pay, for example), a court may conclude that the applicant's rights have been violated.

THE FAMILY AND MEDICAL LEAVE ACT   The FMLA[13] entitles qualified applicants up to 12 weeks of unpaid leave for certain reasons. If an applicant is not hired because he or she had previously exercised his or her rights under the FMLA, a court may conclude that the applicant's rights have been violated. For example, a federal appellate court held that an employer violated the act by failing to hire an applicant because, in the opinion of her employer, she had taken a lot of leave.[14]

THE UNIFORM GUIDELINES ON EMPLOYEE SELECTION PROCEDURES   The UGESP[15] apply to the candidate-choosing process when adverse impact is occurring. The UGESP require firms to either eliminate adverse impact or justify it through validation studies. The UGESP generally state that cut scores should be set no higher than the level necessary for new hires to perform proficiently. Determining the minimum proficiency level is up to the company. This is consistent with the method of determining cut scores that Valtera, the company described in the vignette for Chapter 8, uses. The UGESP also state that "the way in which normal expectations of proficiency within the workforce were determined and the way in which the cutoff score was determined" should be described.

As we explained in earlier chapters, to deal with adverse impact problems, the UGESP also discuss the use of "alternative procedures" that cause less adverse impact but that have similar validity to the problematic procedure. A cognitive ability test may do a good job predicting job success but it may result in adverse impact. In contrast, using a structured interview and a work sample may have the same validity without generating adverse impact. The UGESP do not relieve a company of any of its affirmative action obligations, and "encourage the adoption and implementation of voluntary affirmative action programs" for organizations that do not currently have any.

AN EMPLOYER'S PREFERENCE FOR DIVERSITY The Equal Employment Opportunity Commission (EEOC) encourages voluntary affirmative action and diversity efforts to improve opportunities for racial minorities in order to carry out the congressional intent of Title VII, which prohibits discrimination due to race, color, religion, sex, and so forth. According to the EEO commission, "persons subject to Title VII must be allowed flexibility in modifying employment systems and practices to comport with the purposes" of the statute.[16] That said, firms need to carefully implement affirmative action and diversity programs to avoid the potential for legal trouble.[17]

So, for example, when a company wants to increase the demographic diversity of its workforce, can it make a hiring decision based on a person's qualifications and a protected characteristic such as age, race, or gender, or must the decision be based solely on the person's qualifications? A common question is whether and under what conditions it is ever legally permissible for a legally protected characteristic to be a factor in candidate choice. Recent court rulings involving public institutions (police forces and universities) indicate that among candidates who are minimally qualified for a job, race can be used as a "plus" factor if an "operational need" justifies the employer's voluntary affirmative action efforts.[18] Whether this ruling will be expanded to cover private employers is unknown.[19] The U.S. Supreme court has not ruled on the issue.[20]

It is never permissible to hire a nonqualified minority candidate over a qualified nonminority candidate, however. In one case, a court held that a downsizing school district could not choose to retain a black employee instead of a white employee of equal seniority, ability, and qualifications, solely on the grounds of diversity, even though black employees were underrepresented in the school district.[21] As you can see, it is important to consult legal counsel before using any legally protected characteristic as an employee selection factor.

Pursuing diverse candidates should not begin during the assessment stage of the hiring process. As we have indicated, if qualified diverse candidates are not recruited and, therefore, do not become part of the applicant pool, no selection system can identify them. If a firm's sourcing and recruiting activities identify and attract qualified, diverse applicants, then applying a valid assessment system that has little to no adverse impact should generate quality, diverse hires. Successfully attracting qualified diverse applicants eliminates the need for firms to consider any protected characteristic as a plus factor in candidate choice.[22]

JOB OFFER STRATEGIES

Given the importance of choosing the right candidates and the time and money invested in the staffing process, it is amazing how little thought often goes into the job offer process. When a decision is made to extend a job offer, the focus should shift from evaluating the candidate to communicating your enthusiasm for him or her and persuading the person to choose to work for your company. Whether the job offer is standardized or whether a finalist will receive an enhanced offer because he or she has exemplary credentials, some thought should go into both the content of the job offer and its presentation. The goal of a job offer is not only to get the finalist to accept the offer, but also to strengthen his or her commitment to the firm, enhance his or her enthusiasm for joining the company, and reinforce the company's desired image as an employer. It is important to note that this does not mean misleading the finalist about the job or firm. Indeed, one of the best times to present a realistic job preview (discussed in Chapter 7) is after a job offer has been made and before it is accepted.[23]

Particularly for firms with a talent philosophy of viewing employees as investors rather than assets, the job offer should maximize the employee value proposition offered to the finalist. As you learned in Chapter 4, the employee value proposition is the balance between the intrinsic and extrinsic rewards an employee receives by working for a particular employer. It is often impossible to list all a job's rewards. Nonetheless, the job offer should be crafted to appeal to the finalist's needs and values and closely mirror the rewards most important to the finalist.

To entice the best and brightest talent to join its workforce, Google offers its employees perks including free cafeteria meals, free use of laundry machines, a child care center, dog-friendly offices, and an on-site doctor. Engineers are also able to devote 20 percent of their time to projects of their choice.[24]

Of course, before extending a job offer to a finalist, it is always a good idea to verify the truthfulness of any statements made by the applicant that were relied upon in assessing the person—for example, his or her grade point average, prior work experience, and so forth. It is also wise for a firm to try to determine what the finalist's prior salary was. Finally, it is a good idea to identify a backup hire in case your first choice does not take the job.

Creating a Job Offer

The type of job as well as organizational, applicant, external, and legal factors all influence the content of a job offer. Next, we discuss each of these factors.

THE TYPE OF JOB   The type of job influences the content of a job offer. Job offers vary depending on whether the position is full or part time, exempt or nonexempt from overtime pay, and the level of the position. Job offers for lower-level positions are often shorter and less detailed than the job offers made to fill executive positions.

ORGANIZATIONAL FACTORS   The organizational factors that can influence the content of a job offer include the firm's business strategy, staffing and compensation strategy and policy, internal equity, the company's need to hire someone immediately, and union contracts. For example, a firm pursuing a cost leadership or operational efficiency strategy will likely try to keep its labor costs down. As a result, the company might be less willing to enrich a job offer than a company pursuing a differentiation or innovation strategy for which hiring top talent is a priority. The job offer must also be tied to the firm's compensation strategy. For example, if a company has a policy of extending only standard job offers—in other words, if it doesn't allow the employment terms to differ among different new hires—then the choice of what to include in a job offer is constrained. This has a number of implications, including the amount that a hiring manager can offer a finalist. The hiring manager might also have to get approval from someone else in the organization before making and/or negotiating a wage offer.

Some companies feel that it is important to preserve *internal equity* to ensure that the employment terms of a firm's current employees are as good or better than the terms offered to new hires. For example, around the millennium, Java programming skills were in short supply. One way companies hired Java programmers was by offering them benefits and salaries that in many cases were higher than what existing employees were getting. This can, of course, create hard feelings and lead to morale problems and turnover.

Sometimes a new hire should not be given an enhanced job offer due to internal equity, but business necessity may require giving the person a higher salary. For example, the person could be essential to leading an important project or have special credentials. In the short term, this will help the firm maintain its staffing levels and meet an important short-term need. However, in the long term, it can be costly if the company's current employees threaten to resign if their pay is not increased to the new employee's level of pay.

If a company needs to fill a position immediately, it might decide to enrich a job offer to increase the likelihood that it will be accepted. By contrast, if a company can afford to wait, it might decide to present a more standard offer. Union contracts can also dictate many of the terms and conditions of the employment relationship and affect what must be included in a job offer.

FACTORS RELATED TO THE FINALIST   Factors related to a finalist can affect the content of a job offer. These factors include the finalist's fit with the job and organization, compensation and reward requirements, qualifications and experience, previous compensation package, values and needs, and whether the finalist has other job offers pending. If a finalist has good job offers from other firms and needs to make a decision soon, an enticing job offer might need to be presented to the person relatively quickly. Firms sometimes make a new job offer to a current employee in response to an offer he or she received from another employer (a counteroffer). Counteroffers often try to at least match what is being offered by the competitor.

TABLE 11-3	Resource Reference Table: Determining Market Compensation Levels

America's Career Infonet: www.acinet.org
College Grad Job Hunter: www.collegegrad.com
Jobstar: http://jobstar.org
O*Net: http://online.onetcenter.org
Places Rated: www.bestplaces.net
Salaries Review: www.salariesreview.com
Salary.com: www.salary.com
Salary Expert: www.salaryexpert.com
The Riley Guide: www.rileyguide.com
Wageweb: www.wageweb.com

EXTERNAL FACTORS   As we have indicated, a number of external factors can affect the content of a job offer. These factors include the tightness of the labor market, the cost of living in an area, the risk and cost of a finalist being hired by a competitor, and the market level of compensation and rewards for the position. If the finalist is the only finalist the organization wishes to hire, it might make a more generous offer to increase the likelihood of the person accepting it. If the area in which the new hire will live is expensive, some firms enrich the job offer to accommodate this additional expense. If the finalist has skills that could jeopardize the company's competitive position if he or she was acquired by a competitor, enhancing the job offer to increase the chances it will be accepted can be strategic. For example, when a hiring manager in a well-known investment banking firm announced he had just hired away the competitor's best salesperson, he was asked, "But what will he do for us?" The hiring manager immediately responded, "I'm not sure, but he won't be making $50 million a year for the competitor!"[25]

A firm can determine external factors, such as the cost of living and typical compensation levels, via salary surveys, consulting with trade associations, reading employment ads, and visiting competitors' Web sites. Trade associations and trade magazines, employment agencies, and college placement offices can also provide helpful comparative salary information, as can the job offers finalists receive from other companies. Table 11-3 lists some Web resources that can be useful in determining market compensation levels. This information can help identify appropriate market-based salary ranges, but the firm must still decide what it wants its starting salary range and average to be for a given position. To ensure its starting pay offers are fair and consistent, the firm should develop a *starting pay policy*. An example of a starting pay policy is:

> When determining starting salaries, a hiring department in consultation with the divisional Human Resources Office or human resources manager will consider the applicant's prior experience and/or education directly related to the position to ensure internal equity. A department may pay starting salaries up to the market reference point or salary range midpoint of a job, or up to the average salary of similar university positions provided internal equity is observed. With appropriate justification and documented approval by the divisional Human Resources Office or human resources manager and by the appropriate dean or vice president, a hiring official may offer higher starting salaries.[26]

LEGAL FACTORS   Equal employment opportunity and affirmative action goals are the two primary legal factors that influence the content of a job offer. If a firm has an affirmative action plan or if it is actively pursuing diversity, its progress toward these goals might influence how high a job offer should be. If a company is having trouble getting some subgroups of finalists to accept job offers, enriched offers might be necessary. At the same time, organizations must ensure that job offers are comparable across protected characteristics to avoid charges of discrimination.

Figure 11-1 illustrates the factors that can influence the content of job offers.

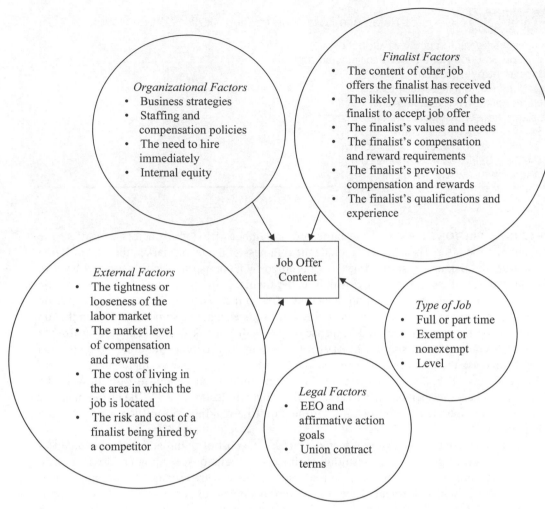

FIGURE 11-1 Factors That Affect the Content of Job Offers

Compensation Decisions

How, precisely, do you decide what to offer finalists? As we have explained, the type of job, a firm's business strategy, and staffing and hiring policies can affect the decision. So can external factors, such as tightness or looseness of the labor market and the finalist's situation. A company with a low-cost strategy may offer finalists a salary at or slightly below market, bonuses tied to the individual's and the company's performance, and a standard benefits package. A company pursuing a differentiation strategy, such as MarineMax featured in the opening vignette, might offer a very desirable hire an above-market salary, generous benefits package, personalized inducements such as a company car, extra vacation time, or flexible work hours, and a sign-on bonus. If the labor market is tight and it is difficult to attract and hire qualified candidates, a higher total rewards package and hiring inducements may be required. Companies are also often willing to be more generous and flexible with job offers for leadership and key positions than for entry-level positions that often involve a more standardized job offer. The total rewards package should reinforce the firm's human resource and staffing strategies as well as its desired image and reputation as an employer.

Another important job offer decision is whether to make a low, competitive, or high job offer, and whether to leave room for further negotiation. A **low job offer** is one that keeps the employer's costs as low as possible by offering a below-market total rewards package, including compensation and benefits. Further negotiation of the offer may or may not be allowed. Although firms pursuing a cost-leadership strategy might be tempted to pursue this strategy to contain labor costs, it is not consistent with a talent philosophy of viewing employees as investors and encouraging employees to stay with the firm for long-term careers. High-quality finalists are also

low job offer

a job offer that consists of a below-market rewards package less likely to accept low job offers. Low offers are often inappropriate for key positions, particularly in firms pursuing a differentiation strategy or a competitive advantage based on innovation that requires top talent. Because of the importance of having quality talent in leadership roles in any organization, low job offers are not likely to be effective for leadership positions in general. For positions in which higher rates of turnover are acceptable, or when the quality of the people hired is not critical, perhaps for low-skilled or temporary work, this strategy can generate new hires, although at potential risk to the firm's image and reputation as an employer.

A **competitive job offer** is one that offers a total rewards package that is competitive with the market for that position. In other words, the salary, benefits, and inducements are about the same as what competitors are offering similarly qualified candidates for similar positions. Further negotiation may or may not be allowed. Although they are not likely to offend anyone, competitive job offers are less likely to entice top finalists to accept the jobs offered them.

competitive job offer
a job offer in which the total rewards package offered is competitive with the market offer

A **high job offer** is one that offers a total rewards package that is above the market. Further negotiation may or may not be allowed. High job offers have the potential to increase an organization's attractiveness among workers who value material rewards and enhance a firm's image and reputation as an employer. To avoid morale problems among their current employees, some firms prefer to offer one-time inducements such as sign-on bonuses, early performance reviews for new hires to speed up their salary increases, and greater relocation allowances while keeping new hires' long-term rewards packages in line with those of their other employees.

high job offer
a job offer in which the total rewards package is above the market offer

When a firm makes a **maximum job offer**, it is extending the finalist its absolute best and final offer. The finalist is informed that this is the firm's best job offer and that no further negotiation is possible. A maximum job offer can be a low, competitive, or high offer. By telling the finalist that the company is offering all that it can afford or equitably do, the firm is communicating its sincere interest in the finalist and, it hopes, reducing or eliminating any negative feelings that might result from the offer being below what the finalist expected. This can be a good strategy if the firm wants to hire someone whose current total rewards package exceeds what the company can offer the person.

maximum job offer
the company's best and final offer

Presenting a high maximum job offer can help fill a position quickly or entice a top finalist to join the firm. Such an offer makes sense when a finalist has received a job offer and needs to make a decision quickly. As is the case with a high job offer, a maximum job offer has the potential to damage morale among a firm's current employees who have lower total rewards packages.

THE EMPLOYMENT CONTRACT

Employment contracts can be verbal, written, or a combination of both. Written statements generally supersede verbal statements. However, in the absence of contrary written statements, an employer is open to legal challenges if it breaks verbal promises. To be enforceable, any contract that cannot be performed or fulfilled within one year must be in writing under the statute of frauds. Every employee has an employment contract. As you learned in Chapter 3, at-will employment is an employment relationship in which either party can terminate the employment relationship at any time, for any legal reason, with no liability as long as there is no contract for a definite term of employment. Even if an employee is hired on an "at will" basis without anything communicated in writing, there is still an oral contract in place that in most instances would be just as enforceable as a formal written agreement. The big difference between the two is that the terms of a written agreement tend to be easier to prove than those of an oral one.[27]

Legally Binding Contracts

A legally binding and enforceable employment contract arises when there is an offer, acceptance of that offer, and sufficient "consideration" to make the contract valid.[28] An *offer* contains the terms and conditions of employment as proposed by the employer, and possibly specific requirements for the offer's acceptance, such as a deadline. A job offer's terms must be definite and certain, and allow the job candidate to reasonably expect that the business is willing to be bound by the offer on the terms proposed. Simply telling a person to "come work for me next week" is too vague to be a valid offer.

An *acceptance* is a clear expression of the accepting party's agreement to the terms of the offer. The offer must be accepted as specified in the offer, and not propose any changes. If the offer requires written acceptance by a certain date, the acceptance must be on time and in writing to be valid. Stating, "I'll accept the offer for an additional $5,000 per year" is a counteroffer, and it becomes the employer's choice to accept or reject it.

Consideration is the bargained-for exchange between the contract parties. In other words, something of value must pass from one party to the other for consideration to have occurred. Each party to the contract must gain some benefit from the agreement and incur some obligation in exchange for that benefit. Typically, this involves an exchange of labor for pay.

Common Contract Content

Employment contracts often focus more on termination issues than on employment. The termination provisions of a contract can include provisions for outplacement assistance, career counseling, and supplemental benefits, such as the ability to continue investing in the firm's 401(k) retirement plan after a person is terminated. However, if a company has a formal severance policy, a separate severance agreement might be unnecessary. For some candidates, the severance terms of the employment contract are a very important factor. This is especially true for CEOs who frequently negotiate for "golden parachutes," or significant benefits including large severance pay packages if their employment is terminated. One chief information officer based his decision on the severance he negotiated. When one company offered three years' pay if the job didn't work out, he accepted it because most executives at that level only receive a year's severance.[29]

Additional Agreements

restrictive covenant
a clause in a contract that requires one party to do, or refrain from doing, certain things

Restrictive covenants are contract clauses that require one party to do, or to refrain from doing, certain things. To stay competitive, many companies must protect their most precious assets—human capital, client relationships, and trade secrets.[30] Almost all companies require employees who have access to confidential information and technical employees involved in research and development to agree not to divulge trade secrets. The company also often retains the *rights to employee inventions and patents*. This can be particularly important for companies pursuing a competitive advantage based on innovation who need to own and protect their discoveries. *Nondisclosure agreements* are intended to stop a current or former employee from giving away trade secrets or using confidential data, like customer lists, for a competitor's benefit. Nondisclosure agreements can be particularly important for companies relying on innovation or a proprietary technology as a competitive advantage. An example of a nondisclosure clause is, "After expiration or termination of this agreement, [employee name] agrees to respect the confidentiality of [company name] patents, trademarks, and trade secrets, and not to disclose them to anyone."[31]

Two additional ways to protect these assets are through nonsolicitation and noncompete agreements. Before their actual departure dates, employees have the right to notify their current customers that they are leaving their companies. However, many firms include *nonsolicitation agreements* in their employment contracts to prevent departing employees from actually soliciting their customers for business on behalf of their new employers. (What constitutes "solicitation" is interpreted on a case-by-case basis.) However, after their employment has ended, employees are generally free to do so, provided they do not divulge their former employers' trade secrets in the process.[32]

Noncompete clauses prevent an employee who has resigned from joining a competitor for a certain period of time. For example, before H. J. Heinz lured Daniel O'Neill away from a senior-level job at Campbell Soup, O'Neill had signed an agreement with Campbell that prohibited him from working for a competitor for 18 months after his departure. Because Campbell Soup wasn't willing to let him go, the two companies eventually reached a settlement stating that O'Neill could not work at Heinz for seven more months. When he finally began his new position, O'Neill had to keep a daily log of his business meetings for 11 months (which were monitored by an independent auditor) to assure no transfer of trade secrets or confidential information.[33]

In order to be legally enforceable, the terms of the noncompetition should be as detailed as possible as to time, geographic area, and type of business activity. The agreements can include not taking after-hours jobs with competitors or in any other way competing with one's former company. Trade secrets, confidential information, customer lists, or the firm's unique services

TABLE 11-4	Employment Contract Content

Although the content of employment contracts varies, depending on the industry and the particular employee, here are some examples of topics frequently covered by employment contracts:[34]

- *The job's title, description of position, and job duties.* The contract should outline the position and its duties, or a reference should be made to a specific job description also provided to the finalist. An employer also should include language allowing the company to assign additional duties, as appropriate, to the new hire.
- *The start date.* The start date is typically at least two weeks from the offer acceptance date if the finalist needs to resign from his or her current job.
- *The job's compensation, benefits, and incentive pay.* If any.
- *Any hiring inducements.* Sign-on bonuses, relocation expenses, and so forth.
- *The offer's acceptance procedures.* The firm needs to spell out that by signing the contract, the finalist accepts the employment terms and conditions offered by the employer, subject to the conditions listed in the agreement. The firm should also insist that the acceptance of the job offer be in writing. An acceptance deadline should be included to allow the company to move on to the next finalist if the offer has not been accepted by a certain date.
- *The duration of the contract.* If it's for a limited period of time.
- *Hours of work.* The contract should outline the job's work hours via a statement like the following: "The regular workday shall consist of eight (8) hours of work between 9 A.M. and 5 P.M." or be worded to provide maximum flexibility: "Hours of work will vary and be scheduled as needed."
- *Disclaimers.* A disclaimer explicitly limits an employee right, such as his or her right to employment, and reserves it for the employer. One of the most common disclaimers is a provision that the employment is at will if it is not for a specific time period. A statement to the effect that by accepting the offer, the employee agrees that the organization has not made any promises other than those in the written offer is also a disclaimer.
- *The rights to the employee's inventions and work products.*
- *Termination criteria.* If the contract is not on an at-will basis, it should spell out any specific grounds for termination.
- *An explanation of how disputes will be handled.* One way to avoid the expense of going to court is to agree to arbitrate any future disputes with the employee. Arbitration is also generally much faster than formal court proceedings.

generally qualify as legitimate business interests that can be protected with noncompete clauses. An example of a noncompete agreement is as follows:

(a) [Employee name] agrees not to compete with [company name] in the practice of [type of business or service] while working for [company name] and for a period of [number and measure of time (e.g., "six months" or "10 years")] after termination of employment within a radius of [number] miles of [company name and location].

(b) For purposes of this covenant not to compete, competition is defined as soliciting or accepting employment by, or rendering professional services to, any person or organization that is or was a client of [company name] during the term of [employee name]'s work with [company name].[35]

Noncompete agreements that are too broad in the scope of their time period, geographical reach, or type of work tend to be overturned by the courts if challenged.[36] Because state laws differ, it's important to check your state's noncompete covenants. Despite the difficulty of enforcing noncompete provisions, many firms include them in their contracts as a deterrent.[37] Offering a consulting contract to departing employees can also prevent them from working for a competitor.

Table 11-4 summarizes some of the content commonly contained in an employment agreement.

Written employment agreements may be multipage contracts or simple letters—both are legally binding. Large organizations often limit contracts to upper management and give other finalists offer letters that reflect the terms they negotiated.[38] An **offer letter** states in clear and precise terms exactly what the compensation structure and terms of the employment will be. Offer letters are often drafted, approved by lawyers, and amended as needed. Figure 11-2 shows an example of a job offer letter.

offer letter
a written letter describing in clear and precise terms exactly what the compensation structure and terms of an employment contract will be

(Date)

Dear Ms. Lopez,

Welcome to ABC Company! On behalf of ABC Company it is my pleasure to extend the following offer of employment to you. This offer is contingent upon your passing our mandatory drug screen.

Title:

_____

This position will report to:

_____

A job description is attached. An annual base salary of $55,000 will be paid in equal biweekly installments consistent with the company's payroll practices, subject to deductions for taxes and other withholdings as required by law. Upon satisfactory completion of the first 90 days of employment, you may be eligible for a bonus based on your meeting the goals and objectives agreed to in the performance development planning process with your manager within two weeks of your start date. The bonus plan for this year and beyond, should such a plan exist, will be based on the formula determined by the company for that year.

As discussed during your interview, ABC Company offers employees and their eligible dependents participation in its health and other benefit plans. Your compensation package includes full medical and dental coverage through our company's employee benefit plan, and fringe benefits including a 401(k) and tuition reimbursement as covered in the enclosed pamphlet. Your employee contribution to payment for benefit plans is determined annually. Twelve paid personal days, which are to include vacation days, sick days, and personal emergency days, are accrued annually at a rate of one per month.

I would like to note that your employment with ABC Company will be "at will," meaning that either you or the company may terminate your employment at any time, for any or no reason, and with or without notice.

By signing below you acknowledge that this offer letter, along with any referenced documents, represents the entire employment agreement between you and ABC Company, and that no verbal or written agreements, promises, or representations that are not specifically stated in this offer, are or will be binding upon ABC Company. This offer is valid for 10 business days and our standard noncompete agreement must be signed and returned before this contract will be considered valid.

We look forward to your arrival at our company and are confident that you will play a key role in our company's expansion into new markets. Please let me know if you have any questions or if I can do anything to make your arrival easier.

Signatures:

_____

(For ABC Company)   Date

_____

(Candidate's name)   Date

FIGURE 11-2   A Sample Job Offer Letter

Source: Adapted from Heathfield, S. M., "Job Offer Letter," Humanresources.about.com, 2006, http://humanresources.about.com/cs/policysamples/a/joboffer_2.htm. Accessed November 23, 2006; Texas Workforce Commission, Job Offer Letter, 2006, www.twc.state.tx.us/news/efte/job_offer_letter.html. Accessed November 23, 2006; HR Document Center, Job Offer Letter—Exempt Position, August 1, 2002, http://service.govdelivery.com/service/document.html?code=HRDOC_146. Accessed November 23, 2006.

Statements on a job application blank (e.g., a statement that providing false information is grounds for termination), statements in employee handbooks, and statements in other documents can be interpreted as enforceable contracts. Accordingly, it is important to check them for consistency and to include a statement in the offer letter similar to "no verbal or written agreements, promises, or representations that are not specifically stated in this offer, are or will be binding upon (company)." Consult legal counsel about all contract wording.

PRESENTING A JOB OFFER

A job offer can be presented to a finalist *in writing* via a formal letter like the one in Figure 11-2. The terms and conditions of employment are outlined, and the finalist is asked to either accept or reject the offer as is. In this situation, no personal contact is made with the finalist and further negotiation is not permitted. The finalist must either reject the offer or accept it as is. This approach can be successful for companies doing a lot of hiring. For example, perhaps a firm has opened a new location and hundreds or even thousands of people need to be hired in a short period of time. However, such an offer is not an effective way to persuade undecided finalists to accept the offers made to them. Neither is the written offer likely to enhance a finalist's enthusiasm for joining the company.

As we have indicated, the other alternative is to present the job offer *verbally*, either face-to-face or by phone. A typical verbal job offer begins with an HR professional or hiring manager congratulating the finalist and letting him or her know that the company is enthusiastic about having them onboard. The job and its salary and benefits are described as well as the work hours and perhaps when the finalist can expect to be evaluated and given a merit raise. The finalist is asked about any reservations he or she may have about accepting the offer or if he or she has any other questions about the job. To persuade a finalist to accept your job offer, it is important to appeal to the finalist's priorities and to address any personal concerns he or she might have. Be sure to respond to any finalist requests for more information. Lastly, the finalist should be given at least 48 hours to consider the offer. A phone offer should also be followed up with a written offer, so the finalist can be sure that the details of the written offer match those conveyed over the phone.

NEGOTIATING

For every employment term and condition, the firm must decide if it is willing to negotiate it and if so, what the lower and upper bounds will be. Similarly, job candidates often establish a lower bound for what they are willing to accept on key dimensions such as pay, benefits, and work hours. So, what terms are negotiable? One survey found that the vast majority of HR professionals believe salaries are negotiable. Roughly one-half of HR professionals believe relocation expenses, flexible work schedules, early salary reviews, paid time off, and sign-on bonuses are negotiable. And at least 20 percent of respondents felt that professional development opportunities, bonuses and incentives, number of work hours per week, and educational assistance are negotiable.[39]

Indeed, the shift in how people view employment contracts over the past 15 years has given employees and applicants greater individual bargaining power. A Towers Perrin study found that today's workforce is more sophisticated, better informed, and more individualistic than ever before.[40] Clearly, employers are feeling more pressured to negotiate with workers as a result. As Edward Lawler, a compensation expert, noted: "It is increasingly likely that organizations will be making individual deals with a large number of their employees. This is particularly likely to be true in the case of knowledge workers and managers. At the executive level, organizations already have elaborate individual contracts that are difficult to compare and evaluate."[41]

Another study found that students who negotiated their job offer received 7 to 8 percent more than their initial offer. But while 52 percent of the men negotiated, only 12 percent of the women did.[42] By not negotiating their salaries, many women sacrifice more than an estimated $500,000 by the end of their professional lives. Women also tend to use a more cooperative negotiation style than do men, although the difference is fairly small.[43] The fact that there can be gender differences in negotiation behaviors and outcomes[44] is not only important for job seekers, particularly females, but also for companies. Because starting salaries are set in part through the new hire's negotiations, gender-based wage disparities can result and grow quite significant over time. This can put firms at the risk of being sued for discrimination.

TABLE 11-5	Negotiable Job Offer Elements

Salary

Sign-on bonuses and other one-time inducements

Nonsalary compensation: performance bonuses, profit sharing, deferred compensation, severance package, and stock options

Relocation expenses: house-hunting expenses and closing costs, temporary living allowances, travel expenses, and spousal reemployment expenses

Benefits: vacation, sick, and personal days (number, amount paid, and timing), conference attendance, tuition reimbursement, professional memberships, product discounts, and short-term loans

Job-specific elements: the timing of the employee's first performance review and potential raise; the job's title, roles, and duties; the location of the work (e.g., whether telecommuting is allowed), work hours and if they are flexible, and the start date

An increasing number of employers are offering flexible benefit packages with different options. Often the packages give employees a variety of choices regarding their benefits, including their health, dental, and disability insurance coverage. Severance pay, stock options, and profit-sharing plans can also be negotiable. Table 11-5 summarizes some commonly negotiated elements of a job offer.

Negotiating with New Hires

The degree to which a salary is negotiable depends on the position, the manager, the organization, and your perceived value. The salaries for most entry-level positions are subject to little, if any, negotiation. Likewise, most state and federal government jobs also have rigid, nonnegotiable salary scales based on one's education and experience. However, for mid-level positions in the private sector, employers will generally negotiate within a job's salary range. For example, a job paying $40,000 a year might have a salary range of between $36,000 and $44,000, and employers will allow a candidate to negotiate between the two. An exceptional finalist might occasionally be offered a salary that exceeds the high end of the range, but only with the approval of the firm's higher-level managers. Higher-level management and executive positions generally offer the greatest opportunities for negotiation. Figure 11-3 shows the bargaining zone for an annual salary.

It should be noted that managers do not always act in the best interests of their employers when they're negotiating starting salaries. Depending on the strength of a manager's desire to hire the finalist and his or her motivation to influence the final compensation package (perhaps to preserve internal equity), the manager's negotiation tactics and goals may differ from those of the firm, and can be costly. For example, some hiring managers might make higher job offers than necessary in an effort to hire a desired candidate or to reduce the time spent negotiating. Consequently, when it comes to negotiating employment packages, organizations need to align the interests of their managers with the firm's goals to ensure that managers negotiate as they're supposed to. If the organizational policy does not allow salary flexibility, being flexible in other

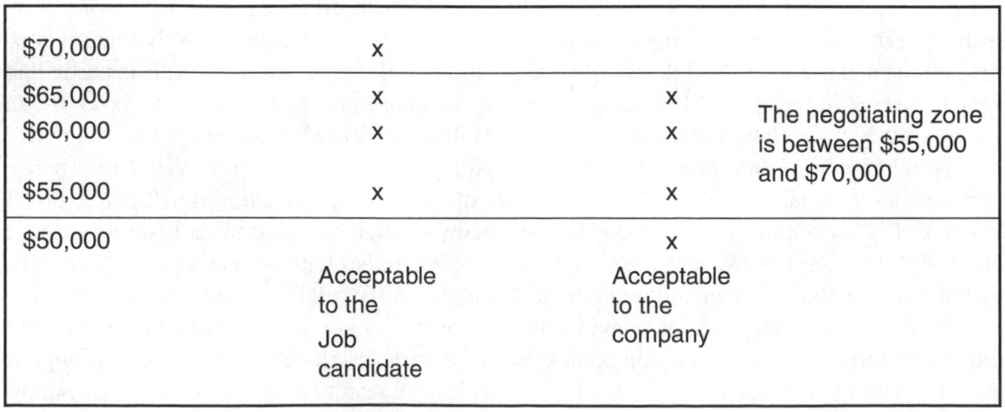

$70,000	x		
$65,000	x	x	The negotiating zone is between $55,000 and $70,000
$60,000	x	x	
$55,000	x	x	
$50,000		x	
	Acceptable to the Job candidate	Acceptable to the company	

FIGURE 11-3 Salary Negotiating Zone

areas, such as working hours, relocation expenses, and sign-on bonuses, will increase the likelihood that the agent will act in the best interest of the organization.[45] People negotiating on behalf of the company should also be given rewards associated with their outcomes (completing the deal on time, negotiating terms the firm desires, controlling salary costs, and so forth).[46]

To successfully negotiate a job offer, you should try to focus on the things that matter most to the finalist. If the person is a middle manager about to put three children through college, money may be important. Often, however, nonmonetary factors, including career advancement opportunities, the opportunity to learn new skills, the community's quality of life, and flexible work hours, are also important to many people. Computer engineers might be most excited about the opportunity to work with the latest technologies. A finalist who has just been laid off might put job security at the top of the list. Selling the opportunity based on the content of the job rewards analysis can be helpful, particularly when done in the context of finalists' own needs and desires.[47] This chapter's Develop Your Skills feature gives you some tips on negotiating a job offer.

Renegotiating Contracts

When a person's job responsibilities change, for example, due to a promotion or reorganization, the terms and conditions of his or her employment are also likely to change. Employment contracts are frequently renegotiated to reflect these changes. Some renegotiated employment contracts simply consist of a letter from the employer announcing the change of conditions. Other employment contracts include the terms and processes for renegotiating an employee's conditions of employment, for example, during an annual performance review.[48]

Legally, before the contractual terms of a person's employment can be changed, there must be an offer made to the person, which he or she accepts. If the employee disagrees with the new terms, negotiating will probably be required.[49] However, if the employee says nothing about the proposed change, he or she will have tacitly agreed to the change, which will become binding on both parties.[50]

If an **explicit employment contract** (written or verbal) does not exist, an **implicit employment contract** or an understanding that is not part of a written or verbal contract, can still exist.[51] Roughly half of the *Fortune* 500 CEOs work under implicit contracts.[52] Most small business employees are also hired without the formality of a written contract. Although explicit employment contracts are not limited to union members, in 2006 12 percent of employed people in the United States were union members and thus covered by explicit employment contracts.[53] In some cases, labor unions allow workers to coordinate their actions in response to a firm's breaching of the implicit contract it has with its workers.[54] Implicit employment contracts tend to be the norm for most positions in most firms.

explicit employment contract
a written or verbal employment contract

implicit employment contract
an understanding that is not part of a written or verbal contract

---

DEVELOP YOUR SKILLS
Job Offer Negotiation Tips

Because employment is an ongoing relationship between the employee and the employer, negotiating needs to be done in a way that results in a win-win outcome for both parties. Here are some experts' suggestions for being an effective negotiator:[55]

- *Do not look at a negotiation as an either/or proposition.* Negotiating is about compromise. Focus on your goals, not on winning.
- *Identify what you can and cannot part with.* Identify the things most important to you (e.g., your salary, career development, or a signing bonus) and those things that are less important (e.g., receiving a prestigious job title). Establish minimum requirements for the critical issues.
- *Try to identify and use sources of leverage. Leverage* is anything that can help or hinder a party in a bargaining situation. For example, an employer who must hire quickly is at a disadvantage. Therefore, you might be able to negotiate a better offer. Multiple job offers can also increase your leverage.
- *Suppress your emotions.* Negotiations can stir emotions. Constantly reminding yourself of your goal can help you achieve an appropriate level of detachment so that you continue to see the deal clearly.
- *Know your BATNA.* BATNA is an acronym for "best alternative to a negotiated agreement." It is what you could have done had no negotiation taken place, or what you will do if you can't reach an agreement. The purpose of negotiations is to see if your needs can be better met by negotiating an agreement, compared to this next best alternative.[56] If the negotiations stall, letting the other side know that you're prepared to accept another company's job offer or decline their job offer can also help to get the process started up again.

(Continued)

- *Take time to evaluate the offer.* Consider the total value of the job offer, including the job's benefits. Be prepared before negotiating and ask for what you want in one session. If you keep saying, "I forgot something," you'll appear disorganized, and it can negatively influence the firm's expectations of you as an employee.
- *Be realistic.* Research your market value and typical salary ranges and benefits packages before you begin negotiating. As we have explained, entry-level salaries are less negotiable than mid-level or executive salaries. Some 311 organizations have little flexibility in terms of what they can offer. Others have a lot.
- *Practice your negotiation skills with a friend.*
- *Document and be prepared to discuss your skills and accomplishments.* Employers are also more likely to meet a request if you can demonstrate why you need it.

- *Be appreciative and respectful.* Begin the negotiation by briefly expressing your appreciation for the offer you've been given. Cite specifics about your positive impressions of the organization and reinforce your good fit with the job and company. Don't be greedy or unreasonable, and know when to quit bargaining. Overnegotiating can dampen a company's enthusiasm for hiring you.
- *Remember that employment is an ongoing relationship.* Job negotiations are the foundation of your career with the company. If you get too little, you will be at a disadvantage throughout your career there. However, pushing too hard can damage your relationship with your employer before it even begins.

Although written contracts help to ensure that the employer and employee have shared expectations and curtail future disputes, few employers provide true written contracts to the majority of their employees. If employees receive anything, it is a letter of agreement, which is less detailed and addresses more basic elements of the employment relationship, including a person's job title and responsibilities, salary and benefits, and start date. Written contracts are usually reserved for higher-level positions and are rarely used for entry-level jobs.

Because binding contracts for employment or for future compensation can be created verbally, great care should be taken during discussions with prospective new hires. Do not make any promises regarding the duration of the person's employment or his or her compensation unless the promises are intended to be contractually binding. An *agent* authorized by the receiver, such as a professional agent for a celebrity or a professional athlete, can negotiate on any finalist's behalf, and agents authorized by the organization, such as executive recruiters and search consultants, can negotiate on behalf of the company. All employees are agents of their firms. If a hiring manager tells a candidate what salary will be offered, it's a binding offer even if the manager is mistaken about what the firm wanted to offer.

CLOSING THE DEAL

While they are considering the offer following negotiations, it is a good idea to stay in contact with finalists to reinforce your enthusiasm about hiring them, and to ensure that they base their acceptance or rejection decision on facts rather than assumptions. Find out how the finalist prefers to be contacted (e.g., via phone or e-mail) and how often. To prevent overwhelming the finalist with a barrage of messages, an HR representative should coordinate any calls and e-mails sent by different people in the company, including the finalist's potential coworkers and hiring manager. When possible, a call from the CEO can also send the message that the finalist is valued and that the CEO cares about the company's employees.

While awaiting an answer from the job finalist, do not turn down your second choice. If the second choice finalist was told of a deadline for making a decision, be sure to contact the finalist before the deadline has passed to say that the position is still open and to update the timeline. Be careful not to make the second or third choice finalist feel like a consolation hire. Treat them with enthusiasm—they are strong finalists to have advanced this far in the hiring process. Even if your first choice finalist accepts your offer, your company may want to try to hire the other finalists in the future.[57]

The senior executives at Cisco Systems often take top candidates out to dinner to show the company's strong interest in them.[58] Offering high-level job offer recipients and even their spouses a tour of the area in which they will be working can help them understand what life will be like if they accept the offer. Employees want to feel respected and assured that the company is a good fit for them. Showing your company as a unique or exciting place to work can also help close the deal. Emphasizing the selling points of the job itself and the career development opportunities that exist, as well as selling the company's image and brand can increase the appeal of the opportunity. The job rewards analysis should help identify some of a job's most attractive features.

Once a job offer has been accepted, the recruiter's role is to begin building the new hire's commitment to the company and enhancing his or her ability to succeed on the job. (It can also be helpful to future hiring efforts to ask what persuaded the person to say "yes," and what he or she thought of each company contact and the hiring process.) Many companies send company handbooks, work materials, and other job and company information that can ease the new hire's transition. Sending a welcome package of apparel, pens, etc., with the company name or logo can help the new hire feel that his or her decision is "official" and help build commitment.

If the new hire is not scheduled to begin work for a few months, as is often the case with people who are about to graduate from college, regular calls from the new hire's coworkers and hiring manager can help maintain the person's enthusiasm for the position. If the new hire lives within a reasonable distance, inviting the new hire to celebrations, meetings, and other activities can help the person begin transitioning to his or her new job.

FAIRNESS PERCEPTIONS AND REJECTIONS

A person's perceptions of fairness will affect how the applicant reacts to the firm's hiring choices, including the person's willingness to accept the job offer, recommend the company to others,[59] continue patronizing the company, or file a discrimination or other lawsuit.[60]

Attending to a person's perceptions of procedural and interactional fairness will increase the finalist's willingness to accept a job offer and reduce the negative spillover effects that can occur when applicants are turned down for a job. Many job offer recipients use the job offer and negotiation process to further assess the organization's commitment to them and evaluate what it would be like to work at the company.

As you learned in Chapter 7, there are three types of fairness.[61] Distributive fairness focuses on the perceived fairness of the outcomes received. Candidates receiving a job offer or promotion are more likely to feel that the hiring outcome is fair than those who do not. Given that most applicants for a position do not ultimately get the job, their perceptions of distributive fairness are often low. Procedural fairness addresses the perceived fairness of the policies and procedures used to determine the hiring outcome. If an applicant believes that she was not given a fair chance of being promoted because the hiring manager had a "favorite" candidate, her sense of procedural fairness will be low. The firm's selection procedures, particularly the perceived job relatedness of the selection method used, the opportunity the method afforded the candidate to demonstrate his or her abilities, and the propriety of the questions asked will all affect a candidate's sense of procedural fairness.[62] If the selection method seems unrelated to the job (lacks face validity)[63] or if inappropriate or illegal questions are asked, this particularly increases applicants' perceptions of unfairness.[64] In short, candidates prefer selection methods that are definitive, valid, job related, and not personally invasive.[65]

The third type of fairness, interactional fairness, relates to the respect and interpersonal treatment candidates perceive they received. For example, if the person negotiating the employment contract seems unreasonable or unhelpful, a candidate's interactional fairness perceptions are likely to be low. For example, we know of one faculty job offer recipient who was very interested in accepting a position until she began negotiating the offer with the dean of the school. Every request she made was quickly met with a "No, we can't do that." The dean made no attempt to negotiate with the candidate nor explain why she wouldn't do so. Ultimately, the professor was so turned off, she declined the job offer—a job offer that she had previously been very excited about.

Rejecting

Companies and job seekers can each reject the other. Rejecting happens when the organization rejects an applicant, candidate, or finalist or vice versa.

WHEN THE COMPANY REJECTS THE CANDIDATE   Rejections should be handled carefully and respectfully. After all, the company might want to recruit those whom it rejected for other job opportunities later. As we have explained, too, the firm wants to avoid any negative spillover effects that could result from how a candidate was rejected. Some companies often do not give rejected external candidates specific reasons for their rejection lest they be perceived as discriminatory.[66] By contrast, in an effort to reduce the negative feelings rejected external candidates often have, other firms provide their external candidates feedback on why they weren't chosen and how they could have done better. In one case, a college dean gave a candidate feedback to the effect that he did not have the necessary nonacademic work experience the college valued. The rejected candidate appreciated the dean's candor and the professional development feedback. Three years later the dean hired the candidate after he had worked with outside organizations and built up the skill set he had previously lacked. Developmental plans can be created for internal candidates to help them gain experience and improve their qualifications.

Rejecting internal candidates has additional issues as these candidates are usually even more aware of the selection procedures, have greater familiarity with other candidates for comparisons, and have more invested in the process than do external applicants. Internal candidates who are not selected or promoted are also retained as employees in their current jobs. Consequently, internal applicant reactions could profoundly impact important organizational outcomes including job satisfaction, morale, retention, and performance.[67]

A firm's human resource department should be sure to keep appropriate records of all applicants for equal employment opportunity and affirmative action (EEO/AA) computation purposes, such as applicant flow. If a rejected applicant is qualified for a different position or if they might be hired in the future for the job to which he or she applied, this can help facilitate the future sourcing and recruiting of prequalified applicants. It is important to note that an individual's data cannot be warehoused for future recruiting purposes without the individual's permission to access it every time.

WHEN THE CANDIDATE REJECTS THE COMPANY   When a candidate turns down a job offer, the person that made the offer should try to find out whether the person might be willing to accept a better offer if the firm were willing to negotiate one. If the negotiation process breaks down thereafter, the candidate's rejection should be promptly and respectfully acknowledged. One human resources expert suggests that the primary reason many people turn down jobs is because they were treated poorly during the hiring process. Although a candidate might initially give a reason for rejecting the firm, it may not be the real cause. The expert suggests waiting six months before asking candidates precisely why they turned down a job offer.[68] At this point, they might be willing to talk more candidly about their recruiting experience.

Reneging

reneging
backing out of a contract after it is accepted

Job seekers should never accept a job offer, even verbally, unless they are willing to commit to it. Backing out of a contract after it is accepted is called **reneging**, and is unethical. Many schools actively discourage reneging among their graduating students by threatening to revoke their ability to apply with other on-campus recruiters or revoking their alumni privileges.[69] Employers should never pressure candidates to renege on other employers. Although reneging is sometimes unavoidable due to a candidate's changing health or family circumstances, it should not be taken lightly.

Employers sometimes renege on the job offers they have extended candidates—sometimes even after the offers have been accepted. Perhaps an employer's business environment changes unexpectedly, the firm experiences a slump, or it is being reorganized, sold, or shut down. Often companies that renege on a job offer will give the job offer receiver compensation for breaking the contract. Instead of reneging, it may be possible to defer the new hire's start date and offer the person a partial salary in the interim. Alternately, it might be possible to hire the individual as a consultant or temporary employee and convert him or her to a full-time hire as soon as possible (e.g., after a hiring freeze is lifted). When many law firms extended job offers to summer interns before the economic downturn and found that they could not use them after all, many paid the associates a reduced salary to delay their start date or a lump sum to cancel the employment contract.[70] Being honest and treating the new hire with respect during the reneging process can soothe the anger and feelings of inequity the person is likely to experience, protect the employer's reputation and brand, and keep the individual interested in working for the firm in the future.

HIRING TOP PERFORMERS AT MARINEMAX

To control its fixed labor costs, MarineMax needs to persuade top talent to accept its job offers without paying them more than it has to. Because successful boat retailing depends on developing relationships with customers, and because the company focuses on premium brands, attracting, keeping, and developing its employees are MarineMax's top priorities. The yacht maker knows that its people are critical to its success. As a result, it constantly tries to hire the best candidates to help it achieve its anticipated future growth.[71] MarineMax pays more than its competitors do, but the company also provides intangibles, such as challenging work and advancement opportunities.

MarineMax tries to tailor its job offers to each finalist. The company is willing to pay what it takes to get top performers. However, to avoid overpaying employees, MarineMax requires candidates to provide the company a full salary history. MarineMax then uses salary surveys and market information to shape each job offer. To avoid having high fixed labor costs, the company uses performance-based pay programs and sometimes negotiates guaranteed performance bonuses for an employee's first year to lure top talent. The company is also willing to use stock options to persuade some top candidates to accept its job offers, which is uncommon in the industry.[72]

Top service technician candidates are enticed with a guaranteed opportunity to bill out a certain amount of work and increase their hourly rate by obtaining additional credentials. This signals to top technicians that a job at MarineMax will pay well. MarineMax's standard benefits package includes health benefits, a 401(k) plan with an employer match, an employee stock purchase plan, and an attractive discount on its boats.[73] Its flexible approach to creating job offers that best appeal to its top candidates has helped make MarineMax a leader in its industry.

Summary

There are different ways to combine candidates' scores on different assessments and make a final choice of whom to try to hire. The choice of these methods should be based on the nature of the job, which job elements are essential, and the importance of involving job experts in the final choice. The quality of a strategic staffing system is largely determined by the people who ultimately accept job offers and become employees. Regardless of the quality of a company's sourcing, recruiting, and assessment methods, if it cannot entice the best candidates to join the company, the staffing system is not as successful as it could be. Although compensation is often cited as an important factor in job choice, other elements of a job offer, including career development opportunities, flexible work schedules, and severance terms, are also important to many candidates. The content of the job offer and its presentation should reinforce the organization's image as an employer as well as its talent philosophy, human resource strategy, and staffing strategy.

Takeaway Points

1. Candidates' scores on different assessment methods can be combined in two different ways. One way is to use a multiple hurdles approach whereby candidates must receive a passing score on an assessment before being allowed to continue on in the selection process. The second way is to use a compensatory approach whereby a candidate's high scores on some assessments can compensate for low scores on other assessments.

2. A final choice can be made using cut scores, which establish a minimum score candidates must exceed; rank ordering, which orders candidates from the highest to lowest depending on their scores; or banding, which assigns candidates to groups based on their overall scores. (After being banded, all candidates in each group are considered to have performed the same on the assessments.)

3. The factors that influence the content of a company's job offer include the type of job as well as the organization, applicant, and external and legal factors.

4. The three compensation strategies firms can choose from are a low strategy (below-market compensation), competitive strategy (at-market compensation), and high strategy (above-market compensation). A maximum strategy (compensation that is nonnegotiable) can be used with any of these three compensation strategies to present a company's best offer.

5. Applicants' perceptions of the distributive, procedural, and interactional fairness of the selection process will influence how they will react when they are offered jobs and rejected for jobs. This can affect whether or not they accept the job offers, recommend the company to others, continue patronizing the company, or file a discrimination, or other, lawsuit.

Discussion Questions

1. Which approach to combining candidates' assessment scores would you favor for choosing candidates? Why?
2. Is it ethical for some new hires to receive different levels of pay and benefits than other new hires? Why or why not?
3. If you received a job offer via e-mail, with no phone or personal contact, how would you feel? Would it influence your decision to accept the offer?
4. If you received a very appealing job offer one week after accepting a different job offer with another company, what would you do?
5. Think about different job offers you have received. What made some of them better than others?

Exercises

1. *Strategy Exercise:* Imagine that you are the manager of a McDonald's restaurant. You are pursuing a low-cost, high-quality service strategy. You believe that the assistant manager you hire is critical to executing your strategy because the person will have a great deal of contact with both your employees and customers. You have just finished interviewing the five finalists for the position. One candidate really stands out: Pat Edwards has three years of relevant work experience and a collaborative and service-oriented style that will fit your restaurant's culture very well. She also scored high on the interview, job knowledge, and simulation assessments.

    Your previous assistant manager had been hired with no job experience and had not done nearly as well during the assessment process. He had been hired six months ago for an annual salary of $26,000 with two weeks paid vacation, a standard health benefits package, and a $1,000 sign-on bonus. You had to let him go last week after his disappointing performance failed to improve. You would like Edwards to accept your offer and start work as soon as possible. Your assignment is to write a job offer letter to Edwards using what you have learned in this chapter.

2. *Develop Your Skills Exercise:* This chapter's Develop Your Skills feature provided several tips on negotiating a job offer. In this exercise, you and a partner will use these tips to role-play a job offer negotiation. When you have finished, switch roles and negotiating partners so that you each have a chance to be the company representative and a chance to be the finalist with someone else. Your instructor will provide you each with more information and goals for your role.

3. *Opening Vignette Exercise:* In this chapter's opening vignette, you learned how MarineMax tries to tailor its job offers to specific candidates. Working in a group of three to five students, reread the vignette and be prepared to share with the class your answers to the following questions:
    a. Do you think that it is ethical for MarineMax to give different new hires for the same job different amounts of pay and benefits?
    b. Should MarineMax use a low, competitive, or high job offer? Why? Should the company present a maximum job offer or leave room to negotiate? Why?
    c. What can MarineMax do to increase the likelihood that the top sales candidates it recruits will accept its job offers?

CASE STUDY

Hiring FBI Agents

The FBI is one of the six bureaus of the U.S. Department of Justice and the primary criminal investigative agency of the federal government. The special agents who work for the FBI investigate people and organizations who violate federal statutes. These violations can be related to organized crime, white-collar crime, financial crime, civil rights violations, bank robberies, kidnapping, terrorism, foreign counterintelligence, and fugitive and drug trafficking matters. Special agents also work with other federal, state, and local law enforcement agencies. The work performed by special agents has a daily impact on the country's security and the quality of life of all U.S. citizens.[74]

The FBI has validated a series of assessment methods for its special agent positions. To effectively utilize the assessments, it uses a combination of multiple hurdles and cut scores to make its hiring decisions:[75]

1. *Application Checklist for the Special Agent Position:* A preliminary application is used to determine if applicants meet the minimum qualifications of the position, including the applicants' citizenship, age, education, work experience, and geographic mobility.[76] Factors including felony convictions and the use of illegal drugs disqualify an applicant.[77]
2. *Special Agent Qualifications Questionnaire/Applicant Background Survey:* Applicants passing the first hurdle are evaluated on factors including their education, work experience, and the needs of the FBI.

3. *Phase I Testing:*[78] Applicants passing the second hurdle are given three tests: A biodata inventory, a cognitive ability test, and a situational judgment test. Candidates whose scores exceed a predetermined cut score advance to the next phase.
4. *Application for Employment:* Candidates passing the third hurdle of Phase I testing are asked to submit a detailed application by a specific date. Only the most competitive applicants, based on the hiring needs of the FBI, are scheduled for Phase II Testing.
5. *Phase II Testing:*[79] Candidates' performance on a structured interview and a written exercise are compared to a cut score. If the applicant's score is at or higher than the cut score, he or she passes Phase II. Candidates who pass this hurdle are sent a letter informing them that they passed and that they might also receive a conditional letter of appointment, based on the determination of their competitiveness and the needs of the FBI. The final offer of employment is contingent upon successfully completing the final screening process.
6. *Final Screening Process:* A job offer is made contingent on passing the following:
    • A Personnel Security Interview—Candidates are questioned about their foreign travel and contacts, the extent of any drug use, the status of their financial obligations, and other security issues.

- A polygraph examination—The information candidates provided during their Personnel Security Interviews is often verified via a polygraph examination.
- A drug test.
- A background investigation—This includes running credit and criminal checks on candidates; interviewing their associates, personal and business references, current employers, and neighbors; and verifying their birth, citizenship, and educational achievements.
- A preemployment physical examination.

QUESTIONS

1. What are the advantages and disadvantages of the FBI using a multiple hurdles approach to select special agents?
2. Would such a lengthy selection process appeal to you or turn you off to working at the FBI?
3. What might the FBI do to increase the chances that the applicants it wants to hire accept the job offers extended to them?

Semester-Long Active Learning Project

Describe how candidates' assessment scores will be combined into a single score that can be used to compare candidates. Describe how you will reduce the candidate pool to a group of finalists and how you will decide which of your finalists will receive a job offer. Using what you learned in Chapter 4, identify how your decision-making plan will enable the company to comply with EEO and other legal requirements.

Case Study Assignment: Strategic Staffing at Chern's

See the appendix at the back of the book for this chapter's Case Study Assignment.

Endnotes

1. "MarineMax Investor Relations," MarineMax, 2007, www.marinemax.com/investor. Accessed May 29, 2007.
2. Ibid.
3. "Join Our Team," MarineMax, 2007, www.marinemax.com/Page.aspx/pageId/106/Join-Our-Team.aspx. Accessed May 29, 2007.
4. Hansen, F., "Negotiating Starting Salaries for Top Performers," *Workforce Management Online*, July 2006, www.workforce.com/archive/feature/24/44/60/index.php. Accessed May 25, 2007.
5. Smart, B., *Topgrading: How Leading Companies Win by Hiring, Coaching, and Keeping the Best People*, Paramus, NJ: Prentice Hall, 1999.
6. Federal Bureau of Investigation, "Phase I Testing," *Applicant Information Booklet*, September 1997.
7. Martinez, M., "Screening for Quality on the Web," *Employment Management Today*, 9, 1 (Winter 2004), www.shrm.org/ema/emt/articles/2004/winter04cover.asp. Accessed October 11, 2006.
8. Federal Bureau of Investigation, "Your Guide to Getting Started," *Applicant Information Booklet*, September 1997.
9. See Bobko, P., Roth, P. L., and Nicewander, A., "Banding Selection Scores in Human Resource Management Decisions: Current Inaccuracies and the Effect of Conditional Standard Errors," *Organizational Research Methods*, 8 (2005): 259–273.
10. Cascio, W. F., Dutz, J., Zedeck, S., and Goldstein, I. L., "Statistical Implications of Six Methods of Test Score Use in Personnel Selection," *Human Performance*, 4 (1991): 233–264.
11. Cascio, R., Alexander, A., and Barrett, G. V., "Setting Cutoff Scores: Legal, Psychometric, and Professional Issues and Guidelines," *Personnel Psychology*, 41 (1988): 21–22.
12. See U.S. Department of Labor, "Compliance Assistance-Fair Labor Standards Act (FLSA)," www.dol.gov/esa/whd/flsa. Accessed July 25, 2007.
13. Ibid.
14. *Smith v. BellSouth Telecommunications, Inc.*, 273 F.3d 1303 (11th Cir. 2001).
15. See, U.S. Department of Labor, "Uniform Guidelines on Employee Selection Procedures," 1978, www.dol.gov/esa/regs/cfr/41cfr/toc_Chapt60/60_3_toc.htm. Accessed July 25, 2007.
16. EEOC Guidelines on Affirmative Action, 29 C.F.R. § 1608.1(c).
17. See, for example, *Frank v. Xerox Corp.*, 347 F.3d 130, 137 (5th Cir. 2003).
18. See, for example, *Petit v. City of Chicago*, 352 F.3d 1111, 1115 (7th Cir. 2003); *Reynolds v. City of Chicago*, 296 F.3d 524, 530–31 (7th Cir. 2002); *Talbert v. City of Richmond*, 648 F.2d 925, 931–32 (4th Cir. 1981); *Cotter v. City of Boston*, 323 F.3d 160, 172 n.10 (1st Cir. 2002); U.S. Equal Employment Opportunity Commission, "EEOC Compliance Manual: Section 15: Race and Color Discrimination," April 19, 2006, www.eeoc.gov/policy/docs/race-color.html#N_115_. Accessed November 30, 2006.
19. U.S. Equal Employment Opportunity Commission, "EEOC Compliance Manual: Section 15: Race and Color Discrimination."
20. See, e.g., Appel, R. N., "Affirmative Action in the Workplace: Forty Years Later," *Hofstra Labor and Employment Law Journal*, 22 (Spring 2005): 571–574; Foreman, M. L., Dadey, K. M., and Wiggins, A. J., "The Continuing Relevance of Race-Conscious Remedies and Programs in Integrating the Nation's Workforce," *Hofstra Labor and Employment Law Journal*, 22 (Fall 2004): 101–104; Frymer, P., and Skrentny, J. D., "The Rise of Instrumental Affirmative Action: Law and the New Significance of Race in America," *Connecticut Law Review*, 36 (Spring 2004): 677, 693–697.
21. *Taxman v. Board of Education of the Township of Piscataway*, 91 F.3d 1547, 1557–58 (3d Cir. 1996).

22. Mathiason, G. G., "The Plus Factor," *Workforce Management,* August 2004: 14–16.

23. Phillips, J. M., "Effects of Realistic Job Previews on Multiple Organizational Outcomes: A Meta-Analysis," *Academy of Management Journal,* 41 (1998): 673–690.

24. Kopytoff, V., "How Google Woos the Best and Brightest," *San Francisco Chronicle,* December 18, 2005: A1.

25. Sullivan, J., "Predatory Hiring: The Best Hire Is Your Competitor's Top Talent," Ere.net, July 2001, www.ere.net/ articles/db/377396CF745111D582 FA00105A12D660.asp. Accessed December 4, 2006.

26. Johns Hopkins University, "Section 5: Salary Administration Program," Personnel Policy Manual, June 26, 2001, http://hrnt. jhu.edu/elr/pol-man/section5.cfm#E. Accessed July 16, 2010. Reprinted with permission from The Johns Hopkins University.

27. Bennett, S., "Negotiating Employee Contracts," Lawyers.com, http://labor-employment-law.lawyers.com/employment-contracts/Negotiating-Employee-Contracts.html. Accessed November 28, 2006.

28. Bennett-Alexander, D. D., and Hartman, L. P., *Employment Law for Business* (5th ed.), Boston: Irwin/McGraw-Hill, 2005; Spray, Gould & Bowers, LLP, "Business and Contract Disputes," 2005, SGBLaw.com, www.sgblaw.com/pages/contract.htm. Accessed May 29, 2007.

29. Mende, B., "Controlling Risk with Employment Contracts," CareerJournal.com, January 26, 1998, www.careerjournal.com/ myc/negotiate/ 19980126-mende.html. Accessed December 1, 2006.

30. Weiss, J. A., "Non-Competition Agreements: Their Lifespan and Other Methods to Protect a Company's Most Valuable Commodities," *Workforce Management Online,* December 2006, www.workforce.com/section/03/feature/24/61/03/index .html. Accessed December 19, 2006.

31. "Sample Noncompete Agreements," Vault.com, 2000, www. vault.com/nr/newsmain.jsp?nr_page=3&ch_id=402&article_ id=51431&cat_id=1244. Accessed May 25, 2007.

32. Bifulco, L., "Non-Compete and Non-Solicitation Agreements," National Association of Women Business Owners, 2001, www. nawbo-oc.com/articles/Noncompete.html. Accessed December 19, 2006.

33. Hetzer, B., "Beware the Ties That Bind," *BusinessWeek,* June 15, 1997, www.businessweek.com/1997/11/b3518128.htm. Accessed May 25, 2007.

34. Adapted from Bennett, S., "Negotiating Employee Contracts"; Yenerall, P. M., Radack, D. V., and Myers, J. J., "Making the Most of Employment Contracts," *HR Magazine,* August 1998; Burke, M., "Demystifying Common Terms in Employment Agreements," *Family Practice Management,* June 2003, www.aafp.org/fpm/ 20030600/38demy.html. Accessed December 9, 2006; Larkin, Hoffman, Daly and Lindgren Ltd., *What Goes Into an Employment Contract . . . And Why,* 1999, http://library.findlaw.com/1999/Jun/1/ 128351.html. Accessed December 9, 2006.

35. "Sample Noncompete Agreements," Vault.com.

36. Garcia, L., "Can a Non-Compete Clause Be Too Competitive?" Washingtonpost.com, April 26, 2007, www.washingtonpost .com/wp-dyn/content/article/2007/04/26/AR2007042601163 .html. Accessed May 25, 2007.

37. Mende, "Controlling Risk with Employment Contracts."

38. Ibid.

39. Esen, E., *Job Negotiation Survey Findings: A Study by SHRM and* CareerJournal.com, Alexandria, VA: Society for Human Resource Management, 2004.

40. Towers Perrin, *The Towers Perrin Talent Report: New Realities in Today's Workforce,* Towers-Perrin, 2001.

41. Lawler, E. E., "Research Directions," *Human Resource Management Review,* 10 (2000): 309.

42. Weiss, T., "A Woman's Guide to Making More Money," Forbes.com, June 29, 2006, www.forbes.com/careers/2006/06/ 28/leadership-business-basics-cx_tw_0629womennegotiating .html. Accessed May 25, 2007.

43. Walters, A. E., Stuhlmacher, A. F., and Meyer, L. L., "Gender and Negotiator Competitiveness: A Meta-Analysis," *Organizational Behavior and Human Decision Processes,* 76, 1 (1998): 1–29.

44. Stuhlmacher, A. F., and Walters, A. E., "Gender Differences in Negotiation Outcome: A Meta-Analysis," *Personnel Psychology,* 52, 3 (1999): 653–677.

45. Rau, B. L., and Feinauer, D., "The Role of Internal Agents in Starting Salary Negotiations," *Human Resource Management Review,* 16 (2006): 47–66.

46. Ibid.

47. Hirschman, C., "Five Mistakes to Avoid," *HR Magazine,* April 2002: 75.

48. APESMA, "Designing, Managing and Re-negotiating Your Employment Contract," *Professional Update,* 7, 9 (October 1997), www.apesma.asn.au/newsviews/professional_update/ 1997/october/article12.htm. Accessed November 15, 2006.

49. Ibid.

50. Ibid.

51. See Mende, "Controlling Risk with Employment Contracts."

52. Gillan, S., Hartzell, J. C., and Parrino, R., "Explicit vs. Implicit Contracts: Evidence from CEO Employment Agreements," March 30, 2006, American Finance Association 2006 Boston Meetings.

53. Bureau of Labor Statistics, "Union Members Summary," January 25, 2007, www.bls.gov/news.release/union2.nr0.htm. Accessed May 23, 2007.

54. Hogan, C., "Enforcement of Implicit Employment Contracts Through Unionization," *Journal of Labor Economics,* 19 (January 2001): 171–195.

55. Kaplan, M., "How to Negotiate Anything," *Money,* May 2005: 116–119; Miller, L., "Eleven Commandments for Smart Negotiating," CareerJournal.com, 2006, www.careerjournal.com/ myc/negotiate/19980410-miller.html. Accessed November 22, 2006; Mende, "Controlling Risk with Employment Contracts"; Johnson, R., and Schall, J., "Pay Up: Soft-Sell Strategies for Negotiating a Higher Starting Salary," Graduating engineer.com, 2006, www.graduatingengineer.com/articles/feature/09-01-03g.html. Accessed November 22, 2006; Loeb, M., "When It Comes to Job Offers, It Pays to Ask for More Money," CareerJournal.com, 2006, www.careerjournal.com/salaryhiring/ negotiate/20060830-loeb.html. Accessed November 22, 2006.

56. Fisher, R., Ury, W. L., and Patton, B., *Getting to Yes: Negotiating Agreement Without Giving In,* New York: Penguin, 1991.

57. "Closing the Deal: How to Get Prospective Employees to Sign On," AllBusiness.com, October 20, 2004, www.allbusiness .com/human-resources/workforce-management-hiring/363-1.html. Accessed November 23, 2006.

58. Hirschman, C., "Closing the Deal," *HR Magazine,* April 2002: 68–75.

59. Hausknecht, J. P., Day, D. V., and Thomas, S. C., "Applicant Reactions to Selection Procedures: An Updated Model and Meta-Analysis," *Personnel Psychology,* 57, 3 (2004): 639–683.

60. Fodchuk, K. M., and Sidebotham, E. J., "Procedural Justice in the Selection Process: A Review of Research and Suggestions for Practical Applications," *Psychologist-Manager Journal,* 8, 2 (2005): 105–120; Truxillo, D. M., Steiner, D. D., and Gilliland, S. W., "The Importance of Organizational Justice in Personnel Selection: Defining when Selection Fairness Really Matters," *International Journal of Selection and Assessment,* 12 (2004): 39–53; Truxillo, D. M., Bauer, T. N., Campion, M. A., and Paronto, M. E., "Selection Fairness Information and Applicant Reactions: A Longitudinal Field Study," *Journal of Applied Psychology,* 87 (2002): 1020–1031.

61. Gilliland, S. W., "Effects of Procedural and Distributive Justice on Reactions to a Selection System," *Journal of Applied Psychology,* 79 (1994): 691–701; Greenberg, J., "Organizational Justice: Yesterday, Today, and Tomorrow," *Journal of Management,* 16 (1990): 399–432.

62. Gilliland, S. W., "The Perceived Fairness of Selection Systems: An Organizational Justice Perspective," *Academy of Management Review,* 18 (1993): 694–734; Truxillo, Steiner, and Gilliland, "The Importance of Organizational Justice in Personnel Selection"; Cropanzano, R., and Wright, T. A., "Procedural Justice and Organizational Staffing: A Tale of Two Paradigms," *Human Resource Management Review,* 13, 1 (2003): 7–39.

63. Gilliland, "Effects of Procedural and Distributive Justice on Reactions to a Selection System."

64. Bies, R. J., and Moag, J. S., "Interactional Justice: Communication Criteria of Fairness," *Research on Negotiation in Organizations,* 1 (1986): 43–55.

65. Smither, J. W., Reilly, R. R., Millsap, R. E., Pearlman, K., and Stoffey, R. W., "Applicant Reactions to Selection Procedures," *Personnel Psychology,* 46 (1993): 49–76.

66. Hansen, F., "Recruiting on the Right Side of the Law," *Workforce Management Online,* May 2006, www.workforce.com/section/06/feature/24/38/12/. Accessed June 30, 2006.

67. Ford, D. K., Truxillo, D. M., and Bauer, T. N., "Rejected But Still There: Shifting the Focus in Applicant Reactions to the Promotional Context," *International Journal of Selection and Assessment,* 17 (2009): 402–416.

68. Hirschman, "Closing the Deal."

69. Scott, N., "Reneging—The Hot Economy's Dirty Secret," Vault.com, 2006, www.vault.com/nr/newsmain.jsp?nr_page=3&ch_id=421&article_id=19572&cat_id=81. Accessed December 7, 2006.

70. Cappelli, P., "Buying Options on Lawyers," *Human Resource Executive Online,* May 26, 2009, http://www.hreonline.com/HRE/story.jsp?storyId=212747437&topic=Main. Accessed April 6, 2010.

71. "MarineMax 2004 Annual Report," 2004, http://media.corporate-ir.net/media_files/NYS/HZO/reports/HZO04AR.pdf. Accessed May 25, 2007.

72. Hansen, "Negotiating Starting Salaries for Top Performers."

73. Ibid.

74. Federal Bureau of Investigation, "FBI Special Agent Selection Process: General Information," *Applicant Information Booklet,* September 1997.

75. Federal Bureau of Investigation, "Your Guide to Getting Started."

76. Federal Bureau of Investigation, "FBI Special Agent Selection Process: General Information."

77. Ibid.

78. Federal Bureau of Investigation, "Phase I Testing."

79. Ibid.

Outline

LEARNING OBJECTIVES
After studying this chapter, you should be able to:

- Discuss ways to make socialization more effective.
- Describe the six different types of turnover.
- Discuss employee retention strategies.
- Discuss various ways of downsizing a company's workforce.
- Describe how to effectively terminate an employee.

Improving Onboarding at Hilton[1]

With over 500 hotels worldwide, Hilton depends on its call center reservations and customer care representatives to manage reservations and customer concerns. Hilton felt that it was a desirable employer, offering employees travel benefits, a strong brand, and the opportunity for some representatives to work from home. But Hilton also realized that the annual turnover rate of 55 percent among these employees was expensive and resulted in lost productivity.

After investigating its turnover patterns in greater detail, Hilton learned that half of all of its reservations and customer care representative hires left before 90 days of employment. This early turnover suggested that its selection and onboarding process could be improved.

Imagine that the company asks for your opinion as to how it can decrease the early turnover of its reservations and customer care representatives and improve their retention and performance. After reading this chapter, you should have some good ideas to share with the firm.

Because strategic staffing manages the flow of people into, through, and out of the organization, it does not end when job offers are accepted. As we have explained, once a person has agreed to be hired, a company's human resource department turns its attention to enhancing the employee's commitment to the organization. Even simple things like following up with new hires prior to their start dates can be useful. One study found that when firms telephoned their new hires to encourage them to maintain their commitment to their new jobs, fewer of them failed to report to work.[2]

Of course, once employees report to work, they need to "learn the ropes" of their new jobs. Corning Glass Works found that employees who attended a structured orientation program were 69 percent more likely to remain with the company after three years than those who did not go through such a program. Texas Instruments found that employees whose orientation process was carefully attended to reached full productivity two months earlier than did other new hires.[3] One expert says, "With a thorough orientation and 'onboarding' process, the probability of achieving the goals of the business and the employee are greatly increased. Without it, the probabilities of disappointment, employee turnover, rework, and dissatisfied clients all grow unnecessarily."[4]

In addition to smoothing the transition of new hires into the company and getting them productive as quickly as possible, it is also necessary to manage the movement of people into different projects and jobs throughout the company. Separations, including terminations, layoffs, and downsizings, are another important part of strategic staffing and talent management. In this chapter, you will learn how to integrate new hires into their work groups and the company, manage the flow of talent throughout the organization, and manage employee separations. After reading this chapter, you should have a good understanding of how to manage the flow of talent into, through, and out of a firm.

ORIENTING AND SOCIALIZING NEW EMPLOYEES

Many organizations invest more money in hiring new employees than in helping them acclimate and become productive. Most new hires want to get off to a good start but need help doing so. Even in restaurants and hotels, it can take about 90 days for a new employee to attain the productivity level of an existing employee.[5] On average, the time for new external hires to achieve full productivity is eight weeks for clerical jobs, 20 weeks for professionals, and more than 26 weeks for executives.[6]

Employers have only one opportunity to make a good first impression on new employees. The best sourcing, recruiting, and staffing practices are useless if the people who are hired cannot be retained. Because most turnover occurs during the first few months on the job, firms can increase the retention rates of their new employees by helping them adjust to their companies and jobs.[7] Because organizations have little opportunity to recover the return on their investment in new employees who quit, newcomer turnover is problematic and expensive. Many managers, in fact, say that high turnover rates are the biggest obstacle to their companies' growth efforts.[8]

Orientation, or *onboarding*, is the process of completing new hires' employment-related paperwork, providing them with keys, identification cards, workspaces, and technology such as computers, company e-mail addresses, and telephone numbers. It also includes introducing the new hires to their coworkers (who will be important to their success), and familiarizing them with their jobs and with the company's work policies and benefits. Orienting new employees can

orientation
the process of completing new hires' employment-related paperwork and familiarizing them with their jobs, coworkers, work spaces, work tools, and the company's policies and benefits

average of 65 percent. Because turnover costs amount to about 30 percent of a reservation agent's salary, these retention rates have had a big impact on JetBlue's bottom line.[85] At one point, the company's annual turnover costs were just 6 percent of the costs experienced by similar firms, or just $327,600 compared to the industry average of $6,084,000![86]

Telecommuting can also improve the productivity of employees if it makes them more content with their jobs. JetBlue's at-home reservationists are 30 percent more productive on average, which makes it more viable for JetBlue to hire domestic workers for the position, rather than outsourcing the jobs to lower labor-cost countries. Customers contacting the reservationists also experience fewer language barriers this way.[87] In fact, JetBlue receives only one complaint for every 300,000 reservation calls made to the company—an industry best. This has saved JetBlue a considerable amount of money when you consider the fact that it costs six times more to gain a new customer than it does to retain an old one.[88] To combat the isolation that home-sourced workers can feel, the company has developed several measures: All homesourced reservation agents must come into JetBlue's regional offices in Salt Lake City for a minimum of four hours each month, which allows them to interact with their fellow employees and with management. Workers are also kept up-to-date with the most recent events occurring at JetBlue.[89]

CHOOSING A GOOD LOCATION   Locating near companies that employ similar talent can be strategic. For example, a technology company in Silicon Valley will likely be able to more easily acquire the talent it needs than if the firm were located in, for example, Fargo, North Dakota. The possible high turnover rate given the ease with which employees can switch employers can help keep a firm's ideas fresh, too. However, as we explained earlier in the book, the same high turnover rate could compromise a research and development company that needs employees to remain working on projects for a long time. Also, there are clearly ethical and strategic issues surrounding the "poaching" of employees from other organizations. Moreover, if you poach employees from other employers, you must be prepared, in turn, to be poached from!

Establishing a separate long-term research facility in a location where the skills of the team are not in as high demand, such as a rural community, can increase employee retention rates, although, as we indicated, initially attracting candidates can sometimes be more challenging. However, the strategy worked for the semiconductor company Intersil. When the turnover rate for the semiconductor industry for a whole was at 20 percent, the turnover at Intersil's semiconductor facility in rural Pennsylvania averaged only 2 percent.[90] Also, as we explained in Chapter 6, when GE had trouble finding people willing to move to "Dreary Erie, Pennsylvania," the company began recruiting junior military officers. Previously used to sitting in foxholes, these employees found Erie less of a limitation.[91]

PROVIDING COMPETITIVE WAGES AND BENEFITS   Competitive pay and benefits will help attract and retain employees, of course. However, even if a company has good benefits, if employees don't understand or appreciate those benefits, then the benefits are unlikely to affect their retention. An analysis by the consulting firm Watson Wyatt found that companies that offer rich benefits but have poor communication practices had an average turnover rate for top-performing employees of 17 percent. Companies that offered less costly benefits but successfully communicated them had an average top talent turnover rate of 12 percent. The best situation, combining rich benefits and effectively explaining them to employees, was associated with an even lower 8 percent turnover rate for top performers.[92] A pay-for-performance plan can also help reduce the turnover of top performers and improve the company's return on what it pays employees.[93]

Capital One believes that executing its business strategy necessitates hiring the best talent. To help attract and retain that talent, the company developed an extensive work-life program. Programs ranging from concierge services and fitness centers to child care subsidies and discounted ticket sales reduce stress and save employees' time. The company tracks the usage of each work-life benefit and conducts a cost–benefit analysis of all such initiatives to identify which are having the most impact on the company's goals. Employees are also surveyed twice a year about how they feel about their workspaces—for example, how they feel about the lighting, functionality, privacy, cleanliness, conveniences, food services, break facilities, recreation facilities, and meeting spaces they use. The bank believes that working on the issues identified by the survey helps it retain employees.[94]

HOLDING MANAGERS ACCOUNTABLE   Rewarding managers and holding them accountable for retaining top performers and ensuring that their subordinates have clear, consistently monitored professional growth plans will increase the chances that the managers will engage in these behaviors. Designing retention training for managers can improve their ability to retain good performers, too. Remember, however, that retaining top performers is not the same as retaining poor performers, which can actually cost a company money.

When Deloitte wanted to reduce attrition among its high performers, it learned from its exit survey data that lack of flexibility was the number one reason women were leaving the company and the number two reason for men. This was despite the fact that Deloitte had 69 different flexible work arrangements ranging from telecommuting to compressed workweeks. Deloitte replaced the flexible work arrangements with a work customization program that allows employees to ask their managers to periodically "dial up" or "dial down" their careers based on career pace, workload, location/schedule, and role. Although not all requests can be approved, one out of three requests have been to dial down, and employee satisfaction with "overall career/life fit" increased by 25 percent as turnover fell.[95]

PROVIDING EMPLOYEES WITH SUPPORT   Helping employees balance their work and their lives can improve their retention. The Marriott Corporation hotel chain has been an industry leader in reducing employee turnover. Through its Pathways to Independence program, Marriott trains welfare recipients for the workforce. In some locations, Pathways alumni are 50 percent less likely to quit than the average employee. The program's unique structure combines internal and external support for the company's welfare-to-work employees. Marriott's supervisors help employees manage their professional lives, while Marriott "case workers" help employees manage their personal lives.[96]

Sonesta Hotels, a family-run chain of 18 properties, developed a formal program to acclimate new hires throughout their first 100 days on the job. The main goal is to rerecruit employees on their 30-, 60-, and 90-day anniversaries. At 30 days, the human resources director sits down with new employees to check if their expectations are being met and whether they have all the tools they need to perform their work. At 60 days, a second orientation called the "Booster" is given with a focus on developing the employees' communication and service skills. Feedback is solicited about the employees' training, and the new employees are asked what else they need to be successful. At 90 days, the new employees formally meet with their managers to set joint goals for the rest of the year.[97]

mobility barriers
factors that make it harder for employees to leave an organization

CREATING MOBILITY BARRIERS   **Mobility barriers** are factors that make it harder for an employee to leave an organization. Mobility barriers can include stock options that vest in the future, requiring employees to stay with the company to receive their full financial value; extensive training in a company's processes and procedures that are unique to that company; or desirable work attributes that competing employers lack. Mobility barriers other than financial incentives to stay, which can sometimes be matched by other organizations, embed employees in the company in such a way that their value is greater inside than outside the firm due to firm-specific knowledge. If the perceived cost of leaving is greater than the expected gain of joining a different organization due to a person's commitment to his or her work group, team, or company, he or she is less likely to resign.[98]

CREATING A STRONG CORPORATE CULTURE   If a company is able to create a strong culture that employees find attractive, it can enhance employees' commitment to the company. Companies like the outdoor clothing and equipment company Patagonia, whose goal is to produce the highest-quality products while doing the least possible harm to the environment, have developed values-based mission statements that appeal to recruits and employees alike. The appeal of the corporate culture helps retain employees with similar values.[99]

Mergers and Acquisitions

Retaining key employees during a merger or acquisition and integrating those employees into the company is critical if the new organization is to succeed. One way to improve the retention of important employees is to create financial agreements with key talent that serve as *golden handcuffs* that create mobility barriers for them. As we just explained, financial incentive packages, such as retention bonuses or stock options that mature over time, can help the firm retain its essential employees and increase their commitment to making a merger successful. To keep talent from leaving prematurely, companies also sometimes increase the value of the severance packages they offer workers who stay until a merger or acquisition is completed. These types of agreements are typically formalized in a written contract that specifies the financial incentives that the employee will receive if he or she stays with the company for a specified time.

Mergers and acquisitions create a lot of job uncertainty for employees—and top performers often have other job opportunities. Consequently, it is important that the employer clearly communicate with employees about their future with the company—what their jobs will entail, where they will be located, and so forth, assuming this information is known. Many companies create special retention strategies for their key personnel during mergers and acquisitions.

Managing Succession

As you learned in Chapter 10, succession management plans for the replacement of employees in key positions and creates a talent pipeline in the company. There are some positions in almost every company that are very costly to the organization if left unfilled. These positions are often at the executive level, but other positions are often critical as well. In smaller organizations, one person might be key to the performance of an entire unit. This is often true for researchers in firms pursuing an innovation strategy, but can be true for companies pursuing a customer intimacy strategy as well. If the employee responsible for managing an important customer leaves, the company's relationship with that customer might deteriorate.

Mobility policies dictate how people can move between jobs within an organization. A mobility policy should clearly state both employees' and supervisors' responsibilities for employee development. On the one hand, employees might be responsible for identifying the training programs they need to enroll in to qualify for promotions and request that their supervisors give them time away from their jobs to complete this training. On the other hand, supervisors might be responsible for regularly coaching and providing feedback to their subordinates, providing accurate assessments of their readiness to be trained and promoted, and helping them use and further develop the skills they acquired during their training. Mobility policies also clearly document the rules surrounding the posting of job openings, the eligibility qualifications for jobs, and the compensation and benefits associated with them. Mobility policies should be well developed, clearly communicated, and perceived as fair by employees. Not every employee who desires a promotion or wishes to transfer to a different position will be able to do so. But if the process used to determine who does and does not get promoted is perceived to be fair, those who aren't able to do so will feel less animosity toward the organization and be more willing to remain with it.

mobility policies
policies that dictate how people can move between jobs within an organization

Redeploying Talent

Workforce redeployment involves moving employees to other parts of the company or to other jobs the company needs filled. Workforce redeployment applies the supply-chain management principles used to optimize inventory management, planning, and production to optimize the utilization of a firm's employees. For firms trying to maximize the efficiency of their workforces, which is particularly important for companies pursuing low-cost strategies, optimizing their workforces is critical.

IBM's Workforce Management Initiative borrows many of the same concepts of supply-chain management, such as capacity planning, supply and demand planning, and sourcing. To manage 100,000 global employees and about as many subcontractors in its Global Services division, the firm built a structure that outlines the company's internal and external skills and provides a real-time view of IBM's labor-supply-chain activities. The system catalogs employees' skills, creating common descriptors around what people do, what their competencies are, and what experiences and references they have.[100] One global pharmaceutical company uses a labor supply chain to better catalog its own employees' talents to help it make better decisions about when to use its own employees and when to call in contractors.[101]

Hewlett-Packard uses workforce redeployment to provide employees some measure of employment security. When the company had 400 surplus workers at its Loveland, Colorado, facility after closing its fabrication division, it redeployed many of them to other locations within the region, loaned employees to other divisions with short-term hiring needs, and permitted

workforce redeployment
moving employees to other parts of the company or to other jobs

employees to be reclassified to lower pay levels and accept other jobs if they chose to. As a result, the company retained more than 50 percent of its surplus employees.[102]

INVOLUNTARY EMPLOYEE SEPARATIONS

Involuntary employee separations are inevitable. Downsizing and terminations are two of the most common reasons for involuntary employee separations. We discuss each next.

Downsizing

downsizing
the process of permanently reducing the number of a firm's employees so as to improve the efficiency or effectiveness of the firm

Downsizing is the process of permanently reducing the number of a firm's employees so as to improve the efficiency or effectiveness of the firm.[103] Downsizing is a popular way for organizations to attempt to improve their flexibility by reducing their bureaucratic structures, giving employees who have been retained by the firm the power to make decisions more quickly, and improving communication within the firm. A downsizing can also be done in response to a merger or acquisition, revenue or market-share loss, technological and industrial changes, a restructuring, and inaccurate labor-demand forecasting.[104]

Labor costs are a large part of many firms' expenses. Thus, private-sector employers often downsize to reduce their costs, maximize the returns their shareholders earn, and to remain competitive in an increasingly global economy. Public-sector downsizings often occur when technological improvements allow fewer workers to do the same amount of work or when governments reduce their operating budgets.[105]

TYPES OF DOWNSIZING   If the choice of which employees to downsize is not constrained by a collective bargaining agreement (which usually mandates that union members with the most seniority be retained), there are several ways to choose who to target in a downsizing. *Across the board* downsizing requires all of a company's units to reduce their headcount by the same percentage. *Geographic* downsizing targets specific locations for employee reductions, perhaps due to the loss of an important customer. *Business-based* downsizing targets only certain segments of a business. In addition, downsizing can target specific *functions* or departments that need to be reduced, or specific *positions* or jobs that are overstaffed. *Performance-based* downsizing targets poor performers. When downsizing is *seniority based*, the last people hired are the first people let go. If cost cutting is a goal of the downsizing, *salary-based* downsizing can help a firm reach this goal. This method involves targeting a firm's most highly paid employees. *Competency-based* downsizing involves retaining employees with the competencies the company expects to need in the future and downsizing employees who lack them. Downsizing can also be done through *self-selection*, if a firm offers its employees inducements to leave, such as early retirement packages or buyouts. Table 12-5 summarizes these downsizing targeting methods.

Firms need to fully plan their downsizing efforts if they want to reduce the related negative consequences that can occur. A downsizing benchmarking study identified seven typical downsizing activities, each of which must be planned for:[106]

1. Conducting a workforce demographics review including an assessment of the age, diversity, and skills of the workforce as well as a projection of the number of employees expected to resign, be terminated, or retire;
2. Assessing the firm's alternatives to downsizing, including implementing a hiring freeze and offering employees buyouts, early retirement, retraining, and relocation packages;
3. Outlining the number of employees slated to be downsized per month, year, location, business unit, department, and occupation;
4. Conducting the downsizing or reduction in force;
5. Providing career transition/job placement assistance to separated employees;
6. Providing assistance for the firm's remaining employees; and
7. Ensuring that an adequate retraining program is in place.

UNINTENDED OUTCOMES OF DOWNSIZING   Firms often experience unintended outcomes of downsizing including the voluntary turnover of their most valuable employees, efficiency losses, and the greater cost and difficulty of hiring new employees and training them amid a downsizing effort. Lower morale and a lack of motivation among a firm's employees can become pervasive, as

TABLE 12-5	Downsizing Targeting Methods
Targeting Method	**Description**
Across-the-board downsizing	All units reduce their headcount by the same percentage.
Geographic downsizing	Specific locations are targeted for downsizing.
Business-based downsizing	Only some segments of the business are targeted (e.g., employees associated with one product line).
Position-based downsizing	Specific jobs are targeted (e.g., accountants or salespeople).
Function-based downsizing	Specific functions are targeted (e.g., the firm's human resources department might be downsized), usually during an organizational redesign.
Performance-based downsizing	Poor performers are targeted for separation.
Seniority-based downsizing	The last people hired are the first downsized.
Salary-based downsizing	The most highly paid employees are targeted.
Competency-based downsizing	Employees with the competencies the company expects to need in the future are retained, and employees without those competencies are targeted.
Self-selection downsizing	The firm encourages employees to self-select out of the company by offering them inducements, such as buyouts or early retirement packages.

can increased employee absenteeism, stress, and uncertainty. In particular, companies need to address *survivor syndrome*, or the emotional effects the downsizing has on employees who are being retained. The emotional aftereffects these employees experience include fear, anger, frustration, anxiety, and mistrust, which can threaten an organization's very survival. Survivors often feel guilty about retaining their jobs and are preoccupied by fears of further layoffs.[107] This can increase the chances that they will quit, be less committed to the firm, and be less flexible—that is, less willing to go out of their way to help the company work toward its long-term goals.[108]

The evidence regarding how layoffs affect survivors' actual productivity is mixed. Some studies suggest that employees who have been retained work harder as a result of "survivor's guilt,"[109] Other studies suggest that survivors feel so insecure that their productivity falls.[110] One study of Boeing employees during a decade when the company laid off tens of thousands of employees found that the laid off employees were less depressed and drank less than those who remained. Employees who experienced survivor's guilt and the stress of not knowing if they would be next experienced the worst stress.[111]

The value of a firm's shares can also fall during a downsizing, and its reputation as an employer can suffer. As a result, firms often have to pay higher wages to attract top talent after they downsize.[112] In addition, when a company's separated employees take advantage of unemployment insurance, the firm's future premiums rise. Also, the employer's costs for job placement services, career and résumé coaching, and skills training designed to assist separated employees rise. The costs of downsizing include:

- Outplacement services (job training, job placement services, and career coaches for downsized employees)
- Higher unemployment insurance premiums in future periods
- Severance pay
- Pay for accumulated but untaken employee vacation time
- The costs related to hiring and training future replacement employees
- Higher staffing costs due to a less desirable postlayoff or postdownsizing employer image.

There is no convincing evidence that downsizing leads to long-term, superior organizational performance or enhanced shareholder value.[113] There are studies that have attempted to measure and evaluate the medium- and long-term effects of downsizing. During the initial stages of a downsizing, the organization doing so usually incurs extraordinarily large costs related to the severance packages, early retirement packages, outplacement services, and so forth designed to help separated employees. Management can evaluate downsizing by preparing a cost–benefit analysis to identify the short-term financial implications of the downsizing and the expected long-term savings or losses.

CONDUCTING A DOWNSIZING Workforce planning, which you learned about in Chapter 5, is an essential part of evaluating whether or not a downsizing effort should be undertaken.[114] Some firms go through the pain of downsizing only to have to upsize a few years later. Downsizing should begin only after the firm's short- and long-term strategic goals have been established and downsizing will clearly help the firm meet both of those goals. Given that downsizing is a traumatic event, no matter how well prepared a firm's workforce is, the process should be carried out in the most expedient manner possible. Companies often make the mistake of spreading out their downsizing efforts over a period of months and even years. This can cause employees a great deal of long-term stress.[115]

During a downsizing, it is important to stay focused on the organization's strategy by consistently reminding employees that restructuring activities are part of a plan to improve the organization's performance and are key to the organization's future success. One expert believes that "a downsizing plan should be included in the strategic management plan of all organizations, regardless of whether they plan to downsize or not. By including such a plan, the organization will be better prepared to begin the staff-reduction process should it be forced to do so in response to environmental changes"[116] Sharing the firm's growth plans and renewal strategies with employees can also ease the anxiety they are likely to feel.

For ethical reasons, companies should always have a working plan of how to conduct a downsizing in a way that is consistent with the company's values and talent philosophy. Without clear policies and procedures set up in advance, it is more difficult to do the right thing when a downsizing is imminent. Given the traumatic nature of a downsizing, every communication and every action should be consistent with the firm's values. If showing employees respect and communicating openly are important values, these become particularly important during a downsizing. What and how the company communicates with separated employees sends a strong message about how it will treat the people who are being retained and outside stakeholders as well. Potential suppliers, current investors, and potential employees reading about unethical or poorly handled layoffs will be wary of doing business with a company that does not properly treat its employees during a downsizing.

Perceptions of fairness are important during a layoff or any type of downsizing. When Royal Philips Electronics had to dismiss about 30,000 employees, it tried to do so in a socially responsible way. The company first continued to invest in training, education, and job search counseling for people put on a dismissal list. The goal was to make the situation as acceptable as possible to the employees staying as well as leaving. As the company's president and CEO Gerard Kleisterlee said, "The people who stay in the organization—although they know as well as the people who leave that you have to do that for the sake of a healthy company—want to see that the people are treated like people want to be treated. I always say, 'Treat somebody else like you want to be treated yourself. Then you will do a good job.' "[117]

When used as a component of an overall reengineering or restructuring strategy, a downsizing effort can be effective. One survey of 531 large companies that had downsized revealed that well over half of them had achieved their goals of reducing costs and expenses. However, less than half had achieved their goals of increased profitability, productivity, and customer satisfaction.[118] In one case, a unionized technology services company that tried to pursue a low-cost strategy by downsizing ended up with significantly above-market labor costs because its union contract required it to retain many longer-term, higher-paid employees. The higher labor costs interfered with the company's ability to compete successfully on price. Table 12-6 summarizes some of the best ways to conduct an effective downsizing.

Measuring the effectiveness of a downsizing effort can be done in a variety of ways, including:[119]

- Meeting the firm's authorized full-time employee headcount goals
- Increasing the firm's ratio of supervisors to employees

TABLE 12-6	Best Downsizing Practices

The following is a summary of some of the best ways to conduct a downsizing:[120]

- *The firm's senior leaders should play a vital role.* They should become involved early and continue to participate actively in the process as well as remain visible and accessible to employees. Employees also need to believe that their managers are a source of credible information.
- *Engage in frequent two-way communication.* Employees want honest and open communication about what is happening to the organization during the downsizing. In other words, the communication must flow both ways—between both managers and their employees. When managers are communicating with employees who are facing termination, they should do so face-to-face, not via e-mail or letters.
- *Involve the right people in downsizing planning.* The firm's senior leaders, human resource executives, and labor representatives should all be involved in planning the downsizing.
- *Identify work processes that will not be needed in the future organization.* This will help sustain those processes that are key to the organization's future.
- *Incentives such as early retirement and buyouts work well and are popular with employees.* Because buyouts and early retirement incentives allow employees to retire with either full or reduced pension benefits at an earlier age than normal, they can be a good best-practices option—one that helps the firm achieve its goals as well as employees achieve their goals.
- *Using multiple strategies and techniques to accomplish a firm's downsizing goals can help leverage the outcome.* Downsizing strategies don't always work exactly as planned. Using multiple strategies helps to ensure the effort is a success.
- *Provide career transition assistance to both separated and surviving employees.* This can include career counseling, personal counseling, career/skill and career transition training, relocation assistance, outplacement assistance, résumé writing assistance, access to office equipment, paid time off, child care, financial counseling, and access to job fairs and Internet job placement sites.
- *Monitor the process's progress.* Take the time to periodically review your firm's downsizing procedures, learn from your mistakes as well as successes, and document this information so that future downsizings can be completed more effectively.
- *Survivors are the key.* The success or failure of a downsized organization depends on the workforce that remains after the downsizing. A well-planned and managed downsizing process that employees believe was administered fairly and humanely will help them believe in and work toward the future success of the organization.

- Employee loss due to attrition versus personnel loss due to incentive programs
- Demographics of buyout recipients
- Impact on diversity goals
- Ability to meet budgetary limits
- Productivity changes
- Reduction in total cost of wages and salaries
- Number of grievances, appeals, or lawsuits filed
- Number of voluntary participants in incentive and career transition programs

Layoffs

A **layoff**, also known as a reduction in force, is a temporary end to employment. Unlike downsizing, which is a permanent separation of employees, the company intends to rehire laid-off employees when business picks back up. Employers tend to dislike layoffs compared to other downsizing methods. Like downsizings, sometimes layoffs are forced by law due to budget cuts, which is the case with most public-sector layoffs. At other times, economic conditions result in layoffs. If a firm is unionized, union members with seniority must usually be retained prior to more junior union members. Unfortunately, this won't guarantee that the firm will end up retaining the right competencies it needs to compete more successfully. Seniority-based layoffs such as this can also have a negative impact on employee diversity, since they disproportionately affect women and minorities, who, on average, are less likely to have seniority. Like downsizings, layoffs often have a negative impact on the reputation of firms as employers—especially young firms that have not yet established positive employer reputations.[121]

layoff
temporary end to employment

In addition to EEOC compliance, the Age Discrimination in Employment Act applies to layoffs as does the Worker Adjustment and Retraining Notification (WARN) Act. The WARN Act is a federal law requiring employers of 100 or more full-time workers to give employees 60 days advance notice of closing or major layoffs.[122]

Alternatives to Layoffs

attrition

the normal reduction of a firm's workforce due to the retirement, death, or resignation of employees

hiring freeze

a policy whereby no new employees are hired for a certain period of time

Instead of layoffs, organizations often reduce their employee headcount in other ways. **Attrition** is the normal reduction of a firm's workforce due to the retirement, death, or resignation of employees. Combining natural attrition with a **hiring freeze**, which involves not hiring any new employees to replace departing employees, can result in a sufficient amount of headcount reduction if the attrition is high enough and the freeze can be imposed for a long enough period of time. Attrition and hiring freezes can protect the jobs of survivors, but there needs to be a plan in place to redistribute the work among them to avoid their being chronically overworked.

Early retirement and buyout incentives are a good way to achieve attrition and are often well received by employees. Companies often fund early retirement and buyout incentives with money they save during hiring freezes. Another way to reduce the size of a company's workforce is to encourage employees to take a leave without pay. Although an employee's benefits are usually reduced during the leave, the company guarantees that the employee can return at the end of a designated period. Leaves without pay can appeal to some employees who need to complete their education, care for family, or transition to another career. When the company wants to downsize to cut its costs rather than meet a mandated reduction in the number of employees, this can be a good strategy.

Flexible work arrangements, such as telecommuting, part-time employment, and job sharing, which we discussed earlier in the chapter, in conjunction with retention strategies can also be used to downsize a company's workforce without resorting to layoffs. The arrangements can decrease absenteeism and turnover, improve a firm's ability to recruit and retain talent, and can increase employees' health, morale, and productivity as they achieve better work-life balances.[123]

As we mentioned earlier in the chapter, rather than layoffs, it's sometimes possible to redeploy targeted employees to other parts of the company or to other jobs the company needs filled. Cross training employees in different competencies and jobs and retraining employees can better enable their redeployment as well.

Firms can also avoid laying off employees by reducing their work hours or reducing their pay. This way, all the employees share the pain of the cutback but no one loses his or her job. When the economy pulled back, casino operator Wynn Resorts Inc. cut the wages of its salaried Las Vegas workers and reduced full-time hourly employees' workweeks to avoid cutting jobs.[124]

Firms might reduce employees' pay but give them company stock in exchange. Oftentimes firms rely on temporary employment and contract employment arrangements to protect the jobs of their regular, full-time employees. Temporary and contract workers are simply hired and let go as needed.

Discharging Employees

Rather than separating multiple people from the company, as happens with downsizing or layoffs, discharging focuses on the termination of individual employees. Although this is not a favorite part of the job for most managers, discharging employees for reasons ranging from poor performance to misconduct is an essential part of managing. Not only does disrespectful or unprofessional treatment of employees increase the likelihood of a lawsuit, it also risks damaging the company's employer brand and future recruiting ability. As an example of a poor way to dismiss an employee, at one university the authors have worked, an assistant to a program director was looking over the next year's budget and noticed that her position was not included in it. When she asked if this was an oversight, she was told that actually she was about to lose her job. This is clearly not a way that anyone would like to learn that they are soon to be unemployed.

Discharges can happen immediately after a policy violation or other job misconduct—for example, a safety violation or the failure of an employee to renew a professional license. Alternatively, a discharge can occur after a long pattern of poor performance. Most organizations use some form of progressive discipline for poor performers to give them a chance to improve. The typical progression of steps in progressive discipline is as follows:

1. A verbal warning
2. A written warning
3. Suspension
4. Discharge

As is the case with downsizing, discharge decisions should be well thought out rather than made emotionally, or in the heat of an argument. Whenever possible, employees need a chance to correct the problems they are having prior to their supervisors taking action. Asking employees to sign that they have read and understand the company policies they must follow is also helpful.

When an employee is being told that he or she is being discharged, the manager's main task is to be respectful but clear in letting the employee know that he or she has been terminated and why. During the meeting, a manager needs be sure to describe all the relevant facts about the employee's dismissal and be prepared to explain how the employee violated the company's policies or failed to meet his or her job requirements, despite persistent attempts to help him or her do so. A human resources professional should write a simple letter that outlines the employee's date of discharge, any contractual obligations owed to the employee, such as severance pay, continuing benefits, and so forth, and the name of the manager who approved the discharge. The HR professional should then send copies of the letter to the discharged employee's immediate supervisor, payroll and benefits department, compliance officers, any labor organization to which the employee belongs, and to the employee. Even if there is an employment-at-will agreement between the two parties, it is important for a company to document all discharges and keep thorough and accurate records regarding their causes.[125]

Having discharged (or downsized) employees sign a *severance agreement* that includes a *release* stating that the departing employee gives up some or all of his or her rights to sue the company can reduce its risk of future litigation. Employee releases are used most often when a company does not have the proper documentation to fire an employee but wants to end the employment relationship with him or her and reduce the possibility of a lawsuit.[126] To be most effective, the release needs to involve some sort of exchange between the two parties, usually money beyond any standard severance agreement. The employee needs to be given an appropriate amount of time to consider the offer and even change his or her mind after signing it. Finally, the employee should be able to negotiate some of the agreement's contents to show that the agreement was not coerced unwillingly.[127] HR professionals should seek legal counsel before drafting a release.

Some common discharging errors include doing it publicly, writing a positive letter of reference after a termination for cause (this opens up the company to charges of having given a negligent referral), trying to document a discharge for a just cause case that doesn't exist, firing an employee after a merit raise or favorable performance review, and stating that the person conducting the discharge disagrees with it. Juries have also looked unfavorably at discharges that were done at the end of a workday or workweek, after the employee returns from a business trip, or at the beginning of a holiday.

Dealing with the Risk of Violence

The potential exists for strikes or even violence during and after a discharge, layoff, or downsizing.[128] Supervisors need to be able to spot the warning indicators for employee violence, including anger, depression, paranoia, withdrawal or isolation, and drug or alcohol abuse, on the part of employees. Many companies now conduct training to help supervisors recognize these signs. Can the employee control his or her behavior? If not, this is a warning sign. Managers should pay attention to how the employee's coworkers react to him or her and listen to their concerns. Coworkers often get a good look at each other's behaviors that their supervisors don't. Any and all threats should be taken seriously. It's possible that the employee may need to utilize the organization's resources including an employee assistance program. If the employee is fired, he or she may need posttermination monitoring and counseling.

This chapter's Develop Your Skills feature provides some tips for conducting an effective meeting when discharging an employee.

DEVELOP YOUR SKILLS
Discharging Tips

Discharging an employee is a part of every manager's job. Like it or not, at some point as a manager, you will probably have to fire someone. Your main task during a termination meeting is to be clear in letting the employee know he or she is being terminated and to reduce the employee's desire to pursue any lawsuit against the company. Here are some tips to help you conduct a discharging meeting professionally and effectively:

- Remain impartial, calm, and in control of the conversation; be respectful at all times.
- Listen to employee requests for severance terms, but reserve final decisions for a later time; being heard and considered will increase the employee's perceptions of fairness.
- Be clear and don't send mixed messages.
- The shock of being fired can prevent the employee from listening to all of what you are saying; repeat yourself if you feel your message is not being heard.
- Don't give career advice to someone you've just fired.
- If the person is being terminated, don't say "laid off" because it implies the possibility of return.

- Hold the meeting in a private, neutral location.
- Deliver information without engaging in an argument; use prepared notes if necessary. Do not ramble, make promises, or say a mistake is being made.
- Be empathetic but do not apologize.
- Discuss the effective termination date, any severance package, and so forth; have the details of the termination and any severance package in writing so the employee can take them with him or her along with the details of the termination.
- Be aware of legal compliance issues.
- Write up an accurate record of the termination interview and provide a copy to the employee.
- Be sure to cover the practical matters such as returning company identification cards and keys, and how the employee will receive a final paycheck.
- If necessary, involve company security but have them keep a low profile until they are needed.
- Notify all relevant parties after discharge that the employee has been terminated.

IMPROVING ONBOARDING AT HILTON[129]

To improve the retention of its reservations and customer care representatives, Hilton built a retention strategy around why employees tend to stay with the company, including the strong brand, travel benefits, and working from home. Core job skills were identified and interviewers were trained to conduct structured interviews with a special focus on retention. Removing technology experience as a job requirement and training it instead expanded the applicant pool to include older workers who have the other core job skills and who tend to have lower turnover rates. Hilton also developed a realistic job preview to promote attrition at the applicant stage rather than post-hire.

Hilton now assigns the best supervisor at each location to be responsible for each newly hired team member immediately after training, and holds them accountable for retaining their teams until the 90-day mark. Trainers and supervisors also discussed which employees were likely to stay or leave based on either their performance or preference to decide who to coach and who to terminate based on poor performance. New hires are also given color-coded badges to encourage other employees to welcome them. This also leads to a celebration after completing 90 days on the job when the new hires receive a regular identification badge. Hilton also adopted new metrics for its call center directors, including at least 75 percent of new hires reaching the 90-day mark and half of all new hires coming from employee referrals due to their higher retention rates.

Hilton's improved staffing and onboarding processes are working. Turnover declined at least 20 percent each month for the first four months, and business metrics, including quality, cost per call, and average handle time, improved.

Summary

Managing the flow of talent into, through, and out of the company is an important part of strategic staffing. Socialization helps new hires understand exactly what the company is, what it does, how it makes money, and what its norms and culture are. By reinforcing new hires' role in the company and its business strategy execution, socialization helps get them up to speed faster and enhances business strategy execution. Properly socializing employees, retaining top performers, and managing the turnover rate of underperforming or undesirable employees are important to getting the right people in the right jobs at the right time and enhancing the execution of any business strategy.

Takeaway Points

1. Orientation and socialization work together to acclimate new hires to an organization.

2. The socialization process can be improved by socializing new employees as a group, using formal activities and materials in a predetermined order within a specified time frame, giving new employees access to role models or mentors, and providing them with social support.

3. The six different types of turnover are voluntary, involuntary, avoidable, unavoidable, functional, and dysfunctional. Voluntary turnover is when the separation occurs when an employee chooses to leave the firm of his or her own accord. Involuntary turnover is when the separation is due to the organization asking the employee to leave. Functional turnover is the departure of poor performers. Dysfunctional turnover is the departure of effective performers the company would have liked to retain. Avoidable turnover is turnover that the employer could have prevented by addressing the cause of the turnover. Unavoidable turnover is turnover that could not have been prevented by the employer.

4. A firm's employee retention strategies can range from increasing employees' pay and benefits, challenging them on the job, developing better managers to supervise them, offering the employees work flexibility, creating accountability among managers for retaining valued talent, and locating the company in a desirable area or in an area where there are few firms competing for the same talent.

5. Reducing a firm's headcount so as to trim the company's labor costs can be accomplished via downsizing, layoffs, attrition and hiring freezes, by offering employees early retirement and buyout incentives or leaves without pay, creating flexible work arrangements for them, redeploying employees, reducing their work hours and/or pay so that all employees share the pain of a cutback but no one loses his or her job, and relying on temporary and contract workers.

6. Discharging an employee requires clearly communicating the message that the person's employment is being terminated and attempting to lessen the person's desire to pursue any legal action against the company. Asking the employee to sign a severance agreement that includes a release is one measure that can be taken. It is important for the firm to treat the employee with respect, hold the termination meeting in a private place, clearly communicate the reasons for the termination and any severance package being offered, and give the employee a termination letter.

7. Supervisors need to be able to spot the warning indicators for employee violence, including anger, depression, paranoia, withdrawal or isolation, and drug or alcohol abuse, on the part of employees. Many companies now conduct training to help supervisors recognize these signs.

Discussion Questions

1. Think of the time you first joined an employer. In what ways did the company and your coworkers socialize you? What could have been done to enhance your socialization experience?

2. How do you think technology can be used best to socialize new employees and get them productive as quickly as possible? When would using technology *not* be a good way to socialize employees?

3. What are the factors that would make you most likely to quit your current job (assuming you are currently working)? What could your organization do to keep you?

4. What downsizing targeting methods do you feel are the most effective? Which are the least effective, and why?

5. If you had to discharge an employee who you thought had the potential for violence, what would you do?

Exercises

1. *Strategy Exercise:* California-based IndyMac Bank, the largest savings and loan in Los Angeles and the ninth-largest mortgage originator in the United States, focuses on building customer relationships and pursues a growth strategy.[130] The overall turnover rates at the Pasadena, California, office are 500 to 10 percentage points above industry benchmarks, ranging from over 40 percent for sales and operations to the low teens for professionals and management. Traditional turnover analysis suggests that IndyMac should be hemorrhaging money. Instead, the company substantially outperforms its competitors.[131]

How can this be true? The answer lies in the bank's understanding of the costs and benefits of different types of turnover. In fact, the company calculates the break point where the financial benefits of the firm's turnover outweigh the costs. For example, higher turnover is acceptable for low-impact, nonexempt operating positions. When an employee leaves one of these jobs, IndyMac pockets the savings when other employees pick up the workload for the 30 to 60 days that the average position is open, plus additional savings when an annual bonus is not paid out to the person who left or when a replacement employee is brought in at a slightly lower salary level. On the other hand, turnover among the firm's high-impact professional and managerial employees can cause a six-month delay on a multimillion-dollar project and cost IndyMac millions of dollars.[132]

Optimal turnover rates are measured within a green-yellow-red range and differ for each job category and for performance levels within each category. The turnover rates in the green band are financially beneficial for the firm; the turnover rates within the yellow band (the broadest band) are cost-neutral and have minimal impact on the company. By contrast, turnover rates that climb into the red band begin to significantly hurt the organization.[133]

After calculating the break point of turnover for different job categories, IndyMac turned its attention to understanding the drivers of turnover and analyzed data on many of its 5,000 employees to identify what matters most to specific segments of its workforce.[134] It plans to use the results of these analyses to better retain top performers. The bank also uses steep performance-based pay differentials to maintain desired turnover rates among its high and low performers.[135]

   a. What financial benefits does IndyMac Bank receive as a result of its turnover?

   b. What are some of the financial costs of turnover for IndyMac?

   c. What will be the long-term consequences of the bank's turnover strategy?

   d. If you were in charge of improving the retention of IndyMac's bank managers, what process would you use to do this?

2. *Develop Your Skills Exercise:* This chapter's Develop Your Skills feature presented you with some tips on how to terminate an employee. Identify a partner and choose who will be the first to be terminated. Imagine that the person being terminated has been a front desk manager for Sunrise Hotel for three years. After performing very well the first year, the manager earned mediocre performance reviews last year, and even lower reviews this year. After going to two development programs in the last year to improve the front desk manager's customer service skills, his or her performance continued to worsen and the company has decided to terminate the manager. The termination is effective immediately, and the hotel is willing to offer two weeks of pay as severance if the manager is willing to sign a release of his or her legal rights to sue for wrongful discharge. The person doing the firing is the hotel's general manager and has been the front desk manager's supervisor for the entire three years. In fact, the two of you have become friends.

Using the additional background information your instructor gives you and the tips in this chapter's Develop Your Skills feature, conduct the termination interview. The person getting fired should resist the news and try to make the termination interview as realistic as possible. Don't make it too easy for the general manager!

When you are finished, the person being fired should give the person doing the firing feedback on what he or she did well, what could have improved the termination interview, and how you were made to feel during the process. Now switch partners with another group and do the exercise again playing the other role.

3. *Opening Vignette Exercise:* This chapter's opening vignette illustrated how Hilton socializes its new call center reservations and customer care employees. Reread the vignette, and answer the following questions:

   a. What are the strengths of Hilton's socialization program and why?

   b. Do you think that it is appropriate for Hilton to hold supervisors accountable for employee retention during the first 90 days? Why or why not?

   c. What additional ideas do you have to quickly socialize new employees into a company focused on customer service?

CASE STUDY

Tuition Assistance at Garden Gate

During the past 14 years, Garden Gate Inc. has grown from a small local garden supply company into a diversified corporation with stores in 36 states and net sales of almost $1.4 billion. The company currently employs 26,500 people and has been expanding at a 12 percent annual rate. Garden Gate expects to continue this pace of growth for at least five more years. The company has a talent philosophy of treating its employees as investors and spends heavily on their training and development. The firm also has a generous tuition-aid program that allows qualified employees to pursue bachelor's and master's degrees part-time if the degree they are pursuing is consistent with their career plans established in conjunction with their supervisors.

Last year the company spent $350,000 on tuition aid and recently decided to more closely evaluate the program's effectiveness. The evaluation was prompted by the recent departure of Jill Ises, who stated that her reason for leaving was that she had not been promoted in the year since she had received her MBA degree. Her career plan had been to become a senior accountant in one of the company's regional offices, and she received high performance appraisal evaluations while earning good grades in the accounting program. Five regional accounting manager positions (the job in between Jill's current job and her desired senior accountant position) had been filled in the past year, and Jill had not been contacted about any of them. Further investigation identified 17 other tuition-aid beneficiaries who had left in the past year. Like Ises, these people said that their lack of being promoted after earning their degrees was the primary reason for their leaving. The following table describes the 18 employees who received tuition aid but left the company because they had not been promoted.

	Name	Gender	Race*	Age	Last Job Held	Degree Earned with Tuition Aid	Position Taken Outside Garden Gate
1	Joe Bandy	M	C	42	Data Processor	BS, Accounting	Accountant
2	Camryn Donley	F	C	33	Administrative Assistant	BS, Management	Sales Manager
3	Lauren Sciano	F	B	35	Brand Manager	MBA	Regional Manager
4	Hui Shi	F	A	31	Legal Assistant	MBA	Financial Analyst
5	Jose Diaz	M	H	39	Administrative Assistant	MBA	Marketing Manager
6	Therese Day	F	B	28	Customer Service Manager	BS, Accounting	Management Trainee
7	Ida Crowe	F	H	33	Administrative Assistant	BS, Marketing	Brand Manager
8	Ron Brown	M	B	27	Project Manager	MBA	Plant Manager
9	Maria Cortina	F	H	45	Compensation Analyst	MS, HR	HR Manager
10	Deb Sandy	F	H	24	Data Processor	BS, Accounting	Accountant
11	Linda Winter	F	B	28	Trainer	MS, Adult Education	Training Director

(continued)

12	Danny Chen	M	C	24	Customer Service Manager	BS, Finance	Financial Analyst
13	Mia Bandy	F	B	33	Administrative Assistant	BS, Marketing	Creative Director
14	Dana Elison	F	C	38	Marketing Analyst	MBA	Financial Analyst
15	Zhana Ames	F	H	30	Sales Manager	BS, Advertising	Account Manager
16	Jill Ises	F	B	41	Accountant	MBA	Accounting Director
17	Alec Smith	M	B	26	Administrative Assistant	BS, Finance	Management Trainee
18	Sally Masino	F	C	28	Payroll Clerk	BS, Management	Store Manager

*For race, A = Asian, B = Black, C = Caucasian, H = Hispanic.

The company's review of its internal hiring policy identified three primary sources for identifying internal talent, and some problems with them:

1. Supervisors are asked to nominate employees they feel are qualified for openings in the company, but there are often dozens of open positions, and many supervisors do not regularly review the internal job postings.
2. The firm's HR professionals try to match open positions with employees who fit the criteria for them by looking at the company's skills inventory database. Unfortunately, the information in the database is often outdated or incomplete.
3. The departments that have openings recommend employees they feel are promotable.

Garden Gate's management is concerned that it is not realizing a sufficient return on its considerable investment in its tuition-aid program, and is considering discontinuing the program.

QUESTIONS

1. Describe the key problems with the tuition-aid program.
2. Does the information in the table indicate any special problems or issues? What do you suggest Garden Gate do about them?
3. Should Garden Gate discontinue its tuition-aid program?
4. Create a plan to improve the retention of tuition-aid recipients.

Semester-Long Active Learning Project

Develop a socialization plan for the person hired for your chosen position based on the socialization choices presented in Table 12-1. Justify your recommendations. Be sure to reflect on the company's culture when developing your socialization plan. Also recommend appropriate staffing technologies that you feel would benefit the plan.

Case Study Assignment: Strategic Staffing at Chern's

See the appendix at the back of the book for this chapter's Case Study Assignment.

Endnotes

1. Finnegan, R. P., *Rethinking Retention in Good Times and Bad*, Mountain View, CA: Davies-Black, 2010; "About Hilton," 2010, http://www.hilton.com/en/hi/brand/about.jhtml. Accessed April 7, 2010; Finnegan, R., "On-Board to Retain," *Talent Management Magazine*, March 26, 2010.
2. Ivancevich, J. M., and Donnelly, J. H., "Job Offer Acceptance Behavior and Reinforcement," *Journal of Applied Psychology*, 55 (1971): 119–122.
3. Lee, D., "How to Avoid the Four Deadliest Onboarding Mistakes," Electronic Recruiting Exchange, November 22, 2005, www.ere.net/articles/db/3F9DEDC4BD074E23A72AD 98B938382CA.asp. Accessed December 19, 2006.
4. Ibid.
5. Mullich, J., "They're Hired: Now the Real Recruiting Begins," *Workforce Management Online*, January 2004, www.workforce.com/section/06/feature/23/59/60. Accessed November 27, 2006.
6. Williams, R., *Mellon Learning Curve Research Study*, New York: Mellon Corp., 2003.
7. Cascio, W. F., *Managing Human Resources*, New York: McGraw-Hill/Irwin, 2003.
8. Martin, C., *Managing for the Short Term: The New Rules for Running a Business in a Day-to-Day World*, New York: Doubleday, 2002.
9. "2007 Training Top 125," *Training Magazine*, March 2007, www.trainingmag.com/managesmarter/images/pdfs/2007Top125.pdf. Accessed May 23, 2007.
10. "Our Customers," *Silanis*, 2006, www.silanis.com/site/corporate/our_customers.php?doc=116. Accessed December 20, 2006.
11. Lee, D., "Onboarding That Welcomes and Inspires," ERE.net, April 10, 2008, http://www.ere.net/2008/04/10/onboarding-that-welcomes-and-inspires/. Accessed February 11, 2010.
12. Ibid.
13. Van Maanen, J., and Schein, E. H., "Toward a Theory of Organizational Socialization," *Research in Organizational Behavior*, 1 (1979): 209–264.
14. Noe, R. A., *Employee Training and Development*, New York: McGraw-Hill/Irwin, 2005.
15. Ibid.
16. Van Maanen and Schein, "Toward of Theory of Organizational Socialization."

17. Ibid.

18. Ibid.

19. Bauer, T. N., Bodner, T., Erdogan, B., Truxillo, D. M., and Tucker, J. S., "Newcomer Adjustment During Organizational Socialization: A Meta-Analytic Review of Antecedents, Outcomes, and Methods," *Journal of Applied Psychology*, 92 (2007): 707–721.

20. Chao, G. T., O'Leary-Kelly, A. M., Wolf, S., Klein, H. J., and Gardner, P. D., "Organizational Socialization: Its Content and Consequences," *Journal of Applied Psychology*, 79, 5 (1994): 730–743.

21. Mullich, "They're Hired: Now the Real Recruiting Begins."

22. Lee, "How to Avoid the Four Deadliest Onboarding Mistakes."

23. Cascio, *Managing Human Resources*.

24. Sullivan, J., "Best Recruiting Practices from the World's Most Business-Like Recruiting Function, Part 3," Electronic Recruiting Exchange, October 3, 2005, www.ere.net/articles/db/C04428C2C066492982C27 A0FF3BC8B9E.asp. Accessed August 23, 2006.

25. In Lee, "How to Avoid the Four Deadliest Onboarding Mistakes."

26. Wyatt, W., *Weathering the Storm: A Study of Employee Attitudes and Opinions, Watson Wyatt Worldwide*, 2002, www.watsonwyatt.com/research/resrender.asp? id=W-557&page=6. Accessed January 17, 2007.

27. Noe, *Employee Training and Development*.

28. "2007 Training Top 125," *Training Magazine*.

29. Van Maanen and Schein, "Toward a Theory Organizational Socialization."

30. Gruman, J. A., Saks, A. M., and Zweig, D. I., "Organizational Socialization Tactics and Newcomer Proactive Behaviors: An Integrative Study," *Journal of Vocational Behavior*, 69, 1 (2006): 90–104.

31. See Rosenbaum, J. E., "Tournament Mobility: Career Patterns in a Corporation," *Administrative Science Quarterly*, 24, 2 (June 1979): 220–241.

32. Van Maanen, J., "People Processing: Strategies of Organizational Socialization," *Organizational Dynamics*, 7, 1 (Summer 1978): 29–30.

33. Ibid.

34. Ibid.

35. "The Top 50," *BusinessWeek*, September 14, 2009: 40–41.

36. Van Maanen and Schein, "Toward a Theory of Organizational Socialization."

37. Levering, R., "Warmer Welcomes, Fatter Profits," *Fortune*, January 10, 2006, http://money.cnn.com/2006/01/09/news/companies/bestcos_welcomerituals/index.htm. Accessed November 22, 2006.

38. Based on Chao et al., "Organizational Socialization: Its Content and Consequences"; Dubinsky, A. J., Howell, R. D., Ingram, T. N., and Bellenger, D. N., "Salesforce Socialization," *Journal of Marketing*, 50 (1986): 192–207; Fisher, C. D., "Organizational Socialization: An Integrative Review," *Research in Personnel and Human Resource Management*, 4 (1986): 101–145.

39. Sullivan, J., "From Average to World-Class: A Checklist to Transform Your Onboarding/Orientation Program, Part 1," Electronic Recruiting Exchange, October 23, 2006, www.ere.net/articles/db/013BB620F 1B64C8FA9B85757D230ACCB.asp. Accessed November 27, 2006.

40. Levering, "Warmer Welcomes, Fatter Profits."

41. Saloner, G., and Chang, V., "Capital One Financial Corp.: Setting and Shaping Strategy," *Harvard Business Case*, December 17, 2004, Product #SM135.

42. Arend, M., "Campus Culture," *Site Selection Magazine*, June 28, 2001.

43. Ibid.

44. Moscato, D., "Using Technology to Get Employees On Board," *HR Magazine*, April 2005: 107–109.

45. Ibid.

46. Frauenheim, E., "IBM Learning Programs Get a Second Life," *Workforce Management*, December 17, 2006, www.workforce.com/section/00/article/24/61/08.html. Accessed December 19, 2006.

47. Wesson, M. J., and Gogus, C. I., "Shaking Hands with a Computer: An Examination of Two Methods of Organizational Newcomer Orientation," *Journal of Applied Psychology*, 90, 5 (2005): 1018–1026.

48. Griffeth, R. W., and Hom, W., *Retaining Valued Employees*, Thousand Oaks, CA: Sage, 2001; Allen, D. G., "Do Organizational Socialization Tactics Influence Newcomer Embeddedness and Turnover?" *Journal of Management*, 32, 2 (2006): 237–256; Cooper-Thomas, H. D., and Anderson, N., "Organizational Socialization: A Field Study into Socialization Success and Rate," *International Journal of Selection and Assessment*, 13, 2 (2005): 116–128.

49. SHRM Weekly Online Survey, August 22, 2006.

50. Deloitte, *Talent Management Strategies Survey*, New York: Deloitte, 2005.

51. Cascio, *Managing Human Resources*.

52. Hanson, F., "The Turnover Myth," *Workforce Management*, June 2005: 34–40.

53. Boudreau, J. W., and Berger, C. J., "Decision-Theoretic Utility Analysis Applied to Employee Separations and Acquisitions," *Journal of Applied Psychology*, 70, 33 (1985): 581–612.

54. Dalton, A., "Applebee's Turnover Recipe," *Workforce Management Online*, May 2005, www.workforce.com/archive/article/24/05/60.ph. Accessed July 10, 2006.

55. Hanson, F., "Overhauling the Recruiting Process at CDW Corp.," *Workforce Management Online*, April 2007, www.workforce.com/section/06/feature/24/85/32/index.html. Accessed June 3, 2007.

56. Ibid.

57. U.S. Department of Labor Bureau of Labor Statistics, "Job Openings and Labor Turnover Survey (JOLTS)," www.bls.gov/jlt. Accessed July 25, 2007.

58. U.S. Department of Labor Department of Labor Statistics, "What Is JOLTS?" www.bls.gov/jlt/jltwhat.htm. Accessed July 25, 2007.

59. See Griffeth and Hom, *Retaining Valued Employees*.

60. March, J. G., and Simon, H. A., *Organizations*, New York: Wiley, 1958; Griffeth and Hom, *Retaining Valued Employees*; see also Mitchell, T. R., Holtom, B. C., Lee, T. W., and Graske, T., "How to Keep Your Best Employees: Developing and Effective Retention Policy," *Academy of Management Executive*, 15, 4 (November 2001): 96.

61. Porter, L. W., and Steers, R.M., "Organizational, Work, and Personal Factors in Employee Turnover and Absenteeism," *Psychological Bulletin*, 80 (1973): 161–176.

62. Phillips, J. M., "Effects of Realistic Job Previews on Multiple Organizational Outcomes: A Meta-Analysis," *Academy of Management Journal*, 41 (1998): 673–690.

63. Campion, M. A., and Mitchell, M. M., "Management Turnover: Experiential Differences Between Former and Current Managers," *Personnel Psychology,* 39 (1986): 57–69.

64. Boyens, J., "Turnover Revolves Around Rewards, Respect, and Requirements," *Nashville Business Journal,* September 22, 2006, http://nashville.bizjournals.com/nashville/stories/2006/09/25/smallb5.html. Accessed December 28, 2006.

65. McEvoy, G. M., and Cascio, W. F., "Do Good or Poor Performers Leave? A Meta-Analysis of the Relationship Between Performance and Turnover," *Academy of Management Journal,* 30, 4 (1987): 744–762.

66. Griffeth, R. W., Hom, P. W., and Gaertner, S., "A Meta-Analysis of Antecedents and Correlates of Employee Turnover: Update, Moderator Tests, and Research Implications for the Next Millennium," *Journal of Management,* 26, 3 (2000): 463–488.

67. Reprinted with permission from *Aligning Rewards with the Changing Employment Deal: 2006/2007 Strategic Rewards Report,* © 2007 Watson Wyatt Worldwide. For more information, visit watsonwyatt.com.

68. Ibid.

69. Agnvall, E., "Exit with the Click of a Mouse: Exit Interviews Go High-Tech," *Society for Human Resource Management,* October 2006, www.shrm.org/hrtx/library_published/nonIC/CMS_018960. Accessed December 19, 2006.

70. Zimmerman, E., "What to Ask Before Employees Leave," *Workforce Management Online,* September 2005, http://www.workforce.com/archive/article/24/16/93.php. Accessed January 21, 2010.

71. "UPS' 37 Principles for Managing People," *Workforce Management Online,* May 2005, www.workforce.com/archive/article/24/03/43. Accessed December 21, 2006.

72. Marquez, J., "Business First," *Workforce Management,* October 23, 2006: 23.

73. Giacalone, R. A., and Duhon, D., "Assessing Intended Employee Behavior in Exit Interviews," *Journal of Psychology,* 125 (1991): 83–90; Griffeth and Hom, *Retaining Valued Employees.*

74. Merritt, J., and Lavelle, L., "It's Time to Plug Talent Leaks," *BusinessWeek Online,* February 2, 2005, www.businessweek.com/careers/content/feb2005/ca2005022_4650_ca004.htm. Accessed June 20, 2006.

75. "2007 Training Top 125," *Training Magazine.*

76. Guthridge, M., Komm, A.B., and Lawson, E., "Making Talent a Strategic Priority," *McKinsey Quarterly,* January, 2008, http://www.mckinseyquarterly.com/Organization/Talent/Making_talent_a_strategic_priority_2092. Accessed February 22, 2010.

77. Subramaniam, M., and Youndt, M.A., "The Influence of Social Capital on the Types of Innovative Capabilities," *Academy of Management Journal,* 48 (2005): 450–463; Broysberg, B., Nanda, A., and Nohria, N., "The Risky Business of Hiring Stars," *Harvard Business Review,* 82 (2004): 93–100.

78. Guthridge, M., Komm, A. B., and Lawson, E., "Making Talent a Strategic Priority," *McKinsey Quarterly,* January, 2008, http://www.mckinseyquarterly.com/Organization/Talent/Making_talent_a_strategic_priority_2092. Accessed February 22, 2010.

79. Hansen, "Overhauling the Recruiting Process at CDW Corp."

80. "Retention Tips from the Trenches," *BusinessWeek Online,* February 2, 2005, www.businessweek.com/careers/content/feb2005/ca2005022_0110_ca006.htm. Accessed December 20, 2006.

81. Stern, G.M., "A Company's Recipe for Entry-Level Staff Chipotle Reaps Rewards by Promoting from Within," *Investor's Business Daily,* September 8, 2009, http://www.allbusiness.com/labor-employment/human-resources-personnel/12885825-1.html. Accessed January 15, 2010.

82. Stern, G.M., "A Company's Recipe for Entry-Level Staff Chipotle Reaps Rewards by Promoting from Within," *Investor's Business Daily,* September 8, 2009, http://www.allbusiness.com/labor-employment/human-resources-personnel/12885825-1.html. Accessed January 15, 2010.

83. See Whitener, E. M., Brodt, S. E., Korsgard, M. A., and Werner, J. M., "Managers as Initiators of Trust: An Exchange Relationship Framework for Understanding Managerial Trustworthy Behavior," *Academy of Management Review,* 23, 3 (1998): 513–530.

84. Keating, M., "Phone Home," *Guardian,* October 15, 2005: D1.

85. Ibid.

86. Autor, D., Katz, L. F., and Krueger, A. B., "Computing Inequality: Have Computers Changed the Labor Market?" *Quarterly Journal of Economics,* 113, 4 (1998): 1169–1213.

87. Nevius, C. W., "For Better or Worse There Is No Place like Home—Sort of," *San Francisco Chronicle,* November 19, 2004: A34.

88. "Call Centers in the Rec Room," *BusinessWeek,* January 23, 2006: 14–15.

89. Friedman, T., *The World Is Flat,* New York: Farrar, Straus and Giroux, 2005.

90. Cappelli, P., "A Market-Driven Approach to Retaining Talent," In Harvard Business Review, *Harvard Business Review on Finding and Keeping the Best People,* Boston: Harvard Business School Publishing, 2001: 27–50.

91. Grow, B., "Renovating Home Depot," *BusinessWeek,* March 6, 2006: 50–58.

92. "Poor Health Benefits Communication Hurts Retention," *Employee Benefit News,* March 2005: 18.

93. Sturman, M. C., Trevor, C. O., Boudreau, J. W., and Gerhart, B., "Is It Worth It to Win in the Talent War? Evaluating the Utility of Performance-Based Pay," *Personnel Psychology,* 56 (2003): 997–1035.

94. Arend, "Campus Culture."

95. Marquez, J.T., "Tailor-Made Careers," Workforce Management, January 2010: 16–21.

96. Weinberg, C. R., "Stop the Job Hop!" *Chief Executive,* 122 (1997): 44–47.

97. Mullich, "They're Hired: Now the Real Recruiting Begins."

98. Purcell, J., "Business Strategies and Human Resource Management: Uneasy Bedfellows or Strategic Partners?" *University of Bath Working Paper Series,* 2005, #2005.16.

99. Hamm, S., "A Passion for the Plan," *BusinessWeek,* August 21–28, 2006: 92–94.

100. Malykhina, E., "Supplying Labor to Meet Demand," *InformationWeek,* March 21, 2005, www.informationweek.com/shared/printableArticleSrc.jhtml?articleID=159902302. Accessed October 14, 2006.

101. Ibid.

102. Pfeffer, J., "The Real Cost of the Virtual Workforce," *Stanford Graduate Business School,* 1998, www.gsb.stanford.edu/community/bmag/sbsm0398/feature_virtualworkforce.html. Accessed June 21, 2006.

103. Freeman, S., and Cameron, K. S., "Organizational Downsizing: A Convergence and Reorientation Framework," *Organization Science,* 4 (1993): 10–29.

104. Datta, D. K., Guthrie, J. P., Basuil, D., and Pandey, A., "Causes and Effects of Employee Downsizing: A Review and Synthesis," *Journal of Management,* 36 (2010): 281–348.

105. "Serving the American Public: Best Practices in Downsizing," *National Performance Review*, September 1997, http://govinfo.library.unt.edu/npr/library/papers/benchmrk/downsize.html#7. Accessed December 27, 2006.

106. Ibid.

107. Muirhead, S., "Compassionate Downsizing: Making the Business Case for Education and Training Services," *The Conference Board/Across the Board* (January–February 2004).

108. Greenhalgh, L., and Jick, T. D., "The Relationship Between Job Insecurity and Turnover, and Its Differential Effects on Employee Quality Level," 1979, Paper presented at the annual meeting of the Academy of Management, Atlanta; Sutton, R. I., "Managing Organizational Death," *Human Resource Management,* 22 (1983): 391–412; Staw, B. M., Sandelands, L. E., and Dutton, J. E., "Threat-Rigidity Effects in Organizational Behavior: A Multilevel Analysis," *Administrative Science Quarterly,* 26 (1981): 501–524.

109. Brockner, J., Davy, J., and Carter, C., "Layoffs, Self-esteem, and Survivor Guilt: Motivational, Attitudinal, and Affective Consequences," *Organizational Behavior and Human Decision Processes,* 36 (1985): 229–244; Brockner, J., Greenberg, J., Brockner, A., Bortz, J., Davy, J., and Carter, C., "Layoffs, Equity Theory, and Work Motivation: Further Evidence for the Impact of Survivor Guilt," *Academy of Management Journal,* 29 (1986): 373–384.

110. Greenhalgh, L., "Maintaining Organizational Effectiveness During Organizational Retrenchment," *Journal of Applied Behavioral Science,* 18 (1982): 155–170.

111. Greenberg, E. S., Grunberg, L., Moore, S., and Silora, P. B., *Turbulence: Boeing and the State of American Workers and Manages,* New Haven, CT: Yale University Press, 2010.

112. Kucynski, S., "Sweetening the Pot," *HR Magazine*, March 2000: 60–64.

113. Cascio, W. F., Young, C. E., and Morris, J. R., "Financial Consequences of Employment-Change Decisions in Major US Corporations," *Academy of Management Journal,* 40, 5 (1997): 1175–1189; De Meuse, K. P., Bergmann, T. J., Vanderheiden, A., and Roraff, C. E., "New Evidence Regarding Organizational Downsizing and a Firm's Financial Performance: A Long-Term Analysis," *Journal of Managerial Issues,* 16, 2 (2004): 155–177; Zyglidopoulos, S. C., "The Impact of Downsizing on the Corporate Reputation for Social Performance," *Journal of Public Affairs,* 4, 1 (2004): 11–25.

114. See Cascio, W. F., and Wynn, P., "Managing a Downsizing Process," *Human Resources Management,* 43, 4 (Winter 2004): 425–436.

115. Boroson, W., and Burgess, L., "Survivors' Syndrome," *Across the Board,* 29, 11 (1992): 41–45.

116. Davis, J. A., "Organizational Downsizing: A Review of Literature for Planning and Research," *Journal of Healthcare Management,* 48, 3 (2003): 181–199.

117. "Views from the Top," *HR Magazine,* November 2006, www.shrm.org/hrmagazine/articles/1106/1106ceoex. Accessed January 10, 2007.

118. In "Serving the American Public: Best Practices in Downsizing," *National Performance Review,* September 1997, http://govinfo.library.unt.edu/npr/library/papers/benchmrk/downsize.html#7. Accessed December 27, 2006.

119. Ibid.

120. Reprinted with permission from *Aligning Rewards with the Changing Employment Deal: 2006/2007 Strategic Rewards Report,* © 2007 Watson Wyatt Worldwide. For more information, visit watsonwyatt.com.

121. Flanagan, D. J., and O'Shaughnessey, K. C., "The Effect of Layoffs on Firm Reputation," *Journal of Management,* 31, 3 (2005): 445–463.

122. "The Worker Adjustment and Retraining Notification Act," *U.S. Department of Labor Employment and Training Administration Fact Sheet,* www.doleta.gov/programs/factsht/warn.htm. Accessed December 28, 2006.

123. In "Serving the American Public: Best Practices in Downsizing," *National Performance Review.*

124. Beasley, D., "Wynn Resorts Cutting Salaries, Bonuses to Save Jobs," Reuters, February 3, 2009, http://www.reuters.com/article/idUSN0354442320090204. Accessed December 11, 2009.

125. Panaro, J., "Avoiding Litigation in Hiring and Termination Situations," Association Management, August 2003, www.asaecenter.org/PublicationsResources/AMMagSidebarDetail.cfm?ItemNumber=9505.Accessed December 29, 2006; Larson, A., "Wrongful Termination of At Will Employment," ExpertLaw, September 2003, www.expertlaw.com/library/employment/at_will.html. Accessed December 29, 2006.

126. CCH, "Releases and Severance Agreements," Business Owner's Toolkit, www.toolkit.cch.com/text/P05_8243. Accessed December 29, 2006.

127. Ibid.

128. This section is based on Lynn, J., "The Good Fire," *Entrepreneur Magazine,* March 2000, www.entrepreneur.com/magazine/entrepreneur/2000/march/19230.html. Accessed May 31, 2007; Johnson, D. L., King, C. A., and Kurutz, J. G., "A Safe Termination Model for Supervisors," *HR Magazine,* May 1996, http://findarticles.com/p/articles/mi_m3495/is_n5_v41/ai_18372603/pg_1. Accessed May 31, 2007.

129. Finnegan, R.P., *Rethinking Retention in Good Times and Bad,* Mountain View, CA: Davies-Black, 2010; "About Hilton," 2010, http://www.hilton.com/en/hi/brand/about.jhtml. Accessed April 7, 2010; Finnegan, R., "On-Board to Retain," *Talent Management Magazine,* March 26, 2010

130. "Corporate Profile," Indymac Bank, http://investors.indymacbank.com/phoenix.zhtml?c=118924&p=irol-irhome. Accessed December 29, 2006.

131. Hansen, "The Turnover Myth."

132. Ibid.

133. Ibid.

134. Babcock, P., "Find What Workers Want," *HR Magazine,* April 2005: 50.

135. Hansen, "The Turnover Myth."

13 Staffing System Evaluation and Technology

Outline

LEARNING OBJECTIVES
After studying this chapter, you should be able to:

- Describe the effects staffing activities have on applicants, new hires, and organizations.
- Explain the different types of staffing metrics and how each is used best.
- Describe a balanced staffing scorecard.
- Explain how digital staffing dashboards can help managers monitor and improve the staffing process.
- Describe how staffing technology can improve the efficiency and effectiveness of the staffing function.

Staffing Technology at Osram Sylvania[1]

Headquartered in Danvers, Massachusetts, and employing over 11,000 people, Osram Sylvania has provided lighting solutions for homes, businesses, and vehicles for over 100 years. As a manufacturing organization, the effectiveness of the company's processes determines its success.

The company recognizes that its recruiting process is costing it unnecessary time and money as it fills 80 or more open positions a month. Osram Sylvania's recruiters gather e-mail résumés from the company Web site and various job boards, then cut, paste, and forward them to hiring managers. Each recruiter spends 6–10 hours per week just cutting, pasting, and forwarding the e-mail résumés. The company also lacks a standard recruiting process across its 26 North America locations.

As a government contractor, Osram Sylvania is subject to the Office of Federal Contract and Compliance Program's (OFCCP) Internet Applicant Guidelines that it is finding difficult to meet without some form of technology. The company wants to streamline its recruiting processes, provide a common structure for all 26 locations, and incorporate external staffing vendors to effectively source and hire quality employees.

Imagine that Osram Sylvania asks you for advice on how it can better incorporate technology to create a more effective staffing system. After reading this chapter, you should have some good ideas.

Executing a business strategy is often harder than creating one. One study found that of the 90 percent of 1,800 large companies that had detailed strategic plans, only about one in eight achieved their strategic goals.[2] Why so few? Not tracking performance is one reason.[3] Another reason goals go unmet is because it's unclear who within the firm is accountable for their execution.[4] The same is true for the staffing function. A key goal of strategic staffing is to get the right people with the right competencies into the right jobs at the right time. But doing so requires that the effort be continually monitored, tracked, and evaluated.

Few companies make investment decisions about recruitment and staffing based on hard data, rather than anecdotal evidence. Yet some companies do successfully use data to create a competitive staffing advantage. Corning Inc. is one such company. Corning gets monthly reports from its recruiting vendor showing the number of applicants versus hires from each recruiting source, including all major and niche job boards. This helps Corning to decide what percentage of its budget to spend on each sourcing channel. Corning believes that it would spend 50 percent more on its recruiting function if it didn't analyze this information regularly because it would throw money at the wrong sources.[5]

To maximize the effectiveness of a staffing system and the investment made in it, evaluating the process is critical. A **staffing evaluation** enables a firm's human resource department to justify what it has done and to identify how its activities contribute to the organization's bottom line. Part of making sure that the human resource department is effective is showing a firm's top managers the hard numbers related to the company's staffing. Measuring and evaluating the staffing function can also provide a firm with feedback about how well its various policies are being implemented. For example, many firms claim to have a "promotion from within" policy, but don't actually promote many employees. Unfortunately, these firms continue to claim success because they lack systematic information about actual internal promotion rates. Additionally, as we discussed in Chapter 8, things that are measured are more likely to be attended to and addressed.[6] The feedback provided by the evaluation effort is necessary to refine and further develop a firm's staffing policies and practices, as well as to learn how well they are achieving their intended results.

We have discussed aspects of staffing evaluation at various points in the book. The purpose of this chapter is not to review them but to discuss the broader issues related to evaluating a staffing system. We first describe different types of staffing outcomes, and then discuss the techniques and tools used to evaluate them as well as the staffing system as a whole. We then describe the role technology plays in terms of the staffing and evaluating process. After reading this chapter, you should understand why evaluation is critical to strategic staffing, how to evaluate staffing systems, and how to leverage technology to improve the effectiveness of staffing systems.

staffing evaluation
the analysis of a staffing system to assess its performance and effectiveness

STAFFING OUTCOMES

How far-reaching are the effects of staffing activities? Staffing activities extend far beyond simply hiring and promoting people. An organization's staffing activities affect a firm's applicants, new hires, customers, and the organization as a whole. Before they ever become employees, the strategic staffing process influences people's willingness to apply and stay in the candidate pool, their expectations about the job and organization as an employer, perceptions of fairness, and willingness to recommend the employer to others and accept its job offers. The influence of strategic staffing on a candidate does not end once a candidate is hired. For example, if the firm recruits and screens for the wrong candidate characteristics, it will hurt its chances that a new hire who accepts the company's offer will succeed in the organization. It will also mean that the talents and efforts the organization needs will be missing. The negative spillover effects related to poor staffing practices can hurt the organization's future recruiting success and image as an employer as well. As a result, it may take longer for the firm to fill jobs, create higher turnover and lower new hire quality, reduce the firm's supply of internal leadership talent, and lower the return on the company's staffing investment.

By contrast, hiring the right people allows the organization to leverage the contributions of its employees right away rather than having to invest the time and resources necessary to change how they behave and think. Performing staffing activities strategically reduces the time to fill open positions by increasing the number of employees qualified for promotion. It also increases the return on the investment a company has made in its staffing system. Figure 13-1 shows how effectively designed staffing systems can create a positive cycle of employee outcomes that enhance an organization's effectiveness. Similarly, poorly designed systems can create a negative cycle that can derail an organization's expansion efforts, impede its strategic implementation, and limit its long-term profitability. Granted, other factors including training, the supervisor's management skills and style, and compensation can also influence some of the new hire outcomes listed in Figure 13-1. However, staffing practices can strongly influence these outcomes, and the ways in which they do so are relevant to strategic staffing.

Both good and bad staffing practices have financial consequences for organizations. A firm often incurs large **direct costs** if critical positions are unfilled for longer than necessary, for example. Direct costs are those charges incurred as an immediate result of some staffing activity. For example, poor hiring increases a firm's direct costs in the areas of training, supervision, turnover, and lower productivity. Direct costs are relatively easy to measure and track over time.

Indirect costs are those not directly attributable to staffing activities, such as lost business opportunities, missed deadlines, lost market share, cost overruns, reduced organizational flexibility, and declines in the morale of a firm's workforce. The indirect costs of poor hiring can be even more significant than the direct costs but more difficult to measure. Conducting a staffing

direct costs
costs incurred as a direct result of a staffing activity

indirect costs
costs not directly attributable to staffing activities (e.g., lost business opportunities and lower morale)

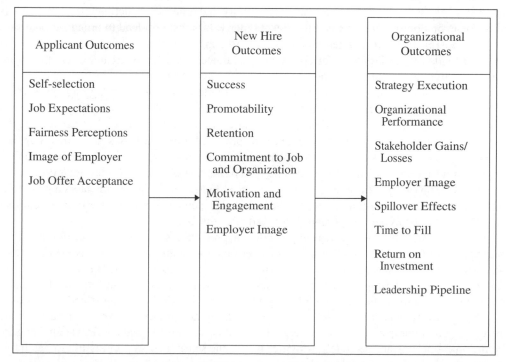

Applicant Outcomes	New Hire Outcomes	Organizational Outcomes
Self-selection	Success	Strategy Execution
Job Expectations	Promotability	Organizational Performance
Fairness Perceptions	Retention	Stakeholder Gains/ Losses
Image of Employer	Commitment to Job and Organization	Employer Image
Job Offer Acceptance	Motivation and Engagement	Spillover Effects
	Employer Image	Time to Fill
		Return on Investment
		Leadership Pipeline

FIGURE 13-1 Strategic Staffing Outcomes

evaluation can help a firm calculate both the direct and indirect costs of its staffing system and identify ways to improve the company's return on its staffing investment.

EVALUATING STAFFING SYSTEMS

As we have explained, evaluating a staffing system allows a firm to objectively assess how well its different staffing initiatives are working and to subsequently improve them. As you learned in Chapter 8, regularly measuring key pieces of information and correlating different staffing measurements can be extremely valuable. Tracking data and making comparisons over time is one way to do this. For example, tracking turnover rates for the organization as a whole and for its individual departments and jobs can help a company identify trends in its staffing; so will tracking the firm's headcount in combination with other factors, such as its revenue or production volumes. This will allow the firm to identify how closely one factor leads or lags another and understand how the firm's staffing activities affect the rest of the organization's operations. Establishing meaningful trends and relationships enables a firm to make more accurate projections and action plans as well. Next, we discuss key performance indicators, staffing metrics, the role Six Sigma can play in terms of improving the staffing process, and how the staffing evaluation process is implemented.

Key Performance Indicators

key performance indicators (KPIs)
measurable factors critical to the firm's success and long- and short-term goals

Staffing evaluation begins with an understanding of the requirements of the company's business strategy, talent philosophy, human resource strategy, and staffing strategy. These factors determine what the firm's most important staffing outcomes are. Once we identify these outcomes, we identify **key performance indicators (KPIs)** that are measurable factors critical to the firm's success and long- and short-term goals.[7] KPIs are the outcomes against which the effectiveness of the staffing system is evaluated.

To design effective KPIs, it is essential to understand what is important to the business and what key business measures exist.[8] Many factors can be useful to measure and track. However, the KPIs that will result in an organization's success are those best able to enhance a firm's strategy execution. These KPIs can include things such as financial measures of revenue growth, customer satisfaction, innovation, and a firm's globalization efforts.[9] For example, an evaluation that demonstrates that a new staffing system increased a firm's revenue because the company's new hires were of higher quality and generated revenue more quickly shows how staffing can contribute to the bottom line. In this example, the KPI is employee revenue generation, and the related staffing evaluation metrics are new hire quality and time to productivity. It is also important to focus on company culture and the stakeholder values that will lead to organizational success in choosing KPIs. If a stated business objective is to develop a diverse workforce, it is important to identify and track underrepresented candidates and employees and where they were recruited so that those sources can be leveraged.

lagging indicator
a factor that becomes known only after a staffing decision has been made

In terms of evaluating staffing systems, it is important to understand lagging and leading indicators. A **lagging indicator** is a factor that becomes known only after a staffing decision has been made. A lagging indicator might be a measure of a recruiting source's effectiveness, the time to fill a position, or the fit, performance, or promotability of a firm's new hires. Lagging indicators measure various aspects of the success or failure of a staffing system but do not help a company improve its staffing efforts midstream. That is, the indicators do not identify exactly what went wrong or right, or indicate how to improve. In general, lagging indicators are not useful for managing staffing on a day-to-day basis but can identify areas of a staffing system that should be further analyzed and perhaps improved after the fact.[10]

leading indicator
a factor that precedes or predicts a staffing outcome

By contrast, a **leading indicator** precedes or predicts a staffing outcome. For example, lower applicant quality and fewer applications per position often precede negative staffing outcomes such as longer time to fill, new hires who take longer to contribute to the firm, and higher turnover. Leading indicators are useful for monitoring the progress of a staffing effort. In other words, they can provide the firm with timely information it can use to adjust and improve the company's staffing outcomes midstream. For example, if the number of applications a company is receiving and their quality are below target levels, this can indicate that the firm should engage in additional sourcing and recruiting activities before the staffing effort progresses too much further, and the risk of a poor candidate being hired increases.

Some indicators can be both leading and lagging indicators. This, of course, can complicate a staffing evaluation effort. For example, the number of applicants is often used as a leading time-to-fill indicator. However, the number of applicants that apply for a position can also be a lagging indicator of a company's employer image. Table 13-1 describes several indicators and some of the outcomes they can lead or lag.

When an organization lacks the luxury of a dedicated staff to develop, track, and analyze the firm's staffing metrics, it must make careful choices about which metrics and indicators best serve its needs. In one small company of 400 employees that sells and leases health care equipment to hospitals, a human resources director and an assistant track the metrics that best reflect the company's culture and strategic goals to ensure that employee costs track favorably against the firm's revenues and profits. Four of the metrics tracked and benchmarked against prior years are lagging indicators: employee cost divided by sales revenue, employee cost divided by net income before taxes, turnover, and ratings of human resources' performance. Absenteeism and time to fill are leading indicators.[11]

Linking people measures to KPIs in a reliable way can require large amounts of data for large companies, such as American Express. American Express keeps a close eye on 15 to 20 different metrics associated with its key positions, including how long it takes to fill the positions, how many offers the company makes before a position is filled, and retention rates. Successfully launching such an evaluation depends heavily on the firm being able to use technology to gather the data. To gather the information and metrics sought, a firm's human resource department must work closely with the company's information technology and finance departments. Evaluating a large amount of data also requires both trial and error and patience on the part of those conducting the evaluations.

Staffing Metrics

Because people pay attention to what gets measured, carefully selecting key metrics to track can help focus employees on key behaviors and outcomes. But too much information makes it difficult to focus attention on the metrics and outcomes that are the most important. To evaluate its staffing success, telecommunication company Avaya sets goals for how many experienced employees it intends to acquire from its competitors. The company also measures the performance of individuals who move internally from one business to another compared with the average performance of employees in that division. One company representative says, "Most companies will say their recruitment is successful if they retain the people that they hire. We look beyond that and set very specific goals for ourselves."[12]

Staffing metrics can be thought of as long term or short term, and can be efficiency or effectiveness oriented. Next, we discuss these different types of metrics and how they are best used.

LONG-TERM AND SHORT-TERM METRICS Metrics can be tracked over many different time periods. Short-term metrics help a firm evaluate the success of its staffing system in terms of the recruiting and new hire outcomes achieved. These metrics include:

- The percentage of hires for each job or job family coming from each recruiting source and recruiter
- The number of high-quality new hires coming from each recruiting source and recruiter

TABLE 13-1	Leading and Lagging Staffing Indicators
Staffing Indicator	**Outcome(s)**
Leading Indicators	
Employer image	Application rates, applicant quality, new hire quality, staffing ROI
Applicant quality	Time to fill, new hire quality, turnover, the satisfaction of hiring managers, leadership skills in an organization, staffing ROI
Applicant quantity	Ability to hire, quality of hire, time to fill, hiring manager satisfaction
Lagging Indicators	
Employer image	Poor hiring decisions, poor staffing process, poor recruiting
Turnover	Poor hiring decisions, poor sourcing, poor recruiting
Job success	Poor planning, sourcing, recruiting, and selection

- The number of diverse hires coming from each recruiting source and recruiter
- The average time to start (by position, source, and recruiter)
- The average time to contribution (by position, source, and recruiter)

Long-term metrics help a firm evaluate the success of its staffing system in terms of the outcomes that occur some time after employees are hired. These metrics include:

- Employee job success by recruiting source and by recruiter
- Employee tenure by recruiting source and by recruiter
- Promotion rates by recruiting source and by recruiter

Short-term metrics are useful as leading indicators of a company's ability to have the right people in the right jobs at the right time to execute its business strategy and to meet its immediate staffing goals. Long-term metrics are useful as lagging indicators. They are best used for evaluating the effectiveness of the firm's long-term staffing system—for example, the long-term, on-the-job success of employees and their turnover and promotion rates.

staffing efficiency
the amount of resources used in the staffing process

STAFFING EFFICIENCY METRICS   **Staffing efficiency** refers to the amount of resources used in the staffing process. Efficiency metrics are analyzed to make process improvements designed to minimize the amount of resources needed to staff a firm—specifically, the firm's *hiring costs* and *replacement costs*. A firm's *hiring costs* include sourcing, recruiting, screening, referral bonuses, travel expenses, advertisements, the cost of assessing and doing background checks on candidates, and the meals and transportation associated with their recruiting processes. *Replacement costs* include hiring costs as well as the productivity losses that occur while positions remain unfilled. Staffing efficiency metrics include the cost per hire, the time to fill positions, and the number of requisitions handled per full time equivalent (FTE) staffing member. Many firms also calculate onboarding costs, such as training and time-to-contribution costs, which can also be used as indicators to measure a firm's staffing efficiency.

The critical factor to remember when tracking staffing efficiency metrics is that it is necessary to be efficient but also meet the needs of a firm's customers. On the one hand, time-to-fill rates that are below a certain benchmark might reflect that the firm is staffing itself efficiently. On the other hand, the same rates might indicate that hiring managers are not spending enough time interviewing enough candidates to ensure that they are hiring the best ones.

One way to compute staffing efficiency is as a percentage of the amount of new hires' compensation. The *staffing efficiency ratio* can be calculated by dividing a firm's total staffing costs by the total compensation of its new hires recruited, and then multiplying the result by 100. For example, a staffing efficiency of 12 percent means it costs $0.12 cents to bring in $1.00 of compensation, or $12,000 to hire someone who makes $100,000 a year.[13] An organization that hires 400 employees annually, each with a compensation of $40,000 annually, would save about $320,000 in staffing costs every year by improving its staffing efficiency by just 2 percent (400 × $40,000 = $16 million total compensation recruited; 2 percent of $16 million = $320,000). By relying more on technology to source, recruit, and screen their employees, many firms could easily achieve such a 2 percent savings.[14]

staffing effectiveness
how well the staffing process meets the needs of a firm's stakeholders and contributes to the organization's strategy execution and performance

STAFFING EFFECTIVENESS METRICS   Strategic staffing is not simply hiring a large number of people or hiring them quickly or cheaply. Strategic staffing is hiring people who become successful in the job, are a good fit with the company, and stay with the organization. Although efficiency and cost are often the initial focus of a firm's staffing evaluation efforts, many companies subsequently shift their focus toward measuring their **staffing effectiveness**.[15] Staffing effectiveness relates to how well the staffing process meets the needs of a firm's stakeholder needs and contributes to the organization's strategy execution and performance. Staffing effectiveness metrics help answer questions such as "Is the number and caliber of finalists being sent to hiring managers meeting their needs?" and "Is the hiring experience and speed acceptable to candidates?" Staffing efficiency is often easier to measure and evaluate than staffing effectiveness. For example, it is relatively easy to measure how many jobs each recruiter is filling (staffing efficiency), but what is often more important is whether the jobs are being filled with the right people (staffing effectiveness).

There are many possible measures of staffing effectiveness. Perhaps the most obvious measure of staffing effectiveness is new hire *job success*. Job success refers to job performance as well as the new hire's fit with his or her work group, unit, and organization, and the degree to which his or her values are consistent with the company's culture and values. Tracking this metric by recruiting source, recruiter, and hiring manager can help improve a company's future staffing efforts. *The quality of hire* reflects whether the company hired the people it set out to as defined by hiring managers' predetermined job performance requirements. New hire job success starts with the quality of the people hired. The quality of hire can be assessed using new hires' performance ratings after an appropriate time on the job, hiring manager satisfaction surveys, objective employee productivity measures, and even safety, absenteeism, and turnover rates. New hire quality matters when it comes to an organization's performance. The *War for Talent* study, published in 2001 by McKinsey & Co., revealed that high performers in operations roles increased the productivity of their firms by 40 percent; high performers in managerial roles increased their firms' profits by 49 percent; and high-performing salespeople created 67 percent more revenue for their firms than average or low-performing employees.

Overall *retention or turnover rates* might seem like good metrics, but remember that retaining poor performers can actually impose a cost on the firm. Tracking the *voluntary turnover rate of top performers* as well as measuring the *turnover rate of bottom performers*, as we discussed in the last chapter, can provide more meaningful information. Tracking monthly turnover by hiring manager, department, or business unit and by race, gender, or age group need not take a lot of time and can reveal patterns that might suggest poor staffing or poor management. Measuring the turnover of employees based on the sources from which they were hired can help identify the return on investment (ROI) from each source. Jeff Cottle, senior vice president of human resources and organizational strategy at SCT, a global information-technology company, tracks turnover by employee type to assess controllable voluntary turnover and understand what's causing it. Says Cottle, "Our perspective on the use of metrics . . . is based on our belief that human-capital metrics have a direct correlation to financial metrics."[16]

Evaluating the *value of top performers* can also be a useful metric. When a competitor was pursuing one of its top technical employees, Texas Instruments (TI) wanted to find out what the employee was worth. TI added up all the ideas that the employee had generated for the company, and what those ideas were worth in terms of patents. TI decided that the employee was probably fairly valued at about $25 million and decided it was worth its trouble to get him to stay. TI gave him a nice amount of stock, structured in a way that provided him an incentive to stay another decade. The company even arranged for a week of private golf lessons for his wife and him at a famous golf resort.[17]

Measuring what a top employee is worth, and comparing that to what an average employee is worth, can be a useful indicator. McDonald's knows that a top manager is worth 35 percent more in profits than an average manager.[18] Calculating the value of a company's top performers can help managers justify what it is worth to invest more in recruiting, hiring, and retaining them. TI doesn't track, and isn't concerned about, what it spends to hire key technology workers. The company understands that these employees will produce far more for the company than what they're paid, and believes that hiring costs are too small a percentage of an employee's value to worry about.[19]

Many other metrics are possible. To identify which divisions in the company are creating new talent, Cisco Systems uses a metric that tracks *why* a person moved within the company rather than simply how many people moved. High performers tend to want to take on new challenges so tracking their movement inside the company is a way to make sure managers serve as talent "launching pads," rather than talent hoarders. Once identified, those managers who "launch" talent are rewarded accordingly.[20]

Some of the key staffing metrics utilized by Valero Energy include:[21]

- *Brand-related metrics.* Valero measures the value of its employment brand by calculating the cost savings related to the positions it fills via its corporate Web page, community referrals, and nonemployment-related TV ads. The recruiting department estimates that the Valero brand saved the company $4,309,005 in recruiting costs.
- *Staffing efficiency metrics.* Valero utilizes the staffing efficiency measure developed by Staffing.org, an independent and nonproprietary nonprofit corporation that develops

standard human resource performance metrics. Valero calculates its staffing efficiency by dividing the firm's total recruiting costs by the total compensation for all the positions it fills annually (the sum of the base starting salaries for each external hire during their first year). Staffing efficiencies in the range of 5 to 9 percent are considered excellent, and those above 16 percent indicate inefficiency.[22] However, these ranges can vary by industry, organizational size, and region.

- *Sourcing channel metrics.* Some of the measures Valero applies to each sourcing channel are:
  - The staffing cost of the source
  - The percentage of the firm's budget the source represents
  - The percentage of applicants recruited via the source
  - The percentage of positions filled via the source
  - The source's speed
  - The source's efficiency
  - The turnover at 12 months of new hires recruited from the source
  - The dependability of the source
  - The average salary of the position filled via the source
- Internal recruiters are also monitored on the previous metrics.

RETURN ON INVESTMENT   As we have stressed throughout this book, staffing costs are an investment. When using metrics and evaluating staffing activities, it can be easy to focus on staffing efficiency and lose sight of staffing effectiveness. If a firm is only concerned with hiring enough people quickly and cheaply, as is often the case during periods of rapid expansion and labor shortages, the firm is not likely to pay much attention to employee-quality requirements. At one point, the human resources department of the telecommunication company GTE (now a part of Verizon) was under pressure to focus largely on efficiency and cost reduction. To hire people faster, recruiters started sourcing from temporary agencies and job banks rather than graduating college students and experienced professionals. This change improved GTE's staffing efficiency. One region of the company reduced its time to fill a position to 50 percent below GTE's company average, and the cost per hire was very low. Unfortunately, the turnover rate in the region rose to twice the company's average and customer service levels in the region fell. Instead of hiring experienced professionals and new graduates, sourcing through temporary agencies and job banks was less selective.[23] For GTE, the previous higher staffing costs and longer times to fill had been good investments.

A cautionary note is in order here: If the only goal an organization pursues is hiring the highest-quality people, its staffing program might not produce enough hires or might produce them at an unacceptable cost. Indeed, a common hiring mantra of organizations is to hire the best talent available. However, as we have explained, not all business strategies require the best talent for all jobs. Architectural Support Services, a computer-aided design company providing technical support for architects, is a case in point: When the company was relatively young, it hired the best and brightest professionals available. However, poor morale and high turnover caused by infighting among the high-powered staff compromised its operations. The organization realized that it did not need to fill all of its positions with the most talented graduates from elite four-year institutions, and started recruiting from community colleges instead. The company was rewarded with a much more loyal and committed workforce, and its results improved.[24] The lesson here is that a balance must be struck between staffing efficiency and staffing effectiveness.

A firm can calculate the ROI for its individual staffing activities, such as the ROI of different recruiting sources or assessment methods, or for the staffing system as a whole. Although many companies have no idea which candidate sources produce the best employees, others have turned the evaluation of their hiring sources into a science. This helps the companies determine the degree to which their recruiting investments are paying off, which allows the firms to cut out poor-performing sources, and to negotiate better contracts with outside recruiters based on the results they produce.

With that said, measuring a firm's overall staffing ROI is not always easy. Nonetheless, if the associated measurements are made carefully, the effectiveness and ROI of staffing initiatives can be demonstrated.[25]

Six Sigma Initiatives

Developed in the 1980s at Motorola, and now practiced by many large corporations, including GE and Dow Chemical, **Six Sigma** is a data-driven quality initiative that uses statistics to measure and improve business processes and their outcomes to near perfection.[26] The central principle of Six Sigma is to measure defects, identify and remove the sources of error, and to reduce defects to near zero. Six Sigma was developed in a manufacturing environment, but the principles and process can be used to improve any process, including staffing.

Six Sigma
a data-driven quality initiative that uses statistics to measure and improve business processes and their outcomes to near perfection

Six Sigma can be used to improve a variety of staffing outcomes, such as:

- Lowering turnover among high performers
- Improving the quality of applicants
- Improving the fit of new hires with a firm's corporate culture
- Reducing the time to fill positions
- Increasing the return on the company's staffing investment

GE Medical Systems used Six Sigma processes to develop its recruitment Web site.[27] Microsoft aligned its recruiting efforts with the rest of its company's implementation of Six Sigma, and even created a senior "manager of quality improvement" position to help improve the processes the company uses to hire its technical employees.[28]

Six Sigma methodology begins with a process map that defines and graphically maps out the process to be improved. The process map, which encompasses the entire process, helps firms identify the important metrics that need to be analyzed. After identifying the source of any defects in the system, an improvement program is created to remove the cause of the defects. To improve the quality of a staffing process, each step of the process must maximize the probability that the selected candidate meets the hiring manager's expectations by maximizing the chances that unqualified candidates are screened out at each step, and enhancing the interest qualified candidates have in the job and the organization as an employer. Figure 13-2 illustrates a staffing process map.

Dow Chemical measures Sigma for its staffing processes on a global basis to improve its processes and yield higher productivity. Dow Chemical's Human Resources Information Technology Global Director Jon Walker states,

> Best practices and proven methodologies are key to improving the staffing process enterprise-wide. Since we've been able to engineer new processes and staffing management technology, we have achieved an increase in Sigma by at least 50 percent. . . . An increase in Sigma will typically result in bottom-line efficiency and cost reduction of five percent or more. As it relates to staffing management, we attribute our productivity gains to finding quality candidates faster, faster time to contribution and a reduction in cycle-time by forty percent.[29]

When local unemployment was a low 2 percent, one Colorado manufacturer was paying a substantial amount of overtime to its experienced workers because it was having trouble recruiting for positions in its 24/7 operation. The company applied Six Sigma quality tools to the staffing process and found that because hiring was taking six weeks—candidates had to apply one week, test the next, interview the next, undergo a blood test, then receive an offer—many quality candidates found jobs elsewhere. By mapping the process and removing barriers, the manufacturer shortened its hiring time to one week, improving hiring rates and reducing the overtime and higher salaries the firm had previously had to pay while the positions were unfilled.[30]

Six Sigma and other quality methodologies focus on not just measuring activities but also understanding the variables that affect those metrics and then systematically attempting to control those variables. The DMAIC (define, measure, analyze, improve, and control) process of Six Sigma can be applied to existing internal processes, and the DMADV (define, measure, analyze, design, and verify) method can be effectively used in creating new processes. In more detail, these processes are:[31]

DMAIC (Define, Measure, Analyze, Improve, and Control)

- *Define the problem.* Reduce unwanted turnover among high performers.
- *Measure.* Identify key measurements underlying turnover, such as the turnover rate among high versus low performers.

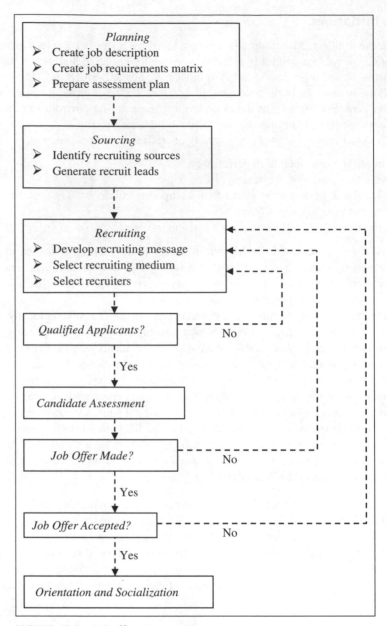

FIGURE 13-2 A Staffing Process Map

- *Analyze.* Understand the key factors and trends that create turnover, such as low employee engagement, the dissatisfaction of employees with their supervision or pay, and high outside demand for the employees' skills.
- *Improve.* Identify and execute a plan to address those factors.
- *Control.* Implement controls to lower turnover on an ongoing basis.

DMADV (Define, Measure, Analyze, Design, and Verify)

- *Define* project goals and customer deliverables, such as improved new hire quality.
- *Measure.* Determine hiring managers' needs, such as their need to hire good employees quickly.
- *Analyze* the process of sourcing, recruiting, screening, and making job offers.
- *Design* the staffing process to screen out undesirable candidates and maximize the quality of new hires.
- *Verify* the performance of the process and its ability to meet the needs of hiring managers.

Although some areas of sourcing, recruiting, and selection are more art than science, if an area can be measured, Six Sigma can be applied to it. For example, by increasing its spending on validated selection tools, a firm can weed out more undesirable candidates and reduce the interviewing and travel expenses related to further screening them. Not only can the tools reduce the firm's recruiting expenses, they can improve the quality of candidates hired and increase employee retention.

The Balanced Scorecard Approach

Good performance is about more than bottom-line financial results. The **balanced scorecard** is a tool used to monitor, assess, and manage the performance of employees as well as align their interests with a firm's key business objectives by assigning them both financial and nonfinancial goals.[32] In other words, the balanced scorecard approach "balances" a firm's strategic, operational, financial, and customer-related goals. The approach also helps managers monitor and assess the performance of their employees so as to quickly take corrective action when needed. After all, financial results are historical measures. Thus, focusing solely on them when evaluating a firm's staffing process is limiting because they reveal only how the company has done in the past—not how it will do in the future. Monitoring nonfinancial measures, including how applicants and employees react to the firm's staffing process and how satisfied hiring managers are with it, for example, can warn a firm about problems that might lie ahead. For example, a dip in employee satisfaction ratings might prompt a manager to say, "because low employee satisfaction leads to higher turnover and weakens our image as an employer, we should address declining employee satisfaction now."

Balanced scorecards help organizations:[33]

- Compare and track the performance trends of different business units, departments, and employees within the organization
- Benchmark the organization against other organizations
- Identify the company's best performers and its best practices

Corporate scorecards are first developed to define the goals and agenda for the entire organization. Each business unit then looks to the corporate scorecard for guidance in creating their own balanced scorecards that support the broader goals and strategies of the organization. Once business unit scorecards are created, each support unit—including a firm's human resource management and staffing department—can create its own scorecard to clarify its goals and track its progress toward meeting them.

A **balanced staffing scorecard** contains objectives, targets, and initiatives for each activity that adds value to the staffing process. Using software, such as Oracle's Balanced Scorecard package, managers can more easily compare the staffing performance of different units, and benchmark it against the firm's budgets, historical data, and peer firms within the industry. From their computers, managers can then click on any indicator to conduct more detailed analyses of the data. If there are problems with the staffing process, the system allows employees to collaborate online to analyze the causes and to take corrective action. It also helps managers see how their decisions impact the company's strategy.

A company's goals and strategies should guide the development of the firm's staffing scorecard. Most of the measures should focus on staffing effectiveness—that is, creating value for the firm. A smaller number of measures should focus on staffing efficiency and cost control. The choice of scorecard criteria should be based not only on the company's strategy and goals, but also the challenges the company anticipates, such as a tightening labor market or changing workforce demographics. The criteria of the scorecard can also be chosen to address any current problems the firm is experiencing—for example, if the firm is having difficulty staffing its key leadership positions.

Assume that every unfilled sales representative position costs a hypothetical retailer $8,000 per day in lost revenue. The company has about 2,000 sales representatives, and averages 120 openings at any given time. The company wants to minimize the time sales representative positions are vacant. In addition, the time hiring managers spend on the sales floor with their representatives adds 20 percent to the revenues the representatives generate. Thus, the retailer wants its managers to balance their sales floor time with the time they spend recruiting and interviewing candidates. To ensure that it is being sufficiently selective, the company would like its hiring managers to interview four to seven candidates per hire. The firm also wants to ensure that it

balanced scorecard
a tool used to monitor, assess, and manage the performance of employees as well as align their interests with a firm's key business objectives by assigning them both financial and nonfinancial goals

balanced staffing scorecard
contains objectives, targets, and initiatives for each activity that adds value to the staffing process

is hiring a diverse sales force and controlling turnover to reduce replacement expenses and lost sales.

Accordingly, the company might create the monthly staffing scorecard as shown in Figure 13-3. Note that the columns to the right show the performance metric being tracked for each region and the goal for each metric is shown in the first row of each column. The data cell for each region is coded green when a metric is consistent with its target, yellow when the metric is becoming problematic, and red when it is out of its target range. The company tracks the time hiring managers spend and number of interviews they conduct per sales representative hire to make sure that enough, but not too much, time is being spent recruiting. The company, of course, also tracks the amount of time it takes to fill a position. If a high percentage of sales positions are vacant, this signals that urgent action is needed. Turnover rates are tracked to identify where retention efforts might be appropriate. The diversity of applicants and candidates hired is also tracked to ensure that the firm is complying with EEO laws and that the company's commitment to diversity is being supported.

It doesn't require a massive effort to improve a firm's staffing metrics. One way to begin is by identifying a problem area and determining how to start measuring and improving it. If the turnover of new hires is a problem, for example, start tracking it by manager and uncover the reasons why people are leaving. Track the information back to the firm's staffing activities, identify areas for improvement, and then make changes and track their results. If new hires are leaving after a year because they don't see a clear career path for themselves in the company, add realistic job preview and career information to the recruitment and socialization process, and incorporate career planning into employees' annual performance discussions. Subsequently track the turnover rates of new hires and see if they improve. If not, reassess what is causing the turnover problem and try again. The metrics used shouldn't be too complex or numerous to understand or explain to others.

Because Nokia wants each of its new hires to fit in with its culture and be able to continually learn and adapt to the company's changing business needs, human resources and hiring managers partner to carefully assess the match between what Nokia needs and can offer new hires and what each candidate needs, wants, and can contribute to the company. Tracking the attrition of new hires at the 12-month mark helps indicate where problem areas might lie, and signals Nokia's human resources personnel to devise corrective measures to address the underlying issues. Nokia further evaluates its staffing effort by conducting focus groups or using other methods designed to identify the reasons why attrition is too high. The reasons could be the hiring process, the hiring manager's skills, HR issues, and the overselling of jobs or the organization. Nokia is careful not to micromanage with staffing metrics. To reinforce its culture, additional metrics are collected only when performance and attrition metrics indicate that a problem is occurring. Nokia is also careful to tailor any staffing metrics it utilizes to different employee populations and problems.[34]

It is often a good idea to implement a staffing evaluation program incrementally rather than taking on the entire staffing system at once. Evaluate one component of the system at a time by calculating its impact on relevant KPIs, such as a division's productivity, employee tenure, performance, labor costs, and employee promotions. For example, a company pursuing a cost-leadership strategy based on an operational excellence competitive advantage might be very concerned about

Region	New Hires	Hiring Manager Hours per Hire	Hiring Manager Interviews per Hire	Time to Fill the Position	Diversity Compliance	Staffing Level	Annualized Turnover Rate
Goal for each metric		15–20 hours	4–7 interviews	<60 days	Full	>95%	<10%
1	15	12	5	55	Compliant	98	6
2	22	14	8	38	Females	95	8
3	30	9	3	21	Hispanics	92	12
4	19	24	14	82	Compliant	97	9
5	27	15	7	19	Males	96	8

FIGURE 13-3 Monthly Balanced Staffing Scorecard
Source: Reprinted with permission from GlaxoSmithKline.

its labor costs. This, of course, would be a good component to track. The direct and indirect cost savings of better recruiting, hiring, and onboarding, as well as the costs of open jobs, such as those associated with severance and unemployment pay, overtime, and the cost of hiring temporary employees, can also be factored in. You can also involve other units of the company, like its finance and operations departments, to acquire the information and data you need. This process helps build the case that staffing activities influence important organizational outcomes and can secure the buy-in needed to make staffing improvements and increase the scope of the evaluation program.

It is important to match a firm's staffing metrics to the different people responsible for them in the hiring process. For example, Nokia tracks the performance of its newly hired executives to the recruiter or search agency that referred them. At lower levels in Nokia, the performance of new hires is tracked to both employees' hiring managers and their recruiters.[35]

Staffing Evaluation Ethics

Ethical issues must be attended to in staffing evaluation. The data used to conduct a staffing evaluation must be high quality. Thus, it is important that everyone responsible for collecting the data ensure that it is accurate. It is also important to keep personal information about applicants and employees private. Any personal information about an employee, including the person's performance and salary information, should be kept confidential and secure. In addition, if applicants or employees are told that the information collected about them will be used in a particular way, the data must be used only in that way. It is also important to realize that some performance comparisons between different recruiters can be unfair. Some recruiting is more difficult because there are fewer diverse, qualified individuals or fewer qualified individuals in general. Recruiting for certain job families can also be more difficult if there is a labor shortage related to those jobs. Nursing and truck-driving jobs are good examples. These positions can be very difficult to fill. One expert recommends that to be fair, recruiter comparisons should be limited to year-to-year comparisons within the same job family and within the same geographic region.[36]

TECHNOLOGY AND STAFFING EVALUATION

One expert says, "When the war for talent is fought over the Internet, corporations will be won and lost over staffing technology."[37] To be sure, the Internet has changed staffing practices in dramatic ways. For example, recruiting employees online costs only about 5 percent of what it costs to recruit them through "help wanted" ads and other traditional means. Online recruiting, application submission, and résumé screening have reduced the average 43-day hiring cycle by more than two weeks.[38] Technology, such as the Internet, has helped companies reach larger numbers of qualified applicants worldwide.

Using technology doesn't merely mean using the Internet to source and recruit applicants, though. Databases and analytical software have made it substantially easier for companies to gather and organize volumes of information about applicants and employees throughout their careers, for example.[39] Technology can also facilitate the administration of employee surveys that can help evaluate the effectiveness of the staffing system. Bernard Hodes's QTrac software assesses the ROI of a firm's employment branding and staffing efforts. An online survey is administered to new hires after 30 days on the job and again at 90 days, 180 days, and 365 days. The survey for each period asks different questions that are most relevant to a new hire at that time to identify any weakness in the recruiting, onboarding, training, and new hire experience and enhance effective recruiting and retention. The home improvement retailer Lowe's uses the monthly reports its QTrac software generates to improve the company's recruiting techniques and the experience of its job candidates. After only two months of QTrac reporting, information was learned that Lowe's translated into tangible plans for improving the process.[40]

Thus, technology helps companies evaluate their staffing functions in terms of their effectiveness and efficiency and better manage their internal labor talent. Next, we discuss some of the most commonly used staffing technologies and tools: résumé screening software, applicant tracking systems, and human resource information systems and how they are used. We then discuss a company's Web site as a critical staffing technology, followed by digital dashboards.

Résumé Screening Software

Résumé screening software screens résumés for certain words or phrases so that recruiters do not have to look at every résumé. This software saves recruiters a lot of time and makes Internet recruiting much more manageable for companies that receive thousands of responses to their job postings. However, relying too heavily on software can result in a firm overlooking highly qualified candidates who do not match specific criteria. As one expert says, "In some cases, the best candidate might not have a specific skill but can learn it."[41] If a company does not invest enough time and resources fine-tuning a system to uncover the best candidates, recruiters might pull up too many résumés matching the desired keywords but too few that are outstanding.[42]

It is important to be careful when selecting résumé screening software—depending on how the software works, it may disproportionately exclude groups of people from various protected categories. For example, a lawsuit filed against one company alleged that the firm's screening software disproportionately screened out African Americans. Rather than deleting résumés, the software identified those that had the words or phrases the company was looking for. It was argued that the words used by the screening software were not the same words that members of the African American community would use to convey that information despite being very well qualified for that job. The case was settled relatively quickly, and there is very little information on what the words were.[43] Nonetheless, the case highlights the importance of being an informed consumer and fully understanding how a software package works.

Applicant Tracking Systems

applicant tracking system
software that allows a database with applicant information and job information to be maintained so that matches between the two are easier to make

An **applicant tracking system (ATS)** is software that allows a database with applicant information and job information to be maintained so that matches between the two are easier to make. First-generation applicant-tracking systems only collected résumés and offered basic search capabilities. Today's systems, whether they're used in-house or in tandem with job boards, allow human resources and line managers to oversee the entire recruitment and staffing process—everything from mining résumés, to conducting background checks, and facilitating the onboarding of new hires. Some ATSs are able to generate detailed profiles of candidates that include their education, background, skills, behavioral attributes, work history, and salary requirements. ATSs not only reduce costs but also help to speed up the hiring process and improve the company's ability to find people who fit the firm's success profile.[44]

ATSs can also provide managers with interview and selection guidelines and even help prescreen applicants by administering online prescreening tests or questionnaires to them. For example, Continental Airline's flight attendant candidates answer 41 questions online before being allowed to complete a formal application.[45] Because ATSs store candidate-related data inside a database, searching, filtering, and routing applications is faster and more effective. This frees up recruiters' time to source and communicate with candidates, and can reduce inefficiencies, costs, and the time it takes to fill positions. Reporting tools that help facilitate a firm's EEOC compliance are often included, as are tools for managing communications with applicants.

ATSs are made by large software firms such as PeopleSoft, SAP, and Oracle, and firms such as HR Diagnostics, RecruitPro, and Hirebridge. Their cost ranges from a few hundred dollars to millions of dollars, depending on their complexity. Training end users to properly use the systems is critical for success, as is selecting the best reporting metrics to incorporate, and carefully testing the usability of the system's functions. The more integrated the various functions are, the more usable the system will be.

Attracting and retaining diverse, high-quality talent is central to ConAgra Food's strategy for continued growth. To make its staffing process more strategic, ConAgra realized that one of the most powerful ways to enrich and diversify its talent pool was to leverage the Internet in a way that would allow the company to find external candidates. The company's ATS now automatically stores all applications and résumés submitted to the company via the Internet, and ConAgra's HR managers review only those that are prescreened by the system. This eliminates hours of research by recruiters. More than 50 percent of ConAgra Foods' recruiting and staffing activities are now done through the Internet and its internal résumé database, and the company has seen an increased flow of quality talent. Including a metrics system also allowed the company to implement actionable recruiting goals to measure the quality and diversity of its candidates.[46]

According to experts, at a minimum an applicant tracking system should be able to:[47]

- Scan résumés
- Generate mailing labels and letters that can be sent to accepted and rejected applicants
- Generate EEO reports
- Schedule and track interviews
- Store the firm's job descriptions
- Generate staffing statistics by activity, recruiter, and recruiting sources
- Generate a job requisition analysis
- Generate a staffing cost analysis
- Create applicant profiles
- Generate mailing labels
- Allow managers' notes regarding different candidates and the staffing process to be stored online

Figure 13-4 shows a screen shot from HR Diagnostics's applicant tracking system. The system shows the number of candidates at each stage in the hiring process, and the menu at the left gives managers easy access to reports, testing outcomes, and other information about candidates and the hiring process.

HUMAN RESOURCES INFORMATION SYSTEMS A **human resources information system (HRIS)** is a system of software and supporting computer hardware specifically designed to store and process all HR information and keep track of all employees and information about them. Also known as human resources management systems (HRMS), these systems support most modern HR departments. An HRIS combines separate HR systems into a centralized database that performs the majority of HR transactions,[48] including reporting capabilities. Some systems are able to track applicants before they become employees. The better HRIS systems help to

human resources information system (HRIS)
a system of software and supporting computer hardware specifically designed to store and process all HR information and keep track of all employees and information about them

FIGURE 13-4 An Example of an Applicant Tracking System (ATS)

From http://www.hr-diagnostics.com.

Source: Reprinted with permission from HR Diagnostics.

manage all employee information, report and analyze employee information, manage applications and résumés, and facilitate employee onboarding.

Human resources information systems usually include each employee's:[49]

- Department
- Job title
- Job grade
- Salary
- Salary history
- Position history
- Supervisor
- Training completed
- Special qualifications
- Ethnicity
- Date of birth
- Disabilities
- Veteran status
- Visa status
- Benefits selected

Company Web Sites

You have probably noticed that many companies feature on their Web sites special careers sections dedicated to the firm's employment opportunities. In fact, corporate Web sites have become the primary way most students research companies and evaluate career opportunities. In addition to providing information about current job openings, the careers site can also contain information about a firm's corporate culture and mission. Many companies are able to accept applications and administer prescreening tests online. Thoughtfully developed careers sites can also result in more effective interviews because applicants' basic questions will already have been answered by Web site content, and poor fits are more likely to have self-selected out after learning more about the organization and job opportunity online.

It is critical that the path to career sites be easy to find, and that career sites be kept usable. When one insurance company buried a jobs link at the bottom of its homepage, requiring users to scroll past unrelated information, job-related inquiries submitted to the firm dropped by 80 percent. Other companies are working on creative ways to grab a candidate's attention as they build their recruiting pages.[50] Goldman Sachs's interactive careers Web site at www 2.goldmansachs.com/careers/index.html is a good example. Organizations can use as much space as they feel they need to communicate their unique employer brand and showcase their employment opportunities. Search functions can help visitors identify the job opportunities they wish to pursue and their desired work locations, and self-assessment inventories can help applicants decide which opportunities are best for them. Drop-down menus and résumé builders can allow visitors to submit their background information in a standardized manner, facilitating the screening and record keeping of this information.

If done professionally and in an easy-to-navigate manner, Web sites can help establish and maintain an organization's image as a good employer. Although a high-quality Web site can be expensive to build, it should be thought of as an investment that will be amortized over the large numbers of people likely to see and use it. The investment is also likely to reduce hiring times and other staffing-related costs.

Despite the benefits of staffing technology, there can be some dysfunctional or unintended consequences related to it as well.[51] Computerized recruiting and staffing systems can depersonalize the hiring process and make it less flexible, negatively impacting applicant attraction and retention rates. If some subgroups lack access to computerized systems or the skills needed to utilize them, online recruiting can result in adverse impact. Privacy concerns sometimes make applicants less willing to use e-recruiting systems.[52] Some research has shown that e-recruiting doesn't always attract the most qualified job applicants and, in fact, has a tendency to attract individuals who switch jobs frequently.[53]

The following are some experts' guidelines for e-staffing:[54]

- The Internet should not be the only recruiting source a company uses.
- E-recruiting should be used when large numbers of candidates are needed, when fairly high education levels are required, and to target applicants in specific labor markets, such as high-technology employees, students seeking part-time work, or new graduates seeking full-time work.
- E-recruiting systems should provide applicants with accurate information about a company's unique characteristics and give a realistic preview of the company.
- Company Web sites should promote values that most new employees will find attractive.
- E-staffing systems should be aligned with the company's strategic goals and enable firms to attract applicants who can help them meet their strategic objectives.
- Feedback should be regularly collected from job applicants about the types of implicit and explicit messages a company's Web site conveys about the firm and its culture.
- To attract diverse applicants, e-staffing systems should be culturally sensitive and possibly include special features (e.g., be presented in multiple languages and an option for large font to accommodate the needs of individuals with vision disabilities).
- To protect applicants' privacy, e-staffing systems should be governed by privacy protection policies that (a) restrict data access, (b) restrict data disclosure, and (c) ensure that only job-relevant data are collected for decision-making purposes. For privacy reasons, all medical information must be kept separate from the employee's other information, in a place where managers cannot see it.

Digital Staffing Dashboards

Just as the dashboard of a car gives the driver indicators of the car's performance and warns when there is danger, **digital staffing dashboards** are interactive computer displays that indicate how a staffing function is meeting its goals, using whatever metrics the user chooses. The metrics are often those from the balanced staffing scorecard but can include other metrics as well. Digital dashboards reflect the idea that a picture is worth a thousand words: The dashboards display large amounts of data in a clear and user-friendly format, usually with charts and graphs, and are interactive, allowing the user to break high-level data down into more detailed reports. Like automobile dashboards, digital dashboards usually present important information in a way that grabs the manager's attention. For example, if a staffing initiative is over budget, a graph related to it might display a red blinking light. SAS's Strategic Performance Management package is such a system.[55]

digital staffing dashboards
interactive computer displays that indicate how a staffing function is meeting its goals

Digital staffing dashboards can include a variety of information including the names of top recruiters and their performance, the number of positions a firm has open, the number of candidates at each stage in the selection process, employee skill sets, turnover rates, diversity statistics, staffing expenses, and many other metrics. Well-crafted staffing dashboards help companies monitor and manage their workforces and chart their progress toward meeting strategic and tactical staffing objectives. Capital One Financial Group uses dashboards to identify its top performers. Erickson Retirement Communities of Baltimore uses dashboards to identify which retirement complexes are having trouble retaining staff members and which complexes have seen employee satisfaction ratings dip.[56] Chicago's Northwestern Memorial Hospital uses dashboards to track its turnover, open positions, number of hires, the reasons why applicants are rejected or decline an offer, and other metrics.[57] Digital dashboards can also keep employees aware of how well they are performing. Thus, if an employee receives a poor performance review at the end of the year, the person is less likely to be surprised and upset by it.[58] Digital dashboard technology is also scalable, allowing even small- and medium-sized companies to use the technology, and contains safeguards to protect sensitive employee data.

ABN AMRO Bank, one of the largest banks in Europe, implemented a digital staffing dashboard to better understand the effects its human resource policies were having on its recruitment and retention efforts and to provide better visibility of the firm's workforce trends and events. In addition to providing a global overview of the company's HR operations (such as the firm's headcount and average employee compensation) by respective quarters and years, the dashboard-based application also gives end users the option of examining KPIs in greater detail, for instance, to evaluate employee compensation by age groups.[59]

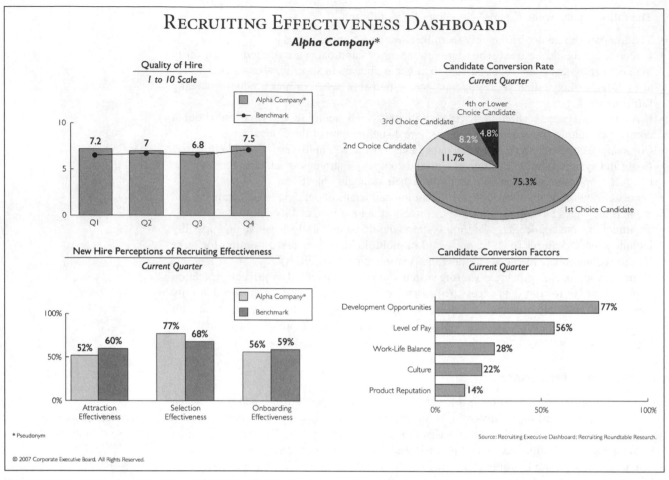

FIGURE 13-5 Recruiting Effectiveness Dashboard

Source: Recruiting Executive Dashbaord, Recruiting Rountable Research © 2007 Corporate Executive Board. All rights reserved. Reprinted with permission.

Figure 13-5 illustrates a recruiting effectiveness dashboard developed by Recruiting Roundtable Research for Alpha Company (a hypothetical company). The dashboard allows Alpha Company to track its hiring quality, candidate conversion rates, new hires' perceptions of the firm's recruiting effectiveness, and candidate conversion factors, or the reasons new hires gave for accepting job offers with Alpha Company.

Because what gets measured gets managed, digital dashboards help keep managers focused on the key factors that drive company success. Creating an effective dashboard takes some planning. Utilizing it can take time, require managers to adapt how they manage, and even alter a firm's corporate culture. This chapter's Develop Your Skills feature provides some tips for creating a good dashboard.

DEVELOP YOUR SKILLS
Creating a Digital Staffing Dashboard

Creating digital staffing dashboards requires time, expertise, and an understanding of what drives a firm's staffing success.[60] Here are some tips for creating a digital staffing dashboard:

1. *Identify the factors that determine a firm's staffing and business success.* The factors might include:[61]
    - The firm's talent depth in its key positions
    - The job success of the firm's new hires (including their performance, fit with the organization, and promotion rates)

- The recruiting sources of top performers (e.g., the colleges top performers attended)
- The retention and absenteeism rates of hires from different sources and different supervisors
- The cost per hire
- The average time to fill a position
- The time to productivity (the time it takes a new hire to achieve a minimum level of output)
- The top five nonmonetary reasons that people accepted the firm's job offers

- Vacancy percentages in key positions
- The time it takes HR personnel to refer résumés to hiring managers
- The time it takes to interview candidates after they have applied with the firm
- The time between a candidate's interview and the offer made to him or her
- The percentage of bad hires
- The percentage of diverse hires
- Applicants' and managers' satisfaction levels with the hiring process
- The five primary reasons top performers leave the firm
- The turnover rate of top performers

2. *Set specific goals.* Each metric should be associated with a target level or range that reflects a business priority (e.g., hiring and retaining more top performers or promoting from within) or financial return (e.g., reducing turnover and saving money).[62]

3. *Prioritize the information.* Dashboards are ineffective if they contain too much information. Identify which metrics are critical, and put them on the main dashboard page. Creating drill-down pages with more detailed information and additional metrics can help limit the amount of information presented on any single dashboard.

4. *Identify how best to present the data.* Bar charts, tables, pie charts, graphs, and even speedometer-style displays are all possible. Managers and employees can be asked to test different formats to identify what works best.

5. *Assess users' comprehension of the data.* Ensure that users are not misinterpreting the data and that they can quickly and clearly understand the information being communicated.

6. *Consider including dynamic capabilities.* Dynamic capabilities on the dashboard will allow managers to plan for different scenarios and growth projections.[63]

7. *Create data entry accountability.* If the data used by the system are not entered accurately or on time, the dashboard will not be accurate.[64] Assess and reward managers for maintaining the database.

STAFFING TECHNOLOGY AT OSRAM SYLVANIA[65]

Osram Sylvania adopted staffing technologies that automatically cross-posts position requisitions to both internal and external career sites, as well as to their five top-producing job boards. Embedded URL tracking and a staffing dashboard that monitors results help save time and increase résumé flow.

To manage the increased number of candidates, the company uses custom candidate prescreening questions that are embedded in the application process for each job. Now when hiring managers log into the system, their candidates are presented in ranked order based on their answers to the prescreening questions. Managers also use mail merge templates to communicate with candidates and set up interviews. And everything is tracked and visible to both recruiters and hiring managers. Employee referrals that come in both through the external Web site as well as the intranet are also tracked.

Osram Sylvania's staffing dashboard and built-in reporting now keep track of key statistics like time to hire and EEO compliance. Diversity is monitored at every stage of the hiring process, so managers can proactively spot if and at what hiring stage certain protected groups are dropping off. Regular diversity reports that used to take several hours are now completed with four mouse clicks, saving substantial time.

The company claims a weekly savings of $4,000 from the automation of its resume processing. Automated job board posting and source tracking have also increased candidate quality, quantity, and time to hire. The company is in compliance of OFCCP rules on Internet candidate searches, and hiring managers are more involved in the recruiting process. Osram Sylvania feels that its new staffing system has also enabled it to hire more effectively.

Summary

Surprisingly few organizations currently evaluate the effectiveness of their recruiting and hiring efforts, making this a high-potential area in which human resources can contribute to the organization's bottom line. One of the biggest challenges in staffing is often the reluctance of hiring managers to rely on the type of strategic staffing system presented in this book, despite its proven effectiveness. Managers often feel that they are good judges of people, and prefer to "trust their gut" and use their instincts in determining where to recruit and who to hire. Understanding and applying the strategic staffing process presented in this book provides a company a strategic staffing advantage over firms that prefer to use an unscientific method based on instinct. Staffing professionals with these skills are also more valuable than those who lack them.

A variety of staffing sources, methods, and skills is usually required if a staffing program is to be effective in meeting all of its goals. Available staffing methods must be analyzed and chosen because they are appropriate to staffing the current vacancy. As the importance of quality and quantity goals change relative to each other, the staffing function must be prepared to change its evaluation strategy as well. In order to measure, we must have clear goals and objectives that are based on the business strategy and the firm's objectives.

Utilizing statistical and software tools for analyzing and predicting staffing outcomes is an important part of maximizing a staffing system's quality and its return on investment. For a staffing system to consistently produce new hires who fit an organization's unique definition of success, quality data as well as training in the tools and processes needed to analyze and interpret this information are necessary to make data-based decisions and create a culture that supports the continual evaluation and improvement of the staffing system.

Today, the increasing demand for HR technology parallels increasing interest in evaluating staffing systems and improving staffing ROI. Technology systems are becoming a critical tool in enhancing the value staffing creates for an organization, and in enhancing the efficiency and effectiveness of the staffing function. While initially used primarily by large organizations, more small and midsize companies now use software products to both effectively measure human capital investment and track a wide range of HR metrics.[66]

As you learned in Chapter 1 and as we have stressed throughout this book, employees are the key to every organization's performance and survival. Strategic staffing involves the movement of people into, through, and out of the organization in future-oriented and goal-directed ways that support the organization's business strategy and enhance organizational effectiveness. Planning, measurement, and continuous evaluation and improvement are important to the success of any staffing system. Staffing must be tied to business strategy and reinforce the company's competitive advantage. It must also be aligned with the other functional areas of human resource management, including training, compensation, and performance management. By partnering with hiring managers and positively influencing the flow of talent into, through, and out of an organization, staffing professionals play an important strategic role in organizations.

Takeaway Points

1. A firm's staffing activities can affect the willingness of applicants to stay in the hiring process and accept job offers as well as their willingness to recommend the employer to others. Staffing can also affect new hires' job expectations, motivation and job engagement, performance, and retention, and influence the organization's performance, strategy execution, and leadership capabilities.

2. Staffing metrics can be short-term or long-term and efficiency or effectiveness oriented. Short-term metrics can be used as leading indicators to gauge a company's ability to have the right people in the right jobs at the right time. Long-term metrics are best for evaluating the effectiveness of the staffing system because they drive the financial impact of staffing on the organization. Staffing efficiency metrics assess the resources used in the staffing process, and staffing effectiveness metrics measure how well the staffing process meets the needs of a firm's stakeholders and contributes to the company's strategy execution and performance.

3. A balanced staffing scorecard is a tool for managing employees' performance and for aligning their incentives with the firm's key business objectives. The scorecard balances a firm's strategic, operational, financial, and customer goals and helps managers monitor and assess the performance of employees so as to quickly take corrective action when needed.

4. Digital staffing dashboards are interactive computer displays of indicators of how the staffing function is meeting its goals, using whatever metrics the user chooses. By continually monitoring selected staffing metrics and alerting managers when goals are not being met, dashboards help managers monitor and improve the staffing process.

5. Staffing technology can improve the efficiency and effectiveness of the staffing function by creating a database of applicant and employee information and automating many of the steps of the staffing process. This can save firms time and money. Because technology allows data to be stored and reports to be generated automatically, it can also facilitate the staffing evaluation process.

Discussion Questions

1. What might prevent organizations from evaluating their staffing systems, and what can be done to remove these barriers?

2. In your opinion, what three metrics might a university use to evaluate the effectiveness of its efforts to fill instructor positions?

3. If your manager was reluctant to invest in an applicant tracking system, how would you persuade him or her to make the investment?

4. As an applicant, how would you feel knowing that technology were used to make an initial decision to screen you out of the hiring process?

5. What information do you want to see when you visit the careers section of a potential employer's Web site?

Exercises

1. *Strategy Exercise:*   Metrics are only information—it is up to you to interpret and use them. Interpret the following metrics and identify what they might mean by addressing the questions that follow them.

   a. Compare the following two recruiting sources:

	Source X	Source Y
Cost	$200,000	$200,000
Number of New Hires	20	10
Cost per Hire	$ 10,000	$ 20,000

   1. Which program do you conclude is better?
   2. If the hires from source X are retained for two years, and the hires from source Y are retained for five years, would your conclusion change?
   3. What additional information would you need to make a recommendation about the source that's preferable?

   b. The turnover rates of different employee subgroups of a firm are as follows:

Employee Group	Turnover Rate (%)
Under 6 months' tenure	85
6 months to 1 year tenure	60
1 to 2 years	30
Over 2 years	12
High performers	25
Moderate performers	20
Low performers	10

   1. In what ways is turnover a problem for this company?
   2. How could the company address the situation?

2. *Develop Your Skills Exercise:*   In this chapter's Develop Your Skills feature, we gave you some tips for creating a digital staffing dashboard. Using this information, create a dashboard for Osram Sylvania (featured in this chapter's opening vignette) reflecting the following metrics. Use color coding to indicate whether or not a metric is within the parameters the company desires.

   Metrics:
   * Top five staffing vendors
   * Job applicant quantity
   * New hires' time-to-contribution rates by recruiting source
   * Diversity by recruiting source
   * Osram Sylvania's staffing efficiency ratio

3. *Opening Vignette Exercise:*   This chapter's opening vignette illustrated how Osram Sylvania used technology to improve its staffing system. Reread the vignette, and answer the following questions:

   a. In what ways did technology improve the company's staffing function?
   b. Do you think it is appropriate for Osram Sylvania to rank-order applicants based on their answers to the online prescreening questions? Why or why not?
   c. If you were a hiring manager at Osram Sylvania, what metrics would you most want to have available about your hires?

CASE STUDY

Staffing Evaluation at Hallmark Cards

Hallmark Cards, founded in 1910, is the largest U.S. manufacturer of greeting cards and the owner of Binney & Smith, the maker of Crayola Crayons.[67] The company pursues a differentiation and innovation strategy and uses creativity and emotion to help people connect to its products, including its stationery, party goods, photo albums, home decor, collectibles, and books.[68] Hallmark Cards employs 4,500 individuals at its corporate headquarters in Kansas City, Missouri, and another 13,500 around the world.

To hire quality people more consistently, Hallmark needed a tool to help it focus its staffing efforts on what is most relevant to the company—that is, on business-relevant criteria that would allow it to more consistently hire quality employees to best execute its strategy.[69] However, Hallmark didn't want the tool to be too complex. To launch the effort, Hallmark created a staffing index to evaluate the quality of the firm's past hires so as to source and screen candidates more effectively.

Upon hiring a new employee, the person's line manager makes an immediate assessment of the employee's intrinsic abilities and desirability. To avoid using complex formulas that require a specialized background to understand, the ratings are simple and focused on measuring the quality and timeliness of Hallmark's hiring system.[70] The possible new hire ratings are: [71]

1 = Average
2 = Above Average
3 = Good
4 = Very Good
5 = Walk-On-Water Good

After six months, the hiring manager uses the same five-point scale to evaluate whether its initial expectations have been realized. The data are used to compare new hires who consistently get top ratings with those who don't to identify any distinguishing factors that can be used to make the hiring process more effective.[72]

According to one expert, Hallmark is on the right track by keeping its system simple and not getting too wrapped up in the numbers and by focusing on the end result of making good hires. Hallmark views the staffing index only as a means to an end and knows that ultimate staffing success will be gauged not by these metrics, but by the organization's performance.[73]

QUESTIONS

1. Critically evaluate Hallmark's staffing index. What are its pros and cons?
2. What additional criteria do you think Hallmark should track, and how should it be measured?
3. Why might an employee rated "walk-on-water good" at the time of hire not live up to expectations? What can a company do to help new employees realize their potential?

Semester-Long Active Learning Project

Propose an evaluation system to assess the effectiveness of your recruiting and selection suggestions. How will you know if your new recruiting and selection system is working? Identify potential barriers to the effective implementation of your recruitment and selection system and propose strategies for coping with them.

Case Study Assignment: Strategic Staffing at Chern's

See the appendix at the back of the book for this chapter's Case Study Assignment.

Endnotes

1. Alexander, I. and Anderson, S. J., "Osram Sylvania Shines New Light on Recruiting With Automation," *Talent Management Magazine*, April 2008: 54–64; Cytiva, Inc., "Osram Sylvania Shines a Light on Their Recruiting Efforts with 'Robustly Configurable' SonciRecruit," 2008, http://www.sonicrecruit.com/press_room/sylvania_case.pdf. Accessed April 7, 2010; "Osram," 2010, http://www.osram.com/osram_com/Consumer/index.html. Accessed April 7, 2010.

2. Kaplan, R., and Norton, D., "The Office of Strategy Management," *Harvard Business Review* (October 2005): 72–80.

3. Mankin, M., and Steele, R., "Turning Great Strategy into Great Performance," *Harvard Business Review* (July–August 2005): 65–72.

4. Dessler, G., and Phillips, J., *Managing Now*, New York: Houghton-Mifflin, 2007.

5. Zimmerman, E., "Keeping Tabs on Productivity of Recruiting Tools," *Workforce Management Online*, March 2005, www.workforce.com/section/06/feature/23/98/25/index.html. Accessed January 3, 2007.

6. Pfeffer, J., "Producing Sustainable Competitive Advantage Through the Effective Management of People," *Academy of Management Executive*, 9 (1995): 55–69.

7. See Lockwood, N., "Maximizing Human Capital: Demonstrating HR Value with Key Performance Indicators," *Society for Human Resource Management*, September 2006, www.shrm.org/research/quarterly/2006/0906RQuart_essay.as. Accessed January 14, 2007.

8. Ulrich, D., and Brockbank, W., *The HR Value Proposition*, Boston, MA: Harvard Business School Press, 2005.

9. Lockwood, "Maximizing Human Capital."

10. Denton, D. K., "Measuring Relevant Things," *Performance Improvement*, 45, 3 (March 2006): 33–38.

11. Lockwood, "Maximizing Human Capital."

12. Marquez, J., "When Brand Alone Isn't Enough," *Workforce Management*, March 13, 2006: 39–41.

13. Group, D., and Joseph, J., *2005–2006 Recruiting Metrics and Performance Benchmark Report*, Willow Grove, PA: Staffing.org and Washington, DC: BNA Inc., August 2005.

14. See Group and Joseph, *2005–2006 Recruiting Metrics and Performance Benchmark Report*.

15. Sullivan, J., "Best Recruiting Practices from the World's Most Business-Like Recruiting Function, Part 4," Electronic Recruiting Exchange, October 10, 2005, www.ere.net/articles/db/D89CC5F6881B4A24A9A344D6E5FF0D37.as. Accessed August 23, 2006.

16. Barkley, M., "The First Three Things That HR Should Measure," *Workforce Online*, February 2003, www.workforce.com/archive/article/23/40/07. Accessed January 11, 2007.

17. Raphael, T., "Cost Per Hire—Don't Even Bother," *Workforce*, June 2002: 112.

18. Ibid.

19. Ibid.

20. Schneider, C., "The New Human-Capital Metrics," *CFO Magazine*, February 15, 2006, www.cfo.com/article.cfm/5491043/1/c_2984284?f=archives. Accessed August 23, 2006.

21. Sullivan, "Best Recruiting Practices from the World's Most Business-Like Recruiting Function, Part 4."

22. Quartana, L., "How to Assess the Effectiveness of Recruiting," Net-Temps.com, www.net-temps.com/careerdev/crossroads/print.htm?id=150. Accessed June 3, 2007.

23. Becker, B. E., Huselid, M. A., and Ulrich, D., *The HR Scorecard: Linking People, Strategy, and Performance*, Boston, MA: Harvard Business School Press, 2001, 48.

24. Cappelli, P., "A Market-Driven Approach to Retaining Talent," In Harvard Business Review, *Harvard Business Review on Finding and Keeping the Best People*, Boston, MA: Harvard Business School Publishing, 2001, 27–50.

25. Singh, R., "The Emperor's New Metrics, Part 2," Electronic Recruiting Exchange, September 8, 2005, www.ere.net/articles/db/001D8B71AF754FA18E074813EB6ADD8A.asp. Accessed January 24, 2007.

26. See Harry, M., and Schroeder, R., *Six Sigma*, New York: Random House, 2000.

27. See http://savelives.gecareers.com.

28. Weston, S., "Six Sigma in Recruiting, Part Two," Electronic Recruiting Exchange, April 29, 2003, www.ere.net/articles/db/3669F629B43644DC825FE6D1250890C4.as. Accessed February 22, 2007.

29. Snell, A., "Applying Six Sigma Principles to Corporate Staffing Departments," Taleo.com, www.taleo.com/research/articles/strategic/applying-six-sigma-principles-corporate-staffing-32.html. Accessed January 5, 2007.

30. Heuring, L., "Six Sigma in Sight," *HR Magazine*, March 2004, www.shrm.org/hrmagazine/articles/0304/0304Heuring.asp. Accessed January 10, 2007.

31. Weston, "Six Sigma in Recruiting."

32. Kaplan, R. S., and Norton, D. P., *The Balanced Scorecard: Translating Strategy into Action*, Boston, MA: Harvard Business School Press, 1996; see also Becker, Huselid, and Ulrich, *The HR Scorecard.*

33. Monina, J., and Morre, K., "Backroom to Boardroom: Bridging People Gaps with Saratoga," PriceWaterhouse Coopers, July 2006, www.pwc.com/Extweb/pwcpublications.nsf/docid/B5E93EADE6 D40A7E8025723C003168E1/$file/PwC_Saratoga.pdf. Accessed January 11, 2007.

34. Based on an interview with Jose Conejos, Nokia's vice president of global HRD and resourcing, and Jadwiga Zareba, head of resourcing for Nokia Worldwide, June 7, 2007.

35. Based on an interview with Jose Conejos, Nokia's vice president of global HRD and resourcing, and Jadwiga Zareba, head of resourcing for Nokia Worldwide, June 7, 2007.

36. Sullivan, J., "The Recruiter's Scorecard: Assessing the Effectiveness of Individual Recruiters," Electronic Recruiting Exchange, October 27, 2003, www.ere.net/articles/db/61A88 F9BB9CB463FAA8312AB2D518837. Accessed June 4, 2007.

37. Sullivan, J., "Best Recruiting Practices from the World's Most Business-Like Recruiting Function, Part 5," Electronic Recruiting Exchange, October 17, 2005, www.ere.net/articles/ db/4EDDC98223964CD 5B5BA718AB0CF0F59.asp. Accessed August 23, 2006.

38. Cappelli, P., "Making the Most of Online Recruiting," *Harvard Business Review* (March 2001): 139–146.

39. Schneider, "The New Human-Capital Metrics."

40. Hansen, F., "Lowe's Builds Its Employment Brand," *Workforce Management Online*, January 2007, www.workforce.com/ section/06/feature/24/62/85/index.html. Accessed January 11, 2007.

41. Greengard, S., "Smarter Screening Takes Technology and HR Savvy," *Workforce*, June 2002: 57–60.

42. Ibid.

43. Flynn, G., "E-Recruiting Ushers in Legal Dangers—Legal Insight," *Workforce*, April 2002, www.findarticles.com/p/ articles/mi_m0FXS/is_4_81/ai_85698986. Accessed January 12, 2007.

44. Greengard, "Smarter Screening Takes Technology and HR Savvy."

45. Hansen, F., "Continental's Recruiting Reach," *Workforce Management Online*, December 2005, www.workforce.com/ archive/article/24/23/41.php. Accessed January 17, 2007.

46. "BrassRing Revealed Recruitment Trends at Summit," May 22, 2006, Wpsmag.com. Accessed July 5, 2006.

47. *Applicant Tracking*, Hr-guide.com, www.hr-guide.com/data/ 201.htm. Accessed January 17, 2007.

48. "Human Resource Information Systems," Lycos.com, www.lycos.com/info/human-resource-information-systems.html. Accessed January 12, 2007.

49. Reh, F. J., "Human Resources Information System," About.com, http://management.about.com/cs/peoplemanagement/g/HR infosys.htm. Accessed January 12, 2007.

50. Pont, J., "State of the Sector: Recruitment and Staffing," *Workforce Management*, May 2005: 49–56.

51. Stone, D. L., Stone-Romero, E. F., and Lukaszewski, K., "The Functional and Dysfunctional Consequences of Human Resources Information Technology for Organizations and Their Employees," In D. L. Stone (ed.), *Advances in Human Performance and Cognitive Engineering Research*, Greenwich, CT: JAI Press, 2003, 37–68; Stone, D. L., Lukaszewski, K. M.,

and Isenhour, L. C., "E-Recruiting: Online Strategies for Attracting Talent," In H. G. Gueutal and D. L. Stone (eds.), *The Brave New World of eHR: Human Resources Management in the Digital Age*, San Francisco, CA: John Wiley and Sons, 2005.

52. Harris, M. M., Van Hoye, G., and Lievens, F., "Privacy and Attitudes Toward Internet-Based Selection Systems: A Cross-Cultural Comparison," *International Journal of Selection and Assessment* 11 (2003): 230–236; Stone, Stone-Romero, and Lukaszewski, "The Functional and Dysfunctional Consequences of Human Resources Information Technology for Organizations and Their Employees."

53. Stone, Lukaszewski, and Isenhour, "E-Recruiting: Online Strategies for Attracting Talent."

54. Ibid.

55. www.sas.com, January 2006.

56. Onley, D. S., "Using Dashboards to Drive HR," *HR Magazine*, April 1, 2006: 109.

57. Creelman, D., "Metrics in Recruiting: The Real World," Human Capital Institute, March 2005, www.hrshopper.com/Management/ fileuploads/2005Metricsin Recruiting.pdf. Accessed December 12, 2006.

58. Onley, "Using Dashboards to Drive HR."

59. Hall, C., "Business Intelligence for Managing the Workforce," Cutter Consortium Business Intelligence Advisory Service, January 1, 2005, www.cutter.com/content-and-analysis/resource-centers/business-intelligence/sample-our-research/biau0502.html.

60. Creelman, "Metrics in Recruiting."

61. Based on Sullivan, J., "Develop an Employment Dashboard and Index," Electronic Recruiting Exchange, April 2001, ourworld.compuserve.com/homepages/gately/pp15s149.htm.

62. Shapiro, J., "6 Tips to Customize Your HR Dashboard," Hodes iQ, www.hodes.com/aboutus/pressroom/sponsorship/pdfs/Dashboardi Q_2.pdf. Accessed January 5, 2007.

63. See, for example, The Dashboard Spy, "A Staffing Dashboard—Xcelsius Calculator for HR Staffing Levels," April 3, 2006, http://dashboardspy.wordpress.com/2006/04/03/ a-staffing-dashboard-xcelsius-calculator-for-hr-staffing-levels. Accessed January 5, 2007.

64. Creelman, "Metrics in Recruiting."

65. Alexander, I. and Anderson, S.J., "Osram Sylvania Shines New Light on Recruiting With Automation," *Talent Management Magazine*, April 2008: 54–64; Cytiva, Inc., "Osram Sylvania Shines a Light on Their Recruiting Efforts with 'Robustly Configurable' SonciRecruit," 2008, http://www. sonicrecruit.com/press_room/sylvania_case.pdf. Accessed April 7, 2010; "Osram," 2010, http://www.osram.com/osram_ com/Consumer/index.html. Accessed April 7, 2010.

66. Lockwood, "Maximizing Human Capital."

67. "Strategic Partners," Crown Media Holdings Inc., http://phx. corporate-ir.net/phoenix.zhtml?c= 103320&p=irol-strategic-partners. Accessed January 4, 2007.

68. "Hallmark Cards, Inc.," Answers.com, www.answers.com/ topic/hallmark-cards-inc. Accessed January 4, 2007.

69. Ibid; Hallmark Card's Staffing Index is available at www.workforce.com/tools/staffing_index.pdf.

70. Dalton, A., "Hallmark's Quality-of-Hire Initiative," *Workforce Management Online*, May 2005, www.workforce.com/archive/ article/24/04/76.ph. Accessed July 4, 2006.

71. Hallmark Card's Staffing Index is available at www. workforce.com/tools/staffing_index.pdf.

72. Dalton, "Hallmark's Quality-of-Hire Initiative."

73. Ibid.

APPENDIX

Strategic Staffing at Chern's: A Case Study

CHERN'S COMPANY HISTORY AND ORGANIZATION

Siblings Ryan and Ann Chern founded Chern's, an upscale shoe and handbag store, 20 years ago after the two of them each graduated with their MBAs. The pair had planned to launch their own company for years, and refined their business model after each spent a great deal of time learning about the retail industry by working in different retail organizations. The product mix and high-quality products Chern's sells made it rapidly successful, and the company developed a loyal following. The firm quickly expanded its product line and became a full-scale clothing retailer 15 years ago. Ryan and Ann have turned their basic idea of providing customers with the best service, selection, quality, and value into a thriving business. The two are now co-presidents of Chern's: Ryan serves as the company's chief executive officer; Ann serves as the company's chief operating officer.

Twelve years ago, Chern's began pursuing an aggressive growth strategy. Currently the company has 140 stores in 28 states on the East Coast and in the Midwest. Chern's employs an average of 19,000 full- and part-time employees. Providing superior customer service has been the company's main business strategy and has successfully differentiated it from its competitors. Although the company's products are expensive, the high product quality and excellent customer service have made the company successful. Because customers' tastes can differ from one store to the next, the company tries to be as decentralized as possible. Therefore, it gives its store managers a considerable amount of discretion in terms of how they run their stores. Likewise, each manager runs his or her own department as a small business and is rewarded according to the department's and the store's overall success.

Because customer service lies at the heart of the company's business strategy, it is a core part of the corporate culture of Chern's. Ann and Ryan believe that customer service is the essence of selling and that because the firm's sales associates are in direct contact with customers, they are the core drivers of the company's performance. Both department managers and assistant department managers support the sales associates. Besides giving the sales staff their full support, the department managers at Chern's are, in turn, supported by their store managers, assistant department managers, buyers, and merchandising managers. Figure A-1 illustrates these relationships.

Core values are an essential part of the Chern's brand and are the foundation of its culture. The company's family ownership contributes to its desire to make every employee and customer feel valued and cared for. The firm is known for its strong and unique culture, which it feels is due to its belief that the best approach to business is to hire good people. As such, Chern's tries to identify and select the right people, train them, and give them the tools and autonomy they need to succeed. Successful employees are rewarded with above-market base salaries and generous bonuses.

The management philosophy at Chern's is based on empowerment. Chern's believes that by hiring well it can trust its employees to use their own judgment. Consequently, the firm gives them a considerable amount of freedom in terms of how they do their jobs. By striving to create a fair and positive environment and giving each employee the tools and autonomy he or she needs to succeed, the company feels it has created an environment in which its sales associates can truly excel. In fact, last year, 42 Chern's sales associates sold at least $1,000,000 in merchandise—a company record.

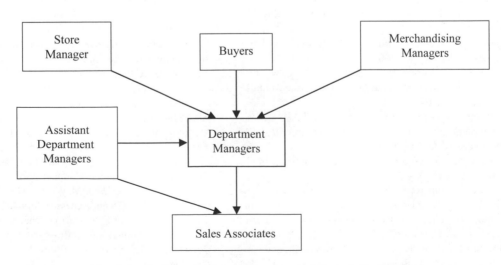

FIGURE A-1   The Sales Support Relationships Among Chern's Staff Members

Because Chern's has a strong reputation for customer service, quality, and selection, it enjoys very positive brand recognition among its targeted customers. It is consistently named one of the top three retailers in regional customer surveys and has been listed among *Fortune* magazine's top 100 best companies to work for. Last year the company ranked number 72 on *Fortune*'s list, down from 44 the previous year. It was the second-highest retailer on the list, behind Nordstrom's. It also ranked as having the best customer service among retailers for the past three years in customer surveys developed by the National Retail Federation.

In addition to focusing on customer service, selection, quality, and value, Chern's has invested heavily in information-technology tools to improve its inventory management and help its sales associates make efficient transactions with customers. The company recently implemented a Perpetual Inventory System to help its buyers react more quickly to the feedback given them by its sales associates and to track inventory to quickly adjust each store's product mix and clothing sizes available. The technology has helped the company increase its efficiency and lower its costs as well as add value for its customers.

CHERN'S FINANCIAL PERFORMANCE

Chern's has enjoyed a strong financial performance over the last few years. Over the past five years, the company's share price has increased 134 percent and the company's revenues have grown at an annualized rate of 9 percent. Revenues and net income have grown as all of the firm's stores have reported sales increases every year over the past three years. Growing revenues and income have provided the company with the financial base and stability it needs for further expansion. Chern's' five-year growth strategy is to open 15 new stores a year and to continue to grow at an annual rate of 9 percent. Figure A-2 shows the company's revenue, gross profit, and net income trends for the last three years.

The company's good financial performance has translated into strong operating cash flow, giving it the option of reinvesting in its business, buying back shares, or passing some of its earnings to investors in the form of dividends. Figure A-3 shows Chern's' operating cash flow trend over the past three years.

Chern's has funded its expansion using its earnings rather than by taking on debt. The company believes that its conservative debt policies and strong cash flow help create shareholder value by enabling it to expand into new markets.

CHERN'S HUMAN RESOURCES

Chern's averages 1 store manager, 8 department managers, 8 assistant department managers, and approximately 100 full-time and 25 part-time sales associates per store. Full-time employees

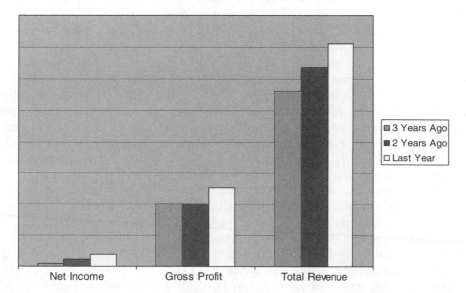

FIGURE A-2 Three-year Revenue, Gross Profit, and Net Income Trends for Chern's

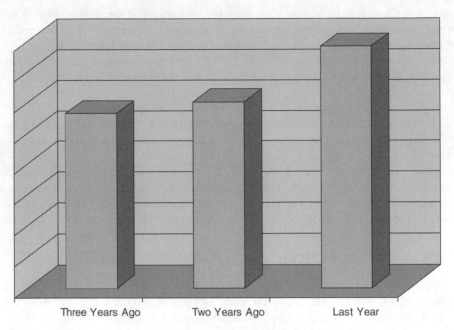

Three Years Ago   Two Years Ago   Last Year

FIGURE A-3   Three-Year Cash Flow Trend for Chern's

receive a generous benefits package, two weeks paid vacation, and are eligible for bonuses. Part-time employees are considered members of the core workforce and receive prorated benefits and bonuses. Because it feels that they would not reinforce its culture, Chern's does not currently utilize temporary or contingent workers of any kind. Turnover among its full-time sales associates has been relatively stable, averaging 20 percent over the past three years. Turnover among the company's part-time sales associates has also been relatively low compared to similar retail operations, averaging 15 percent over the past three years. The part-time sales associates are used to increase the number of sales associates on the floor during peak periods.

The human resources department at Chern's generally does a good job supporting the company's business strategy. The company's compensation, performance management, and training are all designed to get sales associates up to speed and selling quickly. The base pay they earn is 20 percent above the market average, and Chern's matches in their 401(k) plans up to 10 percent of their base pay. Twenty percent of a sales associate's bonus is tied to the person's customer service performance as rated by his or her department manager, 40 percent is based on individual sales performance in relation to that person's sales target, and 40 percent is based on overall store sales. New employees have a reduced sales target for their first year. Sales associates can earn up to 150% of their base pay in bonuses based on both sales and customer satisfaction ratings. Top performers at Chern's earn well above the market average in pay.

Semiannual performance evaluations assess sales associates' initiative, customer service behaviors, coworker support behaviors, and leadership. Raises to an associate's base salary include a cost-of-living adjustment based on inflation, and from 0 to 10 percent based on the department manager's perception of the sales associate's performance, adherence to company values, and leadership contributions. Sales associates are also given 10 personal days, including sick days, and generous health and dental benefits. If a sales associate refers a candidate to Chern's, and the person is hired, the company gives the employee a $1,000 referral bonus after the new hire passes the six-month mark with strong performance.

Chern's largely focuses its training and development activities on its new hires. New hires undergo a two-day orientation. Each then receives on-the-job training from his or her department manager and shadows another sales associate for one week. Employees receive additional training only if they fail to reach their sales quotas two months in a row. Sales associates who fail to reach their quotas four months in a row are given a warning. Those who fail to meet their quotas five months in a row are terminated.

Sales associates can use the store's technology to identify how they are performing relative to their quotas. Chern's expects its employees to be relatively "tech savvy" and be willing and able to quickly learn its systems. Customer information, including information about their previous purchases and fashion preferences, is stored in the company's computer for fast retrieval. Chern's also uses technology to give its buyers feedback about its customers' preferences and purchasing trends. The company's sales associates are also required to record information about customers' inquiries and unfilled requests for particular types of clothing. This is critical because it helps each department better track its inventory and quickly adjust its product mix and sizes to meet the changing demands of its customers. Sales associates can also use the store's computers to check inventory at other Chern's locations to better assist clients in locating desired products.

THE COMPETITION CHERN'S FACES

Chern's primary competitors include Nordstrom, Dillard's, Barney's, Nieman Marcus, and Saks Fifth Avenue. Table A-1 shows the previous and current year's sales, net income, and employee headcount for Chern's relative to its competitors.

At Chern's, sales associates execute the company's customer service strategy by building long-term relationships with their clientele. Sales associates feel empowered, and their business freedom is strongly supported by the corporation as long as the employees work hard and do their best. Chern's tries to hire sales associates with an entrepreneurial spirit, a drive to be successful, and a desire to make money. The sales force's accountability for results and Chern's high expectations of them means that Chern's wants to hire only elite sales associates.

The levels of customer service excellence and sales skills required by Chern's employees are not the same for most other retail firms. High-end retailers, such as Neiman Marcus and Nordstrom, tend to compete more directly with Chern's for hires than do competitors such as Dillard's and Federated Department Stores, which focus less on customer service. The quality of Chern's sales force has enabled it to offer employees considerable upward mobility within the company, which is unusual for a retailer. Chern's fills 75 percent of its department manager and assistant department manager positions internally, whereas most of its competitors fill their management positions externally; 80 percent of the current store managers at Chern's once worked as sales associates for the firm. Promotion from within is important to the company. Both Ryan and Ann strongly believe that internal hires reinforce the company's strong culture.

In order to provide the highest-quality customer service and capture market share, Chern's knows it needs to hire the right sales associates. Although the company's strong culture and high quality initially attracted a sufficient number of talented sales associates who shared the firm's values, the competition for talented sales associates has been heating up. As a result, Chern's is finding it harder to staff and retain the level of sales talent it needs. The sales associates at

TABLE A-1   One-Year Performance of Chern's Relative to Its Competitors

	Chern's	Nordstrom	Dillard's	Barney's	Nieman Marcus	Saks Fifth Avenue
Previous Year's Sales ($ millions)	3,800	8,111	8,525	326	4,390	2,249
Current Year's Sales Growth (%)	9.7	9.9	(.9)	2.3	6.9	8.2
Previous Year's Net Income ($ millions)	193.4	672.5	242.2	24.2	247.8	164.2
Current Year's Income Growth (%)	9.0	6.9	.8	(.6)	6.0	6.4
Previous Year's Headcount (full- and part-time)	19,000	56,500	54,300	1,400	17,900	11,750
Current Year's Headcount Growth (%)	9	2.9	(1.2)	.9	4.1	3.9

Chern's are usually the top performers in the retail industry, so they are never easy to find. Because of the importance of hiring the right salespeople, and their expectation that staffing this important position will become more difficult in the future, Ann and Ryan have decided to launch a strategic analysis of how Chern's staffs its sales associate positions and have asked for your help.

STRATEGIC STAFFING AT CHERN'S: CHAPTER-BY-CHAPTER CASE ASSIGNMENTS

At the end of each of the chapters in this book, you will have an assignment for the case study that applies concepts from that particular chapter. The entire list of assignments can be found at the end of this appendix, just before the candidate résumés are presented. The assignments put you in the role of an external staffing consultant hired by Chern's. Your job is to conduct a strategic analysis of how it staffs its sales associate positions. Your final product will require you to combine each of the assignments into a cohesive report, including a table of contents and any necessary appendices. Format your report as a professional product that you would give to the organization. Chern's is decentralized, which means that your report will be distributed to many store managers, many of whom are unfamiliar with staffing terminology and jargon. Write your report so that they understand and adopt your recommendations and are committed to implementing the changes you've suggested. You might want to keep a copy of the final report to show potential employers the type of strategic staffing work you are capable of performing.

Chapter 1: Strategic Staffing

In this chapter, you learned that the strategic staffing process is guided by hiring goals that are clearly linked to an organization's strategies and objectives. The goal of strategic staffing is to enable the organization to better execute its business strategy. There are two types of staffing goals: process goals and outcome goals. *Process goals* relate to the hiring process itself, and *outcome goals* apply to the product of the hiring effort. Table 1-2 gives examples of both types of staffing goals, and Table 1-3 gives you some questions to consider in setting appropriate staffing goals.

Your consulting assignment for Chapter 1 is to identify realistic long-term and short-term process and outcome goals for staffing of sales associate positions at Chern's. Be sure to relate your goals to the firm's business strategy and explain why each is important and should be adopted by the company.

Chapter 2: Business and Staffing Strategies

In this chapter, you learned about how a firm's business strategy and talent philosophy shape its HR strategy, which then influences the firm's staffing strategy. After Ryan and Ann learned about this process, they felt that the company needed to develop a more formal talent philosophy of its own to shape its HR and staffing strategy. They have asked you for your recommendations.

Chapter 2 and Tables 2–4 and 2–5 should help you identify key components of an appropriate talent philosophy, human resource strategy, and staffing philosophy for Chern's. Be sure to consider the company's business strategy and competitive advantage, life stage, and the company's values and culture when making your recommendations. You should also clarify how putting the right talent in the company's sales associate positions can create a competitive advantage for Chern's.

In addition to developing a formal talent philosophy, HR strategy, and specific staffing strategy, you also need to explain how Chern's should address each of the nine strategic staffing decisions listed in Table 2–6 for the sales associate position, and justify your reasoning. For example, the first decision is whether Chern's should establish a core or flexible sales associate workforce. Describe in your report if Chern's should focus on a core or flexible workforce and to what degree. Be sure to explain why they should follow your recommendations. Do this for the other eight strategic staffing decisions as well, taking into account the chapter material as well as the information provided about Chern's in the beginning of the appendix.

Chapter 3: The Legal Context

Although Ann and Ryan have always known that it is important to comply with equal employment opportunity legislation and other relevant employment laws, it has been eight years since they conducted any sort of discrimination analyses at their company. They ask you to evaluate the sales associate position for any evidence of discrimination based on gender or ethnicity. The first level of disparate impact analyses are typically done at the establishment level, which for Chern's is a single store. Chern's asks you to focus on its flagship store—its largest—which has 140 full-time and 50 part-time sales associates. Chern's gives all department and store managers bias and diversity training, and has never been sued for disparate treatment. Because it knows that adverse impact is still a risk, the company asks you to analyze its full-time sales associate hiring data for evidence of adverse impact.

Tables A-2, A-3, and A-4 summarize the data you will need to use in your analyses. The data for the sales associate flow statistics are based on the previous five years of staffing at Chern's flagship store. Evaluate the stock and concentration statistics and use the four-fifths rule to analyze the flow statistics. In addition to your disparate impact analyses, be sure to recommend strategies that Chern's can use to alleviate any discrimination you may find.

Chapter 4: Strategic Job Analysis and Competency Modeling

Referring to the information presented in the chapter and case, by researching the "retail salesperson" position on O*Net (http://online.onetcenter.org), and by interviewing a sales associate in

TABLE A-2	Sales Associate Statistics Compared to the Relevant Population

Job Category: Sales Associates

	Current Sales Associates (%)	Availability of Sales Associates in Relevant Population (%)
Females	55	60
Males	45	40
Whites	20	25
Blacks	20	25
Asians	32	25
Hispanics	28	25

TABLE A-3	Sales Associate Flow Statistics	
	# Applicants	# Hired
Men	1,000	100
Women	1,400	120
Whites	600	55
Blacks	600	48
Asians	600	67
Hispanics	600	50

TABLE A-4	Sales Associate Concentration Statistics		
	Sales Associates (%)	Department Managers (%)	Store Managers (%)
Female	55	30	40
Male	45	70	60
White	20	20	24
Black	20	15	40
Asian	32	30	16
Hispanic	28	35	20

a similar company if possible (an associate at Saks Fifth Avenue, Nieman Marcus, Nordstrom, and so forth), create a job requirements matrix for the sales associate position at Chern's. Be sure to consider the company's business strategy and corporate culture in creating job duties and identifying competencies or KSAOs. For each competency or KSAO, decide if Chern's should hire people who already possess the characteristic or if the firm should train them to develop it. Also, estimate to the best of your ability how important each characteristic is relative to the others as well as the relative time associates spend on each job duty. You may have to use some judgment to come up with the answers to these questions. You will use this information later to determine how to weight the assessment information obtained on each job candidate.

Given the information contained in the Chern's case description and your own knowledge of this type of position, create a job rewards matrix for the sales associate position. If possible, interview a sales associate in a similar company to obtain additional job rewards information.

Chapter 5: Forecasting and Planning

Chern's has never examined its internal labor market. The company asks you to perform a transition analysis for full-time sales associates. It asks you to conduct relevant analyses to describe the internal labor market for its flagship store.

Summarize the flagship store's internal labor market and highlight any trends or forecasted gaps based on the transition probability matrix in Table A-5. The probabilities are based on annual rates that are averaged over a span of three years. In other words, they are the average rate per year. If Chern's wants to keep its flagship store staffed with 140 full-time sales associates, how many full-time sales associates should it expect to have to hire from outside the company annually?

Traditionally, 30 percent of the store's job applicants for sales associate positions become job candidates, and 15 percent of them receive job offers, 75 percent of which are accepted. Chern's asks you how many applicants it will need to generate each year to acquire the number of new hires you forecasted.

Chern's asks you to research the external labor market for sales associates because the company is concerned about their availability in the future. Using O*Net, choose a state in the United States and research the expected demand for sales associates in that state over the next 10 years. To do this:

1. Go to www.online.onetcenter.org.
2. Search for job 41-2031.00—Retail Salespersons.
3. Scroll to the bottom and find "Wages and Employment Trends."
4. Select a state from the "State and National" drop-down menu and hit "go."
5. Compare the forecasted employment trends in your chosen state with those of the entire United States for the retail salesperson position.
6. Print out the results of your state search and include it with your report.
7. There is also a "Career Video" available on the state results page of your search that you can view for additional information about the work sales associates do.

Now research the employment trends of retail sales workers using the U.S. Department of Labor Bureau of Labor Statistics Web site at www.bls.gov and other resources you identify.

| TABLE A-5 | The Transition Probability Matrix for Chern's Flagship Store |

Transition Probabilities Based on the Past three Years

Job Category	FTSA (%)	PTSA (%)	DEP (%)	BUY (%)	MER (%)	Exit (%)	Current # of Employees
Full-Time Sales Associates (FTSA)	**50**	15	5	5	5	20	140
Part-Time Sales Associates (PTSA)	30	**50**	0	5	0	15	30
Department Manager (DEP)	5	0	**75**	0	0	20	16
Buyers (BUY)	0	0	0	**65**	5	30	5
Merchandising Managers (MER)	0	0	0	0	**80**	20	8

Consider this information when forecasting future gaps or surpluses. You might also consider targeted skill sets or demographics and determine if you can obtain information about skill or demographic trends in your targeted area.

If you forecast a gap between the anticipated supply of qualified sales associates and Chern's anticipated demand for them, determine whether the gap is temporary or permanent. Then, make some recommendations about how Chern's can best address the gap. Be sure to reread the relevant section of Chapter 5 before you do.

Chapter 6: Sourcing: Identifying Recruits

Chern's currently uses six different sources for sales associate applicants: colleges, employee referrals, Cherns.com, a search firm, walk-ins, and local newspaper ads. The company just finished analyzing the effectiveness of each of these sources, and the results are summarized in Table A-6.

Chern's asks you to prioritize its recruiting sources to maximize the effectiveness of the company's future hiring initiatives. Based on what you have read in this case, prioritize the staffing outcomes and rank order the recruiting sources based on their ability to maximize the company's staffing goals for the sales associate position.

Ryan and Ann have heard a lot lately about using the Internet to source passive job candidates. The two are wondering how well this technique would work for its sales associate positions. Referring to the Develop Your Skills feature in Chapter 6, choose an area of the country. First, provide some suggestions on how the Internet might be more effectively used to source and recruit applicants. Second, conduct a Boolean search to source two promising sales associate applicants using the Internet. You may need to try different search engines and different syntax, as highlighted in the chapter. You can also try x-raying and flipping. For example, on Yahoo.com you could try "linkdomain:ffany.org shoes blog" to pull up blogs linked to the Fashion Footwear Association of New York with the word "shoes" in the blog. You should experiment with searches based on your own ideas. Include the various search engines and search terms you used for your final search and provide information about your two leads in an appendix to your final report. Justify each recommendation.

To best serve its diverse clientele and to establish the most positive employer image possible, Chern's wants to hire diverse sales associates. The company also asks you how it can improve the diversity of its applicant pool.

Chapter 7: Recruiting

Develop an outline for a recruiting guide for the sales associate position based on the material you read in this case and what you learned in Chapter 7. The outline should include the company's policies and procedures, budgets, activities, timelines, responsible staff, legal issues, and steps to be taken in recruiting for the position. You do not have time to write an entire recruiting guide. However, Chern's has asked for your help in identifying what it should include in one. Chern's also asks you to make recommendations about what the company can do to increase applicants' fairness perceptions of the process and reduce any negative spillover effects related to it.

TABLE A-6   The Effectiveness of the Sources Used to Recruit Chern's Sales Associates

	Hiring Speed	Cost per Hire	Culture Fit	Average First Year Financial Return	First Year Turnover Rate
College Hiring	5 months	$4,000	Good	$30,000	20%
Employee Referrals	2 months	$2,600	Very good	$38,000	10%
Cherns.com	2 months	$1,500	Good	$38,000	20%
Search Firm	3 months	$5,200	Average	$20,000	15%
Walk-Ins	1 month	$1,500	Poor	$5,000	30%
Newspaper Ads	2 months	$2,000	Poor	$4,000	25%

Chern's would also like to reinforce its employer brand among potential applicants. Ryan and Ann would like to create a stronger employer brand, and ask you for advice on what the company's employer brand should be and how to effectively and consistently market and reinforce it throughout the staffing process. Make some recommendations and explain why your approach would be effective for Chern's.

Chapter 8: Measurement Chapter 9: Assessing External Candidates

Remember to write your report so that the various measurements you learned about in these chapters will be understandable to the firm's store managers and department managers. These employees do not have a staffing or statistics background. Consequently, many of the concepts you discuss in the report will be unfamiliar to them. Be sure you thoroughly explain the concepts and their importance. This will be particularly important when completing the next part of the assignment, which spans Chapters 8 through 11.

Chern's is in the middle of hiring two sales associates for its flagship store and has reduced the initial applicant pool to eight candidates. Because it is the company's flagship store, it is important that all sales associates who work at the store excel at customer service and embody the company's values, and they need the new people to get up to speed quickly. Although Chern's often invests in the training and development of new employees, in this case they would like the two new hires to arrive with the knowledge, skills, abilities, competencies, and other characteristics required to be immediately successful. They also would like the newly hired sales associates to be strong candidates for future management positions.

Ryan and Ann ask you to become involved in the assessment and hiring process. Nearly 80 percent of Chern's sales associates are considered successful. However, Chern's would like the percentage to be at least 85 percent. Ryan and Ann feel that improving the company's assessment and selection system will help it accomplish this goal. Use this opportunity to help Chern's develop a new sales associate assessment and selection system. This is a pilot project to determine how well you are able to improve Chern's staffing process.

All eight candidates are already scheduled to participate in one structured and one unstructured interview that you are asked to view and score. After deducting the costs of the initial applicant screening and the two scheduled interviews for each candidate from the initial budget, the store has $4,000 left to apply to this staffing initiative. It's up to you to decide how to spend the money. What other assessment methods should you use? (The costs of the two interviews are not to be included in your $4,000 budget.)

The assignment for Chapter 8 is to read the case assignment spanning Chapters 8 through 11 and review the eight candidates' résumés at the end of the appendix. You then need to develop an assessment plan that does not exceed your $4,000 budget.

Your goals in developing your sales associate assessment system are threefold:

1. Maximize the return on investment of your assessment system
2. Maximize the job success of the new sales associates hired (in terms of their sales, turnover, and levels of customer service)
3. Maximize the fit of the new sales associates hired (including their customer service orientation and leadership skills) with the company's culture

Table A-7 summarizes the possible assessment methods you can use and their costs.

Next is an overview of the steps you will need to take in completing the next parts of the assignment and the chapter in which each part is assigned. The work will be spread out over the next few chapters.

1. Develop a sales associate assessment and selection plan that does not exceed the remaining $4,000 budget. Justify your proposed selection system using the determinants of the effectiveness of an assessment method identified in Chapter 8. These determinants include:
   a. *Validity*—how well the assessment method predicts relevant components of a person's job performance. Table 9–3 describes typical validities for various assessment tools across many different occupations. You can look at Table 9–3 and consider the results of your job analysis/competency model to determine which assessment is most likely to predict job performance at Chern's.

TABLE A-7 Potential Assessment Methods and Their Costs		
Assessment Method	**Scale of Assessment**	**Cost**
Cognitive Ability Test (measures a candidate's ability to learn, process, and apply information rapidly; verbal, spatial, and mathematical abilities)	Typical scores range from 85 to 130 (mean and standard deviation for this sample are 112.5 and 8.02, respectively).	$70 per candidate
Conscientiousness (measures a candidate's persistence, dutifulness, order, attention to detail, and achievement motivation)	Possible scores range from 1 to 6 (mean = 4.38, std. dev. = 1.06).	$100 per candidate
Openness (measures a candidate's openness to new ideas and situations and intellectual curiosity)	Possible scores range from 0 to 60 (mean = 42.50, std. dev. = 7.07).	$30 per candidate
Sales Interest (measures a candidate's interest in sales as a career; vocational interest inventory)	Possible scores range from 1 to 5 (mean = 3.63, std. dev. = .92).	$50 per candidate
Desire to Avoid Failure (measures a candidate's need to avoid failure and desire to avoid taking risk)	Possible scores range from 1 to 4 (mean = 2.88, std. dev. = .83).	$30 per candidate
Technology Skills Test (measures a candidate's ability to become proficient with the company's various technology tools)	Possible scores for this test range from 0 to 80 (mean = 58.13, std. dev. = 7.99).	$70 per candidate
Job Knowledge Test (measures a candidate's knowledge of sales techniques, understanding of effective customer service practices, and awareness of related issues in the retail industry)	Possible scores for this test range from 0 to 50 (mean = 36.88, std. dev. = 7.04).	$150 per candidate
Simulation (measures a candidate's leadership, sales, judgment, and customer service skills using a work simulation)	Possible scores for the simulation range from 0 to 70 (mean = 43.75, std. dev. = 10.61).	$250 per candidate
Integrity Test (measures a candidate's trustworthiness, integrity, and honesty)	Possible scores for this test range from 1 to 5 (mean = 3.50, std. dev. = 0.93).	$70 per candidate
Fashion Knowledge Test (measures a candidate's knowledge of fashion trends, styles, and fabrics as they apply to a variety of customers)	Possible scores for this test range from 0 to 60 (mean = 38.75, std. dev. = 8.76).	$50 per candidate
Handwriting Analysis (measures a candidate's trustworthiness, personal drive, dependability, sociability, and desire to achieve)	Possible scores for this analysis range from 0 to 10 (mean = 5.38, std. dev. = 3.38).	$150 per candidate

b. ***Return on investment***—the extent to which the assessment method generates a financial return that exceeds the cost associated with using it.

c. ***Applicant reactions***—the extent to which applicants perceive the assessment methods to be job related and fair.

d. ***Selection ratio***—the extent to which the selection ratio is low. A low ratio means hiring only a few applicants, which allows an assessment method to have maximal impact in terms of improving the performance of the people hired.

e. *Usability*—the extent to which people in the organization are willing and able to use the method consistently and correctly.

f. *Adverse impact*—the extent to which an assessment method predicts job performance and other important hiring outcomes without discriminating against members of a protected class.

2. Before viewing the interviews for the next part of the selection process, develop a scoring key for each structured interview question and create a formula to combine the three scores into an overall structured interview score (Chapter 8). The three structured interview questions are as follows:

a. A disgruntled customer is returning a damaged suit jacket he bought the previous week that he needed for an event that night. He is extremely upset. What do you do?

b. A person walks into your store and mentions that she has just moved into the area and that this is the first time she has visited your store. What would you do to make her a customer now and a loyal customer in the future?

c. You're working alone because two people called in sick. Suddenly, five customers walk into your department at once. What do you do?

Additionally, create a scoring key for the unstructured interview based on your expected determinants of success at Chern's. The scoring keys for both types of interviews should reflect the KSAOs or competencies assessed by the questions or interview, not the answers to the questions themselves. Then view the eight structured and eight unstructured interviews available on the book's Web site or if your instructor prefers, view them as a part of the class (Chapter 9).

3. Before or during your next class, submit your assessment plan to your instructor. Your instructor will then give you the candidates' scores on the assessments you choose to utilize (Chapter 9). If your instructor agrees, you can use a multiple hurdles, compensatory, or combined approach for your assessment plan.

4. Using your interview score results, candidate résumés, and scores on the assessment methods you included in your assessment plan, determine which two candidates should receive an offer and submit this information along with the rationale for your choice to your instructor. Write a job offer letter to your top chosen candidate, who is currently considering two other job offers from competitors (Chapter 11).

At the end of the case, your instructor will give you feedback on the job success of your two new hires.

For now you will work on step 1. Submit your assessment plan to the instructor by the deadline the instructor gives you to receive candidates' scores on the assessments you choose to utilize. This request should be sent as your instructor prefers. One possible approach is to format it in the way shown in Table A-8. Use as many columns as necessary to provide a space for your instructor to record each candidate's scores.

Chapter 10: Assessing Internal Candidates

STRATEGIC STAFFING CASE STUDY   As explained earlier, 75 percent of the department managers and assistant department managers at Chern's have been promoted from the company's sales associate staff based on their supervisors' recommendations and structured

TABLE A-8	Format for Requesting Candidates' Assessment Scores			
Candidate	Name of Assessment 1	Name of Assessment 2	Name of Assessment 3	Name of Assessment 4
Alex Turing				
Ben Hirsch				
Chris Prender				
Julia McKnight				
Maria Cruz				
Parvathi Naryan				
Sharon Simmons				
Vera Levitt				

interviews. Unfortunately, Chern's recently analyzed its turnover data and found that a disproportionate number of good sales associates who would have been potentially strong candidates for department manager and assistant department manager positions have left the organization. The exit interviews with these people revealed that the firm's efforts to communicate its promotional opportunities and succession planning intentions to the high-potential sales associates have been insufficient. Many of the sales associates said that they were leaving because they had poor career planning visibility to the managerial positions they sought. The company currently does not tell its high-potential sales associates that they have been flagged for future promotion opportunities, believing that this would demoralize those not on the list.

Because the company's talent philosophy is to promote from within, it feels that it could improve its internal promotion practices. The company asks you to recommend ways that it can identify and develop sales associates who have the potential to become department managers.

Chapter 11: Choosing and Hiring Candidates

You will now continue your assessment and selection process for the two new hires. Develop a rational way of combining the scores on the assessment methods you recommended in your report for Chapter 9. How should Chern's choose which candidates to hire? Do you recommend a multiple hurdles, compensatory, or combined approach? What weights should each assessment score receive when calculating each candidate's overall score? Your job requirements matrix should help you make this judgment. Using your interview score results, candidate résumés, and scores on the assessment methods you included in your assessment plan, identify which two candidates should receive an offer and submit this information, along with the rationale for your choice, to your instructor. Also, explain what additional information you would like to have had before making a hiring decision.

Ann and Ryan believe that in addition to the promotional opportunities Chern's has to offer, the nonfinancial rewards of the job, including the extensive training and development new hires receive and the supportive work climate they experience, have not been sufficiently communicated to candidates. Not only does this explain why good sales associates are leaving the firm, it could also explain why its sales associate job offer acceptance rates have been trending slightly downward. Write a job offer letter to your top chosen candidate, who is currently considering two other job offers. You would very much like to hire your top choice, but she or he has to decide on the other offers within one week. Be sure to use any relevant information from the job rewards analysis you conducted in Chapter 4 as well as the information contained in the initial case description. You can also use the information about Chern's presented in this Appendix.

Your instructor will give you feedback on the outcomes for the two candidates you chose. Each candidate's profile was evaluated by staffing experts and given a job success score of 1 to 10. The scores correspond with the individual financial returns to the company presented in Table A-9 (which were based on a combination of sales performance and a new hire's fit with the company's culture).

TABLE A-9	The First Year Financial Value of Different Job Success Levels
Candidate's Job Success Score	**First Year Financial Return to Chern's**
10	$50,000
9	$40,000
8	$30,000
7	$20,000
6	$10,000
5	0
4	($10,000)
3	($20,000)
2	($30,000)
1	($40,000)

Calculate the ROI of your staffing investment in the new hires' first year based on the financial return realized by your chosen hires and the cost of your assessment system. In addition to the assessment costs you incurred, assume that recruitment and the initial applicant screening cost the company $20,000, and the 16 interviews cost the company an additional $14,800. You can either calculate a net return or an ROI ratio. To compute the net return you will sum the financial return realized by your two hires and subtract the total cost of the selection system. To compute the ROI ratio, you will sum the financial return and divide it by the total cost of the selection system. Interpret either or both of these values.

Chapter 12: Managing Workforce Flow

Chern's asks you to develop an onboarding and socialization strategy for its newly hired sales associates. Using Table 12–1 as a guide, write a report recommending appropriate onboarding and socialization strategies, and explain why you are making each recommendation.

Chern's recently completed a turnover analysis for sales associates at different performance levels and found that functional turnover begins at a performance level that currently covers the lowest-performing 15 percent of its sales associates. It also discovered that the top-performing 10 percent of its sales associates are responsible for 20 percent of the company's sales. Unfortunately, the turnover rate of its top performers is almost twice the turnover rate of its low performers. Ann and Ryan ask you to develop a retention plan for the company's top performers. Because they have developed good relationships with customers, sales associates who have been with the store more than 18 months tend to be the highest performers.

Recall that in their exit interviews, many sales associates who resigned say they are leaving Chern's because they believed they lacked promotional opportunities. Quite a few other top performers would have liked to continue working for Chern's but could not adequately balance their school and family demands because their work hours as sales associates were fixed. The third most common reason top performers gave for leaving Chern's was the lack of training and development opportunities. The company recently conducted an employee engagement survey, which reinforced the fact that employees found these three issues the most pressing. However, the company's sales associates also reported being satisfied with their pay and benefits and very satisfied with the company culture and the support they receive from their department managers.

Chern's has been growing steadily, but its conservative financial goals also create a need to be prepared for unexpected changes in its environment. Chern's believes that the economy is likely to stay strong, fueling its expansion strategy. However, the company wants to be prepared in the event that the economy cools and the demand for its products declines. Although Chern's tries to protect its employees, it recognizes that in the event of an economic downturn, it will need to downsize its sales force to control costs. Chern's asks you to recommend a downsizing strategy in the event that it needs to quickly reduce its number of sales associates by 15 percent.

Chapter 13: Staffing System Evaluation and Technology

Chern's wants a way to find out whether your recommendations helped it reach the following goals:

1. Attracting a more diverse set of qualified applicants
2. Complying with equal employment opportunity and affirmative action guidelines
3. Hiring sales associates who:
   a. Are better able to execute its business strategy
   b. Sell more merchandise
   c. Develop higher-quality relationships with the firm's customers
   d. Stay with the company longer
   e. Are more promotable to department manager positions
   f. Reinforce the company's customer service–oriented culture and make every employee and customer feel valued and cared for
4. Realizing a meaningful positive return on its investment in your recommendations

To help it track its staffing performance, Chern's asks you to create a digital staffing dashboard that contains the five most important staffing indicators to which its store managers need to pay attention in terms of the sales-associate hiring and evaluation process.

Chern's has always been willing to invest in technologies and tools that improve its performance. It asks you to recommend various staffing technologies it should consider adopting to enhance the performance and efficiency of its staffing system. Because the company is financially conservative and is willing to invest in compelling technologies but does not want to waste its money, be sure to thoroughly explain your recommendations and persuade the company to consider adopting them.

With your completed set of recommendations, write an executive summary that describes your overall recommendations for the entire staffing system at Chern's (covering Chapters 1 through 13). This summary should cover the entire project yet it should be concise enough (maybe one to three pages long) to go at the front of the report to highlight the most important recommendations you have made.

SUMMARY OF ASSIGNMENTS

The following is a compiled list of all assignments to be completed in the case study. The specific details are found in each chapter assignment.

1.
   a. Identify realistic long-term and short-term process and outcome goals.
   b. Ensure goals are related to business strategy and explain why each is important.
2.
   a. Develop a formal talent philosophy, HR strategy, and specific staffing strategy.
   b. Address each of the nine strategic staffing decisions.
   c. Explain each of your recommendations for the nine decisions.
3.
   a. Use stock, flow, and concentration statistics to determine if any evidence of discrimination exists.
   b. Recommend strategies to alleviate any discrimination you find.
4.
   a. Using O*Net and other sources of data, create a job requirements matrix.
   b. For each competency or KSAO, decide if it should be used to hire or plan to develop.
   c. Estimate how important each characteristic is relative to the others as well as the relative time spent on each job duty.
   d. Create a job rewards matrix.
5.
   a. Conduct a transition analysis.
   b. Summarize the internal labor market and highlight any trends or forecasted gaps.
   c. Based on the transition probability matrix, calculate how many new full-time sales associates should be hired externally.
   d. Calculate the number of applicants needed to acquire the number of new hires you forecasted.
   e. Use multiple sources of data to describe the current and future labor market for retail salespeople. If you forecast a gap, determine whether the gap is temporary or permanent. Make some recommendations to address the gap.
6.
   a. Rank order the recruiting sources based on their ability to maximize the company's staffing goals.
   b. Provide recommendations on how the Internet might be more effectively used to source and recruit applicants.
   c. Conduct a Boolean search to source two promising applicants using the Internet. Include the search engines and exact Boolean commands used. Provide information about your two leads in an appendix. Justify each recommendation.
   d. Determine how Chern's can improve the diversity of its applicant pool.
7.
   a. Develop an outline for a recruiting guide.
   b. Determine how to increase fairness perceptions of the recruiting process and reduce any negative spillover effects.
   c. Determine what the employer brand should be.
   d. Make recommendations for how the brand can be marketed and reinforced throughout the staffing process.
   e. Explain why your approach would be effective.
8.
   a. Read the next few parts then evaluate the eight candidates' résumés.
   b. Create a scoring key for the interviews.

9. **a.** Develop an assessment and selection plan that does not exceed the remaining $4,000 budget.
   b. Justify your proposed selection system.
   c. Submit your assessment plan to your instructor. Receive scores from your instructor.
   d. Use the scoring key you developed for the structured interviews to view and score the eight structured interviews. Also view and score the eight unstructured interviews.
10. **a.** Improve internal promotion practices.
    b. Recommend ways to identify and develop sales associates who have the potential to become department managers.
11. **a.** Develop a rational way of combining the scores on the assessment methods you recommended. Recommend either a multiple hurdles, compensatory, or combined approach and explain.
    b. Describe the weights for each assessment method when calculating the overall score.
    c. Using your interview score results, candidate résumés, and scores on the assessment methods you included in your assessment plan, identify which two candidates should receive an offer.
    d. Submit this information along with the rationale for your choices.
    e. Explain what additional information you would like to have had before making a hiring decision.
    f. Write a job offer letter to the top candidate of your two selections.
    g. Receive feedback from your instructor on the outcomes for the candidates you chose.
    h. Calculate the ROI or net return of your staffing investment for the two people you selected. Interpret the ROI or net return.
12. **a.** Write a report recommending appropriate onboarding and socialization strategies, and explain why you are making each recommendation.
    b. Develop a retention plan for the company's top performers.
    c. Identify a downsizing strategy to reduce the number of sales associates by 15 percent.
13. **a.** Create a digital staffing dashboard with the five most important indicators of the overall staffing process.
    b. Recommend various staffing technologies to enhance the performance and efficiency of the staffing system.
    c. Thoroughly explain your recommendations and persuade the company to consider adopting them.
    d. Write an executive summary of the entire set of recommendations and place it at the front of the report.

RÉSUMÉS

Julia McKnight

OBJECTIVE	To obtain a position that will offer the opportunity to enhance my clerical and customer service skills within a stable working environment. Looking for a long-tem career in sales.

SKILLS Excellent organizational skills. Strong leadership skills. Hard working. Deep capabilities in the use of technology and software including data entry, Web site programming, and the use of packages like Microsoft Office.

EDUCATION **Concordia High School**
Graduated with honors

WORK EXPERIENCE

Apex Financial
Office Manager
- Oversaw accounting with billing and end-of-the-month closing.
- Managed the local administrative team.
- Answered and directed incoming calls for senior managers.
- Met with customers to assess their needs and direct them to appropriate service agents
- Assisted in other areas in office as needed.

Port Halliback Pontiac
New/Used Sales Officer
- Interacted with customers to show new and used vehicles to meet their needs.
- Processed incoming orders, coordinated shipments, and handled customer-related issues.
- Responsible for managing and tracking inventory allocations for the entire dealer.

Macy's
Customer Service and Sales
- Showed merchandise to customers
- Engaged in financial transactions
- Continually improved sales and service

Alex Turing

Education:
Cornell University, Fiber Science and Apparel Design, College of Human Ecology

Objective: To secure a career in the retail sales industry

Strengths:
—Dedicated and self-motivated team player/builder.
—Loyal and hardworking
—Keen interest in a career in sales
—Able to connect with customers
—Strong skills in the use of technology
—Familiar with sales techniques and methods of addressing customer needs
—Highly ethical and honest

Weaknesses:
—Limited managerial experience
—Still learning about fashion trends

Experience:
The Fashion Place (3 years)   *Customer Sales*
• Communicated and worked as an involved team member
• Consistently increased average annual sales and sales per transaction
• Developed and maintained an extensive clientele by providing exceptional customer service and preserving customer relationships
• Delivered superior sales performance by knowing the product, understanding customer needs, and maintaining a positive attitude

The Suit Suite (2 years)   *Clothing Sales Associate*
• Reliably assisted customers by demonstrating suits of various styles from different designers and highlighting how to properly accessorize for different occasions
• Ensured customer satisfaction by placing and tracking customer orders, contacting customers as orders arrived, and responding to customer feedback as necessary

University Experience:
Cornell Design League
• Member of the executive board of a student-run organization focused on textiles, design, and fashion
• Regularly developed and implemented plans for fashion-related activities, membership drives, etc.

I am a very quick study, with an ability to easily grasp and put into application new ideas, concepts, methods, and technologies. I want a career in retail management and simply need the opportunity to demonstrate what I am capable of doing for your company.

Vera levitt

OBJECTIVE:
To secure a full-time career with an emphasis on retail sales and marketing for high-end clientele

---

EDUCATION:

Michigan State University (GPA: 3.1/4.0)
Bachelors in Arts, *Art History and Visual Culture*

EXPERIENCE:

NEIMAN MARCUS (2 years)
Retail Sales Associate
- Experienced and accomplished every duty and task that can be encountered in a retail environment
- Successfully acted as store manager on a temporary basis
- Worked with others on the sales team to create a shared motivation to succeed

OLD NAVY (1 year)
Retail Sales Associate
- Worked in a fast-paced retail environment
- Utilized fashion knowledge when working with guests to assist them in locating merchandise, identifying prices, checking inventory for additional products, and marketing promotional items
- Our store was ranked number one in sales in 9 of 12 months

OFFICE OF CAMPUS ACTIVITIES
New Student Orientation Co-coordinator
- Volunteer position
- Developed and administered training for orientation staff who delivered new student orientations on campus
- Led orientation advisors who worked directly with new students and assisted them when necessary
- Delivered presentations to large audiences of orientation staff

BIG BROTHERS/BIG SISTERS
Mentor
- Volunteer position
- Demonstrated poise, compassion, and trust to children in need of positive role models
- Provided mentoring and shared life experiences to encourage young people to set and work toward important life goals

PROFESSIONAL STRENGTHS:

- Flexible team player committed to persuading others to action
- Extensive experience in sales
- Dependable and hardworking
- Deeply interested in fashion
- Highly proficient in the use of software applications, such as Microsoft Office (Word, Excel, PowerPoint, FrontPage, Publisher)
- Knowledge of software programming in Visual Basic and the use of automated macros in Microsoft Office

Benjamin Hirsch

Education:
Milton High School

Objective: To become the leading sales representative for your company

Personal Attributes:
- Agreeable and friendly
- Never-fail mentality
- Superior work attitude
- Interested in fashion

Work Experiences:
Dollar Tree Stores, Inc. (2 years)
Assistant Manager
I was originally employed as a day cashier, but within a short period of time I was promoted to assistant store manager. Duties included opening and closing the store, making store deposits, supervising up to 10 employees, managing the cash vault, weekly stock deliveries and merchandising, balancing cash drawers, and running various store reports.

Wal-Mart, Inc. (2 years)
Area Manager
I was employed as an associate in the lay-away department during the busy holiday season. I was promoted shortly after the holidays to the front cash office. Duties included handling large amounts of cash, deposits, and various store reports. Eventually I was promoted to area manager.

As you can see, I have had four years of retail management experience.

CHRIS PRENDER

OBJECTIVE

Contribute to your company's efficiency, growth, and profitability by working in a challenging full-time position in the areas of marketing, sales, advertising, or management

PROFESSIONAL STRENGTHS

- Strong Sense of Customer-Centered Care in the Retail Environment
- Proven Leadership Skills
- Deep Knowledge of Fashion and Fashion Trends
- Able to Devise and Execute Marketing Plans and Strategies

EDUCATION

Bachelor of Arts in Anthropology
Lehigh University

RELATED EXPERIENCE

Coach, Assistant Manager (1 year to current)
- Successfully managed retail team and delivered exceptional results as an assistant to the store manager
- Trained three new associates in store policies and procedures who immediately performed at a high level

Ann Taylor, Sales Associate (1 year)
- Provided superior customer experiences for a quality clothing company
- Placed displays
- Managed and stocked inventory

The FUTURE Magazine, Marketing Intern (6 months)
- Evaluated magazine content
- Conducted market research
- Maintained business reply database
- Assembled media kits

Soles, Merchandising Customer Assistant (1 year)
- Provided quality customer experiences for a luxury brand shoe company
- Fostered deep customer networks by developing trust, building relationships, and enhancing the customer shopping experience
- Ensured merchandise was presented in a visually appealing manner
- Assisted in catalog sales and marketing
- Assisted in work scheduling and planning during high workload periods (e.g., winter holidays)

University Bookstore, Purchasing Intern (6 months)
- Assisted the book purchasers with purchasing decisions, merchandise orders, and faculty contact
- Received shipments and completed merchandise purchase orders
- Maintained visual quality through effective store organization and appropriate merchandise displays

Telemarket Associates, Marketing Sales Representative Intern (1 year)
- Used strong interpersonal communication ability to effectively market advertising opportunities to business owners
- Developed sales experience including scheduling, maintaining a positive mental attitude, and achieving goals

Sports Central, Sales Associate (1 year)
- Promoted apparel for local sports teams by distributing memorabilia throughout the community
- Played music for sport exhibitions
- Conducted half-time promotions at local sports events

ACADEMIC PROJECTS

- Developed an Internet marketing plan for Pizza Hut
- Marketing team consultant for a retail golf franchise
- Provided marketing research to determine the demand for personal concierge services in New York City
- Formulated a team integrated marketing plan for a solar-powered vacuum cleaner

OTHER ACTIVITIES

- Volunteer for Habitat for Humanity
- Volunteer coordinator for low-income child care providers

Sharon Simmons

Summary

I am a dedicated professional sales executive with five years of successful experience in key areas of sales including development of customer relationships, growth of clientele, management of business, and maintenance of inventory control.

- Superb communication and interpersonal skills
- Experienced at communicating with people of various backgrounds
- Strong sense of entrepreneurship
- Superior leadership strengths
- Demonstrated ability to develop customer relationships
- Proven interest and success in a career involving sales and marketing

Objective

To find a customer/client care position in which I can apply my strengths to enhance the customer experience. I would like long-term growth opportunities that will improve your business and enhance my career potential.

Work Experience

The Furniture Place (2 years)   *Assistant Manager*
- Assisted in the management of a 1,200 sq. foot store with daily sales averaging $4,100.00
- Encouraged seven employees to exceed sales goals through effective communication and motivation techniques
- Ranked first out of all employees in region in customer service and product knowledge as judged by a secret shopper evaluation
- Utilized loss prevention techniques to reduce shrinkage and control inventory
- Executed company merchandise directives including design and implementation of floor sets and window displays
- Launched new customer loyalty program
- Completed opening/closing procedures, which included counting cash and bank deposit
- Developed customer relationships by meeting their needs and resolving customer service issues

Victoria's Secret (2 years)   *Sales Specialist*
- Applied the "Engage, Show, Provide" sales strategy to meet sales goals
- Completed regular merchandise directives following the company brand guide
- Promoted Victoria's Secret "Angel Rewards" credit card program and benefits
- Communicated with customers to effectively inform them about products and services
- Consistently one of the top-rated specialists in sales productivity for the store

The GAP Inc. (1 year)   *Sales Associate*
- Assisted customers in product search and addressed customer needs on an ongoing basis
- Engaged in customer transactions
- Assisted in inventory management
- Implemented window displays
- Cleaned, tagged, and organized clothes
- Performed computer work and operated cash register
- Provided a fun shopping experience

Education

New York University, *B.A. Communications*
GPA 3.85 of 4.00

Personal Interests

Yoga   Jazz   Design   Art

MARIA CRUZ

OBJECTIVE	To obtain a career in retail management and apply my background in the field of dramatic arts and fashion

EDUCATION

Vista Lane High School
The New School, NYC: AAS in Fashion Marketing from the Parsons School of Design

ACHIEVEMENTS

Japanese Mastery Levels III and IV	High Honor Roll
Magna Cum Laude	National Honors Society

INTERNSHIP

Assistant Director, Summer Acting Series, Mount Korko Theatre
- Developed series of dramatic plays for summer theatre
- Assisted in set design and construction
- Helped with role development and coached actors
- Created and applied makeup design
- Identified appropriate staging and location

WORK EXPERIENCE

Retail Sales Associate, *Brooks Brothers*
(2 years sales associate)
- Hired as a sales associate to advance new business development initiatives and oversee merchandising efforts for this specialty clothing store.
- Inventory, merchandising, and customer service
- Stocked shelves and organized the merchandise in the various departments
- Worked with manager to maintain superior levels of guest interaction/satisfaction and ensure smooth overall operations
- Consistently achieved and exceeded monthly sales goals and objectives

Retail Sales Associate, *Target Corporation*   (1 year)
- Restocked shelves and organized the merchandise in the various departments
- Educated customers on merchandise and assisted customers with purchasing decisions

Deli Clerk, *Heroes and Legends*   (1 year)
- Prepared sandwiches, salads, and desserts
- Delivered food to tables
- Bussed, cleaned, and set tables

COMMUNITY SERVICE

Help for Homeless Animals
Tended and cared for animals, cleaned cages

ACTIVITIES

Running and biking	Cooking

PERSONAL PROFILE

A hardworking, honest, motivated person who is interested in applying her sense of art and drama to retail sales. A globally aware person and quick learner who is eager to succeed and able to develop an emotional connection with customers.

REFERENCES

Available upon request.

Parvathi Naryan

Objective   To obtain a stable position in retail sales to further advance my
                   knowledge and skills in the area of retail management

Education   Syracuse University
                   School of Visual and Performing Arts
                   Retail Management major, Management Studies minor
                   GPA: 3.4

Experience

                   Sales Associate
Rothmans   (2 years)
                   • Showed merchandise, consulted with customers and facilitated sales
                     including identifying client needs, making product recommendations,
                     and assisting with selections.
                   • Did custom fittings and advised customers in an effort to ensure their
                     specific needs were being met.
                   • Personal shopper for a large number of repeat customers; produced
                     excellent referrals for the business.
                   • Managed all aspects of client relations and built relationships to
                     provide total quality customer service

                   Fashion Representative
Delia's   (1 year)
                   • Assisted in the opening and set up of new store
                   • Created several visual merchandise displays
                   • Used strategic selling techniques to promote the sale of products

Activities *Treasurer*
Syracuse University Retail Association
Managed financial matters, such as banking, collecting membership dues, and
organizing spreadsheets

GLOSSARY

Ability A more stable and enduring capability to perform a variety of tasks than a skill allows.

Action plan Strategy to proactively address an anticipated surplus or shortage of employees.

Active job seekers People who need a job and are actively looking for information about job openings.

Adverse (disparate) impact When an action has a disproportionate effect on a protected group, regardless of the employer's intent.

Affirmative action The proactive effort to eliminate discrimination and its effects, and to ensure nondiscriminatory results in employment practices in the future.

Alternate or parallel form reliability Indicates how consistent scores are likely to be if a person completes two or more forms of the same measure

Applicant tracking system Software that allows a database with applicant information and job information to be maintained so that matches between the two are easier to make.

Assessment plan Describes which assessment method(s) will be used to assess each of the important characteristics on which applicants will be evaluated, in what sequence the assessments will take place, and what weight each assessment will receive in determining an overall score for that characteristic based on the importance of each characteristic to job performance.

Attrition The normal reduction of a firm's workforce due to the retirement, death, or resignation of employees.

At-will employment An employment relationship in which either party can terminate the employment relationship at any time for just cause, no cause, or any cause that is not illegal with no liability as long as there is no contract for a definite term of employment.

Avoidable turnover Turnover an employer could have prevented.

Background check An employee screening method that assesses factors such as a person's personal and credit information, degrees held, character, lifestyle, criminal history, and general reputation.

Balanced scorecard A tool used to monitor, assess, and manage the performance of employees as well as align their interests with a firm's key business objectives by assigning them both financial and nonfinancial goals.

Balanced staffing scorecard Contains objectives, targets, and initiatives for each activity that adds value to the staffing process.

Banding Assigning the same score to applicants who score in a range on the assessment.

Base rate The percent of employees who are defined as currently successful performers.

Behavioral interviews Interviews that use information about what the applicants have done in the past to predict their future behaviors.

Biodata Information about candidates' interests, work experiences, training, and education.

Bona fide occupational qualification (BFOQ) A characteristic that is essential to the successful performance of a relevant employment function.

Boolean searches An Internet search technique that allows a search to be narrowed by using special terms before the key words.

Brand A symbolic picture of all the information connected to a company or its products.

Business necessity An important business objective of the employer.

Business process outsourcing Relocating an entire business function to an independent service provider.

Business strategy How a company will compete in its marketplace.

Career planning A continuous process of career-oriented self-assessment and goal setting.

Career sites Pages on an organization's Web site devoted to jobs and careers within the company.

Centralized staffing A situation in which all of an organization's staffing activities are channeled through one unit.

Central tendency The midpoint, or center, of the data.

Clinical assessments Assessments that rely on trained psychologists to subjectively analyze a candidate's attributes, values, and styles in the context of a particular job.

Cognitive ability tests Tests that assess a person's general mental abilities, including their verbal and mathematical reasoning, logic, and perceptual abilities.

Collective socialization A socialization process whereby newcomers go through a common set of experiences as a group.

Combined approach A combination of centralized and decentralized staffing.

Compensatory approach An approach whereby high scores on some assessments can compensate for low scores on other assessments.

Competencies More broadly defined components of a successful worker's repertoire of behavior needed to do a job well.

Competency modeling A job analysis method that identifies the necessary worker competencies for high performance.

Competitive job offer A job offer in which the total rewards package offered is competitive with the market average.

Complementary fit When a person adds something that is missing in the organization or work group by being different from the others.

Concentration statistics Statistics that compare the percentages of men, women, or minorities in various job categories to see if men, women, or minorities are concentrated in certain workforce categories.

Construct-related validation The process of demonstrating that a measure assesses the construct, or characteristic, it claims to measure.

Contamination error Occurs when other factors unrelated to whatever is being assessed affect the observed scores.

Content-related validation The process of demonstrating that the content of a measure assesses important job-related behaviors.

Contest socialization A socialization process whereby each stage is a "contest," and each new hire earns a track record, or "batting average," after each stage.

Contingent assessment methods Methods whereby a job offer is made contingent upon a candidate passing the assessment.

Contingent work Any job in which an individual does not have a contract for long-term employment.

Core workforce Longer-term, regular employees.

Correlation The strength of a linear relationship between two variables.

Correlation coefficient A single number that ranges from −1 to +1; it reflects the direction (positive or negative) and magnitude (the strength) of the relationship between two variables.

Cost-leadership strategy Be the lowest cost producer for a particular level of product quality.

Criterion data Information about important outcomes of the staffing process.

Criterion-referenced measures Measures in which the scores have meaning in and of themselves.

Criterion-related validation The process of demonstrating that there is a statistical relationship between scores from a measure (the predictor) and the criterion (the outcome).

Critical incidents technique A job analysis method that identifies extremely effective and ineffective behaviors by documenting critical incidents that have occurred on the job.

Culture Norms, values, behavior patterns, rituals, language, and traditions that provide a framework that helps employees interpret and understand their everyday work experiences.

Customer intimacy Delivering unique and customizable products or services that better meet customers' needs and increase customer loyalty.

Data The numerical outcomes of measurement.

Data analytics The process of using data and analytical systems to arrive at optimal decisions, including statistical analyses of data.

Decentralized staffing The different business units of a company each house their own staffing functions.

Deficiency error Occurs when you fail to measure important aspects of the attribute you would like to measure.

Deployment Assigning talent to appropriate jobs and roles in the organization.

Desirable criteria Job candidate criteria that may enhance the new hire's job success, but that are not essential to adequate job performance.

Differentiation strategy Developing a product or service that has unique characteristics valued by customers.

Digital staffing dashboards Interactive computer displays that indicate how a staffing function is meeting its goals

Direct costs Costs incurred as a direct result of a staffing activity.

Disjunctive socialization A socialization process whereby newcomers are left alone to develop their own interpretations of the organization and situations they observe.

Disparate treatment Intentional discrimination based on a protected characteristic.

Distributive fairness The perceived fairness of the hiring or promotion outcome.

Divestiture socialization Tries to deny and strip away certain personal characteristics.

Downsizing The process of permanently reducing the number of a firm's employees so as to improve the efficiency or effectiveness of the firm.

Dysfunctional turnover Turnover due to the departure of effective performers.

Employee Someone hired by another person or business for a wage or fixed payment in exchange for personal services, and who does not provide the services as part of an independent business.

Employee development The training of employees to extend their capabilities and prepare them to assume other jobs and roles in the firm.

Employee engagement The degree to which employees are engaged in their work and how willing they are to put in extra effort.

Employee profiling A process that helps a firm identify what its successful current employees like to do and how people like them can be recruited.

Employee referrals A practice by which current employees identify and refer promising recruits.

Employee value proposition The balance between the intrinsic and extrinsic rewards an employee receives by working for a particular employer in return for the employee's job performance.

Employer brand Reflects what a company offers as an employer and helps manage internal and external perceptions of what it is like to work there.

Equal employment opportunity (EEO) Employment practices are designed and used in a "facially neutral" manner.

Essential criteria Job candidate characteristics that are critical to the adequate performance of a new hire.

Essential functions The fundamental duties or tasks of a position.

Evaluative assessment methods Methods that evaluate the pool of job candidates to determine who will be hired.

Exit interviews Interviews in which separated employees are asked about why they are leaving the firm. The goal is to acquire information that can be used to improve the working conditions of the firm's current employees.

Explicit employment contract A specific written or verbal employment contract.

External recruiting sources Target people outside the firm.

External talent focus A preference for filling jobs with new employees hired from outside the organization.

Extrinsic rewards Rewards that have monetary value.

Face validity A subjective assessment of how well items seem to be related to the requirements of the job.

Fixed socialization A socialization process whereby new hires are informed in advance when their probationary status will end.

Flexible workers Temporary, leased, part-time, or contract workers, or independent contractors employed for shorter periods by firms as needed.

Flextime An arrangement that allows employees to work hours other than a typical eight-hour shift.

Flip searching Finding people who link to a specific Internet site.

Flow statistics Statistics that compare the percentage of applicants hired from different subgroups to determine if they are significantly different from each other.

Formal socialization A structured socialization process conducted outside of the work setting using specifically designed activities and materials.

Fraudulent recruitment Misrepresenting the job or organization to a recruit.

Functional turnover Turnover that results in the departure of poor performers.

Future-oriented job analysis A technique for analyzing new jobs or how jobs will look in the future.

Geographic targeting Sourcing recruits based on where they live.

Global sourcing Sourcing employees on a global basis.

Graphology Any practice that involves determining personality traits or abilities from a person's handwriting.

Growth strategy   A strategy to expand the company either organically or via acquisitions.

High job offer   A job offer in which the total rewards package is above the market average.

Hiring freeze   A policy whereby no new employees are hired for a certain period of time.

Hiring yields   The percent of applicants ultimately hired.

Human capital advantage   Acquiring a stock of quality talent that creates a competitive advantage.

Human process advantage   Superior work processes that create a competitive advantage.

Human resources information system (HRIS)   A system of software and supporting computer hardware specifically designed to store and process all HR information and keep track of all employees and information about them.

Human resource strategy   the linkage of the entire human resource function with the company's business strategy.

Image   A general impression based on both feelings and facts.

Implicit employment contract   An understanding that is not part of a written or verbal contract.

Independent contractor   Performs services wherein the employer controls or directs only the result of the work.

Indirect costs   Costs not directly attributable to staffing activities (e.g., lost business opportunities, lower morale).

Individual socialization   A socialization process whereby newcomers are socialized individually, as in an apprenticeship.

Informal socialization   An unstructured, on-the-job socialization process conducted by a new hire's coworkers.

In-house sourcers   Employees who rely on their own contacts and research and the organization's database of potential applicants to source potential recruits.

Integrity tests   Tests that measure people's trustworthiness, honesty, moral character, and reliability.

Interactional fairness   People's perceptions of the interpersonal treatment and amount of information they received during the hiring process.

Internal assessment   The evaluation of a firm's current employees for training, reassignment, promotion, or dismissal purposes.

Internal consistency reliability   Indicates the extent to which items on a given measure assess the same construct.

Internal job posting systems   Systems that publicize a firm's open jobs to the company's employees.

Internal recruiting sources   Locate people who currently work for the company who would be good recruits for other positions.

Internal talent focus   A preference for developing employees and promoting from within to fill job openings.

Internet data mining   Searching the Internet to locate passive job seekers with the characteristics and qualifications needed for a position.

Internet job boards   Internet sites that allow employers to post jobs and job seekers to post résumés and use a search engine to find one another.

Inter-rater reliability   Indicates how consistent scores are likely to be if the responses are scored by two or more raters using the same item, scale, or instrument.

Interval measurement   A measurement in which the distance between scores on an attribute has meaning.

Intrinsic rewards   Nonmonetary rewards derived from the work itself and from the organization's culture.

Investiture socialization   A socialization process that reaffirms newcomers' self-confidence and reflects the fact that the organization's senior members value the knowledge and personal characteristics of the newcomers.

Involuntary turnover   Turnover due to the organization asking an employee to leave.

Job   A formal group or cluster of tasks.

Job analysis   The systematic process of identifying and describing the important aspects of a job and the characteristics a worker needs to do it well.

Job applications   forms that require applicants to provide written information about their skills and education, job experiences, and other job relevant information.

Job description   A written description of the duties and responsibilities associated with a job.

Job duty   A set of related tasks that are repeated on the job.

Job elements method   A job analysis method that uses expert brainstorming sessions to identify the characteristics successful workers currently have.

Job fairs   Sourcing and recruiting events at which multiple employers and recruits meet with each other to discuss employment opportunities.

Job family   A grouping of jobs that either call for similar worker characteristics or contain parallel work tasks.

Job knowledge tests   Tests that measure candidates' knowledge (often technical) required by a job.

Job-oriented staffing   Hiring to fill a specific job opening.

Job rewards analysis   A job analysis technique that identifies the intrinsic and extrinsic rewards of a job.

Job sharing   An arrangement whereby two people work together to fill one job.

Job simulations   Simulations that measure people's job skills by having them perform tasks similar to those performed on the job.

Job task   An observable unit of work with a beginning and an end.

Judgmental forecasting   Relying on the experience and insights of people in the organization to predict a firm's future employment needs.

Key performance indicators (KPIs)   Measurable factors critical to the firm's success and long- and short-term goals.

Knowledge   An organized body of factual or procedural information that can be applied to a task.

Labor unions   Legally represent workers, organizing employees and negotiating the terms and conditions of union members' employment.

Lagging indicator   A factor that becomes known only after a staffing decision has been made.

Layoff   Temporary end to employment.

Leadership development programs   A specific type of employee development that develops the leadership skills of employees seen as having leadership potential.

Leading indicator   A factor that precedes or predicts a staffing outcome.

Leased workers   Employees of a company (also called a professional employer organization) who take on the operation of certain functions, or staff an entire location on a contractual basis for a client company.

Low job offer   A job offer that consists of a below-market rewards package.

Maximum job offer   The company's best and final offer.

Mean   A measure of central tendency reflecting the average score.

Measurement   The process of assigning numbers according to some rule or convention to aspects of people, jobs, job success, or aspects of the staffing system.

Median   The middle score, or the point below which 50 percent of the scores fall.

Mentoring   A dynamic, reciprocal relationship between a more-experienced employee (mentor) and a more junior employee (protégé) aimed at promoting the career development of both.

Mixed motive   When an employer is accused of having both a legitimate and an illegitimate reason for making an employment decision.

Mobility barriers   Factors that make it harder for employees to leave an organization.

Mobility policies   Policies that dictate how people can move between jobs within an organization.

Mode   The most commonly observed score.

Multiple hurdles approach   A scoring approach whereby candidates must receive a passing score on an assessment before being allowed to continue on in the selection process.

Multiple regression   A statistical technique that predicts an outcome using one or more predictor variables; it identifies the ideal weights to assign each predictor so as to maximize the validity of a set of predictors; the analysis is based on each predictor's correlation with the outcome and degree to which the predictors are themselves intercorrelated.

Multisource assessments   Performance reviews that involve an employee's supervisor as well as other people familiar with the employee's job performance.

Negligent hiring   When an employer hires an applicant it knows or should have known that could harm a third party.

Negligent referral   Misrepresenting or failing to disclose complete and accurate information about a former employee.

Networking   The process of leveraging your personal connections to generate applicants.

Nine box matrix   A combined assessment of an employee's performance and potential.

Nominal measurement   A measurement in which numbers are assigned to discrete labels or categories.

Normal curve   A curve representing the bell-shaped symmetrical distribution of some factor.

Normal distribution   The distribution of scores under the normal curve.

Norm-referenced measures   Measures in which the scores have meaning only when compared to the scores of others.

Objectivity   The amount of judgment or bias involved in scoring an assessment measure.

Observation   Watching people working in similar jobs for other companies to evaluate their potential fit with your organization.

Offer letter   A written letter describing in clear and precise terms exactly what the compensation structure and terms of an employment contract will be.

Offshore labor   Employees living and working in other, usually lower-cost, countries.

Operational excellence   Maximizing the efficiency of the manufacturing or product development process to minimize costs.

Optimal turnover   The turnover level that produces the highest long-term levels of productivity and business improvement.

"Other" characteristics   Characteristics that do not fall into the knowledge, skill, or ability categories; they include a person's values, interests, integrity, work style, and other personality traits.

Ordinal measurement   A measurement in which attributes are ranked by assigning numbers in ascending or descending order.

Orientation   The process of completing new hires' employment-related paperwork and familiarizing them with their jobs, coworkers, work spaces, work tools, and the company's policies and benefits.

Outlier   A score that is much higher or lower than most of the scores in a distribution.

Passive job seekers   People who are currently employed and are not actively seeking another job but could be tempted by the right opportunity.

Percentile score   A raw score that has been converted into an expression of the percentage of people who score at or below that score.

Person-group fit   The match between an individual and his or her work group, including the supervisor.

Person-job fit   The fit between a person's abilities and the demands of the job and the fit between a person's desires and motivations and the attributes and rewards of a job.

Person-organization fit   Fit between an individual's values, beliefs, attitudes, and personality and the values, norms, and culture of the organization.

Person specification   Summarizes the characteristics of someone able to perform the job well.

Person-vocation fit   The fit between a person's interests, abilities, values, and personality and his or her chosen occupation, regardless of the person's employer.

Physical ability tests   Tests that assess a person's physical abilities including strength, flexibility, endurance, and coordination.

Polygraph test   Measures and records physiological factors thought to be indicators of anxiety, including a candidates' blood pressure, respiration, pulse, and skin conductivity while the person answers a series of questions.

Position analysis questionnaire (PAQ)   A copyrighted, standardized job analysis questionnaire that can be used for just about any job.

Practical significance   An observed relationship that is large enough to be of value in a practical sense.

Predictive data   Information about measures used to make projections about outcomes.

Predictor variable   A variable used to predict the value of an outcome.

Proactive staffing   Done before situations or issues arise.

Procedural fairness   People's beliefs that the policies and procedures that resulted in the hiring or promotion decision were fair.

Product innovation   Developing new products or services.

Protected class   A group of people who share a particular characteristic that is protected by federal and/or state employment discrimination laws.

Psychomotor tests   Tests that assess the capacity of a person to manipulate and control objects.

Race norming   Adjusting scores on a standardized test by using separate curves for different racial groups.

Raiding competitors   The practice of hiring top talent away from competitors.

Random error   Error that is not due to any consistent cause.

Random socialization   Socialization steps are ambiguous or changing.

Range   The difference between the highest and lowest observed score.

Ratio measurement   A measurement in which the distance between scores has meaning; it includes a true and meaningful zero point.

Rational weighting   A weighting method whereby experts assign a different subjective weight to each assessment score.

Raw scores   The unadjusted scores on a measure.

Reactive staffing   Done in response to situations or issues.

Realistic job previews (RJPs)   Provide both positive and potentially negative information to job candidates.

Reasonable accommodation   Reasonable steps to accommodate a disability that do not cause the employer undue hardship.

Recruiting   All organizational practices and decisions that affect either the number or types of individuals willing to apply for and accept job offers.

Recruiting guide   A formal document that details the process to be followed when a firm recruits for an open position.

Recruiting yield analysis   Tracks the recruiting sources that produced each applicant and evaluates each recruiting source on the basis of relevant criteria including the number and proportion of qualified applicants coming from each source and their demographic characteristics.

Reliability   How dependably, or consistently, a measure assesses a particular characteristic.

Reneging   Backing out of a contract after it is accepted.

Replacement chart   Visually shows each of the possible successors for a job and summarizes their present performance, promotion readiness, and development needs.

Replacement planning   The process of creating backup candidates for specific senior management positions.

Resource-based view of the firm   Proposes that a company's resources and competencies can produce a sustained competitive advantage by creating value for customers by lowering costs, providing something of unique value, or some combination of the two.

Restrictive covenant   A clause in a contract that requires one party to do, or refrain from doing, certain things.

Résumé databases   Searchable collections of prescreened résumés submitted to the company.

Reviewer profile   A profile of the skills, characteristics, and backgrounds of the most effective recruiters for different positions.

Role   An expected pattern or set of behaviors.

Sampling error   The variability of sample correlations due to chance.

Scatter plot   Graphical illustration of the relationship between two variables.

Screening assessment methods   Methods that narrow a pool of job applicants down to a smaller group of job candidates.

Search firms   Independent companies that specialize in the recruitment and placement of particular types of talent.

Selection   Assessing job candidates and deciding whom to hire.

Selection errors   Not hiring someone who would have been successful at the job or hiring someone who is not successful at the job.

Selection ratio   The number of people hired divided by the number of applicants.

Semi-passive job seekers   People who are interested in a new position but only occasionally look actively for one.

Sensory tests   Assess visual, auditory, and speech perception.

Sequential socialization   A socialization process that follows a specific sequence of steps.

Serial socialization   A socialization process whereby supportive organizational members serve as role models and mentors for new hires.

Situational interviews   Asking people how they might react to hypothetical situations.

Situational judgment tests   Measures of noncognitive skills; short scenarios are presented verbally, in writing, or in videos, and candidates are asked what they believe is the most effective response, or to choose the best response from a list of alternatives.

Six sigma   A data-driven quality initiative that uses statistics to measure and improve business processes and their outcomes to near perfection.

Skill   The capability to perform tasks accurately and with ease; skills often refer to psychomotor activities.

Skills inventory   A company-maintained list outlining which employees have certain skills, competencies, and other relevant job characteristics.

Socialization   A long-term process of planned and unplanned, formal and informal activities and experiences through which an individual acquires the attitudes, behaviors, and knowledge needed to successfully participate as an organizational member and learns the firm's culture.

Sourcing   Locating qualified individuals and labor markets from which to recruit.

Sourcing plan   Prioritizes which recruiting sources should be used to staff a given position to best meet staffing goals.

Specialization strategy   Focusing on a narrow market segment or niche and pursuing either a differentiation or cost-leadership strategy within that market segment.

Spillover effects   The indirect or unintended consequences of an action.

Staffing effectiveness   How well the staffing process meets the needs of a firm's stakeholders and contributes to the organization's strategy execution and performance.

Staffing efficiency   The total cost associated with the compensation of the newly hired employees.

Staffing evaluation   The analysis of a staffing system to assess its performance and effectiveness.

Staffing quotas   Establish specific requirements that certain numbers of people from disadvantaged groups be hired.

Staffing ratio   A mathematical way of calculating the number of employees a firm needs to produce certain levels of output.

Staffing strategy   The constellation of priorities, policies, and behaviors used to manage the flow of talent into, through, and out of an organization over time.

Staffing yields   The proportion of applicants moving from one stage of the hiring process to the next.

Standard deviation   The positive square root of the variance; it is conceptually similar to the average distance from the mean of a set of scores.

Standard error of measurement (SEM)   The margin of error that you should expect in an individual score because of the imperfect reliability of the measure.

Standardization   The consistent administration and use of a measure.

Standard scores   Converted raw scores that indicate where a person's score lies in comparison to a referent group.

Statistical significance   The degree to which the observed relationship is not likely due to sampling error.

Statistical weighting   A weighting method using a statistical technique, such as multiple regression, to assign a different weight to each assessment score.

Stereotype threat   Awareness of subgroup differences on standardized tests creates frustration among minority test takers and ultimately lower test scores.

Stock statistics   Compare the percentage of men, women, or minorities employed in a job category with their availability in the relevant population of qualified people interested in the position.

Strategic staffing   The process of staffing an organization in future-oriented, goal-directed ways that support the business strategy of the organization and enhance its effectiveness.

Strategy   A long-term plan of action to achieve a particular goal.

Structured interview technique   A job analysis method in which subject matter experts provide information about the job verbally in structured face-to-face interviews.

Structured interviews   Interviews in which candidates are asked a series of standardized, job-related questions with predetermined scores for different answers.

Structured questionnaire method   A job analysis method that involves using a list of preplanned questions designed to analyze a job.

Subject matter expert   A person who exhibits expertise in a job.

Succession management   The ongoing process of recruiting, evaluating, developing, and preparing employees to assume other positions in the firm in the future.

Succession management plans   Written policies that guide the succession management process.

Supplementary fit   When a person has characteristics that are similar to those that already exist in the organization.

Systematic errors   Error that occurs because of consistent and predictable factors.

Talent inventories   A detailed record or database that summarizes each employee's skills, competencies, and qualifications.

Talent management   Attracting, developing, retaining, and utilizing people with the required skills and aptitudes to meet current and future business needs.

Talent-oriented staffing   Recruiting and even hiring without a specific job opening.

Talent philosophy   A system of beliefs about how a firm's employees should be treated.

Task inventory approach   A job analysis method in which job experts generate a list of 50 to 200 tasks grouped into categories reflecting the job's major functions; the functions are then evaluated on dimensions relevant for selection purposes.

Telecommuting   An arrangement whereby employees work from a location other than their employer's facilities, such as their homes.

Temporary workers   Nonpermanent workers who can be supplied by staffing agencies or directly hired by the company.

Test-retest reliability   Reflects the repeatability of scores over time and the stability of the underlying construct being measured.

Total rewards   A combination of the intrinsic and extrinsic rewards related to a particular job.

Tournament socialization   A socialization process whereby each stage is an "elimination tournament" and a new hire is out of the organization if he or she fails.

Trade fairs   Events that gather people from a particular industry to learn about current topics and products in their field.

Transition analysis   A quantitative technique used to analyze internal labor markets and forecast internal labor supply.

Trend analysis   Using past employment patterns to predict future needs.

Unavoidable turnover   Turnover an employer could not have prevented.

Unit weighting   Giving multiple assessments equal weight when computing a candidate's overall score.

Unlawful or discriminatory employment practices   Employment practices that unfairly discriminate against people with characteristics protected by law.

Unstructured interview   Questions that vary from candidate to candidate and that differ across interviewers.

Validation   The cumulative and ongoing process of establishing the job relatedness of a measure.

Validity   How well a measure assesses a given construct and the degree to which you can make specific conclusions or predictions based on observed scores.

Validity coefficient   A number between 0 and +1 that indicates the magnitude of the relationship between a predictor (such as test scores) and the criterion (such as a measure of actual job success.

Validity generalization   The degree to which evidence of validity obtained in one situation can be generalized to another situation without further study.

Variability   A measure that describes the "spread" of the data around the midpoint.

Variable socialization   A socialization process whereby employees receive few clues as to when to expect their probationary periods to end, and the timeline isn't necessarily consistent across employees.

Variance   A mathematical measure of the spread based on squared deviations of scores from the mean.

Voluntary turnover   Turnover due to an employee's choice.

Walk-ins   People who apply directly with companies.

Web crawlers   Web sites that continually search the Web for information about people with desirable talents and sell access to their database of potential recruits.

Weighted application blank   A job application on which different information receives different weights.

Whole-person approach   The practice of using a variety of measures and procedures to more fully assess people.

Workforce planning   The process of predicting an organization's future employment needs and the availability of current employees and external hires to meet those employment needs and execute the organization's business strategy.

Workforce redeployment   Moving employees to other parts of the company or to other jobs.

Workload-driven forecasting   Forecasting based on historical data on the average number of hires typically made per recruiter or the average number of recruits processed per recruiter over a given period.

Work samples   Require a candidate to perform observable work tasks or job-related behaviors to predict future job success.

X-raying   Searching for pages that are all on the same host site.

NAME INDEX

Note: The locators followed by 'n' refers to note numbers cited in the text.

Aaker, J. L., 183n
Adams, G. A., 185n
Adelson, A., 154n
Adler, L., 158n
Adnett, N., 61n
Agnvall, E., 330n
Agrawal, V., 117n
Aitchinson, C., 284n
Alderfer, C. P., 172n
Alexander, A., 300n
Allaire, J. J., 237
Alvarez, P. H., 183n
Anders, G., 237n
Anderson, N., 327n
Andre, C., 62n
Andrews, D. R., 137n
Appel, R. N., 301n
Arend, M., 129n, 326n
Arnold, D. W., 252n
Arthur, M. B., 3n
Arvey, R. D., 170n, 238n
Asch, B. J., 181n
Ashford, S. J., 235n
Ash, R. A., 105n
Atwater, L., 280n
Austin, J., 173n
Autor, D., 333n
Avis, J. M., 206n
Axelrod, B., 115n

Babcock, P., 115n, 343n
Baird, L.13n, 33n
Baker, D., 28n
Bakke, Allan, 63n
Ballmer, Steve, 22
Barada, P. W., 72n
Barbee, A. P., 251n
Barber, A. E., 12n, 158n, 160n, 161n, 162n, 169n, 171n, 173n, 181n, 185n, 253n
Bar-Hillel, M., 256n
Barkley, M., 355n
Barney, J., 23, 23n, 24n
Barrett, G. V., 300n
Barrick, M. R., 99n, 246n, 250n, 255n
Barrow, S., 182n
Bartram, D., 241n
Battista, M., 105n
Bauer, T. N., 313n, 314n, 323n
Beatty, R. W., 26n, 279n
Bechet, T. P., 117n, 274n
Becker, B. E., 13n, 42n, 158n, 356n
Bedeian, A. G., 8n
Beeson, J., 284n
Bell, Charlie, 284
Bellenger, D. N., 326n
Belt, J. A., 185n
Ben-Abba, E., 256n
Bennett, S., 305n, 307n
Bennett-Alexander, D. D., 305n
Ben-Shakar, G., 256n
Berger, C. J., 328n
Bergeron, C., 274n
Bergmann, T. J., 170n, 337n
Berkshire, J. C., 152n
Bernardin, H. J., 279n
Bessey, Kerry, 22
Bevier, C. A., 249n
Bianchi, A., 256n

Biddle, B. J., 85n
Bies, R. J., 313n
Bifulco, L., 306n
Blum, Y., 256n
Bobko, P.249n, 261n, 241n, 299n
Bogumil, W. A. Jr., 153n
Bolles, R. N., 288n
Bond, G., 118n
Bono, J. E., 250n
Borman, W. C., 279n
Boroson, W., 338n
Bortz, J., 337n
Bossidy, Larry, 33
Boudreau, J. W., 3n, 40n, 178n, 328n, 333n
Boxall, P., 42n
Boyens, J., 329n
Boyle, M., 152n, 274n
Brauer, D., 117n
Braverman, E. P., 241n
Bray, I. M., 72n
Breaugh, J. A., 8n, 11n, 62n, 157n, 172n, 186n
Brennan, Jack, 326
Brett, J. M., 162n
Bretz, R. D. Jr., 8n, 170n, 185n, 212n
Brockbank, W., 352n
Brockner, A., 337n
Brockner, J., 337n
Brodt, S. E., 332n
Brutus, S., 288n
Buford, J. A. Jr., 8n
Burgess, L., 338n
Burke, M., 307n
Burkholder, N., 134n
Busse, T. V., 246n
Butler, J. E., 115n
Byham, W. C., 179n
Byrnes, N., 153n

Caldwell, D. F., 234n
Caldwell, D. V., 235n
Cameron, K. S., 336n
Campion, M. A., 170n, 250n, 251n, 253n, 255n
Canoni, J. D., 251n
Cantalupo, Jim, 284
Caplan, J., 40n, 233n
Cappelli, P., 150n, 158n, 314n, 333n, 356n, 361n
Carbonara, P., 144n, 234n, 260n, 282n
Carlson, J. F., 220n
Carr, E., 259n
Carr, L., 105n
Carrig, K., 209n
Carroll, S. A., 186n
Carson, K. P., 86n
Carter, C., 337n
Cartwright, S., 250n
Cascio, R., 300n
Cascio, W. F., 299n, 321n, 329n, 337n, 338n
Caudron, S., 290n
Chambers, E. G., 33n, 288n
Chambers, John, 326
Chang, Lucy, 183
Chang, V., 326n
Chao, G. T., 10n, 241n, 247n, 280n, 323n
Chapman, D. S., 173n, 186n
Charan, R., 283n
Chatman, J., 235n
Chen, H., 157n
Chung, Y., 13n, 33n

Clark, H., 284n
Cleveland, J., 279n
Cobb-Walgren, C. J., 183n
Collins, C. J., 23n, 144n, 186n
Collison, J., 129n
Colquitt, J. A., 250n
Conejos, Jose, 360n, 361n
Conger, J. A., 287n
Conlin, M., 248n, 259n
Connerly, M. L., 170n
Coon, Murray, 109
Cooper, K. C., 105n
Cooper-Thomas, H. D., 327n
Copeland, Douglas, 188
Copeland, M. V., 22
Costa, P. T. Jr., 250n
Cottle, Jeff, 355
Coyle, B. W., 172n
Coyne, I., 241n
Crane, A. B., 260n
Creelman, D., 365n, 366n, 329n
Crispin, G., 85n
Crockett, J., 106n
Cronin, B. E., 249n
Cronshaw, S. F., 255n, 241n
Cropanzano, R., 313n
Cucina, J. M., 206n
Cummings, L. L., 4n
Cunningham, M. R., 251n
Curry, Eddy, 79n

Dadey, K. M., 301n
Dalton, A., 328n, 330n
Davidson, B., 134n
Davis-Blake, A., 338n
Davis, G. M., 65n
Davis, J. A., 127n
Davis, K., 127n
Davy, J., 337n
Day, D. V., 241n
Delaney, K. J., 234n
Deloitte, 327n
DeMarco, T., 233n
DeMers, S. T., 33n
De Meuse, K. P., 337n
Denton, D. K., 354n
Dessler, G., 350n
Devanna, M. A., 177n
DiCesare, C. B., 179n
Digman, J. M., 206n
Dineen, B. R., 188n
Dipboye, R. L., 250n, 251n
Director, S. M., 129n
Doherty, Mary, 199n, 224n
Donald, Jim, 22
Donnelly, G., 2n
Donnelly, J. H., 321n
Dougherty, T. W., 191n
Downs, C. W., 191n
Drasgow, F., 33n
Dreiband, Eric, 77
Drotter, S., 282n
Drucker, P., 159n
Dubinsky, A. J., 326n
Duff, M., 169n
Duhon, D., 331n
Dunnette, M. D., 246n, 251n

SUBJECT INDEX

Note: The page numbers with 'b', 'f' and 't' refers to boxes, figures and tables cited in the text

ORGANIZATION INDEX

Note: The locators followed by 'n' refers to note number cited in the text.